Delimiter—setting off elements/separating them from the inde

- *Introductory phrases*

  After getting a draft done, I can revise at my leisure. (Wisem

- *Introductory dependent (subordinate) clauses*

  Though I no longer get up at four, I do try to write at the sam........ every morning.
  (Robinson 84)

- *Parenthetical modifiers (to set off additional or qualifying information)*

  Not for me, and I regret it, the ability to use a spare half hour to start a poem—I need total
  concentration, no need to look at my watch, nothing coming up. (Wiseman 111)

- *Non-restrictive relative clauses (commenting—the material is extra, non-essential)*

  My solution has been to write in retreats, where I can focus fully. (Wiseman 111)

- *Direct address*

  Knowing what I've learned at this stage in my career, what would I say to my younger self,
  starting out as a writer? Work out more, Brad, drink less, don't let the mediocritists pull
  you down and stop pretending you know everything. (Brad Fraser 37)

- *Direct quotations*

  Bob Stallworthy wrote, "There will always be writers who are better than you are and
  writers who are worse; there is little satisfaction in comparing yourself to either." (94)

DASH

- *Appositive*

  That kind of jitteriness—the shaky handheld camera—does, I think, lend itself well to the
  themes of dislocation that I wish to explore. (Rajinderpal S. Pal 72)

- *Interruption within a sentence*

  I get up very early—before sunrise—while there is still some life in last-night's coals.
  (Wayne Grady 41)

- *Emphasis (occasionally can replace colon or semicolon to join sentences or announce lists)*

  Get edgy, get busy and don't worry about failing—it's only one step away from creating.
  (Nicole Markotic 55)

HYPHEN

- *Compounds (do not confuse with dash: a dash **separates**, a hyphen **combines** words into one)*

  It is in disrupted spaces that I tend to begin most of my poems: at airports, in hotels, in
  those thirty-minute coffee shop breaks between appointments. (Pal 72)

SEMICOLON

- *Conjunction of sentences (with or without a conjunctive adverb)*

  Writers don't make words; they shape them. (Richard Harrison 44)

  I find the first draft the easiest because there are no rules, just write what comes; however,
  overall, writing for me requires a lot of revising, something I find tiring and frustrating but
  ultimately rewarding. (Robert Hilles 49)

- *Separation in a series that includes internal punctuation*

  For the younger writer: read, read, read—everything; talk with other artists, photogra-
  phers, sculptors, film-makers, painters, musicians, composers, dancers, writers; know that
  the process of creativity is familiar to all disciplines and, therefore, you are not alone.
  (Louise Halfe 43)

Conversations *about* Writing

Eavesdropping,

Inkshedding,

and Joining In

M. Elizabeth Sargent
University of Alberta

Cornelia C. Paraskevas
Western Oregon University

NELSON EDUCATION

NELSON EDUCATION

Conversations about Writing: Eavesdropping, Inkshedding, and Joining In

by M. Elizabeth Sargent and Cornelia C. Paraskevas

Associate Vice-President, Editorial:
Evelyn Veitch

Executive Editors:
Anne Williams, Rod Banister

Senior Developmental Editor:
Mike Thompson

Permissions Coordinator:
Nicola Winstanley

Senior Production Editor:
Bob Kohlmeier

Copy Editor:
Sandra Braun

Proofreader:
S. J. Robertson

Indexer:
Dennis A. Mills

Production Coordinator:
Ferial Suleman

Creative Director:
Angela Cluer

Interior Design:
Peter Papayanakis

Cover Design:
Peter Papayanakis

Cover Image:
Bumboking, by Michael Earle/Open Studio

Compositor:
VISU*TronX*

Printer:
Transcontinental

Library and Archives Canada Cataloguing in Publication

Sargent, M. Elizabeth, 1948–
Conversations about writing : eavesdropping, inkshedding, and joining in / M. Elizabeth Sargent and Cornelia C. Paraskevas.

Includes bibliographical references and index.
ISBN 0-17-641498-3

1. English language—Rhetoric—Textbooks. I. Paraskevas, Cornelia C. (Cornelia Catherine), 1958– II. Title.

PE1408.S29 2004   808'.042
C2004-904411-7

A RIFF ON EAVESDROPPING
(courtesy of the *Oxford English Dictionary*)

Definitions:

Eavesdrip/eavesdrop (noun): "the space of ground which is liable to receive the rainwater thrown off by the eaves of the building"

Eavesdrip/eavesdrop (verb): "to stand within the eavesdrop of a house in order to listen to secrets" or "to listen secretly to conversation"

Eavesdropper (noun): "one who listens secretly to conversation"

Examples:

1584 – "There must be some **eves-dropers** with pen and inke behind the wall."

1606 – "We will be bold to **evesdroppe**."

1622 – "to **eave-drop**, to prie into men's actions or courses"

1641 – "**Evesdroppers** are such as stand under wals and windowes . . . to heare news."

———————————

The meanings of the word, like its spellings, have shifted over time. Yet all of them grow from the root physical image: a bold someone trying to stay dry outside in the cold while listening for useful news or stories or information (and someone who might have "pen and inke" handy). Of course, a new definition will need to be added because of computers: "eavesdropping" is usually what people do on listservs, eavesdrop first and then join in—without any necessity for getting either wet or cold.

CONTENTS

CONVERSATION 5: THE GRAMMAR-AS-STYLE DEBATE: DOES GRAMMAR INSTRUCTION HURT OR HELP STUDENT WRITING? 237

CONVERSATION 6: ORGANIZATION AND GENRE 284

CONVERSATION 7: AUDIENCE, EVALUATION, AND RESPONSE 326

ACKNOWLEDGMENTS

We've had lucky lifetimes in terms of conversations about writing with friends, family members, colleagues, and students, so we have many people to thank. This book had its start in generative conversations with Anne Williams, who knows how to encourage a book proposal out of somebody (as well as how to get them to revise and fine-tune it). Then Mike Thompson received the torch from Anne as the book went into the next stage of development; finally, Bob Kohlmeier shepherded us through copy editing and production. Of course, others at Thomson Nelson have been working on our behalf as well: to name a few, Rod Banister, Heidi Winkelmann, Sandra Braun, Lisa Rahn, S. J. Robertson (proofreader extraordinaire) and Nicola Winstanley, who handled the complicated task of permissions.

We are also grateful to all the reviewers who took time to read the proposal, then sample chapters, and later the final manuscript and who suggested so many ways to make this text work better for students: Jim Andersen, University College of the Fraser Valley; Kim Blank, University of Victoria; Richard Coe, Simon Fraser University; Susan Drain, Mount Saint Vincent University; Deirdre Flynn, University of Toronto; Dale Jacobs, University of Windsor; Jaqueline McLeod Rogers, University of Winnipeg; Katharine Patterson, University of British Columbia; Carolyn Pittenger, McGill University; Tiffany Potter, University of British Columbia; Marlene Sawatsky, Simon Fraser University; Judy Segal, University of British Columbia; John Spencer, York University; Wendy Strachan, Simon Fraser University; Georgia Wilder, University of Toronto; and Katherine Yuk, Seneca College.

The University of Alberta and Western Oregon University have supported this project by granting sabbatical leaves and release time; and University of Alberta supported it even further by granting the help of hardworking RAs who read and responded to possible selections (Marlene Wurfel), who prepared clean photocopies of the readings (Rebecca Babcock), and who worked tirelessly on scanning and proofreading many of the articles (Laura Davis). Sue Payton of Western Oregon University patiently taught us how to scan the rest. Nancy Barry of Luther College, Decorah, Iowa, read and responded in detail to the introductions to each chapter, giving us an instructor's perspective. Hanne Bjornstad, graduate student in English at Concordia University, Montreal, read the entire manuscript, catching typos as well as giving us a student's perspective. Tania Smith, University of Calgary, responded via e-mail to serve as a resource for further readings; and Lahoucine Ouzgane (University of Alberta) and Carmen Schmersahl (Mount Saint Mary's College) both contributed to our thinking about this project at a crucial early stage. We also learned much from the work of the late Wendy Bishop and her conviction that the real subject of any writing course is writing.

At the risk of sounding ridiculous, we want to thank each other: we've been carrying on a conversation about writing and language since we first met in 1989, a conversation that has nourished and changed our teaching. We're grateful for the powers of e-mail, which allowed us to continue that conversation even after twelve hundred miles separated us and to extend that conversation to other colleagues. Indeed, during this past year we were able to consult many of them at once when we were undecided about possible titles. Their quick and thoughtful responses revealed yet again what we already knew to be true—that our colleagues are expert at carrying on a generous and lively conversation about writing: Chris Anderson, Chris Anson, Ted Bishop, Lisa Ede, Peter Elbow, Pamela Farvolden, Toby Fulwiler, Jean Howard, Marg Iveson, Ingrid Johnston, Carol Long, Jill McClay, Sondra Perl, Robert Root, Carmen Schmersahl, Tania Smith, Ann Staley, Jane Theilsen, and Alice Weldon. Further, how anyone in composition and rhetoric ever managed without the online resources of Chris Anson's *Teaching Composition* website, the WPA (Writing Program Administrators) listserv, the discussion list of the Inkshed community (CASLL—Canadian Association for the Study of Language and Learning) and the *Inkshed* website (maintained by Russell Hunt), or Rich Haswell's *CompPile* is beyond us. We consulted *CompPile* frequently to double-check our sources and to locate new ones: we want to acknowledge that debt, especially since we've never seen it acknowledged elsewhere.

We want to thank not only the students who gave us permission to include their work in this volume, but all the students who have entrusted us with their writing over the years and from whom we have learned so much about the teaching of writing and the writing process.

Any project like this one puts extreme burdens on family members. Cornelia Paraskevas wants particularly to thank Meropi and Zambeta—for taking care of the practical, day-to-day matters so she could devote time to the book—and Frank Nevius, for intellectual, moral, and practical support (giving feedback, encouraging, and making sure the printer had lots of paper and ink), all of which became doubly important while she was recovering from back surgery in Athens during the last month of work on the manuscript. M. Elizabeth Sargent wants to thank Garry Watson, who read every chapter introduction (usually through several drafts), as well as all inkshedding prompts, new practices, essay ideas, and many introductions to individual readings, catching everything from major confusions to minor typos. His doing so, in addition to his uncomplaining fetching of food and coffee over a period of many months, took time away from his own writing: she is grateful.

We owe a debt to our children, with whom we continue to have conversations about writing that surprise and educate us: Hannah and Molly Wallace, Sophie and Martin Watson, Alexander Paraskevas-Shepard and Athena Paraskevas-Nevius. And we want to dedicate this book to our parents—Margaret and George Sargent, Meropi Violaki-Paraskeva and Andreas Paraskevas. Our fathers, like most engineers, wrote constantly (primarily technical and consulting reports); but they also both recited poetry to us from the time we were little, in love not just with the meanings, but also with the sounds and rhythms of words. Our mothers, both published writers (one freelance, the other in medicine), emphasized the ability of words to do important work in the world, to comfort and heal, and to strengthen family and preserve memory. Together, our parents taught us to love language(s) and to respect the power of writing.

M. Elizabeth Sargent
Cornelia C. Paraskevas

PREFACE:

A Letter to Instructors Using This Book

Dear Colleagues,

When we teach writing, we regularly debate whether or not students in a writing course should read other texts—that is, texts in addition to the ones students create themselves. Some argue that students should read *only* their own and each other's writing as they bring rough pieces through a workshop process to a more finished state. Others contend that the weaknesses of student writing are largely due to the infrequency and narrow range of student reading, that students need to read good essays as models for their own writing. Still others maintain that students should be engaging with difficult readings, not to use them as models necessarily, but to struggle with important ideas and issues and to acknowledge the way in which all of our writing inevitably answers to or builds on previous writing. And of course a range of other beliefs about appropriate readings for introductory writing classes exists, from using literature anthologies to focusing on particular environmental or political issues for debate.

We've come to realize that these approaches all have one thing in common: they assume that an introductory writing course is a skills-only course. The content bucket is empty. You can fill the content bucket with pretty much anything you choose, as long as you have the students do a lot of writing about it.

Naturally, we agree that the only way to learn how to write is by writing, that students will grow as writers by writing about almost any subject. And exploratory writing about any topic can help the writer learn more about that topic, while—as a side benefit—increasing the writer's fluency and skill overall. But this anthology is based on the premise that students will grow much *more* as writers over the term of a writing course if they read what working writers have to say about writing and what scholars in the field of rhetoric and composition have found out about the writing process.

Imagine, for a moment, an introductory biology course where no contemporary research in biology was ever mentioned or an introductory philosophy course in which no classic readings in philosophy were assigned. Yet year after year we've continued to do the equivalent in first-year writing courses without giving it a second thought. Further, many texts and handbooks in writing courses continue to walk the student through a series of guidelines, rules, and forms for writing that have long been discredited in the scholarship of the field. Even the best of composition texts and rhetorics, ones informed by recent work in the field, fail to alert students to the fact that disagreement still exists about some basic issues—like the nature of academic writing itself, for instance, and the increasing role of narrative, autobiography, and collage in intellectual argument (just to mention three genres that often help clarify the situatedness and limitations of the author).

NEL

At some institutions, explicit attention to first-year writing has been dropped in favour of moving over entirely to upper-level writing-intensive courses in other disciplines. Certainly we believe in the importance of such courses, particularly in a student's major area of study; but we argue that writing-intensive courses should *build on* a substantive introduction to university writing, not *replace* it. And while we understand the political and economic reasons for eliminating first-year composition classes at various institutions (if, for instance, one's university won't fund FYC—first-year composition—adequately and plans to staff all writing courses with underpaid, overworked adjuncts), we cannot agree with it on pedagogical grounds. Consider the richness of our field and what students are missing when they are denied access to its findings. If our students never take a university writing course, there are certain crucial experiences with academic writing that they will never have, certain key concepts and debates they'll never be aware of, certain moments of consciously reflecting on and learning to understand their own writing processes that no other course will ever be able to make time for. As a result, they are likely to struggle with their writing in unnecessary ways throughout their university and professional careers.

We have come to insist that *the subject in an introductory writing course is writing*, that in such classes our students should be reading and writing about some of the most important work to-date on the writing process and the teaching of writing. They should also be reading and reflecting on what a wide range of writers have to say about their own ways of working with language.

What effect might this study of the writing process and of composition theory have on our students' ability to reflect on their own processes, practices, and rhetorical choices as writers? A few students speak for themselves in this volume; we only wish we could simultaneously publish a companion volume of nothing but student writing—inksheds, group inkshed reports and marginalia, loop writing, process writing, e-mails, feedback sheets and feedback reports, collages, creative nonfiction, persuasive essays, traditional and experimental research papers (with cover letters describing the process of research and drafting)—since that book would, by sheer quantity of evidence, make our case much more convincingly than we can do here (check the bibliography in this volume under *Sargent* for some additional published examples of student writing). We've been using many of the selections in this volume in introductory writing courses and, based on our students' reactions, find it increasingly difficult to imagine organizing a writing course in which we would keep this material from our students.

This anthology is designed to bring composition theory into the writing class by introducing students in both first-year and advanced composition courses to some of the major ideas and debates in composition theory and research and to place student writing itself in the context of the ongoing conversations in the field. First-year students are fully capable of appreciating much of this theory and research and in fact have a right to this information. Students reading this material for the first time often ask, "Why didn't anyone ever tell me about this before?"

Since one of us is a linguist and one of us is a writing specialist, we're of course particularly intrigued by the different perspectives and approaches of those two disciplines, differences that are often reflected in competing definitions of key terms, like **grammar**, for instance (see footnote on page 3 about bolded terms in this text). Hardly any writing texts expose students to the work of linguists like Stephen Pinker or consider the changes in writing instruction that arguments like his might bring about. We believe that through an encounter with such research and theory, through our "teaching the conflicts" (as Gerald Graff famously put it [12]), and through a sustained reflection on their own practice, students will come to appreciate the complexity of the writing process. Becoming more informed and conscious writers, more aware what writing can mean to their lives, has helped our students produce writing that is stronger, richer, more authoritative, and less helplessly mimicking of academic forms they don't yet fully understand or control.

Like Reither and Vipond in this volume, we believe that all knowledge-making is collaborative and that writers only ever write compellingly about subjects they know well and care about to an audience that either needs or wants the knowledge they have to share. This doesn't mean, however, that students should be restricted to writing about what they *already* know, but rather that their writing should help them explore the world, to extend the range of subjects they genuinely care about and to learn more about them. We also agree with Reither and Vipond that the first-year writing class works best when the classroom becomes a community of inquiry. Investigating a live intellectual question together, students use their writing to share their findings with each other. Our students have found crucial questions to explore together in the first-year writing course, largely because they bring their own struggles with writing and their own considerable experience with educational systems to the table: Can writing be taught? Can it be learned? If so, how? And is academic writing as completely different from personal writing as we've been led to believe? What is the role of grammar instruction in the teaching of writing?

Our students use the materials we've collected in this anthology as resources to take off from for further research; they also use their own experiences with language and with schooling as resources. When they write in response to these materials and share their essays with each other, they experience the kind of intellectual curiosity and excitement we—their instructors—sometimes experience at academic conferences, discussing subjects crucial to us with other co-investigators in a field. Such writing helps us (students and instructors both) to explore or think through a particular question while simultaneously communicating our discoveries and our remaining puzzlements to colleagues. In James Britton's terms, such writing is deeply expressive and transactional at the same time—it is writing-to-learn and writing-to-get-something-done, to persuade or communicate with others. When students, informed by some of the major work in composition theory over the past forty years, conduct their own research on the writing process (consult Donald Murray's rich list of research ideas on revision in the final Conversation for a range of possibilities on just one topic), they enter the ongoing conversations about writing; when they study their own experiences as readers and writers or study the processes of other writers (see the interview assignment suggested in Conversation 2, pages 104–105), they are developing an expertise of their own from which they can answer back to some of the continuing debates in the field.

This anthology has been put together, then, on the basis of two beliefs:

—the conviction that introductory writing courses *do* have a subject matter of their own, that subject being the writing process itself, plus the raw data collected during term about the writing processes of everyone in the class, including the instructor (this data to include, of course, the *writing* produced by everyone in the class); and

—the conviction that student writers gain the greatest control over their writing when they learn to reflect consciously on themselves as writers and on their ways of writing, a process nourished by their eavesdropping on a conversation/debate that's been going on about them for a long time in the field of composition and rhetoric, a conversation about the writing process and the teaching of writing.

One of the major accomplishments of the composition and rhetoric field in the past forty years is its determination to look closely at how everyone—from published authors to struggling students—*actually* writes, as opposed to how past rhetorical guidelines (often lumped together and labelled "current-traditional") have assumed they *should* write. Researchers like Richard Braddock (focusing on published authors in the mid-1970s) and Sondra Perl (focusing on "The Composing Processes of Unskilled Writers at the College Level" in the late 1970s) published their findings in journals like *Research in the Teaching of English* and revealed that our North American truisms—like "always use an outline" or "always end the first paragraph with a thesis statement" or "start every subsequent paragraph with a topic sentence"—did not describe how professional authors generally worked and were also of little use in teaching writing to anyone except those of us who had always found school and writing (and following instructions) relatively unproblematic anyway.

The composition field is particularly rich not only because of its interdisciplinary nature (drawing on cognitive science, linguistics, psychology, philosophy, and education, as well as literature) and not only because of the central role it assigns to teaching, but because it includes practitioners as well as scholars (and a certain number of individuals, like poet Wendy Bishop and columnist Donald Murray, who have been both). Researchers in composition and rhetoric see the poet, the playwright, the screenwriter, the fiction writer, and the creative nonfiction writer as experts whose expertise is valuable, indeed crucial, to the field. And working writers—especially when they are also teachers of writing—benefit from and rely on the research and theoretical work that composition scholars are producing.

We have tried to honour that balance in this text. In the pieces gathered here, students will have a chance to hear some of the many voices contributing to this field; the research, reflective and theoretical work that these writers and scholars have done can help students understand their own past, present, and future relationship to language, especially to written language, differently. And as students examine their own practices as writers, they'll discover that they have further exploring to do and insights they'll want to bring to this ongoing conversation themselves. They won't be restricted to eavesdropping.

In our introduction ("A Letter to Students Using This Book"), we have emphasized that there is no one right order in which to read through Conversations 1 through 8 (see "A Word about How These Conversations Are Organized," page 7). We intentionally start with readings that deal broadly with the crucial role of language in all learning and thinking (Conversation 1) and with writers reflecting on the writing process (Conversation 2). Subsequent conversations correspond roughly to one way of imagining the sequence of writing an academic paper: invention and exploratory writing, followed by analysis of the academic assignment and of the task of working with sources, followed by considerations of style and register, genre, audience and feedback, revision and proofreading. Yet we can easily imagine beginning with Conversation 3 (on exploratory writing) or beginning with one of the debates in the field (as a way of focusing an entire course—Conversations 4 or 5) or beginning with Conversation 7 (on audience and feedback, particularly in a workshop course so that students could begin trying out a range of descriptive feedback techniques early in the term). Certainly the readings on revision in Conversation 8 could be used as a starting point for a writing course as well. We emphasize throughout that the writing process itself is recursive; it only makes sense that the process of working with this text is likely to be recursive too. However, it's probably a good idea to take a look at the suggested New Practices in sequence, since some of those do tend to build on one another. This book's corresponding website offers additional resources that will be particularly useful for students who want greater control over sentence-boundary problems like fragments and run-ons: see "A Bare Bones Writer's Grammar" and a "Glossary of Key Words for a Writer's Grammar" (both at http://www.sargent.nelson.com).

Wherever you decide to begin, we hope that you and your students find this book a useful point of entry into the many conversations about writing and that you'll write to let us know if there are parts of this book we should change—or not change.

Sincerely,

M. Elizabeth Sargent
Cornelia C. Paraskevas

INTRODUCTION:

A Letter to Students Using This Book

> The writer communicates with the page. The reader also communicates with the page. The writer and the reader communicate only through the page. This is one of the syllogisms of writing as such. Pay no attention to the facsimiles of the writer that appear on talkshows, in newspaper interviews, and the like—they ought not to have anything to do with what goes on between you, the reader, and the page you are reading, where an invisible hand has previously left some marks for you to decipher, much as one of John Le Carré's dead spies has left a waterlogged shoe with a small packet in it for George Smiley. I know this is a far-fetched image, but it is also curiously apt, since the reader is—among other things—a sort of spy. A spy, a trespasser, someone in the habit of reading other people's letters and diaries. As Northrop Frye has implied, the reader does not hear, he overhears.
>
> Margaret Atwood, *Negotiating with the Dead: A Writer on Writing* 125–26

Dear Students,

Writing is so complicated. And it doesn't help matters to realize that not everyone agrees about which words or arrangements of words are correct or appropriate or effective in specific situations. You already know that words have great power—a kind word can make your day, a loving word can change your life, a cruel or careless word can break your heart. And on a wider scale, the words we use every day can affect how we think, how we understand the world, even how nations interact with each other.

Writing is complicated, and *teaching* writing is also complicated. The truth is, we're not entirely sure how to do it. We have learned a lot in the last forty years about how *not* to do it, but there's still uncertainty out there about what exactly to do in a classroom situation to support students (you) as they (you) develop as writers, especially as writers in a university. The conversation that has been going on about this concerns you, but for some unknown reason up until now, it hasn't occurred to writers of textbooks to mention this fact or to let students listen in on this ongoing conversation. Indeed, writing textbooks usually are structured as if this information should be kept *from* you—that is, the information that there's a lively debate going on about how to teach writing and that scholars often disagree about how to do it. We're particularly alert to some of these debates ourselves (the ones between linguists and writing teachers about the role of grammar in the teaching of writing) because one of us is a linguist and the other is a writing specialist; but there are other important debates that affect you as well.

Knowledge of these debates has not been kept from you for evil reasons but mainly because teachers and textbook publishers have assumed that you wouldn't be interested —indeed, that you might even be confused and demoralized to discover that such widespread disagreement existed. Teachers and textbook publishers have also assumed that you're busy and you just want to get on with it, that you want only to be told how to crank out adequate academic writing so you can complete your university work and graduate in good standing and move on to a career or graduate school—even if the how-to information you're sometimes given has been discredited by recent research on the writing process.

We, too, know that you're busy—too busy, in fact, to waste any more time labouring under the delusion that anyone (including us, the editors of this book) knows *exactly* how to teach you to improve your writing. *You* are the only true expert on your own writing. You may not yet fully and consciously know what you know (or trust it); you may not yet be in full possession of your expertise. We're hoping that this text will help you become even more expert than you already are about yourself as a writer. If you learn to attend to what works and doesn't work for you as a writer, to observe what your own writing habits and strategies are, to understand your history as a writer and reader—and if you use writing itself to help you attend, observe, and understand these things—you can gain greater control over the mystery of your own writing processes.

We also believe that if you spend some time listening in on the various conversations going on about writing in our culture, noticing areas where some consensus and agreement exist and other areas where debate and disagreement prevail, you'll begin to get a wider sense of your choices as a writer in university and beyond. We believe that powerful writing comes from having choices and making choices; thus, we believe that eavesdropping on these conversations about writing will help make you a more powerful writer.

OVERVIEW OF KEY TERMS

Eavesdropping

Have you ever experienced the guilty pleasure (or pain and dismay) of eavesdropping on a conversation about yourself? Of course, this particular conversation is not about you as an individual, but you as a member of a group, students in university writing classes. Just as in any conversation you might overhear about yourself, some of the comments being passed around are good ones. You'd like to hear them: they'd help you write with more confidence, help you value more what you have to say and the way you say it. Some of the comments, however, are critical ones—they might hurt your feelings or anger you, you might take them as a dare, or you might feel that they're completely unfair and unjustified. On the other hand, once you get over the initial shock of hearing them, you might find that they too are helpful—that they're a kind of reality check, that they help you adjust your behaviour in productive ways. And finally, you'll discover that just as some of your friends and coworkers might disagree about your strengths and weaknesses, scholars in the field of **composition and rhetoric**[1] disagree about your writing strengths and weaknesses as well. Discovering what some of these disagreements are can be exciting; these are intellectual puzzles, issues that are not yet settled. And you may find that you have something important to contribute to this conversation from your own experience as a writer.

You may be wondering what the field of **composition and rhetoric** is exactly. **Composition** is a familiar enough term: not just writers, but also artists and musicians study composition, the art of putting parts together to form a whole. The word **rhetoric**, however, conjures up confusing or negative connotations: many people assume that it has something to do with "rhetorical" questions, questions to which a person doesn't really expect or want an answer; others assume that it always refers to false or insincere attempts at eloquence, attempts to impress people or to persuade them to do something against their better judgment (as in, "don't try to manipulate me with your fancy rhetoric"). The term doesn't mean either of those things in this book, but simply "the art of effective expression"—with "effective" meaning not persuasive for shady reasons, but persuasive because writers have managed to discover and express what they truly think and feel, what they most want and need to say, and because they've also managed to articulate good reasons for their claims and to put those reasons into an order, a shape, that matches their own deep sense of what's most important in their argument. You might want to return to this definition of rhetoric a few times as you read further.

Why should the ongoing conversations about composition and rhetoric, about writing and teaching writing, interest you or be of any use to you (especially the ones that aren't directly about you)? Writers have been talking to each other about writing for centuries, pretty much ever since writing existed. When you listen to what working writers have to say about their struggles to write and their writing processes, you realize that you're not the only person who worries that the words you have down on paper aren't good enough or that the next time you have to write something, you might be hopelessly blocked, with nothing but inanities to scratch onto the page. You might also find that some of the strategies that working writers turn to in such moments could work for you.

Introductory writing courses have often been taught without any attention at all being paid to what working writers in a wide variety of fields actually *do* when they write. Instead of suggesting various strategies for invention, for collaboration and feedback, for composing, or for revision that working writers have used, some texts have focused on presenting set patterns, formats, or modes for academic or professional

---

[1] A word in boldface indicates a key term that gathers layers of meaning as it is used in various contexts by various authors throughout this text. These terms all appear in the index, where page numbers in boldface indicate a definition or the term being used with important additional connotations or implications. Becoming alert to how keywords gather meaning-with-use in a particular field (something like a snowball rolling downhill—although in some cases a snowball with internal tensions, as if it had a ticking bomb inside) is part of any serious apprenticeship to a disciplinary conversation.

writing. We won't be doing that here. Yes, there are moments in all of our lives when we must follow a strict formula—a five-paragraph theme, a lab report, a business proposal, a legal document—but such formulas are best learned and followed in context, when they are needed, when the writer is actually immersed in the community or situation that calls for that specific form of writing (see Conversation 6 for a discussion on genre). Such forms of writing can be, in fact, much more difficult and complex than they might seem on the surface and can only be learned well or mastered "on the job," so to speak (for an excellent example of challenging workplace writing, see Jamie MacKinnon on writing in the Bank of Canada). For that very reason, such genres cannot and should not be the focus of an introductory writing course or writing text.

What will this book be trying to do instead? Encouraging you to learn some useful writerly habits that can serve you well over a long and varied lifetime—**eavesdropping** on other writers, **inkshedding** to learn whatever you need to learn or explore as part of a community of writers and learners, and then **joining** the wider ongoing conversations about writing yourself.

Inkshedding

What is inkshedding? The briefest possible definition is that it's an informal kind of writing-to-learn, throwaway writing that you do in order to make something happen inside your head or inside the heads of others as you try to figure something out. So much of our writing is done in order to show others what we *already* know, what we have *already* figured out, that sometimes we forget how important writing is as a tool for thinking, exploring, learning, and understanding. Of course, we all know that multiple drafts can help improve a final paper, but inksheds are not necessarily early drafts of a piece of writing. They may be merely think pieces, one or two pages long, raising questions in response to a lecture, a reading assignment, a heated class discussion, or a quiet day of research on a term project. Some inksheds may lead directly into a formal essay, providing early drafts of key passages. Others don't. But they might all be equally necessary for our thinking to move from point A to point B.

Inkshedding is a Canadian term, coined in the early 1980s at St. Thomas University, New Brunswick, by James Reither and Russell Hunt to describe how they were integrating **freewriting** into their teaching more fully, making freewriting less private and more social. Hunt and Reither saw their classrooms as communities of inquiry, and they wanted a way that their students could use writing to talk to each other on the page to further the investigations they were pursuing together. Reither picked the term after finding it defined in the *Oxford English Dictionary* (*OED*) as a "humourous" word meaning "the shedding or spilling of ink; consumption or waste of ink in writing"; he particularly liked a sentence that spoke of something having been accomplished "with no bloodshed . . . but with immense beershed and inkshed" (see Hunt's piece in Conversation 3). Soon, Hunt and Reither began practising inkshedding not only with their students, but with their colleagues throughout Canada in annual (since 1984) Inkshed conferences—so the practice has spread.

You might already be familiar with **freewriting**, a term first used by Ken Macrorie and then further theorized and developed by Peter Elbow in the 1970s (see the introduction to Conversation 3, pages 106–111): freewriting emphasizes writing nonstop, never pausing to correct anything or to censor your words or thoughts. Because freewriting asks you to write whatever is on your mind without censoring anything, Elbow has insisted that freewriting should be private, never graded or corrected, and read only by the person who wrote it (and not even necessarily read at all, ever). The essential moves in freewriting are keeping the pen (or pencil or fingers on the keyboard) moving and getting the words down on paper in complete safety—and indeed, research on the practice of freewriting has shown its value in increasing writer fluency and in helping writers overcome writer's block (see Belanoff et al., *Nothing Begins with N*).

While Reither and Hunt valued the safety and fluency that freewriting made possible, they also wanted to develop a form of public, focused freewriting that involved students in dialogue with each other and with their teachers. In contrast to freewriting, an inkshed does involve some self-censoring—albeit minimal—in that the person inkshedding will not simply free-associate but will keep an object in view. That is, even if distractions intrude and make their mark on the writing ("When is the bell going to ring? I'm so hungry I can hardly think"), the inkshedder will keep trying to return to the given focus of the inkshed ("Okay, so I'm hungry—but for the next few minutes I have to think further about why that reading assignment upset me so much. So, which details triggered my reaction?"). Knowing that others will be reading the inkshed certainly has an effect on the writer—but once group members begin to trust the process and to believe that surface imperfections don't matter and that they won't be graded or evaluated on their spelling or their grammar or their brilliance in an inkshed, they usually relax and enjoy the opportunity to share their early questions, reactions, and ideas with others.

Important as distinctions between inkshedding and freewriting may be, however, throughout this text we will use those two terms interchangeably: that is, we will always assume that freewriting in a classroom situation is meant to be public and shared unless we specifically talk about private writing instead. Private writing is crucial for a writer's development, and we do make room for it in our classrooms; but when we do so, we always make clear to students (to you) ahead of time that the writing will be completely private and that they (you) won't be expected to let anyone else read it or even know what it's about. It would be much worse for you to write something in the belief that no one was going to read it, only to discover that you were supposed to pass it to the person seated next to you—much worse than if you wrote something you *expected* to be public, only to discover that it was allowed to remain private. To eliminate the possibility of the first circumstance, we simply announce that all freewriting in our classes will be considered public and focused unless we say otherwise ahead of time.

Joining In

How can you begin to enter the conversations about writing and the teaching of writing that have been going on without you? Since these are in large part *written* conversations—they are not only *about* writing but much of the conversation is conducted *in* writing—inkshedding turns out to be a good way to start. If we think of the essays in this volume as contributions that various students and teachers and writers have made to an ongoing, international conversation about writing, we want to be thinking about ways to *join* that conversation, not simply to eavesdrop on it.

Think of an online discussion group. Depending on the seriousness and quality of the group, someone might listen in on the conversation for a long time before risking a public contribution. Instead of posting to the entire group, particularly if it was a list-serv whose respect and good opinion was important to you, you might first send an informal e-mail to a few people in the group—people you already knew well and trusted or people whose recent postings you had particularly admired or agreed with. You might share with those people some of your evolving thoughts and questions on that subject. And if they encouraged you to share your e-mail with everyone on the list, adding a few supporting details or qualifications or deleting a paragraph that might confuse or unnecessarily antagonize your readers, you might work on your e-mail a bit more until you felt it was ready for public consumption. If, however, they responded that several months earlier someone had contributed a long and detailed posting on the same ideas that now interested you, you would restrain yourself, deciding not to reveal to everyone your ignorance of the earlier discussion. Instead, you might go to the archives on that discussion list and read the earlier posting—and then you might find yourself wanting to write a slightly different (and now more nuanced and informed) response.

Joining an academic conversation works in much the same way. You need to listen in on it attentively for a while to get your bearings. Clearly, as someone who has been doing writing assignments in school for at least twelve years and who may also have some writing experience in the world of work as well, you have some strong opinions about what does and does not work for you in the writing tasks and instruction you've experienced. You have something to contribute to this conversation—but you probably won't be heard well or taken seriously if you plunge in without doing some ground-work and without listening to what other writers have been saying to one another about these issues before you arrived on the scene, before you even knew there was such a conversation going on.

Conversation 3 covers the theory of writing-to-learn a bit more fully and will give you further ideas about how to use inkshedding in your learning, especially as a way to enter into various academic and professional conversations (see especially the list of strategies on pages 150–153). But from Conversation 1 on, **inkshedding prompts** will appear, suggesting ways to start your exploratory writing. They come at the beginning of each chapter or selection to help you focus your reading and to encourage you to read actively, the way a writer reads: writers are always on the alert, preparing to respond in writing or to capture their thoughts in writing as they read. Of course, you'll probably need to re-read some of the inkshed prompts right before you inkshed (many prompts will make more sense *after* you have finished particular selections), but having the prompts in mind at the beginning of each Conversation will remind you that you're entering as an eventual participant, not someone observing from a safe distance.

Keep in mind, too, that inkshed prompts are a **genre** (a *kind* of writing, a *genus*) unto themselves, with identifying marks as distinguishing as those that might help you tell one kind of butterfly from another. Chief among these are generosity and superfluity: in other words, a prompt may offer way too many ideas for writing, a cornucopia of questions. So here's what we say in Conversation 1, before the very first inkshed prompt in this book: *Don't ever worry about responding to every question in an inkshed prompt: the questions are only meant to strike sparks. Blow on the spark that seems brightest and see if you can get flames or at least some heat out of it. Although your instructor may occasionally require you to follow a particular prompt, at all other times you should feel free to invent your own inkshed idea if the given prompts fail to strike any sparks.* We encourage you to refer back to this description of inkshedding prompts whenever necessary.

Your instructor may or may not require you to inkshed regularly in response to the readings in this book; but of course, you could inkshed even if you weren't required to. Regular inkshedding in response to some of these prompts would accomplish at least three things:

— it would help you read selections in this book actively and to remember the gist of what you had read;

— it would help you leave a track of your evolving thinking about the issues brought up in the readings (so both you and others can return to and re-read your thoughts, if necessary);

— it would help you practise entering the larger conversation about these issues by sharing your questions and ideas openly in the relative safety of the classroom community before writing more formal papers.

If your instructor does assign inksheds in response to specific readings, you may be expected to share them with your fellow students (your colleagues in class) in a variety of ways. So whatever you do, *make sure you create a secure place for saving and organizing all your inksheds throughout the term.* Our students have repeatedly told us how much their inksheds have helped them study for exams and/or prepare a first draft of an assigned paper; they also have told us that reading through their **process inksheds** (that is, freewrites in which they talked about their writing processes, about how a specific writing task went for them—see New Practice 2 in Conversation 1 for more information about **process writing**) has helped them understand their strengths and weaknesses as writers. Your inksheds will be a rich resource for your reading and writing, so hang onto them; and your instructor may expect you to have them readily available for use inside and outside class throughout the term. You might surprise yourself, discovering that you'll want to hang onto these "conversation starters," these accumulating inksheds, long after you've received your final grade for the course.

A WORD ABOUT HOW THESE CONVERSATIONS ARE ORGANIZED

There is no one right order for reading through all the pieces we've gathered here, all the voices we're trying to put into conversation with each other. Indeed, one possible way to approach this material would be simply to read straight through the introductions to each Conversation before you read any of the individual selections at all. The eight Conversation introductions carry the through-line of the book and would all by themselves give you a quick overview of the composition field.

Your instructor will have a plan for how this text will work this year in your class. No instructor will assign *all* of these readings, and some may start with selections near the middle or end of the text, finishing up the term with selections from the beginning. We've done our best to make these selections work well in any order; that is, we don't think you need to have read everything in Conversation 1 to proceed to Conversation 2, for instance. And we often refer forward and backward to related conversations as we go along. You might, however, find it helpful to check out the New Practices introduced in earlier Conversations even if you don't read the selections in a particular chapter; these New Practices are clearly listed in the Table of Contents as well as in a separate index at the back of the book.

Even though we're assuming that readers will work through the book in whatever sequence suits their needs, we do have a reason for the way we've ordered these sections. It made sense to us to start by examining why on earth we should even spend our time thinking about words and language and writing at all (Conversation 1). Then Conversation 2 allows us to eavesdrop on a range of working writers as they reflect on how and why they write. The rest of the Conversations are ordered roughly according to the way we tend to order stages of the writing process in our minds: allowing time for playful exploratory writing and invention before facing our concerns about voice and tone in academic writing, about grammar and style, about what we need to accomplish with a particular piece of writing (what social action we want to perform and therefore what genre and organizational constraints we're facing), about audience issues and feedback, about revising and proofreading.

However, just because these Conversations focus on elements in the writing process and come in this particular order shouldn't imply that writing is a neat linear process. Far from it. We don't go through pre-writing and invention and then, when we've finished with those, decide crisply which tone or genre or format or organizational pattern we're going to use, only then to reflect on what a specific audience needs or wants and how that audience might respond to or evaluate our writing. We tend to mix these things up, to move back and forth between them, always revising as we go and making rhetorical and stylistic choices all along. The only thing we thought we were sure of is that proofreading should come last—but we know that even in our own writing, we sometimes helplessly proofread and polish a passage that we'll eventually cut from the final version. We should know better. But somehow, we just need to do that silly bit of proofreading right then in order to make any headway at all.

What we're trying to say here is that writing is **recursive**: we don't go through a predictable progression or orderly stages when we write something. We tend to circle back on ourselves. So if, at times, you had the feeling you were going around in circles on a particular writing project, you were probably doing what just about every writer does with any serious piece of writing. There's no way to avoid it. Writing is messy. We need to emphasize that.

So while we've tried to order these conversations as sensibly as we could—invention before genre and audience considerations, all of those before revision, and revision before proofreading—even as we hear ourselves lay out that sequence, we can think of many times when we've proceeded in a completely different order to get an important piece of writing done. Thus, you should feel free to dip into the resources in this anthology in any order (and further resources suggested in the bibliography) to help you reflect on your own experiences with writing in and out of school, to investigate current issues in the ongoing conversations about how writing can best be taught and learned, and to advance inquiry into these matters yourself by joining the written conversation that's been going on for some time now. Think of the authors of these essays as if they were in the classroom with you, as if you were giving thoughtful feedback to them face-to-face (as you'll be giving feedback to your peers and as they'll be giving feedback to you). Your instructor and your colleagues in class will be eager to hear what you bring to this conversation: life experiences and insights, a unique mix of family, cultural, spiritual, educational, linguistic and bodily contexts from which only you can speak. Your voices (all of them—and each one of you does have more than one) are needed in this conversation.

Also, do please write to us if you have suggestions for improving this book.

Sincerely,

M. Elizabeth Sargent and Cornelia C. Paraskevas

CONVERSATION 1:
Life Without Language

INTRODUCTION

> Because we had to work hard in the camps [for conscientious objectors to
> World War II] . . . we would be too tired for reading, writing, and study late
> in the evening. So some of us formed a group to use the "library" (a barracks
> where we put our books together), for early morning literary activity. We
> would quietly get up at four A.M. or so and make our way to the gathering
> place, where we could read and write till breakfast call. Then we would
> work all day outside—U.S. Forest Service work or soil conservation—and
> drag back to camp and into bed. We gained alert hours for mental work and
> the rest of the day for work required of us. Since those days, I have had the
> habit of writing in the early morning. That dawn time is precious: the world
> is quiet; no one will interrupt; you are rested and ready.
>
> William Stafford, "William Stafford: 1914–" in *You Must Revise Your Life* 11–12

Sometimes the best way to understand what language means in our lives is to imagine
what life might be like without it—or at least, without some form of language use we
take for granted. And we can best help our imaginative understanding by reading about
individuals who have been forced to live without one or another form of language,
without listening, speaking, reading, or writing (in Helen Keller's case, without all four).
What does it mean for our lives together that we seem to have a "language instinct"
hardwired into our brains just as web spinning is hardwired into spiders, as sonar is
hardwired into bats? Linguist Stephen Pinker stresses how our ability to use language
to "shape events in each other's brains with exquisite precision" has been heightened
throughout the history of humankind precisely because it gives us an evolutionary
advantage. It's something so ingrained, so much a part of us, that we hardly even notice
the sophistication and complexity of the sentences that come out of our mouths.

We've put Pinker's selection last so that you can experience some of the many different ways in which people can be cut off from language or from kinds of language
before you encounter Pinker's theories. Linda Trichter Metcalf and Tobin Simon help us
take in what a mysterious technology writing is. Keller's early life raises questions about
the intimate link between learning language and becoming fully human. Malcolm X,
unlike Keller, could speak and hear—but he could barely read or write and argues that
when he became a powerful reader and writer, he also became another person entirely.
Eva Hoffman tells a different story: she started life with a full and rich immersion in her
native language (Polish), a lover of books who dreamed of being a writer one day. And
then she lost her language—what happens then? Finally, June Callwood describes

Canadians who are struggling with illiteracy: their situation is in some senses worse than that of Malcolm X (except, of course, that most of them haven't been sent to prison for illegal activities) because they cannot read or write at all. Smart and capable people, healthy and active, often fluent talkers and wonderful listeners, they nevertheless feel trapped in a small and dangerous world where even the vital information on road signs is closed to them.

These selections don't cover all of the situations in which the language instinct Pinker talks about can be blocked or constrained (think, for instance, of stroke victims who suffer from aphasia, the loss of language ability)—but they do help us appreciate one element in Pinker's argument: that our powers of language are not optional extras in this business of being human. As Pinker reminds us, no languageless culture has ever been found on planet Earth. Extend and enrich someone's powers of language and you have immediately extended and enriched their very being, their humanity.

George Bernard Shaw played with this idea in his famous play *Pygmalion* (later adapted into the musical *My Fair Lady*): Eliza Dolittle, a cockney flower girl on the streets of London, becomes the subject of a gentlemen's bet that she can be passed off as a duchess at a garden party within the year if her accent is changed. She studies long hours under an unrelenting taskmaster, the linguist Henry Higgins—and she wins the bet for him. But *her* problems have only begun, since in the process she has become someone else: someone she doesn't entirely recognize or understand and someone she's slightly afraid of, but someone she wants to get to know better. In effect, she had been playing with fire—she thought she'd simply warm herself at its beautiful flames and instead she burned her old house down. She thought learning to speak with an elegant accent would be a lark, a hoot, something she could toy with like a cosmetic, changing the surface of her appearance only.

You are preparing, in reading this book, to enter the world of language more fully and to extend your powers as a reader and as a writer. Consider yourself warned.

Linda Trichter Metcalf and Tobin Simon, from "The Sound of a Voice Thinking" in *Writing the Mind Alive*

Linda Trichter Metcalf and Tobin Simon collaborated to develop Proprioceptive Writing Workshops, opening the first Proprioceptive Writing Center in Maine in 1982 and another in New York City in 1996.

What does **proprioceptive** mean? We are all familiar with our five senses—our alertness to sight, sound, smell, taste, and touch—but we have another sense that we talk about less often: our awareness of where our body is in the world and how our body parts are relating to each other. For instance, we can often sense if someone is behind us even if we can't see or hear or smell or touch them. We can sense if we are lifting our right arm up into the air, even if our eyes are closed and we can't see it—and this sense is not a result of our touching that arm with any other part of ourselves. It's the proprioceptive sense that gets confused if a limb is amputated—the person keeps thinking the limb is there, can even feel pain in that limb, long after the limb has been removed. The proprioceptive sense can also be confused if you have local anesthetic for surgery, say, on your leg: you can be watching the surgeon elevate your leg to work on it and find yourself wondering whose leg that is (since you're quite sure that your own leg is still firmly on the table). The root word in the first part of "proprioceptive" is linked to the word for property, that is, ownership; the root word in the second part is linked to the words "concept" and "perception"—thus, "proprioceptive" refers to the sense or perception you have that something belongs to you.

Metcalf and Simon want writers to feel that way about their writing: they want writers to feel that their writing belongs to them. We want the same thing, but feel uneasy with the subtitle of the book from which the following excerpt is taken: *Writing the Mind Alive: The Proprioceptive Method for Finding Your Authentic Voice* (2002). We would argue, in fact, that we each often have *more* than one voice in writing and that each of these voices feels authentic, feels as if it belongs to us. That is, we don't have many fake writing voices and only one authentic voice. We might have one voice for e-mail to our friends, another for an impassioned letter to the editor of the local newspaper, still another for the term paper in history that we need to finish for tomorrow morning, and yet another for that long overdue thank-you note to our grandmother. But we don't need to decide that only one of these voices is authentic and the others are all somehow false.

Each of us has many selves, corresponding to the many roles we choose to fill over a lifetime; and in choosing the appropriate voice for each role and each occasion, we are being true to those varied selves, not phony or dishonest. On the other hand, we know that our close friends might recognize in each one of our multiple written voices some sound that made us recognizable—this sound is probably what Metcalf and Simon have in mind when they speak of "authentic voice." Certainly our close friends might also accuse us of writing something that did *not* sound like us, something that *did* sound insincere or phony; but we don't lose the ability to make that distinction just because we claim each one of us can write in *more than one* authentic voice. In fact, as writing teachers, we want to emphasize for students the important role that different rhetorical situations will play in helping students discover their full range of possible voices; and in turn, ready access to that full range of voices will help students complete successfully many of the writing tasks they'll be faced with in their university and professional careers.

What is a **rhetorical situation**? It's simply the situation that calls for your words, for your thinking in speech or writing. What is the context? Who or what is making me do this writing: my desire to keep a record of my European trip? the boss who wants this report on his desk tomorrow morning? my mother? Who will the audience be: who will read this writing and who will decide if it "works" or not? What do I know: that is, what details and data do I have to work with and what do I believe to be true? What do I want to accomplish and what is at stake: graduating from university? getting or keeping a job? convincing the person I love to sleep with me? letting a close friend three thousand kilometres away at another university know I haven't forgotten her? Each rhetorical situation can call for a different **genre** (kind) of writing, a different format, and a different voice from you—most of those voices all too painfully real as far as you're concerned.

We agree with Metcalf and Simon, however, that a sense of voice in writing is crucial and that something important is lost (to our thinking as well as our feeling) when the sound of a human voice is absent or ignored in a piece of writing. The following passage highlights how our commitment to a visual information culture, a culture in which we're all meant to process way too much information in way too little time, has turned us into scanners, has caused us to separate writing from sound. The technology of writing allows us to treat it as visual medium alone and thus allows us to hold it at a distance, whether we're reading someone else's writing or producing our own. We all have to register sounds bodily, through vibrations on our eardrums, but we can be much more physically detached from things that we experience only through sight (not least because they can be farther away—we only need to think of thunder and lightning to remember that sound travels much more slowly than light). If we treat reading and writing as visual media, we can work much more quickly: truly *hearing* what we're reading or writing slows us down (vibrations on our eardrums take time, just as music takes time). Certainly there are appropriate and necessary times for skimming and working quickly: we can't spend three hours every day on the newspaper or browsing our favourite Internet site. But in serious reading—for example, of a journal article revealing a complex and astonishing discovery in medicine or of a carefully crafted novel or poem or memoir—what we gain in speed we lose in power. We experience what we read more deeply if we slow down and allow ourselves to hear the voice coming up off the page, a voice thinking or feeling its way through something; and when others read our words, we can't draw them into our experience or claim room in their memories if we've written without ever taking the time to *hear* what we've written.

The truth is, whether we have one voice or many doesn't matter much if we don't take the time to hear *any* of them.

INKSHEDDING PROMPTS

INSTRUCTIONS *(refer back to these whenever you need to):*

After you've read this selection, try inkshedding for fifteen to twenty minutes nonstop in response to one of the following prompts. Doing so as soon as possible after completing the reading will help you remember and assimilate what you've just read. Don't ever worry about responding to every question in an inkshed prompt: the questions are only meant to strike sparks. Blow on the spark that seems brightest and see if you can get a flame or at least some heat out of it. Although your instructor may occasionally require you to follow a particular prompt, at all other times you should feel free to invent your own inkshed idea if the given prompts fail to strike any sparks (consult the list of "Strategies for Writing-to-Learn" in Conversation 3, pages 150–153 for other possibilities).

Read through these prompts again once you've finished reading the selection that follows them.

1. Try out, as best you can without having read *Writing the Mind Alive* cover to cover, a version of Metcalf and Simon's Proprioceptive Writing. If you choose to follow this prompt, your inkshed can be private. However, you should still bring it with you to class to show that you completed it; and your instructor is likely to ask you to do some reflective writing *after* your proprioceptive writing session, a piece of inkshedding that you can share with others (see the definition of **process writing** at the end of this prompt).

   Metcalf and Simon suggest beginning by lighting a candle and playing some baroque music for the duration of the writing session (try a Bach or Vivaldi CD with instruments only, no words or human voices). As a bare minimum, make sure you have a comfortable place to write where you won't be interrupted. Of course, this is good advice for any inkshedding session—turn off your cell phone and vow not to answer any other phones or doors until your twenty minutes are up (Metcalf and Simon suggest twenty-five minutes).

   Make sure you have plenty of paper and a spare pen (or that your computer is working properly and your printer has plenty of paper and ink—you'll need to produce hard copy at the end of this writing session). Then pause for a moment to gather your thoughts and feelings before you begin. Ask yourself what's on your mind. Then, as you hear an answer, begin writing it down: Metcalf and Simon suggest that you should "imagine your thoughts as spoken words and write them exactly as if you could hear them, as they occur to you moment by moment" (32). At any point as you write if a word or a phrase you've written catches your attention, write out what Metcalf and Simon call the Proprioceptive Question: "What do I mean by _____?" (the blank to be filled in with whatever word or phrase snagged your attention). And then continue writing by attempting to answer your own question. You might find yourself asking the Proprioceptive Question only once per session or over and over again as your words tumble out. Don't worry about it either way. You want to welcome whatever comes, whatever occurs to you, without judging, censoring, or editing at this point. Once your time is up, put your hard copy of the session in a safe place—not only because you should bring it to class with you, but because it's important that *you* read it yourself at some point.

   Process writing: Your instructor might ask you to do an inkshed you can share about this writing experience, a piece of **process writing** (that is, writing about your writing process itself) that reflects on what that session of proprioceptive writing was like for you and what it was like to read through the written product of that session a day or so later. This inkshed about your writing process *need not mention* at all the subject matter of your proprioceptive writing.

2. Had you ever thought about the technology of writing itself and how it might have astonished a civilization with an oral tradition to encounter written texts for the first time? Clearly Metcalf and Simon feel that writing's ability to remove "thought from its natural habitat in sound" and to lock it "into a visual field forever" is a mixed blessing. How does the visual nature of writing affect your own reading and writing habits? Do you read your own essays out loud at least once before you finish revising them, before you submit them to a professor for a grade? Do you ever slow down to read key passages of a novel or short story or poem or drama out loud so you can get a sense of the author's voice? As children most of us are encouraged *not* to move our mouths as we read (the fear is that we are sounding out each word phonetically as we read, thus slowing ourselves down and interfering with our comprehension). But sounding out each word in order to figure out what the word *is* should not be confused with being able to read a whole passage out loud fluently and expressively, a practice that often increases and enriches comprehension. Do you *hear* the sound of your own thoughts most of the time? hardly ever? Metcalf and Simon emphasize how effective writing can be as a tool to help us hear the *sound* of our thoughts precisely *because* writing slows our thinking down just enough to allow us to create a record of it. Are there times as you write when you *are* aware of listening in on your thoughts, aware of a voice that you might feel comfortable calling your own? When do those times occur? When do they *not* occur?

WRITING THE MIND ALIVE
PUTTING VOICE BACK INTO WRITING

People who attend our workshops bring with them a lot of old baggage about writing. A school-learned task for most, writing was often used as a measure of success or failure, like a test. To sweep away these associations, we sometimes begin a workshop by recontextualizing the act of writing, presenting it for what it is most fundamentally: a technology for storing speech sounds.

Before the invention of writing, the human voice was the only instrument for conveying thought and recording facts. With the invention of writing our way of remembering changed. Using alphabet-based writing, people recorded their thoughts by preserving the sounds of words in combinations of graphic symbols called letters. . . . Little about this basic process has changed to this day: the use of writing to record sound, whether done by hand, computer, or other instrument, preserves thoughts and anything expressed by words, including feelings, observations, and information, such as when wars take place, where people are born and die, and what things cost.

Although we take it for granted now, the introduction of a technology that transcribes the sounds of speech was an astounding invention—on a par with the harnessing of fire, an event that changed forever the relationship humans had to the world. Not long ago we watched a television documentary about the destruction of virgin rain forest in Brazil, in which indigenous people with an oral tradition confronted a written text for the first time in their lives. Two literate men from a first-world country sat in a circle and introduced a little game to the people of the forest. One man, clad in Bermuda shorts, says to the bare-limbed fellow by his side: "Whisper a message in my ear." The bare-limbed man does so, and the man in Bermuda shorts writes it down on a pad, then passes the pad around the circle until it reaches his literate partner on the other side of the room, who reads the message aloud.

The oral folk stare at the paper confused and amazed. On it they see some scraggly lines, some curves and dots, but nothing that transmits information or meaning to them. They pass the pad back and forth. They turn it over. They shake it. They throw it on the ground and lift it up again, press their ears against it, consult each other in hushed and nervous tones: "Can you hear the pad?" they ask. "Does it speak to you?" Each takes a turn listening but the pad does not speak. Why, then, will it speak to the literates? What power do they possess that activates voice without the use of sound? Nothing in nature explains what the forest people have heard and witnessed in the circle.

As the reaction of these oral folk dramatizes, the impact writing has on the psyche represents a new separation of the previously indivisible mind/body unit. This is the subject of *Orality and Literacy*, a remarkable work by Walter J. Ong, S.J., internationally renowned scholar, teacher, and writer, who has written extensively on the shaping influence of the alphabet, writing, and print on human consciousness. As Ong explains, writing removes thought from its natural habitat in sound and locks it permanently into a visual field forever. . . .

[W]riting separates and extends voice *away* from the speaker. Writing nails down on paper the words of the person speaking—*but just the words*. Everything else that pertains to those words, what the actual context communicates, the written message leaves out.

When you write your thoughts in Proprioceptive Writing, you bring to the visual presence of writing the aural presence of speech. We ask you to think of your thoughts in a radically new way (though it's really an ancient way as well). We ask you to imagine giving thought voice as you think it. This is easier than it sounds once you get the knack of it. You just pretend to be speaking on paper. You can always find words for anything in your mind: your ideas, feelings, mental images, beliefs, opinions, doubts, questions, reasons, memories, hopes, fantasies, regrets, disappointments, suppositions, fears, longings, desires, confusions. Every form of thought you can turn into words in your Writes. In Proprioceptive Writing, voice becomes the organ of thought and every human being has his or her own.

AWAKENING THE AUDITORY IMAGINATION

When you make the shift in Proprioceptive Writing from experiencing thought as mere words in your head to a living voice in your ear, your relationship to your thinking changes. You begin to awaken what T. S. Eliot called "auditory inwardness" and what in Proprioceptive Writing we call the *auditory imagination*—the capacity to enter your thoughts in an interested, nonjudgmental way and gain awareness of yourself from them. In terms of your psychological and spiritual well-being, this capacity is one of the most valuable you'll ever develop.

As we saw in the last section, the first step in finding your voice through Proprioceptive Writing is capturing your actual moment-to-moment thoughts in writing. The second, equally important, part is *overhearing* them *as if they were spoken.* Everyone has the innate capacity to do both; what we "say" we can "hear." So why not make full use of that capacity? After all, if we do not hear our own thoughts and gain information from them, we might as well be thinking someone else's. If you practice Proprioceptive Writing, you'll develop an awareness of the sound of your thinking. You'll begin to imagine your thoughts as a persona with a voice.

People often report to us that though a particular story they tell in a Write may be one they've told before, perhaps to their therapists, they have a more complete emotional experience of it in their Writes. Because they hear their thoughts differently *as* they are writing them, they imagine them more fully. And what they imagine most fully, they care most about.

The kind of hearing we do during a Write requires our total and undivided attention. To get a sense of what this attention feels like, imagine for a minute watching a movie about a double agent on the run. To lose himself in a crowd, our hero crashes an elegant cocktail party. We see him in the middle of the screen trying to blend in; we hear the clinking of glasses and the murmur of the guests all around him. Suddenly, the agent remembers an earlier conversation that hinted at the danger in which he now finds himself. To indicate to the audience that the character has withdrawn his awareness from the surrounding crowd and is focused totally on replaying that conversation in his head, the director cuts the sound of everything else. We see the moving mouths of the animated faces in the room but we no longer hear their voices. All we hear is our hero's thoughts—

remembering that conversation, realizing its importance, sensing his current danger, plotting his next move. For us in the audience it's like an intense form of eavesdropping. To overhear ourselves in Proprioceptive Writing, we must give our total attention to the sounds of our thoughts. Like our hero, we cannot hear ourselves think and listen to anything else at the same time.

NEW PRACTICES TO TAKE FORWARD

1. **Private writing:** You may be asked to do lots of public inkshedding—that is, informal writing to share with others—by your instructor. But your instructor probably assumes that you will turn to private writing whenever you need to, whenever you need a safe space for working out your own thoughts and feelings. Your instructors assume you're doing this because it's what most of them do. Students often imagine that any writing done by their instructors or by published authors comes out right the first time; they aren't aware of the uncountable numbers of words and pages and drafts that get scrapped before a piece of writing goes public, of the many pages of rough writing that uphold that final published essay in something like the way that nine-tenths of an iceberg floats underwater holding up the final tenth that pokes out into the air.

   We've begun saving the multiple drafts of our academic articles and books so our students can see the foot-high stacks of paper that pile up when any serious writing project is underway. Occasionally, publishing an article goes so smoothly that only four or five drafts are needed, including final copy edits and galleys; but much more often, we lose track of the number of different versions as editors and readers ask us to rethink key passages or to read and assimilate new material before submitting yet another draft.

   The point is, each time a draft is rethought or reshaped, a lot of private throwaway writing is generated. Of course, we also write privately when we're upset, when we're grieving or angry or trying to work through some emotional upheaval. But we also use private writing to work through difficult and stuck places in our thinking. Occasionally, if we trust someone completely, we might risk sharing our private writing with them to see if they believe we're on to something; but even then, we'll probably revise and clean up our original scrawl a bit so they won't be too distracted by our cryptic asides and abbreviations and notes to ourselves.

   You don't need an instructor to assign something in order for you to do it. If you need to do a bit of private writing, for any reason, go ahead and do it. You can always come back to these few pages to remind yourself of Metcalf and Simon's suggestions about how to hear the sound of your own thoughts. *Create a safe place to keep all your private writing so you can re-read it if you need to.*

Metcalf and Simon also suggest four concluding questions that you can ask yourself and answer in writing each time you finish a private writing session:

What thoughts were heard but not written?

How or what do I feel now?

What larger story is [this piece] part of?

What ideas came up for future writ[ing]? (39–41).

You can always skim through your answers to these questions in your private writing if you're looking for reminders of things to explore further. Keep and use your private writing in whatever way works best for you—after all, it's yours.

2. **Process writing:** Your instructor may from time to time assign pieces of process writing, inkshedding about how your writing went on a particular project or during a particular writing session. Often these will take the form of letters accompanying the final draft of a formal essay you're submitting for a grade. But writing these assigned pieces of process writing will be much easier if you get in the habit of doing a tiny bit of process writing every time you inkshed. Here's how: when your inkshedding time is up, draw a quick straight line under the last line of your inkshed and then reflect for a minute or two about how your writing went during that inkshed. Were you tired or alert? hot or cold? attentive or distracted by something? too hungry or too full? *Where* were you writing—in a quiet protected place, in a noisy café, in a computer lab, in front of a TV with the volume turned up loud? How do you feel about the writing session—frustrated? contented? relieved to have it over with? wishing you had more time, feeling you still had lots more to say? What were you writing with—a favourite pen? a clunky old computer with several keys sticking as you type?

Over time you'll discover what factors actually make a difference to you. You'll notice recurring features when writing goes well or badly. But you can't notice them if you don't catch them immediately; you can't notice patterns in data you didn't collect. Think of yourself as an anthropologist studying yourself and your writing habits. Try to notice details you might initially think unimportant—like the time of day when you're writing. Perhaps you'll discover that you never manage to write anything interesting until after midnight—or the exact opposite, that you're so tired from 7:00 p.m. onward that you might as well just give up and go to bed and start again in the morning.

Try writing longer process pieces as well whenever you think they'll help. Collect them in a process writing folder. We know of one entire book that grew from random pieces of process writing: one frustrated writer simply jotted down bits of process writing every time he got stuck and then threw those bits into a manila folder. The book ended up being called *Writing Without Teachers* and having a major influence on the field of composition and rhetoric. First published in 1973, it remains one of the best-selling books on writing; a second edition came out in 1998.

We're not suggesting, though, that you need to make a published book from your process writing—only that you can find process writing a great help in figuring out what works and what doesn't work for you as a writer. Getting into the habit of reflecting on your writing process is one of the most effective things you can do to improve your writing and the way you feel about the writing tasks you have to face.

Helen Keller, from *The Story of My Life*

Helen Keller (1880–1968) was not born blind or deaf, but a severe disease when she was nineteen months old left her permanently without sight or hearing. Her own account (in Chapters 4 and 6 of *The Story of My Life*) of her trapped and frustrated years before the arrival of her teacher, Anne Sullivan, has never been surpassed in its ability to capture the exact moment when a life without language turned into a life exhilarated and transformed by language. The play *The Miracle Worker* (a fine old film of it exists with Patty Duke as Helen and Anne Bancroft as Anne Sullivan) also focuses on that exact moment and presents vividly the same question raised by Keller's autobiography: to what extent does our very humanity depend on language? If Helen had only been deaf, she could at least have entered language visually: reading, writing, and of course, primarily signing would have been accessible to her. If she had only been blind, she would have learned to speak: aural language would have been her natural medium. But unable to see *or* to hear, she was locked inside her body with no connection beyond touch, taste, smell, and the vibrations and temperature changes she could sense around her. She was also locked inside the present without a way to conceptualize the future or reflect on the past. Clearly, she was a human being—but one so isolated, so cut off from her *own* mind let alone anyone else's, that her parents feared for her.

The two letters that follow Keller's account give Anne Sullivan's perspective on the same events. Sullivan, who lost her own sight at an early age and who trained at the Perkins Institution for the Blind, wrote these letters to a former teacher of hers there (Sullivan's sight had been partially restored by the time she became Helen's teacher of

Braille and sign language). We can see through Sullivan's words the wild child Helen coming moment by moment into fuller ownership of her human birthright, a full life in language, revealing to her teacher how closely our ways with words are connected with our ways of being human.

INKSHEDDING PROMPTS

1. Are there any experiences in your own life that come to mind as you read Helen Keller and Anne Sullivan's words? Tell whatever memory comes to you, whether it's about your own early struggles with learning to read or write, about disabilities of your own or those of someone close to you, or about what language has meant to you.

2. Helen Keller's *The Story of My Life* leads us to think about the role of words in our interactions with others and in our relation to the world around us— but there are other forms of "language" and expression available to us. Perhaps if Keller had never learned to speak or read or write or sign, she might have thrown herself into the language of dance or sculpture or drumming or mathematics or athletics—if she could have somehow come to know that these other "languages" existed. Which of those options might she have learned without hearing or sight or access to verbal language? What symbol systems or non-verbal modes of expression and communication are important in your life? Describe one of them in enough physical detail so we can inhabit it for a moment and understand from the inside what it means to you as a way to think and to express yourself.

THE STORY OF MY LIFE

CHAPTER IV

The most important day I remember in all my life is the one on which my teacher, Anne Mansfield Sullivan, came to me. I am filled with wonder when I consider the immeasurable contrast between the two lives which it connects. It was the third of March, 1887, three months before I was seven years old.

On the afternoon of that eventful day, I stood on the porch, dumb, expectant. I guessed vaguely from my mother's signs and from the hurrying to and fro in the house that something unusual was about to happen, so I went to the door and waited on the steps. The afternoon sun penetrated the mass of honeysuckle that covered the porch, and fell on my upturned face. My fingers lingered almost unconsciously on the familiar leaves and blossoms which had just come forth to greet the sweet southern spring. I did not know what the future held of marvel or surprise for me. Anger and bitterness had preyed upon me continually for weeks and a deep languor had succeeded this passionate struggle.

Have you ever been at sea in a dense fog, when it seemed as if a tangible white darkness shut you in, and the great ship, tense and anxious, groped her way toward the shore with plummet and sounding-line, and you waited with beating heart for something to happen? I was like that ship before my education began, only I was without compass or sounding-line, and had no way of knowing how near the harbour was. "Light! give me light!" was the wordless cry of my soul, and the light of love shone on me in that very hour.

I felt approaching footsteps. I stretched out my hand as I supposed to my mother. Some one took it, and I was caught up and held close in the arms of her who had come to reveal all things to me, and, more than all things else, to love me.

The morning after my teacher came she led me into her room and gave me a doll. The little blind children at the Perkins Institution had sent it and Laura Bridgman had dressed it; but I did not know this until afterward. When I had played with it a little while, Miss Sullivan slowly spelled into my hand the word "d-o-l-l." I was at once interested in this finger play and tried to imitate it. When I finally succeeded in making the letters correctly I was flushed with childish pleasure and pride. Running downstairs to my mother I held up my hand and made the letters for doll. I did not know that I was spelling a word or even that words existed; I was simply making my fingers go in monkey-like imitation. In the days that followed I learned to spell in this uncomprehending way a great many words, among them *pin, hat, cup* and a few verbs like *sit, stand* and *walk*. But my teacher had been with me several weeks before I understood that everything has a name.

One day, while I was playing with my new doll, Miss Sullivan put my big rag doll into my lap also, spelled "d-o-l-l" and tried to make me understand that "d-o-l-l" applied to both. Earlier in the day we had had a tussle over the words "m-u-g" and "w-a t-e-r. " Miss Sullivan had tried to impress it upon me that "m-u-g" is *mug* and that "w-a-t-e-r" is *water*, but I persisted in confounding the two. In despair she had dropped the subject for the time, only to renew it at the first opportunity. I became impatient at her repeated attempts and, seizing the new doll, I dashed it upon the floor. I was keenly delighted when I felt the fragments of the broken doll at my feet. Neither sorrow nor regret followed my passionate outburst. I had not loved the doll. In the still, dark world in which I lived there was no strong sentiment or tenderness. I felt my teacher sweep the fragments to one side of the hearth, and I had a sense of satisfaction that the cause of my discomfort was removed. She brought me my hat, and I knew I was going out into the warm sunshine. This thought, if a wordless sensation may be called a thought, made me hop and skip with pleasure.

We walked down the path to the well-house, attracted by the fragrance of the honeysuckle with which it was covered. Someone was drawing water and my teacher placed my hand under the spout. As the cool stream gushed over one hand she spelled into the other the word *water*, first slowly, then rapidly. I stood still, my whole attention fixed upon the motions of her fingers. Suddenly I felt a misty consciousness as of something forgotten—a thrill of returning thought; and somehow the mystery of language was revealed to me. I knew then that "w-a-t-e-r" meant the wonderful cool something that was flowing over my hand. That living word awakened my soul, gave it light, hope, joy, set it free! There were barriers still, it is true, but barriers that could in time be swept away.

I left the well-house eager to learn. Everything had a name, and each name gave birth to a new thought. As we returned to the house every object which I touched seemed to quiver with life. That was because I saw everything with the strange, new sight that had come to me. On entering the door I remembered the doll I had broken. I felt my way to the hearth and picked up the pieces. I tried vainly to put them together. Then my eyes filled with tears; for I realized what I had done, and for the first time I felt repentance and sorrow.

I learned a great many new words that day. I do not remember what they all were; but I do know that *mother, father, sister, teacher* were among them—words that were to make the world blossom for me, "like Aaron's rod, with flowers." It would have been difficult to find a happier child than I was as I lay in my crib at the close of that eventful day and lived over the joys it had brought me, and for the first time longed for a new day to come.

CHAPTER VI

I had now the key to all language, and I was eager to learn to use it. Children who hear acquire language without any particular effort; the words that fall from others' lips they catch on the wing, as it were, delightedly, while the little deaf child must trap them by a slow and often painful process. But whatever the process, the result is wonderful. Gradually from naming an object we advance step by step until we have traversed the vast distance between our first stammered syllable and the sweep of thought in a line of Shakespeare.

At first, when my teacher told me about a new thing I asked very few questions. My ideas were vague, and my vocabulary was inadequate; but as my knowledge of things grew, and I learned more and more words, my field of inquiry broadened, and I would return again and again to the same subject, eager for further information. Sometimes a new word revived an image that some earlier experience had engraved on my brain.

I remember the morning that I first asked the meaning of the word "love." This was before I knew many words. I had found a few early violets in the garden and brought them to my teacher. She tried to kiss me; but at that time I did not like to have anyone kiss me except my mother. Miss Sullivan put her arm gently round me and spelled into my hand, "I love Helen."

"What is love?" I asked.

She drew me closer to her and said, "It is here," pointing to my heart, whose beats I was conscious of for the first time. Her words puzzled me very much because I did not then understand anything unless I touched it.

I smelt the violets in her hand and asked, half in words, half in signs, a question which meant, "Is love the sweetness of flowers?"

"No," said my teacher.

Again I thought. The warm sun was shining on us.

"Is this not love?" I asked, pointing in the direction from which the heat came, "Is this not love?"

It seemed to me that there could be nothing more beautiful than the sun, whose warmth makes all things grow. But Miss Sullivan shook her head, and I was greatly puzzled and disappointed. I thought it strange that my teacher could not show me love.

A day or two afterward I was stringing beads of different sizes in symmetrical groups—two large beads, three small ones, and so on. I had made many mistakes, and Miss Sullivan had pointed them out again and again with gentle patience. Finally I noticed a very obvious error in the sequence and for an instant I concentrated my attention on the lesson and tried to think how I should have arranged the beads. Miss Sullivan touched my forehead and spelled with decided emphasis, "Think."

In a flash I knew that the word was the name of the process that was going on in my head. This was my first conscious perception of an abstract idea.

For a long time I was still—I was not thinking of the beads in my lap, but trying to find a meaning for "love" in the light of this new idea. The sun had been under a cloud all day, and there had been brief showers; but suddenly the sun broke forth in all its southern splendour.

Again I asked my teacher, "Is this not love?"

"Love is something like the clouds that were in the sky before the sun came out," she replied. Then in simpler words than these, which at that time I could not have understood, she explained: "You cannot touch the clouds, you know; but you feel the rain and know how glad the flowers and the thirsty earth are to have it after a hot day. You cannot touch love either; but you feel the sweetness that it pours into everything. Without love you would not be happy or want to play."

The beautiful truth burst upon my mind—I felt that there were invisible lines stretched between my spirit and the spirits of others.

From the beginning of my education Miss Sullivan made it a practice to speak to me as she would speak to any hearing child; the only difference was that she spelled the sentences into my hand instead of speaking them. If I did not know the words and idioms necessary to express my thoughts she supplied them, even suggesting conversation when I was unable to keep up my end of the dialogue.

This process was continued for several years; for the deaf child does not learn in a month, or even in two or three years, the numberless idioms and expressions used in the simplest daily intercourse. The little hearing child learns these from constant repetition and imitation. The conversation he hears in his home stimulates his mind and suggests topics and calls forth the spontaneous expression of his own thoughts. This natural exchange of ideas is denied to the deaf child. My teacher, realizing this, determined to supply the kinds of stimulus I lacked. This she did by repeating to me as far as possible, verbatim, what she heard, and by showing me how I could take part in the conversation. But it was a long time before I ventured to take the initiative, and still longer before I could find something appropriate to say at the right time.

The deaf and the blind find it very difficult to acquire the amenities of conversation. How much more this difficulty must be augmented in the case of those who are both deaf and blind! They cannot distinguish the tone of the voice or, without assistance, go up and down the gamut of tones that give significance to words; nor can they watch the expression of the speaker's face, and a look is often the very soul of what one says.

LETTERS FROM ANNE SULLIVAN

April 5, 1887

I must write you a line this morning because something very important has happened. Helen has taken the second great step in her education. She has learned that *everything has a name, and that the manual alphabet is the key to everything she wants to know.*

In a previous letter I think I wrote you that "mug" and "milk" had given Helen more trouble than all the rest. She confused the nouns with the verb "drink." She didn't know the word for "drink," but went through the pantomime of drinking whenever she spelled "mug" or "milk." This morning, while she was washing, she wanted to know the name for "water." When she wants to know the name of anything, she points to it and pats my hand. I spelled "w-a-t-e-r" and thought no more about it until after breakfast. Then it occurred to me that with the help of this new word I might succeed in straightening out the "mug-milk" difficulty. We went out to the pump-house, and I made Helen hold her mug under the spout while I pumped. As the cold water gushed forth, filling the mug, I spelled "w-a-t-e-r" in Helen's free hand. The word coming so close upon the sensation of cold water rushing over her hand seemed to startle her. She dropped the mug and stood as one transfixed. A new light came into her face. She spelled "water" several times. Then she dropped on the ground and asked for its name and pointed to the pump and the trellis, and suddenly turning round she asked for my name. I spelled "Teacher." Just then the nurse brought Helen's little sister into the pump-house, and Helen spelled "baby" and pointed to the nurse. All the way back to the house she was highly excited, and learned the name of every object she touched, so that in a few hours she had added thirty new words to her vocabulary. Here are some of them: *Door, open, shut, give, go, come,* and a great many more.

P.S.—I didn't finish my letter in time to get it posted last night; so I shall add a line. Helen got up this morning like a radiant fairy. She has flitted from object to object, asking the name of everything and kissing me for very gladness. Last night when I got in bed, she stole into my arms of her own accord and kissed me for the first time, and I thought my heart would burst, so full was it of joy.

April 10, 1887

I see an improvement in Helen from day to day, almost from hour to hour. Everything must have a name now. Wherever we go, she asks eagerly for the names of things she has not learned at home. She is anxious for her friends to spell, and eager to teach the letters to everyone she meets. She drops the signs and pantomime she used before, as soon as she has words to supply their place, and the acquirement of a new word affords her the liveliest pleasure. And we notice that her face grows more expressive each day.

I have decided not to try to have regular lessons for the present. I am going to treat Helen exactly like a two-year-old child. It occurred to me the other day that it is absurd to require a child to come to a certain place at a certain time and recite certain lessons, when he has not yet acquired a working vocabulary. I sent Helen away and sat down to think. I asked myself, *"How does a normal child learn language?"* The answer was simple, "By imitation." The child comes into the world with the ability to learn, and he learns of himself, provided he is supplied with sufficient outward stimulus. He sees people do things, and he tries to do them. He hears others speak, and he tries to speak. *But long before he utters his first word, he understands what is said to him.* I have been observing Helen's little cousin lately. She is about fifteen months old, and already understands a great deal. In response to questions she points out prettily her nose, mouth, eye, chin, cheek, ear. If I say, "Where is baby's other ear?" she points it out correctly. If I hand her a flower, and say, "Give it to mamma," she takes it to her mother. If I say, "Where is the little rogue?" she hides behind her mother's chair, or covers her face with her hands and peeps out at me with an expression of genuine roguishness. She obeys many commands like these: "Come," "Kiss," "Go to papa," "Shut the door," "Give me the biscuit." But I have not heard her try to say any of these words, although they have been repeated hundreds of times in her hearing, and it is perfectly evident that she understands them. These observations have given me a clue to the method to be followed in teaching Helen language. *I shall talk into her hand as we talk into the baby's ears.* I shall assume that she has the normal child's capacity of assimilation and imitation. *I shall use complete sentences in talking to her,* and fill out the meaning with gestures and her descriptive signs when necessity requires it; but I shall not try to keep her mind fixed on any one thing. I shall do all I can to interest and stimulate it, and wait for results.

A NEW PRACTICE TO TAKE FORWARD

1. **Marking up your text as you read:** Most of us had it hammered into our heads from first to twelfth grades that we should *never* mark up our textbooks, especially if they didn't belong to us and had to be returned to the school district at the end of each year. But a big change takes place in university when this habit needs to be unlearned (except, of course, with library books). When students buy textbooks, it's a false economy to keep these purchased texts in pristine unmarked condition in the hope of increasing their resale value at the end of term. After all, students buy texts in order to be fully participating members of each class they're taking, in order to learn as much as they possibly can.

    If you're taking a writing course or any kind of course that is asking you to do a lot of writing and to think about your writing processes, you'll need to practise reading like a writer. And *writers mark up the texts they read.* They roll up their sleeves and get down there in the trenches and mess around with the words and the sentences. They mark lines they love and want to remember for qualities of sound or style or meaning or all three together. They mark things they hate and write "good grief!" in the margin. They fill up the blank space at the end of a chapter with a quick summary of what went on in there—or with a heated argument showing why they disagree. They make connections and contrasts ("but look at what she says on page 23, the exact opposite!" or "link this up with the example on page 101"). By the time they've finished reading a book, they could probably write a quick, detailed response to it based on their **marginalia** (the comments they've written in the margins) alone, without even re-reading the book first—though any serious author would read someone else's book several times before publishing anything about it.

    Those who learn to read like writers are *active* readers. They're shaping the meaning of the text as they read it, literally "making sense" of it, actively constructing meaning. They don't just run their eyes across the print. And when they re-read, they interact with their previous selves through that marginalia—sometimes many years later and shocked to see how their reactions have changed. Believe us, we know—one of us is still embarrassed by a huge "good grief" from thirty-four years ago, a "good grief" that now marks one of her favourite passages. The margins of the books we read are a reading history of our lives and are a great resource for us as writers.

    Be warned that from this point on your instructor might do a spot check of your texts during class just to see who is actually marking up the readings and who is not. No points whatsoever are given for neatness or beautifully blank margins. It is of course possible that a university bookstore might pay a bit more for an unmarked text (if they are willing to buy the text back at all—many texts come out in new editions every few years, and yours will have absolutely no resale value if a new edition is due for the following September). But many students *like* buying used texts with comments in the margin—they find the marginalia intriguing, sometimes helpful, and often companionable: marginal comments make them feel as if they have company while they read the text for the first time. Of course, there's always the chance that if you allow yourself to wrestle with a book, to make your mark on the readings in it, you may get attached to it. You may find it's become an important extension of your mind and that you want to hang onto it.

But that decision isn't the important one. What's crucial is getting what's inside the book to go inside your head in the first place—and that rarely happens if you fail to interact physically with the words on the page as you read. Of course, an added bonus is that inkshedding is much easier if you've marked or highlighted a text while you were reading it. All you need to do to get an inkshed started is to glance back at what you've marked, pick a highlighted passage or one of your marginal comments, and start writing from there. If your mind grinds to a halt mid-inkshed, just glance back at the reading again and jump off from yet another highlighted passage. Try it.

Malcolm X, from "Saved" in *The Autobiography of Malcolm X*

Born in Nebraska in 1925, Malcolm X moved frequently as a child because various white groups (among them the Ku Klux Klan) repeatedly threatened and harassed his family. Malcolm's father, the Reverend Earl Little, was an outspoken supporter of the Universal Negro Improvement Association. In 1929, in Lansing, Michigan, four-year-old Malcolm awoke one night to pistol shots, yelling, and fire: his "earliest vivid memory" is of standing outside in the dark with his parents, brothers, and sisters to watch his home burn to the ground.

After an early life of street hustling and crime in Harlem and Boston, he found himself in prison as a convicted thief—and this is where the following selection takes over. Reading Steven Pinker's piece at the end of this Conversation, one is tempted to speculate that once Malcolm's basic needs (for food and shelter) were supplied and he had illegal drugs out of his system, his instinct for language kicked in big-time.

Malcolm X left prison a changed man and a devout follower of Elijah Muhammad, the leader of the Temple of Islam. He had dropped his father's last name—since he now knew it was not his true name, but a name given to his family by white slave owners—and became a spokesman for black Americans. However, as a result of a trip to Mecca in the early 1960s, he made known his new conviction that the Nation of Islam differed significantly from the Muslim faith. He was assassinated in New York City on February 21, 1965. Controversy still exists over who actually killed him, but a few members of the Nation of Islam were convicted of the crime.

In 1963, Alex Haley—who had published an interview with Malcolm X in *Playboy* the previous year—had begun work on *The Autobiography of Malcolm X*, the book from which this selection is taken. Malcolm X met frequently with Haley and read and approved the final manuscript, but didn't live to see it published; after Malcolm X's death, Haley wrote an epilogue for the book describing the assassination and the last weeks of Malcolm's life, including one of Malcolm's last memories (exactly one week to the day before he was killed), the early morning fire bombing and destruction of the small house in which he, his pregnant wife, Betty, and his four little daughters lived. One the most famous and influential autobiographies of the 20th century, Haley and Malcolm X's collaborative work had a profound effect on the Civil Rights movement in the United States. And not least among its effects is the book Alex Haley later came to research and write, *Roots*—the account of one black man who *was* finally able to discover the exact village in Africa from which his family had been taken and, thus, his true family name.

INKSHEDDING PROMPTS

1. What do you think of Malcolm X's claim that a prison is a better place to learn than a university? Inkshed about the distractions of college or of your family responsibilities—what's frustrating about them, what's good about them? Are there any that you could eliminate or reduce in order to focus more fully on the reading, thinking, and writing you want to do while you're still a student? Would several months in prison—assuming it was a safe place for you to be, with adequate privacy and an established routine—allow you to concentrate in a way you can't do now?

2. Is there a passage in this selection that irritated or upset you? Identify it by page number and then use your fifteen to twenty minutes of writing to look at it sentence by sentence, even word by word, if necessary. Can you find the exact spot that gives you the most difficulty or makes you the most resistant? Where do you think your reaction comes from?

3. Have you ever known anyone to read a dictionary cover to cover in the way Malcolm X does? or known a person who could not be pried "out of books

with a wedge"? Inkshed about that person and their reading habits, even if (*especially* if) that person happens to be you.

THE AUTOBIOGRAPHY OF MALCOLM X
from SAVED

It was because of my letters that I happened to stumble upon starting to acquire some kind of a homemade education.

I became increasingly frustrated at not being able to express what I wanted to convey in letters that I wrote, especially those to Mr. Elijah Muhammad. In the street, I had been the most articulate hustler out there—I had commanded attention when I said something. But now, trying to write simple English, I not only wasn't articulate, I wasn't even functional. How would I sound writing in slang, the way I would *say* it, something such as, "Look, daddy, let me pull your coat about a cat, Elijah Muhammad—"

Many who today hear me somewhere in person, or on television, or those who read something I've said, will think I went to school far beyond the eighth grade. This impression is due entirely to my prison studies.

It had really begun back in the Charlestown Prison, when Bimbi first made me feel envy of his stock of knowledge. Bimbi had always taken charge of any conversations he was in, and I had tried to emulate him. But every book I picked up had few sentences which didn't contain anywhere from one to nearly all of the words that might as well have been in Chinese. When I just skipped those words, of course, I really ended up with little idea of what the book said. So I had come to the Norfolk Prison Colony still going through only book-reading motions. Pretty soon, I would have quit even these motions, unless I had received the motivation that I did.

I saw that the best thing I could do was get hold of a dictionary—to study, to learn some words. I was lucky enough to reason also that I should try to improve my penmanship. It was sad. I couldn't even write in a straight line. It was both ideas together that moved me to request a dictionary along with some tablets and pencils from the Norfolk Prison Colony school.

I spent two days just riffling uncertainly through the dictionary's pages. I'd never realized so many words existed! I didn't know *which* words I needed to learn. Finally, just to start some kind of action, I began copying.

In my slow, painstaking, ragged handwriting, I copied into my tablet everything printed on that first page, down to the punctuation marks.

I believe it took me a day. Then, aloud, I read back, to myself, everything I'd written on the tablet. Over and over, aloud, to myself, I read my own handwriting.

I woke up the next morning, thinking about those words—immensely proud to realize that not only had I written so much at one time, but I'd written words that I never knew were in the world. Moreover, with a little effort, I also could remember what many of these words meant. I reviewed the words whose meanings I didn't remember. Funny thing, from the dictionary first page right now, that "aardvark" springs to my mind. The dictionary had a picture of it, a long-tailed, long-eared, burrowing African mammal, which lives off termites caught by sticking out its tongue as an anteater does for ants.

I was so fascinated that I went on—I copied the dictionary's next page. And the same experience came when I studied that. With every succeeding page, I also learned of people and places and events from history. Actually the dictionary is like a miniature encyclopedia. Finally the dictionary's A section had filled a whole tablet—and I went on into the B's. That was the way I started copying what eventually became the entire dictionary. It went a lot faster after so much practice helped me to pick up handwriting speed. Between what I wrote in my tablet, and writing letters, during the rest of my time in prison I would guess I wrote a million words.

I suppose it was inevitable that as my word-base broadened, I could for the first time pick up a book and read and now begin to understand what the book was saying. Anyone who has read a great deal can imagine the new world that opened. Let me tell you something: from then until I left that prison, in every free moment I had, if I was not reading in the library, I was reading on my bunk. You couldn't have gotten me out of books with a wedge. Between Mr. Muhammad's teachings, my correspondence, my visitors—usually Ella and Reginald—and my reading of books, months passed without my even thinking about being imprisoned. In fact, up to then, I never had been so truly free in my life.

The Norfolk Prison Colony's library was in the school building. A variety of classes was taught there by instructors who came from such places as Harvard and Boston universities. The weekly debates between inmate teams were also held in the school building. You would be astonished to know how worked up convict debaters and audiences would get over subjects like "Should Babies Be Fed Milk?"

Available on the prison library's shelves were books on just about every general subject. Much of the big private collection that Parkhurst had willed to the prison was still in crates and boxes in the back of the library—thousands of old books. Some of them looked ancient: covers faded, old-time parchment-looking binding. Parkhurst, I've mentioned, seemed to have been principally interested in history and religion. He had the money and the special interest to have a lot of books that you wouldn't have in general circulation. Any college library would have been lucky to get that collection.

As you can imagine, especially in a prison where there was heavy emphasis on rehabilitation, an inmate was smiled upon if he demonstrated an unusually intense interest in books. There was a sizable number of well-read inmates, especially the popular debaters. Some were said by many to be practically walking encyclopedias. They were almost celebrities. No university would ask any student to devour literature as I did when this new world opened to me, of being able to read and *understand*.

I read more in my room than in the library itself. An inmate who was known to read a lot could check out more than the permitted maximum number of books. I preferred reading in the total isolation of my own room.

When I had progressed to really serious reading, every night at about ten P.M. I would be outraged with the "lights out." It always seemed to catch me right in the middle of something engrossing.

Fortunately, right outside my door was a corridor light that cast a glow into my room. The glow was enough to read by, once my eyes adjusted to it. So when "lights out" came, I would sit on the floor where I could continue reading in that glow.

At one-hour intervals the night guards paced past every room. Each time I heard the approaching footsteps, I jumped into bed and feigned sleep. And as soon as the guard passed, I got back out of bed onto the floor area of that light-glow, where I would read for another fifty-eight minutes—until the guard approached again. That went on until three or four every morning. Three or four hours of sleep a night was enough for me. Often in the years in the streets I had slept less than that.

The teachings of Mr. Muhammad stressed how history had been "whitened"—when white men had written history books, the black man simply had been left out. Mr. Muhammad couldn't have said anything that would have struck me much harder. I had never forgotten how when my class, me and all of those whites, had studied seventh-grade United States history back in Mason, the history of the Negro had been covered in one paragraph, and the teacher had gotten a big laugh with his joke, "Negroes' feet are so big that when they walk, they leave a hole in the ground."

This is one reason why Mr. Muhammad's teachings spread so swiftly all over the United States, among *all* Negroes, whether or not they became followers of Mr. Muhammad. The teachings ring true—to every Negro. You can hardly show me a black adult in America—or a white one, for that matter—who knows from the history books anything like the truth about the black man's role. In my own case, once I heard of the "glorious history of the black man," I took special pains to hunt in the library for books that would inform me on details about black history. . . .

Ten guards and the warden couldn't have torn me out of those books. Not even Elijah Muhammad could have been more eloquent than those books were in providing indisputable proof that the collective white man had acted like a devil in virtually every contact he had with the world's collective non-white man. . . .

I have often reflected upon the new vistas that reading opened to me. I knew right there in prison that reading had changed forever the course of my life. As I see it today, the ability to read awoke inside me some long dormant craving to be mentally alive. I certainly wasn't seeking any degree, the way a college confers a status symbol upon its students.

My homemade education gave me, with every additional book that I read, a little bit more sensitivity to the deafness, dumbness, and blindness that was afflicting the black race in America. Not long ago, an English writer telephoned me from London, asking questions. One was, "What's your alma mater?" I told him, "Books." You will never catch me with a free fifteen minutes in which I'm not studying something I feel might be able to help the black man.

Yesterday I spoke in London, and both ways on the plane across the Atlantic I was studying a document about how the United Nations proposes to insure the human rights of the oppressed minorities of the world. The American black man is the world's most shameful case of minority oppression. What makes the black man think of himself as only an internal United States issue is just a catch-phrase, two words, "civil rights." How is the black man going to get "civil rights" before first he wins his *human* rights? If the American black man will start thinking about his *human* rights, and then start thinking of himself as part of one of the world's great peoples, he will see he has a case for the United Nations.

I can't think of a better case! Four hundred years of black blood and sweat invested here in America, and the white man still has the black man begging for what every immigrant fresh off the ship can take for granted the minute he walks down the gangplank.

But I'm digressing. I told the Englishman that my alma mater was books, a good library. Every time I catch a plane, I have with me a book that I want to read—and that's a lot of books these days. If I weren't out here every day battling the white man, I could spend the rest of my life reading, just satisfying my curiosity—because you can hardly mention anything I'm not curious about. I don't think anybody ever got more out of going to prison than I did. In fact, prison enabled me to study far more intensively than I would have if my life had gone differently and I had attended some college. I imagine that one of the biggest troubles with colleges is there are too many distractions, too much panty-raiding, fraternities, and boola-boola and all of that. Where else but in a prison could I have attacked my ignorance by being able to study intensely sometimes as much as fifteen hours a day?

A NEW PRACTICE TO TAKE FORWARD

Using the dictionary and keeping a word hoard: Not many of us decide to improve our reading comprehension by copying out entire dictionaries, page by page, as Malcolm X did. But most powerful readers and writers have a good dictionary by their side as they work and they consult it frequently—if not *while* they're reading something, then immediately afterwards.

For instance, we often read pretty quickly through an essay the first time, trying to pick up from the overall context clues to the meaning of words we don't recognize or understand. If we don't consult a dictionary immediately as each strange word comes up, we usually mark those words in some way as we read on (perhaps with a question mark in the margin) and then come back to them after we've finished the whole piece. When we look them up at that point, we might write a brief definition in the margin and perhaps re-read a whole passage if the dictionary definition makes a difference in how we would interpret the passage. Also, even if we thought we already knew the meaning of a word, if the word snagged our attention as being used in a new way or with a subtle connotation we weren't familiar with, we might mark it and look it up. Sometimes even ordinary words can begin to seem more complex and worth examining in the *OED* (the *Oxford English Dictionary*) to see if there's something going on in the history of a word or its past uses that we weren't yet aware of. Consider, for instance, the use of the word "honest" in Shakespeare's *Othello,* a word that most of us think we understand, but that Shakespeare uses to (among other things) underscore class differences, insult underlings ("honest Iago"), create irony, and accuse Desdemona of adultery.

If you haven't yet used the *OED,* now is the time. The online version is especially easy to use, but be prepared for a whole new dictionary experience. The *OED* is not for quick look-ups, but for thoughtful research into the world of each word. A rule of thumb: the shorter and more common the word, the longer the definition is likely to be. Some definitions can go on for many pages (and we're talking *big* pages, single-spaced, small print).

How can this be? The goal of the *OED* is to show how writers have used a word with changing gradations of meaning throughout the history of the English language. So each time a word was used for the first time with a new shade of meaning, the *OED* tries to capture that moment; it registers the first sentence in which lexicographers were able to find that word in print, used in that exact way (obviously, the *OED*—while the brainchild of one man initially—is written and updated by a huge team of scholars; the man who started it all, James A. H. Murray, died in 1915, thirteen years before the full first edition was published). Therefore, since each definition includes many sentences in which the word is used (with separate sections for each possible meaning of that word), words with long histories and words that are frequently used take up lots of space. Certain authors or works of literature, not surprisingly, show up again and again as having been the first to ever use a certain word in writing or the first to use it with a certain meaning: William Shakespeare, Geoffrey Chaucer, Charles Dickens, and Jane Austen appear over and over, as does the King James Bible.

Some words or meanings of words gradually die out (and these are labelled "archaic" in the dictionary); and new words and new meanings of existing words are constantly coming into being—which means the exhausted editors of the *OED* had about one day to celebrate their achievement in 1928 and then had to get back to work starting on the first of many huge supplements to record recent changes in the language. English never stands still.

In the early 1970s, there was a professor in England who kept the multi-volume set of the *OED* handy on a large window seat in his living room. With supplements, it had grown to fourteen huge volumes, each one roughly the size and weight of a concrete block. At a dinner party in his home, a graduate student, trying to be witty, joked that it must make entertaining reading on rainy winter evenings. And not joking at all, he replied, "Well, it does get a lot better as it goes along." When asked to explain, he said, "Well, D is much better than A, for example." This particular professor's life could have been described as the exact opposite of Malcolm X's— but he too found nourishment in picking up a good dictionary and reading it through sequentially, page by page. And he's not alone—writer and professor of neurology Oliver Sacks claims that when he first got his *OED* volumes, he read them through from A to Z.

We *don't* expect you to follow suit, reading the *OED* from *aardvark* to *zymurgy*. What we *will* say without apology, however, is that you can't be a serious university student and you certainly can't expect to grow as a writer unless you have a good dictionary by your side and use it. Your instructor can help if you're unsure about what exactly a "good" dictionary might be. Obviously, you can't lug a copy of the *OED* around in your backpack (though you can sometimes arrange to work close to one in the library or close to a computer terminal with access to the *OED* online or on CD-ROM). But neither can you rely on a pocket dictionary that is nothing more than a tool for checking the spelling of common words. At the very least, a decent dictionary should give some information about the **etymology** of each word (i.e., which language and which root word or words it came from).

If you have to choose between purchasing a thesaurus or a dictionary, there's no contest—forget the thesaurus. It can often lead to unintentionally funny and immediately recognizable "thesaurus writing" anyway, writing in which students— attempting to avoid repetition or to sound more scholarly—use big or odd or fancy words with connotations they don't understand, assuming that the bigger word is an exact synonym for the word it's replacing.

Get a dictionary. Use it. Look up any words in this volume that you don't understand. And then if you still need help figuring out how those words are being used, show your instructor the dictionary definitions you've found and ask for further help. Keep a list of these new words and definitions in a section of your binder—hoard them (you never know when you might need them; *hoard*, by the way, is fun to track down in the *OED*, a word that's at least a thousand years old and carries with it, mainly from *Beowulf*, images of monsters and buried treasure). From this point on, we'll assume one thing: that we'll never read another inkshed in which a student complains that an author is using words that students can't understand. We do some-times get inksheds with such complaints, and they always puzzle us: if someone wanted to encounter *only* familiar words, why would he or she attend university? Why not just stay home and read only romances, murder mysteries, and fan maga-zines? A text containing unfamiliar words is an opportunity, not a curse: it's a chance for your vocabulary to grow richer and fuller, for your powers with language to increase. Rejoice! Open that dictionary with delight and anticipation—the world is yours.

Pop Quiz: What Is a Lexicographer?

By the way, the word **lexicographer** is a good test for determining whether your dictionary is adequate for university work. A decent dictionary should at least have the word "lexicography" (with the "er" form listed after it, if not in a sepa-rate entry of its own). It should also signal to you that the two parts of the word come from the Greek words for "word" and "to write"—hence, a lexicographer is a person who writes words down, who collects words.

Further Information on the OED:

http://www.oed.com/about/history.html. This site gives a quick history of the project from its beginnings in 1857.

http://www.oed.com/about/facts.html. Here you can find basic facts—for instance, the longest entry is 60,000 words (think of a typed-up term paper approximately 200 pages long), for the word "set," which has 430 different meanings.

Eva Hoffman, from *Lost in Translation: A Life in a New Language*

Eva Hoffman grew up in Poland but immigrated in 1959, when she was thirteen—with her parents and her nine-year-old sister—to Vancouver, British Columbia. Thirty years later, in her book *Lost in Translation: A Life in a New Language*, Hoffman wrote about the desolation of her first months as a teenager in Canada. In an interview with Harry Kreisler of Berkeley's Institute of International Studies (2000), Hoffman described it as the "loss of a physical voice" and reflected on her experience:

The main impact of immigration for me was my sense of the enormous importance of language. I think that for a while I was, in effect, without language, because Polish lost its relevance to this new world and there were very few people with whom I could speak Polish, and I hadn't yet come into English. And I understood that to be without language is to live in a very dim world, a very dim external world and a very dim interior world. Language is not only something that we use instrumentally, but it is something that truly shapes us, and that truly shapes our perceptions of the world. I always did love language as I was growing up. I loved books. I loved language as much as music. But that sense of losing language was a very, very powerful and potent lesson in the importance of language. And so, indeed from then on, my struggle was for English to inhabit me and to acquire enough command of it so that it would articulate the world and so that it would express the world— both exterior and interior. . . . [W]riting at some point does begin to shape you and define you and to speak back to you, so to speak. And so, in a sense . . . I started constructing myself . . . shaping myself, creating myself through these exercises in writing in English, . . . trying to find any voice at all, a voice in which I could speak, . . . speak English from within, and then write in English from within. (2)

Eva Hoffman lost her birth language but adopted English with all the energy and self-discipline she could muster—and, as she acknowledges, it helped that she was young (just fourteen years old) when she received the diary in which she began writing in English. Twenty years after her arrival in North America, she took a job writing at *The New York Times*.

INKSHEDDING PROMPTS

1.   Is English your first language? If not, what is? What is it like for you to attend university and study and write in a language you did not learn as a child at home? Which of Hoffman's experiences seem similar to your own? Write about some of your own experiences trying to live and learn in a second language and relate them to one or two of hers.

2.   If English is your first language, are you able to imagine from certain passages in Hoffman's writing what her experience must have been like? Which passages help you inhabit her experience—which words, phrases, details in particular? Mention passages that you find especially moving or memorable

and try to explain in as much detail as you can why they work for you. If you prefer, identify a passage or two that confused or bothered you and write in detail about those passages, trying to figure out why they had that effect on you.

3. If you're bilingual, how has your experience with language been different from Hoffman's? Inkshed in detail about some of your stories as a speaker/thinker/writer in two languages, both of which you get to keep and use your whole life long. What's good about being bilingual? not so good? confusing?

LOST IN TRANSLATION: A LIFE IN A NEW LANGUAGE

By the time we've reached Vancouver, there are very few people left on the train. My mother has dressed my sister and me in our best outfits—identical navy blue dresses with sailor collars and gray coats handmade of good gabardine. My parents' faces reflect anticipation and anxiety. "Get off the train on the right foot," my mother tells us. "For luck in the new life."

I look out of the train window with a heavy heart. Where have I been brought to? As the train approaches the station, I see what is indeed a bit of nowhere. It's a drizzly day, and the platform is nearly empty. Everything is the colour of slate. From this bleakness, two figures approach us—a nondescript middle-aged man and woman—and after making sure that we are the right people, the arrivals from the other side of the world, they hug us; but I don't feel much warmth in their half-embarrassed embrace. "You should kneel down and kiss the ground," the man tells my parents. "You're lucky to be here." My parents' faces fill with a kind of naïve hope. Perhaps everything will be well after all. They need signs, portents, at this hour. . . .

*

For the few days we stay at the Rosenbergs', we are relegated to the basement, where there's an extra apartment usually rented out to lodgers. My father looks up to Mr. Rosenberg with the respect, even a touch of awe due to someone who is a certified millionaire. Mr. Rosenberg is a big man in the small . . . community of Polish Jews, most of whom have made good in junk peddling and real estate—but none as good as he. Mr. Rosenberg, who is now almost seventy, had the combined chutzpah and good luck to ride on Vancouver's real-estate boom—and now he's the richest of them all. This hardly makes him the most popular, but it automatically makes him the wisest. People from the community come to him for business advice, which he dispenses, in Yiddish, as if it were precious currency given away for free only through his grandiose generosity.

In the uncompromising vehemence of adolescence and injured pride, I begin to see Mr. Rosenberg not as our benefactor but as a Dickensian figure of personal tyranny, and my feeling toward him quickly rises to something that can only be called hate. He had made stinginess into principle; I feel it as a nonhuman hardness, a conversion of flesh and feeling into stone. His face never lights up with humour or affection or wit. But then, he takes himself very seriously; to him too his wealth is the proof of his righteousness. In accordance with his principles, he demands money for our train tickets from Montreal as soon as we arrive. I never forgive him. We've brought gifts we thought handsome, but in addition, my father gives him all the dollars he accumulated in Poland—something that would start us off in Canada, we thought, but is now all gone. We'll have to scratch out our living somehow, starting from zero: my father begins to pinch the flesh of his arms nervously.

Mrs. Rosenberg, a worn-faced nearly inarticulate, diffident woman, would probably show us more generosity were she not so intimidated by her husband. As it is, she and her daughter, Diane, feed us white bread with sliced cheese and bologna for lunch, and laugh at our incredulity at the mushy textures, the plastic wrapping, the presliced convenience of the various items. Privately, we comment that this is not real food: it has no taste, it smells of plastic. The two women also give us clothing they can no longer use. I can't imagine a state of affairs in which one would want to discard the delicate, transparent bathrobes and the Angora sweaters they pass on to us, but luscious though these items seem—beyond anything I ever hoped to own—the show of gratitude required from me on receiving them sours the pleasure of new ownership. "Say thank you," my mother prompts me in preparation for receiving a batch of clothing. "People like to be appreciated." I coo and murmur ingratiatingly; I'm beginning to master the trick of saying thank you with just the right turn of the head, just the right balance between modesty and obsequiousness. In the next few years, this is a skill I'll have to use often. But in my heart I feel no real gratitude at being the recipient of so much mercy.

On about the third night at the Rosenbergs' house, I have a nightmare in which I'm drowning in the ocean while my mother and father swim farther and farther away from me. I know, in this dream, what it is to be cast adrift in incomprehensible space; I know what it is to lose one's mooring. I wake up in the middle of a prolonged scream. The fear is stronger than anything I've ever known. My parents wake up and hush me up quickly; they don't want the Rosenbergs to hear this disturbing sound. I try to calm myself and go back to sleep, but I feel as though I've stepped through a door into a dark place. Psychoanalysts talk about "mutative insights," through which the patient gains an entirely new perspective and discards some part of a cherished neurosis. The primal scream of my birth into the New World is a mutative insight of a negative kind—and I know that I can never lose the knowledge it brings me. The black, bituminous terror of the dream solders itself to the chemical base of my being—and from then on, fragments of the fear lodge themselves in my consciousness, thorns and pinpricks of anxiety, loose electricity floating in a psyche that has been forcibly pried from its structures. Eventually, I become accustomed to it; I know that it comes, and that it also goes; but when it hits with full force, in its pure form, I call it the Big Fear.

After about a week of lodging us in his house, Mr. Rosenberg decides that he has done enough for us, and, using some acquired American wisdom, explains that it isn't good for us to be dependent on his charity; there is of course no question of kindness. There is no question, either, of Mrs. Rosenberg intervening on our behalf, as she might like to do. We have no place to go, no way to pay for a meal. And so we begin.

*

"Shut up, shuddup," the children around us are shouting, and it's the first word in English that I understand from its dramatic context. My sister and I stand in the schoolyard clutching each other, while kids all around us are running about, pummelling each other, and screaming like whirling dervishes. Both the boys and the girls look sharp and aggressive to me—the girls all have bright lipstick on, their hair sticks up and out like witches' fury, and their skirts are held up and out by stiff, wiry crinolines. I can't imagine wanting to talk their harsh-sounding language.

We've been brought to this school by Mr. Rosenberg, who, two days after our arrival, tells us he'll take us to classes that are provided by the government to teach English to newcomers. This morning, in the rinky-dink wooden barracks where the classes are held, we've acquired new names. All it takes is a brief conference between Mr. Rosenberg and the teacher, a kindly looking woman who tries to give us reassuring glances, but who has seen too many people come and go to get sentimental about a name. Mine—"Ewa"—is easy to change into its near equivalent in English, "Eva." My sister's name—"Alina"—poses more of a problem, but after a moment's thought, Mr. Rosenberg and the teacher decide that "Elaine" is close enough. My sister and I hang our heads wordlessly under this careless baptism. The teacher then introduces us to the class, mispronouncing our last name—"Wydra"—in a way we've never heard before. We make our way to a bench at the back of the room; nothing much has happened, except a small, seismic mental shift. The twist on our names takes them a tiny distance from us—but it's a gap into which the infinite hobgoblin of abstraction enters. Our Polish names didn't refer to us; they were as surely us as our eyes or hands. These new appellations, which we ourselves can't pronounce, are not us. They are identification tags, disembodied signs pointing to objects that happen to be my sister and myself. We walk to our seats into a roomful of unknown faces, with names that make us strangers to ourselves.

When the school day is over the teacher hands us a file card on which she has written, "I'm a newcomer. I'm lost. I live at 1785 Granville Street. Will you kindly show me how to get there? Thank you." We wander the streets for several hours, zigzagging back and forth through seemingly identical suburban avenues, showing this deaf-mute sign to the few people we see, until we eventually recognize the Rosenbergs' house. We're greeted by our quietly hysterical mother and Mrs. Rosenberg, who, in a ritual she has probably learned from television, puts out two glasses of milk on her red Formica counter. The milk, homogenized, and too cold from the fridge, bears little resemblance to the liquid we used to drink called by the same name.

*

Every day I learn new words, new expressions. I pick them up from school exercises, from conversations, from the books I take out of Vancouver's well-lit, cheerful public library. There are some turns of phrase to which I develop strange allergies. "You're welcome," for example, strikes me as a gaucherie, and I can hardly bring myself to say it—I suppose because it implies that there's something to be thanked for, which in Polish would be impolite. The very places where language is at its most conventional, where it should be most taken for granted, are the places where I feel the prick of artifice.

Then there are words to which I take an equally irrational liking, for their sound, or just because I'm pleased to have deduced their meaning. Mainly they're words I learn from books, like "enigmatic" or "insolent"—words that have only a literary value, that exist only as signs on the page.

But mostly, the problem is that the signifier has become severed from the signified. The words I learn now don't stand for things in the same unquestioned way they did in my native tongue. "River" in Polish was a vital sound, energized with the essence of riverhood, of my rivers, of my being immersed in rivers. "River" in English is cold—a word without an aura. It has no accumulated associations for me, and it does not give off the radiating haze of connotation. It does not evoke.

The process, alas, works in reverse as well. When I see a river now, it is not shaped, assimilated by the word that accommodates it to the psyche—a word that makes a body of water a river rather than an uncontained element. The river before me remains a thing, absolutely other, absolutely unbending to the grasp of my mind.

When my friend Penny tells me that she's envious, or happy, or disappointed, I try laboriously to translate not from English to Polish but from the word back to its source, to the feeling from which it springs. Already, in that moment of strain, spontaneity of response is lost. And anyway, the translation doesn't work. I don't know how Penny feels when she talks about envy. The word hangs in a Platonic stratosphere, a vague prototype of all envy, so large, so all-encompassing that it might crush me—as might disappointment or happiness.

I am becoming a living avatar of structuralist wisdom; I cannot help knowing that words are just themselves. But it's a terrible knowledge, without any of the consolations that wisdom usually brings. It does not mean that I'm free to play with words at my wont; anyway, words in their naked state are surely among the least satisfactory play objects. No, this radical disjoining between word and thing is a desiccating alchemy, draining the world not only of significance but of its colours, striations, nuances—its very existence. It is the loss of a living connection.

*

The worst losses come at night. As I lie down in a strange bed in a strange house—my mother is a sort of housekeeper here, to the aging Jewish man who has taken us in in return for her services—I wait for that spontaneous flow of inner language which used to be my nighttime talk with myself, my way of informing the ego where the id had been. Nothing comes. Polish, in a short time, has atrophied, shrivelled from sheer uselessness. Its words don't apply to my new experiences; they're not coeval with any of the objects, or faces, or the very air I breathe in the daytime. In English, words have not penetrated to those layers of my psyche from which a private conversation could proceed. This interval before sleep used to be the time when my mind became both receptive and alert, when images and words rose up to consciousness, reiterating what had happened during the day, adding the day's experiences to those already stored there, spinning out the thread of my personal story.

Now, this picture-and-word show is gone; the thread has been snapped. I have no interior language, and without it, interior images—those images through which we assimilate the external world, through which we take it in, love it, make it our own—become blurred too. My mother and I met a Canadian family who live down the block today. They were working in their garden and engaged us in a conversation of the "Nice weather we're having, isn't it?" variety, which culminated in their inviting us into their house. They sat stiffly on their couch, smiled in the long pauses between the conversation, and seemed at a loss for what to ask. Now my mind gropes for some description of them, but nothing fits. They're a different species from anyone I've met in Poland, and Polish words slip off of them without sticking. English words don't hook on to anything. I try, deliberately, to come up with a few. Are these people pleasant or dull? Kindly or silly? The words float in an uncertain space. They come up from a part of my brain in which labels may be manufactured but which has no connection to my instincts, quick reactions, knowledge. Even the simplest adjectives sow confusion in my mind; English kindliness has a whole system of morality behind it, a system that makes "kindness" an entirely positive virtue. Polish kindness has the tiniest element of irony. Besides, I'm beginning to feel the tug of prohibition, in English, against uncharitable words. In Polish, you can call someone an idiot without particularly harsh feelings and with the zest of a strong judgment. Yes, in Polish these people might tend toward "silly" and "dull"—but I force myself toward "kindly" and "pleasant." The cultural unconscious is beginning to exercise its subliminal influence.

The verbal blur covers these people's faces, their gestures with a sort of fog. I can't translate them into my mind's eye. The small event, instead of being added to the mosaic of consciousness and memory, falls through some black hole, and I fall with it. What has happened to me in this new world? I don't know. I don't see what I've seen, don't comprehend what's in front of me. I'm not filled with language anymore, and I have only a memory of fullness to anguish me with the knowledge that, in this dark and empty state, I don't really exist.

* * *

For my birthday, Penny gives me a diary, complete with a little lock and key to keep what I write from the eyes of all intruders. It is that little lock—the visible symbol of the privacy in which the diary is meant to exist—that creates my dilemma. If I am indeed to write something entirely for myself, in what language do I write? Several times, I open the diary and close it again. I can't decide. Writing in Polish at this point would be a little like resorting to Latin or ancient Greek, an eccentric thing to do in a diary, in which you're supposed to set down your most immediate experiences and unpremeditated thoughts in the most unmediated language. Polish is becoming a dead language, the language of the untranslatable past. But writing for nobody's eyes in English? That's like doing a school exercise, or performing in front of yourself, a slightly perverse act of self-voyeurism.

Because I have to choose something, I finally choose English. If I'm to write about the present, I have to write in the language of the present, even if it's not the language of the self. As a result, the diary becomes surely one of the more impersonal exercises of that sort produced by an adolescent girl. These are no sentimental effusions of rejected love, eruptions of familial anger, or consoling broodings about death. English is not the language of such emotions. Instead, I set down my reflections on the ugliness of wrestling; on the elegance of Mozart, and on how Dostoyevsky puts me in mind of El Greco. I write down Thoughts. I Write.

There is a certain pathos to this naïve snobbery, for the diary is an earnest attempt to create a part of my persona that I imagine I would have grown into in Polish. In the solitude of this most private act, I write, in my public language, in order to update what might have been my other self. The diary is about me and not about me at all. But on one level, it allows me to make the first jump. I learn English through writing, and, in turn, writing gives me a written self. Refracted through the double distance of English and writing, this self—my English self—becomes oddly objective; more than anything, it perceives. It exists more easily in the abstract sphere of thoughts and observations than in the world. For a while, this impersonal self, this cultural negative capability, becomes the truest thing about me. When I write, I have a real existence that is proper to the activity of writing—an existence that takes place midway between me and the sphere of artifice, art, pure language. This language is beginning to invent another me. However, I discover something odd. It seems that when I write (or, for that matter, think) in English, I am unable to use the word "I." I do not go as far as the schizophrenic "she"—but I am driven, as by a compulsion, to the double, the Siamese-twin "you."

*

My voice is doing funny things. It does not seem to emerge from the same parts of my body as before. It comes out from somewhere in my throat, tight, thin, and matte—a voice without the modulations, dips, and rises that it had before, when it went from my stomach all the way through my head. There is, of course, the constraint and the self-consciousness of an accent that I hear but cannot control. Some of my high school peers accuse me of putting it on in order to appear more "interesting." In fact, I'd do anything to get rid of it, and when I'm alone, I practice sounds for which my speech organs have no intuitions, such as "th" (I do this by putting my tongue between my teeth) and "a," which is longer and more open in Polish (by shaping my mouth into a sort of arrested grin). It is simple words like "cat" or "tap" that give me the most trouble, because they have no context of other syllables, and so people often misunderstand them. Whenever I can, I do awkward little swerves to avoid them, or pause and try to say them very clearly. Still, when people—like salesladies—hear me speak without being prepared to listen carefully, they often don't understand me the first time around. "Girls' shoes," I say, and the "girls'" comes out as a sort of scramble. "Girls' shoes," I repeat, willing the syllable to form itself properly, and the saleslady usually smiles nicely, and sends my mother and me to the right part of the store. I say "Thank you" with a sweet smile, feeling as if I'm both claiming an unfair special privilege and being unfairly patronized.

It's as important to me to speak well as to play a piece of music without mistakes. Hearing English distorted grates on me like chalk screeching on a blackboard, like all things botched and badly done, like all forms of gracelessness. The odd thing is that I know what is correct, fluent, good, long before I can execute it. The English spoken by our Polish acquaintances strikes me as jagged and thick, and I know that I shouldn't imitate it. I'm turned off by the intonations I hear on the TV sitcoms—by the expectation of laughter, like a dog's tail wagging in supplication, built into the actors' pauses, and by the curtailed, cutoff rhythms. I like the way Penny speaks, with an easy flow and a pleasure in giving words a fleshly fullness; I like what I hear in some movies; and once the Old Vic comes to Vancouver to perform *Macbeth*, and though I can hardly understand the particular words, I am riveted by the tones of sureness and command that mold the actors' speech into such majestic periods.

Sociolinguists might say that I receive these language messages as class signals, that I associate the sounds of correctness with the social status of the speaker. In part, this is undoubtedly true. The class-linked notion that I transfer wholesale from Poland is that belonging to a "better" class of people is absolutely dependent on speaking a "better" language. And in my situation especially, I know that language will be a crucial instrument, that I can overcome the stigma of my marginality, the weight of presumption against me, only if the reassuringly right sounds come out of my mouth.

Yes, speech is a class signifier. But I think that in hearing these varieties of speech around me, I'm sensitized to something else as well—something that is a matter of aesthetics, and even of psychological health. Apparently, skilled chefs can tell whether a dish from some foreign cuisine is well cooked even if they have never tasted it and don't know the genre of cooking it belongs to. There seem to be some deep-structure qualities—consistency, proportions of ingredients, smoothness of blending—that indicate culinary achievement to these educated eaters' taste buds. So each language has its own distinctive music, and even if one doesn't know its separate components, one can pretty quickly recognize the propriety of the patterns in which the components are put together, their harmonies and discords. Perhaps the crucial element that strikes the ear in listening to living speech is the degree of the speaker's self-assurance and control.

As I listen to people speaking that foreign tongue, English, I can hear when they stumble or repeat the same phrases too many times, when their sentences trail off aimlessly—or, on the contrary, when their phrases have vigor and roundness, when they have the space and the breath to give a flourish at the end of a sentence, or make just the right pause before coming to a dramatic point. I can tell, in other words, the degree of their ease or disease, the extent of authority that shapes the rhythms of their speech. That authority—in whatever dialect, in whatever variant of the mainstream language—seems to me to be something we all desire. It's not that we all want to speak the King's English, but whether we speak Appalachian or Harlem English, or Cockney, or Jamaican Creole, we want to be at home in our tongue. We want to be able to give voice accurately and fully to ourselves and our sense of the world. John Fowles, in one of his stories in *The Ebony Tower*, has a young man cruelly violate an elderly writer and his manuscripts because the legacy of language has not been passed on to the youthful vandal properly. This seems to me an entirely credible premise. Linguistic dispossession is a sufficient motive for violence, for it is close to the dispossession of one's self. Blind rage, helpless rage is rage that has no words—rage that overwhelms one with darkness. And if one is perpetually without words, if one exists in the entropy of inarticulateness, that condition itself is bound to be an enraging frustration. In my New York apartment, I listen almost nightly to fights that erupt like brushfire on the street below—and in their escalating fury of repetitious phrases ("Don't do this to me, man, you fucking bastard, I'll fucking kill you"), I hear not the pleasures of macho toughness but an infuriated beating against wordlessness, against the incapacity to make oneself understood, seen. Anger can be borne—it can even be satisfying—if it can gather into words and explode in a storm, or a rapier-sharp attack. But without this means of ventilation, it only turns back inward, building and swirling like a head of steam—building to an impotent, murderous rage. If all therapy is speaking therapy—a talking cure—then perhaps all neurosis is a speech dis-ease.

June Callwood, "Why Canada Has to Beat Its Literacy Problem"

Born in Ontario in 1924, June Callwood moved from being editor of her school newspaper into a career in journalism. At the age of twenty, she already had a reporting job at Toronto's *Globe and Mail*; because *The Globe* had a policy of not hiring married women, she had to keep her marriage two years later a secret and write under her maiden name. As a mother of four children, she continued writing freelance, publishing many of her pieces in *Maclean's* magazine and also ghostwriting books on the lives of several prominent Americans, including Charles Mayo, Otto Preminger, and Barbara Walters. The first book she wrote under her own name (*Love, Hate, Fear and Anger*) came in the 1950s, resulting from research she did after a bout of serious depression.

Callwood hosted CBC's television program *In Touch* from 1975 to 1978 and co-hosted a recent series called *Caregiving*, a program designed to provide assistance to the many people serving as sole caregivers for loved ones—for aged parents, children with disabilities, or partners with AIDS. Callwood has founded or co-founded over fifty social action organizations and was awarded the Order of Canada in 1986 in recognition of her extensive volunteer work.

The selection that follows dates from 1990, but the problems Callwood describes persist today not just in Canada but throughout North America.

INKSHEDDING PROMPTS

1. Do you know anyone who cannot read or write? If so, write about your relationship with that person or persons (feel free to create a false name for them if you feel uncomfortable letting others in class know who they are) and how their struggles with illiteracy affect their lives and/or your relationship with them. Judging by your own experience, is Callwood exaggerating their difficulties?

2. Try writing a letter to someone in government or to a newspaper about this problem and what you think should be done about it. A word of warning, however—in order to be convincing in writing such a letter, you need to be both restrained (in your emotional tone) and detailed (that is, you'll probably need to do a bit of research). You certainly could quote from Callwood's essay in your letter, but you would need to update her statistics by checking the most recent available data on illiteracy. If you do inkshed such a letter, consider getting some feedback on it so you can revise and polish it before mailing it to a local paper or government agency.

3. The people Callwood describes are not without language; unlike the young Helen Keller, they can speak and listen with no problem. It's *written* language that is beyond their reach—reading and writing. It's tempting to focus on how much better off they are than someone like Keller as a child, that is, Keller before Anne Sullivan: they aren't locked in a solitary world in the same way. But instead, inkshed about the details of their lives revealed to you in Callwood's piece, details that you might not have thought about or

known about before, details that emphasize why reading and writing are so important and why they *can't* simply be replaced by attentive listening and speaking. After all, Helen Keller did herself grow up to be a powerful reader and writer as well as a sought-after guest lecturer; could she have been, then, in some ways luckier, inhabiting a larger world, than some of the illiterate Canadians Callwood describes?

4. Inkshed about the tone of Callwood's piece and her purpose. What do you think she's trying to get us to do? Do you feel moved to do something after finishing her piece? And if so, moved to do *what*? Or do you feel resistant and angry, forced to do something or to feel a certain way? Explore your reactions by describing in detail which passages—specific sentences and words—triggered those reactions, as best you can figure out.

5. What could you do to help change the problem Callwood describes? If you feel at times that university involves you in too many words, too much talk and too little action, use this inkshed to develop an action plan to *do* something and to make a public commitment to follow through.

6. Did Callwood's piece remind you of any struggles of your own in learning to read or to write? or in learning to read or write in a second language? Describe these struggles in as much detail as possible, giving us a scene on a particular day, a scene of you trying to read or to write; don't forget to catalogue your five senses—sight, sound, smell, taste, touch—so we can begin to enter your experience, even if we can do this only in a brief and preliminary way (after all, you only have fifteen to twenty minutes).

WHY CANADA HAS TO BEAT ITS LITERACY PROBLEM

Carole Boudrias shudders when she remembers the time she almost swallowed Drano because she thought it was Bromo. Even more painful to recall is the time she mistook adult pain-killers for the child-size dose and made her feverish child much sicker.

"When you can't read," she explains, "it's like being in prison. You can't travel very far from where you live because you can't read street signs. You have to shop for food but you don't know what's in most of the packages. You stick to the ones in a glass jar or with a picture on the label. You can't look for bargains because you can't understand a sign that says `Reduced.' I would ask the clerk where is something and the clerk would say aisle five. Only I couldn't read aisle five. I'd pretend that I was confused so they'd lead me right to the shelf."

Carole Boudrias is able to read now, at last. She's a 33-year-old single parent who lives with her five children in a handsome townhouse on Toronto's harbourfront and holds a steady job. But her struggle with illiteracy is all too vivid in her memory. "You can't get a job," she says earnestly. "You can't open a bank account. You have to depend on other people. You feel you don't belong. You can't help your children. You can't help yourself."

Six years ago when her oldest child started school, the boy floundered. Because he had been raised in a household without books, print was strange to him. He would point to a word in his reader, that classic, endearingly silly *Dick and Jane*, and ask his mother what it was. She was as baffled as he, so he'd check with the teacher the next day and that evening would proudly read the new word to his mother. She began to absorb the shape of the words he identified. She found she could recognize them even days later.

That was astonishing. As a child she had been labelled mentally retarded and confined to "opportunity classes" where reading wasn't taught. She grew up believing that she wasn't intelligent enough to learn. Nevertheless, she was learning. The vocabulary of words she could read in her son's reader was growing. She began to think maybe the experts were wrong. Then, one miraculous day, she realized she was learning to read even faster than her son was.

"My son was my first teacher," she grins. She had never allowed herself to believe that it was possible that she could learn to read. She hadn't even tried: no one whose life is made up of poverty and failed relationships is ready to take on, voluntarily, the potential for another defeat, another kick in the self-esteem. She hesitated a long time but the evidence was persuasive—she was beginning to read. Her welfare worker had always been kind, so she summoned the nerve to ask her where she could find help.

That led her to Beat the Street, a program that helps people who are illiterate for all the reasons that befall sad children: unrecognized learning disabilities, emotional stress, too many schools, scorn and belittling, terribly bad teachers. She was linked with a volunteer tutor, and they came to admire each other deeply.

"Now I can read, I can read books, anything. I can write. In English and French."

Carole Boudrias has written a book, *The Struggle for Survival*, which tells of her tortured childhood lacerated with incest and violence, and her triumphant recovery from illiteracy. Last summer she was the poet laureate of the annual golf tournament hosted by Peter Gzowski, the beloved and respected heart of CBC Radio's *Morningside*. He has befriended the cause of literacy in Canada and over the past four years has raised a quarter of a million dollars for Frontier College, one of the first organizations in the country to tackle the problem of illiteracy.

"Learning to read," Carole Boudrias says quietly, "was like a second birth, this time with my eyes open. Before I could read, I was a blind person."

Canada has nearly five million adult citizens who are described as functionally illiterate, which means that they can recognize a few words, such as washroom signs and exits, but they can't read dense print at all. They can't decipher directions, for instance, or application forms, or warning labels. The world of newspapers, posters, advertising, books, menus, recipes, and instructions for assembly that literate people take for granted is barred to them; they lead a life of bluff, anxiety, embarrassment, and isolation.

A good many Canadians are as profoundly illiterate as Carole Boudrias was. People who meet illiterate adults are struck by the similarity of their textural experiences. All of them liken the inability to read and write with being disabled or chained in a prison. Edwin Newman, a U.S. broadcaster who writes about language, calls illiteracy "death in life."

The sense of being caged and blinded is not morbid fantasy. People who can't read may be able to walk freely but they can't go far. Subway stops rarely have pictures to guide them and the destinations bannered across the front of buses and streetcars are meaningless. If they ask for directions, well-intentioned people tell them, "Go along Main Street to Elm and turn left." Consequently, they must travel by taxi or stay home, even though they usually are the poorest of the poor.

Almost every job, even simple manual labour such as street-cleaning, requires an ability to read. Personnel managers don't take kindly to people who can't fill out an application, or when asked, can't spell their own addresses.

The divide between the literate and illiterate has never been wider. In this half of the century North America has become a world of forms and documents and instructions, written warnings, posted rules, leaflets, and vital information circulated in brochures. Two generations ago, illiteracy was prevalent but not such a great disadvantage. Someone functionally illiterate could fake it through an entire lifetime and still hold a good job. Employment skills were acquired by watching someone else; apprenticeship was the accepted teacher, not two years in a community college.

Today inability to read is a ticket to social segregation and economic oblivion. A poignant example is the skilled house-painter who turned up one day in the crowded quarters of the East End Literacy Program in Toronto. He said he wanted to read. The counsellor asked him, as all applicants are asked, what he wanted to read. "Directions on paint cans," he answered promptly. "I'm losing jobs. I can't read how to mix the colours."

Many who are illiterate can't read numbers. When they are paid, they don't know if they are being cheated. Because she couldn't fill out bank deposit slips, Carole Boudrias used to cash her welfare cheque in a storefront outlet which clips poor people sharply for no-frills service. To pay for goods, she would hold out a handful of money and let the cashier take what was needed—and perhaps more, she never knew. Once she would have been short-changed $50 she could ill afford if a stranger who witnessed the transaction hadn't protested.

The common emotional characteristic of people who can't read is depression and self-dislike. All feel at fault for their situation: with few exceptions, they went through school with bright little girls exactly their age who leaped to their feet to recite and smart little boys who did multiplication in their heads. Everyone else in the world, it seemed, could learn with ease; for them, even C-A-T looked a meaningless scribble. Teachers called them stupid. Worse, so did other children.

"Stupid" may just be the cruelest word in the language. It consumes confidence, on which the ability to learn relies. Seven-year-olds having trouble with reading will frolic at recess with an edge of glee; 11-year-olds who can't read have bitter faces and scarred souls.

Loss of hope for oneself is a descent into desolation without end. It causes men to rage in fury and women to wound themselves. People who can't read come readily to view themselves as worthless junk, and many feel they must grab what they can out of life and run. Canada's prisons are full of young men who can't read. The Elizabeth Fry Society estimates that close to 90 per cent of the women in Kingston's infamous prison for women are illiterate.

Because Canada has five million people who can't read, the political shape of the country and the priorities of governments are not influenced greatly by the needs of the poor. Since illiterates are effectively disenfranchised, the political agenda is written by the more powerful. Candidates rarely find it advantageous to uphold the causes that matter most to Canada's illiterate—an end to homelessness and the need for food banks, welfare payments that meet the poverty line, and better educational and job-training opportunities. Few votes would follow any politician with such a crusade. The electorate that can't read won't be there to ruffle the complacent on election day.

Their silence costs this country severely. Education is free in Canada because it was recognized that democracy isn't healthy unless all citizens understand current events and issues. Five million Canadians can't do that. Voters, most of them literate, choose candidates who help their interests; those who don't vote, many of them illiterate, by default get a government that does not need to know they exist.

The result is a kind of apartheid. The government has lopsided representation, which results in decisions which further alienate and discourage the unrepresented. The gap between the haves and have-nots in Canada is already greater than at any time in this century, and widening. Urban apartment houses are the work places of crack dealers, the streets are increasingly unsafe, and households have installed electronic security systems. The poor, if asked, would have better answers than guard dogs. The best, most lasting responses to crime and addiction and violence are literacy programs, coupled with job training and full employment.

Schools are a disgrace, with a failure rate of fully one-third of all high school students. A soup company with such a record would be out of business in a day. The educational system has managed to exacerbate the class differences which are developing in this country. Canada's millions of illiterates went through school the required number of years, give or take time-out for truancy, illness, running away from abuse, and confinement in detention homes. These human discards, identified promptly in the first years of elementary schools, will ever after drift around disconsolately. They are surplus people, spare parts for which society has no use. Unless there is a war.

Carole Boudrias is working on a project, Moms in Motion, to help young mothers to get off welfare rolls. She says to them, "What do you want?" They reply, "To go back to school."

Another chance. Five million Canadians need another chance. Maybe they can become literate. Maybe they can become healed and whole. What a lovely goal for the 1990s.

Stephen Pinker from "An Instinct to Acquire an Art" and "Chatterboxes" in *The Language Instinct: How the Mind Creates Language*

Born in 1954 in Montreal, Quebec, Steven Pinker studied experimental psychology as an undergraduate at McGill University and did his doctoral work at Harvard. From 1982 until 2003, he taught at MIT; currently he is the Johnstone Family Professor of Psychology at Harvard. An experimental psychologist interested in all aspects of language and mind, he has published a number of books for a non-specialist audience: *The Language Instinct: How the Mind Creates Language* (1994), *How the Mind Works* (1997), *Words and Rules: The Ingredients of Language* (1999), and most recently *The Blank Slate: The Modern Denial of Human Nature* (2002).

Even though the excerpt from *The Language Instinct* that follows was not aimed at an audience of trained linguists, you may find more technical and grammatical terms than you're used to. We suggest that you not worry about these (you certainly won't be expected to memorize them) but simply read for the gist of Pinker's argument. If you come across a word you don't know that intrigues you, try Malcolm X's tactic—look it up in a good dictionary and keep a list of such words and their definitions for your own use.

Pinker himself defines two terms that appear near the end of this excerpt: **pidgin** and **creole**. A pidgin is created when "speakers of different languages have to communicate to carry out practical tasks but do not have the opportunity to learn one another's languages" (as when slaves were brought from many different parts of Africa to the southern United States): in such a situation, "they develop a makeshift jargon . . . choppy strings of words borrowed from the language of the colonizers or plantation owners, highly variable in order and with little in the way of grammar." A pidgin can become a creole, that is, a full complex language, in one generation: "all it takes is for a group of children to be exposed to the pidgin at the age when they acquire their mother tongue." A creole is "the language that results when children make a pidgin their native tongue" (*Language Instinct* 20–21).

INKSHEDDING PROMPTS

1. On the basis of the following excerpts, what do you think the rest of *The Language Instinct* will be about? Early in this selection, Pinker promises to convince us of many astonishing things in the rest of his book. Does his opening make you curious to read the rest of the book? Do you think he can pull it off? What convinces you the most so far? the least? When Pinker lists many of the common opinions we have about language and then goes on to say that all of them are wrong, were you surprised? irritated? intrigued? What did you think of that tactic as a rhetorical move—risky? effective? ineffective? Did it work for you? Why or why not? Were any of those common opinions ones you believed yourself? (They certainly were for one of us, the non-linguist!) Which ones?

2. Is there a passage you found difficult to understand? Identify it by page number and then use your fifteen to twenty minutes of writing to look at it sentence by sentence, even word by word, if necessary. Can you find the exact spot that gives you the most difficulty or makes you the most resistant? Inkshedding on passages you don't understand has the advantage of alerting your fellow students and your instructor to confusions they might be able to help clear up for you; often if two people swap inksheds written on this prompt, they can help each other—since they rarely stumble over exactly the same passage.

3. Pretend you are Helen Keller, Malcolm X, Eva Hoffman, or June Callwood and write a letter to Pinker as if you've just finished reading this introduction to his book. What do you want to say to him on the basis of your life experience?

4. If you feel overwhelmed by all the ground Pinker has covered in this opening to his book, write a fast inkshed in which you simply try to state in your own words everything you can remember from the reading—what were his main claims? Which stories or details or bits of reported research stuck in your mind the most? Inkshedding on this prompt only works if you do it immediately after reading. Feel free to stop once or twice (but *only* once or twice in your fifteen to twenty minutes!) to look back at passages you marked in the text if you need to jog your memory.

THE LANGUAGE INSTINCT: HOW THE MIND CREATES LANGUAGE

from AN INSTINCT TO ACQUIRE AN ART

As you are reading these words, you are taking part in one of the wonders of the natural world. For you and I belong to a species with a remarkable ability: we can shape events in each other's brains with exquisite precision. I am not referring to telepathy or mind control or the other obsessions of fringe science; even in the depictions of believers these are blunt instruments compared to an ability that is uncontroversially present in every one of us. The ability is language. Simply by making noises with our mouths, we can reliably cause precise new combinations of ideas to arise in each other's minds. The ability comes so naturally that we are apt to forget what a miracle it is. . . .

In any natural history of the human species, language would stand out as the preeminent trait. To be sure, a solitary human is an impressive problem-solver and engineer. But a race of Robinson Crusoes would not give an extraterrestrial observer all that much to remark on. What is truly arresting about our kind is better captured in the story of the Tower of Babel, in which humanity, speaking a single language, came so close to reaching heaven that God himself felt threatened. A common language connects the members of a community into an information-sharing network with formidable collective powers. Anyone can benefit from the strokes of genius, lucky accidents, and trial-and-error wisdom accumulated by anyone else, present or past. And people can work in teams, their efforts coordinated by negotiated agreements. As a result, Homo sapiens is a species, like blue-green algae and earthworms, that has wrought far-reaching changes on the planet. Archeologists have discovered the bones of ten thousand wild horses at the bottom of a cliff in France, the remains of herds stampeded over the clifftop by groups of Paleolithic hunters seventeen thousand years ago. These fossils of ancient cooperation and shared ingenuity may shed light on why saber-tooth tigers, mastodons, giant woolly rhinoceroses, and dozens of other large mammals went extinct around the time that modern humans arrived in their habitats. Our ancestors, apparently, killed them off.

Language is so tightly woven into human experience that it is scarcely possible to imagine life without it. Chances are that if you find two or more people together anywhere on earth, they will soon be exchanging words. When there is no one to talk with, people talk to themselves, to their dogs, even to their plants. In our social relations, the race is not to the swift but to the verbal—the spellbinding orator, the silver-tongued seducer, the persuasive child who wins the battle of wills against a brawnier parent. Aphasia, the loss of language following brain injury, is devastating, and in severe cases family members may feel that the whole person is lost forever. . . .

I [am] writing not about the English language or any other language, but about something much more basic: the instinct to learn, speak, and understand language. For the first time in history, there is something to write about it. Some thirty-five years ago a new science was born. Now called "cognitive science," it combines tools from psychology, computer science, linguistics, philosophy, and neurobiology to explain the workings of human intelligence. The science of language, in particular, has seen spectacular advances in the years since. There are many phenomena of language that we are coming to understand nearly as well as we understand how a camera works or what the spleen is for. I hope to communicate these exciting discoveries, some of them as elegant as anything in modern science, but I have another agenda as well.

The recent illumination of linguistic abilities has revolutionary implications for our understanding of language and its role in human affairs, and for our view of humanity itself. Most educated people already have opinions about language. They know that it is man's most important cultural invention, the quintessential example of his capacity to use symbols, and a biologically unprecedented event irrevocably separating him from other animals. They know that language pervades thought, with different languages causing their speakers to construe reality in different ways. They know that children learn to talk from role models and caregivers. They know that grammatical sophistication used to be nurtured in the schools, but sagging educational standards and the debasements of popular culture have led to a frightening decline in the ability of the average person to construct a grammatical sentence. They also know that English is a zany, logic-defying tongue, in which one drives on a parkway and parks in a driveway, plays at a recital and recites at a play. They know that English spelling takes such wackiness to even greater heights— George Bernard Shaw complained that *fish* could just as sensibly be spelled *ghoti* (*gh* as in *tough*, *o* as in *women*, *ti* as in *nation*)—and that only institutional inertia prevents the adoption of a more rational, spell-it-like-it-sounds system. . . .

I will try to convince you that every one of these common opinions is wrong. And they are all wrong for a single reason. Language is not a cultural artifact that we learn the way we learn to tell time or how the federal government works. Instead, it is a distinct piece of the biological makeup of our brains. Language is a complex, specialized skill, which develops in the child spontaneously, without conscious effort or formal instruction, is deployed without awareness of its underlying logic, is qualitatively the same in every individual, and is distinct from more general abilities to process information or behave intelligently. For these reasons some cognitive scientists have described language as a psychological faculty, a mental organ, a neural system, and a computational module. But I prefer the admittedly quaint term "instinct." It conveys the idea that people know how to talk in more or less the sense that spiders know how to spin webs. Web-spinning was not invented by some unsung spider genius and does not depend on having had the right education or on having an aptitude for architecture or the construction trades. Rather, spiders spin spider webs because they have spider brains, which give them the urge to spin and the competence to succeed. Although there are differences between webs and words,

I will encourage you to see language in this way, for it helps to make sense of the phenomena we will explore.

Thinking of language as an instinct inverts the popular wisdom, especially as it has been passed down in the canon of the humanities and social sciences. Language is no more a cultural invention than is upright posture. It is not a manifestation of a general capacity to use symbols: a three-year-old . . . is a grammatical genius, but is quite incompetent at the visual arts, religious iconography, traffic signs, and the other staples of the semiotics curriculum. Though language is a magnificent ability unique to Homo sapiens among living species, it does not call for sequestering the study of humans from the domain of biology, for a magnificent ability unique to a particular living species is far from unique in the animal kingdom. Some kinds of bats home in on flying insects using Doppler sonar. Some kinds of migratory birds navigate thousands of miles by calibrating the positions of the constellations against the time of day and year. In nature's talent show we are simply a species of primate with our own act, a knack for communicating information about who did what to whom by modulating the sounds we make when we exhale.

Once you begin to look at language not as the ineffable essence of human uniqueness but as a biological adaptation to communicate information, it is no longer as tempting to see language as an insidious shaper of thought. . . . Moreover, seeing language as one of nature's engineering marvels—an organ with "that perfection of structure and co-adaptation which justly excites our admiration," in Darwin's words—gives us a new respect for your ordinary Joe and the much-maligned English language (or any language). The complexity of language, from the scientist's point of view, is part of our biological birthright; it is not something that parents teach their children or something that must be elaborated in school . . . . A preschooler's tacit knowledge of grammar is more sophisticated than the thickest style manual or the most state-of-the-art computer language system, and the same applies to all healthy human beings, even the notorious syntax-fracturing professional athlete and the, you know, like, inarticulate teenage skateboarder. Finally, since language is the product of a well-engineered biological instinct, we shall see that it is not the nutty barrel of monkeys that entertainer-columnists make it out to be. I will try to restore some dignity to the English vernacular, and will even have some nice things to say about its spelling system.

The conception of language as a kind of instinct was first articulated in 1871 by Darwin himself. In *The Descent of Man* he had to contend with language because its confinement to humans seemed to present a challenge to his theory. . . . Darwin concluded that language ability is "an instinctive tendency to acquire an art," a design that is not peculiar to humans but seen in other species such as song-learning birds.

A language instinct may seem jarring to those who think of language as the zenith of the human intellect and who think of instincts as brute impulses that compel furry or feathered zombies to build a dam or up and fly south. But one of Darwin's followers, William

James, noted that an instinct possessor need not act as a "fatal automaton." He argued that we have all the instincts that animals do, and many more besides; our flexible intelligence comes from the interplay of many instincts competing. Indeed, the instinctive nature of human thought is just what makes it so hard for us to see that it is an instinct:

> It takes . . . a mind debauched by learning to carry the process of making the natural seem strange, so far as to ask for the *why* of any instinctive human act. . . .

> [W]e may be sure that, however mysterious some animals' instincts may appear to us, our instincts will appear no less mysterious to them. And we may conclude that, to the animal which obeys it, every impulse and every step of every instinct shines with its own sufficient light, and seems at the moment the only eternally right and proper thing to do. What voluptuous thrill may not shake a fly, when she at last discovers the one particular leaf, or carrion, or bit of dung, that out of all the world can stimulate her ovipositor to its discharge? Does not the discharge then seem to her the only fitting thing? And need she care or know anything about the future maggot and its food?

> [James, *Psychology* 394]

I can think of no better statement of my main goal. The workings of language are as far from our awareness as the rationale for egg-laying is from the fly's. Our thoughts come out of our mouths so effortlessly that they often embarrass us, having eluded our mental censors. When we are comprehending sentences, the stream of words is transparent; we see through to the meaning so automatically that we can forget that a movie is in a foreign language and subtitled. We think children pick up their mother tongue by imitating their mothers, but when a child says *Don't giggle me!* or *We holded the baby rabbits*, it cannot be an act of imitation. I want to debauch your mind with learning, to make these natural gifts seem strange, to get you to ask the "why" and "how" of these seemingly homely abilities. Watch an immigrant struggling with a second language or a stroke patient with a first one, or deconstruct a snatch of baby talk, or try to program a computer to understand English, and ordinary speech begins to look different. The effortlessness, the transparency, the automaticity are illusions, masking a system of great richness and beauty.

In this century, the most famous argument that language is like an instinct comes from Noam Chomsky, the linguist who first unmasked the intricacy of the system and perhaps the person most responsible for the modern revolution in language and cognitive science. In the 1950s the social sciences were dominated by behaviorism, the school of thought popularized by John Watson and B. F. Skinner. Mental terms like "know" and "think" were branded as unscientific; "mind" and "innate" were dirty words. Behavior was explained by a few laws of stimulus-response learning that could be studied with rats pressing bars and dogs salivating to tones. But Chomsky called attention to two fundamental facts about language. First, virtually every sentence that a person utters or understands is a brand-new combination of words, appearing for the first time in the history of the universe. Therefore a language cannot be a repertoire of responses; the brain must contain a recipe or program that can build an unlimited set of sentences out of a finite list of words. That program may be called a mental grammar (not to be confused with pedagogical or stylistic "grammars," which are just guides to the etiquette of written prose). The second fundamental fact is that children develop these complex grammars rapidly and without formal instruction and grow up to give consistent interpretations to novel sentence constructions that they have never before encountered. Therefore, he argues, children must innately be equipped with a plan common to the grammars of all languages, a Universal Grammar, that tells them how to distill the syntactic patterns out of the speech of their parents. . . .

By performing painstaking technical analyses of the sentences ordinary people accept as part of their mother tongue, Chomsky and other linguists developed theories of the mental grammars underlying people's knowledge of particular languages and of the Universal Grammar underlying the particular grammars. Early on, Chomsky's work encouraged other scientists . . . to open up whole new areas of language study, from child development and speech perception to neurology and genetics. By now, the community of scientists studying the questions he raised numbers in the thousands. . . . The best place to begin is to ask why anyone should believe that human language is a part of human biology—an instinct—at all.

from CHATTERBOXES

By the 1920s it was thought that no corner of the earth fit for human habitation had remained unexplored. New Guinea, the world's second largest island, was no exception. The European missionaries, planters, and administrators clung to its coastal lowlands, convinced that no one could live in the treacherous mountain range that ran in a solid line down the middle of the island. But the mountains visible from each coast in fact belonged to two ranges, not one, and between them was a temperate plateau crossed by many fertile valleys. A million Stone Age people lived in those highlands, isolated from the rest of the world for forty thousand years. The veil would not be lifted until gold was discovered in a tributary of one of the main rivers. The ensuing gold rush attracted Michael Leahy, a footloose Australian prospector, who on May 26, 1930, set out to explore the mountains with a fellow prospector and a group of indigenous lowland people hired as carriers. After scaling the heights, Leahy was amazed to see grassy open country on the other side. By nightfall his amazement turned to alarm, because there were points of light in the distance, obvious signs that the valley was populated. After a sleepless night in which Leahy and his party loaded their weapons and assembled a crude bomb, they made their first contact with the highlanders. The astonishment was mutual. Leahy wrote in his diary:

> It was a relief when the [natives] came in sight, the men . . . in front, armed with bows and arrows, the women behind bringing stalks of sugarcane. When he saw the women, Ewunga told me at once that there would be no fight. We waved to them to come on, which they did cautiously, stopping every few yards to look us over. When a few of them finally got up courage to approach, we could see that they were utterly thunderstruck by our appearance. When I took off my hat, those nearest to me backed away in terror. One old chap came forward gingerly with open mouth, and touched me to see if I was real. Then he knelt down, and rubbed his hands over my bare legs, possibly to find if they were painted, and grabbed me around the knees and hugged them, rubbing his bushy head against me. . . . The women and children gradually got up courage to approach also, and presently the camp was swarming with the lot of them, all running about and jabbering at once, pointing to everything that was new to them.

That "jabbering" was language—an unfamiliar language, one of eight hundred different ones that would be discovered among the isolated highlanders right up through the 1960s. Leahy's first contact repeated a scene that must have taken place hundreds of times in human history, whenever one people first encountered another. All of them, as far as we know, already had language. Every Hottentot, every Eskimo, every Yanomamö. No mute tribe has ever been discovered, and there is no record that a region has served as a "cradle" of language from which it spread to previously languageless groups.

As in every other case, the language spoken by Leahy's hosts turned out to be no mere jabber but a medium that could express abstract concepts, invisible entities, and complex trains of reasoning. . . .

The universality of complex language is a discovery that fills linguists with awe, and is the first reason to suspect that language is not just any cultural invention but the product of a special human instinct. Cultural inventions vary widely in their sophistication from society to society; within a society, the inventions are generally at the same level of sophistication. Some groups count by carving notches on bones and cook on fires ignited by spinning sticks in logs; others use computers and microwave ovens. Language, however, ruins this correlation. There are Stone Age societies, but there is no such thing as a Stone Age language. . . .

To pick an example at random of a sophisticated linguistic form in a nonindustrialized people, the linguist Joan Bresnan recently wrote a technical article comparing a construction in Kivunjo, a Bantu language spoken in several villages on the slopes of Mount Kilimanjaro in Tanzania, with its counterpart construction in English. . . . The English construction is called the dative and is found in sentences like *She baked me a brownie* and *He promised her Arpège*, where an indirect object like *me* or *her* is placed after the verb to indicate the beneficiary of an act. The corresponding Kivunjo construction is called the applicative, whose resemblance to the English dative, Bresnan notes, "can be likened to that of the game of chess to checkers." The Kivunjo construction fits entirely inside the verb, which has seven prefixes and suffixes, two moods, and fourteen tenses; the verb agrees with its subject, its object, and its benefactive nouns, each of which comes in sixteen genders. (. . . To a linguist, the term *gender* retains its original meaning of "kind," as in the related words *generic, genus,* and *genre.* . . .) Among the other clever gadgets I have glimpsed in the grammars of so-called primitive groups, the complex Cherokee pronoun system seems especially handy. It distinguishes among "you and I," "another person and I," "several other people and I," and "you, one or more other persons, and I," which English crudely collapses into the all-purpose pronoun *we.*

Actually, the people whose linguistic abilities are most badly underestimated are right here in our society. Linguists repeatedly run up against the myth that working-class people and the less educated members of the middle class speak a simpler or coarser language. This is a pernicious illusion arising from the effortlessness of conversation. Ordinary speech, like color vision or walking, is a paradigm of engineering excellence—a technology that works so well that the user takes its outcome for granted, unaware of the complicated machinery hidden behind the panels. Behind such "simple" sentences as *Where did he go?* and *The guy I met killed himself,* used automatically by any English speaker, are dozens of subroutines that arrange the words to express the meaning. Despite decades of effort, no artificially engineered language system comes close to duplicating the person in the street, HAL and C3PO notwithstanding.

But though the language engine is invisible to the human user, the trim packages and color schemes are attended to obsessively. Trifling differences between the dialect of the mainstream and the dialect of other groups, like *isn't any* versus *ain't no, those books* versus *them books,* and *dragged him away* versus *drug him away,* are dignified as badges of "proper grammar." But they have no more to do with grammatical sophistication than the fact that people in some regions of the United States refer to a certain insect as a *dragonfly* and people in other regions refer to it as a *darning needle,* or that English speakers call canines *dogs* whereas French speakers call them *chiens.* It is even a bit misleading to call Standard English a "language" and these variations "dialects," as if there were some meaningful difference between them. The best definition comes from the linguist Max Weinreich: a language is a dialect with an army and a navy.

The myth that nonstandard dialects of English are grammatically deficient is widespread. In the 1960s some well-meaning educational psychologists announced that American black children had been so culturally deprived that they lacked true language and were confined instead to a "non-logical mode of expressive behavior." The conclusions were based on the students' shy or sullen reactions to batteries of standardized tests. If the psychologists had listened to spontaneous conversations, they would have rediscovered the commonplace fact that American black culture is everywhere highly verbal; the subculture of street youths in particular is famous in the annals of anthropology for the value placed on linguistic virtuosity. . . .

[A] project of [linguist William] Labov's involved tabulating the percentage of grammatical sentences in tape recordings of speech in a variety of social classes and social settings. "Grammatical," for these purposes, means "well-formed according to consistent rules in the dialect of the speakers." For example, if a speaker asked the question *Where are you going?*, the respondent would not be penalized for answering *To the store*, even though it is in some sense not a complete sentence. Such ellipses are obviously part of the grammar of conversational English; the alternative, *I am going to the store*, sounds stilted and is almost never used. "Ungrammatical" sentences, by this definition, include randomly broken-off sentence fragments, tongue-tied hemming and hawing, slips of the tongue, and other forms of word salad. The results of Labov's tabulation are enlightening. The great majority of sentences were grammatical, especially in casual speech, with higher percentages of grammatical sentences in working-class speech than in middle-class speech. The highest percentage of ungrammatical sentences was found in the proceedings of learned academic conferences.

The ubiquity of complex language among human beings is a gripping discovery and, for many observers, compelling proof that language is innate. But to tough-minded skeptics . . . it is no proof at all. Not everything that is universal is innate. Just as travelers in previous decades never encountered a tribe without a language, nowadays anthropologists have trouble finding a people beyond the reach of VCR's, Coca-Cola, and Bart Simpson T-shirts. . . . To convince you that there is a language instinct, I will have to fill in an argument that leads from the jabbering of modern peoples to the putative genes for grammar. The crucial intervening steps come from my own professional specialty, the study of language development in children. The crux of the argument is that complex language is universal because children actually reinvent it, generation after generation—not because they are taught, not because they are generally smart, not because it is useful to them, but because they just can't help it. . . .

[For example, u]ntil recently there were no sign languages at all in Nicaragua, because its deaf people remained isolated from one another. When the Sandinista government took over in 1979 and reformed the educational system, the first schools for the deaf were created. The schools focused on drilling the children in lip reading and speech, and as in every case where that is tried, the results were dismal. But it did not matter. On the playgrounds and schoolbuses the children were inventing their own sign system, pooling the makeshift gestures that they used with their families at home. Before long the system congealed into what is now called the Lenguaje de Signos Nicaragüense (LSN). Today LSN is used, with varying degrees of fluency, by young deaf adults, aged seventeen to twenty-five, who developed it when they were ten or older. Basically, it is a pidgin. Everyone uses it differently, and the signers depend on suggestive, elaborate circumlocutions rather than on a consistent grammar.

But children like Mayela, who joined the school around the age of four, when LSN was already around, and all the pupils younger than her, are quite different. Their signing is more fluid and compact, and the gestures are more stylized and less like a pantomime. In fact, when their signing is examined close up, it is so different from LSN that it is referred to by a different name, Idioma de Signos Nicaragüense (ISN). . . . ISN appears to be a creole, created in one leap when the younger children were exposed to the pidgin signing of the older children. . . . ISN has spontaneously standardized itself; all the young children sign it in the same way. The children have introduced many grammatical devices that were absent in LSN, and hence they rely far less on circumlocutions. . . . Thanks to such consistent grammar, ISN is very expressive. A child can watch a surrealistic cartoon and describe its plot to another child. The children use it in jokes, poems, narratives, and life histories, and it is coming to serve as the glue that holds the community together. A language has been born before our eyes. . . .

When deaf infants are raised by signing parents, they learn sign language in the same way that hearing infants learn spoken language. But deaf children who are not born to deaf parents—the majority of deaf children—often have no access to sign language users as they grow up. . . . When deaf children become adults, they tend to seek out deaf communities and begin to acquire the sign language that takes proper advantage of the communicative media available to them. But by then it is usually too late; they must then struggle with sign language as a difficult intellectual puzzle, much as a hearing adult does in foreign language classes. Their proficiency is notably below that of deaf people who acquired sign language as infants, just as adult immigrants are often permanently burdened with accents and conspicuous grammatical errors. Indeed, because the deaf are virtually the only neurologically normal people who make it to adulthood without having acquired a language, their difficulties offer particularly good evidence that successful language acquisition must take place during a critical window of opportunity in childhood.

A NEW PRACTICE TO TAKE FORWARD

Keeping a reading log: Since the beginning of this text, you've been prompted to inkshed in various ways about the selections you've been reading. However, confronted with excerpts from the early chapters of Pinker's book, you may be feeling that the density of his material overwhelms a mere twenty-minute inkshed.

Certainly, if you were going to write a formal paper about Pinker's work or if you were going take an exam on it, you'd need to do quite a bit more than inkshed—perhaps take detailed notes and then write, slowly and carefully, as accurate a summary as you could of the ground he covered. But you're *not* facing an examination on Pinker's ideas, at least not yet. And believe it or not, an inkshed can help you grasp and remember the gist of a complex and detailed article—certainly much better than if you didn't write about it at all.

Prompt 4 is, in a sense, asking you to write a deft summary of what you've just read (it corresponds to the first item in the list of "Strategies for Writing-to-Learn" in Conversation 3, pages 150–153). When you attempt such a summary in an inkshed, you'll get out of it exactly what you put into it. That is, if you spend time carefully preparing before your inkshedding session begins, looking over the reading and at your marginalia on it, re-reading lines you highlighted, jotting down a few page numbers and ideas you want to cover—and if the inkshedding feels strenuous while you're doing it, as if you're running uphill and breathing hard—chances are you're making things happen in your brain that wouldn't have happened otherwise. You're making connections and doing intellectual work that will stand you in good stead when you want to talk about Pinker's writing with someone else later or when you want to explore some of his ideas in an essay near the end of term, relating them to something else you've read or experienced.

The energy you put into an inkshed can make a huge difference when you try to recall what a particular piece of writing was about. That is, if you turn to one of your inksheds for help a month later—hoping to get a glimmer of what was going on in a particular article, hoping you won't simply have to re-read the entire article all over again—and your inkshed is primarily one long grousing session about how tired you were that day and how irritated you were at the big words Pinker was using, you're in trouble. You'd have to start from square one, re-reading from the first word to the last. But if you had tried hard to figure out what Pinker was up to the first time you read his words and had done your best to quote key passages, to summarize his major claims, and to quickly mention some of the key examples he uses, you'd be amazed how that level of detail helps bring the whole piece to mind in a matter of moments. Putting the effort in up front is well worth it, especially if some of your formal essays for the course are going to evolve from your readings and your inksheds. We've had students tell us that an essay practically wrote itself when they returned to their inksheds and read through them weeks or months later.

One problem, however, is that it can get boring to make most of your inksheds into summaries. Also, although summaries are formidable intellectual tools, helping us hold huge amounts of material in mind at once, good ones (thorough, attentive, detailed) are hard work and can take a lot of time to create (see the New Practice in Conversation 4 for more information on writing effective summaries; also see example summaries by Marta Currah in Conversation 3 and by Kelly Davidson in Conversation 6). Keep in mind that inksheds can take many forms (see Conversation 3 for examples) and allow yourself to be playful and to experiment when you can. A reading log is a collection of inksheds in a variety of forms, all written in response to what you've read, but not necessarily all written as summaries.

Whatever form your inksheds take (and of course at times your instructor may require an inkshed to have a particular focus or approach), *make sure to save all of them in a reading log for the term.* This could simply be a section in a notebook, but date each inkshed at the top and keep them all in order by date, a practice that will help you get a sense of your development as a writer from the beginning of the course to the end. Also, put a short identifying title at the top of each inkshed: usually the name of the author you're writing about will do, though a key word from the title might be useful in case you read more than one essay by the same author. This way you can quickly locate any particular inkshed you need.

And consider inkshedding after *any* serious hour of reading you do, for *any* course. As a form of writing-to-learn, inkshedding can help deepen and extend your understanding of difficult material in any subject area. *Remember, you don't have to wait for an instructor to tell you to inkshed.* Once you've learned this skill and this way of learning (and of remembering what you've read), you can use it to study anything more effectively, from biology to music to business.

Try an experiment with this anthology. Some instructors may require you to inkshed about every piece you read, but others may ask you to inkshed only once a week or only on particular readings. If that's your situation, figure out a way to quiz yourself on the readings after the term is over (perhaps you and a class member could do this for each other) and see if you can remember the readings you did *not* inkshed about as clearly as the ones you *did.* But don't sacrifice your learning for the sake of this experiment: whether your instructor assigns inksheds or not, you can still inkshed about everything you read in this text, for your own sake.

ESSAY IDEAS

Interview one or more people about the role of computers in their writing. If you prefer, gather information through a combination of web and library research. Consider, for a moment, the differences between Nancy Mairs (see her pieces in Conversation 6 and Conversation 7, pages 301–308 and 342–343) and Helen Keller. Mairs can see and hear and speak (so far), but her multiple sclerosis has made it impossible for her to type on her computer keyboard any longer. By the time she had published *Voice Lessons* in 1994, she was learning to use voice-recognition software in order to continue writing by using only her voice. Keller, who had full and free use of her limbs, could not hear or see—and only learned to talk after great effort and training. Computer technology, e-mail, and the Internet were not available to Keller, Malcolm X, or the young Eva Hoffman. What difference could computer technology have made in their lives? Keeping in mind that you'd have to sharpen your own focus further as you gather material, that you'd have to come up with a central question to explore, consider one of the following essay possibilities as a starting point:

1. Imaginatively rewrite one of the pieces in this section in the voice of the author (probably Keller, Malcolm X, or Hoffman), making one major change: they have access to our current level of computer technology. Would that make any difference? What opportunities for language use might have been possible? What frustrations might these new technologies have presented? (Don't answer these questions directly as you write—just keep them in mind and see what details emerge in the revised stories that these voices have to tell.)

2. Interview a person with a disability (or several people with different kinds of disabilities). How has computer technology affected their ability to communicate with others through writing, if at all?

3. Interview one or more senior citizens who don't use computers. Why have they avoided computer technology? What kinds of writing have they done in their lives? What kinds of writing do they do now or want to do? How do they do this writing, using what tools? Do they think the computer would be useful in any of these current or projected writing tasks? Have they used e-mail or the Internet? How do they think of e-mail in relation to traditional letters sent by post? (Feel free to turn this one around and instead interview senior citizens who *have* learned to use computers.)

4. Interview several students, asking detailed questions about computer use. How much do they use e-mail? Do they think of e-mail as writing or as

something else, maybe just speaking made visible? How much does correctness matter to them in e-mail? Do they participate in chat rooms or online discussion groups? Do they think writing in these situations is improving their academic writing or making it worse?

5. Has our dependence on computers made life even more difficult for those Callwood describes, adults who can neither read nor write? How? If you can, interview one or more individuals who struggle with illiteracy in order to gather a range of detailed responses to these questions.

6. Write an essay about your own experiences with computers. Giving as much detail as possible, argue that computer technology has affected your writing (for good or for ill—it's up to you). If you were trying out the proprioceptive writing practice described by Metcalf and Simon, would you want to compose at a keyboard or with pen and paper? Why? Consider all uses of computer technology for your writing, from research to e-mail to online discussion groups to word processing to spell checking to printing to designing graphics.

CONVERSATION 2:

Reflecting on the Writing Process

INTRODUCTION

There was a physicist who played the violin. One morning he took his fiddle
to the lab, wrapped it green with felt, clamped it gently in a vise, and trained
the electron microscope close on the spruce belly, just beside the sound hole,
where a steel peg was set humming at a high frequency. Through the microscope, once he got it focused right, he saw the molecular surface of the wood
begin to pucker and ripple outward like rings on a pond, the ripples rising
gradually into waves, and the steel peg a blur at the heart of play.

When he drew the peg away, the ripples did not stop. In twenty-four hours,
the ripples had not stopped. He saw, still, a concentric tremor on the molecular quilt of the wood. The violin, in the firm embrace of the vise, had a
song, a thing to say.

In another twelve hours, the ripples flattened and the wood lay inert.

Musicians know this without a microscope. An instrument dies if not played
daily. A guitar, a violin, a lute chills the air for the first fifteen minutes of
fresh play. It will need to be quickened from scratch. But the fiddle played
every day hangs resonant on the wall, quietly boisterous when first it is lifted
down, already trembling, anxious to speak, to cry out, to sing at the bow's
first stroke. . . .

Writers know this when they are writing daily.

Kim Stafford, "Writing Daily, Writing in Tune" 1–2

In this chapter, writers write about writing. You may think that writing about writing is
like writing about nothing. But in fact, for many of these writers, the work they do at
the computer keyboard or with pen and paper is the most terrifying work they can
think of. Many of them feel called to do it, even though they find it painful—that is,
they would stop doing it if they could. Others delight in it because they discover so
much about themselves and about the world by writing. For writers in either group,
writing seems to be as terrifying or as important or as pleasurable as climbing mountains or performing open-heart surgery or making love (see Natalie Goldberg's piece
below on "The Rules of Writing Practice" if you don't believe us).

Of course, not all writers write about writing. Some poets and fiction writers absolutely refuse to reflect consciously on their writing processes: they believe they might destroy the magic if they examine their writing processes too closely. But such fears are unwarranted. Consider the analogy of childbirth: an expectant mother doesn't need to fear that the mystery of creation and childbirth will be destroyed if she spends some time reflecting consciously on her condition, learning in detail what happens during labour and delivery and finding out how other women have experienced those processes. She may, in fact, be able to face the hard work of labour and delivery with less fear and less pain if she knows what to expect. But there's no chance that her child or the birth of her child will ever be identical to anyone else's. Nor is there any chance that she'll ever feel *completely* in control or that the magic will be gone.

Many authors (female *and* male) use the childbirth analogy to talk about their writing, seeing their books as their offspring and talking about the labour pains they endured to give birth to their stories or poems or essays, to bring them into the world. You may even feel that way about some of the academic papers you've written (even if you didn't love them very much once they were born). So, think of listening to other authors reflecting on the writing process as if you were listening to a Lamaze instructor teach you how to face childbirth without fear.

It's helpful to eavesdrop on what other writers have to say about writing—not, we hasten to add, because we think we ought to abandon our own practices in order to imitate theirs. But because their attention to the writing process can help us learn to pay conscious and careful attention to our own writing processes, to notice details about our ways of working that we had perhaps never noticed before. In other words, we don't read books about writing as "how-to" books; instead, such books help strengthen in us a habit of reflection on our own writing processes.

So, while reading what these working writers have discovered about their ways of working, make detailed notes about your own—when does writing go well for you? When does it go badly? Reflecting consciously on your writing processes helps you gain some measure of understanding about how you work and why. Inkshedding on how or why you write—and sharing those inksheds (referred to as "process writing") with each other—can help even more (see the suggested inkshedding prompts in this section).

And as you read what various poets and fiction writers have to say about their work, don't assume that their comments have nothing to do with the writing you're struggling to produce in your academic courses. Look for the similarities and take what you can use. We'll look more closely at crucial genre and audience issues later, but for now, just keep in mind that *all* writing and *all* knowledge production are deeply creative (jump ahead to Conversation 6 and read what John C. Polanyi, professor of chemistry at the University of Toronto and winner of a Nobel Prize in chemistry, has to say about the creativity of science, if you have your doubts). The struggles of writers—to get words on the page (or computer screen) daily, to attend to and learn from those words, and to get those words wrestled into some coherent shape for a particular audience—have certain things in common whether the writer is drafting an engineering report or a poem.

INKSHEDDING PROMPTS

After you've read some of the selections in this chapter, record your reactions—questions, irritations, insights, any memories stirred up by the reading. But read the last prompt in this section before you decide how to focus your inkshed, since you can incorporate any of the other prompts into Prompt 9.

1. Tell the story of a specific writing event in your life—perhaps a time writing went well for you or a time writing was a complete disaster (it could be something that happened years ago or just last night). As you write about this experience, give as much detail as you possibly can: What was the rhetorical situation? Was this writing you *had* to do or writing you *chose* to do? Who was the audience? How did you go about preparing to do the writing? Did you start months ahead or several hours before the writing had to be finished? Also, give as much physical data as you can, whether you think it's important or not—what time of day were you usually writing? Where were you writing? What tools were you using: a computer? your favourite pen and favourite notebook? Were you rested or tired, full or hungry, relaxed or nervous, overflowing with information or empty-headed? Don't try to decide what the data means—just inkshed as fast as you can and get it all down on paper. You can read through it later and see if any patterns jump out at you.

2. How would you describe your usual writing process to someone else? That is, if someone asked you how you would usually proceed—from the moment of receiving a writing assignment (or accepting or choosing one, as in agreeing to give a speech at a friend's wedding or a relative's funeral) to the moment of completing it—what general patterns of behaviour could you describe? Think of yourself as an anthropologist observing your own behaviour from a distance. What would you see? Someone making notes in a notebook the very first day the writing task was assigned, analyzing the rhetorical situation and brainstorming? Someone running to the library to take out twenty-five books on the topic and feeling overwhelmed because there wasn't time to read them all? Someone trying to ignore the impending task, hoping that inspiration would come sometime closer to deadline? And what sensory details would you record in your anthropologist's notebook—a writer who always worked with mugs of hot black coffee nearby? or late into the night in a special quiet location, using hunger and thirst to stay alert? or early mornings in a local café with lots of noise around and inspirational pastries and big pots of herb tea? Kim Stafford's piece in this section can suggest the kinds of sights, sounds, smells, tastes, and textures you

might want to notice, including more subtle influences connected with memory or family or place. Again, resist drawing any conclusions at this point. Just record the data, as much of it as you can.

3.   Read Godwin's piece and then inkshed about your own watcher. Create a rough but detailed word portrait; draw a cartoon of this watcher to post over your desk. If this gets too scary, read Goldberg and then invent/describe your internal coach, your writing "sweetheart." Or write out a heated discussion between your watcher and your sweetheart.

4.   Painstakingly describe your methods of procrastination: try writing them up as instructions, as if they were special skills we should all be trying to develop on purpose. Or tell in detail your funniest (or scariest) procrastination story.

5.   Inkshed about the physical activity you love or need the most; then draw as many analogies between it and writing as you can. Goldberg talks a bit about running and writing, so that's a possibility—but consider weightlifting and writing, or dance and writing, or snowboarding and writing, whatever physical activity you know intimately from long experience. Put us on the dance floor with you or on the ski slope or on the balance beam.

6.   After reading through selections in this chapter, especially Donald Murray's piece, inkshed about some writing habits or practices that sound good to you—which ones do you want to remember and to start trying out yourself? Brainstorm about ways to remember them and to trick yourself into doing them on a regular basis.

7.   What surprised you in these selections? Inkshed about anything unexpected, behaviours or feelings that you didn't think professional writers would have.

8.   Inkshed about one or two of these pieces as writing. That is, pick the piece you enjoyed the most and ask yourself what made it work as a piece of writing. How did the beginning of it capture your attention? How did it pull you along from paragraph to paragraph? Start your inkshed by copying out a few of your favourite sentences from that piece; then inkshed about why you like those sentences. Would any of them be good to put on a three-by-five card above your writing desk? (This is a practice Ray Carver describes in Conversation 8, putting important lines from other writers on index cards above his desk.)

9. After reading Natalie Goldberg's pieces "The Power of Detail" and "One Plus One Equals a Mercedes-Benz," inkshed for fifteen minutes a letter to your classmates, introducing yourself to them (start "Dear Members of __[course title]__"). Give as much biographical data as you like, whatever you think it would be useful for your peers to know about you as you work together on one another's writing. Also let your colleagues know, in as much detail as you can, about your writing processes, your feelings about writing, your experiences with writing in the past—in fact, any of the writing you might have done for Prompts 1–8 in this section can be incorporated into this letter. These two short pieces of Goldberg's seem to conflict with one another—one suggests that you should honour the details as they are, the other that you should perhaps go underneath them or beyond them into metaphor. We suggest that you do both things: trust the details of your life and of your writing stories, but if you feel the urge to play with those details or to explore them metaphorically or to speak in images at times, do that too. This particular prompt works best if everyone in the class, including the instructor, writes such an introductory letter and if everyone gets a chance to read everyone else's (or at least five or six of them). Don't forget to sign your letter at the end.

Natalie Goldberg, from *Writing Down the Bones* and *Wild Mind*

Natalie Goldberg lives in northern New Mexico where she writes novels, paints, teaches, and meditates. As anyone who has read her three books on writing will know, she seamlessly integrates her long practice of Zen Buddhism into her work as a writer, seeing writing as a disciplined form of meditation (see her *Writing Down the Bones: Freeing the Writer Within*, 1986; *Wild Mind*, 1990; and *Thunder and Lightning: Cracking Open the Writer's Craft*, 2000). Goldberg is such a phenomenon that even *The Oprah Winfrey Show* has done a segment on her. Goldberg's encouragement of writers and artists everywhere, not just through her books but in countless workshops, has resulted in *Writing Down the Bones* selling over one million copies and being translated into nine languages. The first five selections below have come from that book, and the final two are from *Wild Mind*.

WRITING DOWN THE BONES
WRITING AS A PRACTICE

This is the practice school of writing. Like running, the more you do it, the better you get at it. Some days you don't want to run and you resist every step of the three miles, but you do it anyway. You practice whether you want to or not. You don't wait around for inspiration and a deep desire to run. It'll never happen, especially if you are out of shape and have been avoiding it. But if you run regularly, you train your mind to cut through or ignore your resistance. You just do it. And in the middle of the run, you love it. When you come to the end, you never want to stop. And you stop, hungry for the next time.

That's how writing is, too. Once you're deep into it, you wonder what took you so long to finally settle down at the desk. Through practice you actually do get better. You learn to trust your deep self more and not give in to your voice that wants to avoid writing. It is odd that we never question the feasibility of a football team practicing long hours for one game; yet in writing we rarely give ourselves the space for practice.

When you write, don't say, "I'm going to write a poem." That attitude will freeze you right away. Sit down with the least expectation of yourself; say, "I am free to write the worst junk in the world." You have to give yourself the space to write a lot without a destination. I've had students who said they decided they were going to write the great American novel and haven't written a line since. If every time you sat down, you expected something great, writing would always be a great disappointment. Plus that expectation would also keep you from writing.

My rule is to finish a notebook a month. (I'm always making up writing guidelines for myself.) Simply to fill it. That is the practice. My ideal is to write every day. I say it is my ideal. I am careful not to pass judgment or create anxiety if I don't do that. No one lives up to his ideal.

In my notebooks I don't bother with the side margin or the one at the top: I fill the whole page. I am not writing anymore for a teacher or for school. I am writing for myself first and I don't have to stay within my limits, not even margins. This gives me a psychological freedom and permission. And when my writing is on and I'm really cooking, I usually forget about punctuation, spelling, etc. I also notice that my handwriting changes. It becomes larger and looser.

Often I can look around the room at my students as they write and can tell which ones are really on and present at a given time in their writing. They are more intensely involved and their bodies are hanging loose. Again, it is like running. There's little resistance when the run is good. All of you is moving; there's no you separate from the runner. In writing, when you are truly on, there's no writer, no paper, no pen, no thoughts. Only writing does writing—everything else is gone.

One of the main aims in writing practice is to learn to trust your own mind and body; to grow patient and nonaggressive. Art lives in the Big World. One poem or story doesn't matter one way or the other. It's the process of writing and life that matters. Too many writers have written great books and gone insane or alcoholic or killed themselves. This process teaches about sanity. We are trying to become sane along with our poems and stories.

Chögyam Trungpa, Rinpoche, a Tibetan Buddhist master, said, "We must continue to open in the face of tremendous opposition. No one is encouraging us to open and still we must peel away the layers of the heart." It is the same with this way of practice writing: We must continue to open and trust in our own voice and process. Ultimately, if the process is good, the end will be good. You will get good writing.

A friend once said that when she had a good black-and-white drawing that she was going to add color to, she always practiced first on a few drawings she didn't care about in order to warm up. This writing practice is also a warmup for anything else you might want to write. It is the bottom line, the most primitive, essential beginning of writing. The trust you learn in your own voice can be directed then into a business letter, a novel, a Ph.D. dissertation, a play, a memoir. But it is something you must come back to again and again. Don't think, "I got it! I know how to write. I trust my voice. I'm off to write the great American novel." It's good to go off and write a novel, but don't stop doing writing practice. It is what keeps you in tune, like a dancer who does warmups before dancing or a runner who does stretches before running. Runners don't say, "Oh, I ran yesterday. I'm limber." Each day they warm up and stretch.

Writing practice embraces your whole life and doesn't demand any logical form: no Chapter 19 following the action in Chapter 18. It's a place that you can come to wild and unbridled, mixing the dream of your grandmother's soup with the astounding clouds outside your window. It is undirected and has to do with all of you right in your present moment. Think of writing practice as loving arms you come to illogically and incoherently. It's our wild forest where we gather energy before going to prune our garden, write our fine books and novels. It's a continual practice.

Sit down right now. Give me this moment. Write whatever's running through you. You might start with "this moment" and end up writing about the gardenia you wore at your wedding seven years ago. That's fine. Don't try to control it. Stay present with whatever comes up, and keep your hand moving.

THE POWER OF DETAIL

I am in Costa's Chocolate Shop in Owatonna, Minnesota. My friend is opposite me. We've just finished Greek salads and are writing in our notebooks for a half hour among glasses of water, a half-sipped Coke, and a cup of coffee with milk. The booths are orange, and near the front counter are lines of cream candies dipped in chocolate. Across the street is the Owatonna Bank, designed by Louis Sullivan, Frank Lloyd Wright's teacher. Inside the bank is a large cow mural and beautiful stained-glass windows.

Our lives are at once ordinary and mythical. We live and die, age beautifully or full of wrinkles. We wake in the morning, buy yellow cheese, and hope we have enough money to pay for it. At the same instant we have these magnificent hearts that pump through all sorrow and all winters we are alive on the earth. We are important and our lives are important, magnificent really, and their details are worthy to be recorded. This is how writers must think, this is how we must sit down with pen in hand. We were here; we are human beings; this is how we lived. Let it be known, the earth passed before us. Our details are important. Otherwise, if they are not, we can drop a bomb and it doesn't matter.

Yad Vashem, a memorial for the Holocaust, is in Jerusalem. It has a whole library that catalogues the names of the six million martyrs. Not only did the library have their names, it also had where they lived, were born, anything that could be found out about them. These people existed and they mattered. *Yad Vashem*, as a matter of fact, actually means "memorial to the name." It was not nameless masses that were slaughtered; they were human beings.

Likewise, in Washington, D.C., there is the Vietnam memorial. There are fifty thousand names listed—middle names, too—of American soldiers killed in Vietnam. Real human beings with names were killed and their breaths moved out of this world. There was the name of Donald Miller, my second-grade friend who drew tanks, soldiers, and ships in the margins of all his math papers. Seeing names makes us remember. A name is what we carry all our life, and we respond to its call in a classroom, to its pronunciation at a graduation, or to our name whispered in the night.

It is important to say the names of who we are, the names of the places we have lived, and to write the details of our lives. "I lived on Coal Street in Albuquerque next to a garage and carried paper bags of groceries down Lead Avenue. One person had planted beets early that spring, and I watched their red/green leaves grow."

We have lived; our moments are important. This is what it is to be a writer: to be the carrier of details that make up history, to care about the orange booths in the coffee shop in Owatonna.

Recording the details of our lives is a stance against bombs with their mass ability to kill, against too much speed and efficiency. A writer must say yes to life, to all of life: the water glasses, the Kemp's half-and-half, the ketchup on the counter. It is not a writer's task to say, "It is dumb to live in a small town or to eat in a café when you can eat macrobiotic at home." Our task is to say a holy yes to the real things of our life as they exist—the real truth of who we are: several pounds overweight, the gray, cold street outside, the Christmas tinsel in the showcase, the Jewish writer in the orange booth across from her blond friend who has black children. We must become writers who accept things as they are, come to love the details, and step forward with a yes on our lips so there can be no more noes in the world, noes that invalidate life and stop these details from continuing.

WRITERS HAVE GOOD FIGURES

What people don't realize is that writing is physical. It doesn't have to do with thought alone. It has to do with sight, smell, taste, feeling, with everything being alive and activated. The rule for writing practice of "keeping your hand moving," not stopping, actually is a way to physically break through your mental resistances and cut through the concept that writing is just about ideas and thinking. You are physically engaged with the pen, and your hand, connected to your arm, is pouring out the record of your senses. There is no separation between the mind and body; therefore, you can break through the mind barriers to writing through the physical act of writing, just as you can believe with your mind that your hand won't stop at the wood, so you can break a board in karate.

After one writing class a student, in amazement, said, "Oh, I get it! Writing is a visual art!" Yes, and it's a kinesthetic, visceral art too. I've told fourth-graders that my writing hand could knock out Muhammad Ali. They believed me because they know it is true. Sixth-graders are older and more skeptical. I've had to prove it to them by putting my fist through their long gray lockers.

When I look around at people writing, I can tell just by their physical posture if they have broken through or not. If they did, their teeth are rattling around in their mouth, no longer tight in their gums; their hearts might be pounding hard or aching. They are breathing deeply. Their handwriting is looser, more generous, and their bodies are relaxed enough to run for miles. This is why I say all writers, no matter how fat, thin, or flabby, have good figures. They are always working out. Remember this. They are in tune, toned up, in rhythm with the hills, the highway, and can go for long stretches and many miles of paper. They move with grace in and out of many worlds.

And what great writers actually pass on is not so much their words, but they hand on their breath at their moments of inspiration. If you read a great poem aloud—for example, "To a Skylark" by Percy Bysshe Shelley—and read it the way he set it up and punctuated it, what you are doing is breathing his inspired breath at the moment he wrote that poem. That breath was so powerful it still can be awakened in us over 150 years later. Taking it on is very exhilarating. This is why it is good to remember: if you want to get high, don't drink whiskey; read Shakespeare, Tennyson, Keats, Neruda, Hopkins, Millay, Whitman, aloud and let your body sing.

ONE PLUS ONE EQUALS A MERCEDES-BENZ

I always tell my students, especially the sixth-graders, the ones who are becoming very worldly-wise: Turn off your logical brain that says 1 + 1 = 2. Open up your mind to the possibility that 1 + 1 can equal 48, a Mercedes-Benz, an apple pie, a blue horse. Don't tell your autobiography with facts, such as "I am in sixth grade. I am a boy. I live in Owatonna. I have a mother and father." Tell me who you really are: "I am the frost on the window, the cry of a young wolf, the thin blade of grass."

Forget yourself. Disappear into everything you look at—a street, a glass of water, a cornfield. Everything you feel, become totally that feeling, burn all of yourself with it. Don't worry—your ego will quickly become nervous and stop such ecstasy. But if you can catch that feeling or smell or sight the moment you are one with it, you probably will have a great poem.

Then we fall back on the earth again. Only the writing stays with the great vision. That's why we have to go back again and again to books—good books, that is. And read again and again the visions of who we are, how we can be. The struggle we go through as human beings, so we can again and again have compassion for ourselves and treat each other kindly.

BE AN ANIMAL

When you are not writing, you are a writer too. It doesn't leave you. Walk with an animal walk and take in everything around you as prey. Use your senses as an animal does. Watch a cat when he sees something moving in the room. He is perfectly still, and at the same time, his every sense is alive, watching, listening, smelling. This is how you should be when you are in the streets. The cat's mind is not thinking about how much money he needs, or whom to write a post card to when he visits Florence: he is watching the mouse or the marble rolling across the floor or the light reflecting in crystal. He is ready with all of him to pounce. Now, you don't have to get down on all fours and twitch your tail. Only be still—some part of you, at least—and know where you are, no matter how busy you are.

My friend who went with me to Europe had a phobia about getting lost. She'd never learned to read a city map or pick up simple signals, like "We were in this piazza yesterday. There, across the street, is the Savoy Hotel, where we bought concert tickets, so that must be the turn." Because she was scared, she lost all touch with her common sense, with the natural senses that we rely on as our survival tools. That place in us that is aware and that is always awake. Katagiri Roshi said: "You are Buddha right now!" Only we forget when we are busy or frightened, as my friend was. Afraid of being lost, she became lost.

As writers we have to walk in the world in touch with that present, alert part of ourselves, that animal sense part that looks, sees, and notices—street signs, corners, fire hydrants, newspaper stands.

Also, right before you are planning to write, a good preparation is to become an animal. Move slowly, stalking your prey, which is whatever you plan to write about, no matter what else you might be doing at the moment—taking out the garbage, walking to the library, watering the garden. Get all your senses intent. Turn off your logical mind— empty, no thoughts. Let your words come from your belly. Bring your brain down to your stomach and digest your thoughts. Let them give nourishment to your body. Have a round belly, like Buddha, breathing all the way inside. Don't hold in your stomach. Be patient and measured. Let the writing percolate below the level of thought forms, in the subconscious and through your veins.

Then when you finally pounce, let's say at ten a.m., your designated time to write that day, add the pressure of timed writing. Write for an hour, or twenty minutes, whatever amount you decide, but write for all it's worth. Keep your hand moving, pour out everything, straight from your veins, through your pen and onto paper. Don't stop. Don't doodle. Don't daydream. Write until you're spent.

But don't worry. This isn't your last chance. If you missed the mouse today, you'll get it tomorrow. You never leave who you are. If you are a writer when writing, you also are a writer when you are cooking, sleeping, walking. And if you are a mother, a painter, a horse, a giraffe, or a carpenter, you will bring that into your writing, too. It comes with you. You can't divorce yourself from parts of yourself.

Best come to writing whole with everything in you. And when you're done writing, best to walk out in the street with everything you are, including your common sense or Buddha nature—something good at the center, to tell you the names of streets, so you won't get lost. Something to tell you you can come back to your writing tomorrow and stay with your writing in the hours in between, when you are an animal, out stalking the city.

WILD MIND

THE RULES OF WRITING PRACTICE

For fifteen years now, at the beginning of every writing workshop, I have repeated the rules for writing practice. So, I will repeat them again here. And I want to say why I repeat them: Because they are the bottom line, the beginning of all writing, the foundation of learning to trust your own mind. Trusting your own mind is essential for writing. Words come out of the mind.

And I believe in these rules. Perhaps I'm a little fanatical about them.

A friend, teasing me, said, "You act as if they are the rules to live by, as though they apply to everything."

I smiled. "Okay, let's try it. Do they apply to sex?"

I stuck up my thumb for rule number one. "Keep your hand moving." I nodded yes.

Index finger, rule number two. "Be specific." I let out a yelp of glee. It was working.

Finger number three. "Lose control." It was clear that sex and writing were the same thing.

Then, number four. "Don't think," I said. Yes, for sex, too, I nodded.

I proved my point. My friend and I laughed.

Go ahead, try these rules for tennis, hang gliding, driving a car, making a grilled cheese sandwich, disciplining a dog or a snake. Okay. They might not always work. They work for writing. Try them.

1. *Keep your hand moving.* When you sit down to write, whether it's fourteen minutes or an hour, once you begin, don't stop. If an atom bomb drops at your feet

eight minutes after you have begun and you were going to write for ten minutes, don't budge. You'll go out writing.

What is the purpose of this? Most of the time when we write, we mix up the editor and creator. Imagine your writing hand as the creator and the other hand as the editor. Now bring your two hands together and lock your fingers. This is what happens when we write. The writing hand wants to write about what she did Saturday night: "I drank whiskey straight all night and stared at a man's back across the bar. He was wearing a red T-shirt. I imagined him to have the face of Harry Belafonte. At three a.m., he finally turned my way and I spit into the ashtray when I saw him. He had the face of a wet mongrel who had lost his teeth." The writing hand is three words into writing this first sentence—"I drank whiskey . . ."—when the other hand clenches her fingers tighter and the writing hand can't budge. The editor says to the creator, "Now, that's not nice, the whiskey and stuff. Don't let people know that. I have a better idea: 'Last night, I had a nice cup of warmed milk and then went to bed at nine o'clock.' Write that. Go ahead. I'll loosen my grip so you can."

If you keep your creator hand moving, the editor can't catch up with it and lock it. It gets to write out what it wants. "Keep your hand moving" strengthens the creator and gives little space for the editor to jump in.

Keeping your hand moving is the main structure for writing practice.

2. *Lose control.* Say what you want to say. Don't worry if it's correct, polite, appropriate. Just let it rip. Allen Ginsberg was getting a master's degree from Columbia University. Back then, they were doing rhymed verse. He had a lot of practice in formal meter, and so forth. One night, he went home and said to himself that he was going to write whatever he wanted and forget about formalities. The result was "Howl." We shouldn't forget how much practice in writing he had prior to this, but it is remarkable how I can tell students, "Okay, say what you want, go for it," and their writing takes a substantial turn toward authenticity.

3. *Be specific.* Not car, but Cadillac. Not fruit, but apple. Not bird, but wren. Not a codependent, neurotic man, but Harry, who runs to open the refrigerator for his wife, thinking she wants an apple, when she is headed for the gas stove to light her cigarette. Be careful of those pop-psychology labels. Get below the label and be specific to the person.

But don't chastise yourself as you are writing, "I'm an idiot; Natalie said to be specific and like a fool I wrote 'tree.'" Just gently note that you wrote "tree," drop to a deeper level, and next to "tree" write "sycamore." Be gentle with yourself. Don't give room for the hard grip of the editor.

4. *Don't think.* We usually live in the realm of second or third thoughts, thoughts on thoughts, rather than in the realm of first thoughts, the real way we flash on something. Stay with the first flash. Writing practice will help you contact first thoughts. Just practice and forget everything else.

   Now here are some rules that don't necessarily apply to sex, though you can try to apply them to sex if you like.

5. *Don't worry about punctuation, spelling, grammar.*

6. *You are free to write the worst junk in America.* You can be more specific, if you like: the worst junk in Santa Fe; New York; Kalamazoo, Michigan; your city block; your pasture; your neighborhood restaurant; your family. Or you can get more cosmic: free to write the worst junk in the universe, galaxy, world, hemisphere, Sahara Desert.

7. *Go for the jugular.* If something scary comes up, go for it. That's where the energy is. Otherwise, you'll spend all your time writing around whatever makes you nervous. It will probably be abstract, bland writing because you're avoiding the truth. Hemingway said, "Write hard and clear about what hurts." Don't avoid it. It has all the energy. Don't worry, no one ever died of it. You might cry or laugh, but not die.

I am often asked, "Well, isn't there a time when we need to stop our hand moving? You know, to figure out what we want to say?"

It's better to figure out what you want to say in the actual act of writing. For a long time, I was very strict with myself about writing practice. I kept that hand moving no matter what. I wanted to learn to cut through to first thoughts. Sure, you can stop for a few moments, but it is a tricky business. It's good to stop if you want, look up and get a better picture of what you're writing about, but often I don't stay there. If I give myself a little gap, I'm off for an hour daydreaming. You have to learn your own rhythm, but make sure you do some focused, disciplined "keeping the hand moving" to learn about cutting through resistance.

If you learn writing practice well, it is a good foundation for all other writing.

When I was young, I played tennis. My arm wasn't very strong, and I was impatient. I was so eager to play, I held the racquet up higher on the grip than I was supposed to in order to compensate. Unfortunately, I got used to using the racquet this way. I was a fine tennis player, but no matter how much I played, there was just so far I could improve, because I never mastered one of the important basics: the proper grip on the racquet.

I use this as an example for writing practice. Grow comfortable with it in its basic form before you begin to veer off into your own manner and style. Trust it. It is as basic as drinking water.

Sometimes an interviewer asks me, "So writing practice is old hat? Have you developed something new?"

And I say, "It would be like a Zen master teaching you meditation one year and the next year saying, 'Forget compassion. Standing on our head is what's in.'"

The old essentials are still necessary. Stay with them under all circumstances. It will make you stable—something unusual for a writer.

ACCEPT OURSELVES

I tell students, "Don't throw out your writing. Keep it in a notebook." High-school students especially seem to ball up sheets of paper on their desks as they write. Sometimes I stop and unball one of the papers. Bill's had a date, then his full name scrawled in the upper left-hand corner, then "I remember my mother's"—and that was it. A whole white page with blue lines wasted. I looked down at his notebook, at the page he was working on: Date and name in the upper left-hand corner, then "I remember my mother's hat." Nothing different but the word *hat*. The crumpled paper was his hesitation. My guess is if I hadn't walked by and bent low and whispered in his ear, "Keep going. You're doing fine. Don't cross out. Don't think," another sheet of paper—the one he was working on—would also be crumpled.

I say keep your writing in notebooks rather than on separate sheets of paper or in looseleaf binders because you are less likely to tear out, throw out, or lose those written pages. I say this not so much because I am concerned about the loss of a particular writing—we are all capable of lots of writing—but because it is another practice in accepting the whole mind. Keeping in one notebook the good and bad writing—no, don't even think *good* and *bad*; think instead of writing where you were present or not, present and connected to your words and thoughts—is another chance to allow all kinds of writing to exist side by side, as though your notebook were Big Mind accepting it all. When you reread a notebook and if it has all of your writing, then you have a better chance to study your mind, to observe its ups and downs, as if the notebook were a graph.

We need to learn to accept our minds. Believe me, for writing, it is all we have. It would be nice if I could have Mark Twain's mind, but I don't. Mark Twain is Mark Twain. Natalie Goldberg is Natalie Goldberg. What does Natalie Goldberg think? The truth is I'm boring some of the time. I even think about rulers, wood desks, algebra problems. I wonder why the hell my mother gave me tuna fish every day for lunch in high school. Then zoom, like a bright cardinal on a gray sky, something brilliant flashes through my mind, and for a moment I'm turned upside down. Just for a moment, then the sky is gray again for another half hour or a day or eight pages of writing in my notebook. In rereading your notebook and keeping all your writing in it, you get an opportunity to study your mind. Somehow in seeing the movement of your mind through writing, you become less attached to your thoughts, less critical of them.

We have to accept ourselves in order to write. Now none of us does that fully; few of us do it even halfway. Don't wait for one hundred percent acceptance of yourself before you write, or even eight percent acceptance. Just write. The process of writing is an activity that teaches us about acceptance.

"What did you do for your summer vacation?" That one September long ago my eighth-grade teacher asked my English class to write about this. I began with "I went." Then I thought, "Oh, Nat, can't you think of a better word than *I* to begin with and *went*! Write a better verb." I crossed out "I went." I wrote "She rode." I crossed it out: I began again. "The family visited," then "This summer," then "This past summer," then "Thinking back." Each one was crossed out. What did the first two words matter? I could have rewritten them later anyway, but I should have gotten on with it.

Next I wrote that I played softball all summer. Well, that was a lie. Not once all summer did I play softball, but I thought that was what normal kids did in the summer, so that's what I wrote. I thought it was what the teacher wanted to hear. I also managed to add, "It was fun. I had an interesting summer. It was nice."

Right off, first rule: Don't use *nice, interesting, fun* in your writing. It doesn't say anything.

The truth is, "What I did last summer" could be an interesting topic. (Uh-oh! I just used *interesting* in the last sentence after saying not to. We can also break all rules. It's good to know them, but do what you want with them. After all, who made up the rule anyway? I did in the last paragraph a moment ago as I wrote.) The problem is no one in school ever taught us how to enter a topic or gave us permission to write what really happened. "My father sat at the dinner table in his underwear, drinking beer and swatting mosquitoes, while I sat on the kitchen floor trying to put together a two thousand-piece jigsaw puzzle of the island of Hawaii. I mostly ate Oreos. My brother had a splinter in his thumb that he got from the back screen door. No one could get it out and it became infected, swelled like an elephant. And my mother dyed her hair red and snuck out each night with a man named Charlie after my father got so drunk he couldn't see."

Write the truth. And remember what I whispered in that kid's ear at the beginning of the chapter: "Keep going. You're doing fine. Don't think. Don't cross out." Develop a "sweetheart" inside yourself who whispers in your ear to encourage you. Let's face it. You who have created the editor are also capable of creating the sweetheart, that kind coach who thinks what you do is fine. "But what I do isn't fine." Says who? the editor? Have you murdered anyone in the last day, week, month, year, decade? Probably not. Then don't worry about it. Give yourself a break. You're probably a really fine person. Call up the sweetheart and let him or her give you some compliments.

Donald Murray, "A Writer's Habits"

Donald M. Murray not only taught at the University of New Hampshire for many years and helped establish the graduate program in Composition Studies there—he also worked as a journalist for over half a century. His continuing columns for *The Boston Globe* are available on the web (in the 1990s he was twice named best columnist in Boston), and he has worked for several other newspapers, as well as serving as an editor at *Time*. A Pulitzer Prize for editorial writing (the *Boston Herald* 1954) is only one of his many awards for writing and for teaching.

Murray also publishes fiction and poetry, but his books on the craft of writing and on teaching writing are the ones we know and love the best: *Learning by Teaching, Expecting the Unexpected,* and *The Craft of Revision* (all four editions) are only a few of the titles we keep handy on our shelves for reference and inspiration. We particularly value his insistence that a writer must write daily ("never a day without a line") and that a writer must write badly to write well ("perfect is the enemy of good"). Donald Murray's influential book—*A Writer Teaches Writing*, first published in 1968—helped bring about the new **paradigm** in the teaching of writing (see Hairston's essay in Conversation 3), a paradigm (model) based on the notion that teachers of writing had to write themselves on a regular basis if they were to be of any use to their students, that teachers needed to experience firsthand the struggles and processes that working writers go through. In fact, the title of Murray's famous essay—"Teach Writing as Process, Not Product" (1972)—became a key phrase in the ongoing international conversation about teaching writing.

A WRITER'S HABITS

Habit is the writer's best friend: the habit of the notebook, the habit of placing the posterior in the chair at the writing desk, the habit of using the mail.

I am surrounded by neighbors and friends who want to write and know more than I do, have more to say than I do, are blessed with more talent than I have, but they do not yet have writers' habits.

In trying to help some of them become productive writers recently, I found myself taking inventory of the habits that make me a published writer. I was not born with these habits. They were all acquired years ago for a practical rather than an aesthetic reason: baby needs shoes.

I suppose I hungered for fame, but I wrote to eat. Over the years I have discovered joy in my craft. I delight in my hours alone at my desk when I am surprised by the words that appear on my computer screen. But to arrive at joy I had to develop writing habits.

The following ten habits are essential to my practice of the writer's craft.

The habit of awareness

I am never bored, because I am constantly observing my world, catching, out of the corner of my eye, the revealing detail, hearing what is not said, entering into the skin of others.

I look out my window at snowy woods illuminated by the moon, and the trees seem to move apart: I have a poem. I hear what someone says visiting a sick room: I have a column. I taste my childhood in a serving of mashed potatoes and have a food page feature. I hear Mozart's 16th piano concerto on the FM, hear it again as I heard it when I lay in intensive care, and have another column.

Some of the observations taken in by eye, ear, fingertip, taste bud, or nose are recorded in my daybook or journal, but many more are held in memory. In practicing the habit of awareness, I record more than I know, and that inventory of filed away information surprises me when I write and it appears on the page.

It is almost half a century ago that I was a paratrooper taught how to make myself invisible while crawling forward in a field of grass, bush, and ledge, and, on my last furlough before going overseas, I demonstrated this strange skill for a girl standing at the top of a New Hampshire field. I had forgotten that until a character in my novel edged up that field, and I realized I was not making it up; I was reporting what had rested in a file drawer in my brain all these years.

The habit of reacting

I am aware of my reaction to my world, paying attention to what I do not expect, to what is that should not be, to what isn't that should be. I am student to my own life, allowing my feelings to ignite my thoughts.

That sounds normal, but I have found beginning writers do not value their reactions to their world. They think other people have thought the same way or felt the same way. Perhaps they have, but writers need an essential innocence or arrogance that says, "This experience—observation, thought, or feeling—has not existed until I write it." As writers we must value our response to our world.

I notice my writing habits, and from that grows this article. I see young soldiers poised for combat and write the reactions of an old man who survived combat. I see signs for a house tour, feel an unexpected anger at the smugness of those who invite tours into their homes and end up writing a humorous piece about an imaginary tour through a normally messed up house, ours. I put down my holiday thoughts about the daughter we lost at twenty and find, from readers, that my private reactions speak for them.

I have taught myself to value my own responses to the world—and to share them with readers. I build on my habit of reacting.

The habit of connecting

My wife thinks that my habit of making unexpected connections is my most valuable talent as a writer. Writers see the universal in the particular, they delight in anecdote and parable that reveals a larger story. They treasure metaphor; as Robert Frost says, "Poetry is metaphor, saying one thing and meaning another, saying one thing in terms of another."

I study a painting, read what the artist said about its making, and connect that with a technique essential to effective writing; observe the relationship between the way a child plays and a nation makes war.

Usually, these connections come in a special form I call a "line," that is usually more than a word but not yet a sentence. The line contains an essential tension that will release a text when it is developed in writing. When I have that fragment of language I know I have something to write.

Years ago I wrote in my daybook that "I had an ordinary war," realized what becomes ordinary in combat and began the novel I am writing. More than twenty years ago I wrote "a writer teaches writing" and that phrase became both a book and the title of my first textbook on teaching writing. I wrote "I remember silence," and wrote a poem that recreated the loneliness of my childhood and the way we inflicted pain by turning away. The remembered warning "step on a crack and break your back" turned me into a woman on a circus high wire, and I told her story in a poem.

The habit of rehearsal

The most important part of my writing day may be the twenty-two hours or so when I am *not* at my writing desk. As I leave my writing desk, I start to mull over next morning's writing in my head, and during the hours when I am asleep and awake my conscious, subconscious and unconscious minds combine to prepare next day's pages. I am always rehearsing what I may write.

I walk down the street and I am Melissa confronting Iain in the kitchen of a New Hampshire farmhouse. I see them and hear them. At a stop light I play with the strange, often ironic terminology of financial managers—"redemption," "yield," "trust"—and realize I am writing a column. Sitting in the living room watching the Boston Bruins play Montreal, I am actually weaving an argument for a chapter in a textbook. I am always in the world and out of it, writing what will be written the next morning.

The habit of disloyalty

Graham Greene once asked a profound question—"Isn't disloyalty as much the writer's virtue as loyalty is the soldier's?"—that I often used to describe the relationship of writer to subject, but recently I have realized that I must practice the habit of disloyalty toward myself.

I must be disloyal to what I have written on the same subject before, seeing the familiar anew, willing to contradict what I have said and how I have said it. Writing is an experimental art, and I must conduct new experiments on old questions, digging deeper and deeper into the subject which is often myself. I must be disloyal to the most comforting beliefs and myths of my life.

I find myself, after writing strong columns against war, creating a pastoral poem celebrating a peaceful moment during combat. A character in my novel believes the opposite of what I believe when I am not in that character's skin. I record the anger I feel against my daughter who died early—a rare but momentarily true feeling most survivors experience. I revise my textbooks, changing some of the principles for which I argued strenuously in the last edition.

The habit of drafting

~~nulla dies sine linea. Never a day without a line.~~
~~Each morning I~~
~~I draft~~
~~I write drafts~~

Those who do not write wait until what they want to say is clear in their minds, and when they see it perfectly they write it down. Remember I said that is what those who do *not* write do; writers follow the counsel of André Gide:

> Too often I wait for the sentence to finish taking shape in my mind before setting it down. It is better to seize it by the end that first offers itself, head and foot, though not knowing the rest, then pull: the rest will follow along.

As a trained journalist, I tend to write the first sentence first because it contains the voice, the subject, my point of view toward the subject, the form, the seed from which the writing will grow, but I do it by drafting, grabbing it by "the end that first offers itself," as I did at the beginning of this section, drafting leads until I get one I can follow.

The habit of ease

I live in a community of writers, and I became bored by their grumping, groaning, whining about how hard it was to write. And then I realized I was the leading whiner. If I really felt that way, I told myself, I should take up something more pleasant, perhaps embalming or selling real estate.

The fact is that I have to write, need to write, love—admit it—to write. In recent years I have worked hard to make writing easy. I study the conditions that make it easy to write—

a laptop computer I keep by my living room chair and take on trips, my music on the CD player that helps me concentrate, the information stored on my hard disk to which I can refer in seconds, the community of writer/readers I call on the phone when I need support or stimulus, counsel or a listener for a draft.

I start early, well ahead of deadlines, and when the writing doesn't flow, I step away from it, returning again and again until it comes easily. Unlike the schoolteacher's dictum, "Hard writing makes easy reading," for me, easy writing makes easy reading.

The habit of velocity

I write fast. On a good day I am the boy on the bicycle wobbling downhill so fast his feet are off the pedals, and he is out of control. That's how I want to write, with such velocity that my typing is bad, my grammar ain't, and my spelling is worse; I want to write what I do not know in ways I have not written. I need to speed ahead of the censor and write so fast that my velocity causes the accidents of insight and language that make good writing.

I might write:

> There is tak of land war and I am sitt in a wrm room in my house stil surprised that the dancing shells passed by me [me by?]. Outsde winter woods like the snow woods in whch I fout and I fd my fingers rubb together nervously. What are they doing? I know. It is that bone, smooth, [by yrs?], I find when I dig a foxhole under shell fire, digging like md, crujnhing dwn. It is human, a kull, leg, some part of a man. I remember a txtbk. This was a battlefield in the First World War and this the bone is part of a soldier who fell was killed, shlld?, here in this fld in that war.

I know all that is wrong with that chunk of prose—the typing, the spelling, the awkward language—but it is leading me toward meaning, making me go deeper and deeper into experience. The switch to the present tense, for example, commands me to go back in time until it is immediate and take the reader with me.

I wrote that fast and the speed took me where I did not expect to go. Now I have some writing to do.

The habit of revision

I am in the habit of revision, but I do not try to correct error as much as I try to discover the strength of the draft and try to make it stronger. One of the habits that is most successful for me these days is to layer or overwrite, putting the draft on the computer screen and then writing over it. Here I will demonstrate that technique by saving, with a line drawn through it, what I would simply delete.

~~There is tak of land war and I am sitt in a wrm room in my house~~
~~stil surprised that t~~ The dancing shells ~~passed~~ by ~~me [me by?].~~ this
time. I dig faster, deeper. The shells will return. My shovel hits a rock,
no, something else. I pull it free. It is ~~Outsde winter woods like the~~
~~snow woods in whch I fout and I fd my fingers rubb together nerv-~~
~~ously. What are they doing? I know. It is that~~ bone. I put my
entrenching tool down and rub my hand over it, it is curved, **smooth,**
~~[by yrs?], I find when I dig a foxhole under shell fire, digging like~~
~~md, crujnhing dwn. It is human, a kull, leg, some part of a man.~~ the
back end of a human skull and suddenly I am back in school listening to the professor drone through European History. **I remember**
a place on a map and realize I am there. It was a ~~txtbk. This was~~ a
battlefield in the First World War and in **this** lonely hour in combat
I have found my companion ~~the bone is part of a~~-soldier ~~who fell~~
~~was killed, shlld?, here in this fld in that war.~~ with whom I share the
shell's return.

When I copy it out, you can share the text I found:

> The dancing shells pass by this time. I dig faster, deeper. The shells
> will return. My shovel hits a rock, no, something else. I pull it free.
> It is bone. I put my entrenching tool down and rub my hand over it.
> It is curved, smooth, the back end of a human skull and suddenly I
> am back in school listening to the professor drone through European
> History. I remember a place on a map and realize I am there. It was
> a battlefield in the First World War and in this lonely hour in combat
> I have found my companion soldier with whom I share the shell's
> return.

That may develop into a column, find a place in the novel, become a poem, but now
that I have rediscovered that fragment of bone I am sure it will develop into a piece of
writing—and be revised again to fit its purpose.

The habit of completion

I wrote but did not submit. Then I met Minnie Mae Emmerich. She is of German descent
and does not believe in waste. She sent off something I had thrown away, and it was published. I learned the lesson of completion: A piece of writing is not finished until it is submitted for publication as many times as is necessary for it to appear in print.

I learned the lesson, but I need to relearn it. Forty years later, the poet Mekeel McBride read some poems I had discarded, commanded me to submit them, and some were published. Now I am rededicated to the habit of completion—and submission. I use the mails, submitting what I write to the best market first and, when it comes back, to another and another and another.

Consider my habits, but develop your own by studying what you did when the writing went well, and make what you discover your own writing habits.

Gail Godwin, "The Watcher at the Gates"

You might think that writing ten novels and two collections of short stories would make someone feel completely confident as a writer, but from this short essay it's clear that Gail Godwin understands how frightening the blank page can be and that publishing one book is no guarantee that you'll ever write another. By 1977 (when this piece came out) she already had three novels and a collection of short stories under her belt, plus a nomination for a National Book Award—yet she still had an almost paralyzing fear of failure.

Godwin worked for a while as a reporter for *The Miami Herald* before earning a PhD in English at the University of Iowa (Kurt Vonnegut was one of her teachers). She didn't become widely known until over a decade later when her fifth novel, *A Mother and Two Daughters* (1982), came out; number one on *The New York Times* best-seller list, it earned her a third nomination for a National Book Award.

THE WATCHER AT THE GATES

I first realized I was not the only writer who had a restraining critic who lived inside me and sapped the juice from green inspirations when I was leafing through Freud's "Interpretation of Dreams" a few years ago. Ironically, it was my "inner critic" who had sent me to Freud. I was writing a novel, and my heroine was in the middle of a dream, and then I lost faith in my own invention and rushed to "an authority" to check whether she could have such a dream. In the chapter on dream interpretation, I came upon the following passage that has helped me free myself, in some measure, from my critic and has led to many pleasant and interesting exchanges with other writers.

Freud quotes Schiller, who is writing a letter to a friend. The friend complains of his lack of creative power. Schiller replies with an allegory. He says it is not good if the intellect examines too closely the ideas pouring in at the gates.

> In isolation, an idea may be quite insignificant, and venturesome
> in the extreme, but it may acquire importance from an idea which

follows it. . . . In the case of a creative mind, it seems to me, the intellect has withdrawn its watchers from the gates, and the ideas rush in pellmell, and only then does it review and inspect the multitude. You are ashamed or afraid of the momentary and passing madness which is found in all real creators, the longer or shorter duration of which distinguishes the thinking artist from the dreamer . . . you reject too soon and discriminate too severely.

So that's what I had: a Watcher at the Gates. I decided to get to know him better. I discussed him with other writers, who told me some of the quirks and habits of their Watchers, each of whom was as individual as his host, and all of whom seemed passionately dedicated to one goal: rejecting too soon and discriminating too severely.

It is amazing the lengths a Watcher will go to keep you from pursuing the flow of your imagination. Watchers are notorious pencil sharpeners, ribbon changers, plant waterers, home repairers and abhorrers of messy rooms or messy pages. They are compulsive looker-uppers. They are superstitious scaredy-cats. They cultivate self-important eccentricities they think are suitable for "writers." And they'd rather die (and kill your inspiration with them) than risk making a fool of themselves.

My Watcher has a wasteful penchant for 20-pound bond paper above and below the carbon of the first draft. "What's the good of writing out a whole page," he whispers begrudgingly, "if you just have to write it over again later? Get it perfect the first time!" My Watcher adores stopping in the middle of a morning's work to drive down to the library to check on the name of a flower or a World War II battle or a line of metaphysical poetry. "You can't possibly go on till you've got this right!" he admonishes. I go and get the car keys.

Other Watchers have informed their writers that:

> "Whenever you get a really good sentence you should stop in the middle of it and go on tomorrow. Otherwise you might run dry."

> "Don't try and continue with your book till your dental appointment is over. When you're worried about your teeth, you can't think about art."

Another Watcher makes his owner pin his finished pages to a clothesline and read them through binoculars "to see how they look from a distance." Countless other Watchers demand "bribes" for taking the day off: lethal doses of caffeine, alcoholic doses of Scotch or vodka or wine.

There are various ways to outsmart, pacify or coexist with your Watcher. Here are some I have tried, or my writer friends have tried, with success:

Look for situations when he's likely to be off guard. Write too fast for him in an unexpected place, at an unexpected time. (Virginia Woolf captured the "diamonds in the dustheap" by writing at a "rapid haphazard gallop" in her diary.) Write when very tired. Write in purple ink on the back of a Master Charge statement. Write whatever comes into your mind while the kettle is boiling and make the steam whistle your deadline. (Deadlines are a great way to outdistance the Watcher.)

Disguise what you are writing. If your Watcher refuses to let you get on with your story or novel, write a "letter" instead, telling your "correspondent" what you are going to write in your story or next chapter. Dash off a "review" of your own unfinished opus. It will stand up like a bully to your Watcher the next time he throws obstacles in your path. If you write yourself a good one.

Get to know your Watcher. He's yours. Do a drawing of him (or her). Pin it to the wall of your study and turn it gently to the wall when necessary. Let your Watcher feel needed. Watchers are excellent critics after inspiration has been captured; they are dependable, sharp-eyed readers of things already set down. Keep your Watcher in shape and he'll have less time to keep you from shaping. If he's really ruining your whole working day sit down, as Jung did with his personal demons, and write him a letter. On a very bad day I once wrote my Watcher a letter. "Dear Watcher," I wrote, "What is it you're so afraid I'll do?" Then I held his pen for him, and he replied instantly with a candor that has kept me from truly despising him.

"Fail," he wrote back.

William Stafford, from *Writing the Australian Crawl: Views on the Writer's Vocation* and *You Must Revise Your Life*

Born at the start of World War I (1914), William Stafford spoke out against violence and warfare not just during his life but beyond the grave—*Every War Has Two Losers: William Stafford on Peace and War* (edited by Stafford's son, Kim) came out in 2003, ten years after Stafford's death. During World War II, he was a conscientious objector and worked in the civilian public service camps, an experience he described in *Down My Heart* (1947); when the war was over, he attended the University of Iowa where (like Gail Godwin, but many years before her) he participated in the writing program and earned his PhD in English.

Stafford taught for over thirty years at Lewis & Clark College in Oregon; he retired in 1980 but continued to give readings and workshops and, of course, to write daily up until his death in 1993. Though he has published over fifty volumes of poetry and prose, his first major collection of poems, *Traveling Through the Dark*, didn't come out until he was forty-eight years old, earning him a National Book Award in 1963. He is best known as a poet, serving as Consultant in Poetry to the Library of Congress in 1970 (Poet Laureate); but his books on writing are helpful for *anyone* who wants to write (*Writing the Australian Crawl: Views on the Writer's Vocation*, 1978; *You Must Revise Your Life*, 1986; *Crossing Unmarked Snow*, 1998; and *The Answers Are Inside the Mountains: Meditations on the Writing Life*, 2003). The selections below are from the first two, the ones that came out during his lifetime.

WRITING THE AUSTRALIAN CRAWL

A WAY OF WRITING

A writer is not so much someone who has something to say as he is someone who has found a process that will bring about new things he would not have thought of if he had not started to say them. That is, he does not draw on a reservoir; instead, he engages in an activity that brings to him a whole succession of unforeseen stories, poems, essays, plays, laws, philosophies, religions, or—but wait!

Back in school, from the first when I began to try to write things, I felt this richness. One thing would lead to another; the world would give and give. Now, after twenty years or so of trying, I live by that certain richness, an idea hard to pin, difficult to say, perhaps offensive to some. For there are strange implications in it.

One implication is the importance of just plain receptivity. When I write, I like to have an interval before me when I am not likely to be interrupted. For me, this means usually the early morning, before others are awake. I get pen and paper, take a glance out of the window (often it is dark out there), and wait. It is like fishing. But I do not wait very long, for there is always a nibble—and this is where receptivity comes in. To get started I will accept anything that occurs to me. Something always occurs, of course, to any of us. We can't keep from thinking. Maybe I have to settle for an immediate impression: it's cold, or hot, or dark, or bright, or in between! Or—well, the possibilities are endless. If I put down something, that thing will help the next thing come, and I'm off. If I let the process go on, things will occur to me that were not at all in my mind when I started. These things, odd or trivial as they may be, are somehow connected. And if I let them string out, surprising things will happen.

If I let them string out. . . . Along with initial receptivity, then, there is another readiness: I must be willing to fail. If I am to keep on writing, I cannot bother to insist on high standards. I must get into action and not let anything stop me, or even slow me much. By "standards" I do not mean "correctness"—spelling, punctuation, and so on. These details become mechanical for anyone who writes for a while. I am thinking about such matters as social significance, positive values, consistency, etc. I resolutely disregard these. Something better, greater, is happening! I am following a process that leads so wildly and originally into new territory that no judgment can at the moment be made about values, significance, and so on. I am making something new, something that has not been judged before. Later others—and maybe I myself—will make judgments. Now, I am headlong to discover. Any distraction may harm the creating.

So, receptive, careless of failure, I spin out things on the page. And a wonderful freedom comes. If something occurs to me, it is all right to accept it. It has one justification: it occurs to me. No one else can guide me. I must follow my own weak, wandering, diffident impulses.

A strange bonus happens. At times, without my insisting on it, my writings become coherent; the successive elements that occur to me are clearly related. They lead by themselves to new connections. Sometimes the language, even the syllables that happen along, may start a trend. Sometimes the materials alert me to something waiting in my mind, ready for sustained attention. At such times, I allow myself to be eloquent, or intentional, or for great swoops (Treacherous! Not to be trusted!) reasonable. But I do not insist on any of that; for I know that back of my activity there will be the coherence of my self, and that indulgence of my impulses will bring recurrent patterns and meanings again.

This attitude toward the process of writing creatively suggests a problem for me, in terms of what others say. They talk about "skills" in writing. Without denying that I do have experience, wide reading, automatic orthodoxies and maneuvers of various kinds, I still must insist that I am often baffled about what "skill" has to do with the precious little area of confusion when I do not know what I am going to say and then I find out what I am going to say. That precious interval I am unable to bridge by skill. What can I witness about it? It remains mysterious, just as all of us must feel puzzled about how we are so inventive as to be able to talk along through complexities with our friends, not needing to plan what we are going to say, but never stalled for long in our confident forward progress. Skill? If so, it is the skill we all have, something we must have learned before the age of three or four.

A writer is one who has become accustomed to trusting that grace, or luck, or—skill.

Yet another attitude I find necessary: most of what I write, like most of what I say in casual conversation, will not amount to much. Even I will realize, and even at the time, that it is not negotiable. It will be like practice. In conversation I allow myself random remarks—in fact, as I recall, that is the way I learned to talk—so in writing I launch many expendable efforts. A result of this free way of writing is that I am not writing for others, mostly; they will not see the product at all unless the activity eventuates in something that later appears to be worthy. My guide is the self, and its adventuring in the language brings about communication.

This process-rather-than-substance view of writing invites a final, dual reflection:

1.   Writers may not be special—sensitive or talented in any usual sense. They are simply engaged in sustained use of a language skill we all have. Their "creations" come about through confident reliance on stray impulses that will, with trust, find occasional patterns that are satisfying.

2.   But writing itself is one of the great, free human activities. There is scope for individuality, and elation, and discovery, in writing. For the person who follows with trust and forgiveness what occurs to him, the world remains always ready and deep, an inexhaustible environment, with the combined vividness of an actuality and flexibility of a dream. Working back and forth between experience and thought, writers have more than space and time can offer. They have the whole unexplored realm of human vision.

from WRITING THE AUSTRALIAN CRAWL

Often when my friends pronounce responsibly about the values of creative work I experience a loss of contact. I want at such times to voice what may appear to be an antagonism, maybe even a willful stupidity, about "culture." To "learn the tools of writing," to "understand the essentials of the craft," to "base my practice on models that have proved to be fundamentally sound"—these apparently winsome and admirable phrases put me in a bleak mood. When I write, grammar is my enemy; the materials of my craft come at me in a succession of emergencies in which my feelings are ambivalent; I do not have any commitments, just opportunities. Not the learning of methods, not the broadening of culture, not even the preserving of civilization (there may be greater things than civilizations), but a kind of dizzying struggle with the Now-ness of experience, that is my involvement in writing. And I believe it is this interaction between imagination and its embodiment as it develops which sustains the speaker and the writer—and sustains the artist in other materials.

It is strange to me that we can come to accept the idea that language is primarily learned as speech, is soaked up by osmosis from society by children—but that we then assume the writing down of this flexible language requires a study of linguistics, a systematic checking with lists of standard practices, and so on. Now I realize that we possess many canned arguments about prescription *versus* description and we share many nuances on this subject, from having written and talked about this topic; but I want to take a definite position, and my main plea is for the value of an unafraid, face-down, flailing, and speedy process in using the language.

Just as any reasonable person who looks at water, and passes a hand through it, can see that it would not hold a person up; so it is the judgment of commonsense people that reliance on the weak material of students' experiences cannot possibly sustain a work of literature. But swimmers know that if they relax on the water it will prove to be miraculously buoyant; and writers know that a succession of little strokes on the material nearest them—without any prejudgments about the specific gravity of the topic or the reason-ableness of their expectations—will result in creative progress. Writers are persons who write; swimmers are (and from teaching a child I know how hard it is to persuade a reasonable person of this)—swimmers are persons who relax in the water, let their heads go down, and reach out with ease and confidence. . . .

 . . . [H]ow complex writing can be when viewed from outside, when analyzed. If a person looks at a group of words he can find ideas, sound patterns, all kinds of involuted accomplishments. They are there; human beings are so marvelous in their thinking and in their analyzing that there is no end to the complexity of what can be discovered. This complexity is our opportunity and our triumph: it is not at all my intention to belittle either the existence of or the discovery of these complexities. My point is a slightly different one. I want to plead for the ease of finding and expressing these patterns, these accomplishments which come naturally to the mind. I propose that we start with the assumption that people, even the "shallowest," do have ideas; ideas spring from motion, and the mind is always in motion. Just as the swimmer does not have a succession of handholds hidden in the water, but instead simply sweeps that yielding medium and finds it hurrying him along, so the writer passes his attention through what is at hand, and is propelled by a medium too thin and all-pervasive for the perceptions of nonbelievers who try to stay on the bank and fathom his accomplishment. . . .

 . . . A person writes by means of that meager but persistent little self he has with him all the time. He does not outflank his ignorance by intensive reading in composition class; he does not become brilliant about constructions by learning the history of the language. He is a certain weight of person, relying on the total feeling he has for experience. Consider some implications in writing and in interchanging about it; for instance, a student brings something to discuss, saying, "I don't know whether this is really good, or whether I should throw it in the wastebasket." The assumption is that one or the other choice is the right move. No. Almost everything we say or think or do—or write—comes in that spacious human area bounded by something this side of the sublime and something above the unforgivable. We must accustom ourselves to talking without orating, and to writing without achieving "Paradise Lost." We must forgive ourselves and each other much, in our writing and in our talking. We must abjure the "I wrote it last night and it looked good, but today I see it is terrible" stance. When you write, simply tell me something. Maybe you can tell me how we should live.

* * *

from FINDING WHAT THE WORLD IS TRYING TO BE

(Excerpt from an interview of William Stafford by Sanford Pinsker)

It doesn't sound as if you are troubled by writing blocks.

Writing blocks? I don't believe in them.

But what if somebody has one? Doesn't that person have to believe in them? You may not suffer from them, but surely other people do.

No, I've never experienced anything like that. I believe that the so-called "writing block" is a product of some kind of disproportion between your standards and your performance. I can imagine a person beginning to feel that he's not able to write up to that standard he imagines the world has set for him. But to me that's surrealistic. The only standard I can rationally have is the standard I'm meeting right now. Of course I can write. *Anybody* can write. . . . one should lower his standards until there is no felt threshold to go over in writing. It's *easy* to write. You just shouldn't have standards that inhibit you from writing. . . .

Could you even imagine writing [your poem] "Traveling Through the Dark" as an essay? That is, some prose account of your experience with the deer and the narrow country road?

No. That had to be spare. And to have flying speed as an experience. . . . It makes me nervous to have people say that poems are made of words. Of course, on one level I know I've got to agree. But poems are also made of *contexts*. If you get certain contexts going, you can make mistakes in wording, in diction. That is, *if* you've got flying speed, some kind of momentum. At least the *feeling* I have is not the feeling of great care that everything is going to explode if I don't have the exact word. In fact, I have the opposite feeling: even if I have the *wrong* word, this is going to work. I mean, that's the feeling I have when I do a poem. For me, poetry is *not* like the jeweller's craft . . . polishing, polishing, always rubbing it more and more. It's more like the exhilaration of getting somewhere. It's like running fast and your elbow and knees may not always be exactly right . . . but you're really getting somewhere. That's the sort of feeling writing a poem has. . . .

. . . [M]ost of the poems I write I don't send out at all. And of those I send out, maybe a tenth of them finally get published. So that means an awful lot of them get rejected, even ones I think are all right. I look at it this way: you can run across a log pond—you know, where they're floating the logs at a sawmill—by stepping on one log at a time. And if you don't stay on a given log very long, you can go hopping clear across the pond on these logs. But if you stop on one, it'll sink. Sometimes I feel a writer should be like this—that you need your bad poems. You shouldn't inhibit yourself. You need to have your dreams; you need to have your poems. If you begin to keep from dreaming or from trying to write your poems, you could be in trouble. You have to learn how to say, "Welcome . . . welcome." Welcome, dreams. Welcome, poems. And then if somebody says "I don't like that dream," you can say "Well, it's my life. I had to dream it." And if somebody else says "I don't like that poem," you can say, "Well, it's my life. That poem was in the way, so I wrote it."

* * *

YOU MUST REVISE YOUR LIFE
from FACING UP TO THE JOB

(Excerpt from an interview of William Stafford by Nancy Bunge)

When you talk about writing poetry, you usually talk about letting things happen.

It's a strong impulse of mine to put that into any such conversation about writing because I feel that it's important to let the process of writing bring about things rather than be just the writing down of things that are already brought about. . . . Does this make any sense?

That makes sense, but how do you do it?

I do it in any way I can to keep [people] from feeling that they have to be on guard about what they write or that they have to have it all formulated before they begin or that there are unallowable things in dignified discourse. I'd like to go all out on this and confront as squarely as possible those who make students feel that writing is something that is done with the fully conscious, already accomplished self. I think writing is itself educational, exploratory, and worthy of trust while you're doing it. So if you think of something while you're writing, that's fine. . . .

. . . [T]he product is expendable, but the process is precious. This is what I'd like to say. I keep meeting poets who say something like, "Well, I'm trying to do something that is worthy and lasting and beyond my lifetime," and so on. I think that's just frivolous. That's something only society decides and I don't see that it makes any difference anyway. But the process is the process of living centrally and paying attention to your own life. Surely that's worth doing. If you don't, who will? . . .

[R]eal art, genuine art, comes not from hammering out something for posterity, but from making the discoveries that are yours to be made because of your unique constitution and the unique encounter you have in experience.

Are there ever any days when you don't write?

There are no days I *can't* write.

Are there ever any days you don't write?

There are days I don't write. For instance, I'm headlong from somewhere to somewhere else and full of distractions, and I forgive myself for those days; it's not a fetish, I think, but most days I do write.

Does that change the day at all?

Yes. It changes the day a little bit. For me, for analogy, it's sort of like jogging. If I've done my jogging it's an OK day. If I've done my writing, it's a really OK day. It's a confirming, satisfying activity to do. And it's almost devotional. Maybe that's too strong, but it's as if a day of my life deserves a little attention from life. . . .

Poems and stories and helpfully enhanced discourse of any kind, I think, are results of a trustful, undistorted entry into the language that's natural to yourself. And I suddenly glimpse the possibility of conceptualizing language as something that can be exactly congruent with your mental life. That congruency is menaced by many things: competitiveness, systematic educational distortion toward prizes, maybe even being bullied by those around you so that you just don't have the bounce that it takes to get into your own thought and language. . . . I'd like to have a classroom so people can let that congruency between thought and language have its way with their discourse. I think as human beings, insofar as we cherish each other, we cherish that trust that it's all right to live your own life and even to have your own thoughts and occasionally in a mild way to express them.

Someone asked you when you found out you were a poet and you said that you wondered more about when everyone else stopped.

Yes, yes. The kind of process we are talking about is native to everyone, kids with their hopscotch and so on. Everyone. Everyone I've ever met, everyone, has what to me is the essential element of what we're talking about. They may not write what they call poems, but they make remarks that they like better than other remarks. They have that lip-smacking realization of differences in discourse. But then later they may feel, "I'm a salesman. I'm not allowed to have any lip-smacking impulses about things. I'm going to give it the way it is in the book." And so they quit, as far as I'm concerned, at least that part of their lives. . . . I don't know a time when I wasn't enjoying language. And I guess that's what a poet does. But I think everyone shares in this, and it's artificial to think there's a life without it. They're asking the question from the point of view that poetry is something that you have to nerve yourself to do. I don't think that's true. Not to do poetry is possible, I suppose, but it's hard and I never met anyone who didn't do it in some sense of coursing sounds, of being either delighted or discouraged about how the sentence comes out, by responding or not responding to what somebody says. You're really in a tough spot if you don't have any of those responses. And so they're asking me to enter a universe in which the values I hold dear are reversed when they ask that question. I just don't want to go into that world, so I stop.

* * *

"When I Met My Muse," a poem by William Stafford

I glanced at her and took my glasses
off—they were still singing. They buzzed
like a locust on the coffee table and then
ceased. Her voice belled forth, and the
sunlight bent. I felt the ceiling arch, and
knew that nails up there took a new grip
on whatever they touched. "I am your own
way of looking at things," she said. "When
you allow me to live with you, every
glance at the world around you will be
a sort of salvation." And I took her hand.

Kim Stafford, "My Father's Place" in *Early Morning: Remembering My Father, William Stafford*

Kim Stafford directs the Northwest Writing Institute at Lewis & Clark College in Portland, Oregon; he also helps increase public access to his father's work by serving as literary executor for the William Stafford Archive. Originally focusing on medieval literature (in his University of Oregon doctoral thesis), he has published poetry, creative nonfiction, fiction, children's literature, plus a CD of original songs (*Wheel Made of Wind*, 1997). His most recent work is the book about writing from which the epigraph to this chapter is taken: *The Muses Among Us: Eloquent Listening and Other Pleasures of the Writer's Craft* (2003), the fourth chapter of which is entitled "The Writer as Professional Eavesdropper." The notion of eavesdropping, overhearing, attentive listening, is central to Kim Stafford's vision of the role of writers in our culture: the writer's task is to preserve and record voices that might otherwise be lost.

The selection below is taken from Kim Stafford's memoir of his father, with whom he shares a vision of writing as a gentle but enduring weapon against violence, war, and destruction. The following statement opens Kim Stafford's website:

> We live in a world where a few people could destroy us all, but a few people cannot save us. The math doesn't work that way. We can only be saved when many people—and finally all people—recognize and live by our true interdependence on earth. This means that education, interactive culture, and the expressive arts are the greatest priority of our time. . . . Writers have a place in this essential work—to question, listen, and tell the connecting stories of human experience, the quiet voices of local life everywhere. This is the work I champion, through my own writing and teaching.

MY FATHER'S PLACE

A few days after my father died, I needed to sleep alone at the home place, to go back to the room I shared with my brother when we were young. Mother was away. I came to the house after dark, found the hidden key. In the home labyrinth, your feet know the way. Down the hall in the old garage, I turned into the study my father had built, where I stood a moment: dark walls, dim rows of books, papers on the desk, the making place. Then up two steps to the kitchen, a turn down the hall, and into the room of childhood.

For the first time in years, I slept deeply from the moment I lay down—until I woke at around 4 A.M. Mother had told me that since his death she, too, had been wakened at my father's customary writing time. As I opened my eyes, the moon was shining through the bedroom window. The house was still, the neighborhood quiet. Something beckoned me to rise, a soft tug. Nothing mystical, just a habit to the place. Lines from a poem of his came to mind:

> When you wake to the dream of now
> from night and its other dream,
> you carry day out of the dark
> like a flame.

This beckoning before first light brought a hint from my father's life, and I accepted it:

> . . . Your life you live by the light you find
> and follow it on as well as you can,
> carrying through darkness wherever you go
> your one little fire that will start again.

> —*from* "The Dream of Now"

I dressed and shuffled down the hall. In the kitchen, I remembered how my father would make a cup of instant coffee and some toast. Following his custom, I put the kettle on, sliced bread my mother had made, and marveled at how sharp my father had kept the knife. The plink of the spoon stirring coffee was the only sound, then the scrape of a butter knife. My father's ritual pulled me on: I was to go to the couch and lie down with paper. I took the green mohair blanket from the closet, turned on a lamp, and settled in the horizontal place on the couch where my father had greeted ten thousand early mornings with his pen and paper. I put my head on the pillow just where his head had worn through the silk lining and propped my notebook against my knees.

What should I write? There was no sign, only a feeling of generosity in the room. A streetlight brightened the curtain beside me, but the rest of the room was dark. I let my gaze rove the walls—the fireplace, the dim rectangle of a painting, the hooded box of the television cabinet, a table with magazines. It was all ordinary, at rest. In the dark of the house my father's death had become an empty bowl that filled from below, the stone cavern of a spring. I felt grief, and also abundance. Many people had written us, "Words cannot begin to express how we feel without Bill. . . ." I, too, was sometimes mute with grief. But if my father had taught me one thing about writing, it was that words *can* begin to express how it is in hard times, especially if the words are relaxed, direct in their own plain ways.

I looked for a long time at the bouquet of sunflowers on the coffee table. I remembered sunflowers are the state flower of Kansas. I remembered my father's poem about yellow cars. I remembered how we had eaten the last of his summer plantings of green beans.

I thought back to my father's last poem, the one he wrote the day he died. He had begun with a line from an ordinary experience—a stray call from an insurance agent trying to track down what turned out to be a different William Stafford. The call had amused him, the agent's words had stayed with him. And that morning, 28 August 1993, he had begun to write:

"Are you Mr. William Stafford?"

"Yes, but. . . ."

As he often did, he started his last poem with recent news from his own life before coming to deeper things. But I wasn't delving into his writing now. I was in the cell of his writing time, alive earlier than anyone, more alert in welcome, listening.

The house was so quiet I heard the tap of my heart, felt the sweetness of each breath and the easy exhalation. It seemed my eyes, as in one of my father's poems, had been "tapered for braille." The edge of the coffee table held a soft gleam from the streetlight. The stack of magazines was jostled where he had touched them. Then I saw how each sunflower had dropped a little constellation of pollen on the table. The pollen seemed to burn. The soft tug that had wakened me, the tug I still felt, wanted me awake to ordinary things, to sip my bitter coffee, to gaze about, and to wait. Another of his poems came to mind:

> How still earth stayed that night at first when you didn't breathe.
> I couldn't believe how carefully moonlight came.
>
> —*from* "Letting You Go"

The way moonlight touched the curtain seemed to be instructing me how to breathe, to think, to wonder. My father had said once that time alone would allow anyone to go inward, in order to go outward. You had to go into yourself to find patterns bigger than your life.

I started to write ordinary things. Then I came to the sunflowers. This could be told wrong if I tried too hard. My father's way is not about trying, not about writing poems, not about achievement, certainly not fame. His way is being private before first light, with your breath, the scratch of the pen. His way is something like worn silk, a blanket, and that dusting of pollen from the sunflowers.

My head fit his dent in the pillow. My hand moved easily with the pen:

> pause at the gate to take off the one big shoe of his body, step
> forward light as wind.

In the uninterrupted abundance of my own time, I finished a page, closed my notebook, and rose for the day. As my father would say at such a time, there was much to do but I had done the big thing already.

Who will take my father's place in the world of poetry? No one. Who will take his place in this daily practice of the language of the tribe? Anyone who wishes. He said once the field of writing will never be crowded—not because people can't do important work, but because they don't *think* they can. This way of writing is available to anyone who wishes to rise and listen, to put words together without fear of either failure or achievement. You wake. You find a stove where you make something warm. You have a light that leaves much of the room dark. You settle in a place you have worn with the friendly shape of your body. You receive your own breath, recollection, the blessings of your casual gaze. You address the wall, the table, and whatever stands this day for Kansas pollen in your own precious life.[1]

Alistair MacLeod, "Writing about a Life That Is Fierce, Hard, Beautiful and Close to the Bone"

Long-time professor of English and creative writing at the University of Windsor, Alistair MacLeod spends his summers writing in a cliff-top cabin in Cape Breton. Born in Saskatchewan, he spent the first ten years of his life on the Prairies before his parents moved back east to Nova Scotia. After earning an MA at the University of New Brunswick, he went to the University of Notre Dame for his PhD (1968); he then taught at Indiana University until his return to Canada in 1969. He is known primarily for his novels and short stories—among them, *The Lost Salt Gift of Blood* (1976), *As Birds Bring Forth the Sun* (1986), *No Great Mischief* (1999), and *Island* (2000)—for which he has won many awards.

---

[1] With Kim Stafford's permission, the last few lines of this piece have been taken from the first published version in *Hungry Mind Review*, 1993.

WRITING ABOUT A LIFE THAT IS FIERCE, HARD, BEAUTIFUL AND CLOSE TO THE BONE

From time to time there are writers who come riding out of the hinterlands of this country called Canada. And they are writing about a life that they really know down to its smallest detail. And it is a life that is fierce and hard and beautiful and close to the bone. They are not fooling around, these writers, not counting their phrases, not being coy. And they have not returned from an aimless walk through a shopping plaza "looking for something to write about." They both know what they want to say and how to say it and they go at their task with the single-mindedness of the Ancient Mariner encountering the wedding guest. "Look," he says, "no wedding for you today because I am going to tell you a story. And I am going to hold you here and not with my hand nor with my 'glittering eye' but by the very power of what I have to tell you and how I choose to tell it. I am going to show you what I saw and heard and smelled and tasted and felt. And I am going to tell you what it is like to be abandoned by God and by man and of the true nature of loneliness and of the preciousness of life. And I am going to do it in such a way that your life will never ever again be the same."

STUDENT WRITING

INKSHEDS

Mike Beyrouty first encountered several of the readings now included in this chapter (those by Goldberg, Godwin, and Murray) when he was a first-year student in 1998. He wrote journal entries about those reading selections and later incorporated the resulting inksheds (the ones reproduced below) into a literacy narrative entitled "Emergence of a Writer."

MIKE BEYROUTY

In order to find what is hidden in our minds, we must "outrace the censor," just as Murray says. I've learned to let myself go and not think about anything I might be doing wrong. Let your stinky feet scare away the girls. It doesn't matter what anything or anybody else thinks at that moment. All that matters is that you get it down on paper. Once you've got it there, it is there forever, it can't escape you. It is like a dream. You have a dream that is bright and colorful and takes you to a wonderful world. You think to yourself you will never forget it. You say this right after your dream, but in an hour it's gone forever. The magical place you were, the ideas you had, are gone. If you write it down, though, you *will* have it forever.

The Murray piece talks about writing with speed while Godwin talks of familiarity with the censor. Godwin doesn't call it a censor, though. She calls it a "watcher at the gate." She talks of ways to trick and deceive the watcher so you can get your best ideas out in the open without his knowing it. She puts a face to the thing, the mental block. She calls it an enemy and now because she has something solid to go after, she can look at ways to defeat it—just as doctors and scientists look for ways to treat diseases. They must first have a cause before they can even think about treating the disease. That's what the author is doing. She doesn't know exactly what to call it, so she puts it in a form she can easily visualize—now she can fight it.

* * *

After I read Goldberg's essay "Be an Animal," something started happening to my writing. Everything had come together. I began to write fast and not think about the language. My writing became instinct. Just as for an animal it is instinct to hunt, for me it was instinct to write. I didn't have time to think. Ideas came from the left, then from the right, then they started popping out of the air. Pretty soon these ideas were things the censor would not want to have on paper. But, since the river of ideas had started flowing so furiously, it washed the censor away for the time being.

No, wait—it didn't wash him away, for that would mean he wouldn't come back when the water receded. Let's say he was engulfed under the water. He remained there but unable to function because of the recent flood of ideas. This is why the idea of outrunning the censor is a good one. Your must remember that once you slow, the flood of ideas will also recede with your pace and soon the censor will be in full swing again. It is a constant battle.

Goldberg talks of the writer becoming an animal. She does not talk about familiarizing yourself with the watcher: she talks about the mode you need to be in in order to get past it. The mode she describes reminds me of being in the zone for basketball. When you're in the zone and you have the ball, you know you can't go wrong. There is no hesitation, no doubt. You know you can drain the three or drive past your opponent at will. You know you can break through. Everything else fades and what's left is only the ball, the basket, and you. The defender is irrelevant. He is an undersized speedbump while you are a semi that wouldn't even feel him if you went over him at eighty miles per hour. Being the animal is just like being in the zone. All you can feel is your writing. All you can think about is your writing. All five senses are in tune and in synch while mind and body are one. Nothing can stop you. The watcher at the gate is on lunchbreak, the fog has lifted. You don't hear people walking by. You don't hear the knocking on the door. It's just you and the paper and the words in your head.

NEW PRACTICES TO TAKE FORWARD

1. **Forget about writer's block:** Take William Stafford's advice—if ever you feel yourself unable to write, just lower your standards. You can *always* write: perhaps you can't always write *well*, but you can always write *something*. And keep in mind that if your instructor requires you to bring a rough draft or an inkshed to class, writer's block is no excuse. You aren't required to bring a brilliant draft, just a draft, something that can be worked with or improved. You can't work with or improve something that doesn't exist (i.e., nothing). And even a horrible draft (or—to take a hint from Goldberg—even the worst draft in Edmonton, the worst draft in Canada, the worst draft in North America) qualifies as *something*.

2. **You fill in the blank—choose the new practice you want or need:** Go back to inkshed Prompt 6 at the beginning of this chapter and to Murray's essay. Pick a writing practice (or create one) that you'd like to turn into a habit of your own from now on and describe it here: _____ _____. Try to make it a permanent part of your writing process.

3. **Process writing reminder:** Continue doing a tiny bit of process writing every time you inkshed. (For details, see New Practice 2 on process writing, pages 20–21 in Conversation 1.)

ESSAY IDEAS

Occasionally, we'll suggest an idea for a more extended piece of writing, one you might like to develop at greater length and revise through multiple drafts. These writing ideas may or may not correspond to the formal assignments your instructor requires, but we hope some of them give you ideas for pieces you might enjoy creating on your own, now or in the future, required or not. Our assumption is that, as your inksheds accumulate, you'll discover that you have gathered a lot of material to work with and pieces of writing that might lead somewhere. For instance, the inkshed by Mike Beyrouty at the end of this Conversation ended up becoming part of a longer essay; and the essay by Stephanie Bishop in Conversation 8 grew out of several inksheds she had written during an academic term. Inksheds are obviously just warmups and/or sketches, ways to explore or learn things, not finished or polished pieces of writing on their own. So here are a few suggestions for longer writing projects.

1. **The writing-interview essay:** Interviews with individuals who have more work or writing experience than you do—or experience of a different kind— can generate rich material for essays. In as much detail as possible, ask about their writing history and writing processes. Try choosing interviewees in a field or line of work that interests you: find out what kinds of writing need to be done regularly in that occupation. Ask about every time their fingers touch a keyboard or hold a pen during the day, from the time they rise in the morning until the time they go to sleep at night (in other words, even writing a cheque or a to-do list counts). Ask them to tell you stories about times writing went well for them or times writing went badly. Gather information about their attitudes toward writing, their experience of it in school, and any private or personal writing they've done over the years. Gather more detail than you can use so you can look for emerging themes in your material. Make sure that you allow the data you've collected to suggest a possible shape or structure for your finished piece—you don't want a reader to experience your interview as a random list, just one unrelated detail after another.

   Keep in mind that interviewing just one individual can generate more data than you can use in one essay, so don't interview more than two people no matter what—unless you plan on a book-length project (once people get talking about their writing processes to someone who is genuinely interested, they usually don't want to stop). There are many possible formats interviews can follow: see Mammen's interview of Peter Elbow in Conversation 7 as well as the excerpts from William Stafford interviews in this Conversation. Use the interview to make some discoveries that matter to you—perhaps about the person you've interviewed or about your future career or about your own writing processes in comparison to those of your interviewee.

2. **Interview yourself:** Do everything in Essay Idea 1—except the person you interview should be yourself. Gather as much detail as you can about your own writing history and habits and goals (Inkshedding Prompts 1–9 should help). What you end up with could take many forms: an inventive schizophrenic piece in which you interview yourself; a reaction to some of the pieces you've read so far in this text, entering into conversation with a few of them or putting a few of them into conversation with each other; a literacy narrative (that is, a piece in which you reflect on your relationship to reading and writing and talk about key moments in your growth or deterioration as a writer). Or something we haven't thought of yet and couldn't even have imagined until you created it.

CONVERSATION 3:

Exploratory Writing and Invention: Freewriting, Inkshedding, and Writing-to-Learn

INTRODUCTION

> [F]or the most practical of reasons, Quintilian advises students to write on wax, to facilitate fast and easy-to-erase writing; to leave wide margins for additions, deletions, emendations, notes, and corrections; and to leave plenty of space for other jottings, "for sometimes the most admirable thoughts break in upon us which cannot be inserted in what we are writing, but which on the other hand, it is unsafe to put by, since they are at times forgotten, and at times cling to the memory so persistently as to divert us from some other line of thought" (*Education of the Orator*, c. 94 AD, X.iii.31-3).
>
> Cheryl Glenn, "When Grammar Was a Language Art" 23

Freewriting

You may have lots of experience with freewriting, though it may have been called something else—fast writing, speed writing, inkshedding, **writing-to-learn**. But it's unlikely that you've been introduced to the *theory* of freewriting or to research about it. In our experience, many students are resistant to freewriting because they don't see the point of it. When they've been asked to freewrite, they've often experienced it as busywork, as writing they were required to do for no apparent reason, writing that wasn't even going to be graded.

So it often makes sense to try an experiment, just to highlight the difference between freewriting and other forms of writing.

Take out a pen and a piece of paper. We promise that this will be private writing: you won't be letting anyone read it. But we're asking you to throw yourself into it with the seriousness and intensity, the total concentration, of a child at play; otherwise, you won't get the information or the experience you need from this experiment.

Okay, here are the requirements. First, write about whatever your current obsession is, whatever rises to the surface of your mind these days when you're not being distracted by something else. This obsession can be something sad or glad, it doesn't matter. No one but you will read about it. If you don't have any obsessions today, think of a piece of writing you'd like to get done, or at least started—maybe there's a thank-you note you need to write or a letter to a friend. Pick whatever is on your mind.

Second, however, follow the five rules below *as you write*. By this we mean, don't wait until you have finished writing a whole paragraph before going back and consulting these rules. Think about them from the moment you write your first word and, at the very latest, stop at the end of each sentence to double-check that you have been following them:

1. **Put an exclamation mark after every proper noun.** If you can't remember what proper nouns are, just make your best guess.

2. **Put an asterisk by every preposition.** If you can't remember what prepositions are, again, make your best guess—but here's a short refresher course: put the asterisks *above*, *below*, *in front of*, or *behind* whatever you think is a preposition.

3. **Capitalize every R, S, V, and B *wherever* they appear**—not just at the *beginning* of a word, but at the *end* of a word and also in the *middle*.

4. **Delete every "ing" from any word in which it appears**—not just from verb forms, as in "jumping" or "writing," but also from words like "ring" and "springlike" or "springing" (two "ing" bits to strike out in that last one). There's no need to blacken out or to completely erase the "ing"—simply put one straight line through it after you've seen yourself write it.

5. **Underline every adverbial phrase or clause.** Again, if you've forgotten what those are or you never knew, just take your best shot at it—you won't be handing this in, after all.

This experiment works best if you do it with everyone else in the classroom, including the instructor, so you can keep each other focused for the required five minutes and then talk about the experience afterward. But if that's not possible, go ahead and concentrate as hard as you can for five minutes on your own. Time yourself exactly (this will be important later).

***** When you see these asterisks, *close the book and write for five minutes.*

Now that a full five minutes are up, stop and quickly do a primitive form of proofreading: that is, "correct" what you've written according to the five "rules" above (for this exercise, don't worry about any other rules you've been taught in the past). As you go back through what you've written, make a mental note of which rules you were able to follow most of the time and which ones you forgot. If you're doing this experiment in class, it's fun to find out how others reacted and what rules they found easy or hard to follow and why.

Now pause to reflect on what that writing felt like; especially if you're trying this exercise on your own, take a few minutes to inkshed your reactions to the process of writing according to those rules and also your reactions to proofreading according to those rules once the writing was done (make sure to use a separate piece of paper). Hang onto this inkshed—you'll be comparing it to another one soon.

***** *Close the book and inkshed for a few minutes.*

Now, *before* doing anything else, read the following two passages from Peter Elbow, a major theorist on freewriting:

> The most effective way I know to improve your writing is to do freewriting exercises regularly. At least three times a week. . . . Don't stop for anything. Go quickly without rushing. Never stop to look back, to cross something out, to wonder how to spell something, to wonder what word or thought to use. . . . The easiest thing is just to put down whatever is in your mind. If you get stuck it's fine to write, "I can't think what to say, I can't think what to say" as many times as you want; or repeat the last word you wrote over and over again; or anything else. The only requirement is that you *never* stop.
>
> (*Writing Without Teachers* 3)

> Frequent freewriting exercises help you learn simply to *get on with it*, and not be held back by worries about whether these words are good words or the right words.
>
> Thus, freewriting is the best way to learn—in practice, not just in theory—to separate the producing process from the revising process. Freewriting exercises are push-ups in withholding judgment as you produce so that afterwards you can judge better. . . .
>
> Freewriting helps you learn to write when you don't feel like writing. It is practice in setting deadlines for yourself, taking charge of yourself, and learning gradually how to get that special energy that sometimes comes when you work fast under pressure.
>
> Freewriting teaches you to write without thinking about writing. We can usually speak without thinking about speech—without thinking about how to form words in the mouth and pronounce them and the rules of syntax we unconsciously obey—and as a result we can give undivided attention to what we say. Not so writing. Or at least most people are considerably distracted from their meaning by considerations of spelling, grammar, rules, errors. Most people experience an awkward and sometimes paralyzing *translating* process in writing: "Let's see, how shall I say this." Freewriting helps you learn to *just say* it. Regular freewriting helps make the writing process *transparent.* . . .

Freewriting helps you to think of topics to write about. Just keep writing, follow threads where they lead and you will get to ideas, experiences, feelings, or people that are just asking to be written about.

Finally, and perhaps most important, freewriting improves your writing. It doesn't always produce powerful writing itself, but it leads to powerful writing. . . . [F]reewriting also brings a surface coherence to your writing and it does so immediately. You cannot write really incoherently if you write quickly. You may violate the rules of correctness, you may make mistakes in reasoning, you may write foolishness, you may change directions before you have said anything significant. That is, you may produce something like "Me and her we went down and saw the folks but wait that reminds me of the thing I was thinking about yester oh dam what am I really trying to say." But you won't produce syntactic chaos: language that is so jumbled that when you read it over you are frightened there is something the matter with you. (*Writing with Power* 14–16)

Often we've had students worry that they'll fill pages and pages of freewriting with nothing but "I can't think what to say, I can't think what to say." In practice, that hardly ever happens. Yes, fierce freewriters do end up repeating words or phrases. Some students have actually spooked us with what we call "freewriting mantras" that seem to come out of nowhere. For instance, one barked at herself (on paper, of course) whenever her brain seemed to stick in a groove—"Think, think, think, think"—and invariably, she followed her own orders and thought and more sentences appeared after that point. Another student wrote "deeper, deeper, deeper, deeper" whenever he felt blocked. Other students have simply repeated a key word, a word that linked to what they most wanted to think about.

But the crucial instruction is to keep the pen moving. Robert Whitney, in an essay on the theory and practice of freewriting, described his own experience with students who would hit a kind of freewriting wall (something like the wall a runner can hit during a long race). He would notice a few students in each class who would have no trouble freewriting for the first four or five minutes, but would suddenly freeze when they'd finished transcribing whatever had been on the surface of their brains—the surface static, so to speak. He would invite these students individually to his office so he could work with them one on one. Again he would ask the student to freewrite, again the wall would be hit about four minutes in, and he would ask, "What are you thinking?" The student would look up, terrified, and say "Nothing"—and Whitney would reply, gently but persistently, "No problem—*Nothing* begins with an *N*."

In other words, feel free to write "nothing, nothing, nothing, nothing" as many times as you need to. When *something* finally comes into your head, at least your pen will be moving, ready to catch it.

And something always does come into your head. It may not be earth-shattering—though often what comes after one of these walls is lively and surprising, thought-provoking—but it won't be *nothing*. And even if session after session of freewriting results in what you consider garbage, writing that you always throw away, the practice itself feeds your more serious composing in ways that are difficult to describe.

What is more likely is that you will occasionally discover in your freewriting sentences or ideas that you want to keep and to build on. Powerful writing can't come from nowhere anymore than powerful dancing or powerful ball playing can come from nowhere: months and months of practice can go into preparing for one performance or one important game.

Now that you've read a bit of theory about freewriting, it's time for another writing session. You can continue writing about the same obsession if you like or writing the same letter or whatever you started before. But this time you're not only going to throw out the five rules you were following above; you're going to forget about *any* writing rules you've worried about ever. This doesn't mean that you're going to make mistakes on purpose. If following certain rules is second nature for you (like capitalizing the word at the beginning of a sentence or putting a period at the end), continue to follow those rules. Trying *not* to follow them will distract you. The goal is to have as few distractions between you and your thoughts as possible. Remember to go quickly without rushing—this is not a race, but you also don't want to pause since censors tend to rear their ugly heads during the pauses. Again, this is private writing so no one is going to read it but you. Write nonstop for five minutes, exactly the same amount of time as before so you can easily compare the two pieces of writing.

Begin.

***** *Again, close the book and write for five minutes. (Please time yourself.)*

Now take a look at those two pieces of writing, the one you wrote following those five rules on page 107 and the freewriting you just did. Which one is longer? Which one was easier to do? During which one did you feel in closer contact with the contents of your own mind? If you're doing this exercise on your own, inkshed briefly now on a separate sheet of paper about the experience of freewriting as opposed to what we can now call **unfreewriting**.

***** *Again, put the book aside to inkshed for a few minutes.*

Now that you've done two short pieces of private writing and two pieces of **process writing** ("process writing" is the term that describes the two inksheds about how those sprints of private writing went for you), swap your process writing with some of the other students in your class to see what their reactions were. The point of this exercise is obvious, of course, but not nearly as compelling if you just read about it in a textbook without trying these exercises out yourself, intensely and in good faith. We particularly like having teachers or future teachers try out these two forms of writing, since teachers tend to self-select: that is, they are often people who have found writing unproblematic. If they've never had serious difficulties with spelling or grammar or usage, at least not serious enough to make them frustrated with schoolwork, they can have trouble understanding how their students can struggle with the mechanics of writing. The good thing about these five peculiar and arbitrary rules is that they put everyone on the same footing—*no one* has had any practice writing according to these rules; these rules feel strange and distracting to *everyone*. Thus, it helps give teachers an experience that most of them don't ever remember having but that many of their students *do* have, the experience of worrying so much about following the rules that they can't remember where their sentence was going from one word to the next. These rules also highlight for teachers how arbitrary the rules of English can seem to students for whom these rules are *not* second nature (and that's especially the case for students from other countries, for whom English is a second or third language). We've dubbed writing according to these eccentric rules "unfreewriting," an exercise Sargent developed after first reading the work of Lucy Calkins (199).

Of course, the point of freewriting is *not* to create final drafts by writing nonstop, but simply to become more fluent and more practiced. Freewriting is *never* meant to replace your slower and more considered composing practices; it's something to practise *in addition to* your established writing processes. If you have writing habits and procedures that work for you, whatever you do, *don't change them*. Simply add fifteen minutes of freewriting, at least three times a week, to your schedule: it will nourish you as a writer, no matter what your usual writing processes are. And it will be waiting there on the sidelines, handy, if you ever experience a moment of writer's block and need something to dynamite you out of it.

Inkshedding

In Russ Hunt's piece on inkshedding in this Conversation, it's clear from his very first sentence that inkshedding owes a lot to freewriting—is, in fact, simply a variety of freewriting. The essential distinction, however, is that inkshedding is always public: it's always written with an audience in mind and with the intention of being shared. And it's important that the audience *knows* what freewriting and inkshedding are before you share your raw writing with them. In our culture, people are quick to judge if your writing is full of surface errors—unless they understand the theory and practice of freewriting themselves. Luckily, in a writing class, it doesn't take long to build up a community of writers and learners who understand what exploratory writing is and who trust one another to read and respond to exploratory writing productively (see Conversation 7 on "Audience, Evaluation, and Response" for a range of useful ways to respond to the freewriting of others). Remember, as a class member, never to violate that trust. Don't take a piece written inside the trusting community of the class and share it with anyone *outside* the class unless you have the permission of the author—and, we would argue, unless you have made sure that anyone reading that writing understands the goals and purposes and limits of exploratory writing.

In the autumn 2001 issue of *Inkshed* (the newsletter of CASLL, the Canadian Association for the Study of Language and Learning), Doug Brent of the University of Calgary clarified the differences between freewriting and inkshedding; in doing so, he was summarizing several days' worth of face-to-face conversations at the May 2001 Inkshed Conference, a conference in which Peter Elbow, after giving the keynote address, had been an active participant:

> Inkshedding is more transactional at its core. Although similar in form to freewriting, to the extent that it is produced quickly with little regard for the niceties of scholarly prose, inkshedding is different in that its reason for being is already audience. . . . Inkshedding is designed to be shared, first among the others sitting at the table who exchange the tattered bits of paper, mark them up, annotate them, write exclamation marks and "me too's" in the margin, and later among the entire conference or classroom, whether by being edited and photocopied or merely by being stapled to the wall.

> It is this on-the-wallness that marks a fundamental difference between inkshedding and freewriting. The purpose of inkshedding is to make sure that all voices are heard, in ways that are not possible in a group in which only one can speak at a time and the strongest and most confident voices are generally the ones that get to speak. Inkshedding takes advantage of the asynchronicity of text—the fact that all can write simultaneously, and . . . all can simultaneously read. (1)

Thus when students read each other's inksheds, the focus is to be more on *what* is said, not so much on *how*: students are to read, understand, and answer to the ideas, to the *content* of the inkshed, not try to evaluate or improve the writing itself in any way. Inkshedding, plus reading and responding to the inksheds of others in this way, often improves both writing *and* learning, as Reither and Vipond reveal in their essay in this chapter.

Writing-to-Learn

One of the things that writers and scholars in the field of composition and rhetoric agree on is that writing is a way of figuring out the world, of figuring out what we think and what we know—it is not simply a way of recording and communicating what we *already* know. This is true whether the writing is private or public. We all know that listening, reading, and talking are important ways to learn (lectures, textbooks, and class discussions are based on our assumptions about these modes of learning). But we're now discovering that *writing* is arguably the most effective learning tool available to us. Janet Emig, a major scholar and researcher in the composition field, has been particularly influential in showing how writing is a unique way of knowing. Her well-known 1977 essay, "Writing as a Mode of Learning," argued that out of all verbal acts (speaking, listening, reading, or writing), writing was the most powerful way to learn. Lasting learning needs the hand and the eye, not just the brain, and only writing *requires* us to use all three simultaneously. Writing, according to Emig (125), does three things at once: it allows us to learn (1) by *doing*, by bodily activity (it's "enactive"); (2) by *seeing* marks on a page, a physical track of our thinking (it's "iconic"); and (3) by articulating, *verbalizing* (the process of putting things into words makes writing "symbolic").

Emig focuses in her essay on differences between talking and writing. She notes that writing, unlike speech, is always an artificial, learned activity and that speech and writing (as shown in studies of aphasia in stroke victims) come from different organic sources in the brain. Precisely because writing involves both process *and* a visible graphic product, it leaves a track of our thinking that is "more readily a form and source of learning than talking." Writing—unlike reading, listening, or talking—"uniquely corresponds to certain powerful learning strategies" (122).

Certainly listening and reading are creative and engaged verbal acts; but what distinguishes them from speaking and writing is that they are not "originating"—that is, the words being listened to or read weren't originally supplied or put together by the listener or the reader. Emig highlights the properties of each verbal act in the following list (123; italics ours):

- Reading is creating or re-creating *but not originating* a verbal construct that *is* graphically recorded.

- Listening is creating or re-creating *but not originating* a verbal construct that is *not* graphically recorded.

- Talking is creating *and originating* a verbal construct that is *not* graphically recorded.

- Writing is creating *and originating* a unique verbal construct that *is* graphically recorded.

Thus writing is a more complete and powerful mode of learning than the other three.

Emig's dense and groundbreaking work—drawing on her own research into students' writing processes as well as on the research of linguists, cognitive psychologists, and educators—has had a major impact on the development of **WAC** (**writing-across-the-curriculum**) and **writing-to-learn** programs across North America. Informal, ungraded but required and tightly focused exploratory writing is increasingly used in *all* fields, including math and science, to help students deepen and extend their learning of difficult concepts. Marta Currah's annotation (in this Conversation) of an important essay by Peter Elbow suggests a wide range of such writing-to-learn activities. And Toby Fulwiler's important work on journals owes a lot to Emig's research; he continues to influence the ongoing conversation about WAC, about **writing-intensive courses (WIC)** in all disciplines, and about how first-year writing courses should be taught (see his pieces in this chapter, including the policy statement on journals that he drafted for the National Council of Teachers of English). As Emig puts it, "writing through its inherent re-inforcing cycle involving hand, eye, and brain marks a uniquely powerful multi-representational mode for learning" (125), enabling students not only to *engage* with and dig into texts and materials more actively, but also to *remember* more clearly what they have read and studied. In other words, writing helps all learners learn better no matter what subjects they are studying or at what level.

While the debate may continue about the relative value of private versus public freewriting-to-learn, teachers and researchers agree that *either* practice would help students understand difficult material better than they ever could *without* writing about it at all. Perhaps the more important distinction is the one between low-stakes (ungraded) and high-stakes (graded) writing—informal, ungraded, but required writing-to-learn (often in the form of journals or project logs) has become an essential element in many university courses that take seriously the irreplaceable role writing can play in supporting student learning. For Emig, of course, the operative term is "writing"—public or private, graded or ungraded, *all* writing is an indispensable form of learning, *all* writing is writing-to-learn. Even when we're working on formal papers or major projects that will be graded or evaluated in a way that may affect our lives forever, we are facing opportunities for learning; all writing is, in that sense, exploratory writing, helping us make discoveries about ourselves and about the world.

Invention

How do people get ideas in the first place? How do they get words on the page? How do they find themselves writing passages that surprise them, that they never expected to write when they first sat down and turned the computer on? The process of coming up with words and ideas becomes even more impenetrable, invisible, if—as Duncan Carter points out in this section—we cling to a persistent myth about writing: "You have to know your point before you write."

It might surprise you to learn that some of the **writing-to-learn strategies** you may have been experimenting with in this book (see pages 150–153 in this chapter) could also be called **invention strategies**. Another term for them would be **heuristics** (which is just a word for anything that helps us make discoveries or learn, helps us solve a problem or figure something out). In the past, you may have been told to write essays in certain formats—for instance, "cause and effect" or "compare and contrast." These structures started out as heuristics or invention strategies, aids for thinking, but somehow got solidified into fixed essay forms. Whatever you thought of them as fixed forms, as moulds to pour your ideas into, they still work well as ways to *get* ideas in the first place. You may end up having to create a whole new structure for your finished piece, but it can certainly help you to get started if you use, for instance, a compare and contrast strategy to brainstorm about how two things are alike and then how they are unlike.

As Maxine Hairston points out about the new **paradigm** in the teaching of writing (see her well-known essay in this chapter), we have learned to focus more on invention than we used to, helping students get rough drafts written. Recently, scholars in composition have developed some additional strategies to help us as we begin to compose. Sondra Perl's **Composing Guidelines**, reprinted in this Conversation, can help you get started on a difficult writing task even when you don't have much idea what your topic is. And Peter Elbow's **loop writing** (see Karen Kurt's cartoon on page 154) can be especially productive if you've done such a huge amount of reading and research that you're overwhelmed and can't imagine how to shape all that material into a paper. With either of these forms of exploratory writing, what we find most useful of all is the way they set limits.

Let us explain. Like most procrastinators, we often used to put off starting a writing task because it seemed too big to tackle. We were always waiting for the perfect time to get started—that is, several days (or maybe even just *one full day*) on which we had nothing else planned to distract or interrupt us—a time that, by definition, did not and could not ever exist (perfection being inhuman). But we found that if we planned to spend, say, two hours following the Perl Composing Guidelines or Karen Kurt's loop cartoon, we could make a bargain with ourselves. We *knew* we wouldn't finish; we wouldn't even *try* to finish a piece of writing. We'd only make a start. We also knew that after two hours of intense nonstop writing we could stop and do something else, perhaps reward ourselves by going out with friends or watching a film. But the following day, when we would read through the printout, we'd have something to work with; and because we had written intensely without stopping, we would have generated some of the heat that we usually could experience only when we were panicked at the last minute, working all through the night to meet a deadline. So the writing, messy though it might be, would also have a certain energy. Because of that energy, it would probably have made some necessary mental connections, connections we couldn't have made otherwise.

So keep in mind that the Composing Guidelines and loop writing are powerful heuristics, invention strategies, that can help you to separate the composing process from the editing process, to explore your ideas and your research, and to get those difficult first words on the page.

We've included in this section as well a few excerpts from the process writing of our students as they reflect on their experiences with the Perl Composing Guidelines or with loop writing (more examples of student process writing can be found in Sargent's "Felt Sense in the Composition Classroom"). Our students share our realization that not every invention strategy will work for everyone; further, a strategy that worked for you one month may not work well for you the next. Thus, it's important to try each of these strategies several times to get a feeling for situations when it will be fruitful for you and when it is less likely to be. Of course, none of these strategies can help you if you don't try them—or if you don't try them with concentrated energy and commitment. Risk-taking is always required.

Further, as Karen Burke LeFevre has pointed out, invention itself is not a solitary, individual act, but is collaborative through and through. Everything we write, even our most private exploratory writing, has been shaped and influenced in some way by everything we've ever read or heard or seen in our culture, as well as, more specifically, by the conversations we've been having with our peers in a particular course and by the occasion that is calling our writing forth. In an academic setting, this occasion is most often a required writing assignment, but see the introduction to Conversation 6 for a description of genre as social action and examples of other kinds of occasions.

We've discovered that we can heighten the collaborative nature of invention and increase opportunities for productive collaborative invention by allowing others to read our exploratory writing and to mark or highlight the passages that they think we should keep and/or develop further. We model this process ourselves by reading through at least one long piece of exploratory writing, usually loop writing, from each student early in the term so students (you) can get some good ideas about how to do this effectively for each other (see New Practice 2, pages 173–174 in this section, for further details). After a session of loop writing at white heat together in a computer lab, students hand us the resulting printouts certain that what they've written is complete garbage. Certainly, most loops are messy—but if they're garbage, they're garbage into which diamonds have been thrown. We are eager to sort through them, glad to get our hands dirty. We discover in these loops passages that make us laugh, that move us, that surprise us and make us think, that take our breath away. Often we find the best writing we've ever seen from particular students, especially students who were finding it hard to inkshed nonstop on their own: writing in the group setting pushes them to keep their fingers moving and not to second-guess themselves. And much more often than one might think, we find hints of how a strong essay could take shape: we'll highlight certain passages that each student should keep (writing in the margin comments like "These two sentences had better show up in your final essay exactly as they appear here, or you're in big trouble"), and we're sometimes able to point out what the focus or heart of a future essay could be ("If you start with the question you raise in #8, and then include the discussion from your dialogue section, and then lead into your data with that strong sentence in #2 . . ."). Some loops are so rich we can actually point out three or four possible ways that a lively essay could take shape.

Students are often stunned (in a good way—see Marcie Bonstrom Arnold's process writing in this chapter) to get their loops back with highlighting and with enthusiastic, generative comments all over them. So many of them (and this may be true of you as well, but we're talking right now about our experience with students in the past) have for so long associated marginal comments with *problems* in their writing, we sometimes have to remind them that loop marginalia *never* criticize the writing itself. What would be the point? The writing is obviously rough. It's not meant to be a polished draft. If a gem shows up, our job is to highlight it so that the student doesn't (so you don't) miss it or toss it out—especially since, in our experience, students (you) are way too apt to throw such gems away, assuming that they're not formal or polished enough for academic display. We engage with the ideas and certainly might write a comment in the margin that showed we disagreed or felt an important complication or detail had been overlooked. But the primary goal is to emphasize material the writer can build on, lines that should be kept or developed further. We always assume that much of each loop will be throwaway writing, writing whose sole purpose for being was just to get the good stuff generated and visible so someone could identify it and suggest ways to work with it. And once we have modelled how to heighten the social nature of invention by responding to loop writing, students (you) know how to do it for each other the next time.

Keep in mind that *all* invention strategies, all exploratory writing sessions, are only the first steps in a long roundabout journey. We separate composing from editing in order to generate richer material (and more of it) to work with. But working with that material—through multiple drafts, revising, and editing—will be necessary if any piece of writing is ever to face the world on its own.

INKSHEDDING PROMPTS

1. Duncan Carter describes some common myths about writing. Were you taught any of these myths? Are there some of these beliefs about writing that you're willing or even eager to abandon? others that you want to argue for? Where did these myths come from in your own life—from teachers, your parents, TV, or the culture at large? Try to be as specific as possible pinpointing the source of your beliefs about writing. Has Carter convinced you to change your mind about any of these myths? If so, how? What persuaded you? Has he supported all of his assertions with evidence? If he hasn't convinced you, has he made you curious, made you want to explore some of his assertions further? If so, which ones? Are there some other beliefs that you or others have about writing that you think Carter should have mentioned, beliefs that should also be questioned?

2. A **paradigm** is simply a model or an example. So when scholars talk about **paradigm shifts** in their fields, they're talking about moments when our model of the world changes in important ways. That is, the entire intellectual framework alters for a large group of people, not just a few—though it is often a few pioneers who have risked their careers to bring the new model into being and then to bring it to everyone's attention. The term has been used most often to refer to changes in science: for example, the paradigm shift when everyone came to believe that the earth revolved around the sun, rather than the other way around; or the paradigm shift when everyone came to accept Einstein's theory of relativity.

Such changes do not occur overnight. They may be exciting, but they can also be painful: they can require such a transformation of one's whole belief system and such a questioning of one's lifework that some people can never make the transition. Thomas Kuhn's famous book, *The Structure of Scientific Revolutions*, reveals that some scientists can never accept certain changes: the new paradigm takes hold completely only after a whole generation of scientists has died out.

How well does the analogy of a paradigm shift work for what Hairston (in "The Winds of Change") describes happening in the teaching of writing? As you read through the pieces in this Conversation, note any resistances of your own. What interests and excites you in the new paradigm she talks about ("the process paradigm") in the teaching of writing? What bothers you about it? Do you find Carter any more convincing after reading Hairston? Which piece of writing (Carter or Hairston) persuades you more and why? There's no one right answer to that last question, but inkshedding about it might tell you something about the kind of voice you find most compelling in a piece of academic writing and therefore the kind of academic writing you most want to produce yourself.

3. As you read through the essays in this Conversation, you'll probably start noticing something strange—a lot of these people are dropping names. In fact, they're dropping a lot of the same names, and some of these are the names of authors of essays in this book. But the names overlap in an odd way. Take a look:

    - **Carter** (whose piece is the shortest) still manages to mention two names: Emig and Sommers (on revision).

    - **Hairston** mentions so many, we can list only a few: Emig, Sommers (on revision again), Murray, Elbow, Perl, Britton, Flower, Bruffee.

    - **Fulwiler** mentions Emig, Graves, and Britton.

    - **Hunt** mentions, among others, Elbow, Britton, Flower, Graves, Paré, and Reither.

    - **Reither and Vipond** mention Hunt, Paré, Bruffee, LeFevre, and Frank Smith.

    So what is happening here? These texts answer to each other; they seem to have been written in the presence of these other scholars: they acknowledge their influence and their contributions. One word for this phenomenon is **intertextuality**; and the way in which the references to other scholars overlap and interconnect leads some researchers to refer to the existence of an **intertextual web**, a web we're caught up in from the first minute we begin to work in any particular field. Another way of putting it, the way we've been describing it in this book, is to call it an ongoing conversation— these authors are all in **conversation** with one another, even though they may never have met in person.

Of course, nobody likes name-dropping if it's done just to impress. And perhaps name-dropping is even more irritating if it doesn't impress you but just makes you feel left out—because you don't recognize any of the names. But are these scholars trying to impress us? or to make us feel left out? Perhaps it will help to think of footnotes and endnotes and works-cited lists as address books, made available openly so we can look these people up and get to know them ourselves. Notice that Emig, for instance, is listed by the first three authors. Your reading may have slowed down and you may have gotten a bit bored when, in the introduction to this Conversation, we gave you a few paragraphs of information about Emig and her work—but we were, literally, trying to introduce her to you (to get you to at least shake her hand) so you wouldn't feel so left out when Carter, Hairston, and Fulwiler all mentioned her by name.

Go back to those paragraphs (pages 112–114) now and re-read them. Inkshed a quick summary of her ideas and speculate how they may have influenced not just the work of the three authors who mention her by name, but some of the other pieces in this chapter, including Perl's Composing Guidelines, Elbow's loop writing (see Kurt's cartoon), Sargent's Writing-to-Learn Strategies, and the NCTE guidelines on using journals.

4.   How did you react to Toby Fulwiler's essay? Did anything he had to say about first-year students and about the assumptions and experiences they bring with them from high school irritate you or seem inaccurate or unfair? This piece appeared in *The Chronicle of Higher Education* in 1986 (note the out-of-date reference to "freshmen"), so his primary audience at the time was university teachers and administrators. Why is he writing to them in this way, about these things? That is, what social action do you think he's trying to accomplish? What is he trying to change? Some students have taken his comments as a kind of dare—do you experience them this way? He obviously wasn't expecting students to read his piece. Be as detailed as you can be about the exact sentences that seem to trigger your reactions, positive or negative. Writing-to-Learn Strategies 20 and 21 (see page 152) might be especially appropriate for writing a response to Fulwiler; or inkshed a letter

to him, as in Strategy 23 (Fulwiler loves letters and has in fact written an entire book about them as a tool for learning, *The Letter Book*).

5. After reading Hunt on inkshedding, Sargent's Writing-to-Learn Strategies (which are essentially inkshedding strategies), Marta Currah's summary of Peter Elbow's essay, the NCTE guidelines, and the introduction to Conversation 3 with its summary of Janet Emig's work on writing as a mode of learning (see pages 112–114), check out Mindy Levine's inksheds (pages 168–170). She kept a writing-to-learn log as a way of supporting her studies in Biology 102. After you've read about her experience, pick a course you're currently taking where the material feels daunting; then pick an inkshedding strategy (see pages 150–153) and try one of them to explore a particular concept, lecture, lab, or reading that you're having trouble with (1, 2, 4–9, 14–15, or 18 might work especially well). Consider showing your inkshed to a friend who is also taking the class and who seems to be grasping the material more easily; or you could share it with your instructor, asking for some clarification. You could also read through your inkshed a few days later and then go back to your lecture notes or your textbook to see if you can figure out exactly where your confusion began; another inkshed at this point, to record anything you learn in the process, might be useful. Try keeping an inkshed log for a while in that particular class as a secret weapon to support your learning. If you put a lot of energy into an inkshed log during a semester, you might discover that studying for a final exam is much easier—not only because substantive inksheds can give you quick summaries of lectures and reading assignments to review at exam time, but because, having written about the material week by week, you've actually retained more information all along and have less need to cram for the test.

6. Read through the introduction to Sondra Perl's "Guidelines for Composing" in this section. Then, write for at least one uninterrupted hour following the guidelines themselves, allowing yourself five to ten minutes for each prompt. Even if you have done this once already in class, try it again on your own when you're free to work at your own pace. What you write during this session will be private writing—that is, you won't be asked to let anyone read it—but make sure you have a printout of it. Try if possible not to read it for at least a week. Then, read through it and reflect on these three things in a process inkshed:

    i. What was the experience like for you as you were writing under the Perl Guidelines?

ii. What was it like reading through your writing a week or several days later?

iii. What do you think about the Perl Composing Guidelines themselves, reading them through again after having followed them at least once?

Did you write about something private or did you use the guidelines to get started on a writing assignment for one of your classes? Often, people who write about personal issues during their first Perl Guidelines session assume that the Composing Guidelines could never help them with an intellectual or practical writing task—and vice versa. It helps to read other people's inksheds to get a sense of how differently people make use of the Composing Guidelines. If you've been thinking about possible ways to develop further the writing you started under the Perl Guidelines, discuss those in your process writing if you want to.

7. Write for at least an hour nonstop following the loop cartoon on page 154. Make sure before you begin that you've got lots of new material in your head, reading or research you've been doing to prepare to write about a particular topic. When the loop asks you to make a particular move, connect it somehow to your specific topic. Feel free to have lots of material with you—books, notes, articles with key passages underlined. Whenever your mind goes blank, glance briefly at one of those resources for a key word or image or concept to jog your mind, to remind you of some of the ideas and data you've been working with. Then jump right back into the writing as fast as possible. Let your fingers fly and make a real mess.

Loops are particularly good at getting us to jump quickly into forms we might not otherwise try out (dialogue, narrative, description, epigraph) or into different perspectives (different audiences, voices, time frames, mindsets). They can also clear our minds by forcing us to articulate certain otherwise unspoken assumptions, our prejudices toward the material (biases for or against) or our fears about the assignment itself.

If you're working at a computer, make sure to save after each item in the loop, especially making sure to save your work one final time at the end before you print out. E-mail yourself a copy of what you've written or make sure you have a backup on disk. Also, remember, if you're working on your own, you can work through the loop items in any order—and you can skip a few of the items, especially if you're running out of time. Just don't spend the whole hour writing on only one to three items, and make sure to try the suggestions that seem hardest and strangest to you.

When you're done, if at all possible, swap your loop writing with a colleague who is working on a similar project. See New Practice 2 at the end of this Conversation (page 173) on giving and getting loop feedback.

8. Reither and Vipond organize their classes around a crucial research question that everyone works to explore together throughout the term. Use your fifteen to twenty minutes of nonstop inkshedding to brainstorm a few questions about writing or the teaching of writing that you think are important, questions that have come to you from the readings in this Conversation, questions you might be interested in exploring further. Pick one of your research questions to focus on and sketch all the ways you can think of for conducting this inquiry: describe in as much detail as possible the kinds of interviews, surveys, experiments, library research, or web research you might carry out. If some examples would help, glance at Donald Murray's list of research ideas on revision in Conversation 8 (pages 401–408). Your instructor may ask everyone to pool their research ideas in order to arrive at a few common class goals for inquiry during the term.

Duncan Carter, "Five Myths about Writing"

Posted above our desks is a useful warning we learned from Duncan Carter: don't mark surface errors in students' rough drafts because, first, such a practice sends the wrong message and, second, it's as useless as "shooting fleas off a charging rhinoceros." Whenever we feel tempted to copy edit early drafts, we think of Carter's alarming image and try to restrain ourselves.

Professor of English and Associate Dean of the College of Liberal Arts and Sciences at Portland State University (PSU) in Oregon, Carter directed the writing program at PSU, managed its writing-intensive courses, and developed the Challenge Program, a program giving future high-school teachers experience teaching introductory composition at the college level and thus firsthand knowledge of what their high-school students would need to know to be prepared for university writing. With Sherrie Gradin, he co-authored *Writing as Reflective Action* (2001).

FIVE MYTHS ABOUT WRITING

Learning how to write, students first have a lot to unlearn: all those things they "know" about writing, well, just ain't so. When I teach writing, I fondly hope my students will have gained some distance from these debilitating myths by the end of the term. Here are what one of my Writing 121 classes thought were the most common student myths about writing.

You have to know your point before you write.

Perhaps because they have been told that good writers work only from detailed outlines, students often believe that they have to know their main point before they start writing. (This is precisely why their main point often turns out to be some readily available cultural commonplace: a cliché.) They don't see writing as a process of discovering meaning. A good deal of freewriting, journal keeping, and other informal, ungraded "writing-to-learn" may help them come to see writing as a form of inquiry—as opposed to a method of recording the outcome of inquiry that took place elsewhere.

Good writers always get it right the first time.

Years of well-intentioned English teachers have responded to students' first drafts as if they were supposed to have been perfect. Combined with a pedagogy which suggests that revision is a form of punishment, it is not hard to see where students get the idea that good writers don't have to revise. They don't know that Thoreau wrote seven drafts of *Walden*, or that Hemingway rewrote the last page of *Farewell to Arms* some thirty-five times.

A good piece of writing has five paragraphs: introduction, conclusion, and three paragraphs of support.

The "**five-paragraph theme**" is a student genre so widespread in American schools that Janet Emig, author of a seminal work in composition studies, refers to it as the "fifty-star theme." Granted, even Aristotle knew that a good argument had a beginning, a middle and an end; in his *Rhetoric* he noted that speeches only have two essential parts: "You must state your case, and you must prove it." But the five-paragraph theme is too limited, too inflexible, too constraining for most purposes. What students need to learn in college is that different disciplines structure arguments differently, and that within disciplinary constraints one's argument dictates structure rather than the other way around.

Revision means fixing spelling and grammar.

Wrong, it means having the vision over again. Nancy Sommers, now of Harvard, has done some research comparing the revision habits of student writers with those of more experienced writers. She concluded that students don't rewrite so much as they "reword," rarely engaging in the kind of "global" revision—cutting, adding, rearranging, refocusing, rethinking—that is habitual to experienced writers. Students often seem to stampede to closure; we can help them by teaching them to re-open their papers rather than closing them down prematurely. Peer or teacher feedback on early drafts helps. What students think of as revision is better thought of as editing or even proofreading.

The best paper is one that follows instructions and takes no risks, or correctness is more important than having significant ideas.

Probably a corollary of the four previous myths. The only way we can counter this tragic misconception is to take our students' ideas seriously. Yet when we make twenty remarks on a student's paper, only one of which is a response to the idea and nineteen of which correct spelling and grammar, we are keeping this myth alive.

Additional myths

Good writers always have topic sentences in their paragraphs, usually the first sentence of the paragraph.

You have to have a clear idea of your structure before you start.

The thesis sentence has to go at the end of the first paragraph.

Writing itself is a form of punishment.

Use commas where you would breathe. (What if you're a heavy breather?)

Assume your audience doesn't know anything about the subject.

You cannot use contractions or *I*, parentheses, dashes, the verb *to be*, exclamation marks, colloquialisms, expletives, *I think* (or *I feel*) in formal writing. Nor can you start a sentence with *and, but,* or *however.*

Maxine Hairston, from "The Winds of Change: Thomas Kuhn and the Revolution in the Teaching of Writing"

Maxine Hairston gave us some simple but memorable advice that we try hard to follow when we teach writing: when you read through a student's paper for the first time, sit on your hands. That is, don't mark any errors at all until you've seen the shape of the whole piece, until you see what the student is trying to say and how the student is trying to say it. Read through the piece the first time, as much as possible, *for content only.* The second time through, Hairston maintains, you'll not only notice fewer mistakes—you'll be in a better position to describe the two or three things the student could do to strengthen this particular essay.

Of course, what we've found over time is that this is good way to read *anyone's* writing, not just student papers: we should read with the expectation that the writer has something meaningful to say and that the writer has shaped each sentence carefully in order to express that meaning. Reading with pen or pencil in hand for the purpose of marking mistakes changes the way we read: when we read looking for error, not surprisingly, error is the main thing we find.

In a very specific location, the University of Texas at Austin (UT), Hairston influenced the conversation about writing by directing the composition program and teaching many graduate students, UT being one of the first universities in North America where one could earn a PhD in Rhetoric and Composition (since 1979). Beyond her own university, Hairston became a major voice in the wider conversation about writing through her research and publications and as president (in 1985) of the National Council of Teachers of English. She has authored or co-authored over seven textbooks, texts that have introduced process methodologies to many students and instructors.

In the excerpt below, taken from her most famous essay, Hairston argues that the field of composition and rhetoric has changed drastically since the 1960s. She doesn't argue that this change happened overnight (in fact, it's clear that in many places, it still has *not* happened). In the two sections of her essay which we have not had space to reprint here, she details the many signs of change over time—from the work of linguists like Noam Chomsky; to the insights of psychologists like Carl Rogers; to an important seminar on the teaching of English held at Dartmouth in 1966; to the work of Mina Shaughnessy, facing open admissions at CUNY (City University of New York) in 1970 and trying to figure out ways to be useful to students who were completely unprepared for university writing; to the Bay Area Writing Project in the States, initiated in 1975 (now known as the National Writing Project, with multiple project sites in most states); to the work of scholars like Janet Emig and James Britton, studying the writing processes and abilities of students, and the work of professional writers like Donald Murray, examining their *own* writing processes and insisting that textbooks needed to reveal what working writers went through to produce their work. Murray's influential book, *A Writer Teaches Writing*, first came out in 1968; his 1972 essay, "Teach Writing as Process, Not Product," is—according to Hairston—where that admonition first entered our ongoing conversation about writing.

from THE WINDS OF CHANGE: THOMAS KUHN AND THE REVOLUTION IN THE TEACHING OF WRITING

In 1963, the University of Chicago Press published a book titled *The Structure of Scientific Revolutions*, written by Thomas Kuhn, a University of California professor of the history of science. In the book Kuhn hypothesizes about the process by which major changes come about in scientific fields, and conjectures that they probably do not evolve gradually from patient and orderly inquiry by established investigators in the field. Rather, he suggests, revolutions in science come about as the result of breakdowns in intellectual systems, breakdowns that occur when old methods won't solve new problems. He calls the change in theory that underlies this kind of revolution a paradigm shift. I believe we are currently at the point of such a *paradigm shift* in the teaching of writing, and that it has been brought about by a variety of developments that have taken place in the last 25 years.

Briefly, Kuhn's thesis in *The Structure of Scientific Revolutions* is this.

When a scientific field is going through a stable period, most of the practitioners in the discipline hold a common body of beliefs and assumptions; they agree on the problems that need to be solved, the rules that govern research, and on the standards by which performance is to be measured. They share a conceptual model that Kuhn calls a paradigm, and that paradigm governs activity in their profession. Students who enter the discipline prepare for membership in its intellectual community by studying that paradigm.

But paradigms are not necessarily immutable. When several people working in a field begin to encounter anomalies or phenomena that cannot be explained by the established model, the paradigm begins to show signs of instability. For a while, those who subscribe to the paradigm try to ignore the contradictions and inconsistencies that they find, or they make improvised, *ad hoc* changes to cope with immediate crises. Eventually, however, when enough anomalies accumulate to make a substantial number of scientists in the field question whether the traditional paradigm can solve many of the serious problems that face them, a few innovative thinkers will devise a new model. And if enough scientists become convinced that the new paradigm works better than the old one, they will accept it as the new norm.

This replacement of one conceptual model by another one is Kuhn's paradigm shift. He cites as classic examples the astronomers' substitution of the Copernican model of the solar system for the Ptolemaic model and the development of Newtonian physics. Such shifts are usually disorderly and often controversial, and the period in which they occur is apt to be marked by insecurity and conflict within the discipline.

Kuhn believes that because these shifts are so disruptive, they will occur only when the number of unsolved problems in a discipline reaches crisis proportions and some major figures in the field begin to focus on those unsolved problems. But even with mounting evidence that their conceptual model doesn't work, supporters of the traditional paradigm resist change because they have an intellectual and sometimes emotional investment in the accepted view. They particularly resist abandoning the conventional textbooks that set forth the precepts of their discipline in clear and unqualified terms. Those texts, as Richard Young points out in his essay, "Paradigms and Problems: Needed Research in Rhetorical Theory," are usually so similar that one way to discover the traditional paradigm of a field is to examine its textbooks.[1]

Finally, however, most of the resistance to the new paradigm will dissipate when its advocates can demonstrate that it will solve problems that the traditional paradigm could not solve. Most of the new generation of scholars working in the field will adopt the new model, and the older practitioners will gradually come around to it. Those who cling to the old paradigm lose their influence in the field because the leaders in the profession simply ignore their work. When that happens, the paradigm shift is complete, and the theory that was revolutionary becomes conventional.

This summary of Kuhn's book is sketchy and too simple, but I think it accurately reflects the key points in his theory. When he developed the theory, he considered only the so-called hard sciences, particularly chemistry, astronomy, and physics. He did not claim or even suggest that his model for scientific revolution could or should apply to social sciences or the humanities, where research is not done in laboratories and usually does not involve measurements or formulas. Nevertheless, I believe that composition theorists and writing teachers can learn from Thomas Kuhn if they see his theory of scientific revolutions as an analogy that can illuminate developments that are taking place in our profession. Those developments, the most prominent of which is the move to a process-centered theory of teaching writing, indicates that our profession is probably in the first stages of a paradigm shift.

THE CURRENT-TRADITIONAL PARADIGM AND ITS PROPONENTS

In order to understand the nature of that shift, we need to look at the principal features of the paradigm that has been the basis of composition teaching for several decades. In "Paradigms and Problems" Richard Young describes it this way:

> The overt features . . . are obvious enough: the emphasis on the com-
> posed product rather than the composing process; the analysis of dis-
> course into description, narration, exposition, and argument; the
> strong concern with usage . . . and with style; the preoccupation with
> the informal essay and research paper; and so on.[2]

Young adds that underlying the traditional paradigm is what he calls the "vitalist" attitude toward composing: that is, the assumption that no one can really teach anyone else how to write because writing is a mysterious creative activity that cannot be categorized or analyzed.

In an article in the Winter, 1980, *Freshman English News* James Berlin and Robert Inkster ascribe other features to the conventional paradigm. Basing their conclusions on an analysis of repeated patterns in four well-known and commercially successful rhetoric texts, they add that the traditional paradigm stresses expository writing to the virtual exclusion of all other forms, that it posits an unchanging reality which is independent of the writer and which all writers are expected to describe in the same way regardless of the rhetorical situation, that it neglects invention almost entirely, and that it makes style the most important element in writing.[3]

I would make three other points about the traditional paradigm. First, its adherents believe that competent writers know what they are going to say before they begin to write; thus their most important task when they are preparing to write is finding a form into which to organize their content. They also believe that the composing process is linear, that it proceeds systematically from prewriting to writing to rewriting. Finally, they believe that teaching editing is teaching writing.

It is important to note that the traditional paradigm did not grow out of research or experimentation. It derives partly from the classical rhetorical model that organizes the production of discourse into invention, arrangement, and style, but mostly it seems to be based on some idealized and orderly vision of what literature scholars, whose professional focus is on the written product, seem to imagine is an efficient method of writing. It is a prescriptive and orderly view of the creative act, a view that defines the successful writer as one who can systematically produce a 500-word theme of five paragraphs, each with a topic sentence. Its proponents hold it *a priori*; they have not tested it against the composing processes of actual writers.

At this point some of my readers may want to protest that I am belaboring a dead issue—that the admonition to "teach process, not product" is now conventional wisdom. I disagree. Although those in the vanguard of the profession have by and large adopted the process model for teaching composition and are now attentively watching the research on the composing process in order to extract some pedagogical principles from it, the overwhelming majority of college writing teachers in the United States are not professional writing teachers. They do not do research or publish on rhetoric or composition, and they do not know the scholarship in the field; they do not read the professional journals and they do not attend professional meetings such as the annual Conference on College Communication and Composition; they do not participate in faculty development workshops for writing teachers. They are trained as literary critics first and as teachers of literature second, yet out of necessity most of them are doing half or more of their teaching in composition. And they teach it by the traditional paradigm, just as they did when they were untrained teaching assistants ten or twenty or forty years ago. Often they use a newer edition of the same book they used as teaching assistants.

Out of necessity, apathy, and what I see as a benighted and patronizing view of the essential nature of composition courses, English department administrators encourage this unprofessional approach to the teaching of writing. In the first place, they may believe that they have so many writing classes to staff that they could not possibly hire well-qualified professionals to teach them; only a comparatively few such specialists exist. Second, most departmental chairpersons don't believe that an English instructor needs special qualifications to teach writing. As one of my colleagues says, our department wouldn't think of letting her teach Chaucer courses because she is not qualified; yet the chairman is delighted for her to teach advanced composition, for which she is far more unqualified. The assumption is that anyone with a Ph.D. in English is an expert writing teacher.

I think, however, that the people who do most to promote a static and unexamined approach to teaching writing are those who define writing courses as service courses and skills courses; that group probably includes most administrators and teachers of writing. Such a view, which denies that writing requires intellectual activity and ignores the importance of writing as a basic method of learning, takes away any incentive for the writing teacher to grow professionally. People who teach skills and provide services are traditionally less respected and rewarded than those who teach theory, and hiring hordes of adjuncts and temporary instructors and assigning them to composition courses reinforces this value system. Consequently there is no external pressure to find a better way to teach writing.

In spite of this often discouraging situation, many teachers who cling to the traditional paradigm work very hard at teaching writing. They devote far more time than they can professionally afford to working with their students, but because they haven't read Elbow or Bruffee they have no way of knowing that their students might benefit far more from small group meetings with each other than from the exhausting one-to-one conferences that the teachers hold. They both complain and brag about how much time they spend meticulously marking each paper, but because they haven't read Diederich or Irmscher they don't know that an hour spent meticulously marking every error in a paper is probably doing more harm than good. They are exhausting themselves trying to teach writing from an outmoded model, and they come to despise the job more and more because many of their students improve so little despite their time and effort.

But the writing teacher's frustration and disenchantment may be less important than the fact that if they teach from the traditional paradigm, they are frequently emphasizing techniques that the research has largely discredited. As Kuhn points out, the paradigm that a group of professionals accepts will govern the kinds of problems they decide to work on, and that very paradigm keeps them from recognizing important problems that cannot be discussed in the terminology of their model. Thus teachers who concentrate their efforts on teaching style, organization, and correctness are not likely to recognize that their students need work in invention. And if they stress that proofreading and editing are the chief skills one uses to revise a paper, they won't realize that their students have no concept of what it means to make substantive revisions in a paper. The traditional paradigm hides these problems.

Textbooks complicate the problem further. As Kuhn repeatedly points out, the standard texts in any discipline constitute a major block to a paradigm shift because they represent accepted authority. Many, though certainly not all, of the standard textbooks in rhetoric and composition for the past two decades have been product-centered books that focus on style, usage, and argumentation; Sheridan Baker's *The Practical Stylist* and Brooks and Warren's *Modern Rhetoric* are typical examples. When Donald Stewart made an analysis of rhetoric texts three years ago, he found that only seven out of the thirty-four he examined showed any awareness of current research in rhetoric. The others were, as he put it, "strictly current-traditional in their discussions of invention, arrangement, and style."[4] And textbooks change slowly. Publishers want to keep what sells, and they tend to direct the appeals of their books to what they believe the average composition teacher wants, not to what those in the vanguard of the profession would like to have. . . .

THE EMERGING PARADIGM

But the most promising indication that we are poised for a paradigm shift is that for the first time in the history of teaching writing we have specialists who are doing controlled and directed research on writers' composing processes. Sondra Perl of Herbert Lehman College of the City University of New York and Linda Flower and John Hayes of Carnegie-Mellon University are tape recording students' oral reports of the thoughts that come to them as they write and of the choices they make. They call their investigative strategy "protocol analysis," and they supplement it with interviews and questionnaires to put together composite pictures of the processes followed by working writers. Sharon Pianko of Rutgers University has done a study in which she matched groups of traditional and remedial writers, men and women writers, and 18-year-old and adult writers and compared their composing habits. Nancy Sommers of New York University has done a study comparing the revising practices of college freshmen and experienced professional writers, and Lester Faigley and Stephen Witte of the University of Texas now have a federal grant to do a more comprehensive study on revising. (An article based on this study appeared in the December, 1981, issue of CCC.) Lee Odell of Rensselaer Polytechnic Institute and Dixie Goswami are currently involved in a federally-funded study of the practices of writers in business.

From these and other studies we are beginning to find out something about how people's minds work as they write, to chart the rhythm of their writing, to find out what constraints they are aware of as they write, and to see what physical behaviors are involved in writing and how they vary among different groups of writers. So far only a small amount of data has been collected, and the inferences we can draw from the studies are necessarily tentative. As Linda Flower puts it, because we are trying to chart and analyze an activity that goes on largely out of sight, the process is rather like trying to trace the path of a dolphin by catching glimpses of it when it leaps out of the water. We are seeing only a tiny part of the whole process, but from it we can infer much about what is going on beneath the surface.[10]

What are we finding out? One point that is becoming clear is that writing is an act of discovery for both skilled and unskilled writers; most writers have only a partial notion of what they want to say when they begin to write, and their ideas develop in the process of writing. They develop their topics intuitively, not methodically. Another truth is that usually the writing process is not linear, moving smoothly in one direction from start to finish. It is messy, recursive, convoluted, and uneven. Writers write, plan, revise, anticipate, and review throughout the writing process, moving back and forth among the different operations involved in writing without any apparent plan. No practicing writer will be surprised at these findings; nevertheless, they seriously contradict the traditional paradigm that has dominated writing textbooks for years.

But for me the most interesting data emerging from these studies are those that show us profound differences between the writing behaviors of skilled and unskilled writers and the behaviors of student and professional writers. Those differences involve the amount of time spent on writing, the amount of time preparing to write, the number of drafts written, the concern for audience, the number of changes made and the stages at which they are made, the frequency and length of pauses during writing, the way in which those pauses are used, the amount of time spent rereading and reformulating, and the kind and number of constraints that the writers are aware of as they work. This kind of information enables us to construct a tentative profile of the writing behaviors of effective writers; I have sketched such a profile in another paper, not yet published.

From all this activity in the field, the new paradigm for teaching writing is emerging. Its principal features are these:

1. It focuses on the writing process; instructors intervene in students' writing during the process.

2. It teaches strategies for invention and discovery; instructors help students to generate content and discover purpose.

3. It is rhetorically based; audience, purpose, and occasion figure prominently in the assignment of writing tasks.

4. Instructors evaluate the written product by how well it fulfills the writer's intention and meets the audience's needs.

5. It views writing as a recursive rather than a linear process; pre-writing, writing, and revision are activities that overlap and intertwine.

6. It is holistic, viewing writing as an activity that involves the intuitive and non-rational as well as the rational faculties.

7. It emphasizes that writing is a way of learning and developing as well as a communication skill.

8. It includes a variety of writing modes, expressive as well as expository.

9. It is informed by other disciplines, especially cognitive psychology and linguistics.

10. It views writing as a disciplined creative activity that can be analyzed and described; its practitioners believe that writing can be taught.

11. It is based on linguistic research and research into the composing process.

12. It stresses the principle that writing teachers should be people who write.

PORTENTS FOR THE FUTURE

I believe that important events of the recent past are going to speed the revolution and help to establish this new paradigm in the nation's classrooms. First, the University of Iowa's Writing Institute, which received a $680,000 grant from the National Endowment for the Humanities to train freshman composition directors, has this year completed its work and sent out forty administrators for writing programs who will almost certainly base those programs on the new model. They are bound to have a profound influence on their institutions.

Second, graduate programs in rhetoric are rapidly increasing across the country. The last count in the Spring, 1980, *Freshman English News* showed that fifty-three institutions have added graduate rhetoric courses since 1974, and that was not a complete list. Enrollment in these programs is climbing because students realize that English departments now offer more jobs in rhetoric and composition than in any other specialization. Most of these programs are going to produce young professionals who have been taught by scholars who know recent research and are committed to the new paradigm: Richard Young, Ross Winterowd, Joseph Comprone, James Kinneavy, Andrea Lunsford, Elizabeth Cowan, Linda Flower, to name just a few. When these new graduates go into English departments where the traditional paradigm prevails, they are certain to start working for change.

Third, in many schools, even graduate assistants who are in traditional literary programs rather than rhetoric programs are getting their in-service training from the rhetoric and composition specialists in their departments. They are being trained in process-centered approaches to the teaching of composition, and when they enter the profession and begin teaching lower-division writing courses along with their literary specialities, they are most likely to follow the new paradigm. And, more and more, the methods courses for high-school teachers are also being taught by the rhetoric specialists; that change will have a profound effect on secondary school teaching.

Fourth, we now have process-based texts on the teaching of writing. Shaughnessy's *Errors and Expectations* is well known and widely used. It has been joined by Irmscher's

Teaching Expository Writing and Neman's *Teaching Students to Write.* The authors of both these latter books incorporate research findings and recent developments in the profession into their philosophies of and methodologies for teaching writing.

Fifth, college composition textbooks are changing. Along with their traditional books, most publishers are now publishing at least one process-oriented, rhetorically-based writing text. Several are now on the market and more are forthcoming, most of them written by scholars and teachers who are leaders in the profession. Moreover, many major publishing houses now retain well-known composition specialists to advise them on manuscripts. The publishers sense change in the wind and realize that the new crop of well-informed and committed writing program directors who will be taking over are going to insist on up-to-date textbooks. The change will even reach into some high schools because one large company has hired one of the country's leading rhetoricians to supervise and edit their high-school composition series. Many others will probably follow their example.

But no revolution brings the millenium nor a guarantee of salvation, and we must remember that the new paradigm is sketchy and leaves many problems about the teaching of writing unresolved. As Kuhn points out, new paradigms are apt to be crude, and they seldom possess all the capabilities of their predecessors. So it is important for us to preserve the best parts of earlier methods for teaching writing: the concern for style and the preservation of high standards for the written product. I believe we also need to continue giving students models of excellence to imitate.

Kuhn contends that "the transition between competing paradigms cannot be made a step at a time, forced by logic. . . . Like the gestalt switch, it must occur all at once (though not necessarily in an instant) or not at all."[11] He says, however, that, "if its supporters are competent, they will improve it [the paradigm], explore its possibilities, and show what it would be like to belong to the community guided by it."[12] I see this last opportunity as the challenge to today's community of composition and rhetoric scholars: to refine the new paradigm for teaching composition so that it provides a rewarding, productive, and feasible way of teaching writing for the non-specialists who do most of the composition teaching in our colleges and universities.

Notes

1. Richard Young, "Paradigms and Problems: Needed Research in Rhetorical Invention," *Research in Composing*, ed. Charles Cooper and Lee Odell (Urbana, Illinois: National Council of Teachers of English, 1978), 31.

2. Young, 31.

3. James A. Berlin and Robert P. Inkster, "Current-Traditional Rhetoric: Paradigm and Practice," *Freshman English News*, 8 (Winter, 1980), 1–4, 13–14.

4. Donald Stewart, "Composition Textbooks and the Assault on Tradition," *College Composition and Communication*, 29 (May, 1978), 174.

Notes 5–9 belong to the sections not reprinted here, "Signs of Change" and "The Transition Period," and thus have been omitted.

10. Linda Flower and John Hayes, "Identifying the Organization of Writing Processes," *Cognitive Processes in Writing*, ed., Lee W. Gregg and Erwin R. Steinberg (Hillsdale, NJ: Lawrence Erlbaum Associates, 1980), 9–10.

11. Thomas Kuhn, *The Structure of Scientific Revolutions*, Second Edition (Chicago: University of Chicago Press, 1970), 150.

12. Kuhn, 159.

Russell Hunt, "What Is Inkshedding?"

Russell Hunt has taught at St. Thomas University in New Brunswick (STU) since 1968, serving as department chair several times and once as academic vice-president. As co-organizer of the first Inkshed Working Conference (1984) and as initiator and maintainer of the Inkshed website, he's essentially the horse's mouth for information about inkshedding. His many publications, particularly on collaborative and dialogic teaching, as well as his active presence online—on his own website (http://www.stthomasu.ca/~hunt/), on the CASLL (Canadian Association for the Study of Language and Learning) electronic discussion list, and in the extraordinary conversations going on between students in his classes at STU—have made him a major voice in the conversation about the teaching of writing, especially among Canadian scholars and teachers. The following piece has been posted for several years as an interactive essay on the CASLL/Inkshed website; indeed, in several passages the suggestions of other readers are incorporated and acknowledged.

WHAT IS INKSHEDDING?

"Inkshedding" began as a practice in the early eighties, when Jim Reither and I began trying to make "freewriting" (which we had learned about from writers like Peter Elbow) into something dialogically transactional. Actually, we didn't articulate what we wanted in quite that way, at the time. What we said we wanted was to give writing a social role in a classroom, and thus to create a situation in which the writing was read by real readers, in order to understand and respond to *what* was said rather than to evaluate and "help" with the writing.

We did this in our classes by asking students to freewrite in response to a shared experience—a reading, a class discussion, an event—and then arranging to have the freewritten texts passed around for reading, asking the readers to mark with a vertical line in the margin passages in which the writer said something "striking," something that seemed to them interesting or new or outrageous. We then arranged for the passages marked most often to be transcribed, photocopied, and distributed at the next class meeting.

Jim Reither came up with the word "inkshed," having found it in the *Oxford English Dictionary*. It wasn't exactly a description of what we were doing; the Oxford offers it as a "humourous" word, meaning "the shedding or spilling of ink; consumption or waste of ink in writing." The word had been used earlier by Marvell and Sterne, but our favourite quotation was from Carlyle: "With no bloodshed . . . but with immense beershed and inkshed."

The ways in which inkshedding functions—and the ways in which it has been used and modified in varying situations—have grown and changed profoundly, of course, since then. In some ways, in fact, it has turned out to be a reasonable instance of my general stance as a teacher, which has been focused on finding ways to foster growth in literacy by making it more directly and perceptibly instrumental. Inkshedding turned out to have a number of implications, many of which we hadn't anticipated at all.

For me, maybe the most important of these implications was that texts composed in such a situation are increasingly likely—even with novice writers—to be formed with an anticipation of audience. As oral language is uttered, it is shaped in large part by the need to address a particular interlocutor or discourse situation. James Britton called this "shaping at the point of utterance." Like speech, writing, it has always seemed to me, needs this pressure; inkshedding provides it. It's not always true the first few times a group or individual engages in inkshedding, but over a few experiences you can begin to see telltale evidences of the way audience pressure (which the writer may or may not be conscious of) affects the shape of the text, in things like clarity of handwriting and increased explicitness of reference.

It's also important that during inkshedding ideas, positions, and questions, which would not otherwise attain a hearing, have a better opportunity to get "on the floor" than they would in an oral discussion. A significant force in the original impetus for using inkshedding in classrooms was the perception that classroom discussions tend to be dominated by a few voices. This is natural, as the "bandwidth" for classroom discussion—at least for *whole* class discussions—is very narrow. Only one voice can be heard at any one time: for what *everyone* thought about an event to be articulated and discussed is not only practically difficult (even in a small class), but also socially constraining—the first few utterances tend very strongly to determine and focus the range of discussion, to determine the kinds of questions or issues which will be raised. Anthony Paré, in a comment on an earlier draft of this piece, says, "I've always felt that inkshedding allowed for the individual exploration of a top-of-the-head response before that response is deflected, diminished, or destroyed by the first question or comment spoken out loud. Inkshedding allows each member of the group to 'gather' her/his thoughts before they are scattered by that first, articulate, confident person who gets up to say what you weren't even thinking about."

What written discussion tends to do is broaden the bandwidth—everyone in the room can, as it were, talk at once.

But what is even more important is that every idea or response has a chance not only to be formed in the first place, but also to be "heard."

That "hearing" is important. What is often overlooked in this situation—indeed, in any discussion of student writing—is the importance of *reading*. Writing, of course, had been seen as central from the very beginning, in the origins of the practice as freewriting (which might or might not ever be read). But what differentiates the social practice of inkshedding from what we might call the expressivist practice of freewriting is that the text is *read*. And even more, that the text is read in what we can characterize as "dialogic" ways—that is, read *for what it says, dialogically*, not in order to evaluate it or to help the writer improve her text. And because the reading occurs immediately, and in public, the writer has a good chance to come to realize this. The nature of this reading, and the social transaction it affords, is an issue that has come to seem to me increasingly important. The concept of "transaction"—in the sense defined by Dewey and Bentley, in their *Knowing and the Known*—is central here because it reminds us that no component of the process can be understood or characterized outside the process. The writer is influenced by the reading, and her understanding of that reading, as much as the reader is influenced by the writer, and the whole event itself cannot be understood outside its relation to preceding and subsequent events, in what Peirce called the infinite web of semiosis. As Anthony Paré pointed out in that same commentary, "Texts are located in an intertextual web. This is something students don't (can't) get, since their texts are not linked to other texts. Students eavesdrop on the disciplinary conversation and report what they've heard; they don't *join* the conversation. They are intellectual voyeurs. Inkshedding gets them into the action."

A number of ways of organizing situations to make this reading more central and more influential—more a part of the action—have evolved. At the beginning, we asked for small teams of volunteer editors to read all the inksheds produced on a given occasion, marking with vertical lines in the margin passages which they found "striking." The more people who found a passage striking, the more vertical lines accumulated; a secretary could, in theory, simply transcribe passages in a fairly mechanical way, beginning with those with the most vertical lines. The transcribed passages could be photocopied and distributed for a subsequent meeting of class, to start off a further discussion (or another session of inkshedding) with the ideas that had survived this evolutionary pruning process.

Early on—especially as we began to use inkshedding as a way of structuring discussions at conferences and professional workshops—the decisions of the "editorial committee" became a subject of dispute. Everyone wanted to read everything (or, to be a bit

more cynical, perhaps everyone wanted *her own* writing to be read by everyone else).
One response to this was to post all the inksheds on the wall; what this meant, however,
was that in practice very few were read—in general, only those with extremely clear
handwriting. Another response was to allow a "reading time" immediately after the
inkshedding, in which anyone could read anybody else's and mark "striking" passages for
transcription. As it has turned out, these "reading times" have become what is often one
of the most powerful moments in my own teaching and conference participation, as
people silently exchange sheets of paper and a "discussion" occurs in almost complete
silence, punctuated by *sotto voce* expressions of agreement or outrage, or laughter. There
is something particularly powerful about the fact that the reading and selection is being
done immediately, or as one anonymous commentator on an early version of this text put
it, "in real time."

A further extension of the reading process—especially if there's a pressure for an immediate discussion, rather than waiting for the process of transcription and copying—involves
asking individuals to find one passage from someone else's inkshed to read aloud. This ele-
vates reading to an even more central position and is especially powerful for novice writers.
One of the most important educational aspects of inkshedding, for me, is the way it fore-
grounds and dramatizes the transactional nature of text. For almost all students (and this is
especially important for those who have difficulties, or limited experience, with writing and
reading), text has never been the basis of an authentic social transaction—beyond, perhaps,
a thank you note to a distant grandmother or, more recently, e-mail exchanges with friends.
The process of creating an identity and a role in a group through written text, as they do
every day through oral utterance, is one in which they have only rarely engaged. And it is
my belief that this process is the defining mark of the fully literate person.

Of course, one of the most persistent questions about inkshedding has to do with
ethos: are inksheds signed? Oral contributions to a discussion are, of course, always
"signed"; there's no question whose voice you're hearing when the person is across the
room from you. Inksheds, however, can be signed or not, and there are powerful and persuasive arguments on both sides of the question. On the side of signing them is the argument that taking responsibility for what you've said encourages not only a deepened
reflection about its possible consequences, and thus a more active awareness of the reader
and a more attentive consideration of what might be called the "rhetorical back-pressure,"
the anticipation of response that shapes language at the point of utterance. On the side of
not signing them is the argument that it is one of the characteristic strengths of written language that it needs to create its ethos within the bounds of the text, that—as Socrates
noticed—once you've let that text go it goes around saying the same thing over and over,
beyond your control or influence, to people who don't know you and are unable to read
it with you there to warrant it and immediately respond to misinterpretations. Does it make
a difference? Clearly. Is one better? It depends, it seems to me, on the situation. In

practice, at conferences and workshops, I usually leave it up to the writer.

Inkshedding moved toward becoming an institution when, in response to discussions among Canadian delegates to the Conference on College Composition and Communication, and influenced by the powerful collegial informality of the Wyoming Conference on Freshman and Sophomore English, Jim Reither and I organized the first "Inkshed Working Conference" in Fredericton, in 1984. One of the features of the conference was that we conducted discussions after sessions by means of inkshedding, taking the "edited" inksheds and transcribing, photocopying and publishing the most-marked passages within a few hours of the session. The first morning of the conference, the edited inksheds from the opening evening session were distributed at breakfast, and their impact on the conference was profound.

The next year, Chris Bullock and Kay Stewart at the University of Alberta and Grant MacEwan Community College organized a second conference in Alberta, and within a year or so there was a regular newsletter (edited for the first few years by Jim Reither) and an annual national conference, dedicated not only to exploring literacy and learning, but to extending and testing the limits of the ways in which scholarly or professional conferences can be organized, and attracting writing teachers, English and education professors, public school teachers, graduate students, and others (regularly, the conference and the listserv have included a bracing range of disciplinary perspectives—from writing teachers at the Bank of Canada to professors of religious studies, from tutors in writing centres to cognitive psychologists and professors of engineering).

There is now a national organization, the Canadian Association for the Study of Language and Learning (CASLL); an Inkshed Newsletter (under a floating editorship, currently based at the Nova Scotia College of Art and Design); an annual conference now in its twenty-second year; an occasional publisher of monographs, based at the University of Manitoba and the University of Winnipeg); a website and an international electronic discussion group, CASLL.

A POSTSCRIPT IN PROGRESS: ELECTRONIC INKSHEDDING AND CONTEXTUALIZED READING

What has perhaps been most important about inkshedding for me is the power of its basic idea—that writing written in the expectation of reading and response, especially *immediate* reading and response, will do more to engage the writer in making, using Linda Flower's term, "reader-based" decisions in an active way than writing whose reader has to be imagined up out of whole cloth. It was clear from the moment I began to explore electronic networks as a medium for the exchange of texts that the potential for that immediacy was, at least potentially, powerfully enhanced by electronic mediation.

Thus, the fundamental ideas involved in the practice of inkshedding have extended inexorably into, and shaped, the increasing use of computer-mediated writing and reading in my teaching. As, over the past few years, students arrive in my classes with more and more experience with computers and computer networks, it has become increasingly rare for paper-based pen-and-ink inkshedding to continue in my courses much beyond the second or third week of class. Very quickly, new forms supplant the use of pen and paper.

Such forums present new challenges and opportunities, of course. Contexts for reading can become a powerful and unpredictable force. Some years ago on a now-defunct electronic forum, Roger Graves said, discussing reading and writing that is electronically mediated, "I just read some of the . . . discussion on Will's ["Will's Virtual Restoration and Eighteenth Century Coffeehouse," the electronic forum I often use as part of my eighteenth-century literature class], and I was trying to decide what was different about it—different from face-to-face/classroom talk. I think some of those things wouldn't be said. . . . I think there is a different quality to the talk here, and I think not having to say it to a room of people who might laugh *while you're still physically present* makes it easier for some people to say/write things. So a) this wouldn't have happened without the technology, and b) the quality of critical thought seems measurably better."

In response, I said,

> I think, yes, it does make a difference that people aren't physically present (and that's not always a good difference: it allows people the freedom to say potentially risky things, but it also affords flaming). But I think—I started thinking more seriously about this on the way home from the conference—that a much more important difference is *the way these texts are read.*

> An outsider to this discussion simply can't read the texts the way a member of it can, because the member is reading with the constant knowledge that her role is to *respond.* She's expected to (indeed, she's required to, in some sense: she can choose which to respond to, but if she chooses not to respond at all she essentially eliminates herself from the class).

> I think the knowledge that you're reading *as a member of the discourse community* changes the way you read in ways that are a whole lot more than trivial. It makes you a Bakhtinian reader ("understanding is nothing more nor less than the preparation of a response"[1]—that's not accurately quoted, but it's close enough for government work) with a vengeance. You're a member of the community in the same way that I'm a member of (for instance) the 4Cs

community [CCCC], or—for a better example, maybe, because smaller and more intimate—the Inkshed one. And I think that aware- ness also changes what you'll write, and how.

I've regularly been reminded of this as I've tried to show people a text taken out of such a context—an online discussion board or a class e-mail list, for example—and demonstrate how it exemplifies the sort of discourse produced in such a community. People who aren't members of the community almost always read the text very differently in the new context. A brilliant move in an online conversation, such as a reference to shared experience or knowledge, or a pulling together of previously disconnected ideas, can be seen as arrogant, flippant or incomprehensible in a different, larger conversation. It can be difficult to help people see the way a particular choice represents a move in a spe- cific conversation rather than a "public" text (a move in a larger conversation). This is a more complicated and rich distinction than it seems, stated flatly like that: I'm not simply pointing to things like jocularity of tone or personal references that may be present and vis- ible in the text, but to how a reader who is a member of the group will attend to and fore- ground particular passages because of the conversation of which this inkshed is a part, and someone who isn't, won't.

Does this mean that this sort of writing differs radically from "public" writing? Of course. But it's also true, as all the work in the theory of genres has shown us, that public writing itself varies profoundly from situation to situation. The trick is to get the knack of knowing how to live in new, unfamiliar genres. Inkshedding, I believe, can jump-start that process.

Endnote

[1] The actual quote from Bakhtin is "all real and integral understanding is actively responsive, and constitutes nothing other than the initial preparatory stage of a response" (*Speech Genres* 69).

Acknowledgments

Among the participants at the 16th Inkshed Working Conference who offered me marginal comments on this text in draft, the following signed their marginalia: Marcy Bauman, Doug Brent, Jamie MacKinnon, Kenna Manos, and Anthony Paré. I am equally grateful to those who did not sign.

Works Cited

Bakhtin, M. M. *Speech Genres and Other Late Essays*. Ed. C. Emerson and M. Holquist. Trans. V. W. McGee. Austin: University of Texas Press, 1986.

Britton, James. "Shaping at the Point of Utterance." *Reinventing the Rhetorical Tradition*. Ed. Aviva Freedman and Ian Pringle. Conway, AR: L & S Books, University of Central Arkansas for the Canadian Council of Teachers of English, 1980. 61–65.

Dewey, John, and Arthur F. Bentley. *Knowing and the Known*. Boston: Beacon Press, 1949.

Elbow, Peter. *Writing Without Teachers*. New York: Oxford University Press, 1973.

Flower, Linda. *Problem-Solving Strategies for Writing*. San Diego: Harcourt Brace Jovanovich, 1989.

Graves, Roger. Personal Communication, 1998.

Paré, Anthony. Personal Communication, 1999.

"Welcome to Inkshed." Official website of the Canadian Association for the Study of Language and Learning. <http://www.stu.ca/inkshed/>

* * *

For further reading

Hunt, Russell. "Some Strategies for Embedding Writing in Dialogic Situations." *The Point: The Newsletter of SCENT—UPEI's Senate Committee on the Enhancement of Teaching*. 5.1 (June 1996): 3–4. <http://www.stu.ca/~hunt/strats.htm>

—. "Traffic in Genres, In Classrooms and Out." *Genre and the New Rhetoric*. Ed. Peter Medway and Aviva Freedman. London: Taylor & Francis, 1994. 212–230. <http://www.stu.ca/~hunt/traffic.htm>

—. "Electronic Discussions in Learning and Teaching: Why They Don't Work, and How They Might." *Connexions: The Newsletter of the International Society for the Exploration of Teaching Alternatives* 10.2 (Summer 1998): 1–7. <http://www.stu.ca/~hunt/connexns.htm>

Toby Fulwiler, "Freshman Writing: It's the Best Course in the University to Teach"

Toby Fulwiler is best known for championing the use of journals and writing-to-learn in all disciplines. Professor Emeritus at the University of Vermont, where he was Director of Writing, he's expert not just at teaching writing but at teaching *with* writing:

for the past twenty years he has been conducting, across North America and abroad, teaching-with-writing workshops for faculty in a wide variety of fields. His *The Journal Book* (1987) was so influential that it has sequels: *The Journal Book for Teachers of Technical Programs* and *The Journal Book for Teachers of At-Risk College Writers*, both co-edited with Susan Gardner in 1999. *The Working Writer, College Writing: A Personal Approach to Academic Writing, Teaching with Writing, Writing Across the Disciplines: Research into Practice*, and *The Letter Book* are just a few titles that give a sense of Fulwiler's contribution to the conversation about writing.

FRESHMAN WRITING: IT'S THE BEST COURSE IN THE UNIVERSITY TO TEACH

Some English teachers believe that teaching freshman English is the worst chore in the university. So bad, in fact, that only part-timers and graduate students should have to do it. Or so bad that everyone on the faculty should share The English Teacher's Burden. But there's another way of looking at it.

An English teacher myself, I've always considered teaching writing to be among the very best jobs in the university—best, that is, if you value teaching small classes where your primary business is helping students learn to think imaginatively, reason critically, and express themselves clearly, and where it matters who your students are, where they come from, and what they believe.

Many 18-year-olds arrive at college unprepared for the academic community, where they will be expected to reason dispassionately and autonomously about a wide range of ideas. Instead, they expect 13th grade, where they will be told once again what to do. I'm not quite sure where their misconception comes from, but I have my suspicions. This past fall, for instance, as my freshmen talked with me about writing, they told me a lot about how they viewed learning, as well.

- They described their own writing ability in clear, correct, coherent sentences that began with the words "I can't write because . . ." Why do they believe that writing is a skill they cannot master?

- They asked me to teach them about "thesis statements" and "topic sentences." When I asked them what those were, they taught me. Where did they learn that English classes are an endless series of repetitions?

- Early in the term, they told me that they had nothing important to say about their schools, jobs, families, friends, experiences, ideas, lives; later, they wrote pages about those same subjects. Why did they come to college believing they had nothing to say?

- When I asked them to define good writing, they wrote that it was detailed, focused, supported, and aimed well at an audience; they told me all that in writing that was general, unfocused, unsupported, and aimed at no audience at all. Why did they not practice what they preached?

- They came to my class after being schooled for 12 years, yet they had never learned to write for one another; to read their own writing to others; to listen seriously to what their classmates wrote; to give and receive positive criticism. Who or what taught them that learning is a one-way street?

Freshmen arrive at college with a badly distorted view of writing because they have seldom written anything that mattered to them. Instead, in the name of writing, they have been asked to memorize spelling lists; to fill in blanks in vocabulary workbooks; to compose fragments of thought into practice sentences; to write in arbitrary formats, such as five-paragraph themes. They have been drilled in those activities in spite of research by such scholars as James Britton at the University of London, Janet Emig at Rutgers University, and Donald Graves at the University of New Hampshire, indicating that students, from the first grade through college, learn to write best when they write and rewrite whole compositions on subjects they care about, for audiences who take them seriously.

* * *

Freshmen arrive at college believing writing has more to do with correctness than with communication, with prescription than with imagination, with drill than with critical thought. They believe that writing serves the teacher, not themselves. And they certainly do not believe that the act of writing is either creative or fun. Unfortunately, they expect yet another round of the debilitating criticism that has sapped their confidence and taught them that they have nothing to say. After 18 years of teaching college writing, I've come to believe that American schools do more to discourage serious writing (and learning) than to encourage it.

First-year college students show up in class behaving just like first-year college students. Their writing is not only full of faulty spelling, clumsy grammar, and careless diction; it is also full of sloppy reasoning, unsupported assertions, and weak logic. Those who lament that freshmen write and think like freshmen consider such a course a burden. Those that see the first year of college as a starting point, and understand that all sophomores must be freshmen first, consider freshman English an opportunity.

If writing is the academic activity most likely to reveal faulty reasoning and insufficient knowledge, then re-writing is the activity most likely to correct the inconsistencies and supply the knowledge. A good freshman writing course is essentially a re-reading and re-writing course.

Teaching writing is not the same as teaching subjects such as literature, history, or economics, and that difference is what causes most of the problems for teachers of first-year writing courses. Writing teachers cannot lean on a vast accumulation of bibliographic knowledge or even on last year's lecture notes. Instead, they need to study and understand their own writing process in order to help the students with theirs. The primary "texts" in their classroom will not be published text-books, but rather the corpus of each student's own writing.

* * *

For writing classes to work, teachers must surrender some of the authority to which they are accustomed and pass it, along with the responsibility to use it well, to the students. Teachers must stop taking home their student writing to "correct" or "grade," and start taking it home to read and respond to. Of course, for this to be possible, the students' writing must become interesting to read.

And now we've come full circle. Writing becomes interesting to read only when it becomes interesting to write; and it becomes interesting to write only when the writer has a stake in his or her topic, thinks it's important, and believes someone else will think so, too. When that happens, as it often does, the transition from passive trainee to active learner occurs.

What is a freshman writing course actually like? My current class is fairly typical: I meet 22 students twice a week for 80 minutes. They bring drafts of writing to nearly every class, some of which I read and respond to, some of which they read and respond to among themselves, none of which is graded until the end of the term. In 15 weeks, I ask my freshmen to complete three or four pieces of writing, but for the first seven weeks they write and rewrite only one piece, a personal narrative.

I expect drafts written early in the term to be sketchy and superficial, as the writers try to find out what is expected of them. I tell them that I expect their narratives to recreate for the reader, as believably as possible, each writer's private experience. They are to recast general memories into articulated experience, refocus it, describe it, fill in relevant detail—show, rather than tell—and always answer the question, So what?

Each draft comes in clipped to the previous drafts; each time I read a draft I notice the changes from one to the next. I want revision to become a habit of mind, and so encourage major changes, additions, re-starts—all the time trying to react honestly to what I read. When drafts work right away, the students try out new angles, expand what's there, and work continually on their editing skills. When drafts are not working, I encourage the students to start again, and encourage them to try until something clicks. We pay serious attention to all the work that's written seriously. We use one another's writing—mine as well as theirs—to demonstrate whatever lessons (about leads, titles, editing, for example) we need to learn.

* * *

During the second half of the course we study the relationship between personal experience and more objective, research-based academic writing. In the latter form, too, the problem is believability, but for objective writing the resources are external to the writer. Now they depend on libraries, interviews, and site visits to create credibility, whereas before they relied upon their own experience.

As students write and revise, they learn to shape and reshape meaning in both their personal and their academic lives. In the act of seemingly endless revision, usually without precedent in their secondary-school experience, students begin to transform their understanding of knowledge from something fixed and rigid to something fluid and relative. By the end of the term, they have revised their way to new interpretations of their own experience. They have refocused and reshaped their research projects several times, making it difficult for them to continue to see things as black or white, right or wrong. ("No, what you say here isn't wrong—but what if you approached it this way next time?")

At the end of the term, the students hand in portfolios containing all their written work. They receive one grade on a combination of process (amount of serious revision and risk-taking) and product (completeness, neatness, correctness, and coherence of the final draft).

The opportunity in freshman English, then, is to help students learn to write in their own voices about a variety of issues for different audiences, and to help one another along the way. Not all of them succeed completely, of course, but they are well started. When they do succeed, they have become mature and independent writers. And they have become mature and independent thinkers, as well, members of the academic community at last.

National Council of Teachers of English (NCTE) Commission on Composition "Guidelines for Using Journals in School Settings"

Toby Fulwiler drafted the following document and then revised it after receiving feedback from various other members of the National Council of Teachers of English (NCTE) Commission on Composition. The Commission approved these guidelines on November 28, 1986, making them a policy statement of record for NCTE, the largest professional association of English teachers in North America. Such policy statements are a genre unto themselves; they seldom can be enforced, but they carry real weight as reminders of best practice in a particular field. When members of a professional organization feel a pressing need for guidance on a particular issue, they usually turn to experts on that issue to collaborate and produce a document something like this one—documents that go through an extensive drafting and revision process before being approved by the association. Fulwiler's seven co-authors are acknowledged below.

GUIDELINES FOR USING JOURNALS IN SCHOOL SETTINGS

STUDENT JOURNALS

In recent years teachers in elementary and secondary schools as well as in college have been asking students to keep personal notebooks most commonly called journals, but sometimes called logs, daybooks, think-books, and even diaries. These informal notebooks serve a range of educational purposes, from practice in self-expression to figuring out problems in science classes. Some teachers encourage students to write about whatever they want, while other teachers carefully specify topics. In most cases, students are encouraged to express honestly their personal opinions, take some risks with their thought, and write in their own natural voices.

Because journals give students great freedom to express their thoughts and feelings, students often write about things more private and intimate than teachers are comfortable with—things that more properly belong in personal diaries than in school journals. The problem for teachers is how to encourage students to write personally and frankly about subjects they care about without, at the same time, invading their private lives.

This document will outline some of the assumptions behind journal assignments and suggest guidelines to help teachers avoid the problems of privacy which journals occasionally present.

ASSUMPTIONS ABOUT LANGUAGE AND LEARNING

Students are asked to keep journals for strong pedagogical reasons, based generally on the following assumptions about the connections between thought and language:

1. When people *articulate connections* between new information and what they already know, they learn and understand that new information better (Bruner, 1966).

2. When people *think* and figure things out, they do so in symbol systems commonly called languages, most often verbal, but also mathematical, musical, visual, and so on (Vygotsky, 1962).

3. When people *learn* things, they use all of the language modes to do so— reading, writing, speaking, and listening; each mode helps people learn in a unique way (Emig, 1977).

4. When people *write* about new information and ideas—in addition to reading, talking, and listening—they learn and understand them better (Britton, 1975).

5. When people *care* about what they write and see connections to their own lives, they both learn and write better (Moffett, 1968).

WRITING TO LEARN IN JOURNALS

Teachers assign journals—and logs and think-books and daybooks—for a variety of specific and practical reasons, including the following: (1) to help students find personal connections to the material they are studying in class and textbook, (2) to provide a place for students to think about, learn, and understand course material, (3) to collect observations, responses, and data, and (4) to allow students to practice their writing before handing it in to be graded.

In general, teachers in all subject areas, from history and literature to psychology and biology, have found that when students write about course readings, lectures, discussions, and research materials they understand better what they know, don't know, want to know and how it all relates to them. In elementary classes, as well as in high school and college, when students study science, math, and reading, they log what they are learning about science, math, and reading in their journals. Teachers commonly ask students to read aloud voluntarily from their journals to help start class discussions or clarify for each other points of confusion or differing interpretation. In short, journals are active, methodical records of student thought and opinion during a given term, meant to help students prepare for class discussions, study for examinations, and write critical papers.

In addition, English and language arts teachers commonly assign journals to help students learn to write formal assignments. Here student writers keep journals for many of the same reasons as professional writers: to find and explore topics; to clarify, modify, and extend those topics; to try out different writing styles; to sharpen their powers of observation; to practice fluency; and in general to become more aware of themselves as writers.

In most instances, teachers consider journals to be the students' territory, a place in which students can experiment and try out ideas without being corrected or criticized for doing so. Consequently, while most teachers periodically collect and read journals, they neither correct them for spelling nor grade them for ideas. Instead, they respond personally and positively to selected entries, usually in soft erasable pencil. Sometimes teachers simply respond positively to selected entries; at other times they ask questions or make suggestions in response to student questions; in many cases the journals provide a place where a non-threatening dialogue between teacher and student is possible.

Journals are useful tools for both students and teachers. They can help students prepare for class discussion, study for examinations, understand reading assignments, and write formal papers. In the following section are some of the guidelines for assigning journals which teachers have found helpful in the past.

GUIDELINES FOR ASSIGNING JOURNALS

1. Explain that journals are neither "diaries" nor "class notebooks," but borrow features from each: like the diary, journals are written in the first person about issues the writer cares about; like the class notebook, journals are concerned with the content of a particular course.

2. Ask students to buy looseleaf notebooks. This way students can hand in to you only that which pertains directly to your class, keeping more intimate entries private.

3. Suggest that students divide their journals in several sections, one for your course, one for another course, another for private entries. When you collect the journal, you need only collect that which pertains to your own course.

4. Ask students to do short journal writes in class; write with them; and share your writing with the class. Since you don't grade journals, the fact that you write too gives the assignment more value.

5. Every time you ask students to write in class, do something active and deliberate with what they have written: have volunteers read whole entries aloud; have everyone read one sentence to the whole class; have neighbors share one passage with each other, etc. (In each case, students who do not like what they have written should have the right to pass.) Sharing the writing like this also gives credibility to a non-graded assignment.

6. Count but do not grade student journals. While it's important not to qualitatively evaluate specific journal entries—for here students must be allowed to take risks—good journals should count in some quantitative way: a certain number of points, a *plus* added to a grade, as an in-class resource for taking tests.

7. Do not write back to every entry; it will burn you out. Instead, skim-read journals and write responses to entries that especially concern you.

8. At the end of the term ask students to put in (a) page numbers, (b) a title for each entry, (c) a table of contents, and (d) an evaluative conclusion. This synthesizing activity asks journal writers to treat these documents seriously and to review what they have written over a whole term of study.

Of all writing assignments, journals may be the most idiosyncratic and variable. Consequently, good reasons exist to ignore any of these suggestions, depending on teacher purpose, subject area, grade level, or classroom context. However, these suggestions will help many teachers use journals positively and efficiently in most school settings.

This document was drafted by Toby Fulwiler with considerable help from members of the NCTE Commission on Composition, including Glenda Bissex, Lynn Galbraith, Ron Goba, Audrey Roth, Charles Schuster, Marilyn Sternglass, and Tilly Warnock.

References

Britton, J. et al. (1975). *The development of writing abilities*, 11–18. London: Macmillan Education.

Bruner, J. S. (1966). *Towards a theory of instruction*. Cambridge, MA: The Belknap Press of Harvard University.

Emig, J. (1977, May). Writing as a mode of learning. *CCC*, 28: 122–128.

Moffett, J. (1968). *Teaching the universe of discourse*. Boston: Houghton Mifflin.

Vygotsky, L. (1962). *Thought and language*. Cambridge, MA: MIT Press.

M. Elizabeth Sargent, "Strategies for Writing-to-Learn/Invention Strategies"

M. Elizabeth Sargent earned her BA at Duke University, then her PhD at the University of Kent at Canterbury (in the UK) as a Marshall Scholar. In 1982, her third year of teaching at Gettysburg College, she received—only an hour after handing back the first version in class—an extensively revised, freshly-typed essay from a student who told her he was using the college mainframe computer to write all his papers. Realizing that the way she taught writing—and especially the way she taught revision—was about to change profoundly, she left within the year to work as an educational associate for a small computer company and also to establish and direct the Kaypro Computer Writing Project in the Baltimore County Public Schools, setting up one of the first high-school computer writing labs in North America. She then taught at Western Oregon University for eleven years until taking a position as writing coordinator at the University of Alberta in Edmonton in 1999. She has published two books with the Modern Language Association—*Part-Time Academic Employment in the Humanities* and (with Garry Watson) *Approaches to Teaching the Works of D. H. Lawrence*—and is co-editor of this volume.

The following two selections appeared as appendixes in her piece "'Errors and Expectations'; or, How Composition Scholarship Changed the Way I Ask for and Respond to Student Writing" in the *ADE* (*Association of Departments of English*) *Bulletin* (1994). Both appendixes had appeared previously in *What's Happening with Writing at*

Western Oregon State College?, a monograph edited by M. Elizabeth Wallace (now Sargent), Cornelia Paraskevas, Thomas Rand, Jane Thielsen, and Donald Weiss in 1991. These Strategies for Writing-to-Learn (which owe a debt to the work of Sam Watson at the University of North Carolina at Charlotte) have been lightly edited for inclusion here. The loop cartoon was created by Karen Kurt while she was taking a graduate course from Peter Elbow at the University of Massachusetts Amherst.

STRATEGIES FOR WRITING-TO-LEARN/ INVENTION STRATEGIES

SUMMARIZE/REMEMBER/REFLECT

1. *Write a Summary:* of a lecture, class discussion, seminar, or chapter.

2. *Condense Your Notes:* Read over your notes from a class and then write down what you think were truly the main ideas, the organizing ideas, in that lecture or discussion.

3. *Make a Test:* Read over your notes and design a difficult test for yourself. Several hours or days later, take the test. Include an essay question.

4. *End of Class Observations:* Immediately after class, jot down your impressions of what went on and why the instructor organized the class that way. If you have any confusion, try to explain why or to pinpoint in writing the moment at which your confusion began.

5. *Lab Reflections:* Immediately after a lab session, sit down and write about what you did and what the point of it was.

ZEROING IN—LOOKING CLOSELY AT IMPORTANT PASSAGES/DETAILS OR KEY CONCEPTS

6. *Key Word:* Choose a word that seems important to your reading (one that you don't understand or is repeated or otherwise emphasized) and write about all of its associations with anything else in the text or in your experience. Look it up in a good dictionary and puzzle over the possible implications of its different meanings.

7. *Mapping:* Write a key word from the text or lecture in the middle of a page. Then build upon it by association, jotting down related words and indicating relations with arrows. Continue until you reach terra incognita. Also try Treeing: put a topic at the top or bottom of a page and branch into subtopics.

8. *Extraction of Significance:* Take a statement from your reading or a lecture and exhaust all its possible meanings.

9. *Write Out the Definition:* Pick a key concept or term in your course and try to define it fully, giving illustrations.

10. *Show Off on a Topic:* Pick any topic and write down everything you know about it, no matter how obscure and irrelevant. This is a good way to get started on an assigned paper or to study for a test.

11. *Double-Entry:* Draw a vertical line down the center of a blank page. In the left column, write a few memorable quotations from an assigned reading or a lecture. In the right column, respond positively or negatively to the quotation or write a related idea, something you wish to add, a question raised by the quotation, or a paraphrase.

12. *Character Study:* Begin your analysis of a fictional or historical character by reviewing two or three key passages in the text; then write quickly every detail you can think of about that character, puzzling over which details are the most important or revealing. Pay attention to the way the character is described, what the character says and does, and what other characters say about the character.

13. *Literary Term:* Choose a literary term (like "point of view" or "foreshadowing") that seems to offer a way into the text. Write a brief definition of the term; then look back at the text through the lens of that term to see if any details seem important now that didn't seem all that important before.

MAKING CONNECTIONS—PUSHING YOUR THINKING FURTHER

14. *Ask Yourself a Question:* (a good question, clearly formulated, to which you would truly like a response) and then try to answer it yourself in as many ways, crazy and sensible, as possible.

15. *Particle, Wave, and Field:* Look at your subject from three different perspectives. First, consider it as an entity in itself (particle). Describe its essential characteristics. Next, consider it as part of a process that takes place in time (wave). For example, you might describe its causes or effects. You might explain what is required to keep it going. Finally, consider the subject as part of a whole system that affects things around it (field). What are the other components of the system? How are they related?

16. *Pre-guessing Chapters:* Before you read a chapter in a text, write about what you imagine the chapter might be about, guessing from its title or from material covered in the preceding chapter. (You can also pre-guess a lecture, discussion, or lab.)

17. *Narrow down Your Topic:* Write about an idea for two minutes. Stop. Pick a topic sentence from that paragraph and write for another two minutes about that. Again, pick another topic sentence from the second paragraph and write for another two minutes. The longer you do it, the more specific you become about the topic.

18. *Growing a Problem:* Raise all the questions you have pertaining to a particular concept or assignment. Jot down all thoughts on it, no matter how disordered and fragmented.

19. *Making Connections:* Write on every possible way in which new information can be connected to ideas, beliefs, and information you already have.

20. *Build Contradictions:* State all the oppositions and contradictions in the material you are reading or studying. Argue the pros and cons. Have a debate with yourself.

21. *Doubting and Believing Games:* If you are struggling with a new concept or perspective, write down all the implications for your life if you believed that concept fully. Then, do the opposite: what would the implications be if you doubted the new idea completely?

22. *Metaphor:* Compare something to something else, and then elaborate on the similarities and differences between the two things, e.g., "This hunting story is told in such arty language, it's like a BMW lurching down a bumpy country road." Unpacking such wild comparisons can yield surprising insights.

TEACHING A DIFFICULT CONCEPT TO SOMEONE ELSE

23. *Letter Writing:* Choose a real person to write a letter to about your subject. Experiment with audiences of varying backgrounds and levels of expertise in your subject area (try writing to a precocious nine-year-old who would need an especially clear and simple—yet not condescending—explanation).

24. *Create an Audience:* Pick a fictional or historical character or imagine a person to whom you might want to explain a difficult concept, someone who might be anything from your worst possible to your best possible audience. Describe them with a few deft details to suggest their background, values, physical presence, context, or habitual ways of thinking. Briefly explain why it would be useful or helpful for them to be your audience or to understand this particular concept. Then, with them in mind, do your best to explain the concept and help them understand it. (Example: Tell Sacagawea, the Native woman who helped Lewis and Clark find their way to the Pacific, how a global positioning system works: you'll understand it thoroughly yourself once you're done.)

THE LOOP WRITING PROCESS
(Rx for that tough essay)

by Peter Elbow

as interpreted by Karen Kurt
University of Massachusetts
AMHERST

THE VOYAGE OUT

1. FIRST THOUGHTS! Your pen is on fire. Just write down all thoughts and feelings you have on your subject. NO ERASING.

confused about your reading/ feelings? Tell the chain of mental events back to your-self: "I began to change my mind when X and Y said the woman was demonstrating her rights as an individual, and then I "thought they were wrong"

5. NARRATIVE THINKING.

Give your essay instant life by writing out a dialogue between major players in your essay.

I am the Sun King

Horse-Feathers

4. DIALOGUES.
LOUIS XIV   VOLTAIRE

ooo, MY MIND IS MADE UP.

2. PREJUDICES. Record all of your deep set feelings of why this thing exists, why this is happening how this movement is destroying Canada, etc. Prejudices can be good as well as bad!!

INSTANT VERSION. 3. Pretend you've got all the data you need already. Write a quickie essay knowing you will find the data when you research.

"OH MY GOD - IT'S A MIRACLE!"

6. STORIES. Record your own stories related to the subject. Do you remember a time you were in the same position or a similar one, and acted a certain way? Record related events, anecdotes. Unlock the rich treasury of personal memory. Write down 15-20 stories briefly told. _Private_ examples may support your conclusion.

11. VARY THE TIME! Try writing about your subject to an audience in the past or in the future. or BE a person in the past reflecting on current events & the likelihood of change. How would Canada have seemed to a woman born there in 1670? 1720?

7. SCENES. Focus on individual moments. Record memorable "scenes" or still photos in your mind regarding subject. This will give you insight into the CENTERS OF GRAVITY.

HEY MAN WITHOUT NEEDS A BLACK HOLE HERE!

8. PORTRAITS. WHO COMES TO MIND as you are writing about the French Revolution and the Reign of Terror? Your 3rd grade teacher? Evaluate your novel through a portrait of a character. Insight!!

9. VARY THE AUDIENCE. Say, Explain the French Revolution to your boxing coach.

10. VARY THE WRITER. Pretend you ARE the historical figure and write a self-analysis. Pretend you are the author of the novel in question & explain your characters' or creation.

I GOT TEN MINUTES, KID - GIVE IT TO ME STRAIGHT!

12. ERRORS. Record misconceptions and dangerous ways of thinking you know you have to avoid. This cuts the static in your head.

THE VOYAGE HOME

13. LIES. Write down as many LIES as you can think of about your subject. Some will be silly. Some may clear fog or give you new ideas.

"Return, then, to full consciousness of what your goal is:

Think about
- assignment guidelines
- what you want to do to your audience
- go over everything mark good points
- What do you want your main point to be?
- choose your revision tactics

TOPIC HARBOR
Audience town
Den o' Professional Critics
DMZ

October 15, 1988

James A. Reither and Douglas Vipond, from "Writing as Collaboration"

James A. Reither and Douglas Vipond taught at St. Thomas University (STU) in Fredericton, New Brunswick, for many years, Reither in English and Vipond in Psychology. They've collaborated on several projects, including an issue of *Textual Studies in Canada* (Issue 4, subtitled *Genre, Intertextuality, Collaboration, and Other Struggles*). Vipond has published, among other things, articles on readability theory and, in 1993, a book entitled *Writing and Psychology: Understanding Writing and Its Teaching from the Perspective of Composition Studies*.

Reither is best known in the composition field for his short but influential article "Writing and Knowing: Toward Redefining the Writing Process" (1985), which advanced the novel idea that actually knowing something might play a huge role in motivating someone to write and in making that piece of writing worth reading. Central to his argument in that piece (as it is to his piece here, with Vipond) was the notion that we don't know or inquire or investigate in a vacuum; instead, we belong to communities of inquiry and write for others who share a certain knowledge base with us and who also share the desire to extend that knowledge. If we have researched and explored material that no one else has yet written about in that community, we feel a pull from that community to share what we have discovered/created because they *need* what we know—and that pull is a crucial part of our motivation to write, even if we don't feel comfortable writing for publication. We feel responsible for what we know. It's as if a knowledge gradient exists—the knowledge we have *that no one else yet has* pulls the necessary writing out of us; meanwhile, the knowledge base we share with a particular community makes us aware that members of that community *want* this knowledge. Even if they might argue with it or resist it initially, they may be the only group of people prepared to understand it and carry it forward.

Reither and Vipond believe that if we could set up our classrooms so that writing was seen from beginning to end as a social and collaborative process, motivated by something we knew that others didn't, something that others *needed* to know, the teaching and learning of writing would be transformed.

from WRITING AS COLLABORATION

The topic of writing as social process has been a hot one in the last few years, so much so that it has become a dominant strand in our literature and at our conferences. The result has been a kind of revolution in composition theory. Unfortunately, however, the revolution seems to have been confined pretty much to the literature. Although the case for writing's social dimensions no longer requires arguing—it can be assumed—we would be hard put to point to a corresponding transformation in the ways writing is conceived and dealt with in our classrooms. In fact, even though radical changes in practice seem called for if we believe even some of what has been claimed about the social dimensions of writing, little substantive change in either course design or classroom practice has come about that can be said to result directly from this reconsideration of the nature of writing. With few exceptions, writing courses continue to focus on the production of compositions, on form and structure, topic and mode, disciplinary discourse and formal conventions. . . .

We find it more helpful to think of writing (and knowing) not as social but, more specifically, as collaborative. Instead of asking, "In what ways is writing a social process?" we ask, "In what ways are writers collaborating with others when they write?" Phrasing the question this way brings into focus writers' relationships with other writing and other writers. Thinking of writing as a collaborative process gives us more precise ways to consider what writers do when they write, not just with their texts, but also with their language, their personae, their readers. Most important, this apparently slight adjustment in terminology allows us more readily to tease out some answers to the practical question, "So what if writing is a social process?"

TEACHING WRITING AS COLLABORATION

. . . How does conceptualizing writing as collaboration affect the way we think about teaching writing and other courses in which writing is valued? How can we organize courses so students become engaged in writing that is deliberately collaborative in both long- and short-range realms?

It is not our purpose here to provide a step-by-step guide to setting up such courses. Instead, we will give a brief synopsis of what happens in our courses, which are organized as "Collaborative Investigations." Then . . . we offer some general principles or guidelines for practitioners who have become convinced that writing and knowing are indeed collaborative processes and wish to implement such ideas in their teaching.

In general, we organize a course by setting a question which we ask the students to answer by functioning as a research team whose task it is to divide the labor and carry out the research necessary to answer the question. Library research is always part of the project, although other modes of investigation may be used as well. This organization sets a situation that encourages the students in our writing and content-area courses to establish—through authoring, coauthoring, and workshopping—immediate, local communities of writers-knowers. The writing and knowing in these classroom communities arise primarily out of a relationship between the students in the course and a larger writing-knowing community whose knowing and whose ways of making meaning are manifest in a body of published literature. Therefore, the relationship, and the writing and knowing that develop out of it, begins with reading in that literature. . . .

The aims of the student community-within-a-community are collectively to develop, through reading and writing, its own knowledge claims, and cooperatively to find ways to fit its knowledge claims into the knowledge of the larger community. The relation of the smaller to the larger community is profound insofar as the larger community provides information, terminology, standards, values, persuasive strategies, discourse and audience models, and so on. The relation is acknowledged through presupposition and other forms of imitation and through allusion, quotation, and citation. In our experience, the most powerful way to arrange this kind of situation is to organize a course so that students collaboratively investigate a more or less original scholarly question or field. The teacher sets a long-range research project or question for the class, casting the students as members of a research group. . . .

Once the long-range project is set, the project is divided into chunks and the students organize themselves into investigative teams. Teams are responsible for gathering information, usually from the library, making sense of what they're finding out, writing reports on their findings, and presenting their reports to the group as a whole. As the long-term project proceeds, short-term projects are completed and new ones defined. Needs, circumstances, and directions change. Membership on research teams changes. As the course proceeds, the students take on more and more responsibility for the direction of the research; we also move toward greater formality of presentation, often concluding the course with a student-run conference or by binding and "publishing" a collaboratively written course book. The teacher is responsible for orchestrating and, acting as an expert co-researcher, modeling the process. Except on an ad hoc basis, at "teaching points," the instructor does not attempt to teach research or writing skills explicitly. The students learn most of what they need to know about inquiry, reading, and writing as part of the larger process of joining a post-secondary, academic version of what Frank Smith calls the "literacy club."

In our courses, the sole purpose of the research reports is to advance the overall class research project. These reports are thus not graded (and, in fact, none of the written work produced by the students is graded by the instructor). How then are grades determined? We base evaluation on two criteria. A quantitative criterion refers to the consistency of effort in the course: in addition to attendance, we keep track of the number of times each student participates on a research team, drafts or rewrites a report. A qualitative criterion refers to the extent to which a student contributes to the learning of others; it is assessed by the people who are in the best position to judge—the other students in the course. To obtain these evaluations we have students write confidential assessments of the degree to which they have been helped by each of the other students in the course. The quantitative criteria (sheer effort and participation) and the qualitative criteria (value of contribution, as judged primarily by one's peers) are given roughly equal weight in determining whether a student's performance is below average, average, above average, or outstanding.

Now that we've seen, at least in broad outline, what happens in our courses, we offer the following guidelines to practitioners who wish to implement some of the ideas presented here.

1. Organize the course—whether it's a writing course or a content-area course— as a collaborative investigation of a genuine scholarly field or question. This sets up the conditions that make the course collaborative in the knowledge-making sense.

2. By dividing the students into teams, structure the course so the students regularly come together in plenary to report their findings to and receive suggestions from the others in the research group. This makes the course collaborative in the workshopping sense.

3. If only in the name of efficiency, encourage the students to cooperate in gathering and making sense of information and ideas. The more they work together, the more they learn about the subject under study and about ways of making meaning in the subject. In other words, encourage all forms of coworking, including coauthoring.

Thus, we recommend that practitioners make their courses collaborative in as many realms as possible, having their students work together as coauthors, workshoppers, and knowledge makers. Let us expand on each of these.

Coauthoring

Make the course collaborative in the coauthoring sense by allowing and encouraging various forms of coauthoring as a means of achieving efficiency and quality in reading, writing, and reporting. Coauthoring helps students experience the frustrations of cooperation but also the joys—the synergy that enables a small team to accomplish more than its members could acting individually.

Workshopping

Make the course collaborative in the workshopping sense by having the students report to one another what they're finding out in the sources provided by the larger community outside the classroom. A crucial condition here is that those to and for whom the students write, their fellow student-inquirers, must have uses for the ideas being reported. The students function within a community of "knowledgeable peers" (Bruffee, "Conversation") who, given the cooperative nature of the project, want and need what the others have to offer. When the students report to one another (both orally and in writing) on what they have found out, they are functioning as knowing scholars, as literate persons who can contribute to what others know and believe. That is, they are functioning as teachers. Other students respond by telling them what is understandable and what isn't, what fits and what doesn't, which questions are answered and which ones are raised, and by what is, when it happens, the most powerful feedback of all—using, citing, and building on what they learn from them.

The classroom thus takes on the character of a workshop . . . . One value of a workshop arises out of the fact that, as circumstances and needs change, different people bring to bear different roles, different talents, different modes and areas of expertise. The research projects must therefore be organized to enable the students to develop expertise in the eyes of their colleagues and their teacher. Expertise and authority are strongly promoted when the territory of the scholarly field is divided into more manageable chunks and different people are given responsibility for different territories. This division provides real audiences who have real needs for the writing. The students can become expert researchers, expert note-takers, expert organizers, expert group leaders, expert first-drafters, expert revisers, and so on and on. Their expertise gives them roles and status in the workshop. It gives them authority—something to say, ways to say it, a community to whom to say it, and, thus, reasons for saying it. It makes them valuable to the group, and their sense of their value makes them be and feel important. They need not become experts in all these things; indeed, expertise in just two or three areas is precisely what makes them valuable.

Knowledge Making

Make the course collaborative in the knowledge-making sense by setting a research question and a long-term goal of developing knowledge claims that could find fit in a scholarly field's knowing. Get the students reading in the literature of a field, to listen in on the conversation, to find out who's talking about what, how they're talking about it, why they're talking about it.

Students must be given the opportunity to take part in honest scholarly inquiry, inquiry whose aim is genuinely to make meaning out of and with a genuine scholarly field. As the course progresses and the project takes on logic, direction, and necessity of its own, students must be given greater and greater responsibility for determining what comes next. Decisions about gathering, organizing, and disseminating information and ideas are then given over to the students—unless, of course, the information needed is "of such minor significance that it can be told" (Boomer 12).

In doing their own research, students learn to exploit the resources of the library: archival collections, reference materials, abstracts and citation indexes, as well as books and periodicals. Of these, articles are especially important because they are the chief means academics use to construct and negotiate knowledge claims. Students learn to find articles, but more important, they learn to identify important, useful articles and to separate them from chaff. They learn to conduct article traces using quotation and citation, and they learn the deep significance of quotation and citation in the knowledge-making process. Moreover, they learn to read these articles with greater purpose and skill, because they're reading them for their own uses, to satisfy their own needs. By reading the literature of a given field of study, students learn the values, conventions, forms of argument and evidence of that field. They learn that writing and knowing consist in using and building on others' writing and knowing. In short, they learn to write by reading. Or, more accurately and importantly, since there is no such thing as knowing how to write (there is only knowing how to write in certain genres for certain audiences on certain subjects in certain situations), they learn how to learn how to write. Perhaps most important of all, students learn that writing and knowing are collaborative acts—vital activities people do with other people to give their lives meaning.

Texts are figures that arise out of the ground of others' texts. In one way or another, all writing and knowing, and all learning about writing and knowing, are processes we undertake not alone but with others. We learn to write by using writing, our own and others', to achieve genuine ends. Our most powerful motive for writing is to change and be changed by others with whom we would identify, because the ability to bring about change through language is central to authority and identity within the community. All of us who make meaning through writing and reading—scholars, teachers, students—do so in community with others who share our interests in the knowing and the knowledge-making processes that constitute our fields of inquiry. Writing *is* collaboration. It cannot be otherwise.

We gratefully acknowledge the trusted assessors—the enablers—who helped workshop this paper: Russell Hunt, Anthony Paré, and Karen Burke LeFevre (who still, it should be said, prefers the term *social* to the term *collaborative*). Those who know LeFevre's *Invention as a Social Act* will recognize in this paper an intertextual debt which is but poorly acknowledged in our few direct allusions to that fine book.

Works Cited

Boomer, Garth. "Addressing the Problem of Elsewhereness: A Case for Action Research in Schools." *Reclaiming the Classroom: Teacher Research as an Agency for Change.* Ed. Dixie Goswami and Peter R. Stillman. Upper Montclair, NJ: Boynton/Cook, 1987. 4–13.

Bruffee, Kenneth. "Collaborative Writing and the 'Conversation of Mankind.'" *College English* 46 (1984): 635–52.

Hunt, Russell A., and Douglas Vipond. "Evaluations in Literary Reading." *TEXT: An Interdisciplinary Journal for the Study of Discourse* 6 (1986): 53–71.

LeFevre, Karen Burke. *Invention as a Social Act.* Carbondale, IL: Southern Illinois UP, 1987.

Smith, Frank. *Joining the Literacy Club.* Portsmouth: Heinemann, 1988.

Vipond, Douglas, and Russell A. Hunt. "Point-driven Understanding: Pragmatic and Cognitive Dimensions of Literary Reading." *Poetics* 13 (1984): 261–77.

Sondra Perl, "Guidelines for Composing"

Sondra Perl, a Guggenheim fellow and the first person in composition studies to be named a Professor of the Year by the Carnegie Foundation for the Advancement of Teaching (1996, for the state of New York), is Professor of English at Lehman College and the Graduate Center of the City University of New York. Perl's early research on student writers made a huge impact on the conversation about teaching writing: from close analysis of what students were actually doing while they composed, she discovered that students who had difficulty with writing tended to lose track of their thoughts because of premature editing. Fascinated, as Janet Emig was, with the ways in which writing connected the mind and the body, Perl began working with the insights of Eugene Gendlin, a professor at the University of Chicago, who had developed the notion of "felt sense." In fact, Perl's most recent book is entitled *Felt Sense: Writing with the Body* (2004) and includes a CD version of the Composing Guidelines reprinted below. Perl argues that "felt sense" will help us to better understand something that is a continuing puzzle for most writers—how do new ideas come to us? As you try out Perl's Composing Guidelines, you'll notice immediately that she is asking you to do something that most freewriting and inkshedding instructions warn against: she is asking you to pause. But notice also that the pauses are for a very specific kind of activity—for listening attentively to your body, to your felt sense, for what will come *next*.

Freewriting and inkshedding warn us not to pause because most of us, when we do stop writing, look back over what we have written in order to edit it—and pretty soon, we have jumped off our train of thought and are back in all-too-familiar and all-too-depressing territory (the this-is-no-good, this-is-full-of-typos-and-mistakes territory). So be careful: when the Perl Guidelines ask you to pause, don't use that time to read back over what you have just written. Close your eyes and attend to what's coming. Listen. Trust your body to provide you with language for the next thing. Think not only of Pinker's ideas about our instinct for language (see Conversation 1), but of Eugene Gendlin's reassuring lines:

> *Our bodies imply the next words and actions to carry our situations for-ward. . . .* [O]ur next words "come" from the body, just as hunger, orgasm, and sleep come in a bodily way, and just as food-search comes in an animal. . . . Animals act in new ways very often. With linguistic and cultural elaborations, our bodies imply *what we want to say*, which can be typical or something very new. It can surprise us. . . .
>
> ("How Philosophy Cannot Appeal to Experience,
> and How It Can," 28)

If you follow the Composing Guidelines during an in-class writing session, your instructor will let you know that whatever you produce will be private writing. You may be asked (if you were working on a computer) to print it out and show the instructor that you have a hard copy of your writing, but you will not be asked to let your instructor or anyone else read it. However, hold onto that printout (and either make a disk copy of your writing or e-mail it to yourself, just in case you want to develop that piece of writing further at some point). Your instructor will probably ask you to delay reading what you have written for several days, even a week if you can manage it, so you can get some distance on it. But at that point, you will probably be asked to read what you produced during the Perl Guidelines session and to write a piece of process writing about it (see Inkshedding Prompt 6 in this section).

GUIDELINES FOR COMPOSING

INTRODUCTION

Traditionally, teachers help students with their writing after they produce first drafts. Sometimes we offer our students help before they begin writing by working with them on strategies for planning and organization. Only recently have we known how to help our students *while* they are in the process of writing.

The guidelines for composing are designed to guide writers through the composing process, from finding a topic worth writing about to discovering what to say about it. They consist of a series of questions which ask writers to look back in order to move forward, to question themselves, to search for the right word—to do what many skilled writers do naturally.

The guidelines also direct writers to look for a "felt sense." This term, coined by Eugene Gendlin, refers to the physical sensation that often accompanies barely formed impressions. To Gendlin, a felt sense is always rather murky and puzzling. But as we name this felt sense, as we put words to it, what was formerly inchoate and diffuse comes into focus. At this moment, we experience a "felt shift," the sense of relief that accompanies new understanding.

To explain felt sense, Gendlin gives the example of knowing you have forgotten something but not knowing what it is. You are on your way to work but something keeps nagging at you. What is it? you ask. What did you forget? Notice that you don't know what it is, but you have a physical felt sense. You feel your pockets. Is it your keys? No. You search your mind. The papers you meant to copy? You've forgotten the papers but that's not it. The idea doesn't satisfy the physical sensation. You still have that wordless discomfort. All of a sudden, it comes to the surface: the book you promised to return. That's it. It's still sitting on your desk. You feel a sudden physical relief, an easing inside. You have just experienced what Gendlin calls a "shift" in your felt sense.

A similar process operates when writers write. If we pay close attention, we can notice that the meanings we construct while writing often come to us first in the vague, puzzling way Gendlin describes. We have a sense of what we want to say, but we're not quite sure how to say it. As we write, we begin to make discoveries about our subjects and to clarify what we mean. At such times we often say that we are "on the right track." At other times we hit dead-ends, uncomfortably aware that something is missing but not sure what it is. In these instances, it is our felt sense which often serves as our internal guide, the criterion which helps us judge whether or not our words capture our intended meanings. When they do, we can experience the shift Gendlin describes. When they do not, we need to pause, to consult this complex bodily feeling once again and to continue writing.

The guidelines for composing aid writers in the act of meaning-making described above. Based on the questions, writers normally produce a set of notes which can later be shaped into a draft.

PROCEDURE

If you choose to use these instructions with a class, in a writing workshop, or in a one-to-one tutoring situation, it is useful to inform people ahead of time that you will be inviting them to ask themselves a series of questions and that they will have time to write after each one. Advise them that the questions are meant to be guides; they may not fit everyone's experience. Some questions may be distracting for a particular writer and should be ignored. The writer can tune in again when he or she is ready to listen. Before you begin the guidelines, ask people not to interrupt you and to hold questions. Afterward, give them time to continue writing and then invite them to write about and express their reactions to the exercise. Remember, however, that what people write during the guidelines may be personal or private. The notes they produce are not meant to be shared in a group unless the writers themselves choose to share them.

* * *

The sentences in brackets are meant for teachers. They are not to be read aloud as part of the exercise.

1. Find a way to get comfortable. Shake out your hands, take a deep breath, settle into your chair, close your eyes if you're willing to, relax. [In this first step, you are helping people become aware of their inner states. Being able to do this will make it easier for them to locate a felt sense. As people sit quietly for several minutes, ask them to notice if they feel any tension in their arms and necks. Ask them to pay attention to their breathing as they inhale and exhale. If there is some laughter in the room or some noise outside, ask them to notice it and then to come back quietly to themselves and their breathing.]

2. Ask yourself, what's going on with me right now? [short pause] Is there anything in the way of my writing today? [short pause] When you hear yourself answering, begin to make a list. [Leave time for people to write—about 1 or 2 minutes.] Now that you've noted all the distractions, I'd like you to take that piece of paper and set it aside. Perhaps, now that they are down on paper, those distractions won't intrude so much. If you'll relax and get comfortable again, I'll continue.

3. Ask yourself, how am I right now? [short pause] What's on my mind? [short pause] When you hear yourself answering, begin to make a list. [Leave time for people to write—about 1 or 2 minutes.]

4. Now ask yourself, what else is on my mind? Is there anything I'm interested in that I might write about today? Does a particular person, a place, or an image come to mind? Jot these down. If you came here today with a specific topic in mind, put that on your list too. If you can't think of anything, write the word "nothing." [Again, leave a few minutes for people to write.]

5. Ask yourself, now that I have a list—long or short—is there anything else I've left out, any other piece I'm overlooking, maybe even a word I like, something else I might at some time want to write about that I can add to this list? Jot down whatever comes. [The purpose of #3–5 is to make an inventory of possible topics for writing.]

6. Now, you may have one definite idea or a whole list of things. Look over your list and ask, which one of these items draws my attention right now? Which one seems to stand out? Which one could I begin to write on even if I'm not certain where it will lead? Take the idea or word or issue and put it at the top of a new page. Save your list for another time. If nothing seems to jump out at you, choose something for the sake of the exercise.

7. Now, take a deep breath, relax as we did earlier, and settle comfortably into your chair. Realize that you already know a lot about your particular topic. Without delving into any one part, see if you can jot down all your associations with or thoughts on this topic. For instance, ask yourself, what are all the parts I know about this topic? What can I say about it now? Perhaps you will write a list, a bunch of phrases, notes to yourself, stream of consciousness writing. [This can take about 5 minutes.]

8. Now, I'm going to interrupt you and ask you to set aside all the pieces you already know. I want you to take a fresh look at this topic or issue, to grab hold of the *whole* topic—not the bits and pieces—and ask yourself, what makes this topic interesting to me? What's *important* about this that I haven't said yet? What's the *heart* of the issue? [This can take about 5 minutes.]

9. Wait quietly and see if a word, an image or a phrase comes to you from your felt sense of the topic. Take this word or image and explore it. Ask yourself, what's this all about? Describe the image or word. As you write, let your felt sense deepen. Continue to ask yourself, is this right? Am I getting closer? Am I saying it? See if you can feel when you're on the right track. Notice when you write if you can experience the shift of "Oh yeah, that says it." [Leave at least 5 to 10 minutes here.]

10. If you're at a dead-end, you can ask yourself, what makes this topic so hard for me? Or, what's so difficult about this? And again, pause and see if a word or image or phrase comes to you that captures this difficulty in a fresh way.

11. You can continue along now writing what comes to you. When you stop you can ask, what's missing? What hasn't yet gotten down on paper? And again, look to your felt sense for a word or an image.

12. Ask yourself, where is this leading? What's the point I'm trying to make? Again, write down whatever comes.

13. Once you feel you're near or at the end, ask yourself, does this feel complete? Look to your body for the answer. Again, write down whatever answer comes to you. If the answer is no, pause and ask yourself, what's missing? Then continue writing.

        * * * * *

14. Now you may have anywhere from one to several pages of notes that can form the basis of a piece of writing. Ask yourself, what form would work best for what I'm trying to say? Is this a story? A poem? An essay? Something else? Who's talking? What point of view is this? Is there another point of view I can use? Make some notes about the shape your piece will take.

15. When you feel you have a shape for your piece, begin writing it. [If some time remains in the session, encourage people to continue writing. If there is no time left for writing, proceed to #16.]

(16.) Now, for the next _____ minutes, review your notes from the beginning of the exercise and write about what happened. What was this experience like for you? This last piece of writing will be shared with the group.

*****

During the discussion that follows, people may reveal that they have had strong responses to the guidelines. It is important to allow people time to express their reactions. The guidelines may work differently for each person each time you do them.

Sources

Gendlin, Eugene. *Focusing.* New York: Everest House, 1978.

Perl, Sondra. "Understanding Composing." *College Composition and Communication*, 31:4 (December 1980): 363–69.

STUDENT WRITING
MARCIE BONSTROM ARNOLD

PROCESS WRITING INKSHED: ON LOOP WRITING

In the following piece of process writing, **Marcie Bonstrom Arnold** describes her first experience of loop writing and then reflects on the marginal comments she received from the instructor.

December 3, 2002

When we were asked to read about loop writing, I was instantly made curious as to how the process would work to start our research essay as it seemed a roundabout way to get started (especially the map on the loop writing process seemed confusing and unproductive to me). However, on the night that we did the loop writing in the lab I found that I appreciated using the focused freewriting that loop writing is to get my thoughts flowing on the various articles we examined. The loop writing prompts such as stories, first thoughts, dialogue, etc. weren't asking me to write anything specific which was good because at that point I hadn't really formed specific opinions regarding my essay. I found the dialogue part difficult to do in such a short period of time—I had never dialogued with writing before and it took me awhile to think of what to say (I couldn't just freewrite quickly in this section). Changing audience, writer, and time proved difficult for me because I don't normally do this in my writing—I can see that this may get easier with more loop writing exposure. What I really enjoyed doing that surprised me was writing out my lies, errors or any sayings. I found that I had a lot in my head that wanted to come out.

At the time when I was loop writing I felt embarrassed that the Prof. would be reading my work that night as it seemed jumbled together and really unfocused to me. However after I later read what I wrote I was surprised to see that for the most part it made sense. I was blown away by the Prof.'s comments on my loop writing as she found certain passages quite interesting that I would have normally overlooked. Her suggestions on potential topics for my essay (taken from the loop writing) were great and very helpful. I would never have been able to pull that much thought out of my loop writing as she did—nor would I have had the confidence to see those main points would work together in a piece. She seemed particularly interested in my collaborative writing experiences during my business degree. I tried to capture a lot of my loop writing thoughts on teachers creating a supportive environment for student writing in my essay. On the whole, I think I prefer loop writing to unfocused freewriting when starting a major piece like an essay as I need a bit of focus to get my thoughts rolling out on to the paper.

NILS PETERSON

PROCESS WRITING INKSHED: ON SONDRA PERL'S COMPOSING GUIDELINES

Nils Peterson wrote the following passage of process writing one week after having tried Sondra Perl's Composing Guidelines for the first time.

February 7, 2001

. . . It was surreal looking back on what I wrote over a week ago. I didn't give it a second thought until now, and it surprised me. When I was actually in the lab, writing, I felt a bit uncomfortable and a bit brain dead. There's a lot of "uhhs" and "ummms" in the writing, but what came through was strange. It seemed when I first read it that it was someone else's writing, like I'd taken it from someone else's brain. But as I read it, I had constant flashbacks to what I was thinking and writing then.

When I wrote it, I had just read a really stupid article, and I wrote "I'd love to tear his argument to shreds." It took me a while to figure out what I was talking about at the time. A couple of sentences just totally blew me away when I read them: it was as though a real writer wrote it. . . .

MINDY LEVINE

WRITING-TO-LEARN JOURNAL INKSHEDS: STRATEGY #4—END OF CLASS OBSERVATION

Mindy Levine wrote the following entries in her writing-to-learn journal while a student in first-year composition. The class assignment had been simply to choose one other course the student was taking that term, a course that seemed especially difficult, and to inkshed twice a week in response to the subject matter of that course. The goal was to see if inkshedding about challenging material would help deepen and extend the student's learning of that material.

The writing instructor did not read all of these entries, but scanned them quickly once a week at the beginning of class. This particular entry (February 9, 1990) caught the instructor's eye. Responding to the instructor's suggestion in the margin, the student took the journal entry itself to her biology professor and then wrote about her visit to his office and his reaction (see the entry dated February 16). Both entries could be classified as *End of Class Observations* (see Writing-to-Learn Strategy 4, as described on page 150), although the second describes an individual class, that is, a short tutorial in the professor's office. The student not only learned some information about biology: she also discovered that visiting a professor's office wasn't as terrifying as she had expected it to be, especially since the professor was primarily concerned to support her in her attempts to learn. She also agreed to have her two journal entries reproduced to be distributed to everyone in her first-year writing class as examples of one possible way (out of many) to use a writing-to-learn journal productively.

FEBRUARY 9, 1990

(Good use of fw!)

Journal Entry
BI 102 #13

February 9, 1990

After class today I was really confused! I didn't feel like Dr. Turner explained the concept very well. He didn't space his topics out enough and there wasn't enough time to ask questions when he was done.

I think the point at which I lost him was when he started explaining the origination and the effects of the ozone layer. And how it acts on polymers and protenoids. I understood his example about the chalk, and if you layed all of the pieces out and the radiation struck them it would alter them, this was the analogy too the polymers and protenoids with the ozone layer effecting them.

The reason I think I became confused is I just had a lot of other worries on my mind and I was trying to sort those, plus try and organize the information he was giving me and it was working at all.

But then towards the end of the lecture I started to understand again, and I wasn't thinking so much about my personal worries! I think that he needs to slow down when we get to more complicated stuff. More pauses would maybe encourage people to ask questions. Because when he talks a mile / minute you are constantly writing and nothing can really proces.

Basically, I will need to go back and read the parts I didn't understand. And when I read at my own pace I have a lot better luck with understanding the material.

go see him, show him this, then write me an entry for next week about what you learned, (write PLEASE READ at the top)

FEBRUARY 16, 1990

Journal Entry
Please Read!

Mindy:
Could I make
a copy of this?
Thanks!

February 16, 1990

This is in response to you about when I went in to talk to Dr. Turner to get some confusion straightened out.

I took my journal in there with me and I sat down. The first thing I said was, "You lost me last Friday in the middle of the lecture + I need to get things straightened out before the next test!" So I proceeded to take my writing journal out, explaining that to him, and how I have exactly where I lost it in my writing - to-learn journal of notes. He seemed to be impressed with the fact that I picked Biology for the subject to write on. Then I let him read the whole entry and he smiled the whole time, and it was really bugging me, because I thought he was sort of laughing at me. But when he was done reading it, he said, "Great, I know exactly where I can start explaining things to you." So he pulled some papers out of his desk and told me to start taking notes when he started talking and that should clue me in on what I didn't have in my notes. So I did, and it didn't take long to do that.

After we were done, he asked me if he could look at all my other entries about Biology, and I let him, so he thumbed through them, and he said that he really thought the approach was beneficial to kids who struggle with a certain subject! So I was really glad it went well, because I was nervous to go in, in the first place! :)

MARTA CURRAH

ESSAY SUMMARY/ANNOTATION

Marta Currah drafted the following annotation of an essay by Peter Elbow as part of a class project to build a full annotated bibliography of all articles read during the term about writing and the teaching of writing.

November 16, 2002

Elbow, Peter. "Teaching Writing by Not Paying Attention to Writing." *fforum: Essays on Theory and Practice in the Teaching of Writing*. Ed. Patricia Stock. Upper Montclair, NJ: Boynton/Cook, 1983. 234–239.

In this article Elbow advocates a creative solution to improving student writing while reducing teacher workload. He challenges established teaching doctrines, pointing out that, as important as it is to encourage students to "pay more attention to writing," it is also beneficial to spend time using it "without paying attention to it" (234). In effect, the writing itself ceases to be the point. What becomes important is the writer's ability to "understand or remember something better or see something from a different point of view" (234). When one focuses less on writing as output and more on the mental event the writing brings about (writing as input), the writing becomes easier. Added bonuses are that such writing takes "no time away from the subject matter" (238), assigning it "doesn't require teachers to be experts in writing" (234), and fluency often improves. Elbow offers four ways to "use writing as pure *input*":

1) Shorten lectures by ten minutes and use the time at the end to freewrite.

2) Start each class discussion with ten minutes of freewriting to help students recall the previous class or an assigned reading.

3) If a hard question arises, pause for five or ten minutes of freewriting. This gives students an opportunity to collect their thoughts, which they are then more likely to share with the class.

4) Finally, use freewriting at the end of a seminar to allow students to work out some conclusions so that they can "carry away with them some of the benefit of the discussion" (236).

These activities use writing, yet they do not feel as though the student is "working on writing," but rather on the subject area at hand, whether it be biology, economics, or modern drama. Since students may feel that "writing that does not hurt and does not count" (236) is irrelevant, Elbow believes teachers must use "unambivalent authority" to make such writing happen.

Elbow offers some pointers on writing as a way to "get another job done." While this writing is *"output* for an audience, for communication" (236), it's ungraded and might be thrown away after it's read so we shouldn't worry about perfecting it. Student attention should be "on the job rather than on the writing."

5) Start a course by having both the teacher and students write rough, informal pieces about what they expect to learn from the course, their positive and negative expectations, their requirements of the teacher and each other, and strengths they can offer.

6) At various points during the course, students could be invited to freewrite about how the course is going for them: these freewrites could help teachers make adjustments to the class during term.

7) If students want to drop the class or if the class requires an interview for entrance, students could be asked to take ten minutes to write their reasons out informally.

8) Keep a journal of thoughts and reactions to readings, class sessions, and other course activities.

9) Write a think-piece each week exploring insights or issues about the week's reading or recording "an unsuccessful struggle with a perplexity" (237).

10) Have students write a self-evaluation on their own performance in the course: "what they are proud of . . . what they could do differently next time" (237).

11) Have students write a frank teacher evaluation, not to be read until the final grades are posted.

Elbow also suggests ways to make graded writing more useful and fair, especially emphasizing that term papers should not be left until the end of the term—because learning is minimized if multiple drafts are not allowed and improvement is impossible to judge.

NEW PRACTICES TO TAKE FORWARD

1. The first one is simple: **You now have a well-supplied invention toolbag. Use it.** Keep these heuristics handy, remembering that you have not only Strategies for Writing-to-Learn as a way to support, deepen, and extend your learning in any subject area but also loop writing and Perl's Composing Guidelines and, of course, the bedrock of all these practices—private freewriting. Next time you feel writer's block heading in your direction, especially when you have big writing projects to start, wave one of these invention tools in its grey face and start writing like a mad thing. The block tends to dwindle to pebble size when you're ignoring it. As William Stafford put it, you might need to lower your standards temporarily. You can *always* write; you might not be able to write *well*, but you can always write. And the good stuff, the stuff you can use and build on, tends to come *when* you're writing.

2. **Learn how to give and to ask for productive feedback on your exploratory writing to heighten and take advantage of the social nature of invention.** This is, of course, easier to do if your instructor has the time to model how to give such feedback by reading and responding to a full set of loops, one from each student. But reading and responding to a loop from every student, given class sizes or time constraints during any particular term, may not be possible; it may be necessary, even the very first time, for students to do this for each other. So make sure to look back at the two last pages in the introduction to this Conversation (pages 116–117) for a description of how we, the editors of this book, try to respond to loop writing: that will give you a sense of your goals in giving this feedback and the appropriate receptive spirit in which to enter a piece of rough exploratory writing. We often think of William Stafford's stance whenever we read someone else's loop writing—or indeed, when we loop-write ourselves: "Welcome! Welcome!"

    Read through a loop with a highlighter in hand, marking the passages that jump out at you and responding to the content of the loop in the margins (quarrels, questions, hurrahs, "me too's"—whatever feels appropriate). Don't hesitate to let your colleague know when you don't understand something: most loops have incomprehensible bits, especially if our fingers shifted accidentally to the left or right on the keyboard for a line or two. When you give each other's loops back, feel free to talk about the feedback once you've both read through it. Ask questions, make sure you understand what the feedback means. It's also useful to ask your colleague to tell you more about their topic and their ideas. You may even find yourself able to identify a centre of gravity in the loop, something you want to hear more about, even if it's just a glimpse you caught while reading through the stories or scene sections in the loop. Such a centre of gravity can often become the focus of a more formal academic paper.

If you're giving your loop to someone else to read and that person is not in your writing class, make sure they understand the status of the writing you're giving them. Ask them to read the discussion of invention in the introduction to Conversation 3 (pages 114–117) as well as Inkshedding Prompt 7 on loop writing (pages 121–122) and this New Practice (2) before they begin reading. Nothing can destroy your motivation and energy for writing like destructive feedback at an early, vulnerable stage in the process when your ideas are just hatching. Think of eggs; think of incubators. Your ideas need some warmth and protection in order to develop further, to break out of their various shells and find their legs.

ESSAY IDEAS

CREATE A COLLAGE

1. **An inkshed collage**: By now, you probably have a whole pile of inksheds. You should be keeping all of them organized in a notebook in some kind of order—probably chronological, since many instructors ask you to look back through all your exploratory writing at the end of a course to reflect on how it has changed from the beginning of term to the end. But consider also using your inksheds to make a **collage** (also known as a **segmented essay**). The process is simple. Go back through a group of inksheds, perhaps ones that seem to be related to each other in some way. Highlight the passages you like best. Then type up those passages; if they're already on the computer, do some cutting and pasting. Whatever you do, though, don't destroy the original inkshed, on paper or on disk.

A written collage requires two things: that you arrange these excerpted passages in an order that pleases you, for whatever reason; and that you clearly separate these items by some sort of marker, so readers don't get confused and think they've got a traditional linear essay in front of them. Asterisks work well. Some writers simply number their sections, once they've definitely decided on the order they want. Some use graphic symbols.

Alternate short sections (even as short as a sentence) with longer sections, funny ones with sad ones, narratives with passages of theory or data—whatever contrasts and juxtapositions seem to carry or build meaning for you. Read Robert Root's collage in Conversation 6 or Stephanie Bishop's in Conversation 8 if you'd like to see some examples. If you look at contemporary literary journals or magazines, you'll notice that many published essays are actually collages with sudden breaks between sections; we've all become expert at reading collages because of our exposure to movies, which often work with sudden cuts from one scene to another and with various forms of montage.

When you're done, give your collage a title.

2.   **A collaborative collage**: Collages are fun to do collaboratively as well. You can select the inksheds you want to work with and then swap with colleagues from class. They can highlight what they like best in your work, and you can do the same for them. Then go ahead with the rest of the procedure in Essay Idea 1. Or carry the collaboration a bit further: combine passages and build one longer collage together, one that includes passages from several of you.

3.   **A loop collage**: Follow all the steps in Essay Idea 1 with the one exception that instead of looking through all your inksheds, you simply read through a long piece of your loop writing, highlighting the passages you like best. Loop collages can be especially rich and inventive and fun for others to read because they often include passages in many different genres: narrative, description, dialogue, letters, and epigraphs, just to name a few. But they can also be persuasive arguments if they were written with a focus on a particular subject or with a certain body of reading freshly in mind. Indeed, effective academic essays have been written as collages, even ones incorporating dialogue, narrative, letters, and description (Jane Tompkins's widely anthologized piece, "Me and My Shadow," a critique of academic writing, comes to mind). Loop collages, working by thoughtful juxtaposition and progression, can make the final weight fall in powerful and unforgettable ways, as in a loop collage written by one of Sargent's students, Darci Jungwirth, and published in Elbow and Belanoff's *Being a Writer* (90–93).

CONVERSATION 4:

The Academic Writing Debate: What Is Academic Writing For?

INTRODUCTION

Suppose you tell me something you are excited about, perhaps something personal or a new point in philosophy. Now you are eager to hear from me. Suppose I say only your own words back to you, over and over, with no indication that I have grasped their meaning, and without saying anything further. You would be angry. You want to hear what your point makes me think, how I would move on from it.

Now I oblige you and begin telling you what I think, but you notice that I have not grasped your point exactly. Now you stop me. "Wait," you say. "That wasn't my point." *You do not want to hear my reaction to a misunderstanding of your point.* Now suppose I am very stupid. I might object: "You don't like it if I say what you said, and you don't want something different either. Well then, what do you want?"

But if I am not stupid, I stop the moment you tell me that I have not understood exactly. You say "Let me say what I mean more exactly." Then you say more, or put the point differently, and soon I say "Oh, I see." *Now* you are again eager to hear what I will say, and perhaps this time you see that what I say is *what your exact point* makes me think.

What does the story show? Understanding is more intricate than either a copy or something different. *We need more terms than "same" or "different"! We can generate the needed terms from the intricacy of the story.* You are not eager to hear how I go on from something *different* that you did not say, nor do you want the *same* thing back. You want to hear how I *move from* your point, because I will move in a way you cannot imagine without me, yet may be able to follow as being from your point; if so, you may then move on still further.

Eugene Gendlin, "Reply to Wallulis" 284–85

Do you know what your theory of knowledge is? Chances are you have one, whether you know it or not.

And why would that matter, you might ask?

Because our theories of knowledge shape everything we do, especially in schools—

how we learn, how we write, how we read, how we relate to our fellow students and to our instructors, how we carry on conversations about ideas. Our theory of knowledge is what we believe about how knowledge is created and upheld and what knowledge is for. And, whether you've thought consciously about your theory of knowledge (your **epistemology**) or not, you do have one—probably one that is heavily influenced by the culture at large, where science and technology are so essential that we've learned to operate on the basis of a lot of unexamined assumptions about knowledge.

For instance, we tend to talk about knowledge as if it exists, objective and established, outside of us somewhere—maybe in some publication (an article or a book) or in some database or on the web or in some expert's head. And a lot of us assume that universities exist so that we can listen to such experts give lectures, collect the information from the lectures (by taking copious, detailed, and accurate notes), and then somehow transfer the information into our own heads—where we can hold onto it, we hope, at least until the exam. One theorist, Paulo Freire, has called this "the banking model" of education. This model usually depends on the notion that the role of language in relation to knowledge is simply to get out of the way: that is, language should be as clear and direct as possible and call no attention to itself—it should simply be a windowpane onto the world, letting us see the world and gather knowledge about it.

Others argue that we need to throw out that banking model and instead admit that all knowledge is **socially constructed**; that *there is no knowledge anywhere that was not shaped, created, or upheld by human beings*; that therefore all knowledge is limited and imperfect and provisional, bound to be superseded by subsequent "discoveries." The word "discoveries" is in quotation marks because, from this perspective, nothing is simply "out there" to be discovered—discoveries are actually constructed things, built out of the research, creativity, perceptions, and insights (as well as biases and ideologies) of those who work within a particular knowledge community (and who manage to convince others within that community that they have produced new knowledge). The role of language, according to this social constructionist model, is central: there is no knowledge or thinking *without* language. Language can never be a clear windowpane onto something else: language is all we have, it's what knowledge is made of, and it too is, of course, socially constructed. Persuasive language is especially powerful (and potentially dangerous) since it can determine what large groups of people will come to accept as knowledge.

Happily, as with most truly absorbing dilemmas, we don't have to choose only one of these epistemologies and completely eliminate the other. Any knowledge that we take seriously is simultaneously both things at once, discovered *and* created—though the proportions may be unequal, depending on the kind of knowledge we're talking about. A cure for diabetes might lead us to talk more of discovery, while a work of literary criticism might lead us to talk more of creation; but the scientists involved certainly worked hard over many years to *construct* their shared knowledge about diabetes, while literary critics have to attend long and hard to the texts under discussion, working to *find* important connections between them, and would make arbitrary and unsupported statements about those texts at their peril. We need a theory of knowledge generous enough to include both perspectives, acknowledging that they require each other for balance and completeness.

So, one answer to the question "What is **academic writing** for?" is that it allows us to talk to each other about ideas, to carry on a conversation—and, in Gendlin's terms, to carry that conversation forward, for both the discovery and creation of knowledge. The passage from Gendlin above is itself an example of academic writing. Does it seem particularly difficult or pompous or hard to read? Probably not. But on the very same page of the very same essay, Gendlin wrote sentences that *are* quite difficult to read, that contain specialized terms that he has defined carefully elsewhere. Why? You might grow impatient and wonder why he can't just be clear and accessible (and tell stories) all the time.

Because, as his story makes clear, he is committed to the idea of "carrying forward," of building theories, of generating terms—to the idea, in fact, of turning to the "intricacy" of stories in order to generate *further* terms. Not that he assumes that the only purpose of stories is to provide us with more and more useful terms to use in our theories: he also believes that the better our terms and theories, the better our shared stories will become. He's not the only scholar/writer to point out the rich interaction between story and theory, between abstractions and concrete details, between generalizations and specific examples. In this section, Carolyn Matalene will carry the discussion about such tensions even further in her essay about the difficulties student writers have moving up and down the abstraction ladder as they try to incorporate their own experience into their academic writing.

You may notice that at the very beginning of her essay, by the way, Matalene positions her own piece in an ongoing conversation: this is one of the distinguishing marks of academic writing, clearly acknowledging the ideas of others. She in fact refers to the debate (also included in this section) between David Bartholomae and Peter Elbow about the importance and nature of academic writing—in particular, about the kind of writing that should be taught in universities. We use the word "debate" intentionally here: a debate and a conversation seem to us quite different things in tone and in purpose. Certainly, debate has served as a primary model for academic discourse for a long time: we've at times referred to this model as the *High Noon* school of academic discourse—as in the famous Western of that name, several guys shoot it out on Main Street in front of everyone else and you know that some of them are going to be full of holes and flat on the ground before it's all over. We can, unfortunately, without too much trouble, still find examples of academic writing that get all their heat from attack, from making fun of or shredding the work of another scholar. Reading such pieces, we often get the impression that the only way the authors could work up the energy for intellectual work was to get angry: only by destroying someone else's position could they get their own clearly stated.

If the only alternative to combative debate, however, is bloodless chitchat, a kind of cocktail-party banter where nothing is at stake and everyone pretends to be nice to everyone else, we're no better off. Still, such a situation seems a long way off in an academic culture where the final oral exam required for earning a PhD is still referred to as a "defence," summoning up images of attackers swarming in the PhD candidate's direction.

Clearly, since Bartholomae chooses to subtitle his essay "A Conversation with Peter Elbow," we're meant to feel that the genuine give and take of conversation—a true dialogue—is the goal. As you read through their exchanges, you'll need to be considering how *you* would categorize them. Do these exchanges constitute a debate or a dialogue? Does their printed conversation match the model Gendlin gives us, of two people listening so closely to each other that they grasp *exactly* the point the other is trying to make? And do they reveal their understanding of the other not merely by repeating what he has said, but by carrying it forward? If they do carry the conversation forward together, in ways neither could have done by himself, where exactly is it that we end up? And how does Matalene carry it forward, if she does?

Clearly, none of them—Matalene, Elbow, or Bartholomae—are in *direct* conversation with Patricia Nelson Limerick; but the stereotypes of academic writing she describes are the subtext for their discussion. As Limerick's essay in this section reveals, more than one stereotype of academic writing functions in popular culture: and scholars fighting viciously over intellectual territory are at least more dramatic and interesting (and less foolish) than scholars padding their sentences to protect themselves from attack, although, as Limerick suggests, the two practices seem to be closely related.

What all of these pieces share, however, is a concern with what kind of writing should be taught to students in a university. An easy answer is **academic writing**—if one is to survive, indeed flourish, in the academy, certainly one has to know how to do academic writing. But what *is* that? Do these authors agree on a definition of that animal? Is it one thing or different in every academic discipline? And what kind of academic writing do you *want* to produce? (For a range of possible answers to this question, see the introduction to Conversation 6 on genre). If academic writing needs to change, is it too much to ask of students that they help to bring that change about? Certainly, ignoring set forms and guidelines for academic tasks is risky, and students have a lot to lose in a culture where grades can determine entrance to professional or graduate programs. More importantly, such behaviour—ignoring or flouting conventions of academic writing—could even be misguided: it's all too easy to complain that a piece of writing is bad writing simply because it is difficult. After all, some concepts *are* difficult; the author may have struggled to express them clearly and failed *precisely* for that reason, not because the author was being intentionally murky as a defence against being attacked. If material is complex, writing about it as if it were simple and easy to understand would be misleading.

If academic writing is about carrying on a conversation, and not just carrying it on but carrying it *forward* in some way, then writing a paper that is going to perform this social action, this carrying forward, is no mere dead-end exercise (a "non-form," as Richard Larson has famously called the usual research paper assigned in first-year writing classes). Instead, producing a serious piece of academic writing involves you in a web of social obligations: first, to *eavesdrop* on the conversation long enough (through whatever means are available, reading and interviewing and possibly conducting original observations and experiments of your own) to prepare yourself to participate, to discover what this community of inquiry knows already and what it is longing to know;

then, to *venture some tentative contributions* of your own (drafts, sketches, preliminary findings) to elicit some response, some reality check on where your contributions might fit into the conversation, if they fit at all; and finally, through a recursive process of drafting, revising according to feedback from members of this knowledge community, and exploring along the edge of what is known and what is not yet known, to *risk submitting your contribution for public scrutiny and evaluation.*

Whether or not your contribution to the conversation accomplishes the social action you most hope for (which in a university would primarily be the production of new knowledge, however slight—including, of course, the challenging or re-interpretation of existing knowledge), this way of understanding the process helps make one thing crystal clear—there is never a "perfect" paper. A perfect paper suggests that there might be an end to the ongoing conversation. Some book blurbs may seem to claim that further conversation is pointless if they refer to something as "the definitive work on X"—but scholars are increasingly uneasy calling *any* work "definitive" these days. A *useful*, as opposed to *perfect*, piece of academic writing will allow others to move forward from it, which leaves little time for them to stand around simply applauding in gratitude. There will always be ways in which your paper could have gone further, accomplished more, made connections with X, Y, and Z: thus, happily, there will always be comments your colleagues and your instructor can make about how the conversation extends around your paper—forward, backward, off to the sides—highlighting for you all the things you didn't manage to say.

Don't fret about this. A much more worrying situation is a paper that leaves everyone speechless—because somehow it doesn't seem to connect with the ongoing conversation at any point.

And, finally, a great and comforting truth—substantive knowing *counts* in a piece of academic writing. If you have discovered/created something that other people need to know, they'll work very hard to understand you: *people will put up with a remarkable number of bad sentences in order to get good information*, information they need to live their lives. This truth applies broadly, from scientific journals to romance novels. It may even account for more flawed academic writing than Limerick's theory does. Consider what has been referred to as a tendency for academics to "rush into print" to disseminate information. Often this tendency is attributed simply to a scholar's wish to beat another scholar to the punch, to get credit for a discovery before someone else does. But there is another way to look at it. University professors are trying to balance many tasks each week: teaching, reading and responding to student work, working on departmental committees on curriculum and administrative chores, keeping up with recent publications in their disciplines, *in addition to* doing their own research. Writing up the results of their research is also a pressing obligation, and not only because job security may depend on it: professors feel what all serious scholars feel (a feeling Hunt's piece in the previous chapter underscores), a strong obligation to the communities of inquiry to which they belong. Perhaps, believing that other scholars need their research results or need the theory they've worked out, they rush into print without going through as many drafts as they should. Perhaps they've even procrastinated and are working tight to a publication deadline, unable to revise as much as they would like.

No, that can't be. After all, if students would never do that, why should instructors—right?

INKSHEDDING PROMPTS

1. Look at the list of Strategies for Writing-to-Learn on pages 150–153 in Conversation 3. The first item on the list may seem the most familiar and may also seem deceptively simple: "Write a summary." However, summarizing is never simple or straightforward—it always involves highlighting certain things, minimizing others, or leaving them out completely. And how we summarize can also affect how we remember: if we summarize carelessly, we can easily keep in our minds a memory of a piece of writing that is one-sided or unfair, that seriously misrepresents or idealizes the writing. Trying to summarize in an inkshed is, therefore, especially dangerous, since you're writing quickly and just sketching. A serious summary, even just one or two paragraphs long, can take quite a while to compose and revise. See for instance, Currah's summary of Elbow in Conversation 3 or Davidson's summary of Root in Conversation 6: clearly, neither of those summaries is an inkshed.

    With that in mind, do some careful preparation for this inkshed. Choose an article from this section to summarize; then look back through it, noting key points and passages you marked in some way. Highlight a few crucial sentences that seem to capture some of the major moves in the argument and a few of the details you felt were most convincing. Once you've invested at least five to ten minutes preparing, write your inkshed with the article beside you, allowing yourself to pause once or twice during the inkshed to look back at the marked text so you can copy one of those highlighted sentences or accurately incorporate one or two of the most convincing details. Your inkshed summary will be incomplete and imperfect, but when you re-read it a few weeks later, the energy you invested in trying to state the central ideas and the main argument of the essay will pay off: you'll probably find that your inkshed will immediately bring the whole piece of writing to mind again.

    Such summaries are incredibly useful tools for writing papers (see the New Practice in this chapter) or studying for exams. They aid memory and save time (when you're studying for an exam, for instance, it's much quicker to re-read your summaries than to re-read everything over again in full). And summaries make something happen in your brain that won't happen any other way—writing a summary that is as full and complete and accurate as you can make it gives you a firm grasp on what you've read. It helps you make the material your own, make it part of your mental landscape (we think that part of this is physical—that struggling to condense the material to manageable size, wrestling it down from, say, twenty pages into twenty lines, is an intense bodily process that imprints the key concepts in a way nothing else can). Of course your summaries will leave things out, but if you make a habit of swapping summaries with some of your colleagues, you'll find yourself noticing details that you hadn't picked up on your own at all. Writing inkshed summaries is hard work: they take a lot of mental energy and can feel like running uphill. Like a run uphill, however, or any good workout, they make you stronger.

2.   This prompt works best if you've already tried Prompt 1 on all the pieces in this section—the complete Bartholomae/Elbow exchange plus the Matalene and Limerick essays. But it's revealing to try even if you haven't had time to write detailed summaries beforehand.

Imagine that Bartholomae, Elbow, Matalene, and Limerick are having coffee together in a local café. One of them brings up the topic of academic writing. You're sitting at the next table, eavesdropping. In your trusty note-book, record their conversation for at least twenty minutes. Try to capture the tone of voice you imagine each one of them to have, just from the evidence of the writing you've read by each of them so far.

If, after ten minutes or so, Fulwiler were to step in and join the animated conversation, that would be okay too. If you looked again at his piece in Conversation 3 on teaching first-year writing, you could see how Bartholomae's comments on "sentimental realism" might have gotten Fulwiler's back up; but Matalene might have her own aggravations over Fulwiler's assumption that in academic writing "the resources are external to the writer." Guy Allen might want to fly in from Toronto to join this conver-sation as well; his piece is not in this volume, but you can easily locate its address in the bibliography at the end of this book. His essay has been talking back indirectly to Bartholomae's essay since the day Allen's piece was first published.

3.   Notice that each author in this section characterizes the academic writing dilemma differently. Bartholomae speaks of the personal versus the aca-demic (often characterizing detailed personal writing or narrative as "senti-mental realism"); Elbow speaks of "being a writer" versus "being an academic"; Matalene speaks of centrifugal and centripetal writing (terms

she took from another theorist). How does Limerick characterize the dilemma? If you want to see how one student characterized Elbow and Bartholomae's discussion, see Suzanne LiaBraaten's essay in Conversation 7. Reflect in your inkshedding about what these dichotomies reveal about each author's thinking. Which way of characterizing the issues at stake seems most persuasive to you? Can you brainstorm in your inkshed about more useful ways of talking about the tensions in academic writing, a way that takes all of these voices on the subject into account?

4. This inkshed requires a few minutes of skimming back through the essays in this chapter before you can begin.

Bartholomae writes compellingly about how all serious academic writing means that the page is "crowded with others," and we can easily see in his piece "Writing With Teachers" that many other scholars and thinkers have influenced his thoughts on these matters. The same is true, of course, for many other essays in this volume, including the ones in this chapter. But it's interesting to see how differently Matalene, Elbow, Limerick, and Bartholomae handle their sources. Look through Elbow's piece: unlike Matalene but like Bartholomae, he has no list of works cited at the end. However, he does have a few endnotes, plus a few specific references within the text itself (note, for instance, his citation of Jeanette Harris on page 198 and of William Stafford on page 199). Bartholomae crowds many more "others" onto the page than Elbow does; his "others" even outnumber Matalene's (if we count her works-cited list alone, that is—if we count all the students from whom she quotes, the picture changes).

However, if you—as an apprentice to this conversation—wanted to go to the library to read some of the authors who had influenced Bartholomae, how easy would it be? Who is Fish? Who is Foucault? Even if you found out their first names and enough information to locate them in a library cata-logue or on the web, how would you know which works in particular were relevant to the conversation Elbow and Bartholomae are having? If, as we suggested earlier, works-cited lists or detailed references (in footnotes, end-notes, or in the text itself) serve as address lists so you can locate partici-pants in the conversation on your own, how many detailed addresses can you get from each of the authors in this section?

Inkshed about what this reveals to you about the different attitudes toward academic writing the authors in this section have, keeping in mind that what you notice about the handling of sources may reveal something at odds with the *explicitly stated* views on academic writing in these essays. Also keep in mind that none of these pieces were written for a student audience and all but Limerick's were published in academic journals (where presumably most readers would know—or know how to find out quickly—who Fish and Foucault were).

5. Working with sources is often a matter of summarizing effectively, integrating a complex argument or detailed research findings into your own line of thinking. It's a necessary skill for academic writers to master, and even professors who've been doing it for years can have trouble. Before you inkshed, take a look at two less-than-perfect examples in this volume, both produced by professors of English.

    First, check out how we tried to handle a necessary summarizing moment in the introduction to Conversation 3. Can you remember if, while you were reading that introduction, your attention wandered for a moment? Was there anything that jarred on you, a place where you felt you had to slow down to take in new information? We're willing to bet that, if you *did* have at least some resistance, it was to the section on writing-to-learn and Janet Emig's work that begins on page 112. We knew that her original essay was much too dense to include in this textbook, but also much too influential to ignore. This short summary was our best attempt at a solution (we rewrote it many times in an attempt to integrate it more smoothly).

    Second, take a look at the last two paragraphs of Matalene's essay. How convinced are you by the passages she quotes at length from sociologist Richard Harvey Brown? How well integrated into her text does this material seem to you? What is the force of the "Thus" with which she opens her final paragraph? Why should we believe Brown—simply because he's a sociologist? Matalene talks about students who have difficulty moving up and down the abstraction ladder, but perhaps she's alert to their difficulties because she herself has a hard time occasionally.

    Use this inkshed either (1) to reflect on one or both of these attempts to summarize or (2) to sketch out an alternative solution. That is, try to condense the material on Emig even further without omitting anything essential (feel free to send us your suggestion—we may use it in the next edition of this text). Or rewrite the last two paragraphs of Matalene's essay, not eliminating Brown but perhaps quoting less of him and integrating his ideas more effectively into her argument. (We'd be interested in reprinting creative solutions to Matalene's dilemma too.)

6. Locate the original piece by Elbow that Marta Currah has summarized in Conversation 3. Read her detailed summary first, then his original. What if anything did her summary leave out? Which did you find more convincing and why? If you were to write a summary of his piece yourself, what would

you include that she did not? What would you omit? Inkshed a detailed, accurate summary of Elbow's piece that is not a list and that is at least half the length of hers, maybe even one-third. Is that easy to do?

TWO VOICES IN A CRUCIAL DEBATE:

DAVID BARTHOLOMAE AND PETER ELBOW

David Bartholomae, like Peter Elbow, attributes much of his expertise as a teacher of writing to his own struggles with writing—but with a different emphasis. Because he had to work hard as an undergraduate to learn to make the moves that academics regularly make in their writing, the moves that help academic writers recognize each other and respect serious scholarly work within their **discourse community**, he wants to help his students learn those moves as well. He wants them to be taken seriously in the academy and to become full-fledged members of whatever conversation is going on within their field, the community of inquiry in which they're working to produce knowledge.

Professor and chair of the English department at the University of Pittsburgh, he has published many articles on the teaching of writing. "The Study of Error," part of which is included in this volume (see Conversation 8), received from the Conference on College Composition and Communication (CCCC) the Braddock Award for best essay of the year in 1981. With Anthony Petrosky, also of the University of Pittsburgh, Bartholomae has co-edited four influential textbooks: *Facts, Artifacts, and Counterfacts; Ways of Reading: An Anthology for Writers* (now in its sixth edition); *Ways of Reading Words and Images;* and *Reading the Lives of Others: A Sequence for Writers.* Bartholomae chaired the CCCC in 1988 and has further influenced the ongoing conversation about the teaching of writing in his editorial role for the Pittsburgh Series on Composition, Literacy, and Culture, published by the University of Pittsburgh Press.

Peter Elbow attributes his expertise at teaching writing to his severe early difficulties with writing. How can any student who finds writing difficult learn to write from a teacher who has always found writing easy? Elbow discovered that he couldn't, at any rate: he had to drop out of graduate school because he simply couldn't write the required papers. Over the next few years, he freewrote every time he tried to write and got stuck; and by 1973 he was able to publish the book that had evolved from those many folders of freewrites, *Writing Without Teachers.* (He had also by then been able to return to grad school to complete his PhD) Oxford University Press recently reissued *Writing Without Teachers* along with Elbow's *Writing with Power;* then—two years later—Oxford brought out his major work to date, *Everyone Can Write: Essays Toward a Hopeful Theory of Writing and Teaching Writing* (2000).

Now Professor Emeritus of English at the University of Massachusetts Amherst (UMass), where he has taught since 1987, Elbow continues to write, to lead workshops internationally, and to teach. He directed writing programs (at UMass and at SUNY Stony Brook) and taught at MIT, Franconia College, Evergreen State College, and

Wesleyan University. With Pat Belanoff, he wrote a workshop course in writing, *A Community of Writers*, now also available in a shortened form as *Being a Writer*. His many other publications deal mainly with invention and the theory of freewriting, voice, audience, feedback, evaluation and grading.

The exchanges between Elbow and Bartholomae should probably be read in the order given below, which is the order in which they originally appeared in *College Composition and Communication* in 1995.

DAVID BARTHOLOMAE

WRITING WITH TEACHERS: A CONVERSATION WITH PETER ELBOW

At the 1989 and 1991 meetings of CCCC, Peter Elbow and I began a public conversation about personal and academic writing. We have had several opportunities to continue it in private and we have decided to go public once again, partly because we find it useful to think these questions through in conversation (and partly because the conversation we had in 1989 has been reproduced as the Bartholomae/Elbow debate in ways we would like to challenge or revise). Here are the texts of the talks we gave at the 1991 CCCC in Boston, followed by a brief response from each of us.

Where to Begin?

Most discussions like the one we are about to have begin or end by fretting over the central term, academic writing. It is clear that this is not just a contested term, but a difficult one to use with any precision. If, for example, it means the writing that is done by academics, or the writing that passes as currency in the academy, then it is a precise term only when it is loaded: academic writing—the unreadable created by the unspeakable; academic writing—stuffy, pedantic, the price of a career; academic writing—pure, muscular, lean, taut, the language of truth and reason; academic writing—language stripped of the false dressings of style and fashion, a tool for inquiry and critique.

And so on. I don't need to belabor this point. Academic writing is a single thing only in convenient arguments. If you collect samples of academic writing, within or across the disciplines, it has as many types and categories, peaks and valleys, as writing grouped under any other general category: magazine writing, business writing, political writing, sports writing. Or, I could put it this way: Within the writing performed in 1990 under the rubric of English studies, writing by English professors, you can find writing that is elegant, experimental, sentimental, autobiographical, spare, dull, pretentious, abstract, boring, dull, whatever.

If I am here to argue for academic writing as part of an undergraduate's training, or as a form or motive to be taught/examined in the curriculum, I need to begin by saying that I am not here to argue for stuffy, lifeless prose or for mechanical (or dutiful) imitations of standard thoughts and forms. We need a different set of terms to frame the discussion. It is interesting, in fact, to consider how difficult it is to find positive terms for academic writing when talking to a group of academics, including those who could be said to do it for a living. It is much easier to find examples or phrases to indicate our sense of corporate shame or discomfort.

I don't have time to pursue this line of argument here, but I think it is part and parcel of the anti-professionalism Fish argues is a pose of both the academic right (for whom the prose in our journals is evidence of bad faith, of the pursuit of trends, an abandonment of the proper pursuit of humane values, great books) and the academic left (for whom professional practice is the busy work we do because we are co-opted). For both, academic writing is what you do when you are not doing your "real" work.

My Position, I Think

I want to argue that academic writing is the real work of the academy. I also want to argue for academic writing as a key term in the study of writing and the practice of instruction. In fact, I want to argue that if you are teaching courses in the university, courses where students write under your supervision, they can't not do it and you can't not stand for it (academic writing, that is) and, therefore, it is better that it be done out in the open, where questions can be asked and responsibilities assumed, than to be done in hiding or under another name.

To say this another way, there is no writing that is writing without teachers. I think I would state this as a general truth, but for today let me say that there is no writing done in the academy that is not academic writing. To hide the teacher is to hide the traces of power, tradition and authority present at the scene of writing (present in allusions to previous work, in necessary work with sources, in collaboration with powerful theories and figures, in footnotes and quotations and the messy business of doing your work in the shadow of others). Thinking of writing as academic writing makes us think of the page as crowded with others—or it says that this is what we learn in school, that our writing is not our own, nor are the stories we tell when we tell the stories of our lives—they belong to TV, to Books, to Culture and History.

To offer academic writing as something else is to keep this knowledge from our students, to keep them from confronting the power politics of discursive practice, or to keep them from confronting the particular representations of power, tradition and authority reproduced whenever one writes.

Now—I say this as though it were obvious. Students write in a space defined by all the writing that has preceded them, writing the academy insistently draws together: in the library, in the reading list, in the curriculum. This is the busy, noisy, intertextual space— one usually hidden in our representations of the classroom; one that becomes a subject in the classroom when we ask young writers to think about, or better yet, confront, their situatedness.

And yet, it is also obvious that there are many classrooms where students are asked to imagine that they can clear out a space to write on their own, to express their own thoughts and ideas, not to reproduce those of others. As I think this argument through, I think of the pure and open space, the frontier classroom, as a figure central to composition as it is currently constructed. The open classroom; a free writing. This is the master trope. And, I would say, it is an expression of a desire for an institutional space free from institutional pressures, a cultural process free from the influence of culture, a historical moment outside of history, an academic setting free from academic writing.

Whose desire? That is a hard question to answer, and I will finesse it for the moment. I don't want to say that it is Peter's; I think it is expressed in Peter's work.

I can, however, phrase this question: "Whose desire is this, this desire for freedom, empowerment, an open field?"—I think I can phrase the question in terms of the larger debate in the academy about the nature of discourse and the humanities. The desire for a classroom free from the past is an expression of the desire for presence or transcendence, for a common language, free from jargon and bias, free from evasion and fear; for a language rooted in common sense rather than special sense, a language that renders (makes present) rather than explains (makes distant). It is a desire with a particularly American inflection and a particular resonance at a moment in the academy when it has become harder and harder to cast any story, let alone the story of education, in a setting that is free, Edenic or Utopian.

"I have learned to relinquish authority in my classroom." How many times do we hear this now as the necessary conclusion in an argument about the goals of composition? "I want to empower my students." "I want to give my students ownership of their work." What could it mean—to have this power over language, history and culture? to own it?

Unless it means stepping outside of the real time and place of our writing—heading down the river, heading out to the frontier, going nowhere. Unless it means stepping out of language and out of time. I am arguing for a class *in* time, one that historicizes the present, including the present evoked in students' writing. Inside this linguistic present, students (with instruction—more precisely, with lessons in critical reading) can learn to feel and see their position inside a text they did not invent and can never, at least completely, control. Inside a practice: linguistic, rhetorical, cultural, historical.

As I am thinking through this argument, I read Peter's work as part of a much larger project to preserve and reproduce the figure of the author, an independent, self-creative, self-expressive subjectivity. I see the argument against academic writing, and for another writing, sometimes called personal or expressive writing, as part of a general argument in favor of the author, a much beleaguered figure in modern American English departments. This is one way that the profession, English, has of arguing out the nature and role of writing as a subject of instruction—personal writing/academic writing—this opposition is the structural equivalent to other arguments, arguments about authorship and ownership, about culture and the individual, about single author courses, about the canon.

And these arguments are part of still other arguments, with different inflections, about production and consumption, about reading and writing, about presence and transcendence, culture and individualism—arguments working themselves out in particular ways at conferences and in papers in many settings connected to the modern academy. The desire for an open space, free from the past, is a powerful desire, deployed throughout the discourses of modern life, including the discourses of education.

The Contact Zone

When we talk about academic writing at CCCC, I don't think we are talking about discourse—at least, after Foucault, as discourse is a technical term. We are not, in other words, talking about particular discursive practices and how they are reproduced or policed within the academic disciplines.

I would say that we are talking about sites, possible scenes of writing, places, real and figurative, where writing is produced. This is why so much time is spent talking about the classroom and its literal or metaphorical arrangement of power and authority—where do we sit, who talks first, who reads the papers. Whether we rearrange the furniture in the classroom or rearrange the turns taken by speakers in a discussion, these actions have no immediate bearing on the affiliations of power brought into play in writing. At worst, the "democratic" classroom becomes the sleight of hand we perfect in order to divert attention from the unequal distribution of power that is inherent in our positions as teachers, as figures of institutional/disciplinary authority, and inherent in the practice of writing, where one is always second, derivative, positioned, etc.

I am trying to think about the scene of writing as a discursive space. So let me say that we shouldn't think of ourselves as frontier guides but as managers, people who manage substations in the cultural network, small shops in the general production of readers and writers. We don't choose this; it is the position we assume as teachers. If, from this position, we are going to do anything but preside over the reproduction of forms and idioms, we have to make the classroom available for critical inquiry, for a critique that is part of the lesson of practice. We have to do more, that is, than manage.

If our goal is to make a writer aware of the forces at play in the production of knowledge, we need to highlight the classroom as a substation—as a real space, not as an idealized utopian space. There is no better way to investigate the transmission of power, tradition and authority than by asking students to do what academics do: work with the past, with key texts (we have been teaching Emerson, Rich, Simon Frith on rock and roll); working with other's terms (key terms from Rich, like "patriarchy," for example); struggling with the problems of quotation, citation and paraphrase, where one version of a student's relationship to the past is represented by how and where he quotes Rich (does he follow the block quotation with commentary of his own? can Rich do more than "support" an argument, can a student argue with Rich's words, use them as a point to push off from?).

I want this issue to be precise as well as abstract. You can teach a lot about a writer's possible relations with the past by looking at how and why she uses a passage from an assigned text. This is not, in other words, simply a matter of reproducing standard texts, but of using them as points of deflection, appropriation, improvisation, or penetration (those are Mary Louise Pratt's terms). But you can't do this without making foremost the situatedness of writing, without outlining in red the network of affiliations that constitute writing in the academy.

Let me do this another way. There is a student in my class writing an essay on her family, on her parents' divorce. We've all read this essay. We've read it because the student cannot invent a way of talking about family, sex roles, separation. Her essay is determined by a variety of forces: the genre of the personal essay as it has shaped this student and this moment; attitudes about the family and divorce; the figures of "Father" and "Mother" and "Child" and so on. The moment of this essay is a moment of the general problematics of writing—who does what to whom; who does the writing, what can an individual do with the cultural field? Of course we can help the student to work on this essay by letting her believe it is hers—to think that the key problem is voice, not citation; to ask for realistic detail rather than to call attention to figuration. Almost two hundred years of sentimental realism prepares all of us for these lessons. We can teach students to be more effective producers of this product. We can also teach them its critique. Perhaps here is a way of talking about the real issues in the debate over academic writing? How can you not reproduce the master narrative of family life? How might a student writer negotiate with the professional literature? How and what might it mean to talk back to (or to talk with) Adrienne Rich about family life? What does it mean for a student to claim that her own experience holds equivalent status with Rich's memories as material to work on?

Teachers as Writers

We have several examples of academics announcing that they are now abandoning academic writing. I am thinking of Jane Tompkins' recent article, "Me and My Shadow." I am thinking of other similar moments of transcendence: Mina Shaughnessy's use of Hoggart and Baldwin as writers who could use autobiography to do intellectual work. I am thinking of Mike Rose's book, *Lives on the Boundary*. I am thinking of the recent issue of *PRE/TEXT* devoted to "expressive writing." I am thinking of the roles Gretel Ehrlich or Richard Selzer have played at this conference, or of scholars like Peter and Chuck Schuster. Or that wonderful session of CCCC where Nancy Sommers and Pat Hoy presented extended personal essays as conference papers. I am thinking of Don McQuade's chair's address at the 1989 CCCC. I am thinking of some of Peter's prose. And some of my own.

I seem to be saying that one cannot not write academic discourse, and yet here are examples of the academics pushing at the boundaries in decidedly academic settings. I don't see this as a contradiction. I would say that these are not examples of transcendence but of writers calling up, for a variety of purposes, different (but highly conventional) figures of the writer. These are writers taking pleasure in (or making capital of) what are often called "literary devices"—dialogue, description, the trope of the real, the figure of the writer at the center of sentimental realism. There is great pleasure in writing this way (making the world conform to one's image, exalting one's "point of view"), and there are strategic reasons for not doing academic writing when it is expected—I would say all great academic writers know this. I would call the writing I cited above examples of blurred genres, not free writing, and both genres represent cultural interests (in reproducing distinct versions of experience and knowledge). In my department, this other form of narrative is often called "creative non-fiction" or "literary non-fiction"—it is a way to celebrate individual vision, the detail of particular worlds. There is an argument in this kind of prose too, an argument about what is real and what it means to inhabit the real. The danger is assuming that one genre is more real than the other (a detailed, loving account of the objects in my mother's kitchen is more "real" than a detailed loving account of the discourse on domesticity found in 19th century American women's magazines)—in assuming that one is real writing and the other is only a kind of game academics play. The danger lies in letting these tendentious terms guide the choices we make in designing the curriculum.

A Brief History

Why, we might ask, do we have such a strong desire to talk about schooling as though it didn't have to be schooling, a disciplinary process? I have started one answer—it is part of a general desire to erase the past and its traces from the present.

I would also say that our current conversations are very much a product of an important moment in composition in the early 1970s—one in which Peter played a key role. At a time when the key questions facing composition could have been phrased as questions of linguistic difference—what is good writing and how is that question a question of race, class, or gender?—at a time when composition could have made the scene of instruction the object of scholarly inquiry, there was a general shift away from questions of value and the figure of the writer in a social context of writing to questions of process and the figure of the writer as an individual psychology. If you turn to work by figures who might otherwise be thought of as dissimilar—Britton, Moffett, Emig, Northrop Frye, Jerome Bruner— you will find a common displacement of the social and a celebration of the individual as fundamentally (or ideally) congruent with culture and history. Here is how it was phrased: There is no real difference between the child and the adult (that's Bruner); the curriculum is in the learner (that's Moffett and Britton); we find the universal mind of man in the work of individuals (that's Frye). All find ways of equating change with growth, locating both the process and the mechanism within an individual psychology, equating the learner with that which must be learned. And, as a consequence, schooling becomes secondary, not the primary scene of instruction, but a necessary evil in a world that is not well-regulated, where people would naturally mature into myth or prose or wisdom. School is secondary, instrumental, something to be overcome. And, in a similar transformation, writing becomes secondary, instrumental (to thinking or problem solving or deep feeling or unconscious imaginative forces).

I would say that the argument that produces archetypal criticism produces cognitive psychology, free writing, and new journalism: I've got Bruner, Linda Flower, Peter, Tom Wolfe, and John McPhee all lined up in this genealogy, this account of the modern curricular production of the independent author, the celebration of point-of-view as individual artifact, the promotion of sentimental realism (the true story of what I think, feel, know and see).

Conclusion, or, So How Do I Get Out of This?

I am at the point where I should have a conclusion, but I don't. I could say this is strategic. Peter and I are having a conversation, and so it would be rude to conclude. Let me reimagine my position by rephrasing the questions that allow me access to it. Here is how I would now phrase the questions that I take to be the key questions in the debate on academic writing:

Should we teach new journalism or creative non-fiction as part of the required undergraduate curriculum? That is, should all students be required to participate in a first person, narrative or expressive genre whose goal it is to reproduce the ideology of sentimental realism—where a world is made in the image of a single, authorizing point of view? a narrative that celebrates a world made up of the details of private life and whose hero is sincere?

I don't have an easy answer to this question. It is like asking, should students be allowed to talk about their feelings after reading *The Color Purple*? Of course they should, but where and when? and under whose authority?

I think it is possible to say that many students will not feel the pleasure or power of authorship unless we make that role available. Without our classes, students will probably not have the pleasure or the power of believing they are the figure that they have seen in pieces they have read: the figure who is seeing the world for the first time, naming it, making their thoughts the center of the world, feeling the power of their own sensibilities. This has been true for teachers in the Writing Projects, it will be true in our classes. Unless we produce this effect in our classroom, students will not be Authors.

There is no question but that we can produce these effects. The real question is, should we?

In a sense, I feel compelled to argue that we should. We should teach students to write as though they were not the products of their time, politics and culture, not our products, as though they could be free, elegant, smart, independent, the owners of all that they say. Why should they be denied this pleasure; or, why should it be reserved for some writers in our culture and not for others?

But I can also phrase the question this way: Why should I or a program I stand for be charged to tell this lie, even if it is a pleasant and, as they say, empowering one for certain writers or writers at a certain stage of their education? Why am I in charge of the reproduction of this myth of American life?

Or—is it a matter of stages in a writer's education? Should we phrase it this way: A 19-year-old has to learn to be a committed realist in order later to feel the potential for the critique of this position. People used to say something like this about traditional forms of order in the essay: You have to learn to write like E. B. White before you can learn to write like Gertrude Stein. Picasso couldn't have been a cubist if he hadn't learned to draw figures.

Learn to be **logocentric**?* Learn to celebrate individualism? Learn to trust one's common sense point of view? Who needs to learn this at 18? Well, one might argue that students need to learn to do it well, so that it seems like an achievement. That is, students should master the figures and forms, learn to produce an elegant, convincing, even professional quality narrative before learning its critique and imagining its undoing.

I could phrase the question this way: Should composition programs self-consciously maintain a space for the "author" in a university curriculum that has traditionally denied students the category of author (by making students only summarizers or term paper writers)?

But it is too easy to say yes if I phrase the question like that. What if I put it this way? Should composition programs maintain a space for, reproduce the figure of, the author at a time when the figure of the author is under attack in all other departments of the academy. That is, should we be conservative when they are radical? Should we be retrograde in the face of an untested avante-garde?

Or—are we (should we be) a part of the critique, given our privileged role in the production of authors in the university curriculum, our positions in charge of sub-stations in the culture's determined production of readers and writers?

When I phrase the question that way, the answers become easy. I don't think I need to teach students to be controlled by the controlling idea, even though I know my students could write more organized texts. I don't think I need to teach sentimental realism, even though I know my students could be better at it than they are. I don't think I need to because I don't think I should. I find it a corrupt, if extraordinarily tempting genre. I don't

---

* logocentric: "[believing] that language can be authentic, fully representative and capable of producing fixed or certain meaning" (Green and LeBihan 265).

want my students to celebrate what would then become the natural and inevitable details of their lives. I think the composition course should be part of the general critique of traditional humanism. For all the talk of paradigm shifting, the composition course, as a cultural force, remains fundamentally unchanged from the 19th century. I would rather teach or preside over a critical writing, one where the critique is worked out in practice, and for lack of better terms I would call that writing "academic writing."

PETER ELBOW

BEING A WRITER VS. BEING AN ACADEMIC: A CONFLICT IN GOALS

Perhaps David and others can persuade me that I am wrong, but I fear that there is a conflict between the role of writer and that of academic. I wish there were not. In this essay I will explore how this conflict plays out in a first year writing class. But it will be obvious that I see the issue lurking in a larger dimension—even autobiographically. I am an academic and I am a writer. I've struggled to be able to make those claims, and I am proud of both identities—but I sometimes feel them in conflict. Thus I'm talking here about the relationship between two roles—two ways of being in the world of texts. It is my wish that students should be able to inhabit both roles comfortably.

Note that I'm talking here about roles, not professions. That is, I'm not trying to get first year students to commit to making their living by writing—nor to get a Ph.D. and join the academy. But I would insist that it's a reasonable goal for my students to end up saying, "I feel like I *am* a writer: I get deep satisfaction from discovering meanings by writing—figuring out what I think and feel through putting down words; I naturally turn to writing when I am perplexed—even when I am just sad or happy; I love to explore and communicate with others through writing; writing is an important part of my life." Similarly, I would insist that it's a reasonable goal for my students to end up saying, "I feel like I *am* an academic: reading knowledgeable books, wrestling my way through important issues with fellows, figuring out hard questions—these activities give me deep satisfaction and they are central to my sense of who I am." In short, I want my first year students to feel themselves as writers and feel themselves as academics.

Of course these are idealistic goals; many students will not attain them. But I insist on them as reasonable goals for my teaching, because if I taught well and if all the conditions for learning were good, I believe all my students *could* achieve them. I don't mind high or distant goals. But I'm troubled by a sense that they conflict with each other—that progress toward one could undermine progress toward the other. A distant mountain is a good guide for walking—even if I know I won't get to the top. But I feel as though I am trying to walk toward two different mountains.

In this dilemma, my first and strongest impulse is to be adversarial and fight for the role of the writer against the role of the academic. And I can't pretend I am doing otherwise here. But I'm also trying to resist that adversarial impulse. I'd like to celebrate academics—the other half of my own identity. If *we* don't celebrate academics, no one else will. Therefore I'll try to hold myself open so David or others of you can persuade me that I am misguided in my sense of conflict. Perhaps you can persuade me that if I would only make certain changes I could serve both goals well. Or better yet, perhaps you can assure me that I'm already serving both goals now and my only problem is my feeling of conflict. For I wish I didn't see things this way. Everyone says, "Don't give in to binary thinking. Take a cold shower, take a walk around the block." But I see specific conflicts in how to design and teach my first year writing course. And since I feel forced to choose—I choose the goal of writer over that of academic.

* * *

Let me now explore specific points of conflict in my designing and teaching of a first year writing course—conflicts between my attempts to help students see themselves as academics and see themselves as writers. But my first two points will be false alarms: places where I and others have sometimes been *tempted* to see a conflict but where careful examination shows me there is none. Perhaps some of the other conflicts can be similarly diffused.

(1) Sometimes I've felt a conflict about *what we should read* in the first year writing course. It would seem as though in order to help students see themselves as academics I should get them to read "key texts": good published writing, important works of cultural or literary significance; strong and important works. However if I want them to see themselves as writers, we should primarily publish and read their own writing.

In my first year writing class I take the latter path. I publish a class magazine about four times a semester, each one containing a finished piece by all the students. (I'm indebted to Charlie Moran for showing me how to do this—supporting the practice with a lab fee for the course.) We often discuss and write about these magazines. This may be the single most important feature of the course that helps students begin to experience themselves as members of a community of writers.

But on reflection, I don't think there is any conflict here. It's not an either/or issue. To read both strong important published texts and the writing of fellow students serves both my goals. Academics read key texts and the writing of colleagues; so do writers. In short, I think I could and probably should read some strong important published works in my first year course. I would never give up using the magazines of students' own writing, but that needn't stop me from also reading at least some of the other kind of texts.

(2) Just as I see no conflict about what to read in my first year course, so too about *how to read* these texts. That is, whether I want my students to be academics or writers, it seems crucial to avoid coming at key texts (or at student texts) as models. That is, I must

fight the tradition of treating these readings as monuments in a museum, pieces under glass. We must try to come at these strong important texts—no matter how good or hallowed they may be—as much as possible as fellow writers, as fully eligible members of the conversation—not treat them as sacred; not worry about "doing justice" to them or getting them dirty. To be blunt, I must be sure not to "teach" these texts (in the common sense of that term), but rather to "have them around" to wrestle with, to bounce off of, to talk about and talk from, to write about and write from. Again: not feel we must be polite or do them justice. In taking this approach I think we would be treating texts the way academics and writers treat them: using them rather than serving them. (I take this as one of the lessons of David's *Facts, Artifacts, and Counterfacts.*)

(3) But even if there is no conflict about what to read and how to read, I do see a problem when it comes to the question of *how much to read*. If my goal is to help my students experience themselves as academics, surely I should spend at least as much time reading as writing. Academics are readers. But I don't. I always spend much more of our time writing than reading. I even spend a significant amount of class time writing. Writing in class helps me not just sanction, dignify, and celebrate writing; it helps me frankly *coach* students in various concrete practices and techniques and approaches toward getting words on paper. I could weasel and say that writing is reading—what with all that crucial reading over what you write—and so I'm really serving both goals by emphasizing writing. But academics don't just read over what they write. This is a blunt issue of emphasis: In my course there is a clear emphasis on writing over reading.

It's not that I care absolutely more about writing than reading. I'm simply saying that virtually every other course privileges reading over writing—treats input as central and output as serving input. My only hope, it seems to me, of making students experience themselves as writers while they are in the academy—and a slim hope at that—means hanging on to at least one course where writing is at the center. When other courses in the university make writing as important as reading, I'll respond with a comparable adjustment and give reading equal spotlight in my first year course. I might even make that adjustment if only English department courses made writing as important as reading, but of course they don't. Isn't it odd that most English courses study and honor writing (literature), but seldom treat the act of writing as central? The only course that tends to make writing central is the one course that most English faculty don't want to teach.

(4) But let me tighten the screw a bit. I've been talking as though everything would be dandy if only we had more time, or at least divided up the time equally—as though the interests of reading and writing do not inherently conflict. But I can't help sensing that they do. And I would contend that academics have come to identify with the interests of reading—often identifying themselves against writing.

Let me spell out some of the conflicts I see between the interests of writers and the interests of academics-as-readers.[1] To put it bluntly, readers and writers have competing interests over who gets to control the text. It's in the interests of readers to say that the writer's intention doesn't matter or is unfindable, to say that meaning is never determinate, always fluid and sliding, to say that there is no presence or voice behind a text; and finally to kill off the author! This leaves the reader in complete control of the text.

It's in the interests of writers, on the other hand, to have readers actually interested in what was on their mind, what they intended to say, reading for intention. As writers we often fail to be clear, but it helps us if readers will just have some faith that our authorial meanings and intentions can be found. It helps to listen caringly. If we are lost in the woods, we have a better chance of being found if the searchers think we exist, care deeply about us, and feel there is hope of finding us. And it goes without saying, writers are interested in staying alive. Writers also have interest in *ownership* of the text—and, as with "killing," I want to take this metaphor seriously: Writers have a concrete interest in monetary payment for their labor. But of course the metaphorical meaning is important too. Writers usually want some "ownership," some say, some control over what a text means. Almost all writers are frustrated when readers completely misread what they have written. It doesn't usually help if the readers say, "But the latest theory says that we get to construct our own meaning." Of course there are exceptions here: Some writers say, "I don't care what meaning readers see in my words," but more often it is writers who celebrate presence and readers absence.

Let me be more concrete by using this very text as illustration. I get to decide what I *intended* with my words; you get to decide what you *heard*. But the question of what I "said," what meanings are "in" my text—that is a site of contention between us. And we see this fight everywhere, from the law courts to the bedrooms: "But I said . . ." / "No you didn't, you said . . ." Academics in English are the only people I know who seem to think that the speaker/writer has no party in such discussions.

We see this contest between readers and writers played out poignantly in the case of student texts. The academic is reader and grader and always gets to decide what the student text means. No wonder students withdraw ownership and commitment. I can reinforce my point by looking at what happens when the tables are turned and academics produce text for a student audience—that is, lecturing extensively in class. Here the academic also turns the ownership rules upside down and declares that in this case the writer-lecturer gets to decide what the text means.

Is this just a story of readers being mean and disrespectful to writers? No, it goes both ways. Among writers, there is perhaps even a longer tradition of disdain for readers. (And also, of course, of disdain for academics.) Writers often say, "Readers are not my main audience. Sometimes the audience that I write for is me. For some pieces I don't even *care* whether readers always understand or appreciate everything I write. Sometimes I even write privately. What do readers know!" In response, readers often say, "What do writers know? We're in a much better position than they are to read the text. Let's not be put off by writers' wishful thinking. Intention is a will o' the wisp. Never trust the teller, trust the tale."

In short, where writers are tempted to think they are most important, readers and academics are tempted to think they are the most important party. Readers and academics like to insist that there is no such thing as private writing or writing only for the self. (See, for example, Jeanette Harris, *Expressive Writing,* SMU Press, 1990, 66.) Readers like to imagine that writers are always thinking about them; they are like children who naturally think their parents always have them in mind. Some readers even want to see everything that writers write. But writers, like parents, need some time away from the imperious demands of readers—need some time when they can just forget about readers and think about themselves. Yes, writers must acknowledge that in the end readers get to decide whether their words will be read or bought—just as parents know that in the end the child's interests must come first. But smart writers and parents know that they do a better job of serving these demanding creatures if they take some time for themselves.

(5) Another collision of interests between writers and readers. Writers testify all the time to the experience of knowing more than they can say, of knowing things that they haven't yet been able to get into words. Paying attention to such intuitions and feelings often leads them to articulations they couldn't otherwise find. Readers (and teachers and academics), on the other hand, being on the receiving end of texts, are more tempted to say, "If you can't say it, you don't know it"—and to celebrate the doctrine that all knowledge is linguistic. (Painters, musicians and dancers also have the temerity to question academics who proclaim that if you can't say it in language you don't know it and it doesn't count as knowledge.)

In my first year writing course I feel this conflict between the interests of readers and writers. Yes, my larger self wants them to feel themselves as readers and academics, but this goal seems to conflict with my more pressing hunger to help them feel themselves as writers. That is, I can't help wanting my students to have some of that uppitiness of writers toward readers. I want them to be able to say, "I'm not just writing for teachers or readers, I'm writing as much for me—sometimes even *more* for me." I want them to fight back a bit against readers. I want them to care about their intentions and to insist that readers respect them. I try to respect those intentions and see them—and assume I often can. Yes, I'll point out where these intentions are badly realized, but if my goal is to make students feel like writers, my highest priority is to show that I've *understood* what they're saying. It's only my second priority to show them where I had to struggle.

I want to call attention to this central pedagogical point that writers often understand and readers and academics and teachers often don't: The main thing that helps writers is to be understood; pointing out misunderstandings is only the second need. Thus—and this is a crucial consequence—I assume that students *know* more than they are getting into words. Most of my own progress in learning to write has come from my gradually learning to listen more carefully to what I haven't yet managed to get into words—and respecting the idea that I know more than I can say. This stance helps me be willing to find time and energy to wrestle it into words. The most unhelpful thing I've had said to me as a student and writer is, "If you can't say it, you don't know it."

Imagine, then, how different our classrooms would be if all academics and teachers felt themselves to be writers as much as readers.

(6) Here is a related point of conflict between the role of academic and writer. What kind of attitude about language shall I try to instill in first year students in a writing course? If my goal is to get them to take on the role of academic, I should get them to distrust language. It is a central tenet of academic thinking in this century that language is not a clear and neutral medium through which we can see undistorted nonlinguistic entities.

But in my desire to help my students experience themselves as writers I find myself in fact trying to help them *trust* language—not to question it—or at least not to question it for long stretches of the writing process: to hold off distrust till they revise. Some people say this is good advice only for inexperienced and blocked writers, but I think I see it enormously helpful to myself and to other adult, skilled, and professional writers. Striking benefits usually result when people learn that decidedly unacademic capacity to turn off distrust or worry about language and learn instead to forget about it, not see it, look through it as through a clear window, and focus all attention on one's experience of what one is trying to say. Let me quote a writer, William Stafford, about the need to *trust* language and one's experience:

> My main plea is for the value of an unafraid, face-down, flailing, and speedy process in using the language.
>
> Just as any reasonable person who looks at water, and passes a hand through it, can see that it would not hold a person up; so it is the judgment of common sense people that reliance on the weak material of students' experiences cannot possibly sustain a work of literature. But swimmers know that if they relax on the water it will prove to be miraculously buoyant; and writers know that a succession of little strokes on the material nearest them—without any prejudgments about the specific gravity of the topic or the reasonableness of their expectations—will result in creative progress. Writers are persons who write; swimmers are (and from teaching a child I know how hard it is to persuade a reasonable person of this)—swimmers are persons who relax in the water, let their heads go down, and reach out with ease and confidence. (*Writing the Australian Crawl: Views on the Writer's Vocation*. Ann Arbor: U of Michigan P, 1978, 22–23.)

(7) A large area of conflict: How shall I teach my students to *place themselves* in the universe of other writers? Insofar as I want them to internalize the role of academic, I should teach my students always to situate themselves and what they have to say in the context of important writers who have written on the subject: to see the act of writing as an act of finding and acknowledging one's place in an ongoing intellectual conversation with a much larger and longer history than what goes on in this classroom during these ten or fourteen weeks. In short, I should try to enact and live out in my classroom the Burkean metaphor of intellectual life as an unending conversation. This is what we academics do: carry on an unending conversation not just with colleagues but with the dead and unborn.

But the truth is (should I hang my head?) I don't give this dimension to my first year writing classroom. I don't push my first year students to think about what academics have written about their subject; indeed much of my behavior is a kind of invitation for them to *pretend* that no authorities have ever written about their subject before.

It might sound as though I invite only *monologic* discourse and discourage *dialogic* discourse. That's not quite right. I do invite monologic discourse (in spite of the current fashion of using "monologic" as the worst moral slur we can throw at someone), but I invite and defend dialogic discourse just as much. That is, I encourage students to situate what they write into the conversation of other members of the classroom community to whom they are writing and whom they are reading. Let me mention that the regular publication of the class magazine does more for this dialogic dimension than any amount of theoretical talk. I often assign papers *about* the class publication. In short, I find it helpful to invite students to see their papers as dialogic—parts of a conversation or dialogue; and I also find it crucial to assign dialogues and collaborative papers. But I also find it helpful to invite them to see their papers as monologues or soliloquies. My point here is that both academics and writers seem to me to engage in both monologic and dialogic discourse. (By the way, the classroom publication of student writing also helps me with another kind of "situating"—that is, I try quietly to find moments where I can invite students to be more aware of the positions from which they write—as men or women—as members of a race or class, or as having a sexual orientation.)[2]

In short, the real question or point of conflict here, then, is not so much about whether I should get my first year students to feel their writing as monologue or dialogue, whether to get them to speak to other voices or not, or to recognize their own positions or not. I'm working for both sides in each case. Rather it's a larger more general question: Whether I should invite my first year students to be self-absorbed and see themselves at the center of the discourse—in a sense, credulous; or whether I should invite them to be personally modest and intellectually scrupulous and to see themselves as at the periphery—in a sense, skeptical and distrustful. I recently read an academic critique of a writer for being too self-absorbed, of reading his subjectivity too much into the object he was allegedly examining, of being imperial, arrogant—practicing analysis by means of autobiography. I have to admit that I *want* first year students in my writing class to do that. I think autobiography is often the best mode of analysis. I'm afraid that I invite first year students to fall into the following sins: to take their own ideas too seriously; to think that they are the first person to think of their idea and be all wrapped up and possessive about it—even though others might have already written better about it—I invite them to write as though they are a central speaker at the center of the universe—rather than feeling, as they often do, that they must summarize what others have said and only make modest rejoinders from the edge of the conversation to all the smart thoughts that have already been written. (By the way, I was trained by good New Critics in the 1950s who often tried to get me to write as though no one else had ever written about the work I was treating. Therefore we cannot call this intellectual stance "nonacademic." New Critics may be out of fashion but no one could call them anything but full fledged academics—indeed their distinguishing mark in comparison to their predecessors was heightened professionalism in literary studies.)

Perhaps this sounds condescending—as though I am not treating my students seriously enough as smart adults. I hope not. When I come across a really strong and competent first year writer who is being too arrogant and full of himself or herself and unwilling to listen to other voices—then in my feedback I instinctively lean a bit on that student: "Wait a minute. You're talking as though yours are the only feelings and thoughts on this matter; have you ever considered looking to see what X and Y have said? You will have no credibility till you do." And obviously, when students start to work in their disciplinary major, of course I am happy to force them to situate their writing among all the key positions in the conversation of that discipline. But grandstanding, taking themselves too seriously, and seeing themselves as the center of everything—I don't see these as the characteristic sins of first year students.

Admittedly, first year students often suffer from a closely related sin: naiveté. For being naive and taking oneself too seriously can look alike and can take the same propositional form: implying simultaneously, "Everyone else is just like me" and "No one else in the universe has ever thought my thoughts or felt my feelings." But when we see a paper with these problematic assumptions, we should ask ourselves: Is this really a problem of the writer taking herself too seriously and being too committed and self-invested in her writing? or is it a problem of the writer, though perhaps glib, being essentially timid and tapping only a small part of her thinking and feeling? When I get a strongly felt, fully committed, arrogant paper I am happy to wrestle and try to get tough with the writer. But so often with first year students it is the latter: timidity and lack of deep entwinement in what they are writing.

Am *I* just being naive? Maybe. In any case let me openly acknowledge an arguable assumption underneath all this. I sense it is the distinguishing feature of writers to take themselves too seriously. Writing is a struggle and a risk. Why go to the bother unless what we say feels important? None of us who has a full awareness of all the trouble we can get into by writing would ever write by choice unless we also had a correspondingly full sense of pride, self-absorption, even arrogance. Most first year students have a strong sense of the trouble they can get into with writing, but they tend to lack that writer's corresponding gift for taking themselves too seriously—*pride* in the importance of what they have to say. Look at our experience parenting: Most parents know instinctively that their job is to help their children take themselves more seriously, not less seriously. Once a student can really begin to own and care about her ideas, that will lead naturally to the necessary combat—which will lead to some cultural sophistication in itself.

(8) Here is my last brief point of conflict between the role of writer and academic. We all know that when students write to teachers they have to write "up" to an audience with greater knowledge and authority than the writer has about her own topic. The student is analyzing "To His Coy Mistress" for a reader who understands it better than she does. (Worse yet, the teacher/reader is often looking for a specific conclusion and form in the paper.) Even if the student happens to have a better insight or understanding than the teacher has, the teacher gets to define her own understanding as right and the student's as wrong. Thus the basic subtext in a piece of student writing is likely to be, "Is this okay?"

In contrast to students, the basic subtext in a writer's text is likely to be, "Listen to me, I have something to tell you," for writers can usually write with more authority than their readers. Therefore, unless we can set things up so that our first year students are often telling us about things that they know better than we do, we are sabotaging the essential dynamic of writers. We are transforming the process of "writing" into the process of "being tested." Many of the odd writing behaviors of students make perfect sense once we see that they are behaving as test-takers rather than writers.

How about academics on this score? It would seem as though they would have at least as strong an authority stance as writers do. After all, the academic in her writing has done a piece of research or reflection as a professional and is usually saying things that her readers do not know. But look again. I think you'll notice a curious resemblance between how students write to their teacher-readers and how academics write to their colleague-readers—even if the academic is a tenured professor. Yes, the academic may have data, findings, or thoughts that are news; yet the paradigm transaction in academic writing is one where the writer is conveying those data, findings, or thoughts to authorities in the field whose job is to decide whether they are acceptable. These authorities get to decide whether the writing counts as important or true—whether it is valid—and ultimately whether it counts as knowledge. Have you ever noticed that when we write articles or books as academics, we often have the same feeling that students have when they turn in papers: "Is this okay? Will you accept this?" But damn it, I want my first year students to be saying in their writing, "Listen to me, I have something to tell you" not "Is this okay? Will you accept this?"

Of course some academics manage to send the strong perky message, "Listen to me, I have something to tell you." But the structure of the academy tends to militate against that stance. And of course the structure of the classroom and the grading situation militate even more heavily against it. Therefore I feel I have a better chance of getting my students to take that forthright stance toward readers and their material if I do what I can to make them feel like writers, and avoid setting things up to make them feel like academics.

* * *

Conclusion. Behind this paper, then, I'm really asking a larger cultural question: Is there a conflict in general—apart from first year students or students in general—between the role of writer and the role of academic? Perhaps, my categories are oversimple, but I confess I'm talking also about my own experience. I'm proud of being both an academic and a writer, partly because I've had to struggle on both counts. I'd like to inhabit both roles in an unconflicted way, but I feel a tug of war between them.

I suspect that if we could be more sensible about how we create and define the roles of academic and writer in our culture, the conflict might not be necessary. I have the feeling that the role of academic as we see it suffers narrowness for not containing more of what I have linked to the role of writer. Frankly, I think there are problems with what it means to be an academic. If academics were more like writers—wrote more, turned to writing more, enjoyed writing more—I think the academic world would be better. David, on the other hand, probably believes that the role of writer suffers narrowness for not containing more of what I have associated with the role of academic. So the conflict plays itself out. I am ready to try to be more wise about these roles. I suppose the obvious problem is that I define writer in too "romantic" a fashion. I stand by—nervously—trying to hold myself open to correction on this point. But are you going to make me give up all the features of the role of writer that seem helpful and supportive? I hope you won't make the role of writer more astringent and trying than it already is.[3]

Notes

[1] I am indebted here to a valuable unpublished paper about Polanyi by M. Elizabeth Sargent at Western Oregon University.

[2] It might sound as though my emphasis on student writing means that I'm keeping *authoritative* voices out of the classroom, but I'm not. It's only *academic* voices I don't particularly invite in. For I bring in a *bit* of outside reading. My point is that even timid students find it relatively easy to speak back with conviction to President Bush, to the Pope, to Adrienne Rich, to *The New York Times*; but not to academic or scholarly writers. It's interesting to ask why this should be. It's not because academics and scholars have more authority—especially in the eyes of most students. It must be something about academic discourse. Of course it may be that I should spend more time teaching my students to talk back with authority to academics, and

David gives good direction here in his *Facts, Artifacts, and Counterfacts* but so far I haven't felt it as a high enough priority to give it the time it requires.

[3] Not knowing that David and I were going to publish these talks till fairly recently, I used points numbered 4–6 in my essay "The War Between Reading and Writing— and How to End It." *Rhetoric Review* 12.1 (Fall 1993).

DAVID BARTHOLOMAE

RESPONSE

My sense is that our papers pretty much staked out the terms of our different positions. There is a good bit of common ground. This is inevitable. We are about the same age, both products of a similar moment in English (my teachers were also shaped by the New Criticism), both working inside the same profession. If our conversation is useful, it seems to me it will be for the degree to which it shows where people like Peter and me are nervous, not quite so certain about what we are doing (or not certain that we are, in fact, doing the same things). I am not trying to be contrary in my response; I think the following points of difference are both illustrative and important.

I agree with Peter that there is a conflict between what he has called "the role of the writer and that of the academic." The academic, for him, is a person with an eye to the past (or to books and articles) and with a skeptical, critical attitude towards language. The writer is the person who works with pleasure and authority on his or her own and without being skeptical or distrustful, at least of his or her own language project. As Peter phrases the issue, the question he faces as a teacher is "whether I should invite my first year students to be self-absorbed and see themselves at the center of the discourse—in a sense, credulous; or whether I should invite them to be personally modest and intellectually scrupulous and to see themselves as at the periphery—in a, sense, skeptical and distrustful." This comes very close to the way I would define the issues. Peter comes down on the side of credulity as the governing idea in the undergraduate writing course; I come down on the side of skepticism. Peter wants his students to "trust" language and implies, rightly, that I would teach a form of mistrust. The word I would use for mistrust is *criticism*, and in my article I called academic writing a form of critical writing. Peter argues that he too has tried to unmask the "subtle and sometimes insidious powers of teachers." I think of the problem of the teacher as only a minor version of the larger problem of the forms of knowledge that are presented to students as naturally or inevitably or unquestionably "there" in the academy.

The pedagogical questions in this conversation are both practical and fundamental: Are freshmen ready to think first and primarily about the problems of writing when they write? Is criticism an appropriate point of entry into the college curriculum (and is the

freshman course appropriately conceived of as a point of entry into the college curriculum)? Is it the job of college English to teach students to learn to resist and be
suspicious of writing and the text? I would say yes to all three. I would say that Peter's
answer is "no," although his position is, of course, more complex than I can make it in
summary. You can see Peter working out his position in relation to these questions in *What
Is English?*—where he both reports on and places himself within a larger version of the
debate we represent in our papers. As I said in my article, I think the argument that Peter
makes is part of a larger attempt within the culture to preserve the idea of an independent,
self-determining subjectivity, what I labeled the writer on the frontier. My article is part of
the attack on that figure. At the center of our arguments are two different versions of "the
writer."

Let me move quickly, then, to what is as close to a "real" example as we have—the
writer of the divorce paper whom I allude to in my opening essay. Peter says, "I agree with
you in wanting to understand and acknowledge the cultural forces and voices that enter
into her paper; but I wouldn't be so dismissive of her role: I'd still grant her what we grant
to the literary figures we study, namely that her writing is hers—even if it is over-deter-
mined by countless cultural and psychological forces." In the course that I teach, I begin
by *not* granting the writer her "own" presence in that paper, by denying the paper's status
as a record of or a route to her own thoughts and feelings. I begin instead by asking her to
read her paper as a text already written by the culture, representing a certain predictable
version of the family, the daughter, and the writer. I ask her to look at who speaks in the
essay and who doesn't. I ask her to look at the organization of the essay to see what it
excludes. And I ask her to revise in such a way that the order of the essay is broken—to
write against the grain of the discourse that has determined her account of her family. I
begin by being dismissive.

The course that I am arguing against (and I will not say that it is Peter's, although I
think it is often offered in his name) would begin by not being dismissive. It would begin
by encouraging a student to work that opening essay to its perfection: adding detail, adding
voice and color, improving it as narrative or essay or both. The work of revision, in other
words, would be directed at preserving and perfecting rather than calling into question (or
dismissing) the discourse. Perhaps later, as a point of reflection, the student may read or
think about alternative versions of "the family" or even alternative versions of the "essay"
she has written.

These two courses I have been imagining thus provide a different version of what it
means to say that the writing "is" the writer's. The course I teach makes the moment of possession not the opening moment but a later one, where if the writer is present that presence
can be seen in the work of revision, where the evidence lies in the work directed against
writing (that is, against the culture's desire to tell a certain story about the family and girl-
hood; or against the discourse's desire to hide its origins, its argument, and its seams).

Peter rightly suggests that we probably differ on how much time students should spend reading in a writing course. I would agree, and think that the differences are more fundamental than peripheral. A series of required texts are central to my teaching, usually essays or chapters from books or journals that are said to be "beyond" students' interests or abilities. My goal is to show students how to work with difficult material. There is a practical payoff here, since students, I believe, will at some point be expected to do so and no one else is taking the time to show them how and why they might do the work.

I also want students to be able to negotiate the ways they are figured in relationship to the official forms of knowledge valued in the academy—that is, I want them to be prepared to write themselves out of a rhetorical situation in which their roles are already prepared, where they are figured as simple-minded or not-yet-ready-for serious discussion. I want my students to have a way to begin, to establish their power over the text (and the author); I want them to write essays that do more than summarize or reproduce the words of "authorities." Like Peter, I want students to take pride in their work and to take themselves and their work seriously, to be arrogant, self-absorbed. (*Ways of Reading* is the product of the courses I and my colleagues have been teaching for years.)

My route to this is by teaching students to be able to work closely with the ways their writing constructs a relationship with tradition, power and authority—with other people's words. It is here, in the sentences and paragraphs, that I think we can work on cultural politics (where "ownership" becomes a term that works in a writing class). I think it is very important to be able to work with how a student represents or makes use of or revises or intervenes with or takes possession of (say) Adrienne Rich's argument in "When We Dead Awaken." My experience tells me that without instruction, students will feel they have no way of working with that text, nothing to say beyond what Rich has already said.

I want to teach a student to work on the essay she is writing in parallel with Rich's text, with what she chooses to cite (and what she ignores), with what she does with the passage she quotes. Here, in these places on the page, talking about the choice and positioning of a block quotation (for example), I can help students negotiate the ways in which they are figured in the reading and writing that goes on in the academy. This too, I think, is a way of teaching a student writer to say, "Listen to me; I have something to tell you."

Finally, I would say that it is the idea of "criticism" that most marks our different positions on the role of the teacher. It is important to Peter to appeal to what students can learn "in the absence of instruction." I would never argue that school is the only place one learns or that teachers are the only ones to make learning possible. I would argue, however, that since the point of criticism is to ask questions of the things that seem beyond question, to ask students to see the natural as artificial, it cannot come from within. It will not happen on its own, but only when prompted. That is how I imagine the writing teacher. The writing teacher is the person who not only prompts students to write but who prompts students to revise, to work on their writing in ways that they would not if left to (not their own) but the culture's devices.

PETER ELBOW

RESPONSE

Common Ground

You seem to imply through allusions to my titles and my work that I am more wholly opposed to your work than I am. I wonder if you are prey here to an assumption in academic discourse (and rhetoric too), that discourse means argument and that difference means opposition. So let me start by pointing out significant places where we agree. You argue for "academic writing as a major part of an undergraduate's training." I agree. My only reservation is to say that this training isn't feasible or desirable in a *one* semester first year introductory writing course, but that it should indeed go on in later courses in the major and in other upper level courses. Nothing I've said here is an argument against academic writing—only for something in addition. You say we must make the classroom itself available for critical inquiry; "to hide the teacher is to hide the traces of power." I agree. We mustn't pretend we have less power or authority than we do, and I've tried to write about this so as to help students and teachers see this power and deal better with it. You say it's crucial and necessary to study the past, to be aware of our place in history. Ditto for culture, gender, class, race, sexual orientation. I think I'm an ally on these matters. You insist that individuals are socially constructed. I agree to a significant extent—especially insofar as you make positive arguments about all the voices and forces that help make us who we are and that color what we think and write. But notice that your arguments are mostly negative. That is, you assume without argument that if I celebrate "independent, self-creative, self-expressive subjectivity," I must be against the notion of people as socially constructed. But I am not.

There is a crucial matter of theory here. You say in passing that I can't have it both ways, that I can't stick up for both perspectives on the human condition. But you never give any reason for this theoretical position. I insist I *can* have it both ways. My Chaucer book argues that human life is *both* free and determined. *Embracing Contraries* is entirely devoted to arguing for "both/and" thinking and trying to show the problems with "either/or" thinking— showing how we can validly maintain opposites in various realms of theory and practice. You argue against "academic bashing," whether from the left or right. I agree. Sure, I struggle to make the academic world less pompous and more able to exploit the cognitive power of the believing game and the intelligence of feelings. But this is no attack, it's an attempt to reform. I am proud to be an academic. You say that colleges and universities (and schools too) have tended to deny students a sense of being an author—"making students only summarizers or term paper writers." I agree. You go on to say that we should try to show them that they can be "elegant, smart, independent." However, you feel this would be lying to them, whereas I insist that they *can* in truth be elegant, smart, and independent.

Differences: Utopias and Freewriting

You say that the classroom is "real space, not an idealized utopian space." You seem to be insisting on two things here: that a classroom cannot be utopian, and that utopian spaces are not real spaces. This highlights what may be our most important difference. Let's look at a micro-utopian space that I love: freewriting. This is an activity that permits a classroom space to be at once utopian and real. (Were not Fruitlands and Summerhill real spaces?) Note that freewriting does not involve trying to hide the teacher or her authority. Indeed using it tends to make our authority more naked. Why else would students do something so odd and unnatural as to write for ten minutes—without stopping, no matter what—trying not to worry about the conventions of writing and also assuming that the teacher who orders it won't see it and is urging them not to show it to anyone else?

Nor does freewriting pretend magically to reveal one's pure natural essential self or to escape the effects of culture and the past. Far from it. People who use freewriting tend to notice immediately that it shows more nakedly than other kinds of writing all the junk that culture and the past have stuffed into our heads. Nothing is better than freewriting at showing us how we are constructed and situated. Another way of saying this is that freewriting is the opposite of an attempt to preserve the idea of a self-generated autonomous author. Rather it is an invitation to take a ride on language itself, and (insofar as the phrase has any meaning at all) to "get out of the self": to relinquish volition and planning and see what words and phrases come out of the head when you just kick it and give language and culture a start.

So does freewriting pretend to be free? Yes and no. It is not free from the teacher's authority (until a person takes it over by choice), nor from the forces of culture and language. But it does create freedom in certain crucial ways. It frees the writer from planning, from meeting the needs of readers, and from any requirements as to what she should write about or how her writing should end up—for instance, as to topic, meaningfulness, significance, or correctness of convention. Freewriting then is a paradigm of the real and the utopian: an example of how we can use our authority as teachers in our institutional settings to create artificial spaces that can heighten discovery and learning. It is a way to take ten minutes of a classroom and make certain things happen that don't usually happen given the institutional and cultural forces at work. Students discover that they can write words and thoughts and not worry about what good writing is or what the teacher wants, they discover that their heads are full of language and ideas (sometimes language and ideas they had no idea were there), and they discover they can get pleasure from writing.

Admittedly, my utopianism often takes a different direction from yours—a direction that troubles you, towards non-instruction. You say there is no writing without teachers, not only in school but even out of school. I would acknowledge that there is no schooling without teachers, no assigned writing without teachers, no teaching without authority, and indeed little human interaction anywhere without unequal power or authority. But surely there is plenty of writing without teachers not only outside the academy but even inside. I'm thinking about all the writing that students do unrelated to their school work: diaries, letters, notes, stories, poems, newspaper writing.

But isn't language, above all, the realm where people most blatantly *do* learn without teachers? Children learn more grammar by age five than linguists can yet fully articulate, and get very fluent in its deployment—all without teachers. (If you say that all children have "teachers" in the person of their parents and playmates, you are just aggrandizing a term to destroy it since there would be no way then to distinguish between teaching and non-teaching.) The most striking fact about language acquisition is the absence of teaching. What people need for acquiring language is not teaching but to be around others who speak, to be listened to, and to be spoken to. It may be utopian to carry this principle of learning without teaching from speech to writing, but that is just what I and many other teachers and students have found useful. (An odd, minimal kind of utopianism: simply trying to stop teaching now and then—trying to cultivate in the classroom some tufts of what grows wild outside. But there is plenty of research about how small children learn not just to speak but to write before school—simply by being around writing.) Above all, it is empowering for students to discover that they can learn so much without instruction.

Approaches to Student Writing

You are eloquent about noticing when we and our students are being manipulated by the culture. But couldn't it be said that in making this case you are pursuing the same myth I am? That is, like me, you seem to want to give your student writer more control over her writing, more ability to make her writing her own. But of course you see me as preaching independence and control while actually leading her down the primrose path to being unconsciously or unawarely written, while you are insisting that the way to help her get more control is to help her see how she is being written by the culture and get her to "write against" it or resist it—not to be ruled, not to be taken over. Thus your premise seems to be not that we are *always* written by language and culture, but that we must engage in the critique of language and culture and recognize their power over us so that we can step somewhat out of the path of the bulldozer.

But there is a crucial difference in our concrete approaches to students. That is, even though I agree with your goal of helping students be less manipulated by the culture, I would hold back much more in my critique of this student's writing. I simply want to critique or intervene much less than you do. You may well answer, "That just gives culture more free play over their minds." But here I make something of an act of faith or commitment. I feel I must leave students more control, let them make as many decisions as they can about their writing—despite the power of the culture. I must call on some faith in the ability of students to make important choices, decisions and perceptions of their own when I can clear a good space.

Of course, this doesn't always work and I'm often disappointed at how they replay the culture. But my holding back is not just an act of faith; it's also an act of methodological commitment—an insistence on keeping means and ends in harmony with each other. What the culture does—as you point out so powerfully—is to do their thinking for them. Therefore it seems to me that the most precious thing I can do is provide spaces where I don't also do their thinking for them (despite the attendant risks of giving more room for the culture). In contrast, your response to her paper seems to do her thinking for her—that is, you are telling her that she thought she meant X, but really she didn't; she thought she told what she saw and experienced, but really her perceptions and experience were a script written out for her by the culture. It feels important to me *not* to do that. If my end or goal is to get students to think for themselves and not be dupes of others' thinking for them, I don't want to try to seek that end by thinking for them—even if that means I must sometimes look on helplessly while they believe something I wish they would abandon.

Let me try to be more specific about teaching practice—about how I would respond to that student's paper. I would *not* "begin by encouraging the student to work that opening essay to its perfection." (I appreciate how you acknowledge that my own practice might differ from what is sometimes done in my name.) I would try to help her make up her own mind where to take it. So if she wanted to make her paper "perfect" in the problematic genre you describe, I would try to help her. But (and this is crucial for me) I try to remove all pressure to make papers perfect in that way. I'm always trying hard to show students that progress for a paper often means listening for a perplexity or scruple—which often means letting the paper fall radically apart. That's why I have to take out the grading pressure: I'm often trying to encourage students to let their writing get worse.

So if this paper were the first one in a semester, I would give no response at all. For the first third of a semester or so, my goal is for students to write a great deal, to hear their own writing and even see some of it published, hear each others' writing (and some of mine)—but to get little or no feedback. This is no solipsistic, nonsocial vacuum: They are constantly hearing the writing of others and putting their own writing out to others. It's just a vacuum from explicit feedback. I put a lot of faith in the long range benefits of helping students achieve *their* goals—helping them gradually relinquish their conditioned assumption that their job is to accomplish *our* goals.

But I'm *not* saying that I want to leave students completely alone for the culture to play on—with no feedback from me or from other students in the class. For the last two-thirds of the semester I try to set things up so that they hear plenty of feedback from peers and from me. So let me try to describe the kinds of feedback I might give that paper. I might say, in effect, "I don't see your own experience reflected in the main assertions of your paper," or even (gingerly), "I wonder if your own experience might have been partly *caused* by X." But I want to avoid saying, "I don't believe these/your experiences are really yours." I have faith that if students attend more and more closely to their experience, they will gradually be led to sounder questioning and thinking. Perhaps you would say that your comment to her is also an attempt to get her to pay better attention to her experience. But students easily distrust their experience, and we do harm if we try to "correct" them about their own experience. In short, I want students to hear my comments but still be able to resist or deny them. (Needless to say, I'm describing what I try to do. What I actually do at 11:30 p.m. when I'm tired and grouchy is another story.)

Really, I've come back to my original theme of trying to help students see themselves as writers. That is, my goal is that students should keep writing by choice after the course is over—because of my faith that the process itself of engaging in writing, of trying to find words for one's thinking and experience and trying them out on others, will ultimately lead to the kind of questing and self-contradiction that we both seek. But I want them to get there by a path where the student is steering, not me.

Carolyn Matalene, "Experience as Evidence: Teaching Students to Write Honestly and Knowledgeably about Public Issues"

Carolyn Matalene is now Distinguished Professor Emeritus at the University of South Carolina, where she not only pursued her research interests in composition pedagogy, workplace writing, and modern rhetorical theory, but won teaching awards, working to help students "join the conversation yet maintain their own freedom" (as she puts it in the essay below). Her collection of essays, *Worlds of Writing: Teaching and Learning in Discourse Communities of Work* (1989), was built on the groundbreaking work of Lee Odell and Dixie Goswami in *Writing in Nonacademic Settings* (1985). Both books emphasize the ways in which writing teachers should help students think ahead to the writing that is going to be demanded of them in their careers—particularly to the collaborative writing practices taken for granted in the business world. Matalene herself has collaborated with others on her most recent publications—with Katherine Reynolds, *Carolina Voices: Two Hundred Years of Student Experiences* (2001); with Alice Klement, *Telling Stories/Taking Risks: Journalism Writing at the Century's Edge* (1998); and with J. F. Reynolds, J. N. Magnotto, D. Samson, and L. V. Sadler, *Professional Writing in Context: Lessons from Teaching and Consulting in Worlds of Work* (1995). Her 1992 piece in this volume is well known and reveals her characteristic challenge to academic writing: make sense, value the experience of those outside academia, and write (and teach writing) to include them and their expertise.

EXPERIENCE AS EVIDENCE: TEACHING STUDENTS TO WRITE HONESTLY AND KNOWLEDGEABLY ABOUT PUBLIC ISSUES

One of the largest crowds at the Conference on College Composition and Communication in Boston gathered to hear David Bartholomae and Peter Elbow engage in "A Dialogue on Academic Discourse." Their debate, whether writing courses should require students to engage in academic discourse or should allow them to write from their own experience, is clearly a live issue, one that many writing teachers and program directors are struggling with.[1] Focusing on writers or focusing on readers, affirming private visions or encouraging public voices, teaching students or teaching books—which emphasis is more effective, which more responsible? Of course, framing the issue this baldly would be unfair to the intellectual rigor and subtlety that both Bartholomae and Elbow bring to the classroom. Bartholomae doesn't just ask students to write about what they read; rather, they compose their own personal readings of difficult texts. (See *Facts, Artifacts, and Counterfacts.*) And Elbow wants his students to understand the "intellectual practices of academic discourse" although they are working on nonacademic tasks (153). Clearly, Bartholomae and Elbow teach both students and books, and the power of Bartholomae's approach to academic discourse is that it begins with the student.

But the positions represented by Bartholomae and Elbow do not always retain such complexity and inclusiveness when they are voted on by program committees, realized in book adoptions, and then outlined for teaching staffs. Actually, the mere fact of a committee probably means that those who favor emphasis on academic discourse will win the day; in my experience, academics in groups like to sound rigorous (however reified their notion of rigor), like to make students measure up, like to design hard courses for others to teach. Cooper and Selfe share my skepticism about our motives for insisting upon academic writing: ". . . our efforts to instill in our students the specific conventions and values associated with academic discourse may well be designed more to legitimate our own work and our status in the larger society than to teach our students knowledge and skills that will enable them to function as productive members of society" (849). Or perhaps the grave importance we attach to mastering academic discourse has less to do with our belief in it than with the relief it offers us from dealing with the personal. Robert J. Connors finds "a curious discomfort in English teachers' attitudes toward students writing from personal experience. . . . For many teachers, literature and literary analysis provided a way out of the world of personal writing that made them uncomfortable. . . . The question of personal writing is uncomfortable for many teachers because it presents such a clear mirror of one's individual philosophy of education" (178–80).

For whatever reasons, teaching books and emphasizing writing based on information rather than on experience tends to be the fashion in many composition courses, especially in large programs. And as these courses are transformed from abstract philosophies to concrete assignments, so do they seem inevitably to privilege argumentation—often to the exclusion of all other genres. The rationale goes like this: Students need to master academic discourse, which involves making assertions and supporting them; thus, they need to write arguments incorporating outside sources, and learn to cite them correctly. They need to read more and write about what they read; then they will be able to join the academic conversation. And their teachers will be able to hold them to rigorous standards. Thus, English 101 becomes a course in argumentation incorporating a collection of readings on social issues.

I am used to hearing what students need—from parents, teachers, colleagues, administrators, authors, editors, from just about everyone who speaks English. And I am used to hearing what students ought to be made to do, but seldom do I hear what they actually have done, what a semester's worth of their writing actually looks like or sounds like. Sometimes we give them a test to prove a point and call it a research study, but seldom do we bother to look over all of the writing that a class of students has done to see what the currently touted approach to teaching writing actually produces in the way of writing. So I decided to do just that, remembering that Mina Shaughnessy changed our views of basic writers, not by giving us numbers, but by reading students' writing and listening to their voices.

I decided to listen to the voices of 24 freshmen at my university as they fulfilled the requirements for the new "argument track" version of English 101. I am not suggesting that my findings or my conclusions are generalizable, but I do think the method is transferable, probably even a good idea. Reading a batch of writing folders to find out what a particular course design actually yields, keeping in mind what it is supposed to yield, is salutary. I recommend it to anyone who sits on a program committee and designs courses for others to teach.

The students whose papers I read were all in one class taught by an experienced and enthusiastic teacher, Mary, who was the Assistant Director of Freshman English and who had helped design the argument track. Her texts, chosen by a committee, were the *St. Martin's Handbook* and *The Informed Argument,* a reader which includes short pieces on important contemporary issues. Students read these pieces, discussed their construction and use of support, then wrote their own arguments in response. They were to establish their own position, using the material or the ideas of the experts for support. Each student's writing folder contained six arguments on the following topics: competition, animal experimentation, censorship, gun control, a social problem of the student's own choosing, a position paper about reading literature, and a final exam, also an argument on some other issue dealt with in the textbook.

I read, of course, as a complete outsider, not one of the natives, not even a visitor, and not knowing anything of the people who went with these texts. I just wanted to know how they sounded as speakers in the argumentative mode, how comfortable they were with a purpose imposed upon them, how convincing they could be arguing the issues that Robert K. Miller, editor of *The Informed Argument,* had decided were important.

Of course, with or without assignments, no individual speaker or writer has complete freedom; that we have learned from Bakhtin. Because of the restrictions imposed by genre, "the single utterance, with all its individuality and creativity, can in no way be regarded as a *completely free combination* of forms of language" ("Speech Genres" 81). "Any utterance is a link in a very complexly organized chain of other utterances" ("Speech Genres" 69). So no speaker or writer can ever be Adam, starting completely fresh. But some speakers are more adept in joining the conversation yet maintaining their own freedom than others. As Bakhtin puts it: "The better our command of genres, the more freely we employ them, the more fully and clearly we reveal our own individuality in them (where this is possible and necessary), the more flexibly and precisely we reflect the unrepeatable situation of communication—in a word, the more perfectly we implement our free speech plan" ("Speech Genres" 80).

So I read these papers, trying to read like Bakhtin, trying to be sensitive to different voices, trying to determine the students' "command of genres" and the extent to which they could reveal their "own individuality," implement their own "free speech plan."

And what I heard surprised me. I heard repeatedly the strange disjunction, dislocation, or dissonance of public and private voices at odds. I heard student writers, trying to sound like the writers in the text, but unable to write convincingly in the authoritative public voice and unable to negotiate between external evidence and internal experience. Learning to sound authoritative, after all, isn't easy. The worst excesses of bureaucratic prose are committed by insecure writers who try to sound important by using big words, long sentences, passive constructions, redundant modifiers, and abstract nouns as agents. Learning to move up and down the abstraction ladder gracefully isn't easy either. These students were willing to scale the heights, less adept at returning to earth. So some of the dislocations occurred when a writer—here a young man named Patrick—tried to slide down but fell off:

> Competition is a positive human nature that is present in everyone.
> Man will always have the urge to be better than the other guy.

When writing about himself as a soccer player, Patrick sounded like a real person:

> For seven years I played soccer. My participation in the sport made
> me feel more comfortable around the other players and helped me
> learn the positive aspects of competition. We all wanted to win.

When the team played as a unit successfully and we won, a feeling of accomplishment would rush over me.

But then to conclude, the disembodied public voice took over again:

> In today's world competition is becoming more and more important. It is a healthy outlet for one's aims and hopes. I hope that it is looked upon as an important part of growing up and is most helpful. Competition must serve as a tool through life. It cannot become an obsession. It is a positive aspect of life. It should be experienced by everyone.

The disjunction between the private and the public voice seemed most apparent in the papers written on competition. On this subject—more than any other—students had experiences of their own to draw upon, but seldom the awareness that they could and should integrate their own experience into the assignment or the ability to negotiate levels of abstraction smoothly. Consider the dissonance in Tracy's account:

> I kept in mind that practice makes perfect, and then I thought, "practice doesn't always make perfect." Surely, I knew if I listened to my inner thought, I would probably never be able to accomplish anything in life. I did audition, and when the instructor came out, she announced that there were ten dancers being chosen for the Junior Company, I was one of them. There have been some successes and then there have been some failures; but, a performer must be able to deal with the successes and/or failures he/she will encounter.

After Tracy told of her own moment of triumph, she immediately lurched to a higher level of generality, avoiding any linkage.

Sometimes the lurching happened in a single sentence, as in Beth's paper:

> If I did not have the quality of competition, my character wouldn't have enabled me to deal with life's many situations and today's society.

Two of these student writers continue to haunt me. One was a young man named Eric who had mastered bodilessness.

Competition is an important part of life. But how are children affected by competition? Competition can be a growing experience for a child provided influential people in the child's life supply him with the proper motivation and support. This may include anything from a rational discussion with the child about putting his competitive zeal in proper perspective to teaching him the courtesy of winning and losing with a mature disposition.

But on page 5 of his paper, his own experience as a little league umpire came through:

One day I called a kid safe because the first baseman pulled his foot off the bag too early. The coach I made the call against was never really upset with me, but the parents were livid. I was cursed and yelled at for the next hour despite the fact that the game was over forty-five minutes earlier.

Eric went on to draw some conclusions about competition from his experiences; children under nine, he says, should play sports only to learn the basics.

There should be as little emphasis placed on winning as possible, maybe even to the point of not keeping score. [What a fine and original idea.] Children under the age of six should not be allowed to participate in organized sporting events for the simple reason that children under six don't have the attention span necessary to function for an entire game. I've seen five year olds play with bugs in the outfield instead of paying attention to the game.

Those little leaguers catching bugs in the grass were for me the most memorable image I found in all the folders I read. Here I felt was a student ready to become a powerful writer, but he was never encouraged or empowered to be real—that wasn't allowed for in the argument track—and so he didn't. Instead, with his classmates, he moved on to the next "issue." He returned to the world of generalization in all of his subsequent writing and collected an A for so doing. Eric will be ok—at least in the game of getting As.

But how I would like to get my hands on Danielle, and encourage her first to write through her anger and then to integrate the two voices. She began:

Competition within sports is very positive in many ways as well as very negative in other ways

—a line I read so often that it gave me the shakes. But then, Danielle's experience as an athlete and as a woman took over and she presented a long narrative of her life as an athlete. Here are some excerpts: My father believed girls were not put on this earth to do the same things that boys were capable of doing. . . . My father never really pushed me to play sports, but just accepted the fact that his daughter was a tomboy. I really hated to be called that; I was a female athlete who just loved sports. . . . When I was about ten years old, my brothers and I had started to win many trophies. I thought that these trophies would somehow open my father's eyes and see how good I really was. I was wrong; he continued to favor my brother's participation in sports only. . . . I never really let my father get to me so much that I would quit the one thing that I loved most, playing sports. I felt sports were a way to forget about things around me and to escape to a world I loved most. . . . At the end of my senior year, I made it to the top: Scholarships to Princeton and Cornell for soccer and softball, highlights and fame, but it just was not the same without the most important person behind me all my life, my father!

After this effort, Danielle never again spoke in her own voice but tried to manage the public voice of the textbook. Her later paper on censorship ends:

> Again, parents are the ones who have an impact on their children
> not the books they read. The reduction or abolishment of censorship
> can occur in the future if more credit is given to the parents for the
> righteous upbringing of their siblings.

Given what we now know about her father and how she feels about him, these sentences seem both fake and dishonest. What are we doing if we let Danielle get away with this? What are we accomplishing if we ignore her fractured syntax and encourage her to assume this fraudulent tone? Are we really helping her to master academic discourse? Imagine the powerful arguments she could have written about women in sports if she had been allowed to rely on her own expert knowledge—she *is* an expert at being an athlete— instead of on the distant views of those canned experts. I cannot but imagine as well how she might have been changed by presenting her story and her arguments to classmates and hearing their responses.

Most of the students, however many times I read their papers, did not become real for me; I seldom heard what seemed to me an actual human. In fact, I heard some real people turned into strangely unreal people. Cyndie, for example, was herself a ballet dancer, but this is how she wrote about her art:

> Although this type of competition may seem unhealthy to the indi-
> vidual, it is actually a lifeline. This competition makes the dancer's

adrenaline flow. The feeling of accomplishment is so tremendous
that nothing else matters except achieving this sensation again and
again. True the disappointments are hard for the dancer to handle,
but she must take it and turn it into a positive situation the next time.
Usually this does occur.

"Usually this does occur"? How can a ballerina be so bodiless? How can we get this
dancer back into the dance? Instead of making her quote others, which Cyndie dutifully
did, we should be helping her to see that her own experience makes her an authority on
being a ballet student, probably an authority ready to argue about training regimens or
teaching techniques or audition practices. Instead of requiring her to sound like a talking
head, we should be empowering her as a writer. That means we must begin by valuing her
and her experience. If we would teach students as well as books, then we must get over
our fear of feeling—both the feelings of our students and our feelings about them. This
needn't mean being sappy. As Jeanette Harris points out, "Experience-based discourse may
be self-referential, but its primary purpose is not necessarily self-revelation" (157). Harris
concludes her study, *Expressive Discourse,* by asserting, "Rather than privileging either
experience or information as sources of subject matter, we should encourage students to
use both. It is, I believe, this purposeful combination of experience and information that
produces the most effective discourse" (166–67).

The important word here is surely *purposeful.* Is the purpose of the writing to communicate a position to a real audience or to fulfill an assignment in the argument track? If
students believe that hiding their experience is what is being asked of them, if they ignore
their own feelings and try to sound like books, if they discount their private responses and
adopt an elevated, authoritative tone, they are likely to sound just plain weird. Unable to
achieve a "free speech plan," they instead combine bad writing with bad thinking. Here
are some examples.

Dana tried to sound formal:

> Through observation of the many ailments this world is continually
> facing, one can find it increasingly important to incorporate labora-
> tory animal testing with our technology today.

But her syntax went awry:

> Living in a carnivorous world, it is hard to deny that many animals
> are killed each year in order to supply our bodies with a good source
> of protein.

Jennifer, trying to efface herself in order to write academic discourse, managed to sound monstrous:

> Several of my relatives have undergone many different types of major surgery, including open heart surgery. These procedures have been made possible through the availability of animal research. If these technological advances had not been designed many special events would not have been shared with these family members. [No dead people at Thanksgiving dinner]

Sometimes students summoned up abstract agents to solve complex problems effortlessly:

> Although teenage pregnancy seems to be an evergrowing problem, society now seems to be realizing the need for education and starting to take more responsibility in acting on this need.

Sometimes they stayed wondrously high on the abstraction ladder, like David:

> Many things and activities occur in our society today. Some of these contain different views of different topics.

The more papers I read, the louder and more insistent became the generalized voice, the student writer trying to sound like the authorities in the textbook writing for a "general audience." Of course, the essays the students were using as models—as Martin Nystrand has noted—". . . were in their conception addressed to very particular readers for very particular purposes." "No one, after all, actually writes for *The Norton Anthology,* least of all those authors whose works finally reside there" (106).

Certainly, the writers included in *The Informed Argument* often used the first person and often included very specific, very personal experiences, but evidently, what the students picked up on or thought they were supposed to pick up on were the generalizations. I started calling this generalizing voice—a voice willing to draw conclusions about people, competition, technology, society, and the like—the Centripetal voice, a term central to Bakhtin's philosophy of language. Bakhtin sees human activity in language as perpetually locked in a struggle between centripetal, unifying forces, "working toward concrete verbal and ideological unification and centralization" and centrifugal differentiating forces yielding stratification and heteroglossia ("Discourse" 271). As he puts it, "Alongside the centripetal forces, the centrifugal forces of language carry on their uninterrupted work;

alongside verbal-ideological centralization and unification, the uninterrupted processes of decentralization and disunification go forward. . . . It is possible to give a concrete and detailed analysis of any utterance, once having exposed it as a contradiction-ridden, tension-filled unity of two embattled tendencies in the life of language" ("Discourse" 272).

The texts from which I have been quoting, then, can be read as tension-filled examples of two embattled tendencies. In the writing folders for this class, the Centripetal voice out-shouted, out-talked, out-droned the individual one. Many—perhaps most—of my colleagues are pleased and relieved to hear this voice. They can deal with it by correcting syntactic missteps or formal failures. And it doesn't tap their fear of feeling, their embarrassment at dealing with the personal lives of their students. One of my disheartened colleagues says that most teachers don't want to see their students as real people, that they don't want to feel anything about these folks who drift in and out of their lives each semester. Connors' discovery of the longstanding "curious discomfort" that English teachers have toward personal writing supports this view. And, of course, many teachers approach literary texts as occasions for intellectual analyses only. "It's not about feelings, it's an intellectual game," I heard one professor of literature tell a group of graduate students in a workshop on teaching fiction. Certainly, when students are encouraged to write from their own experience, some of their topics will be messy, some of their feelings will leak out. First drafts may well be shapeless outpourings, personal laments, pointless narratives. Now is the time for the teacher/editor to be understanding, sympathetic, and tough. "Why would anyone want to read this? Who cares? What can readers learn from your experience? What do you want us to get? Where could you get this published?" These are hard questions, ones my students tell me keep them up late, but they are the questions that require and enable students to transform their own experience into a structure that has a point for readers. Shaping personal knowledge for public communication is, I am convinced, the writing opportunity that genuinely empowers students.

In a writing class that allows students to choose their topics and their purposes, the teacher's responsibility is to explain the writer's options, to suggest the genres that might be appropriate. Thus—to use examples from such a class—Jason's memory of his mother delivering him to his new stepmother and then of losing that mother too became in the third draft a youthful (and moving) argument against divorce. And Michelle's account of working in a nursing home and the sketches of the new friends she made there became an affirmative portrayal of elderly communal life. Neither of these students, I submit, could have written so effectively or gained so much as writers had they been fulfilling an argument assignment from a list of issues. And in the last analysis, making one's own experiences or inside information into purposeful communication for an audience of peers is surely closer to the actual nature of producing academic discourse than is writing about someone else's topic and manipulating their information. Doesn't the scholarship we really care to read and to write begin from a deeply personal commitment, interest, curiosity?

To permit students their own free speech plans and then to extend their ability to express them by increasing their command of genres can be the ethos of the writing class. This is not to argue that the expressive mode is necessarily more honest than the argumentative, but rather, that a good argument should be the writer's own expression—not someone else's.[2] When our writing courses are based on canned issues, emphasize forms before purposes, affirm the Centripetal voice, and ignore the personal one, they reveal our preference for teaching books rather than students. And they often as well force teachers to react according to rules rather than good sense.

In the class I examined the thrust of the teacher's comments, in keeping with the goals of the course, almost always had to do with "support"—all propositions were to be supported with facts, examples, quotations. Students who could work in quotations from the textbook authors were praised. Of course, using reading to support one's assertions was what the course was all about, so a quotation, even if applied totally out of context, was credited. (I wondered if Martin Luther King had ever intended that his "Letter from a Birmingham Jail" be used to argue against abortion.) Mary [the teacher] tried to encourage and value the use of personal experience for support in limited amounts, but sometimes she got nervous when the personal took over the paper and became more important than the issue—as in Danielle's competition paper. So the course requirements seemed to ask the teacher as well as the students to think more about appearing academic than sounding real.

Two of the students in this class, however, were considerably more experienced or more self-confident than their classmates and had learned how to join the conversation yet maintain their own freedom—as Bakhtin would say. When I came upon their folders, I knew at once that these writers were different. Jeanne had been out of school for twenty-six years raising a family, and whatever the assignment, she simply ignored the top-down or rules-first approach of the course and made each topic her own. Her paper on competition was about her own son:

> At age seven, Bubba started with city football. He was lucky, he played on a team where teaching and playing, not winning, were the goals of his coaches.

Her censorship paper was about her own library:

> In Orangeburg, at least five hundred people a day take advantage of this freedom in our county library. How many of these patrons realize that this essential freedom may be used against them?

And her gun control paper began with local knowledge:

> He was standing behind a jeep holding a very large, unusual gun in
> his hands. Several shrimpers were with him discussing prices. The
> gun was long, like a shot gun, with what appeared to be a large,
> metal canister between the stock and the barrel. A man standing near
> me identified the weapon as a machine gun. He said the owner was
> a gun dealer selling automatic weapons out of the back of his jeep.
> "Why would a shrimper working out of Edisto Beach need a
> machine gun?" I asked myself.

The other writer who startled me in my reading was Paul, a man in his twenties. He
too could make a topic uniquely his own. His paper on censorship was about a homeless
man he had observed and how we censor such people out of our reality:

> . . . without seeing the unpleasantness of people living in the back
> alleys or begging for whatever scrap of food or handout they get;
> without smelling the stench of someone who hasn't bathed or
> washed their clothes for months; without sensing any of these
> unpalatable facts, our reality is easier to swallow. Our lives are more
> pleasant.

Both Paul and Jeanne had been around long enough and perhaps out of school long
enough to have confidence in their own voices, as opposed to the Centripetal voice, and
to believe in their own right to argue about the world, instead of just listening to the arguments of others. Both achieved their own free speech plan, ignoring the Centripetal
voice—and their teacher thought they were great. In fact, when Jeanne added quotations
to her competition paper—because those were the rules—Mary felt they were intrusive.
Both students, however, made her wonder, was she really supposed to let them write like
this? If they relied on the personal, instead of on the authorities, would they sound truly
academic? How could she let them use what they knew but also fulfill the requirements of
this reading-based, issue-oriented course? (Jeanne and Paul, I submit, had more to teach
their fellow students than all of the essays in the reader.)

As the issues marched forward, most students either had no relevant knowledge of
their own or had figured out that sounding impersonal worked the best. So when Mary
brought in a *Newsweek* column at the end of the term, an argument in favor of the Orphan
Drug Act written by a man whose daughter was suffering from an immune system disorder,
a number of the students thought the father's very personal example "weakened" his case.

Composition courses when structured exclusively as courses in argument, though intended to bring students into the academic conversation, can easily become rigid and formal. When the form comes first and the issues are assigned, students' own experiences are likely to be devalued. Most students quickly learn that the easiest, safest, least risky method is to keep private and public separate. That seems to me seriously wrong. To use Bakhtin's terms, as writing teachers we should be dedicated to heteroglossia; we should be encouraging many voices, not turning them all into one. Surely, teaching students that they have the right and the responsibility to add their own unique voices to the American conversation is why we teach argument anyway. Surely, we want to strengthen their individual, private voices so that one day they may speak, not just listen, and act, not just watch. So that one day they will sound like Vaclav Havel, not White House speech writers.

Those of us who value and privilege the experiences of student writers are used to being told that we are not rigorous and not preparing our students to write academic discourse. We are also used to being told by more thoughtful critics that we naively ignore the problematic, contradiction-ridden nature of the personal. No, we are just not afraid of dealing with the problems, not afraid to ask and to help student writers turn personal experience to public account. It is not a question of valuing the personal over the impersonal or academic discourse over personal expression. It is a question of how best to prepare students to be decent and honest in their writing whether they are talking about their grandparents or about euthanasia. Talking about euthanasia IS talking about one's grandparents. And to pretend that this is not so, to suggest that we can draw a line between public and private writing and keep the personal in one compartment and the impersonal in another is not only bad writing instruction, but also immoral.

Sociologist Richard Harvey Brown in his book *Society as Text* analyzes public and private voices in the context of our political culture. And his analysis makes clear to me why our willingness to separate public and private is not a trivial matter, why the genres of the composition course mean more than filling forms and quoting sources. Western culture, which has long affirmed and depended upon the Romantic grammar of the self as a moral agent, is now inhabited as well by the positivist grammar of the self as an "inventory of performance" used in the game of "impression management" (32–34). "Though this modern Western self is an ideal type and is incarnated differently in different classes, and genders, and other groups, its constant characteristic is the loss of positive linkage between person and polity, a bifurcation between a public self defined as a functionary guided by positive, instrumental reason, and a private, affective self that is the locus of arational feelings, values, and emotions. By limiting moral action to the purely private sphere, and by restricting the public sphere to purely instrumental behavior, this bifurcation has engendered a crisis of citizenship, legitimation, and political obligation" (1).

Bifurcation, separation of the private and public—that it seems to me is what the argument track is all about, at least, that is, when students are told what issues to argue and which authorities to depend upon. They can engage in "purely instrumental behavior" shuffling around quotes and sources to fulfill assignments. Jeanne and Paul survived by refusing to separate, by refusing to listen, refusing to be taught. They simply went about their business, turning their own life's experience to rational account. For them, for all effective and mature and honest writers, as Brown explains,

> . . . the formal protocols of reason and decision making function largely as covering accounts for purposive reality constructions that were put together in response to local economic requirements, career pressures, and other nonrational contingencies. All of us—scientists included—are continually engaged as on-the-street or at-the-lab-bench rhetoricians. Thus, rather than being a guiding rule of individual, organizational, or scientific life, rationality turns out to be a rhetorical achievement—a symbolic product that is constructed through speech and actions which in themselves are nonrational. (77)

Thus, we try to *sound* rational as we argue our very personal points of view. Rationality *follows* rhetoric, emerges *from* discourse. We must start with honest, personal writing and move to honest personal writing about public issues. To proceed the other way, starting with distant issues and asking students to go and be rational about them reveals our own fear of feeling, our own discomfort with empowering student writers. It is a practice as insane and bizarre and—alas—common as using the great works of the world's literature to make students memorize the meanings of literary terms.

---

[1] This debate continues in the issue of *PRE/TEXT* 11 (1990) edited by Peter Elbow. In a pyrotechnical display of advanced academic name-calling, Stephen North and David Bartholomae argue their cases, far removed from classrooms. My concern here, however, is with the actual writing of students.

[2] Jim W. Corder reaches the same conclusion—by a very different route—in "Argument as Emergence, Rhetoric as Love," *Rhetoric Review* 4 (1985): 16–32.

Works Cited

Bakhtin, M. M. "Discourse in the Novel." *The Dialogic Imagination.* Ed. Michael Holquist. Trans. Caryl Emerson and Michael Holquist. Austin: U of Texas P, 1981. 259–422.

———. "The Problem of Speech Genres." *Speech Genres and Other Late Essays.* Ed. Caryl Emerson and Michael Holquist. Trans. Vern W. McGee. Austin: U of Texas P, 1986. 66–102.

Bartholomae, David, and Anthony Petrosky. *Facts, Artifacts, and Counterfacts: Theory and Method for a Reading and Writing Course.* Upper Montclair, NJ: Boynton/Cook, 1986.

Brown, Richard Harvey. *Society as Text: Essays on Rhetoric, Reason, and Reality.* Chicago: U of Chicago P, 1987.

Connors, Robert J. "Personal Writing Assignments." *College Composition and Communication* 38 (1987): 166–83.

Cooper, Marilyn M., and Cynthia L. Selfe. "Computer Conferences and Learning: Authority, Resistance, and Internally Persuasive Discourse." *College English* 52 (1990): 847–69.

Elbow, Peter. "Reflections on Academic Discourse: How It Relates to Freshmen and Colleagues." *College English* 53 (1991): 135–55.

Harris, Jeanette. *Expressive Discourse.* Dallas: Southern Methodist UP, 1990.

Lunsford, Andrea, and Robert Connors. *The St. Martin's Handbook.* New York: St. Martin's, 1989.

Miller, Robert K. *The Informed Argument: A Multidisciplinary Reader and Guide,* 2nd ed. New York: Harcourt, 1989.

Nystrand, Martin. *The Structure of Written Communication: Studies in Reciprocity between Writers and Readers.* Orlando, FL: Academic Press, 1986.

Patricia Nelson Limerick, "Dancing with Professors: The Trouble with Academic Prose"

Patricia Nelson Limerick, champion of clear and accessible academic writing, comes—like another well-known teacher and writer, the late Richard Marius, Director of Expository Writing at Harvard—not from the field of English but from history. She earned her PhD in American Studies from Yale (1980) and, after a four-year stint teaching at Harvard, joined the faculty at the University of Colorado (CU) at Boulder as a Western American historian with particular interests in ethnic history and environmental history. *The Legacy of Conquest* is her best-known work and has had a major impact on her field; *Something in the Soil*, focusing on "the atomic west," is one of her most recent books. However, always an advocate for taking academic knowledge outside the bounds of the university, she continues to publish in places like *The New York Times*, *USA Today*, the *Denver Post*, and *The Chronicle of Higher Education*; to speak to audiences as diverse as the Bureau of Land Management Summit Conference and the

International High Level Radioactive Waste Conference; and to serve as adviser for productions like Ken Burns's PBS series, *The West*. Although she has received too many awards and honorary appointments to mention, ranging from Official Fool of the University of Colorado (1987–2008) to MacArthur Fellow (1995), she has made time regularly to teach—as part of CU's Minority Arts and Sciences Program—a summer bridge class on writing for first-year students of colour.

DANCING WITH PROFESSORS: THE TROUBLE WITH ACADEMIC PROSE

In ordinary life, when a listener cannot understand what someone has said, this is the usual exchange:

> Listener: I cannot understand what you are saying.

> Speaker: Let me try to say it more clearly.

But in scholarly writing in the late 20th century, other rules apply. This is the implicit exchange:

> Reader: I cannot understand what you are saying.

> Academic Writer: Too bad. The problem is that you are an unsophisticated and untrained reader. If you were smarter, you would understand me.

The exchange remains implicit, because no one wants to say, "This doesn't make any sense," for fear that the response, "It would, if you were smarter," might actually be true.

While we waste our time fighting over ideological conformity in the scholarly world, horrible writing remains a far more important problem. For all their differences, most right-wing scholars and most left-wing scholars share a common allegiance to a cult of obscurity. Left, right and center all hide behind the idea that unintelligible prose indicates a sophisticated mind. The politically correct and the politically incorrect come together in the violence they commit against the English language.

University presses have certainly filled their quota every year, in dreary monographs, tangled paragraphs and impenetrable sentences. But trade publishers have also violated the trust of innocent and hopeful readers. As a prime example of unprovoked assaults on innocent words, consider the verbal behavior of Allan Bloom in *The Closing of the American Mind*, published by a large mainstream press. Here is a sample:

> If openness means to "go with the flow," it is necessarily an accommodation to the present. That present is so closed to doubt about so many things impeding the progress of its principles that unqualified openness to it would mean forgetting the despised alternatives to it, knowledge of which makes us aware of what is doubtful in it.

Is there a reader so full of blind courage as to claim to know what this sentence means? Remember, the book in which this remark appeared was a lamentation over the failings of today's *students*, a call to arms to return to tradition and standards in education. And yet, in 20 years of paper grading, I do not recall many sentences that asked, so pathetically, to be put out of their misery.

Jump to the opposite side of the political spectrum from Allan Bloom, and literary grace makes no noticeable gains. Contemplate this breathless, indefatigable sentence from the geographer Allan Pred, and Mr. Pred and Bloom seem, if only in literary style, to be soul mates:

> If what is at stake is an understanding of geographical and historical variations in the sexual division of productive and reproductive labor, of contemporary local and regional variations in female wage labor and women's work outside the formal economy, of on-the-ground variations in the everyday content of women's lives, inside and outside of their families, then it must be recognized that, at some nontrivial level, none of the corporal practices associated with these variations can be severed from spatially and temporally specific linguistic practices, from languages that not only enable the conveyance of instructions, commands, role depictions and operating rules, but that also regulate and control, that normalize and spell out the limits of the permissible through the conveyance of disapproval, ridicule, and reproach.

In this example, 124 words, along with many ideas, find themselves crammed into one sentence. In their company, one starts to get panicky. "Throw open the windows; bring in the oxygen tanks!" one wants to shout. "These words and ideas are nearly suffocated. Get them air!" And yet the condition of this desperately packed and crowded sentence is a perfectly familiar one to readers of academic writing, readers who have simply learned to suppress the panic.

Everyone knows that today's college students cannot write, but few seem willing to admit that the professors who denounce them are not doing much better. The problem is so blatant there are signs that students are catching on. In my American history survey course last semester, I presented a few writing rules that I intended to enforce inflexibly. The students looked more and more peevish; they looked as if they were about to run down the hall, find a telephone, place an urgent call and demand that someone from the A.C.L.U. rush up to campus to sue me for interfering with their First Amendment rights to compose unintelligible, misshapen sentences.

Finally one aggrieved student raised her hand and said, "You are telling *us* not to write long, dull sentences, but most of our assigned reading is *full* of long, dull sentences."

As this student was beginning to recognize, when professors undertake to appraise and improve student writing, the blind are leading the blind. It is, in truth, difficult to persuade students to write well when they find so few good examples in their assigned reading.

The current social and political context for higher education makes this whole issue pressing. In Colorado, as in most states, the legislators are convinced that the university is neglecting students and wasting state resources on pointless research. Under those circumstances, the miserable writing habits of professors pose a direct and concrete danger to higher education. Rather than going to the state legislature, proudly presenting stacks of the faculty's compelling and engaging publications, you end up hoping that the lawmakers stay out of the library and stay away, especially, from the periodical room, with its piles of academic journals. The habits of academic writers lend powerful support to the impression that research is a waste of the writers' time and of the public's money.

Why do so many professors write bad prose?

* * *

Ten years ago, I heard a classics professor say the single most important thing—in my opinion—that anyone has said about professors: "We must remember," he declared, "that professors are the ones nobody wanted to dance with in high school."

This is an insight that lights up the universe—or at least the university. It is a proposition that every entering freshman should be told, and it is certainly a proposition that helps to explain the problem of academic writing. What one sees in professors, repeatedly, is exactly the manner that anyone would adopt after a couple of sad evenings sidelined under the crepe-paper streamers in the gym, sitting on a folding chair while everyone else danced. Dignity, for professors, perches precariously on how well they can convey this message: "I am immersed in some very important thoughts, which unsophisticated people could not even begin to understand. Thus, I would not *want* to dance, even if one of you unsophisticated people were to ask me."

Think of this, then, the next time you look at an unintelligible academic text. "I would not *want* the attention of a wide reading audience, even if a wide audience were to *ask* for me." Isn't that exactly what the pompous and pedantic tone of the classically academic writer conveys?

* * *

Professors are often shy, timid and even fearful people, and under these circumstances, dull, difficult prose can function as a kind of protective camouflage. When you write typical academic prose, it is nearly impossible to make a strong, clear statement. The benefit here is that no one can attack your position, say you are wrong or even raise questions about the accuracy of what you have said, if they cannot *tell* what you have said. In those terms, awful, indecipherable prose is its own form of armor, protecting the fragile, sensitive thoughts of timid souls.

The best texts for helping us understand the academic world are, of course, Lewis Carroll's *Alice's Adventures in Wonderland* and *Through the Looking Glass.* Just as devotees of Carroll would expect, he has provided us with the best analogy for understanding the origin and function of bad academic writing. Tweedledee and Tweedledum have quite a heated argument over a rattle. They become so angry that they decide to fight. But before they fight, they go off to gather various devices of padding and protection: "bolsters, blankets, hearthrugs, tablecloths, dish covers and coal scuttles." Then, with Alice's help in tying and fastening, they transform these household items into armor. Alice is not impressed: "'Really, they'll be more like bundles of old clothes than anything else, by the time they're ready!' she said to herself, as she arranged a bolster round the neck of Tweedledee, 'to keep his head from being cut off,' as he said." Why this precaution? Because, Tweedledee explains, "it's one of the most serious things that can possibly happen to one in a battle—to get one's head cut off."

Here, in the brothers' anxieties and fears, we have an exact analogy for the problems of academic writing. The next time you look at a classically professorial sentence—long, tangled, obscure, jargonized, polysyllabic—think of Tweedledum and Tweedledee dressed for battle, and see if those timid little thoughts, concealed under layers of clauses and phrases, do not remind you of those agitated but cautious brothers, arrayed in their bolsters, blankets, dish covers and coal scuttles. The motive, too, is similar. Tweedledum and Tweedledee were in terror of being hurt, and so they padded themselves so thoroughly that they could not be hurt; nor, for that matter, could they move. A properly dreary, inert sentence has exactly the same benefit; it protects its writer from sharp disagreement, while it also protects him from movement.

Why choose camouflage and insulation over clarity and directness? Tweedledee, of course, spoke for everyone, academic or not, when he confessed his fear: It is indeed, as he said, "one of the most serious things that can possibly happen to one in a battle—to get one's head cut off." Under those circumstances, logic says: tie the bolster around the neck, and add a protective hearthrug or two. Pack in another qualifying clause or two. Hide behind the passive-voice verb. Preface any assertion with a phrase like "it could be argued" or "a case could be made." Protecting one's neck does seem to be the way to keep one's head from being cut off.

Graduate school implants in many people the belief that there are terrible penalties to be paid for writing clearly, especially writing clearly in ways that challenge established thinking in the field. And yet, in academic warfare (and I speak as a veteran), your head and your neck are rarely in serious danger. You can remove the bolster and the hearthrug. Your opponents will try to whack at you, but they seldom, if ever, land a blow—in large part because they are themselves so wrapped in protective camouflage and insulation that they lose both mobility and accuracy.

* * *

So we have a widespread pattern of professors protecting themselves from injury by wrapping their ideas in dull prose, and yet the danger they try to fend off is not a genuine danger. Express yourself clearly, and it is unlikely that either your head—or, more important, your tenure—will be cut off.

How, then, do we save professors from themselves? Fearful people are not made courageous by scolding; they need to be coaxed and encouraged. But how do we do that, especially when this particular form of fearfulness masks itself as pomposity, aloofness and an assumed air of superiority?

Fortunately, we have available the world's most important and illuminating story on the difficulty of persuading people to break out of habits of timidity, caution and unnecessary fear. I borrow this story from Larry McMurtry, one of my rivals in the interpreting of the American West, though I am putting this story to a use that Mr. McMurtry did not intend.

* * *

In a collection of his essays, *In a Narrow Grave*, Mr. McMurtry wrote about the weird process of watching his book *Horseman, Pass By* being turned into the movie *Hud*. He arrived in the Texas Panhandle a week or two after filming had started, and he was particularly anxious to learn how the buzzard scene had gone. In that scene, Paul Newman was supposed to ride up and discover a dead cow, look up at a tree branch lined with buzzards and, in his distress over the loss of the cow, fire his gun at one of the buzzards. At that moment, all of the other buzzards were supposed to fly away into the blue Panhandle sky.

But when Mr. McMurtry asked people how the buzzard scene had gone, all he got, he said, were "stricken looks."

The first problem, it turned out, had to do with the quality of the available local buzzards—who proved to be an excessively scruffy group. So more appealing, more photogenic buzzards had to be flown in from some distance and at considerable expense.

But then came the second problem: how to keep the buzzards sitting on the tree branch until it was time for their cue to fly.

That seemed easy. Wire their feet to the branch, and then, after Paul Newman fires his shot, pull the wire, releasing their feet, thus allowing them to take off.

But as Mr. McMurtry said in an important and memorable phrase, the film makers had not reckoned with the "mentality of buzzards." With their feet wired, the buzzards did not have enough mobility to fly. But they did have enough mobility to pitch forward.

So that's what they did: with their feet wired, they tried to fly, pitched forward and hung upside down from the dead branch, with their wings flapping.

I had the good fortune a couple of years ago to meet a woman who had been an extra for this movie, and she added a detail that Mr. McMurtry left out of his essay: namely, the buzzard circulatory system does not work upside down, and so, after a moment or two of flapping, the buzzards passed out.

Twelve buzzards hanging upside down from a tree branch: this was not what Hollywood wanted from the West, but that's what Hollywood had produced.

And then we get to the second stage of buzzard psychology. After six or seven episodes of pitching forward, passing out, being revived, being replaced on the branch and pitching forward again, the buzzards gave up. Now, when you pulled the wire and released their feet, they sat there, saying in clear, nonverbal terms: "We *tried* that before. It did not work. We are not going to try it again." Now the film makers had to fly in a high-powered animal trainer to restore buzzard self-esteem. It was all a big mess; Larry McMurtry got a wonderful story out of it; and we, in turn, get the best possible parable of the workings of habit and timidity.

How does the parable apply? In any and all disciplines, you go to graduate school to have your feet wired to the branch. There is nothing inherently wrong with that: scholars should have some common ground, share some background assumptions, hold some similar habits of mind. This gives you, quite literally, your footing. And yet, in the process of getting your feet wired, you have some awkward moments, and the intellectual equivalent of pitching forward and hanging upside down. That experience—especially if you do it in a public place like a graduate seminar—provides no pleasure. One or two rounds of that humiliation, and the world begins to seem like a very treacherous place. Under those circumstances, it does indeed seem to be the choice of wisdom *to sit quietly on the branch*, to sit without even the *thought* of flying, since even the thought might be enough to tilt the balance and set off another round of flapping, fainting and embarrassment.

Yet when scholars get out of graduate school and get Ph.D.'s, and, even more important, when scholars get tenure, the wire is truly pulled. Their feet are free. They can fly wherever and whenever they like. Yet by then the second stage of buzzard psychology has taken hold, and they refuse to fly. The wire is pulled, and yet the buzzards sit there, hunched and grumpy. If they teach in a university with a graduate program, they actively instruct young buzzards in the necessity of keeping their youthful feet on the branch.

This is a very well-established pattern, and it is the ruination of scholarly activity in the modern world. Many professors who teach graduate students think that one of their principal duties is to train the students in the conventions of academic writing.

I do not believe that professors enforce a standard of dull writing on graduate students in order to be cruel. They demand dreariness because they think that dreariness is in the students' best interests. Professors believe that a dull writing style is an academic survival skill because they think that is what editors want, both editors of academic journals *and* editors of university presses. What we have here is a chain of misinformation and misunderstanding, where everyone thinks that the other guy is the one who demands dull, impersonal prose.

Let me say again what is at stake here: universities and colleges are currently embattled, distrusted by the public and state funding institutions. As distressing as this situation is, it provides the perfect setting and the perfect timing for declaring an end to scholarly publication as a series of guarded conversations between professors.

The redemption of the university, especially in terms of the public's appraisal of the value of research and publication, requires all the writers who have something they want to publish to ask themselves the question: Does this have to be a closed communication, shutting out all but specialists willing to fight their way through thickets of jargon? Or can this be an open communication, engaging specialists with new information and new thinking, but also offering an invitation to nonspecialists to learn from this study, to grasp its importance and, by extension, to find concrete reasons to see value in the work of the university?

This is a country desperately in need of wisdom, and of clearly reasoned conviction and vision. And that, at the bedrock, is the reason behind this campaign to save professors from themselves and to detoxify academic prose. The context is a bit different, but the statement that Willy Loman made to his sons in *Death of a Salesman* keeps coming to mind: "The woods are burning, boys, the woods are burning." In a society confronted by a faltering economy, racial and ethnic conflicts, and environmental disasters, "the woods are burning," and since we so urgently need everyone's contribution in putting some of those fires out, there is no reason to indulge professorial vanity or timidity.

Ego is, of course, the key obstacle here. As badly as most of them write, professors are nonetheless proud and sensitive writers, resistant to criticism. But even the most desperate cases can be redeemed and persuaded to think of writing as a challenging craft, not as existential trauma. A few years ago, I began to look at carpenters and other artisans as the emotional model for writers. A carpenter, let us say, makes a door for a cabinet. If the door does not hang straight, the carpenter does not say, "I will *not* change that door; it is an expression of my individuality; who cares if it will not close?" Instead, the carpenter removes the door and works on it until it fits. That attitude, applied to writing, could be our salvation. If we thought more like carpenters, academic writers could find a route out of the trap of ego and vanity. Escaped from that trap, we could simply work on successive drafts until what we have to say is clear.

Colleges and universities are filled with knowledgeable, thoughtful people who have been effectively silenced by an awful writing style, a style with its flaws concealed behind a smokescreen of sophistication and professionalism. A coalition of academic writers, graduate advisers, journal editors, university press editors and trade publishers can seize this moment—*and pull the wire*. The buzzards can be set free—free to leave that dead tree branch, free to regain their confidence, free to soar.

STUDENT WRITING

Please turn to Suzanne LiaBraaten's essay, "New Beginning," in Conversation 7 for one first-year student's reaction to the Bartholomae–Elbow debate.

A NEW PRACTICE TO TAKE FORWARD

CREATE AN ANNOTATED BIBLIOGRAPHY, PART 1:

One method for writing strong academic papers

You know what a bibliography or list of works-cited is: the list at the end of a paper that lets everyone know which books or articles or newspapers or websites or other sources you drew from to do your writing. You may have thought of such lists as a nuisance late at night, the last mechanical detail that stood between you and an extra hour of sleep before the paper was due—or, even more dismissively, as just an irritating hoop to jump through to prove that you didn't plagiarize and that you did actually do some significant research. You wouldn't be alone either if you found yourself mystified by the cryptic "syntax" required in different disciplines—MLA (Modern Language Association) style for English papers, APA (American Psychological Association) for psychology papers, CBE (Council of Biology Editors) for papers in the biological sciences, and a range of other documentation styles for everything from law to history to medicine.

But you probably have never thought of your bibliography in the way most instructors think of it—as evidence that you've made a serious attempt to recognize and enter into an ongoing conversation. The bibliography literally speaks volumes: it shows that you acknowledge that you're not the first person to be curious about a particular subject, that you recognize some of the major "players" in this particular conversation, that you know something about what everyone agrees on and disagrees about in this particular knowledge community, as well as what they think they know about this subject now and what they all still want to know or to figure out. And as a result, you can position your own contribution to the conversation in a reasonable way, claiming neither too much for it nor too little.

A common mistake some students fall into is assuming that they're simply supposed to summarize and present the research that's been done by everyone else. Of course, a student *can* earn passing grades for writing papers like that—such papers can be plodding, but if they're thorough, they at least show that the student has done some careful reading. But stronger papers realize that, whether or not the instructor already knows the research or the ideas summarized in the paper—in which case the instructor doesn't *need* the summary and may, in fact, be bored by it—an effective piece of academic writing has to go *beyond* summary. This doesn't mean that papers shouldn't occasionally contain moments of summary, but that the summary—when it appears—is always in the service of some higher goal, that of thinking a question through.

Whatever your paper is about, in whatever field, there's one sure-fire way to avoid tedious and meaningless summary. And that's to put all the summaries in your bibliography. We call bibliographies with summaries of each item **annotated bibliographies**. As you do your research, create the bibliography as you go along. Computers make this simple. Start your works-cited file on the computer on the very first day you start your reading and research; find out which format your instructor requires (MLA, APA, Chicago, CBE, whatever) and create a full and complete entry each time you read through something that relates to your project. No matter how much you've jotted on notecards or how much you've underlined a photocopied text, force yourself to inkshed a full and clear *summary*—one or two detailed paragraphs is enough—of what you've read, emphasizing the material that speaks to the focus of your project. Force yourself to make a clear statement of what you think that author's main argument or research conclusions were. Note anything else that's essential to your project: methodology, limitations, special strengths and weaknesses of the work you've just investigated.

By the way, make sure to make backup copies of your bibliography as you go along. Don't ever trust a computer's hard drive entirely; always have backup copies on disks that can be used on another computer in case your own develops sudden problems, which—if it's going to happen—will invariably happen at the worst possible moment, just minutes before you were going to make your first and only backup copy.

When you finally go to write your paper, you'll have summaries of every major source to draw on; you'll be amazed how much easier it is to develop an overview of a piece of intellectual territory with these summaries in your head or close by. If you want to make sure that your instructor appreciates all the research you've done, hand the annotated bibliography in with your final project—your instructor doesn't need to read it, but handing it in will help you realize that you don't need to include any of that summary in your paper. Your paper, instead, can concentrate on developing your own argument, drawing on your sources only as you need to in order to move your argument forward or to critique it.

Meanwhile, when your paper is done and it's time to create the final works-cited list, all you need to do is make an electronic file copy of your full bibliography (make sure to keep the original by changing the filename when you save), delete whatever you didn't use, and then put everything in the proper order. Of course, the proper order will depend on which citation style you're required to use. In MLA citation style, for instance, authors and texts are the most important things, so a works-cited list is alphabetized first by authors' last names and then, if there are several works by the same author, by title. Other styles that emphasize dates over text will list multiple works by the same author chronologically instead of alphabetically. But all the hard work of typing details in the appropriate citation format will have been done bit by bit over a period of weeks—and you won't have any of those last-minute panics of realizing that you no longer have a copy of the material and thus cannot find the necessary citation information. You might even get that extra hour of sleep.

Examples

Annotations can range from detailed and thorough to pithy, and both kinds are valuable—they meet different needs. Marta Currah's annotation of an Elbow essay in Conversation 3 is a good example of a detailed annotation; Kelly Davidson's annotation of Root's essay in Conversation 6 is briefer (but then, so is Root's essay). Keep in mind that useful one-paragraph annotations have been written of 500-page books, however, so there's no mechanical guideline to follow. Authors write the annotations they need to write in specific situations, for specific audiences and purposes.

Ideas for Collaboration

Annotated bibliographies make excellent collaborative projects. Individual class members can be assigned the task of preparing particular annotations by a certain date, say the date on which all annotations are to be combined into one large computer file. Everyone in class can then use that file as a base works-cited list to work from, keying in any necessary additional sources that each individual paper is in conversation with. Or, several students could draft annotations of the same book or article in order to collaborate in the production of one final annotation combining the strengths of their individual attempts: then only their final, jointly produced version would be included in the class bibliography.

ESSAY IDEA

After creating a thoughtful annotated bibliography on a subject that interests you, write an essay that enters into conversation with the authors listed there. Keep reminding yourself as you write that your reader can always refer to the bibliography annotations for a summary of a particular author's work, so include in your essay only those details that are essential to take the reader along on your own line of reasoning.

CONVERSATION 5:

The Grammar-as-Style Debate: Does Grammar Instruction Hurt or Help Student Writing?

INTRODUCTION

> All I know about grammar is its infinite power. To shift the structure of a sentence alters the meaning of that sentence, as definitely and inflexibly as the position of a camera alters the meaning of the object photographed.
>
> Joan Didion, "Why I Write" 7

> Thus all these tiny scratches give us breadth and heft and depth. A world that has only periods is a world without inflections. It is a world without shade. It has a music without sharps and flats. It is a martial music. It has a jackboot rhythm. Words cannot bend and curve. A comma, by comparison, catches the gentle drift of the mind in thought, turning in on itself and back on itself, reversing, redoubling and returning along the course of its own sweet river music; while the semicolon brings clauses and thoughts together with all the silent discretion of a hostess arranging guests around her dinner table.
>
> Pico Iyer, "In Praise of the Humble Comma" 6

> He is an old and experienced man in vice and wickedness he is never found in opposing the works of iniquity he takes delight in the downfall of neighbors he never rejoiced in the prosperity of his fellow creatures he is always ready to assist in destroying the peace of society he takes no pleasure in serving the Lord he is uncommonly diligent in sowing discord among his friends and acquaintances . . . .

The last passage above would be described by most people in our culture as an "ungrammatical" sentence or, another way of putting it, an example of "bad grammar." Part of what we hope to do in this chapter is convince you that, in fact, the **grammar** of this passage is just fine, even though the lines are confusing because they require some further decisions to be made about sentence boundaries and meaning (decisions that will then require us to attend to "details" of punctuation, usage, and mechanics, details that are in this case clearly crucial). But the lines are not meaningless, even if the meaning could go off in one of two directions; they are obviously written by an English speaker who not only knows the *expected* word order of English sentences but knows how to play around with it.

When you hear the word "writing," you probably think of grammar; and you probably think of grammar in terms of mechanical correctness primarily—that is, you probably assume that good writing means having no run-ons, no spelling or capitalization errors, no sentence fragments, and no punctuation mistakes.

You are not alone. A lot of people make those assumptions: they link grammar to correctness and then link grammar-as-correctness to writing. In fact, thinking about what grammar is and what role it should play in the teaching of writing (if any) leads us into one of the major debates in the field of composition, a debate we invite you to join. You might be surprised to learn, for instance, that many writing teachers felt—as Patrick Hartwell did—that this issue was settled by 1985: the conclusions from years of research were in, that the teaching of grammar either had *no* effect on the improvement of student writing or had a *negative* effect (because time given to drills in formal *grammar* instruction was time taken away from *writing* practice and instruction).

But since 1985 another group of scholars has been questioning those research results. Martha Kolln, Cheryl Glenn, Rei Noguchi, Cornelia Paraskevas, and Brock Haussamen (among others) have been arguing that the research didn't focus on teaching grammar the way they themselves teach it. They don't teach grammar as a set of rules writers have to obey; instead, they teach **rhetorical grammar, grammar as style**, a rich resource writers can draw on consciously to create certain powerful effects. They all agreed with Kolln's assessment that the earlier research findings merely concluded "that grammar should not be taught *in isolation*, as an end in itself. . . . not that it should not be taught at all":

> Unfortunately, the result of the research has been to drive grammar instruction out of the composition classroom, rather than into it, where it belongs. (Kolln vi)

To understand the relation between grammar and writing as this second group of scholars understands it, we need to remind ourselves of ancient Greece, a place and time when students were taught grammar as part of a rich language-arts program that included logic, rhetoric, and grammar. As Cheryl Glenn reminds us in her essay "When Grammar Was a Language Art," grammar—the study of the written form of language (*gramma*, after all, just means *letter* in Greek)—was central to the composition classroom in classical times and students, in mastering that art, "were nourished and supported" by it, able to "develop a range of styles that complemented as well as reinforced the substance of their compositions" (27–28). Glenn argues for integrating grammar into the teaching of writing for contemporary students because it can lead "them forward, orienting them toward what they can learn to do well rather than focusing on what they do wrong (the focus of too much contemporary grammar work)" (28).

This ancient tradition of grammar as the study of **style** continued almost unchanged until the 1700s. That's when "the language mavens," as Pinker calls them, decided that the English language needed improvement because it was changing: they noticed, for instance, that the language of their contemporaries was quite different from

Shakespeare's language. For them, change meant corruption; they needed to take measures to fix language (*ascertain* is the term they used) and keep it from changing ever again. So they set up rules that the users of language were supposed to follow, rules that were often based on Latin (which belongs to the Romance language family, whereas English belongs to the Germanic family), rules that were hard to remember because they were unnatural. Here are a couple of them that you undoubtedly know: don't end sentences with a preposition ("this is something I won't put up with" is a sentence they would consider wrong); don't split infinitives (something that is *impossible* to do in Latin, a language in which all infinitives are one word, but that is all too possible in English—"**to** boldly **go** where no one has gone before" is wrong according to these self-appointed guardians of the language).

But these arbitrary rules were obviously never part of the grammar that students had studied for nearly two thousand years in order to write more powerfully. These rules come from a different kind of grammar, a grammar whose purpose is to tell you that there is only one acceptable way of using language and that any deviation from that way is absolutely wrong. These are the rules that Pinker, in this chapter, calls **prescriptive rules** (because they try to "prescribe" how we should write and talk). Pinker clearly prefers **descriptive grammar**, the kind of grammar that linguists are interested in when they do their research and want to "describe" how people actually *do* speak and write. In descriptive grammar, the terms *correct* and *incorrect* as the language mavens would use them are meaningless.

Wait a minute, you may be thinking—are there *three* different kinds of grammar I have to keep track of now—grammar-as-style, descriptive grammar, prescriptive grammar? One was bad enough!

Actually, Patrick Hartwell described *five* different kinds of grammar (but you don't need to keep track of them—they are described briefly, however, in Paraskevas and Sargent's essay in this Conversation, pages 271–273). Linguist Brock Haussamen suggests in a recent essay that we keep track of just *two* kinds of grammar, public and private (see his "Public Grammar and Private Grammar: The Social Orientation of Grammar," posted at the website associated with this text: www.sargent.nelson.com). But there is one of Hartwell's categories that you should know about because it will make you feel much more confident about your writing—Grammar One. The easiest way to describe it is to give the example Hartwell uses himself: he finds that when he asks students to arrange in "natural order" the five words "French, the, young, girls, four," all native speakers quickly arrange the five words in their proper sequence without any difficulty, but none can explain the rules governing this order (189–190). Try it yourself with a group of friends. Hartwell concludes that Grammar One "is eminently usable knowledge—the way we make our life through language—but it is not accessible knowledge; in a profound sense, we do not know that we have it" (190). Nor do we need to know it consciously in order to speak or to write and make sense to other people. All native speakers are powerful "knowers" of Grammar One, just by virtue of their having been born with functioning ears and mouths into a community that uses a particular language. Grammar One is amazing because it allows native speakers to combine words into millions of different complex sentences with embedded structures and to understand and produce sentences they have never heard before. Obviously, Grammar One is what the field of linguistics focuses on, is what linguists are describing when they speak of *descriptive* grammar.

So if we all know Grammar One, why should there be any debate? We shouldn't have to study something we already know, right?

Consider a closely related debate, one that the essays in this section also reflect on. If we stop talking in terms of *prescriptive* grammar, in terms of correctness and error, we still have the question of **register**—that is, what varieties of language are *appropriate* to use in different situations? Many think of this as a conflict between **Standard English** versus "bad English" (and many think their version of English is substandard and is thus bad English). But to a linguist, the term "bad English" is meaningless: it couldn't even refer to garbled "word salad" (Pinker's term for gibberish), let alone to actual varieties of English, since gibberish would be called simply "non-English" by a linguist. Since all native speakers of a language know Grammar One without being aware of their actual knowledge, they generate *meaningful* statements in English, not word salad. You know, for example, how to put the words "child flowers cranky the three bought" in their proper order even though you don't know how you have that knowledge or why the order you chose is the only one possible for English. No native speakers, for example, would say that the order is "three the bought child cranky flowers"; we all agree that the proper order for the words we gave you is "the cranky child bought three flowers."

But what about sentences like "He ain't smart"? Aren't these evidence of bad grammar? Shouldn't the person who said something like that have to take remedial English in order to learn proper English? Well . . . no! Even that sentence is fine from a linguistic perspective; it follows a pattern, a rule, and it is a rule that a lot of native speakers follow when they create English sentences (subject, verb, complement). The issue with this sentence isn't that it is *bad*—it is simply written in non-Standard English. This sentence could be perfect in an e-mail to a friend, yet risky or inappropriate in a job application letter.

Standard English, you may think, is the same as *prescriptive* English. Let's look into this more closely, in order to debunk this myth. Standard English is a fairly flexible variety of English, the variety we find in newspapers and magazines, a variety characterized by the absence of stigmatized forms. It is an idealized form, a public grammar (in Haussamen's terms), a form that we use in public life, the form that "our society approves for general use and defines as literacy" (3). It is not *better* than other forms of English—it is simply the form that by convention we have chosen to use in our public life.

This isn't simply an issue of playing with words. It is a fundamentally different way of looking at language, a way of allowing both dimensions of language—the private and public—into writing. Obviously, every student has the right to learn public grammar because it is the grammar of power: everyone knows how hurtful it can be to be dismissed as ignorant simply because one has accidentally used a non-standard form in a situation where using the standard form mattered. And such incidents can have huge consequences—not being hired for a job, not getting into graduate school, not being considered classy enough to marry into a particular family. But it's not a matter of set rules or prescriptions: it's a matter of decisions and choices. It's not a matter of forbidding certain non-standard forms and expressions (which can be apt or funny or powerful in certain situations, and many of which gradually find their way into standard English over time), but of finding language appropriate for different audiences and occasions.

Style and Register

If we're going to talk about grammar as style, we had better explain what we mean by **style**. And we should perhaps emphasize first what we do *not* mean by it: we don't think of style as the icing on the cake or, to shift similes, the coat of varnish put on after a solid piece of furniture is built. Instead, style is an integral part of any piece of writing from invention on, from the moment words go down on a page in some meaningful order. Close attention to language—to the sounds of words, to the pace and rhythm of sentences, to the directions given by punctuation—doesn't necessarily come last in the writing process: stylistic concerns are never simply cosmetic, never just decoration, something extra. A writer's style—the way a writer puts words in order, the kinds of words that writer tends to work with, even that writer's characteristic punctuation moves—shapes the meaning of the text at a deep level. But also, just as a writer can have many voices, a writer can have many styles depending on genre constraints, on the social action that particular writer wants each text to perform.

Again, it's about choices. Corbett's well-known statement is a good place to begin: "style represent[s] the choices that an author made from the **lexical** and **syntactical resources** of the language" (24—boldface ours). The resources of the language are mainly words (**lexical**) and the arrangements into which those words can be put (**syntactical**). The kinds of words we tend to use and the way we characteristically arrange them may lead people to describe our style as "high" or "low" or "middle" (or to use other more colourful words, "turgid" or "chatty"). Martin Joos described five registers along a continuum from the frozen and the formal to the consultative, the casual, and the intimate (*The Five Clocks*, as cited in Corbett, 24). Some experienced writers can move easily between these five registers, shifting into whichever one feels necessary or appropriate in a certain situation. So we're not locked helplessly into one style: the wider our working vocabulary, the more we know about possible ways to arrange words, the more choices we have and the more easily we can move from one register to another as needed.

Unfortunately, acquiring a wide range of choices—in terms of words or patterns of words—takes time, and we certainly don't have the time or space here to do more than hint at a few stylistic possibilities and concerns. It's obvious that having a rich working vocabulary—the words we actually use in our writing, as contrasted to the words we might recognize in other people's writing—will make it more likely that we'll be able to choose the exact word we want when we're writing. From analyzing Shakespeare's plays, scholars have been able to determine that he had a working vocabulary of over 21,000 words, the largest working vocabulary of any writer to date. And as we discovered in Conversation 1, Malcolm X was able to change his reading and writing abilities by one tactic alone, copying out the dictionary page by page and thus increasing his working vocabulary.

We can do something of the same thing for our dictionary, our lexicon, of **syntactical choices** (a linguist would call it a repertoire of syntactical choices)—that is, our understanding of what arrangements of words are possible and desirable (see Paraskevas and Sargent in this Conversation; also consult Katie Wood Ray's *Wondrous Words* for a wide range of syntactic structures to try out, from Taffy Sentences to See-Saw Sentences to Close-echo Effect Sentences to Runaway Sentences—not to be confused with run-on sentences!). But such sentence structures are not objects that serious writers manipulate mechanically; at times, it can almost seem the other way round, as if the sentence structure chose and shaped the author. As Corbett points out, the theory of knowledge we have, our worldview, tends to influence the characteristic word arrangements (**syntactic structures**) we use:

> Syntactic patterns also tell us something about the way a writer structures his or her thoughts. . . . The frequent occurrence, for instance, of balanced or antithetical patterns in Dr. Johnson's sentences suggests that he tended to structure his thinking in terms of parallel or opposing dichotomies. The many levels of subordination in John Henry Newman's prose suggests that he tended to see things in terms of hierarchies. The stringing together of independent clauses in Hemingway's prose, often with redundant use of coordinating conjunctions, indicates that Hemingway tended to view the phenomenal world as a flux of discrete, coordinate elements. Henry James's heavy use of parenthetical elements reflects a mind disposed to meticulous qualifications. And so on. (27)

But does this mean that there's no point in enlarging our range of choices? that we're helplessly going to write a certain way no matter what?

We don't believe that. We're committed to the idea that the more choices you have, the more fully you can express what you have to say and the more you can *have* to say. That is, your skill with language can *affect* your worldview, your theory of knowledge, what you notice and what you don't. All we have to do is remember Helen Keller's story and Malcolm X's transformation to be reminded of that.

But increasing our range of rhetorical choices depends to some extent on how conscious we are of the choices before us; and becoming more conscious of those choices requires some understanding of what we like to refer to as a "bare bones writer's grammar" (see this book's website at http://www.sargent.nelson.com). As you'll see below when we talk about cutting words out (unnecessary ones) and putting words in (words that will state our meaning more clearly and memorably), you can't get too far in such matters if you can't tell a sentence from a beanbag. Luckily, however, if you're a native speaker of English, you probably have more knowledge about sentence structure than you know you have—our job, as we see it here, is simply to show you how to access it.

As we look at a few stylistic concerns below, then, we'll try to make ourselves useful by focusing tightly on three areas:

eliminating wordiness (Lanham);

crafting sentences;

punctuating rhetorically (i.e., to create certain effects).

Our goal in doing this is not to teach you grammar for its own sake (though the structure of language is a fascinating subject of study), but for the purpose of increasing your range of rhetorical choices as you write.

Cutting Words Out: Eliminating Wordiness

Often as we write, our sentences are windy—unclear. We write the way we think. And if we're struggling to write something academic and difficult, struggling because we're not used to academic writing and its conventions, our language can show signs of stress (see Bartholomae's "Inventing the University" for specific examples). Our language can become stuffy, official, sometimes barely intelligible. Richard Lanham has linked such academic writing to what he calls "the official style," a style characterized by too many nouns and too few verbs, a style that is not active and moving and lively, but static. Sentences written in this style have what he refers to as a high "lard factor"; and Lanham warns us that prose, "unlike beefsteak, does not become more choice when marbled with fat" (12). Lanham offers strategies for making our lard-laden sentences lean, strategies that we're going to lay out for you quickly in this section.

We are not saying, however, that all sentences should be short! After all, as you can see in Paraskevas and Sargent's piece below, certain kinds of long sentences, at least those with interesting syntactic twists, are characteristic of fluent writing. All we—and Lanham—are saying is that every word in each sentence should be carefully placed, that every word should have a clear purpose and meaning. Otherwise, the sentence feels padded. Such sentences can cause readers to lose their way; readers wander about, trying to unpack the meaning, but failing to do so. Instead, they end up frustrated with the writer. In fact, they can quickly stop trusting the writer. Think of it this way: every word you put into a piece of writing is a contract with the reader. You're asking him or her to pay attention to it; by including it, you're implying that it's important. If it isn't necessary or important, you've violated the reader's trust. Each unnecessary word or phrase you cut will help you keep the reader's trust a little bit longer.

But we want to emphasize again—if something is necessary and important, it must be kept.

Here's a sentence Lanham claims has a high lard factor: "One can easily see that a kicking situation is taking place between Bill and Jim" (1). Does this sentence have any energy? You probably notice energy mainly in one word, "kicking." Does this sentence make you want to read on? Probably not. You might be thinking that you would never write such an obviously padded sentence for such a simple meaning—most likely you wouldn't. But we are using this as an extreme example, to show you what happens when padding becomes too much. Even in this case, though, the sentence can be repaired using Lanham's Paramedic Method. There are seven steps to this method of spotting and resuscitating a sick, sluggish sentence (Lanham 21):

1. Circle the prepositions.

2. Circle the "is" forms.

3. Ask, "Who is kicking who?"* [or "Who is doing what?"]

4. Put this "kicking" action [the main event] in a simple active verb [if possible].

5. Start fast—no mindless introductions.

6. Write out the sentence on a blank sheet of paper and look at its shape.

7. Read the sentence aloud with emphasis and feeling.

Let's try these steps or guidelines on the sentence above: "One can easily see that a kicking situation is taking place between Bill and Jim."

1. We have one preposition, "between."

2. We have one "is" or "to be" form: "is taking place."

3. We don't know who is kicking who (the sentence is unclear about this).

4. Since we're trying to "fix" this sentence, we'll make an executive decision that Bill is kicking Jim (note that the original sentence gives us no guidance here): "Bill kicks Jim."

5. Eliminate the mindless introduction: we can probably ditch "One can easily see that."

6. Writing the sentence out and looking at its shape, we notice that whoever is *doing* the kicking is hidden in a prepositional phrase near the end. We also notice that the action, the main event, is tucked away as a modifier in front of the vague noun "situation": "a kicking situation."

7. If we read the original version of fifteen words out loud, emphasis and feeling seem a bit silly. Of course, the slimmed down version of three words—"Bill kicks Jim"— seems a bit thin too, but at least it doesn't take quite so long being thin. And the lard factor is the relationship of the words we cut out (the fat) to the words we started with: twelve words were cut, fifteen were there to start with, so the fat factor was four-fifths or 80 percent. In other words, the original sentence was mostly lard, not much meat.

---

* Lanham usually ignores the who/whom distinction—which is clearly on the way out in Standard English—and uses only "who" throughout his book.

The big question is, have we lost anything important in slimming this sentence down (i.e., not just fat, but something essential like an arm or a leg or a heart or some vital organ)? We would argue no, in this case. But what do you think?

Let's try Lanham's guidelines on a more interesting sentence:

> For the writer, the practice of bad writing is harmful, for it results in an
> inhibition of his responses to intellectual and imaginative stimuli. (29)

1. First, we need to circle all the prepositions. Here, we have five ("for," "of," "in," "of," and "to"). We need to start our Paramedic Method with prepositions because when too many of them string along in a chain (like the three at the end), they can create confusion, dull the sentence, and take its energy/action away.

2. Circle the "be" verbs. There's nothing wrong with these verbs—in fact, they're useful for complex constructions like "are leaving" or "have been seen"; and they're essential to express certain states of being (as in, "He is happy"). Often, however, we can fall into a lazy habit of using "be" verbs as the main verb, the verb used to express the main event in the sentence. It's easy to see that "be" verbs are static (they just *are*, they express a state of being); if possible, we want a verb with movement and energy, a verb that catches our attention. We need to replace "is" with a more specific, accurate verb, a verb that will make the reader stop and take notice.

3. Technically, the "doer" or the subject is "the practice of bad writing"—is the word "practice" essential? Could we try a clearer, stronger subject? Maybe just "bad writing"?

4. What is the main event? It seems to be buried in the noun "inhibition." We need to make that into a verb, a verb that accurately expresses our meaning: perhaps the verb "inhibits" could replace the windy construction "it results in an inhibition"?

5. Opening with a prepositional phrase can work well in certain sentences, but here it seems to slow things down. Can we keep the word "writer" for later, but cut this opening phrase?

6. What does the overall shape of the sentence tell us? It seems to be put together of lots of small units (phrases) averaging three words long ("For the writer" + "the practice" + "of bad writing" + "is harmful" + "for it results" + "in an inhibition" + "of his responses" + "to intellectual and imaginative stimuli"). Five of these units are prepositional phrases, three of them trailing along together at the end. Prepositional phrases can be crucial to strong sentences, but too many of them dissipate the impact of each one—do we need all five?

7. It's hard to read this sentence with much emphasis or feeling—the many small phrases make the pace fairly predictable and broken up.

Let's now rewrite the sentence: Lanham suggests we decide on "Bad writing inhibits a writer's mind and imagination" (30). Thus, by following his own guidelines, Lanham has cut the lard factor by more than half, removing sixteen words from an original twenty-four (a fat factor of 66 percent). But has Lanham lost anything? We think he has. In his eagerness to cut fat, he has created some confusion. *Whose* writing harms the writer? In the first version, it's clearly the writer's own writing (the word "practice" seems to have been playing an important role after all). In the second version, it could be someone else's. Arguably the main event could be not "inhibits" but "harms"—that would depend on our purpose in writing the original sentence. If we were to say "Writing badly inhibits a writer's responses to intellectual and imaginative stimuli," we would be a bit closer to what the original sentence was trying to say (even if the lard factor is now closer to one-half than two-thirds). But we actually would prefer to use the verb "dulls" here instead of either "harms" or "inhibits" (since it seems to capture the meaning of both those verbs). Yet the verb "dulls" didn't appear anywhere in the original at all and perhaps is not exactly what the original author intended.

This business of revising sentences and eliminating wordiness is tricky. Sometimes we think Lanham's method works beautifully. Look at the following sentence and his revision (final lard factor of 66 percent again):

> **Original:** I think that all I can usefully say on this point is that in the normal course of their professional activities social anthropologists are usually concerned with the third of these alternatives, while the other two levels are treated as raw data for analysis.

> **Revision:** Social anthropologists usually concentrate on the third alternative, treating the other two as raw data.

We don't know what the "third alternative" is in either version, yet the second sentence, with its compression, makes more sense even so—the essential contrast has been heightened (between the "third" thing and "the other two"). And Lanham gained a lot here from his guideline about eliminating mindless introductions. We often need those to get ourselves going (like revving the engine of a car first thing in the morning)—but we can also often cut them after we've gotten our engine running. Lanham warns that a similar problem can occur at the ends of sentences, where he calls it "dieselizing—the prose engine continuing to run after the key has been turned off" (13).

The first step then is to analyze our sentences—to see the empty parts, the parts that make our sentences dull, tentative, indefinite. We've been building on a body metaphor so far (bones, muscles, skin, vital organs, fat), but Goldberg uses a different metaphor: "Writing is the act of burning through the fog in your mind. Don't carry the fog out on paper" (See Goldberg's "Make Statements" in this chapter). Choose whatever metaphor is most effective for you, but certainly Lanham's Paramedic Method and Goldberg's memorable advice should help you shape your sentences to be compact and full of energy, to cut to the chase. Remember that the goal of Lanham's Paramedic Method is to help you create tight, muscular sentences with no padding, sentences that reveal rather than hide your thoughts. But cutting just for the sake of cutting can be a danger as well. The need for tight sentences must be balanced against the need for longer, more fluent sentences that show a high degree of craftsmanship and polishing and that embody as much of your intended meaning as possible.

Putting Words Back In: Sentence Craft, Word Craft

The rhythm and pace of a sentence depends on its length, its words and their order. Sometimes we need to lengthen our sentences for greater fluency. But we also need to vary sentence length in order to vary the rhythm of our prose. There are sections in our texts where we want the reader to run with us, to keep our breathless pace—that's when we need tight, short sentences that move the action forward. At other times we want the reader to take time to reflect, to slow down, to follow us as we develop a complex argument and as we try to support our position. This can be done with long sentences that give readers time to think, time to pull all the information together.

As we work with our sentences, we can change or deepen their meaning—we can generate new meaning even very late in the writing process. When we focus on sentence craftsmanship, we can end up tightening sentences and/or lengthening them to make them more graceful. If you've been taught that repetition in your writing is a bad thing, you're in for a surprise—since powerful effects often depend on the judicious use of repeated words or structures (see Paraskevas and Sargent, pages 268–270). By altering structure or pace at the sentence level, we discover ways to tell our readers when to move fast through a piece and when to slow down, when to zoom in on a particular detail and when to look at the general picture.

Part of the rhythm of a sentence depends on its structure. But part also depends on the choice of words—long words slow the reader down. They can also be intimidating since most are Latin- or Greek-based. These are the words that a lot of our readers find prestigious—and we don't disagree with them. They *are* prestigious; but they can make a piece fairly dense and hard to read. Most of the words we use daily are short—because they are original English words, part of the earliest forms of our language. These short words, in general, help the reader: they are not the million-dollar words, as our students say, but are the workhorse words, the words that build a solid foundation. And often powerful effects result when we vary word length (just as powerful effects can result when we vary our sentence lengths). Consider, for example, the effect of these famous lines from *Macbeth*, when Macbeth has just murdered the king and is realizing that all the water in the world will not be able to clean his bloody hands—that in fact, his hands are much more likely to turn all the water in the world into blood (or the colour of blood). We'll italicize the words we especially want you to notice:

> Will all great Neptune's ocean wash this blood
> Clean from my hand? No, this my hand will rather
> The *multitudinous* seas *incarnadine*,
> Making the *green* one *red*. (2.2:58–61)

Notice that nearly every word in this passage is a one-syllable word, a simple workhorse word. Four words have two syllables, but they're all pretty familiar. Therefore, the two words that stand out and slow us down are the Latin words, the five-syllable "multi-tudinous" and the four-syllable "incarnadine" (i.e., turn red); after those two mouthfuls, so close together, the simple colour contrasts and the single syllables of "green" and "red" hit with special force, particularly since that very last phrase ("Making the green one red") restates bluntly the same meaning of the long, Latinate preceding one.

But don't assume that all short words are easy to read, like "red" and "green." There are short words that are actually harder to process than long words. So although long words *can* make a text less readable (especially if they are Latin-based borrowings), short words can make a text less readable too if they're unfamiliar (less familiar words like *schist* being harder on readers than everyday words like *beautiful*). Once more, you need to weigh the risks and benefits of your word choices since those choices will affect the style and readability—and of course meaning—of any piece of writing.

Knowing the **etymology** of a word (the root, the source, the words and language it originally came from) allows you consciously to vary not only word length but derivation. Where a word originally comes from can affect the connotations and the overall flavour of that word since trailing along behind it—like long roots underground—are its original culture and its history. Doing a background check on certain words can allow you to use their full power or to make up surprising and effective word combinations. Also keep in mind that you can often move a word out of its usual position in order to give it special emphasis: because we have such a strong expectation of normal word order in English, even subtle variations draw attention to themselves. Consider two fairly everyday examples of restrained emphasis from a children's book by Libba Moore Gray, a result simply of putting an adjective in a different location (since adjectives usually come *before* nouns, those *following* nouns stand out): "drink lemonade *cold*" (13), "drink hot tea *spiced*" (17, italics ours; see Wood Ray's *Wondrous Words* for further examples and ideas on lexical craftsmanship).

Rhetorical Punctuation

Unless you've read the recent bestseller by Lynne Truss—*Eats, Shoots & Leaves* (which is, depending on how you punctuate it, about either an extremely rude houseguest or a panda bear)—you may never have thought of punctuation as a meaning-making device or of punctuation marks as symbols that could be used for stylistic or rhetorical effect. For most of us, punctuation marks had to be placed mechanically according to rules that handbooks gave us: which mark to use—and when—was supposed to be clear and straightforward. Our experience in teaching writing, however, has shown us that because the rules are not clear—they are tendencies rather than rules—students tend to play it safe by limiting their choices to basic punctuation marks: period, comma, question mark, exclamation mark, with an occasional colon for lists and dashes relegated to informal writing and e-mail. Lewis Thomas's piece in this section has fun with the mistaken notion that punctuation rules are straightforward and emphasizes that punctuation is as much a rhetorical tool as it is a syntactic tool—that is, it has as much to do with making meaning as it does with marking sentence boundaries clearly on the page for readers.

Skilled writers know how to manipulate their punctuation to guide their readers, to give an extra layer of meaning to their words. John Dawkins, in his study of accomplished writers, found out that most of them don't actually follow the handbook rules. Not that their punctuation is wrong—far from it. These experienced writers use various punctuation marks to indicate varying degrees of separation and connection between their ideas: they use this rhetorical function of punctuation to make their meaning clearer to their readers (see Paraskevas, "The Craft of Writing: Breaking Conventions," or better still, "The Place of Run-ons and Dashes in Writing—The Craft of Breaking Conventions," at http://www.sargent.nelson.com, both of which summarize Dawkins's findings).

We're not arguing that all punctuation decisions are up for grabs. Some punctuation mistakes can be serious, especially if they misrepresent your meaning or give others the impression that you have difficulty recognizing basic sentence boundaries (see our "Bare Bones Writer's Grammar" at http://www.sargent.nelson.com if you need a quick reference on sentence boundary issues). For instance, there's only one approach (that we know of anyway) for punctuating the following sentence to get it to make sense:

James where Sam had had had had had had had had had had had the teacher's approval.

(See if you can figure it out; if you're stumped, check this book's website for the answer.)

Not that sentences like that come up very often (or should). Still, you can always check the inside front covers of this book for quick reference on punctuating correctly, especially to indicate syntactic structure and help prevent confusion for your readers, most of whom have a distinct aversion to punctuating other people's sentences for them.

Yet what would be the "correct" way to punctuate the long unpunctuated and unfinished sentence that we used as an epigraph to this Conversation about grammar? Punctuation becomes a good deal more interesting when we also think of it rhetorically, as a stylistic tool, a tool for making meaning and, as Iyer puts it, for scoring "the music in our minds."

Of course, had we world enough and time, we could explore style even further—there are ways of analyzing the style of paragraphs, for instance. And there are stylistic implications to the way entire pieces of writing are structured (see McConnell in Conversation 6 on the style of beginnings, for instance).

All these choices—in words, in sentence structure, in punctuation (as well as in larger structures)—are important because they give you more choices and greater power as a writer. They are not about correctness. They are choices you make about how you want people to hear your words, how you want them to react to your sentences and your ideas. And therefore the question remains, what kind of grammar should be taught in schools? We think that, ideally, school grammars should help students become more aware of their internal grammar, of Grammar One, the grammar they already know so well. If students became more conscious of the knowledge they already have, they would become more and more skillful users of grammar as style, which we believe connects grammar to writing most closely. But what do you think? Should *prescriptive* grammar (language etiquette) be taught in schools as well? instead? We invite you to read these selections and then join the conversation about the grammar/writing/style connection.

INKSHEDDING PROMPTS

INKSHEDDING *BEFORE* READING CONVERSATION 5:

Try inkshedding for fifteen to twenty minutes nonstop in response to one of the following prompts *before* you read any of the readings in this section. Give yourself a chance to jot down some of your own thoughts and feelings about the issues below before you've been influenced by anyone else's ideas. Inkshedding ahead of time will give you a written record of what *your* position was on some of these matters before reading about anyone else's. A written record also makes it easier to go back weeks or months later to see if your position or practice has changed and, if so, how. Inkshedding ahead of time can also make the readings easier to follow: you'll be more tuned in and receptive to the ideas being explored.

Of course, you can inkshed on the same prompt *after* reading any of the pieces in Conversation 5 as well, to explore how the reading has affected your thinking. Inkshedding as soon as possible after completing a reading will help you remember and assimilate what you've just read.

1.   Our experiences with grammar often shape our relationship with writing. Write about your experiences with grammar. First, draw a line down the middle of a page. On the left-hand side, list definitions of grammar—as many as you can think of, goofy or serious—and on the right-hand side, write a brief reaction to each definition. Inkshed on how these definitions have affected you as a writer, how they have shaped the language you use in your pieces.

2.   We all have language prejudices. For example, some of us make quick judgments about a speaker's intelligence from the use of double negatives ("I'm not working here no more"). What specific language prejudices—language pet peeves, as we like to call them—do you have? Give a few detailed examples of expressions (in writing or speech) that make you nuts. How did you develop these pet peeves? Inkshed about some of your prejudices and think how they have affected your own use of language.

3. Spend a few minutes imagining a conversation with your best friend (in person or via e-mail), a conversation where you don't have to worry about your language. Jot down some of the expressions that you would typically use with your friend—they might be single words, short phrases, or whole sentences. Now try to figure out the main characteristics of this private language, its main features. What are they? How do they differ from features of your public language? How does your register change if additional participants join in the conversation?

4. Choose a page or paragraph from one of your favourite writers. Now, consulting a handbook on usage, try to explain the use of every punctuation mark. Does the writer always follow the handbook's advice? Are there any deviations? If so, what effect do those deviations have?

5. How do you understand the term "style" in a piece of writing? How does it reveal itself? Think about a few of your favourite writers in terms of style. What makes their style interesting to you? What is it in the language use that attracts you? Tell the story of how you came to like the style of a particular author. Or, if you prefer, describe *your* writing style. Look back at the development of your style. What characterizes it? How did you develop it? Who served as your model? How did your readings influence your style? Are there any features of your style that you are particularly proud of? Is there a particular aspect of your style you'd like to work on? Is your style different in different pieces? Why? Give some detailed examples, specific sentences or phrases from your past work, that you think reveal your characteristic ways of writing and thinking.

6. Inkshed about your past experiences with writing handbooks—how often do you consult them? When you do consult them, do you have any difficulties finding the help you need? If so, how would you describe those difficulties? What is your favourite writing handbook and why? What's the most useful thing about it?

7. What are your experiences with computer software for commenting on grammar, usage, and mechanics? Which programs do you have experience with? Give as many specific examples as you can of times a particular piece of software was helpful and times it was misleading or irritating. Which word processing program do you use most often? Do you regularly use the grammar-checking function that comes with your word processor? If so, how useful is it?

8.   Do you use emoticons in your e-mails? If so, why? Which ones are your favourites so far? Have you invented any of your own? What do they add to your writing?

INKSHEDDING *AFTER* READING CONVERSATION 5:

Inkshed on one of the prompts above, but this time make clear how the reading(s) has (have) changed your thinking or your practice, if there has been any change. If your thinking or practice has not changed, tell why. Or try one of the additional prompts below, 9–12.

9.   In his piece "Notes on Punctuation," Lewis Thomas has provided us (while amusing us) with basic guidelines for syntactic punctuation, guidelines that he himself uses in this piece. How would his piece change had he punctuated it differently? What happens to our reading of the piece, for instance, if we change every semicolon in it to a period? Or if we change the final mark to a period instead of a comma? Imagine as an audience for your inkshed someone who can't imagine how a punctuation mark could make anyone laugh, let alone how a period put "at just the right place" could "pierce the heart" (as Isaac Babel famously put it): by describing how four or five specific punctuation marks are placed ingeniously in Thomas's short piece, try to change that person's mind (or at least get a smile out of them).

10. Read Stephanie Bishop's segmented essay in Conversation 8; she writes about her initial irritation at the Goldberg selection included in this chapter—until Bishop took the time to analyze her own past writing. Take a page or paragraph of a piece of writing you've done in the past year and analyze it (in detail, giving the kinds of specific examples that we long for in Bishop's piece) in the light of one of the readings in this Conversation. You could focus on the punctuation in your passage (Thomas), on word choice or directness of expression (Goldberg), on sentence length and fluency in that passage (Paraskevas and Sargent), on register or correctness (or anything else that occurs to you after reading Pinker in this chapter or the "Bare Bones Writer's Grammar" at http://www.sargent.nelson.com). You could also use Lanham's Paramedic Method on it, as described in the introduction to this chapter (pages 243–246), and then inkshed about what you discovered, comparing your original to the pared-down result.

11. How do you decide on the punctuation you will use in a particular piece? How do you understand the term "stylistic punctuation"? Are you more likely to use stylistic punctuation early in the writing process or not? Does your exploratory writing give more indications of stylistic punctuation than

your finished writing? What do you find out if you compare the punctuation you use in your exploratory writing with the punctuation you use in your finished pieces? Has reading this Conversation influenced your thinking about how you'll attend to punctuation issues in the future? If so, how?

12. Will any of the materials on grammar, including grammar-as-style, supplied in this section or on the website (http://www.sargent.nelson.com) actually help your writing? Or are grammar considerations just distracting as you compose and revise? Are the glossary (entitled "Key Words for a Writer's Grammar—Language for Talking about Language" and located on the web-site) or the Quick References on the inside covers of this book useful to you? Does the "Bare Bones Writer's Grammar" (located on the website as well) help you understand sentence boundaries and handbooks any better? And if so, will that understanding affect your style or your writing in any way— or at least your editing and proofreading once all your drafting and revising is done? How?

Stephen Pinker, from "The Language Mavens" in *The Language Instinct: How the Mind Creates Language*

In this brief excerpt, Stephen Pinker takes on the self-appointed "grammar police" in our culture; the whole chapter is worth reading for its meticulous exploding of various obsessions about correctness (which turn out not to be correct at all, once the way language works is better understood). See also selections from earlier chapters of Pinker's *The Language Instinct* in Conversation 1.

THE LANGUAGE INSTINCT: HOW THE MIND CREATES LANGUAGE

from THE LANGUAGE MAVENS

Imagine that you are watching a nature documentary. The video shows the usual gorgeous footage of animals in their natural habitats. But the voiceover reports some troubling facts. Dolphins do not execute their swimming strokes properly. White-crowned sparrows carelessly debase their calls. Chickadees' nests are incorrectly constructed, pandas hold bamboo in the wrong paw, the song of the humpback whale contains several well-known errors, and monkeys' cries have been in a state of chaos and degeneration for hundreds of years. Your reaction would probably be, What on earth could it mean for the song of the humpback whale to contain an "error"? Isn't the song of the humpback whale whatever the humpback whale decides to sing? Who is this announcer, anyway?

But for human language, most people think that the same pronouncements not only are meaningful but are cause for alarm. Johnny can't construct a grammatical sentence. As educational standards decline and pop culture disseminates the inarticulate ravings and unintelligible patois of surfers, jocks, and valley girls, we are turning into a nation of functional illiterates: misusing *hopefully,* confusing *lie* and *lay,* treating *data* as a singular noun, letting our participles dangle. English itself will steadily decay unless we get back to basics and start to respect our language again.

To a linguist or psycholinguist, of course, language is like the song of the humpback whale. The way to determine whether a construction is "grammatical" is to find people who speak the language and ask them. So when people are accused of speaking "ungrammatically" in their own language, or of consistently violating a "rule," there must be some different sense of "grammatical" and "rule" in the air. In fact, the pervasive belief that people do not know their own language is a nuisance in doing linguistic research. A linguist's question to an informant about some form in his or her speech (say, whether the person uses *sneaked* or *snuck)* is often lobbed back with the ingenuous counterquestion "Gee, I better not take a chance; which is correct?"

In this chapter I had better resolve this contradiction for you. Recall columnist Erma Bombeck, incredulous at the very idea of a grammar gene because her husband taught thirty-seven high school students who thought that "bummer" was a sentence. You, too, might be wondering: if language is as instinctive as spinning a web, if every three-year-old is a grammatical genius, if the design of syntax is coded in our DNA and wired into our brains, why is the English language in such mess? Why does the average American sound like a gibbering fool every time he opens his mouth or puts pen to paper?

The contradiction begins in the fact that the words "rule," "grammatical," and "ungrammatical" have very different meanings to a scientist and to a layperson. The rules people learn (or, more likely, fail to learn) in school are called *prescriptive* rules, prescribing how one "ought" to talk. Scientists studying language propose *descriptive* rules, describing how people *do* talk. They are completely different things, and there is a good reason that scientists focus on descriptive rules.

To a scientist the fundamental fact of human language is its sheer improbability. Most objects in the universe—lakes, rocks, trees, worms, cows, cars—cannot talk. Even in humans, the utterances in a language are an infinitesimal fraction of the noises people's mouths are capable of making. I can arrange a combination of words that explains how octopuses make love or how to remove cherry stains; rearrange the words in even the most minor way, and the result is a sentence with a different meaning or, most likely of all, word salad. How are we to account for this miracle? What would it take to build a device that could duplicate human language?

Obviously, you need to build in some kind of rules, but what kind? Prescriptive rules? Imagine trying to build a talking machine by designing it to obey rules like "Don't split infinitives" or "Never begin a sentence with *because."* It would just sit there. In fact, we already have machines that don't split infinitives; they're called screw-drivers, bathtubs, cappuccino-makers, and so on. Prescriptive rules are useless without the much more fundamental rules that create the sentences and define the infinitives and list the word *because* to begin with. . . . These rules are never mentioned in style manuals or school grammars because the authors correctly assume that anyone capable of reading the manuals must already have the rules. No one, not even a valley girl, has to be told not to say *Apples eat the boy* or *The child seems sleeping* or *Who did you meet John and?* or the vast, vast majority of the millions of trillions of mathematically possible combinations of words. So when a scientist considers all the high-tech mental machinery needed to arrange words into ordinary sentences, prescriptive rules are, at best, inconsequential little decorations. The very fact that they have to be drilled shows that they are alien to the natural workings of the language system. One can choose to obsess over prescriptive rules, but they have no more to do with human language than the criteria for judging cats at a cat show have to do with mammalian biology.

So there is no contradiction in saying that every normal person can speak grammatically (in the sense of systematically) and ungrammatically (in the sense of nonprescriptively), just as there is no contradiction in saying that a taxi obeys the laws of physics but breaks the laws of Massachusetts. But this raises a question. Someone, somewhere, must be making decisions about "correct English" for the rest of us. Who? There is no English Language Academy, and this is just as well; the purpose of the Academie Française is to amuse journalists from other countries with bitterly argued decisions that the French gaily ignore. Nor were there any Founding Fathers at some English Language Constitutional Conference at the beginning of time. The legislators of "correct English," in fact, are an informal network of copy-editors, dictionary usage panelists, style manual and handbook writers, English teachers, essayists, columnists, and pundits. Their authority, they claim, comes from their dedication to implementing standards that have served the language well in the past, especially in the prose of its finest writers, and that maximize its clarity, logic, consistency, conciseness, elegance, continuity, precision, stability, integrity, and expressive range. (Some of them go further and say that they are actually safeguarding the ability to *think* clearly and logically. This radical Whorfianism is common among language pundits, not surprisingly; who would settle for being a schoolmarm when one can be an upholder of rationality itself?) William Safire, who writes the weekly column "On Language" for *The New York Times Magazine,* calls himself a "language maven," from the Yiddish word meaning expert, and this gives us a convenient label for the entire group.

To whom I say: Maven, shmaven! *Kibbitzers* and *nudniks* is more like it. For here are the remarkable facts. Most of the prescriptive rules of the language mavens make no sense on any level. They are bits of folklore that originated for screwball reasons several hundred years ago and have perpetuated themselves ever since. For as long as they have existed, speakers have flouted them, spawning identical plaints about the imminent decline of the language century after century. All the best writers in English at all periods, including Shakespeare and most of the mavens themselves, have been among the flagrant flouters. The rules conform neither to logic nor to tradition, and if they were ever followed they would force writers into fuzzy, clumsy, wordy, ambiguous, incomprehensible prose, in which certain thoughts are not expressible at all. Indeed, most of the "ignorant errors" these rules are supposed to correct display an elegant logic and an acute sensitivity to the grammatical structure of the language, to which the mavens are oblivious. . . .

[T]he language mavens would have a much better chance of not embarrassing themselves if they saved the verdict of linguistic incompetence for the last resort rather than jumping to it as a first conclusion. People come out with laughable verbiage when they feel they are in a forum demanding an elevated, formal style and know that their choice of words could have momentous consequences for them. That is why the fertile sources of howlers tend to be politicians' speeches, welfare application letters, and student term papers. . . . In less self-conscious settings, common people, no matter how poorly educated, obey sophisticated grammatical laws, and can express themselves with a vigor and grace that captivates those who listen seriously—linguists, journalists, oral historians, novelists with an ear for dialogue. . .

So what should be done about usage? Unlike some academics in the 1960s, I am not saying that instruction in standard English grammar and composition is a tool to perpetuate an oppressive white patriarchal capitalist status quo and that The People should be liberated to write however they please. Some aspects of how people express themselves in some settings *are* worth trying to change. What I am calling for is innocuous: a more thoughtful discussion of language and how people use it, replacing *bubbe-maises* (old wives' tales) with the best scientific knowledge available. It is especially important that we not underestimate the sophistication of the actual cause of any instance of language use: the human mind.

. . . Many prescriptive rules of grammar are just plain dumb and should be deleted from the usage handbooks. And most of standard English is just that, standard, in the same sense that certain units of currency or household voltages are said to be standard. It is just common sense that people should be given every encouragement and opportunity to learn the dialect that has become the standard one in their society and to employ it in many formal settings. But there is no need to use terms like "bad grammar," "fractured syntax," and "incorrect usage" when referring to rural and black dialects. . . . [U]sing terms like "bad grammar" for "nonstandard" is both insulting and scientifically inaccurate. . . .

The aspect of language use that is most worth changing is the clarity and style of written prose. Expository writing requires language to express far more complex trains of thought than it was biologically designed to do. Inconsistencies caused by limitations of short-term memory and planning, unnoticed in conversation, are not as tolerable when preserved on a page that is to be perused more leisurely. Also, unlike a conversational partner, a reader will rarely share enough background assumptions to interpolate all the missing premises that make language comprehensible. Overcoming one's natural egocentrism and trying to anticipate the knowledge state of a generic reader at every stage of the exposition is one of the most important tasks in writing well. All this makes writing a difficult craft that must be mastered through practice, instruction, feedback, and—probably most important—intensive exposure to good examples. . . . [A] banal but universally acknowledged key to good writing is to revise extensively. Good writers go through anywhere from two to twenty drafts before releasing a paper. Anyone who does not appreciate this necessity is going to be a bad writer. Imagine a Jeremiah exclaiming, "Our language today is threatened by an insidious enemy: the youth are not revising their drafts enough times." Kind of takes the fun out, doesn't it? It's not something that can be blamed on television, rock music, shopping mall culture, overpaid athletes, or any of the other signs of the decay of civilization. But if it's clear writing that we want, this is the kind of homely remedy that is called for.

Cornelia C. Paraskevas and M. Elizabeth Sargent, "Understanding Grammar as Style"

Cornelia Paraskevas is originally from Athens, Greece. After finishing her degree there in English/Linguistics, she completed a PhD in Theoretical Linguistics at the University of Kansas, Lawrence, with the help of a Fulbright Scholarship (1987). As she started learning more about composition theory—a process that began when she taught first-year composition at the University of Kansas and had to attend seminars for GTAs (Graduate Teaching Assistants)—she realized that there was no contact zone between linguistics and writing. That's when she decided to focus her energies on finding ways to bridge the gap, to bring linguistics into composition through issues of grammar instruction. As a result, she publishes essays not only on Greek linguistics but on rhetorical grammar and style. Her pieces have appeared in, to name a few periodicals, *Oregon English Journal, Inland,* NCTE's *English Journal,* and *Classmate* (a publication of the Manitoba Association of Teachers of English). She has been teaching linguistics, first-year writing, and composition theory at Western Oregon University since 1989 and is constantly exploring ways to bring discussions about language into the writing classroom. She and **M. Elizabeth Sargent** (see the introduction to Sargent in Conversation 3) taught together for a decade at Western Oregon University and are co-editors of this volume.

UNDERSTANDING GRAMMAR AS STYLE

Forty years after Richard Braddock's research—which revealed the potentially negative effect of grammar instruction on writing—one would think that the discussion about grammar and writing would be history.

But it isn't. In fact, it's heating up again as scholars argue that we must start seeing grammar as inseparable from writing, that we need to see it as a powerful stylistic resource for writing. Can we convince you? See what you think after you've read through the examples that follow. If you have trouble with any of the terms in boldface, refer to the online resources available with this text at http://www.sargent.nelson.com: the glossary ("Key Words for a Writer's Grammar—Language for Talking about Language") and the "Bare Bones Writer's Grammar." But we suspect your considerable competence as a speaker of English is all you'll need.

HOW WE GUIDE THE READER'S ATTENTION: GENERAL PRINCIPLES OF EMPHASIS AND INFORMATION DISTRIBUTION

1. Something Old/Something New: The Principle of the Given-New Arrangement

We write for so many reasons—to convey information, to share feelings, to ask questions, to make statements—but all our wildly different written sentences are nevertheless usually arranged in a similar order, a particular order that most of us have unconsciously learned simply by being readers. First comes the old, given, known information (that means information that can be recovered from earlier sentences or information that is shared knowledge between the readers and the writers) and then comes the new information.

Here's an example of that arrangement, taken from this book (we need at least two sentences in sequence to see how this **given-new** arrangement works):

> One theorist, Paulo Freire, has called this "the banking model" of education. This model usually depends on the notion that the role of language in relation to knowledge is simply to get out of the way.
>
> (Introduction to Conversation 4, page 177)

Look at the second sentence; it starts with the words we have underlined, "this model." As readers, you can interpret what "this" refers to ("the banking model of education") because it appeared in the preceding sentence. This information, then, is known/given to you. The rest of the sentence (the part that begins with "usually") is the new information that the second sentence carries. Look back at these two sentences in context (on page 177) to find out what the "this" in the *first* sentence refers to.

Now, you might ask, does this arrangement of information correspond with the usual word order in English? And the answer is yes: every sentence in English has two parts—the **subject** and the **predicate**, arranged in that order. First comes the subject, then the predicate. This arrangement (we call it **syntactic** arrangement) corresponds with the pattern of information distribution in a sentence: known, given information appears in the subject position; new information appears in the predicate. So looking back at the sentence we analyzed, we see that the old/given/known information "this model" corresponds to the subject and the new information corresponds to the predicate.

As readers, we have figured out this arrangement from our exposure to reading, even though no one has taught it to us. We expect to find it in everything we read—from newspaper and magazine articles to eloquent pieces of literature. Let's see again how this works, using a longer piece this time:

> My chore is to open a bank account and then join my friends Leda and Theo for lunch in Plaka, the lovely, crowded old quarter of Athens, at a restaurant owned by a man who calls himself simply the Mustache, or for specificity, the Mustache from Olympia. The bank is affiliated with my bank in the States, and I explain to the raven-haired representative with the dramatic makeup that I will be here for a year and a bit and would like to open an account. I hand her letters of recommendation and she takes them to her supervisor. When she returns, she says, "We open accounts in dollars under the following conditions . . ." (Storace 22)

The second sentence begins with the **phrase** "The bank"; the **definite article** "the" tells us that somewhere in the preceding sentence there must have been some mention of a "bank." (You know this intuitively—otherwise you would have expected an **indefinite article**, as in "a" bank.) The wording doesn't have to be identical in these two references to banks—as long as our common sense, our knowledge of the world, helps us see that there is a connection between the two. Here, then, we see that "the bank" connects to "the bank account" that was mentioned in the first sentence—after all, bank accounts can be opened only in a bank. So "the bank" is considered to be old, given information. This chain-like arrangement (what is new information in one sentence becoming old/given information in the following sentence) also gives unity (we call that **cohesion** in linguistics) to a text.

Sometimes there may be partial similarity between two expressions that refer to the same thing: "bank" and "bank account." But often there is no similarity between the two expressions, so we have to infer the connection: for instance, "the raven-haired representative" in the second sentence and "her" in the third are completely different in terms of wording. Yet, we understand that "her" refers to "the raven-haired representative" because we assume that the text is cohesive, that the writer uses the **pronoun** "her"—and later "she"—as a shortcut so that she won't have to repeat "the raven-haired representative" every time. Here, by the way, lies the usefulness of pronouns (words like "this" or "her")—they serve as cohesive ties across sentences and keep us from repeating the same expression over and over again. If you really want to confuse someone, try this: take all the pronouns out of a piece you have written and replace them with the expressions they replace—all cohesion breaks down because you have eliminated the cohesive ties.

2. The Principle of End Weight

The basic (**unmarked**, as we say in linguistics) word order in English is subject-predicate. And since the subject usually carries old information, it is usually shorter ("lighter") than the ("heavier") predicate, which carries new information.

Here's a sentence that may take some extra effort to read, even though there's nothing technically wrong with it:

> <u>A law affecting the election of MPs in the less-populated areas of Greece</u> was passed last week.

What makes you have to work a bit harder with this sentence? Do you find it reader-unfriendly because it delays the main event—the **verb** "was passed"— until the end, after you have had to read a lot of information in the subject (the underlined part)? The flow of information is difficult because the subject is so full of new information. If you have difficulty with this sentence, don't feel as if your information-processing ability is impaired. Your innate sense of grammar led you to expect the main event—the one expressed by the verb in the predicate—to come earlier and the new information to come later. The sentence is difficult to process because the subject ("A law affecting the election of MPs in the less-populated areas of Greece") is so much longer than the predicate ("was passed last week"). In general, we expect the weight of a sentence to be in the predicate, where the new information is, and—specifically—towards the end of the sentence. To accomplish this, we can break up the long subject, keeping the key part in the subject position and moving the rest to a position after the predicate, towards the end of the sentence:

> <u>A law</u> was passed last week <u>affecting the election of MPs in the less-populated areas of Greece</u>.

This move, then, has made the flow of information easier because we have the basic event in the beginning of the sentence and all the extra information at the end; the subject is light, as most readers expect it to be, and the weight has shifted to the end of the sentence.

Here's another example to consider: "It is clear that language affects thought." The sentence begins with "it"—and some of you might have been told that this is "bad grammar." Let us tell you something—not only is this not "bad grammar," but as native speakers of the language, this is the best way we have of constructing our sentence to honour the **principle of end weight**. If we try not to use "it," this is what we get: "<u>That language affects thought</u> is clear." This sentence is certainly correct; but it does have a heavy subject (the underlined part), and some readers might find that this construction takes a lot of energy to read, energy they might not be willing to expend.

As writers, remember you have choices—but for each choice you make, there are risks. You'll want to weigh your risks carefully so you won't lose your readers.

3. The Principle of End Focus

In speech, when we want to stress a particular word or phrase, all we have to do is raise our voices; in writing, there is no audible voice. To represent that stress, that emphasis, we need to move the word/phrase towards the end of the sentence, towards the end of the new-information chunk. Consider the following two sentences:

> The London Symphony Orchestra will perform <u>at the Athens Concert Hall</u>   <u>on February 16 and 17, 2004</u>.

> The London Symphony Orchestra will perform <u>on February 16 and 17, 2004,</u>   <u>at the Athens Concert Hall</u>.

Even though the two sentences contain exactly the same information, they differ from each other with respect to emphasis; in the first sentence, the stress is on the date. If you are not sure about that, try the following test. Create a question for sentence one. You'll probably instinctively come up with something like this:

> <u>When</u> will the London Symphony perform?

Now look at the second sentence; here, the emphasis is on the *place* of performance:

> <u>Where</u> will the London Symphony perform?

This is a particularly useful principle to remember as you place two successive prepositional phrases in order: put the most important new information as close to the end of the sentence as possible. The one to appear closest to the end of the sentence will be the one your reader will remember best because it appeared last.

4. The Principle of Emphasis

The last principle is the simplest one. Remember one basic feature about the arrangement of all English sentences: the usual pattern is for the subject to come before the predicate. This is the basic order of words in English—the **unmarked** word order—the order most commonly followed.

Let's pretend you are really angry with someone's behaviour and you want to convey that feeling in your writing. You could write: "I will not tolerate <u>this behaviour</u>." But this sentence doesn't really show how angry you are—how the behaviour has bothered you. Now let's turn the sentence around, moving "this behaviour" to the front of the sentence so that it will be the first thing the reader will see. Read it again and look at what happens: "<u>This behaviour</u> I will not tolerate." By moving that phrase (the **direct object**, as it happens) from the predicate to the front, we have upset the expected structure of the sentence—we have "raised our voice" for emphasis.

If you want to emphasize a part of your sentence, if you want to catch the reader's attention, all you need to do is move the part you want to emphasize out of its normal, expected position into an unexpected one. That move will slow your readers down—but it will also guide their attention to where you want it to be. This works particularly well with expressions of time and place that modify the verb. Their normal, expected position is in the predicate. But let's look at the following sentence:

> <u>All over Greece, but particularly in Athens</u>, the ideal taverna recreates a miniature, perfect dream village in a state of feast. (Storace 98)

It begins not with the subject (not with the usual arrangement, in other words), but with an expression of place—"all over Greece, but particularly in Athens." This is unexpected—as readers of English, we expect to see the subject first thing. Why did the writer do it then? For emphasis. By starting the sentence in an unexpected way, she caught your attention—she tapped you on the shoulder to make you look where she wanted you to look.

The writer had other choices. She could have written, for example,

> The ideal taverna <u>all over Greece, but particularly in Athens</u>, recreates a miniature, perfect dream village in a state of feast.

But in this sentence, we don't feel the shoulder tap. We don't pause in our reading since there are no surprises in the word order—the sentence begins as expected, with the subject.

One way we, as writers, can catch the reader's attention is to make an unexpected move; and everything that appears at the beginning of a sentence other than the subject is an unexpected move.

HOW WE SPEED OUR SENTENCES ALONG: COMPRESSION AND SYNTACTIC FLUENCY

Sometimes we read passages that take our breath away because the writer has such control of the written word, of the structures that characterize the written language (as opposed to the spoken language), and she can use them to scream or to whisper. Part of that control has to do with **fluency**—some texts feel more fluent than others—and fluency, in turn, depends both on length (how many words in a "sentence") and on construction (the order and type of elements in a "sentence").

Why have we used quotation marks around the word "sentence" above? Because we have to be careful: to measure fluency in terms of length, we can't just look at anything that begins with a capital letter and ends with a period. Why not? Well, for one thing, it might not actually *be* a sentence—it could be a **fragment**. And for another thing, we can certainly imagine long sentences that wouldn't necessarily strike us as fluent. How about, for instance, the typical bed-to-bed story of a second grader?

> My Day. First, I got up and then I ate my cereal and then I brushed my teeth and then I got dressed and then I went to school and then I had lunch and then I walked home and then I played with Bobby and then I had a hot dog and corn and then I heard a story and then I went to sleep. The end.

The middle sentence in this story is sixty-four words long. But fluent?

T-Units to the Rescue: Long T-Units versus Long Sentences

So Kellogg Hunt, a scholar who studied the development of writing abilities in children and adults, decided to use a different unit of measure for fluency. He called that unit a **T-unit** (minimal terminable unit), and he defined it as an **independent clause** together with any **dependent** elements in it. According to his way of measuring, then, the long second-grader's sentence above may be only one sentence, but it contains eleven T-units, each one containing an average of six words.

Now let's look at the T-units in the following adult sentence:

> If you have identified problems with grammar or spelling in your work, this book will give you a tool to check your drafts with and protect your investment in your work. (Buckley xvii)

Here we have thirty-one words, but only *one* T-unit: there are two **clauses**, but the first clause—"If you have identified problems with grammar or spelling in your work"—is dependent (it can't stand alone). Remember that each T-unit is an independent clause *plus* any dependent elements; that means that a dependent clause by itself cannot be a T-unit.

Using T-units as the measure, Kellogg Hunt found that adult writing is characterized by longer T-units (at an average of about twenty words per unit) than novice writing (which averaged roughly eight words per unit). Here's a typical example of a child's writing, a sentence containing a single T-unit with seven words:

> Mama, I hope you enjoy this note.

And here's a long adult sentence, a sentence consisting of a single T-unit and fifty words.

> One equivalent might be someone like Arthur Ashe, an artist who was an exemplary figure, whose genius revealed the connection between tennis courts and courts of justice, whose game was brilliant and exciting because it described the world, and who performed the ultimate athletic feat of living what he thought.
>
> (Storace 98)

If you find the second piece—the one by the adult writer—denser, you are right: long T-units often make a piece feel dense. Once again, the choice is yours: you need to choose the construction that best moves your meaning forward, always keeping in mind that each choice has consequences.

If your T-units seem on the short side to you, don't worry; there are various ways to increase the length of a T-unit, to expand your already powerful natural syntactic abilities, so that you can create sentences that are typical of written language, sentences with lots of **modifiers**. Let's see how you can do that: first, start with a basic clause, a sentence that contains a single T-unit of ten words:

> Jane was reading a book about life in Ancient Greece.

You can easily add information about the time of the event either through a simple **adverb** like "yesterday" or through a longer expression of time like "last week" or through a whole dependent clause like "when she called me." You can add even more modifiers, not just around the verb but around the nouns: you could add adverbs and **adjectives** like "beautifully illustrated" or "carefully researched" in front of the word "book"; you could add **appositives/renamers** like "my childhood friend" (after "Jane"); and you could add another modifier, a whole clause—"who has been studying classics for the past two years"—after the appositive you added earlier, "my childhood friend."

Now that you have used expansion techniques, the sentence above has become much longer—still one T-unit but now containing twenty-nine words:

> Last week, Jane, my childhood friend (who has been studying clas-
> sics for the past two years), was reading a beautifully illustrated,
> carefully researched book about life in Ancient Greece.

And these modifiers are not padding—if they're thoughtfully chosen, they make your writing more specific and more memorable, so that readers can see what you want them to see.

By now, you might be asking, "Does Hunt's research imply that, if we want our writing to be fluent like the writing of superior adult writers, we need to write really long sentences? or sentences with really long T-units?" No—it's not that simple. First of all, we know that superior adult writing is characterized by **variety in sentence length**. Second, superior adult writing is characterized by **variety and compression in sentence structure**. For instance, how do we know instantly that the following sentence could not have been written by a second grader?

> I walk through an unexpected piece of countryside, <u>apartment build-
> ings going up on land that clearly belongs to the modest empty farm-
> house still standing</u>. (Storace 40)

Yes, there are twenty-four words in this sentence. But we need to consider other factors besides length when we think of fluency: the number of T-units in each sentence and the internal structure of the T-units, that is, the way the words are put together, their syntactic arrangement.

Simple T-units versus Complex T-units

Adults have longer T-units, but fewer of them per sentence than children. This is exactly what our sentences above show: the child's sentence on page 263 had eleven T-units whereas our adult examples so far have had only one.

But we also need to consider the internal structure of the T-units. The child's T-units, as expected, are syntactically simple and predictable: the subject comes first, then the predicate. And there are no intricate constructions. The adult's sentence, however, contains an arresting construction, a construction we don't normally use in speech but that we do encounter in writing: "apartment buildings going up on land that clearly belongs to the modest empty farmhouse still standing." What happens to the sentence if the construction changes slightly?

> I walk through an unexpected piece of countryside; apartment build-
> ings <u>are</u> going up on land that clearly belongs to the modest empty
> farmhouse still standing.

By simply adding a semicolon and the verb "are," we affected the fluency of the sentence; we made it less interesting and less compressed. Now we have two T-units in the sentence—which is not terrible, of course—but in the process we lost the unusual twist in the sentence, the part that (because it is not used in speech) makes us slow down as readers, catches our eye. This particular construction, by the way, is called an **absolute**.

You might think that these unusual constructions (**appositives, absolutes,** and **participials**) are created only through inspiration—not true! You can easily learn how to create such constructions and thus how to make your writing more fluent. In general, in all three cases, you begin with a full clause and then reduce/consolidate the clause by either eliminating the subject and/or eliminating or changing the verb:

1. **To create an appositive (renamer):** first we write two complete sentences, each with the same subject. One of the sentences needs to use a form of the verb "to be":

   Constantinople fell to the Ottomans in 1453.

   Constantinople <u>was</u> the capital of the Byzantine Empire.

   Then, we eliminate the "be" verb and the subject from one of the two sentences and set it within the other sentence (setting it off with commas):

   Constantinople, <u>the capital of the Byzantine Empire</u>, fell to the Ottomans in 1453.

   Of course, we could have combined the two sentences without creating an appositive—we could have kept the verb and made a dependent clause instead:

   Constantinople, <u>which was the capital of the Byzantine Empire</u>, fell to the Ottomans in 1453.

The meaning remains the same, but the effect is different. The appositive is more compressed; it's a construction we use in writing to tighten our language and to make it move more quickly, a construction that reveals greater control and fluency.

2. **To create an absolute:** The basic principle for creating an absolute is the same as that for an appositive: start with a full clause. Look at the three absolutes underlined in the following sentence:

> All over Greece, but particularly in Athens, the ideal taverna
> recreates a miniature, perfect dream village in a state of feast,
> the tables set out in a plaza under shady thick-trunked old plane trees,
> the moon if possible shining peacefully through their branches,
> the wine flowing from barrels. . . . (Storace 98)

What would the corresponding three full clauses look like? (We're underlining the main verbs that we'd need to add in order to make each absolute phrase into a clause.)

> The tables are set out in a plaza under shady thick-trunked old plane trees.

> The moon if possible is shining (or shines) peacefully through their branches.

> The wine is flowing (or flows) from barrels.

So we can create the absolute constructions simply by eliminating the "be" verb from these clauses or by changing the main verb to a participle modifying the subject—we reduce/consolidate the clauses by turning them into phrases. Absolutes can appear anywhere in a T-unit; their purpose is simple—to focus, to zoom in on a detail. And that's why we often find them in descriptive passages.

3. **To create a participial (or participle):** again, we begin with a full clause, just as with appositives and absolutes. The highlighted constructions below show how the participle started its life as a full clause but was condensed to move more quickly:

Here are brief descriptions of the book's major reference codes, <u>followed by several tutorials</u>. (Hacker v)

Here are brief descriptions of the book's major reference codes, <u>*which are* followed by several tutorials</u>. (This is our version, to show how Hacker's compressed participial phrase could have been written as a full clause.)

All we did is eliminate the pronoun "which" and the verb "are." What we have left is a consolidated/tightened/reduced construction, a participial. The unreduced construction and the reduced construction share the same meaning; yet the consolidated construction brings a sense of greater movement and control to the sentence.

Parallel Structure

By this point, you have probably realized a potential downfall of sophisticated adult fluency—it can create dense prose. We can make it easier for readers to process dense sentences, however, by using another device—**parallel structure**. In simple terms, the principle of parallel structure is this: similar meanings should be expressed with similar structures. Parallel structures facilitate information processing because the order of words (their syntactic arrangement) is the same across the structures—it is only the meaning that differs. But there's another benefit to using parallel structures as well—they create a sense of rhythm in the sentence.

Let's see how these parallel structures help us process a long, fairly dense sentence, one we've looked at earlier:

One equivalent might be someone like Arthur Ashe, an artist
<u>who was an exemplary figure,</u>
<u>whose genius revealed the connection between tennis courts and courts of justice,</u>
<u>whose game was brilliant and exciting because it described the world,</u> and
<u>who performed the ultimate athletic feat of living what he thought.</u>

(Storace 98)

The four clauses following the word "artist" are not only similar in structure, but each one also starts with the same or a similar pronoun ("who" and "whose" belong to the same category). This similarity—this parallel structure, as we call it—gives the sentence a sense of rhythm and balance; it also facilitates our reading since only the *meaning* in each clause changes while the basic pattern doesn't (in other words, our poor brains get a bit of a rest—they don't have to figure out a new pattern as well as a new meaning for each clause). Of course, the sentence is also using other kinds of repetition effectively (repetition obviously plays a role in creating most parallel structures): notice how the repeated word "courts" pulls two ideas together. And the author uses subtle forms of repetition throughout to link athleticism with artistry, game with genius, tennis with justice.

Any construction can play a role in creating parallel structure; in fact, in the following passage (one you've also seen before), the absolutes are in parallel structure:

> All over Greece, but particularly in Athens, the ideal taverna
> recreates a miniature, perfect dream village in a state of feast,
> <u>the tables set out in a plaza under shady thick-trunked old plane trees</u>,
> <u>the moon if possible shining peacefully through their branches</u>,
> <u>the wine flowing from barrels</u>. . . . (Storace 98)

This balanced structure helps us more easily shift our focus from the tables to the moon and finally to the wine—the lens focuses for a second on each of them with equal strength, and we don't have to expend extra energy working out what the syntax is each time. In fact, it's amazing how quickly our brains pick up even a hint of parallel structure. Somehow, once we've taken in the first structure, we're prepared for the second one and the third. What we would find distracting, actually, would be the sudden breaking of the pattern, as in the following sentence:

> Marge stood out in a crowd: <u>she was not only stunning</u>, but <u>her height was over six feet</u>.

We feel something is wrong there, as if we had been happily walking along the sidewalk, taking in the view, and our right foot suddenly hit the ground six inches below our left, off the curb. What were we expecting? Well, something more like this:

> Marge stood out in a crowd: <u>she was not only stunning, but tall</u>.

Or possibly, if the exact height is crucial, like this:

> Marge stood out in a crowd: she was <u>not only stunning</u>, but <u>over six feet tall</u>.

Even in such a short time, in the space of only twelve words at the beginning of the sentence, we had built up an expectation that the sentence then violated (and we could argue that the expectation would be there in only six words—"She was not only stunning, but . . ."—since it's essentially the "not only/but also" construction that calls up our expectation of parallel structure).

The good news about parallel structure is that, out of all these suggestions for **syntactic fluency**, it is the most instinctive. In the most famous play ever written about linguistics, George Bernard Shaw's *Pygmalion* (on which the musical *My Fair Lady* is based), Shaw has fun with our instinctive use of parallel structure: when a linguistics professor takes on a bet that he can change a London street person, Eliza Doolittle, into a duchess simply by changing her language, he has a run-in with her father, Alfred Doolittle, a garbage man. And he's so taken with Mr. Doolittle's natural ability at parallel structure that in the end he somehow manages to get him involved in lecturing all over North America (where presumably we are easily taken in by such things). Here is the string of sentences that first makes Professor Henry Higgins comment on Alfred Doolittle's "natural gift of rhetoric" and "the rhythm of his native woodnotes wild." Professor Higgins is insisting that Doolittle answer a question, and Doolittle replies:

> I'll tell you, Governor, if you'll only let me get a word in. I'm *willing* to tell you. I'm *wanting* to tell you. I'm *waiting* to tell you. (Act II)

By keeping the structure parallel, by keeping every word the same except one in each clause, Doolittle manages to focus our attention on the one word that changes (the words we've italicized—and notice that even *those words* are parallel, each starting with a "w" and ending with "ing," the last two only differing by one letter); the parallel structure here also creates a rhythm that pulls us along. Certainly parallel structure can be overused (at which point it becomes simply amusing and a distracting mannerism). But Shaw's main point is that such skill with language comes naturally to all of us—we don't have to be linguists to claim it as our birthright.

In all these cases of fluency then—as Kellogg Hunt found—writers discover ways to pack more meanings (more propositions, as we say in linguistics) into each sentence; they create constructions that we usually see only in writing, constructions that make us pause and pay attention because they are unusual.

As we've mentioned before, there are risks here—consolidation and compression can create prose so dense that readers resist it, are unwilling to unpack it (although parallel structures can certainly help readers process dense prose more easily). Once again, you will have to weigh the risks against the benefits of your readers' possible other reactions.

GRAMMAR AS STYLE

Was Braddock wrong then? Is there a role for grammar instruction in the teaching of writing? Is there an important connection between grammar and writing?

We, of course, would argue that there is a connection, but we would want to make crystal clear what we meant by the word "grammar" and exactly what kind of grammar instruction we had in mind. Braddock's research was not wrong: the grammar instruction he criticized *deserved* to be criticized. According to one influential article, Patrick Hartwell's "Grammar, Grammars, and the Teaching of Grammar" (1985), there are at least five different ways we talk about grammar (see his pages 108–111), and the kind of grammar instruction Braddock observed would fall under Hartwell's categories 3 and 4 below. Take a look:

> **Grammar 1** = the way we put words together to make meaning;

> **Grammar 2** = the formal study of the ways people in a certain culture usually put words together to make meaning (i.e., linguistics, the study of Grammar 1);

> **Grammar 3** = language etiquette ("good" language behaviour according to what Pinker calls "the language mavens"—often based on unfounded prejudices);

> **Grammar 4** = a teacher's grammar (the grammar that is usually taught in schools);

> **Grammar 5** = a writer's grammar (enough conscious knowledge of Grammars 1 and 2 to deepen a writer's enjoyment of and control over written language).

Obviously, what we hope for is that we can gradually bring about a change in Grammar 4—the grammar taught in schools—so it is more closely related to Hartwell's Grammars 1, 2, and 5 than it is to Grammar 3 (arbitrary rules of language etiquette that have no real basis in studies of language at all). Unfortunately, however, what nearly everyone thinks of when they think of grammar (which, not surprisingly, they try to avoid doing) is Grammar 3 or 4.

Let us offer up an alternative set of **linguistic assumptions** about language, an alternative to Grammars 3 and 4. Most of our colleagues in linguistics and composition would agree that we operate on the basis of the following assumptions these days:

- All speakers intuitively know their native language (Grammar 1). This knowledge, however, is unconscious (that is, native speakers cannot usually *tell* us what they know) but observable. (Linguists observe it, and what they discover makes up Grammar 2.)

- The **syntactic repertoire** available to all speakers is based on this unconscious knowledge; each person's competence, his or her "natural syntactic repertoire" (Glenn), changes and enlarges over time as that person figures out the syntactic patterns of the surrounding language.

- There are certain syntactic patterns/arrangements that mark/characterize mature style (syntactic fluency) and that are found in writing but not in speech. Syntactic fluency is characterized not necessarily by more *words* per sentence but by more *meanings* per sentence (propositions). (Grammar 5 can help here.)

- As teachers, our goal should be to *assist* in the ongoing transformation taking place in our students' language and writing as their syntactic fluency increases over time (in other words, teachers don't bring this change about—it occurs with or without us as students grow as language users in their culture—but we can encourage and support and enrich it).

So, according to these assumptions, what—if any—grammar instruction would be of use to a writer? Obviously, any native speaker already is competent in Grammar 1 and would without any hesitation or problem recognize "A dog barks" as an English sentence and "Barks dog a" as **non-English**. Do writers need Grammar 2? (that is, do all writers need to be linguists?). No. Do they need Grammars 3 and 4? Again, no—though as part of public grammar, Grammars 3 and 4 can take a while to change, so it's often useful to be aware of them, especially if a writer wants to impress certain audiences. But a writer's grammar, Grammar 5, can—as we hope we have convinced you—support writers in their work and give them conscious choices about how they would like to affect their readers.

Understanding grammar as style, then, means being alert to the craft of experienced writers, noticing their skill with compression and parallel structure, and growing in the ability to transform a text from simply readable to elegant and well crafted. Understanding grammar as style means becoming a writer who knows how to scream and how to whisper by shaping fluent and syntactically mature sentences.

The research has yet to be done on whether this new kind of grammar instruction would have a positive or negative impact on writing instruction (it's hard to do research on something that isn't actually taking place yet in most schools!). But we would argue that if teachers start from Hartwell's Grammar 1—our unconscious knowledge of grammar—and then move to a transformed Grammar 4 (ideally, a subset of Grammar 2, with a writer's grammar, Grammar 5, as its goal), they can give developing writers a huge amount of support without burdening them with a correspondingly huge amount of extraneous information or unnecessary rules. A writer's grammar, the basic grammar we need to know in order to be able to understand how to consciously craft sentences, is compact. And such an understanding of grammar as style leads us to answer yes to the question, "Is there an important connection between grammar and writing?" Undoubtedly there *is* a connection if we think of grammar as the conscious understanding of what is possible in written texts.

Works Cited

Buckley, Joanne. *Checkmate*. Toronto: Thomson Nelson, 2003.

Glenn, Cheryl. "When Grammar Was a Language Art." *The Place of Grammar in Writing Instruction: Past, Present, Future.* Ed. Susan Hunter and Ray Wallace. Portsmouth, NH: Boynton/Cook, 1995: 9–29.

Hacker, Diana. *A Canadian Writer's Reference.* 2nd ed. Toronto: Thomson Nelson, 2001.

Hartwell, Patrick. "Grammar, Grammars, and the Teaching of Grammar." *College English* 47.2 (1985): 105–127.

Hunt, Kellogg. "Early Blooming and Late Blooming Syntactic Structures." In Cooper, Charles R., and Lee Odell, Ed. *Evaluating Writing: Describing, Measuring, Judging.* Urbana, IL: National Council of Teachers of English, 1977. 91–106.

Storace, Patricia. *Dinner with Persephone—Travels in Greece.* New York: Vintage Books, 1996.

Natalie Goldberg, from *Wild Mind* and *Writing Down the Bones*

Natalie Goldberg, like many other writers who encourage writing as receptive daily practice, also thinks carefully about revision, style, and the power of individual words. Also like many other writers, she believes we rely on strong, specific verbs to supply "the action and energy of a sentence":

> [B]e aware of your verbs and the power they have and use them in fresh ways. The more you are awake to all aspects of language, the more vibrant your writing will be. You might decide ultimately that *run, see, go,* are for you. That's fine, but then it is a choice you make rather than

some place in your sentence where you are unaware, asleep and snoring. ("The Action of a Sentence" 89)

As much as student Stephanie Bishop had enjoyed earlier Goldberg essays (like the ones in Conversation 2), Bishop disagreed with the second of Goldberg's pieces below (see Bishop's segmented essay in Conversation 8)—that is, she thought she did until she went back and did a quick analysis of some of her own writing.

The software program *Editor*, by the way, agrees with Goldberg in the first piece reprinted here—eliminate those *very*'s and *really*'s whenever you can (*Editor* always flags such empty intensifiers for you and asks if you could perhaps bear to part with them).

WILD MIND

VERY AND REALLY

Be careful of the use of the word *very*. Usually we don't need it. It's a word that emphasizes something that has already been stated. "The boy was *very* timid." It doesn't add that much; and, as a matter of fact, "The boy was timid" gives us a more direct statement. We hear *timid* better without the hoopla of *very*. *Very* lessens the presence of the word it is modifying. "It is very good." Take out *very*. "It is good." This is a brave statement and is rarely used. Simple, direct, to the point. No doilies of lacy *verys* are put around the quality of good. Just *good*. "He was very dead"—let's be honest. Someone's either dead or they're not. There is a clear line between life and death. Let's draw that line. Be aware of *very* and how you use it.

It is the same with the word *really*. "It was *really* fine." It almost sounds as though the writer doesn't believe it was fine—"Really, I promise, it was fine." "It was fine" is a simple, direct statement that you can stand behind. We don't have to fluff it up. Words and sentence structure reflect the integrity of a writer. State clearly what you have to say. Don't be afraid. Step forward.

I find when I speak I use *really* a lot, because underneath I don't trust people's attention. I am trying to get them to "really" listen. Someone is either listening or not. We don't have to get them to "really" do it.

We can just settle back into our bodies and write, neither hiding nor reaching out. Just being present. Then we write out of true emptiness. We write because we write and for no other reason. That is good.

WRITING DOWN THE BONES

MAKE STATEMENTS AND ANSWER QUESTIONS

In the early seventies there was a study done on women and language that affected me deeply and also affected my writing. One of the things the study said was that women add on qualifiers to their statements. For instance, "The Vietnam war is awful, *isn't it?*" "I like this, *don't you?*" In their sentence structure women were always looking for reinforcement for their feelings and opinions. They didn't just make statements and stand behind them: "This is beautiful." "This is terrible." They needed encouragement from outside themselves. (By the way, what they found to be true for women they also mentioned was true for minorities.)

Another thing women did in their speech was to use a lot of words like *perhaps, maybe, somehow.* Indefinite modifiers. For instance, "Somehow it happened." As though the force were beyond understanding and left the woman powerless. "Maybe I'll go." Again, not a clear assertive statement like "Yes, I'll go."

The world isn't always black and white. A person may not be sure if she can go some place, but it is important, especially for a beginning writer, to make clear, assertive statements. "This is good." "It was a blue horse." Not "Well, I know it sounds funny, but I think perhaps it was a blue horse." Making statements is practice in trusting your own mind, in learning to stand up with your thoughts.

After I read the article, I went home and looked at a poem I had just written. I made myself take out all vague, indefinite words and phrases. It felt as though I were pulling towels off my body, and I was left standing naked after a shower, exposing who I was and how I felt. It was scary the first time, but it felt good. It made the poem much better.

So even though life is not always so clear, it is good to express yourself in clear, affirmative statements. "This is how I think and feel." "This is who I am in this moment." It takes practice, but it is rewarding.

But while you are practicing writing, do not worry if you see yourself using those indefinite words. Don't condemn yourself or be critical. Just be aware of it. Keep writing. When you go back over it, you can cut them out.

Another thing you should watch out for are questions. If you can write a question, you can answer it. When you are writing, if you write a question, that is fine. But immediately go to a deeper level inside yourself and answer it in the next line. "What should I do with my life?" I should eat three brownies, remember the sky, and become the best writer in the world. "Why did I feel weird last night?" Because I ate pigeon for dinner and I wore my shoes on the wrong feet and because I am unhappy. "Where does the wind come from?" It comes from the memory of pioneers on the Croix River. It loves the earth as far as the Dakotas.

Don't be afraid to answer the questions. You will find endless resources inside your-self. Writing is the act of burning through the fog in your mind. Don't carry the fog out on paper. Even if you are not sure of something, express it as though you know yourself. With this practice you eventually will.

Lewis Thomas, "Notes on Punctuation"

Lewis Thomas (1913–1993), a physician and biomedical researcher, started writing poetry while an undergraduate at Princeton and continued during his studies at Harvard Medical School. His prose writing, however, had been confined to scientific pieces until 1971, when he was given the opportunity to write essays about nature in a weekly column entitled "Notes of a Biology Watcher." Praised for his clarity and fluency, Thomas won the National Book Award in 1974 for *The Lives of a Cell: Notes of a Biology Watcher.* Other books include *The Youngest Science: Notes of a Medicine-Watcher* (1983), *Et Cetera, Et Cetera: Notes of a Word-Watcher* (1990), and *The Medusa and the Snail: More Notes of a Biology Watcher* (1979), from which this piece is taken.

NOTES ON PUNCTUATION

There are no precise rules about punctuation (Fowler lays out some general advice (as best he can under the complex circumstances of English prose (he points out, for example, that we possess only four stops (the comma, the semicolon, the colon and the period (the ques-tion mark and exclamation point are not, strictly speaking, stops; they are indicators of tone (oddly enough, the Greeks employed the semicolon for their question mark (it pro-duces a strange sensation to read a Greek sentence which is a straightforward question: Why weepest thou; (instead of Why weepest thou? (and, of course, there are parentheses (which are surely a kind of punctuation making this whole matter much more complicated by having to count up the left-handed parentheses in order to be sure of closing with the right number (but if the parentheses were left out, with nothing to work with but the stops, we would have considerably more flexibility in the deploying of layers of meaning than if we tried to separate all the clauses by physical barriers (and in the latter case, while we might have more precision and exactitude for our meaning, we would lose the essential flavor of language, which is its wonderful ambiguity)))))))))))).

The commas are the most useful and usable of all the stops. It is highly important to put them in place as you go along. If you try to come back after doing a paragraph and stick them in the various spots that tempt you you will discover that they tend to swarm like minnows into all sorts of crevices whose existence you hadn't realized and before you know it the whole long sentence becomes immobilized and lashed up squirming in commas. Better to use them sparingly, and with affection, precisely when the need for each one arises, nicely, by itself.

I have grown fond of semicolons in recent years. The semicolon tells you that there is still some question about the preceding full sentence; something needs to be added; it reminds you sometimes of the Greek usage. It is almost always a greater pleasure to come across a semicolon than a period. The period tells you that that is that; if you didn't get all the meaning you wanted or expected, anyway you got all the writer intended to parcel out and now you have to move along. But with a semicolon there you get a pleasant little feeling of expectancy; there is more to come; read on; it will get clearer.

Colons are a lot less attractive, for several reasons: firstly, they give you the feeling of being rather ordered around, or at least having your nose pointed in a direction you might not be inclined to take if left to yourself, and, secondly, you suspect you're in for one of those sentences that will be labeling the points to be made: firstly, secondly and so forth, with the implication that you haven't sense enough to keep track of a sequence of notions without having them numbered. Also, many writers use this system loosely and incompletely, starting out with number one and number two as though counting off on their fingers but then going on and on without the succession of labels you've been led to expect, leaving you floundering about searching for the ninethly or seventeenthly that ought to be there but isn't.

Exclamation points are the most irritating of all. Look! they say, look at what I just said! How amazing is my thought! It is like being forced to watch someone else's small child jumping up and down crazily in the center of the living room shouting to attract attention. If a sentence really has something of importance to say, something quite remarkable, it doesn't need a mark to point it out. And if it is really, after all, a banal sentence needing more zing, the exclamation point simply emphasizes its banality!

Quotation marks should be used honestly and sparingly, when there is a genuine quotation at hand, and it is necessary to be very rigorous about the words enclosed by the marks. If something is to be quoted, the *exact* words must be used. If part of it must be left out because of space limitations, it is good manners to insert three dots to indicate the omission, but it is unethical to do this if it means connecting two thoughts which the original author did not intend to have tied together. Above all, quotation marks should not be used for ideas that you'd like to disown, things in the air so to speak. Nor should they be put in place around clichés; if you want to use a cliché you must take full responsibility for it yourself and not try to fob it off on anon., or on society. The most objectionable misuse of quotation marks, but one which illustrates the dangers of misuse in ordinary prose, is seen in advertising, especially in advertisements for small restaurants, for example "just around the corner," or "a good place to eat." No single, identifiable, citable person ever really said, for the record, "just around the corner," much less "a good place to eat," least likely of all for restaurants of the type that use this type of prose.

The dash is a handy device, informal and essentially playful, telling you that you're about to take off on a different tack but still in some way connected with the present course—only you have to remember that the dash is there, and either put a second dash at the end of the notion to let the reader know that he's back on course, or else end the sentence, as here, with a period.

The greatest danger in punctuation is for poetry. Here it is necessary to be as economical and parsimonious with commas and periods as with the words themselves, and any marks that seem to carry their own subtle meanings, like dashes and little rows of periods, even semicolons and question marks, should be left out altogether rather than inserted to clog up the thing with ambiguity. A single exclamation point in a poem, no matter what else the poem has to say, is enough to destroy the whole work.

The things I like best in T. S. Eliot's poetry, especially in the *Four Quartets,* are the semicolons. You cannot hear them, but they are there, laying out the connections between the images and the ideas. Sometimes you get a glimpse of a semicolon coming, a few lines farther on, and it is like climbing a steep path through woods and seeing a wooden bench just at a bend in the road ahead, a place where you can expect to sit for a moment, catching your breath.

Commas can't do this sort of thing; they can only tell you how the different parts of a complicated thought are to be fitted together, but you can't sit, not even take a breath, just because of a comma,

STUDENT WRITING
HANNE BJORNSTAD

INKSHED

The following brief passage comes from an inkshed **Hanne Bjornstad** wrote after reading several of Cornelia Paraskevas's essays: "Teaching Grammar as Style," "The Craft of Punctuation," and "Sentence Fluency, Sentence Craft."

March 2003

Why does grammar matter? What makes it important? Paraskevas has helped me make this more clear to myself and to understand the usefulness it can have. These essays all concentrate especially on sentence structure and punctuation, not so much on word choice issues (not on things like "I should've gone" vs "I should've went"). This concentration shows how, as writers, we can use grammar to have more control over the meaning of our sentences. She takes the position that grammar and punctuation are not just sets of arbitrary rules like "textiquette" or something (although I also don't think that most etiquette rules are useless). Each punctuation mark, according to Paraskevas, indicates different degrees of separation and therefore gives us control over our ideas. We can make ideas have greater or lesser value. We can vary their placement. We can stick them up at the front, bury them in the middle, tack them at the end. We can use ideas to interrupt other ideas. In this way, punctuation becomes an important rhetorical device instead of just being a random set of strange little rules.

All of a sudden, grammar is understandably important.

A NEW PRACTICE TO TAKE FORWARD

CONSULTING A WRITING HANDBOOK

University instructors usually expect students to be making good use of writing handbooks as they compose formal papers and prepare to submit them for evaluation. In our experience, however, many handbooks are only useful if you *already* know and understand what's in them.

True, a handbook is a reference book, just like your dictionary; and most people have no problem consulting a handbook to check appropriate citation styles for different academic disciplines (see page 324 in Conversation 6) or to locate advice on formatting issues (margins, page layout, title pages, headers and footers, and so on).

But you may have trouble elsewhere. The largest part of every writing handbook is devoted to grammar, punctuation, usage, and mechanics. If you've ever tried to look up information on grammar in a writing handbook so that you could avoid run-ons, for example, there's a good chance that you felt lost. Even if you managed to find the information you were looking for (since it's not always clear from the index or the table of contents what term you should be using to locate a particular section), handbooks assume that you already know basic grammar terms; therefore, they don't take the time to explain them to you. *In fact, handbooks are often clear only if you know a lot about grammar before you open the handbook!* The expression we use in linguistics for this phenomenon is COIK—which stands for "clear only if known." In other words, if you know what a run-on is, then you can understand the information about run-ons given in the handbook; but if you have no idea what a run-on is exactly (though you've been told that you commit them and that you shouldn't), the handbook is of little help.

Let's examine a characteristic situation you might find yourself in. Supposing you look in one well-known handbook because your instructor has given you a page number to consult in order to correct your run-on sentences. You find a clear rule:

> Use a comma before a coordinating conjunction joining independent clauses.
>
> (Hacker 193)

If, however, you don't know what **coordinating conjunctions** are and you can't tell an **independent clause** from a hatbox, you're not much better off. We might like to think that our Quick Reference: Joining Clauses, located inside the back cover of this book, might be more useful than this handbook rule, but it still can't help you identify independent clauses.

You might read on for ten more pages in the handbook, hoping that specific examples would help. The handbook asks if a comma should be used in the following sentence: "They came early and stayed until midnight." The handbook says no (203), but the reason it gives also leaves you confused: "although a comma is used before a coordinating conjunction joining independent clauses, this rule should not be extended to other compound word groups."

There are those two terms again—"coordinating conjunction" and "independent clause." Most handbooks don't expect you to have coordinating conjunctions memorized; those are probably listed in the index (a handy acronym is FANBOYS: For, And, Nor, But, Or, Yet, So). A good dictionary will also list them. But most handbooks *will* expect you to be able to tell clauses from phrases and, further, to tell an independent clause from a dependent one. They may give definitions and examples, but these are unlikely to enable you confidently to tell independent and dependent clauses apart in your own writing.

Before we consider a solution to this problem, let's look at one more characteristic handbook dilemma: your instructor says you have problems with fragments and points you to a handbook for help. All good handbooks have an index at the back. If we look for the term **fragment** or **sentence fragment** in the index of one useful handbook, Joanne Buckley's *Checkmate*, for example, we easily locate the appropriate section and read the following:

> A sentence fragment . . . is part of a sentence that is set off as if it were a whole sentence by a beginning capital letter and a final period or other end punctuation. However, the fragment lacks essential requirements of a grammatically complete and correct sentence. (153)

This is a fairly typical way for handbooks to describe fragments. But since we might have supposed that one quick way to *locate* sentences would be to look for word groups starting with capital letters and ending with periods, such definitions can puzzle us if we don't already know what a fragment is. Further, since fragments can also create problems when they are embedded within longer sentences, far away from periods or capital letters, such definitions can be misleading. Notice that the second sentence assumes that we already know what the "essential requirements of a grammatically complete and correct sentence" are. Again, like most handbooks, this one is making assumptions about our background knowledge: it's assuming we know that a minimum sentence contains at least one independent clause and, in addition, that we know reliably how to tell independent clauses from all other possible word groups.

Obviously, if you *can* reliably identify independent clauses, most handbooks probably make good sense to you already, especially clearly organized ones like Buckley's. But if you can't do this, take a moment to read through the compact "Bare Bones Writer's Grammar" available at http://www.sargent.nelson.com, which is designed to supply some of the basic street smarts you'll need in order to start finding and using the information available in writing handbooks. When you've finished reading through those pages, let's tackle the situations above armed with new tools.

***** Pause here to consult the "Bare Bones Writer's Grammar" at http://www.sargent.nelson.com

After telling us to "use a comma before a coordinating conjunction joining independent clauses," the first handbook has asked if a comma should be used in the following sentence: "They came early and stayed until midnight." Clearly, we're being asked if that sentence contains two separate independent clauses. Now that we have tests that allow us to recognize independent clauses (**Yes-no questions, tag questions**, and **embedding**), we can test the word group that follows the word "and" to see if it qualifies as an independent clause: "stayed until midnight." We can't successfully perform all three of our tests, so we know "stayed until midnight" is not an independent clause: thus, no comma is required before "and."

The second handbook is attempting to help us tell fragments from sufficient minimal sentences. Now that we have tools for identifying independent clauses and we know that

independent clauses = minimum sentences,

we are able to demystify what initially seemed like a circular definition in the handbook. A fragment is a group of words that won't pass our three tests, but is nevertheless masquerading as an independent clause by being punctuated as one and perhaps even starting with a capital letter (although it could be incorrectly punctuated as an independent clause while being embedded in a longer sentence).

Handbooks can be valuable resources for writers; we use them if we're not sure whether we have cited an electronic source properly, if we have doubts about the use of italics or quotation marks, or if we need to find out how to punctuate a particular construction. But to be able to use handbooks, we must understand how to locate and make sense of the information we need. The Quick Reference guides inside the covers of this book can help; so can the "Bare Bones Writer's Grammar." But these tools can't replace a detailed writing handbook or a text-specific computer handbook like *Editor*. Make a practice of consulting good handbooks when you need writing advice and refer to the tools we've introduced here whenever you need to.

Also, if at any point you find yourself confused by particular terms, turn to the glossary available at http://www.sargent.nelson.com, "Key Words for a Writer's Grammar—Language for Talking about Language." It provides enough basic terminology to help you penetrate any additional mysteries a handbook might present. Special terms evolve in all communities of inquiry and expertise, terms that allow people within those communities to think about certain issues more deeply and to talk about those issues efficiently with each other. And *all* writers, no matter what their particular area of expertise and inquiry, will at times need special terms to talk about their writing *as writing*: they'll need *language to talk about language*. To communicate with other writers, to give and receive feedback on our drafts as we revise, we don't need to become linguists—but we do need to understand the working vocabulary that writers use. Doing so will also help us become effective and confident users of writing handbooks.

ESSAY IDEAS

Locate and read Patrick Hartwell's famously persuasive essay, "Grammar, Grammars, and the Teaching of Grammar," and then two more recent pieces, Brock Haussamen's "Public Grammar and Private Grammar" and Laura Micciche's "Making a Case for Rhetorical Grammar." Hartwell can be quite convincing that grammar should not be taught in a writing class: the research results are clear. But Haussamen and Micciche are persuasive too. What do you think now, after reading through the material in this Conversation, especially Pinker's piece, and after consulting the online "Bare Bones Writer's Grammar" (which is based in large part on linguist Rei Noguchi's work—see http://www.sargent.nelson.com)? With all that reading under your belt, you're equipped to join the conversation about these issues, perhaps by trying out one of these essay ideas:

1. How important is "correctness" in one's public grammar and how do these linguists define "correctness"? Taking the disagreements between these five linguists into account, write an essay presenting *your* perspective on what grammar—if any—should be taught as part of a writing class.

2. Start keeping a commonplace book like the *florilegia* (flowers of reading) Micciche describes (724). Keeping in mind the techniques for sentence fluency described in Paraskevas and Sargent (pages 257–271), as well as various strategies for word choice and rhetorical punctuation (see the introduction to Conversation 5 and Paraskevas), write a paper analyzing in some detail elements of rhetorical grammar and rhetorical punctuation in one or two of the passages you've collected, showing how this language has been constructed to work on us, perhaps even to manipulate us, as readers.

CONVERSATION 6:
Organization and Genre

INTRODUCTION

> The advice of the old handbooks just doesn't work: It is *not* a good idea to think a piece through completely before you write. It is *not* a good idea to write an outline and try to stick to it. It is *not* necessary to start each piece with a thesis statement, each paragraph with a topic sentence. Most real writers simply don't do it that way. The best advice about learning to write now is based on the idea that the very act of writing is an act of thinking. It *is* good to start writing and watch where the writing takes you; to digress when you're exploring an idea; to witness your thought, visibly on paper (or computer monitor), and have a dialogue with it—because that helps you find out what you know, what you don't know, and what you need to know.
>
> Toby Fulwiler, "Writing Is Everybody's Business" 23

> Can it be that poetry often allows both writer and reader to swing wide on allusion and hint and loose connection, just because only by such reckless-ness can one reach far out for meanings, with frail helps from language?
>
> William Stafford, "Breathing on a Poem" 51

Organization

What does Toby Fulwiler think he's doing throwing out all our traditional notions about organization? Especially when the one thing students seem to know pretty well before they begin university work is the **five-paragraph theme**, with its clear guidelines on where to put **thesis statements** and **topic sentences**? Surely if we toss those things aside, we'll end up with the recklessness of poetry and connections so loose that we'll fail our university courses.

Perhaps. But perhaps the **genres** of poetry and academic writing are not as distinct as we might think. Both are highly structured forms of human thought in which we have to pay close attention to how material begins to seek its own form.[1] And, as we hope to convince you, decisions about genre and organization can't be made apart from each other. The real problem with the five-paragraph theme is that it short-circuits more serious genre decisions as well as the experience of wrestling with material to discover

---

[1] See, for instance, Art Young's wonderful short piece online about the value of "Writing Poetry in First-Year Composition Courses" as a way of improving student thinking and problem-solving in *all* fields, including science (he also provides a pithy annotated bibliography of additional resources on this subject). http://www.mhhe.com/socscience/english/tc/pt/young/young.htm

what shape it wants to take. Donald Stewart, in an essay entitled "Some History Lessons for Composition Teachers," puts it this way:

> The five-paragraph essay is a formula, not a composition. It is rule-governed, hence easy to mark, but imposing it on every subject one writes about is the equivalent of trying to put a wiggling 110-pound dog, or a barrel of apples, or several gallons of fresh maple syrup, or the unassembled parts of a ten-speed bicycle, or three different type-writers, or a wardrobe for a Florida vacation all in the same size box. . . . the result is that the writer does not submit implicitly to the guidance of his subject, but seeks to manipulate the thought by a pre-conceived scheme devised and imposed from without. (137)

Of course, since Stewart published these comments nearly twenty years ago now, we're not feeling terribly hopeful about the five-paragraph theme relinquishing its hold any-time soon. We should also make clear that there are a few good things to say about it—it emphasizes, at least, the need for an organizing focus for every academic paper. Unfortunately, it often also emphasizes that students shouldn't begin writing until they know for certain what that focus—usually referred to as a **thesis statement**—is. Certainly if *we* always put off writing until we knew what our thesis statement was going to be, we'd never get much of anything written; we tend to figure out our focus *while* we write and then go back later to revise and re-shape, to sharpen that focus so readers will be able to see it as well.

Still, as stressful and prematurely limiting as it may be to come up with a thesis statement *before* writing an essay, it can occasionally be a time-saver (which can be especially handy during an essay exam): the great virtue of a thesis statement is not just that it helps you figure out what to put *into* an essay, but that it helps you figure out what to leave *out*. Or in our case—since we so often write before we know what the thesis statement is going to be and thus end up with too much material—it helps us figure out what to *cut* out.

And there is a way to re-conceive this business of coming up with a thesis statement so that the process is less stressful. Too often we think our thesis has to be a state-ment of something we already know (i.e., "In this paper I will show that . . ."). If, instead, we managed to get ourselves started by declaring what we *wanted* to know (to figure out, puzzle over, wonder about), we'd still get the narrowing benefits of a thesis statement, but we wouldn't need to have written an outline of the whole paper or to have all our research finished, all our data collected, before beginning to write. In this scenario, a thesis statement that essentially states "Okay, here's what I'm going to puzzle over in this piece of writing" has just accomplished several useful things:

1. it has created an oasis, a place of rest, for your mind—because, in stating what you are going to puzzle over, you have also, simultaneously, eliminated hundreds of other things, things that you are *not* (for the time being) going to puzzle over;

2. it has taken the pressure off because you have not promised to prove anything, only to investigate something, to be curious about something;

3. it has helped organize your reading and research—you don't need to read *every-thing* in relation to a particular topic, but only the things that are going to help you figure out this one thing that you're curious about;

4. it has generated some organizational energy that can help hold your essay together—because now you have a story to tell, the story of how you investigated something and how you did or did not figure something out (you may not need to keep this story in your essay once you're done—you may end up simply summarizing your conclusions after all—but the energy of the story will still make itself felt in your final draft).

Let's develop this last item briefly for a moment. In an essay that won the Braddock Prize in 1985, Peter Elbow became interested in the problem of organization in writing: what makes a piece of writing feel coherent, held together, to a reader? Most of the models we have for writing are visual and spatial (the five-paragraph theme, for instance, is a highly visual and symmetrical model, often symbolized by the image of an old-fashioned keyhole). But what if we think of writing as something experienced in time, not space—more like music than like painting, for instance? It makes sense to do this because, as readers of anything over a page long, we can keep only a certain amount of print in view at once. And most of us can read only a sentence or two at a time and need help, as we go along, remembering what was on the previous page once we've moved to the next one. Perhaps this is why the five-paragraph format is so useful for teachers, who have to read so many papers: it gives essentially the same map for every paper, so it helps the reader visualize the overall shape of the piece. Perhaps this is also why teachers have insisted on students putting a clear **topic sentence** at the beginning of every paragraph—even though we've known ever since Braddock's research in 1974 ("The Frequency and Placement of Topic Sentences in Expository Prose") that professional writers rarely do this themselves.

But what holds longer pieces of text together in our minds? We can't, for instance, have a simple visual five-paragraph map for a twenty-page essay, let alone for a whole book. Elbow suggests that we consider how longer pieces of music, like symphonies, work: the music sets up certain patterns of expectation, dissonance, suspense, harmony, promises or hints of further harmony, disappointment, and resolution. Or perhaps a better way to say this is that it sets up certain patterns—an established key, a time signature—precisely in order to break or alter those patterns for emphasis whenever it needs to. A powerful piece of music creates suspense; it pulls us along by challenging or stretching or breaking patterns in sound, offering at times mini-resolutions to tease us along, to keep us listening, eager for the deeper resolution we expect at the end. If a piece of music moves us, we want to hear it more than once because we love going through this experience-in-time, eager to follow that thread of melody again through its variations and through its moments of discord and near dissolution until the satisfaction of the final notes.

Aren't strong pieces of writing held together by essentially the same dynamic in time? Elbow argues that students have been led to believe that essays are for *telling* people things (often things these people don't yet have any desire to know), not for figuring things out, for making a journey through time. The resulting essays have no suspense, what Elbow refers to as a "felt itch"—no tension that carries the reader through time. If, however, the essay created some intellectual suspense at the very beginning, established what the "itch" was—and if the essay pulled the reader through time toward the final scratching of this itch (providing a few mini-scratches along the way, perhaps, to keep the reader hopeful for more)—chances are that the reader would experience the writing as deeply coherent and tightly organized because of the strong forward movement, because of the satisfying and absorbing experience-in-time the author had constructed.

Does it help to think of writing in this way? In the writing we *pay* to read, in books and newspapers and magazines, we expect authors to have figured out some way to pull us through time—often a strong title or a lead sentence, a hook to drag us into a dilemma or perplexity that needs our attention; often a promise of satisfaction beyond discordant obstacles that delay gratification along the way; usually at the end some attempt at resolution (even if nothing more than a statement of further questions that need to be explored). Readers expect some music to be made. Donald Murray puts it this way: your writing has to have an edge, a tension to attract and hold a reader, something that surprises—and you can't surprise a reader if you aren't at least somewhat surprised yourself by what you have written ("Letter" 61). Margaret Atwood claims that good writing takes place at intersections, knots, "places where the society is snarled or knotted up" (cited in Murray, "Letter" 59). Professional writers often seem to think of writing not as a straight line, but as the patient untangling of a knot, a process that takes place over time.

For students, however, the situation is temporarily reversed in that students *actually pay to have someone read and respond to what they write.* So, in truth, there is no obligation for you to make music. But you might want to try it anyway since, first, it might be more fun; second, it might be more of a challenge intellectually (you might learn more); and third, you might get better marks on your papers. We certainly can't promise this last, of course, even though we've noticed, when *we* read student papers, that if we get absorbed in the writing we tend not to notice or mark as many mechanical problems—our attention is focused elsewhere. Whereas if we're *not* being pulled along through time, if we don't feel any intellectual suspense, if we're not on the edge of our seats, we find ourselves marking surface errors almost as a way to keep ourselves awake and useful—even though we sense that those minor infelicities are not the real problem.

You're doubtless realizing by now that no one can give you explicit instructions on how to organize every essay, any more than a musician could tell you one pattern you should follow in writing every song or symphony. But sometimes we can get good ideas from looking at structures others have tried or invented. Before we describe below some possible organizational patterns you could experiment with, however, we want to offer a word of warning. A host of useful, recurring organizational schemes have been offered up as models for essays (a definition essay, a compare/contrast essay, a cause and effect essay, etc.); but *none* of these can work very well if (considering the paragraph from Donald Stewart on pages 284–285) they are imposed on your material from the outside, especially if they don't feel appropriate, if there isn't a good "fit" between your material and the form. Stewart suggests "submitting" to your material instead, which may seem like cryptic advice. Nevertheless, it's *good* advice. You may find yourself needing to invent some structure no one has ever tried before if you're going to honour the richness of the material you've gathered and the complexity of the thinking you've done about it.

So we're offering some alternative patterns here only as **heuristics** (which is the best way to think of the more traditional structures, like compare/contrast, as well)— ways to explore your material, play with it, shape it, and make connections. Hearing of structures you've never tried before can jog you into being more inventive yourself, can get your mind going in a different direction. You might create a hybrid, mixing two or three of these together; or an entirely new form might emerge from the material you're working with.

First, consider trying out some forms from creative nonfiction—perhaps a collage or a meander (see the pieces by Root and Jones in this Conversation). The meander has precedent all the way back to Montaigne's essays in which, in a very real sense, the subject of each essay was primarily the author's mind at work: the reader became absorbed in following the twists and turns of Montaigne's brain as he felt and puzzled his way through a particular question.

Collage is something that film has been exposing us to for a long time (though the technique is most frequently referred to in film as montage); and many essays in well-known magazines like *The New Yorker*, *Harper's*, *The Atlantic*, *Maclean's*, as well as in smaller literary magazines like *The Fiddlehead*, *The Malahat Review*, and *Grain*, are segmented essays (another word for a written collage). Segmented essays don't abandon structure, but create structures required by the content of the piece: they can work by juxtaposition, by parallelism, by accumulation, by journaling, or by some extra-literary kind of patterning appropriate to the subject. What they don't do is work in "prefabricated shapes to be selected off the rack to fit the body of the topic"—in fact, segmented essays make "demands on both the writer and the reader," demanding "that the reader learn to read the structure of the essay as well as its thought" (Root, "Beyond Linearity" 324). Some thinking can be done productively only in a linear format; but some can only be done productively by working in contrasts or mosaic, in multiple scenes or images. Root suggests we think of a parallel in art—paintings with multiple panels, triptychs or polyptychs. If you feel that a segmented essay would do more justice to your material and your thinking than a linear essay, consult with your instructor before proceeding (to see if your intructor believes an alternative form could work and would be welcome, or at least acceptable, for a particular assignment).

Second, consider borrowing or playing with some forms from fiction—and not just traditional fiction, which is in some ways very close to the itch/scratch movement-through-time Elbow talks about (conflict, rising action, climax, denouement, etc.). Diane Lefer, in a piece called "Breaking the 'Rules' of Story Structure," suggests some alternative metaphors (her essay gives specific examples of each one): a mosaic, a wheel, a jazz improvisation, a ballad (with the prose equivalent of stanzas and refrains), a gossip session, instant replay (telling about one specific incident over and over, from different perspectives), a process story (focusing not on *what* happens, but *how*), and finally, "a story that peaks again and again, in which waves of excitement and satisfaction are diffused throughout the text instead of being focused on a single moment near the end" (13–16). These metaphors for writing loomed up out of stories and novels Lefer had read, many of them from other cultures: the wheel image, for instance, came from a Native American piece in which "the heart of the story [was] the hub of the wheel" and "the storyteller move[d] around the circumference a bit, then down one of the spokes to touch the hub, then back to the circumference, approaching the heart again and again from different points." Such non-linear forms are demanding for readers, who are essentially being asked to "share in the effort of creation" (14)—but an active reader has to be better than a bored one.

Yet how effective can the strategies of fiction or creative nonfiction be in a university setting where intellectual argument is the privileged form? We would be naive to deny or ignore the privileged position argument continues to hold in the academic world. Indeed, just as Lefer has been pointing out how obsessed with conflict traditional fiction has been, feminist scholars in the field of composition and rhetoric have been critiquing the genre of academic argument for its focus on conflict and debate. Cynthia L. Caywood and Gillian R. Overing describe the situation in the academy this way (in *Teaching Writing: Pedagogy, Gender, and Equity*):

> certain forms of discourse and language are privileged: the expository essay is valued over the exploratory; the argumentative essay set above the autobiographical; the clear evocation of a thesis preferred to a more organic exploration of a topic; the impersonal, rational voice ranked more highly than the intimate, subjective one. (xii)

Such critiques are not based on a timid fear of debate or a denial/avoidance of conflict. Feminist scholars know as well as anyone else that argument in a university setting is essential and that it's not about open combat or fisticuffs (at least not usually). **Argument** is the word scholars use for a line of careful reasoning, a considered claim that is supported with as much detailed evidence and significant data as possible. However, feminist scholars *have* raised questions about how to acknowledge conflict more usefully and thus make academic argument more effective; and some of them, like Catherine E. Lamb in her 1991 essay, "Beyond Argument in Feminist Composition," have drawn on the field of mediation and conflict resolution to do so.

Lamb's suggestion is that we redefine argument so that we no longer think of academic writing as adversarial (that is, so that we no longer acknowledge the other side's position only in order to refute it) and instead think of academic writing as dialogic, as conversational. In this view, the true task of argument is to create/enlarge a space in which opposing voices can stand in all their fullness and to explore what possible larger understanding could incorporate their conflicting positions. In this view, conflict is not avoided or reduced, but fully recognized: knowledge is seen "as something that people do together rather than something anyone possesses" (Lamb 201, citing Gage 156). The goal is no longer to "win" but to state opposing positions fully and fairly and, as in mediation, "arrive at a solution in a just way that is acceptable to both sides" (201). Power in this framework doesn't belong to either side but (following Hannah Arendt's suggestion about the *polis* in classical Greece) springs up in the created space where people speak and act together (199). That is, true power is revealed by creating such a space in one's writing. Creating the sense of spaciousness Arendt describes in *The Human Condition* is Lamb's goal for academic writing, a goal shared by many other contemporary composition scholars as well (cf. Chris Anderson and Lex Runciman).

Traditional academic argument may still be the privileged form for now, but it is not the only genre we need to concern ourselves with, even in a university (and academic writing itself has been changing and enlarging in the past few decades[2]). Probably the single most useful tool you can learn in a writing class is the principle of genre variation and how to respond to it. That is, if you learn how to be alert to different rhetorical situations, how to analyze them, how to determine the genre constraints you're facing in each situation, you'll have a theoretically grounded practice that will serve you well in *all* the writing you need to do, both in the academy and in your career.

Genre

So what is **genre** anyway? The dictionary definition is pretty simple—it's just a type or a kind (of anything—the root word, the one we use most often for plants and animals, is *genus*; and as Pinker points out in Conversation 1, page 60, the word *gender* comes from the same root). When we talk about genres in writing, we're basically establishing categories; and, while we need categories (patterns, schemes) as ways to organize and talk about things, these categories can help us organize large amounts of information only by leaving a lot of things out. We could put it this way: categories (genres) can be a way to think about something or a way to *avoid* thinking about something (depending on what our categories neglect, fail to describe adequately or account for). Thus, when we use categories to think with, we always need to make clear that they are provisional, "for the purpose of thought" (as D. H. Lawrence once put it, 60).

That said, what *are* some of the taxonomies, categories (**genres**) we've developed to organize our thinking about writing? From school, you're already familiar with poetry, fiction, drama, and nonfiction. Most of the time, unless you sign up for a creative writing course, nonfiction prose is the main genre you end up using for your university work—but that category is huge and needs to be broken down still further: **literary nonfiction** (also called **creative nonfiction**—memoirs, travel writing, biography, meditations on nature, on life, on death, on writing, etc.); **popular nonfiction**

---

[2] Alternative or experimental forms of discourse in the academy are appearing more regularly in academic journals in all disciplines every year. See Bishop (with its debt to Weathers), Bridwell-Bowles, Bizzell, Royster, Tompkins, Helen Fox et al. (*Alt Dis: Alternative Discourses and the Academy*). See also Ede and Lunsford's study of collaborative writing.

(everything from magazine articles to self-help books to the ghost-written autobiographies of movie stars); and **academic nonfiction**.

Academic prose is broken down still further into sub-genres according to subject (science writing versus writing about literature, for example—we'll return to this distinction in a moment), but also according to formal characteristics or according to what the writing wants to achieve. In first-year writing classes, a recurring set of formal categories, referred to as the **modes of discourse—exposition/argumentation/description/narration**—creates one model for classifying types of academic writing. Unfortunately, once these "modes of discourse" found their way into composition textbooks, they took on a life of their own: according to Robert J. Connors in "The Rise and Fall of the Modes of Discourse," these categories are fairly recent and first appeared in print in 1827. Since then, however, "more students have been taught composition using the modes of discourse than any other classification system" (1–2). Connors describes the rise of the modes of discourse in detail, but we're not yet convinced the fall has taken place: we still see assignments being given as if these modes actually existed in some pure form, as if it were possible (or desirable) for an expository essay to be written unadulterated by any traces of argument, narration, or description—even though most of us find ourselves crossing such genre divides, mixing and matching modes, all the time (cf. for instance Joseph Trimmer's *Narration as Knowledge* and Jaqueline McLeod Rogers on "The [Growing] Role of Narrative as Evidence in Academic Writing").

Perhaps more useful is the traditional model of communication, especially since its categories clearly can never exist in pure form, on their own—all four must work together in every successful communicative act, *every time*. We might, in any particular piece of writing, emphasize one more than the others, but all four elements must be present if the act of communication is to take place at all:

sender (the writer);

receiver (the reader, the audience);

code (language, the text itself);

reality (the world, the subject being written about).

Composition scholars have found this traditional **communication model** useful in several different ways. Flower and Hayes used it, for instance, to examine what novice writers struggle with. Novice writers tend to have a hard time because they focus *only* on the topic of their papers (reality, or the world) and the format of their papers (the code, language); experienced writers look at *all parts of the communication model*—not just the subject (the *world*) and the text (the *code*), but also the reader (the *receiver* of the message they were trying to send) and the author (the *sender* of the message). As a result, experienced writers often find new writing ideas emerging from their attention to audience and to voice. As Flower and Hayes put it, experienced writers set different problems to themselves than novice writers do; we can solve only the problems we identify, the problems we give ourselves to solve. Novice writers can't solve writing problems they can't see: "good writers are simply solving a different problem than poor writers" (101, 93).

Composition scholars have also used the model above to talk about problems teachers have when they assign and evaluate writing in different fields (cf. Fulkerson). The four elements of the communication model correspond to four approaches to teaching writing, depending on what a teacher in a particular discipline expects a student writer to emphasize in the traditional model of communication—the *writer* (**expressive**); the *reader* (**persuasive**); *language* (**literary**); or the *subject* (**referential**). Of course, because they're based on the communication model above, all four qualities (**expressive/persuasive/literary/referential**) are also always present in any communicative act: they can usefully describe only matters of emphasis or degree. That is, an article in a prestigious scientific journal may emphasize the **referential** and **persuasive** (focusing on the world, on the data, on the experiment being described, and then trying to persuade other scientists that this data is significant). There may be an attempt to structure such a piece as if the article wrote itself or God wrote it (that is, **expressive** elements are minimized, the first person is not used, the authors [often plural in scientific journals] are not themselves getting any attention); and there may be minimal attention to language itself (to **literary** elements) apart from an attempt to be clear and dispassionate (since, in some settings, one can be persuasive only by absenting oneself, by sounding as if one doesn't have strong feelings about the material being presented). However, this doesn't mean that an expressive element is *absent*—the authors have carefully *created* a certain distanced voice that feels appropriate to the task at hand. And an attention to language is still crucial—the language may not be calling attention to itself, but that is itself a created effect (and a difficult one). If the language were murky and unintelligible or full of gushing phrases about how exciting and important these new findings were, the piece could not persuade the scientific audience toward which it was directed. These categories are most useful, therefore, if we keep reminding ourselves that *every* piece of effective writing needs to take all four of them into account (literary critics have used these categories productively as well—cf. M. H. Abrams).

Yet another important model exists for classifying nonfiction writing. Genre scholars are convinced that we need additional ways to talk about genre, more practical ones. For instance, Carolyn R. Miller suggests (in her well-known piece "Genre as Social Action," 1984) that we should start by talking about genres we're familiar with from everyday life: "the letter of recommendation, the user manual, the progress report, the ransom note, the lecture . . . the eulogy, the apologia, the inaugural, the public proceeding, and the sermon" (155). She argues that a "sound definition of genre must be centered . . . on the action it is used to accomplish" in the world (151). There are certain situations that recur and certain kinds of writing that are called for in those situations—writing that she refers to as "rhetorical action" or "social action."

How can Miller's perspective on genre help? Well, for one thing, we can learn what to do by noticing how others have responded to similar situations. If we're suddenly asked to give the eulogy at an uncle's funeral, we can calm ourselves by thinking about other talks we've heard given at other funerals or by talking to people who have given such talks and who might let us read what they wrote for those occasions. If we can identify certain shared characteristics in these pieces of writing, we can draw on those for guidance as we compose a piece honouring our uncle—a piece which is nevertheless new, speaking specifically to our uncle's unique qualities as well as to whatever is unique in our own situation.

As Lloyd F. Bitzer put it in his description of "The Rhetorical Situation" (1968), over time similar situations recur and call for, demand, similar kinds of written action. These pieces of writing or recurring forms become a tradition that then "tends to function as a constraint upon any new response in the form" (13). Or as Miller says, in particular situations (like funerals or courtroom speeches or application letters, for instance) writers "respond in similar ways, having learned from precedent what is appropriate and what effects their actions are likely to have on other people" (152). We won't try to get into a detailed analysis of what is and isn't a genre according to Miller's way of thinking, but we do agree with her that looking at the *de facto* genres, "the types we have names for in everyday language, tell us something theoretically important about discourse" itself and about our culture (155). These types of writing involve us in social action—we may "recommend one person to another, instruct customers on behalf of a manufacturer, take on an official role, account for progress in achieving goals" (165)—and in doing all of these things we are simultaneously "connecting the private with the public," connecting events that happen only once in our lives with events that happen over and over again in our culture (like the funeral of an uncle, for instance).

Thus, no writing course could ever teach students to write in every genre, to create writing for every situation demanding written action that they might be expected to encounter in a lifetime; no course could even prepare students for every writing demand they were likely to encounter in a university. But a writing course *can* alert you to the principle of genre variation itself. We know that academic writing overall does have some identifiable traditions and constraints because of the action it wants to perform, the work it wants to accomplish in the world, and that these traditions and constraints are not mysterious, but observable and learnable (cf. Giltrow). We also know that each academic discipline has additional traditions and constraints of its own: it's up to you to pay attention to these, to ask your instructors in that discipline for guidance and for models to follow. This is especially true in matters of citation; yet even though citation styles vary from one subject area to another, one thing never varies in academic writing—the need to acknowledge the previous work of others. You are not trapped, however, in repeating what has been done before: just make sure you only experiment, try something new, based on an understanding of what the traditions and constraints of academic writing are and why they exist. Asking yourself what your writing needs to accomplish, what form of social action you want it to be, can help too.

We're not telling you something you don't already know here, by the way. But you may not *know* that you know it: you may not have honoured your knowledge. Not a year goes by without a few of our students saying in exasperation, "There's no such thing as good writing or objective standards for good writing—you just have to find out what specific profs want and then give it to them, and they all want something different." Rephrase that comment a bit and remove the irritation about the situation, the cynicism, and you have a useful truth: "There is no one objective standard for good writing because 'good' writing is writing that works in a specific situation; and since every academic discipline is asking different questions and investigating those questions by different methods, writing strategies that work well in one academic field won't necessarily work well in another. Thus, what I need to do for each academic project is to look at models of effective writing in that field and consult with the instructor to see what traditions and constraints are operative for each specific project or assignment."

It's not as much fun without the tone of disgust and cynicism, without the hands thrown in the air; but it's a pretty accurate description of the situation. And it only makes sense that an English professor is unlikely to be able to teach you how to write well for, say, a biology assignment—because you actually have to *know* biology in order to write biology well. Hence the need for writing-in-the-disciplines, writing-across-the-curriculum, or writing-intensive courses in each major field. What's at stake here is the principle not just of genre variation, but of **discourse communities** or (the term we prefer) **communities of inquiry**—the ways in which people talk to each other and write for each other to carry their investigations forward and produce knowledge.

Academic writing is clearly only one genre among many. If you think of genre as social action, you'll soon realize that the work your writing needs to accomplish will affect both the substance and the shape (the organization) of your writing. Sometimes organizational patterns are rigid, inflexible: a lab report may need to be written in one way only; the same is true of an accident report filed by a police officer. The world is full of fixed forms; in fact, university forms of writing are often quite flexible in comparison. Some report formats will require that your findings and conclusion be clearly stated in the very first sentence or two (allowing busy readers to decide immediately if they need to read any further); other forms will expect you to bring the reader along with you as you think something through, giving your conclusions only at the very end after allowing the reader to reach them with you. Some genres allow, even rely on, a strong authorial voice; others absolutely forbid it. So keep in mind that taking time to reflect on genre-as-social-action, to make thoughtful genre decisions, will often help you solve your organizational problems.

Consider some of the genres most familiar to you—recipes, thank-you notes, weather reports, business letters. Some of these follow predictable forms for good reason; others allow lots of experimentation. Perhaps an inventive business letter once caught your attention by making you laugh; or perhaps you've held onto a particular thank-you note because it was so detailed and imaginative, not just written according to the usual formula. Some genres reflect the gender biases of the culture at large (not surprisingly, if we think of writing as social action): think, for instance, of diaries and recipes, as opposed to project logs and instructions for assembling a bicycle. Forms of writing can also reflect cultural assumptions and limitations: the five-paragraph theme, with its mechanical structure, its insistence on being obvious (tell them what you're going to tell them, then tell them, and then tell them what you've told them) seems insulting and quintessentially North American to scholars from oriental cultures where indirection and subtlety are prized.

We've included in this Conversation a piece by Nancy Mairs that examines a genre she labels "the literature of personal disaster." But how would you categorize *her* piece itself? Is it exposition, argumentation, description, or narration? Is it focused on exploring the topic, or on revealing her personal life, or on persuading the reader to feel a certain way, or on experimenting with language? What social action is it trying to perform?

We've also included two short pieces by Canadian Nobel Prize–winning scientist John C. Polanyi. His scientific papers aren't nearly as accessible to a wide, non-specialist audience as these two pieces are, for obvious reasons. But it's worth noting his expertise in one particular genre here, one all of us are likely to be called on to perform at some point in our lives: the after-dinner speech. The substance of these two short pieces is worth emphasizing as well: artists and scholars in any field, from science to poetry, are always simultaneously creating and discovering reality collaboratively with others. There is no way out of this situation: that is, this activity of creating/discovering reality is always going on in human culture, whether we consciously pay attention to it or not. Writing-as-social-action is one way actively to acknowledge and participate in this work, to play a role in shaping/discovering the kind of reality we need and want to live in, wherever we find ourselves—writing a paper on epistemology for Philosophy 101; drafting an application essay for medical school; adding a tactful, detailed paragraph to a form letter mailed out by the insurance company you work for, a letter explaining why coverage was denied (cf. Schryer); or writing a eulogy for an uncle's funeral. It all counts in the ongoing human conversation about how we want to live together from day to day.

INKSHEDDING PROMPTS

1. Inkshed about the most unusual genre you've ever produced. It could be something you wrote for your family, friends, or significant other. It could be something you had to write for work through a collaborative revising and editing process. Or it could be something you wrote in a school setting. Describe the occasion that demanded that piece of writing and the writing process you had to go through, from start to finish. What social action was that piece of writing meant to perform? Did it work?

2. A related but slightly different inkshedding idea—inkshed about the most unusual written structure you've ever created. It could be something you had to write for work, family, or school. How and why did you come up with the pattern of organization you used? What gave you the idea for it? Describe the occasion that demanded that piece of writing and the writing process you had to go through, from start to finish. Did the unusual structure feel appropriate to the content of the piece—why or why not? Did the piece accomplish what it was supposed to accomplish?

3. One of the most familiar and powerful genres in existence is the letter. This book opens with two letters, and many formal pieces of writing have their beginnings in letters—letters to the editor of the local paper, letters to friends or colleagues explaining why we're upset about something or on fire about a particular topic, query letters to publishers proposing a book or article. Most of us write letters on a regular basis in the form of e-mails. Often, depending on the intended recipient, a letter allows us to write in a more natural voice, with more energy and freedom and less restraint than usual (this can be a good thing or a bad thing).

    Inkshed a letter about some of the readings in this section. State at the top who your intended audience is—an imaginary audience, a real audience (your mom, your best friend, a high-school teacher), one of the authors represented in this book—and give a detail or two that reveals what kind of audience you imagine them to be. Tell them why you have chosen to write to them about what you've read and give them a detailed sense of what the readings are about, quoting any specific passages that particularly struck you or confused you or that you want to quarrel with (look back at lines you marked in the text if you need to). Remember to start out with "Dear _____" and to sign your name at the end. Consider mailing this letter to the intended recipient (but make sure to keep a copy for your inkshedding log).

4. After reading Nancy Mairs's piece on the literature of personal disaster, inkshed on how you would categorize it and why. Is it exposition, argumentation, description, or narration? Is it academic writing, expressive writing, persuasive writing, or literary writing? That is, how would you analyze it in terms of the traditional communication model: is it focused on exploring the topic—the fifteen books she discusses and the genre to which those books belong—or on revealing her personal life, or on persuading the reader, or on experimenting with language? What social action is her piece trying to perform? And do you think it succeeds or not? How is it organized? How is white space used in the piece? Does her opening paragraph serve to pull us into the piece or not?

    Can you imagine her piece as a paper written in response to an assignment in a particular course? If so, what course might that be? What assignment? What grade would you give it? Do you think the literature of personal disaster that she describes could be called a genre? If so, what social action does *it* perform? Do you think readers' reactions to her piece would be determined, or at least influenced, by their gender? (In the excerpt from Mairs's essay "Voice Lessons" in Conversation 7, a piece that also reflects on genre issues, she describes how dismissive a male audience was of her writing about illness and the body—see pages 342–343.)

5. Inkshed about the organization of any piece in this volume, including the introductions to each Conversation, especially any piece whose structure surprised or intrigued you or any piece you felt—as you were reading it—that you yourself would have organized differently. How is it currently structured? How did that work for you? (Be specific). How did it *not* work for you? (Again, be specific.) How did the structure fit or not fit the material the author was working with? How would you change it if you could? Why do you think the author structured the piece in that way? (See Root and Davidson in this Conversation for brief reflections on the inseparability of form from meaning.)

    We struggled for a long time with the introduction to this Conversation on genre. We tried putting the discussion of genre first, organization second. We tried moving the material from the end of the genre section closer to the beginning of that section. We tried to figure out what to cut. If you do inkshed about how you would have organized that introduction (or any of the others), please feel free to send us a copy of your inkshed. We might try your ideas out in the next edition.

6. Look through the table of contents in this volume to remind yourself of the pieces you've read so far. Then inkshed about the genres represented. How would you categorize them? Pick *one* of the schemes for classifying types of nonfiction writing (the modes, the communication model, genre as social action; see pages 290–294) and use that scheme to talk about the variety of readings included in this anthology. Which varieties are not represented well? Which genres do we need more of? less of? If you inkshed on this topic, feel free to send us a copy so we can take your comments into account as we revise for the next edition.

7. We've mentioned before that inkshedding prompts are themselves a unique genre of writing. So are marginalia, that is, the conversations we carry on with authors in the margins of books or on the margins of our colleagues' papers and inksheds as we respond to their ideas. Notice at the end of Russ Hunt's piece (Conversation 3, pages 140–141) that he acknowledges marginalia as well as e-mails (look at his works-cited list to see how he cites unpublished material that was written only for him). What are typical characteristics of marginal commentary? What traditions and constraints affect the comments you write in the margins of inksheds? or of works-in-progress you've been asked to respond to? What traditions and constraints

do you notice in the marginal commentary you receive from instructors? Check out the University of Alberta online document "Learning to Read Instructor Comments and Marks on Essays" (available at http://www.humanities.ualberta.ca/english/marking.html). Does that document help you understand the genre of commentary any better? What social action is the document trying to perform?

8.   One of the characteristics of academic writing as a genre is its commitment to accurate citation. That is, all scholarly work carefully positions the author in an ongoing conversation, one in which the author did not say the first word and will not say the last, and acknowledges previous contributions to that conversation. However, the exact way citations are handled, the details that each academic discipline pays most attention to, varies from field to field. For instance, in the field of English literature, titles and passages of text and authors' names are crucial because they are themselves the subject of study: scholars often quote the exact words of other authors. In the sciences and social sciences, however, date of publication is emphasized; how recent a piece of research is will usually be more important than the exact words the researcher used or the title that researcher gave his article.

Look through the pieces in this volume and inkshed about how many different citation styles you can find examples of (consult *A Note about Citation Styles* at the end of this chapter or a handbook if you need to do so). How are citation styles handled differently in the NCTE piece in Conversation 3 and in the Paraskevas/Sargent piece in Conversation 5, "Understanding Grammar as Style"? What other differences do you notice between different genres, say, between pieces like Ray Carver's (which is a foreword to a book by one of his teachers, John Gardner) and Reither and Vipond's (which is an article in an academic journal), in terms of drawing on the ideas and work of others? We've in fact omitted Pinker's citations, but look at a copy of *The Language Instinct* itself to see the elegant way in which he has handled citations so that the reading text itself is as clean as possible.

Citation styles not only change from field to field and genre to genre; they also change over time. Notice how Mairs in this Conversation and Hairston in Conversation 3 handle citations; how do they handle citations differently from Russ Hunt in Conversation 3? How are their endnotes different from the footnotes in the introductions to Conversations 6 or 7 in this volume? What do you think of the Modern Language Association's (MLA's) move to in-text citations in the last decade or so? What the heck is that "Ibid" in Mairs's last footnote? (see page 308). "Ibid." and "op. cit." are no longer used in MLA citation style; you may run across them in older articles, however, so it's useful to know what they mean (any good dictionary will have a list of abbreviations in which they will appear). Do you think MLA made a good decision when it eliminated the need for them?

9. Find a paragraph in this volume whose in-text citations bothered or puzzled you, maybe because they cluttered up the text or because you experienced them as name-dropping, referring to a lot of writers and works you'd never heard of. Consult the works-cited list at the end of that selection or the bibliography at the end of this book in order to write an inkshed in which you unpack those citations in plain English—what *exactly* do they mean? Think of them as spy code and decode them (obviously, your translation will be longer than the original). Go ahead and write this inkshed as a spoof of academic writing if you like—feel free to have fun with it, as long as you get your information accurate. Your inkshed may help you or a colleague understand what the passage is actually saying.

Rick McConnell, "Beginning to Understand the Beginning"

Rick McConnell, a graduate of the journalism program at the Southern Alberta Institute of Technology (SAIT), wrote the piece below in 1996 as one of his regular columns in the *Edmonton Journal*. Before starting at the *Journal* as a general reporter in 1989, he had covered everything from farm news to city council for several smaller newspapers in Saskatchewan.

BEGINNING TO UNDERSTAND THE BEGINNING

All beginnings are hard.

Novelist Chaim Potok was right when he wrote that. Beginnings are hard. All of them.

Whether you are starting a lifetime of education with your first day of kindergarten, or beginning a friendship, a marriage, or a new job, it's important to get started on the right foot.

Those of us in the writing game know this as well as anyone. Every column, every news story, every short story, even an epic novel, has to get off to a good start. That crucial first sentence is, well . . . just that, crucial. If we don't get you interested right from the start, you might get bored and wander over to the comics page or close the book and flip on the TV.

In the newspaper business we call these first sentences "leads." We agonize over them, sweat over them, talk about them, put them off as long as possible. Sometimes we'll walk around the room and bother other people; if you can't think of a good lead, at least you can keep someone else from getting started on what they're doing while you're not doing what you should be doing.

The best newspaper lead I ever saw was written by James (Scotty) Reston of *The New York Times*. On November 22, 1963, Reston was at the *Times* Washington bureau when word came in that President John F. Kennedy had been assassinated. While the main news stories about the shooting, the arrest of a suspect, and the swearing in of the new president fell to reporters in the field, Reston was asked to sum up the feelings of a nation for the next day's front page. So he sat down at his old manual typewriter and opened a vein, as sportswriter Red Smith liked to put it. This two-sentence lead was the result:

> America wept tonight, not alone for its dead young president, but for itself. The grief was general, for somehow the worst in the nation had prevailed over the best.

I didn't have to look that up to get it right. I know those two lines better than any I have ever written myself. What Reston wrote that day was simply the best beginning to a newspaper story ever. The rest of us can spend the rest of eternity trying to write the second best.

Because I love beginnings so much, I use them as a way to judge all writing. I even shop for books by opening to the first page and reading the opening sentence. If I like it, I'll flip inside and read the beginnings of a couple of other chapters. Then I'll read the blurb on the jacket.

Then I'll take it home and, often as not, find out I bought the same book two years ago and have already read it twice.

Poking through my shelves the other day I found two copies of Norman Mailer's *The Naked and the Dead*. If I lose one, I'll still be able to turn to the opening page and read his first sentence. "Nobody could sleep." That's all it says. I've read that line dozens of times and the whole book three times. It never puts me to sleep.

"In our family, there was no clear line between religion and fly fishing." Maybe not, but Norman MacLean knew there was a line between good writing and boring writing when he used that sentence to open his novella *A River Runs Through It*. I've been hooked on his writing for years.

Here are some other opening lines I love:

"My father said he saw him years later playing in a tenth-rate commercial league in a textile town in Carolina, wearing shoes and an assumed name." (*Shoeless Joe* by W. P. Kinsella.)

"Above the town, on the hill brow, the stone angel used to stand." (*The Stone Angel* by Margaret Laurence.)

Beginnings can be wacky:

"We were somewhere around Barstow on the edge of the desert when the drugs began to take hold." (*Fear and Loathing in Las Vegas* by Hunter S. Thompson.)

Or dramatic:

"She only stopped screaming when she died." (*Kane and Abel* by Jeffery Archer.)

Or they can just set a nice scene:

"When Augustus came out on the porch the blue pigs were eating a rattlesnake—not a very big one." (*Lonesome Dove* by Larry McMurtry.)

"A few miles south of Soledad, the Salinas River drops in close to the hillside bank and runs deep and green." (*Of Mice and Men* by John Steinbeck.)

But the fact remains, all beginnings are hard and good ones are even harder.

That's why I stole the beginning of this column from Chaim Potok. It's actually the first line of his novel *In the Beginning*.

Potok knew what he was talking about. Then again, maybe Clive Barker put it better. He started his 1987 novel *Weaveworld* with this sentence:

"Nothing ever begins."

Hmmm. I'll have to think about that.

Nancy Mairs, "The Literature of Personal Disaster"

Nancy Mairs, poet and essayist, writes about the literature of personal disaster in the selection below as an insider, not only because of her husband's cancer but because of her own long struggle with multiple sclerosis and resulting bouts of suicidal depression. Her MFA (1975) and PhD (1984) are both from the University of Arizona, where she has also taught writing and literature. To date, she has published eight books, among them *Remembering the Bone House* (1989), *Carnal Acts* (1990), *Ordinary Time: Cycles in Marriage, Faith, and Renewal* (1993), *Voice Lessons: On Becoming a (Woman) Writer* (1994), *Waist-High in the World: A Life Among the Nondisabled* (1996), and *Troubled Guest: Life and Death Stories* (2001). She frequently contributes to periodicals like *The Christian Century*, *The Women's Review of Books*, and *The New York Times Book Review*.

The final piece in *Voice Lessons*, the collection of creative nonfiction from which the essay below was taken, is entitled "The Writer's Thin Skin and Faint Heart" and reflects on her annual struggle with rejection. Every year Mairs applied for major fellowships to support her writing; every spring she heard of her failure to receive them. Some rejection letters said, "We hope you'll apply for funding in the future," to which her response was, "Yeah, sure." Yet her examination of voice in that volume took on special force as she contemplated the next writing project she planned to undertake, tentatively titled "Waist-High in the World: (Re)Constructing (Dis)Ability"—a venture that would be, as she put it, dramatically new, using voice-activated equipment now that my fingers are too weak to push a pen or punch a keyboard. . . . With my voice, of all things, I may write a proposal. With my voice I may go on, fellowship or no, to write a book. Stranger things have happened. (149)

THE LITERATURE OF PERSONAL DISASTER

A few days before Christmas 1990, hunched on the edge of a folding cot with my laptop computer on a little table drawn up to my knees, I wrote compulsively, hour after hour, as though capturing my world in detail could defer its end. After every few words, I glanced across the top of the screen at my husband, slit and stitched up and webbed in plastic tubing, so wasted and waxy that I had to keep reminding myself: *This is George. You know him. You have loved him for almost thirty years.* "I suppose there are millions of us at this very moment in just the same pain," I tapped on the keys. "Why do I feel so *singular*?"

Yes, millions keeping bedside vigils, whispering as I whispered over and over, *Come back! Don't leave me! I need you!*, each of us trapped in this profound and irrational solitude, as though walls of black glass had dropped on every side, shutting out the light, deadening all sound but the loved one's morphine-drugged breathing: I was not, in truth, alone. Was it that intuition which had driven me before, and would goad me again, to write intimately about illness, disability, and death? And does the same suspicion provoke others to tell their stories—so much like mine, so absolutely their own? Are we all groping for one another through our separate darks?

Because my books have dealt candidly with my own multiple sclerosis, suicidal depression, and agoraphobia, as well as my husband's melanoma, I am frequently asked to review or endorse works that belong to a distinct though largely unrecognized sub-genre I've come to call, only half-facetiously, the Literature of Personal Disaster. Knowing from painful experience what can happen when one's work falls to a reviewer so unempathic that he wishes not only that one had written some other book but also that one had lived some other life, I'm willing enough to read, on their own terms, first-hand accounts of AIDS (Elizabeth Cox's *Thanksgiving: An AIDS Journal*), freak accidents (Andre Dubus's *Broken Vessels*) and illnesses (Molly Haskell's *Love and Other Infectious Diseases*), manic depression (Kate Millett's *The Loony-Bin Trip*), childbirth gone awry (Anne Finger's *Past Due*), cancer (Susan Kenney's *In Another Country* and *Sailing*), polio (Leonard Kriegel's *Falling into Life*), deafness (Carol Glickfeld's *Useful Gifts*), stroke (May Sarton's *After the Stroke*), widowhood (Rebecca Rice's *A Time to Mourn*), to name only a few. These are serious works of fiction and nonfiction, not the print equivalents of the sensational sagas touted by "Geraldo" or "A Current Affair," and they warrant my attention, if not always my affection.

I consider reviewing a professional obligation, and ordinarily I take the books assigned to me rather than select them myself. Thus, I did not choose to be the kind of connoisseur of catastrophe I have gradually become. But what of other readers, the ones a publisher's marketing staff must have in mind when they give an editor the nod for a journal delineating a mother's slow wasting from pancreatic cancer (Le Anne Schreiber's *Midstream*) or the remembrance of a beloved husband, newly dead (Madeleine L'Engle's *Two-Part Invention*)? If, as I have read, something like a thousand new titles are published each week, what do the bookmongers believe will draw readers to these two? Sorrow? Curiosity? What are they supposed to find there? Solace? Reassurance? Sheer relief that, however wretched their own lives may seem, others are worse?

* * *

In short: Why do I, and others like me, write this stuff? Why does anybody read it? (Or, to put the matter more cynically but no doubt more accurately, why does anybody think any-body else is going to pay good money to read it?) And what, if anything, happens when they do?

In *A Nation of Victims*, a book more wrong-hearted than wrong-headed, which could have been written only by a well-educated young Euro-American male who appears in his jacket photo to be in the pink of condition, Charles J. Sykes complains that, U.S. society having "degenerated into a community of insistent sufferers," our "National Anthem has become The Whine."[1] If so, then one might reasonably expect the works I'm writing about, founded as they are in pain and loss, to form an analogous National Literature. But in truth, virtually no writer I've encountered has sounded more aggrieved than Mr. Sykes himself. Sad, yes. Frightened, yes. Furious, yes. But almost never plaintive.

The true victim—the person set apart from ordinary human intercourse by temporary or permanent misfortune—has little enough time and even less energy for sniveling. Illness and death, whether one's own or a beloved's, take *work*, and I'm not using the word metaphorically. There are hands to be held and basins to be emptied and upper lips to be kept stiff. One has to husband one's resources. Self-pity simply doesn't provide an ade-quate motive for expending precious effort to write about the ordeal. But the work, tough as it is, feels singularly instructive, as though one were taking up a severe and rather odd new discipline, spelunking, perhaps, something that draws one through the stink of bat guano toward an unfathomable abyss. It pricks all one's senses.

The impulse, at least for someone of a writerly persuasion, is not to bemoan this con-dition but to remark it in detail. Initially, one's motives for translating happenstance into acts of language may be quite private. Catastrophe tends to be composed not of a mono-lithic event but of a welter of little incidents, many of which bear no apparent relationship to one another, and language, in ordering these into recognizable patterns, counteracts dis-orientation and disintegration. This process of making sense of a flood of random data also produces the impression—generally quite groundless—of control, which may save one's sanity even though it can't save one's own or anyone else's life.

These therapeutic results provide ample reason for keeping a personal journal, but they don't account for the penchant of some writers (and most of the words I have in mind were written by people who would have been writing *something* anyway) for transforming intimate experience into public artifact. Some may share my aesthetic drive: to transmute dross—my own hastening physical deterioration, my husband's wretched, retching progress through chemotherapy—into lapidary reality. And some may find, as I have done, that they thereby write their way into better behavior than they believed themselves capable of. I am forever publishing brave statements that I must then make good on if I am to be a woman of my word.

I can't always do so, of course, but sometimes I can. And since I possess no extraordinary existential gifts, I assume that you can, too. You will need to, I know. All of us who write out of calamity know this before all else: there is nothing exceptional about our lives, however these may differ in their particulars. What we can offer you, when the time comes, is companionship in a common venture. It's not a lot, I know, but it may come in handy. The narrator of personal disaster, I think, wants not to whine, not to boast, but to comfort. As one of the sufferers interviewed in Cheri Register's *Living with Chronic Illness*[2] points out, it is possible to be *both* sick *and* happy. This good news, once discovered, demands to be shared.

This underlying drive to console may account for the fact that more women than men seem attracted to the genre and that the works of women tend to be more intimate and immediate than those of men. This gender difference is not essential but circumstantial: women have traditionally been accorded social permission both to suffer and to mitigate suffering, especially messy suffering, the kind involving fevers, excreta, compresses, and nursery puddings. Men, by contrast, have been supposed to pretend that nothing hurts or frightens them, not the bully's rabbit punches on the playground, not the black tumor gnawing at the entrails, *nothing*, and to sneer at pain and terror in others. Choosing to speak publicly about affliction is risky for both, but for different reasons: for the woman, because the behavior (public utterance) is culturally impermissible; for the man, because the condition (physical or mental weakness) is proscribed. Clearly, the woman who undertakes to publish a book about her miseries, or about anything else, has already decided to transgress, at whatever cost, the taboo on female speech; thus, she has resolved the crucial issue before beginning her project. But a man, who is expected to speak publicly but not to expose his infirmities, may have to struggle with this conflict of (self)interest in the writing itself.

The approved resolution to his problem is to distance the authorial subject from the suffering subject. The author—highly intelligent, perceptive, above all in control—may then scrutinize and explain and interpret pain without ever appearing to fall victim to it. This use of intellect to divorce self from experience may account for the peculiar deadness of a book on madness like William Styron's *Darkness Visible* when contrasted with the third, "depressed" section of *The Loony-Bin Trip*, which forces the reader to pace Kate Millet's narrow, grimy kitchen along with her as she subsists on soda crackers and coffee, unable to write, unable to speak, her attention contracted to a single point: "Oneself. In danger."[3]

That intellectualization is not a strictly gender-bound coping strategy is made clear by Susan Sontag's brilliant but icy *Illness as Metaphor,* which bears no trace of the author's personal encounter with cancer. I don't condemn nonpersonal analysis; on the contrary, I for one need *Illness as Metaphor* to be exactly as it is. But the drawback to an approach like Styron's—openly self-referential yet without intimacy—is that it also distances the reader from an experience she or he may have no other means for understanding. I've *been* mad in just the way Styron has, and even I couldn't figure out from his book what such a state feels like.

Which happens to be fine with me, since I already know. (Not that great, no matter what poets of disaster like Sylvia Plath and Anne Sexton suggest.) But what of the woman who wrote to me after her lover had shot herself to death? She didn't need a description of depression (she was a psychiatrist) but a means of fathoming suicidal despair. She needed to enter and endure it with me. Those writers who seek to console and hearten must make themselves and their anguish wholly transparent, revealing not illness as metaphor but illness as illness, in order to persuade the skeptical reader, through the very writing, that survival (at least till the last page) is possible.

* * *

With the exception of the strictly private journal, which lies outside any literary discussion unless its author later decides to change its status, the sense of isolation I mentioned earlier figures powerfully in the writer's impulse to record calamitous events intending to make them public. Publication of any sort is an intrinsically social act, "I" having no reason to speak aloud unless I posit "you" there listening; but your presence is especially vital if I am seeking not to disclose the economic benefits of fish farming in Zaïre, or to recount the imaginary tribulations of an adulterous doctor's wife in nineteenth-century France, but to reconnect myself—now so utterly transformed by events unlike any I've experienced before as to seem a stranger even to myself—to the human community.

The "you" required by such an "I" must be unusually vivid and available, I know as a writer. That is, in writing I construct an ideal reader possessing these characteristics. But I don't expect real readers to share them. Real readers, in fact, puzzle me a bit, the way women puzzled Freud, and I'm terrifically grateful to the ones who write and tell me what they want, which tends to be advice (sometimes), sympathy (often), and (every now and then) the chance to give me pieces of their minds, some of these more palatable than others. Many want simply to thank me for putting their feelings into words. These voices, lending materiality to my readerly ideal, transform monologue into intercourse.

When I take up the role of reader myself, I sense a discrepancy between my own readers, both imagined and actual, who are generally smart, sensitive, and sympathetic, and those some publishers have in mind for their releases. (Or do they have readers, as distinct from consumers, in mind at all?) I don't read the most disastrous disaster narratives, I'm sure, since these never make it as far as the reviewer's desk. Only once have I had to tell a publisher that not only would I not endorse the book he sent me, if I were he I wouldn't even publish it. (He did, and went belly up not long afterward, which gave me less satisfaction than I would have anticipated.) I read nothing written in pop-psyche-speak, on principle, and I lack the background to comment on books, good or bad, dealing with sexual or substance abuse. All the same, too much of what I do read is poorly conceived, clumsily written, and carelessly edited.

Although bad books are published in every genre, I know, I mind these more, perhaps because I feel a certain defensiveness about personal disaster as an authentic literary subject. As people with disabilities who were once shuttered by shame and superstition move out into productive roles in society, and as society is enriched by their participation, we will all benefit from the increase in awareness and information their works provide; and surely we can all use the solace derived from knowing that the grief and fury we feel when "bitten by bad nature," as Sylvia Plath puts it,[4] has been endured by at least one other person. We must take care, however, not to condescend subtly to such authors by lowering the literary standards to which we hold them out of a cynical or sentimental misreading of readers' needs and expectations.

What, if not misplaced pity, prompted an editor to accept for publication a manuscript in the first chapter of which a psychiatrist likens the challenge of psychoanalyzing the raving paranoiac who has just showed up in his tastefully accoutred Central Park office to "trying to make par on a long and winding hole where you cannot see the green as you tee off." The entire book turns out to be just as shallow as its founding metaphor would suggest. Did the editor consider writers about madness too inept to produce literature of quality? Did he believe that only voyeuristic or prurient readers would be drawn to a book on such a topic, and that they merited whatever they got? Less cynically, did he regard schizophrenia as so urgent a subject that the usual standards ought to be waived in order to broadcast as much information as possible?

Although in some instances (I wonder whether AIDS might be a contemporary case) such a documentary function might justify publication, it cannot by itself make books in this genre work as literature. It's not enough to feel bad nature's bite: to find yourself, having stopped to help two stranded motorists, catapulted by a speeding car into the night, from which you wake to a new life without the use of your legs; to flounder about, baffled and bitter, for some way to prepare your young children for their father's death; to drag yourself, in an ill and aging body, from bed to desk and back again until you weep and wish for death. These are central situations in some of the best work being done in this genre, but by themselves they're merely horrific, not redemptive. Misery, no matter how mysterious and poignant, is not enough to make a book, and if an editor and the marketing strategists who drive editorial decisions think it is, somebody (or preferably a lot of somebodies) has to tell them otherwise.

The trick, with this as with any genre, is to satisfy its requirements while escaping its confines. The writing about personal disaster which functions as literature tends not to be "about" disaster at all. That is, whatever adversity provides the grounds for the project must be embedded in a context both enigmatic and elaborate: the insistent everyday world. For this reason, perhaps, writers already experienced in other genres are apt to accomplish most in this one. The works of the writers I have in mind transcend their separate ordeals to speak generally, and generously, of the human condition.

Andre Dubus, a critically acclaimed writer of short fiction, was indeed struck by a car and crippled permanently in 1986. But *Broken Vessels* is extraordinary not because it depicts physical and emotional trauma but because it demonstrates tacitly, by collecting essays written between 1977 and 1990, the spiritual maturation that suffering can force: "After the dead are buried, and the maimed have left the hospitals and started their new lives, after the physical pain of grief has become, with time, a permanent wound in the soul, a sorrow that will last as long as the body does, after the horrors become nightmares and sudden daylight memories, then comes the transcendent and common bond of human suffering, and with that comes forgiveness, and with forgiveness comes love. . . ."[5] The life that leads one to this point can no longer be termed in any sense disastrous.

Susan Kenney, who has chosen to treat the issues raised by her husband's cancer in fictional form, delineates a similar progress toward sympathetic wisdom as her central characters, Sara and Phil, move ambivalently and ambiguously toward Phil's death. One of the great virtues of both *In Another Country* and *Sailing* lies in Kenney's eye and ear for the comic in even quite grisly situations, as when Phil, in the throes of chemotherapy's nausea, performs spectacularly in front of a traffic cop, thereby sparing Sara a speeding ticket. The memory of this scene buoyed me through many a gastric eruption during George's chemotherapy. The truth is that those of us in calamitous circumstances laugh a good deal, not just because Norman Cousins has told us to, though his was excellent advice, but because funny things go on happening to people no matter what. Kenney's capacity for capturing life's clutter—the way cancer has to fit in among children's tantrums and Christmas shopping and the pressures of work and the death of the old dog—shows suffering in its proper scale, not inconsequential, by any means, but not insurmountable either.

Like Dubus and Kenney, May Sarton captures and celebrates the commonplace, in her poems and novels but especially in her journals, of which *Endgame* is the most recent. Over the years, she has drawn her audience into her world—the cats, the lilacs and daylilies and tree peonies, the bottles of Vouvray and champagne, and always the dogged work of a prolific writer—so meticulously that when I was given the chance to call on her last summer, I stepped into a landscape already familiar, salt meadow joining the yellow house with the sweep of the sea. There I met at last the woman who had been teaching me what to love about solitude, about company, for years. She gave me chilled wine and *gaufrettes* and one white rose from her garden.

As Sarton's health has failed, wearing her to translucency, infirmity has surfaced, gradually and naturally, as a major theme in her recent work. In permitting it to emerge instead of painting it over, she communicates a harsh lesson: aging is the one disaster that, if we escape all others, will claim us in the end. As luck and the actuarial tables would have it, most of "us" will be women, many of whom, having endured the grievous loss of a life partner, will suffer both the lack of "the tangible 'we' when two people live together in amity" and loneliness "in essence for the *self*,"[6] the former resilient and responsive self, who now creeps crablike across the ice to the car for yet another trip to the doctor who will never again make her well. Eventually, each will say, "I want to die, there's no doubt about that. When you have as much pain as I have and there's no way out you *do* want to die, if you're as old as I am. . . . There is that hope that someday, while you're asleep, the old heart will stop beating."[7]

Yet, in spite of her admission that now "everything hurts," Sarton casts aside "fantasies of suicide as a way out of the constant chronic pain. . . . I feel one must have one's death, one must not make one's own death. One must let death come when the time has come." In the meantime, she writes, not so much about being old and ill as about what matters moment by moment: not a "really appallingly frail and old-looking woman" but the person within, "seeing an awful lot, being aware of an awful lot"—a friend's thick, savory soup, and Pierrot the Himalayan, who looks "like a Roman emperor in cat form," and the house filled with dewy pale pink roses, purple anemones, white and lavender tulips, blue asters. . . .[8] These are books about going on. All the way. To our common destination.

To which none of us wants to go ignorant and alone. Hence, into the dark, we write.

Endnotes

[1] Charles J. Sykes, *A Nation of Victims: The Decay of the American Character* (New York: St. Martin's Press, 1992), p. 15.

[2] Cheri Register, *Living with Chronic Illness: Days of Patience and Passion* (New York: The Free Press, 1988).

[3] Kate Millett, *The Loony-Bin Trip* (New York: Simon and Schuster, 1990), p. 285.

[4] Sylvia Plath, "Blue Moles," *The Colossus* (New York: Vintage Books, 1968), p. 49.

[5] Andre Dubus, *Broken Vessels* (Boston: David R. Godine, 1991), p. 138.

[6] May Sarton, *After the Stroke* (New York: W. W. Norton, 1988), pp. 75–76, 42.

[7] May Sarton, *Endgame* (New York: W. W. Norton, 1992), pp. 277–78.

[8] Ibid., pp. 282, 186, 157.

Robert Root, "This Is What the Spaces Say"

Robert L. Root taught English for twenty-eight years at Central Michigan University (CMU) after earning both his MA (1971) and PhD (1975) in English from the University of Iowa. He kicked off his recent retirement from CMU by moving to Colorado, taking on a two-week artist's residency in Rocky Mountain National Park (August 2004), and serving as organizer and keynote speaker for "Mapping Nonfiction," a conference in Estes Park sponsored by AEPL (the NCTE Assembly for Expanded Perspectives on Learning). He plans to focus even more fully in retirement on writing both creative nonfiction and studies of nonfiction. His numerous books include *Working at Writing: Columnists and Critics Composing (1991)*; *Those Who Do, Can: Teachers Writing, Writers Teaching—A Sourcebook* (co-authored with Michael Steinberg, 1996); *Wordsmithery: A Guide to Working at Writing*, 2nd ed. (1998); *E. B. White: The Emergence of an Essayist* (1999); *Recovering Ruth: A Biographer's Tale* (2003); and *The Fourth Genre: Contemporary Writers of/on Creative Nonfiction*, 3rd ed. (co-edited with Michael Steinberg, 2005). The essay below was presented at the Conference on College Composition and Communication on March 15, 2001, and gives a quick sense of Root's important role in exploring the possibilities and the history of the **segmented essay**. His well-designed website (http://www.chsbs.cmich.edu/Robert_Root/) is a rich resource on creative nonfiction and also supplies a link to view the polyptych mentioned in this selection (*The Ghent Altarpiece* by Jan Van Eyck).

THIS IS WHAT THE SPACES SAY

> Each person we meet, each place we visit, each event in our lives, and for that matter the universe itself in its far-flung glory, all confront us as bits of perception and memory, inklings and intuitions, and we seem compelled . . . to bind these scraps into a whole that makes sense.
>
> (Scott Russell Sanders, "The Warehouse and the Wilderness,"
> Unpublished Essay: 5)

Beyond an expanding recognition of nonfiction as a literary genre, the most significant change in the nature of nonfiction in our time has been the use of space as an element of composition. Most literary journals and mainstream publications regularly publish segmented essays—and consequently so do many composition readers, although only few textbooks display any awareness of the form. **Segmented essays**—sometimes called **collage essays** or **disjunctive essays** or **paratactic essays**—depend on space, usually expressed as numbers or rows of asterisks or squiggly lines or white breaks in text, as a fundamental element of design and expression. Knowing what the spaces say is vital for understanding the nonfictionist's craft and appreciating the possibilities of this contemporary form; it also helps us to better understand the nature of truth in the segmented essay.

* * *

The segmented essay is like an oratorio or a concerto. The spaces are like the intervals of silence between the separate elements. Sometimes the segments of prose in an essay can be recitative, aria, duet or trio, chorus; they can be *allegro non troppo, allegro appassionato, andante, allegretto grazioso.* This is what the spaces say: In this interval of silence hold onto what you have just heard; prepare yourself to hear something different; ponder the ways these separatenesses are part of a whole. Like musical compositions, nonfiction need not be one uninterrupted melody, one movement, but can also be the arrangement of distinct and discrete miniatures, changes of tempo, sonority, melody, separated by silences. This is what the spaces say.

* * *

The segmented essay is like a medieval altarpiece, composed of discrete panels that create a series of balances and juxtapositions rather than one continuous, unified image. Think of a triptych like Hieronymus Bosch's three-part masterpiece, *The Garden of Earthly Delights,* with its large central section displaying "The World before Noah," one side panel depicting "The Marriage of Adam and Eve," the other depicting "Hell." Think of a polyptych like Jan Van Eyck's twenty-part masterpiece, *The Ghent Altarpiece,* which can be displayed opened or closed, its pairs of parallel panels widely separated, each panel framed and bordered, all set off starkly from one another. Sometimes the segments of prose in an essay can be figure studies, landscapes, allegories, separated pairs of portraits, images of context and consequence thematically linked to a central scene.

This is what the spaces say: Stand up close and ponder each image on its own; stand further back and connect each panel to another panel that completes it as a pair or contrasts with it as an opposite; encompass all of it, remaining always aware of the borders and the individual panels but inviting an impression of the whole through its parts. Like a polyptych painting, nonfiction need not be one self-contained and harmonious picture but can also be an arrangement of separate images, a retable or reredos of scenes and portraits collectively viewed but separated by borders and frames. This is what the spaces say.

* * *

The spaces in a segmented essay are like the blackouts between scenes in a motion picture, like the fade-out/fade-in, the imageless transition between disparate sequences of images, the slow dissolve that introduces a flashback, the crosscutting to parallel events. The spaces in a segmented essay are like the silences between songs on a recording, the use of emptiness in photographs to highlight or foreground images, the time lapse between two hyperlinks on a website, the time it takes to shift focus from one facet of a multi-faceted object to another, the breaks between poems in a sonnet sequence. We learn what we learn, we know what we know, we experience what we live in segments and sections, fragments, moments, movements, periods, disjunctions and juxtapositions. This is what the spaces say.

* * *

The issue of truth, which seldom surfaces in other literary genres, perplexes nonfictionists. We begin in reality, in the hope of achieving some better understanding of the actual through writing. The inventions and manipulations of character and plot that are the hall-mark of the novelist's creativity are the barriers of the nonfictionist's psychology; the will-ingness to settle for the fictionist's "higher truth through fabrication" negates the nonfictionist's chances of even visiting the vicinity of the kind of earthbound and actual truth that is nonfiction's special province. The truth is hard to know, and it's hard, ulti-mately, to explain, perhaps especially about our own lives, what we experience as partic-ipants, what we observe as spectators.

In a segmented essay the truth may come in bursts, in the segments of prose that are the visible text. The segmented essay is not all continuous argument, all evidence and explanation; instead, it's a combination of pause and epiphany, silence and revelation, emptiness and edifice. This is what the spaces say: arrange the viewing of the panels so that you see their relationships in the juxtapositions rather than in a unified unbroken whole; linger your thoughts on the melody just ended before you hear the one about to begin; expect to know whatever this essay is about in the same way you know anything else, in fragments of certainty and segments of supposition, surrounded by gaps in your knowledge and borders of uncertainty. You need not fill every bit of space in order to say that you know enough; you need not write unsegmented prose in order for what you write to be truth enough. This is what the spaces say.

Mary Paumier Jones, "Meander"

Mary Paumier Jones started writing short nonfiction after taking a class in 1991 with Judith Kitchen, a faculty member at SUNY Brockport. With Judith Kitchen, she has co-edited two books—*In Short: A Collection of Brief Creative Nonfiction* (1996) and *In Brief: Short Takes on the Personal* (1999), both published by Norton.

MEANDER

A *Nova* show about the forms of nature prompts me to look up "meander." Having always used the word to refer to walking, I am surprised to learn that it comes from water. Rivers and streams meander, verb, have meanders, noun. "Meander", in fact, comes from the name of a river, one in ancient Phrygia, now part of Turkey—the Meander, now the Meanders. Change of name notwithstanding, the waters still flow from the Anatolian plateau to the Aegean Sea. A namesake, a Meander River, meanders in northern Alberta.

In what we do on foot, meandering implies an aimless wandering, with the pleasant connotation that the very aimlessness of the wander is something freely, even happily, chosen.

The meanders of water seem equally aimless, but are, it turns out, very regular in their irregularity—although if you were walking along the bank of a meandering river, you might find that hard to believe. You would head in one direction, and then curve around until you are going the opposite way, and then around again, following a path which turns upon itself and makes no sense. Could a helicopter or fairy godmother, though, raise you high enough, you would see that what seems like chaos below actually forms a regular repeating pattern of serpentine flexuosity.

The shortest distance between two points may be a straight line, but a river neither knows nor cares. It seldom flows straight for a distance of more than about ten times its width. A river erodes its banks, and the way of the world is such that one side invariably erodes faster than the other. It eventually collapses and its sediment is carried along and deposited downstream. Two curves are thus begun: the erosion point becomes the outside of one; the sediment pile, the inside of the next.

The water on the outside has to flow faster to keep up, causing more erosion, more sediment movement. The outsides get deeper, the insides shallower. At any point, the shape of the river shows its history. If other forces do not prevent, the bends over time work toward becoming perfectly elliptical. "Ellipse" comes from the Greek for "to fall short," an ellipse falling as it does short of a perfect circle.

This has all been observed in nature and shown experimentally in laboratories, and is thought by many to be sufficient explanation for meanders.

Others disagree, especially now that infra-red images from satellites show that ocean currents—which have no erodable banks—also meander. The jet stream appears to meander as well. Mathematicians have calculated that the most probable path between two points on a surface is in fact a meander. Meanders then may be the norm, not the exception. The question may be not why some rivers meander, but why every river we see does not.

* * *

There might be particular essays whose shape is more akin to one of the other basic natural forms—a sphere or hexagon, a spiral, say, or helix or branch—but on the whole, I think, what essays do best is meander. They fall short of the kind of circular perfection we expect of fiction or poetry. They proceed in elliptical curves, diverging, digressing.

We can float or row or swim or speed or sail along the meandering course of an essay. We can meander on foot on the river bank with the essayist. We expect only to go somewhere in the presence of someone.

Perhaps we will end up close to where we started, perhaps far away. We will not see the shape of our journey until we are done, and can look back on it whole, as it were, from the air. But we will, and very quickly, come to know the shape of our company—the mind, the sensibility, the person, with whom we are traveling. That much seems necessary to essay structure—one individual human speaking to another who wants to listen.

* * *

Flattened out, the thin human cortex, the gray matter of the brain, is much too large for the skull within which it must fit. The problem has been elegantly solved by intricate pleating and folding, as if the cortex were a piece of thick fabric gathered in tightly to fit. In anatomy books, we can see pictures of cross-section slices of the gathers. The shape is unmistakable, like a close-packed river shot from above, meandering within.

John C. Polanyi, "Science and the Arts: Two Ways of Seeing" and "Confessions of a Scientist"

John Charles Polanyi was born in 1929 in Germany to Hungarian parents, Magda and Michael Polanyi. When John was four, his father became Professor of Chemistry at Manchester University, England; thirteen years later, John entered Manchester University himself, just in time to attend his father's last lectures on chemistry, given to first-year students. That same year, 1946, Polanyi senior transferred to the Department of Philosophy where he focused on writing *Personal Knowledge*, his major work in epistemology.

John Polanyi described himself as impatient with "the large number of rules that one must master before one can play the game of science." He was more interested in politics and history and only gradually realized—after earning his PhD in 1952 (working under a research supervisor who was a spirited ex-student of his father's) and doing postdoctoral work at the National Research Council in Ottawa and at Princeton University—what his life's work in chemical physics was going to be. As he puts it, the story of his slow apprenticeship to science illustrates "that in the choice of a career, as in other major decisions, a lifelong commitment need not start with a love affair."

Eventually his study of chemical reactions, assisted by his graduate students over many years at the University of Toronto, led to his being awarded a Nobel Prize in Chemistry in 1986, one of the few Nobel Prizes ever awarded to a Canadian.

Like his father before him, he has throughout his career been a major spokesperson for academic freedom, particularly for the freedom of basic science to ask its own questions and pursue truth according to its own standards, not according to standards of usefulness or of the immediate promise of practical application. In his own case, for instance, studies of barely detectable chemical luminescence led to the development of the most powerful lasers in existence. But no one could have foreseen that outcome even when his research was being awarded the Nobel Prize, let alone when it was just getting started in the 1950s. Polanyi has continually stressed that high-quality science is a necessary investment in the future. To the cry for relevance in basic science, he has responded that "nothing is more irredeemably irrelevant than basic science."

Polanyi has received too many awards and honours to list, including over thirty honorary degrees from universities in six different countries. He is convinced that scientists should involve themselves in public affairs; in 1978 he chaired an international symposium on "The Dangers of Nuclear War" that led to his co-editing a book of that title. He has been an active member of the American Academy's Committee on International Security Studies and of the Canadian Centre for Arms Control and Disarmament; has served on the Prime Minister of Canada's Advisory Board on Science and Technology; has published over seventy articles on such issues; and has given many times that number of talks.

In the two short pieces below—one written for a symposium of Nobel Prize winners, the other delivered as a speech thanking the medical doctors who had presented an award for Polanyi's crucial work leading to laser technology—we glimpse two different genres and get a strong sense of audience and of occasion. While most of Polanyi's science writing speaks the language of specialists, his public writing is shaped by the necessity to communicate with those who are *not* researchers in chemical physics. In these selections, Polanyi's goal is to convince his listeners that science is an art. He claims that all writing, all art, all intellectual work, is creative in that it involves faith, commitment, discovery, and active shaping; it involves being willing to dive into the work without knowing precisely what the results will be. All such work is also limited, imperfect, and provisional (because it is done by human beings). Scientists, artists, and scholars in the humanities are—in their determination to search for truth according to uncompromising standards they set to themselves—more alike than we commonly surmise.

SCIENCE AND THE ARTS: TWO WAYS OF SEEING

The artist and the scientist have a common aim: to give shape to the world around them. They do this by searching for patterns—patterns that link the previously unconnected. Such patterns can be made evident in paint, words, numbers, or with the aid of the symbols of mathematics. But a brush-stroke or word is also a symbol.

Artist and scientist are impelled by the same fundamental human impulse: the wish to live, and hence to experience. They experience by making contact, by embracing the world. But whether physically or intellectually, one can only embrace what has shape. That is why the giving of shape is central to existence. We call it "discovery."

Though discovery can become a high art, it is clearly not the exclusive provenance of the artist or the scientist. It is a general pursuit that begins with the onset of consciousness, ending only with death.

The demands made on the beginning discoverer, the infant, are so remarkable that one could argue for distribution of Nobel prizes at birth. The infant is required to invent a system of physics embodying such profound concepts as number, form, colour, taste, size and permanence. It does so through the same procedure as its adult counterpart, namely through play tempered by logic.

The requirements for play and logic are different. Each must be given its due. Happily the human mechanism is a blend of the controlled and the haphazard that opens the way to discovery.

Implicit in these statements is the claim that science is one of the arts. More precisely it is implied here that the act of discovery is an act of creation. The scientist, calculator in hand, is seen to be painting the natural world as surely, and as unsurely, as the painter, brush in hand.

Relativity was not there lying in wait for its discoverer any more or less than *Guernica* was there waiting for its creator. Both scientist and artist made a culturally-conditioned commitment to a world-view; relativity and *Guernica* were the outcome. It was in the tests that they applied to their views that scientist and artist to some extent differed.

Both scientist and artist made a valid statement of truth for their time. Both made their assertions on the basis of such evidence as was available to them. These assertions, since they embodied elements of the truth, were timeless, but, since they were less than the whole truth, were of their time. We conclude that both individuals, our prototypical scientist and artist, drew on the culture of the age and contributed to it. Without the other neither could have been what they were, nor done what they did.

CONFESSIONS OF A SCIENTIST

(RESPONSE OF THE RECIPIENT OF THE AMERICAN LARYNGOLOGICAL ASSOCIATION AWARD)

The many occasions that I and my wife have shared with the medical community are a testimonial to your generosity. I am not thinking here of generosity in kind, but of mind. More than any profession that I know, you reach out to other disciplines. You feel a kinship, I think, with others, such as myself, who attempt to understand the world and then, having failed to understand it, are foolhardy enough to try to improve it. I chose to make my career in the inanimate sciences. We all strike a variety of Faustian bargains. In mine it was simply that in order to find an area of study that was more tractable than yours, I was obliged to choose one that was less significant. Living things, as you rightly judged in your own career choice, are much the most interesting. They are also the most resistant to dependable generalizations—which are the very stuff of science.

It may, however, come as some comfort to you to realize that the pursuit of understanding, even at the boundary between chemistry and physics where I have spent my scientific life, is a pretty desperate undertaking. This is the case despite the fact that molecules generally keep their appointments and lead fairly regular lives. Notwithstanding these advantages, it commonly takes decades in my own field of chemical physics to recognize a recurrent pattern of behavior in the midst of the confusion of unknown, and hence uncontrolled, variables.

When my graduate students knock at my office door it is seldom in order to announce a discovery, but rather to explain to me in agonizing detail why it is that they are nowhere near making one. The only source of satisfaction that these callers have is in noting that once again the physician-in-chief, myself, has proved his incompetence by prescribing a treatment to which the molecules failed to respond.

This failure on my part leads to an interesting question. How in fact does a research director differ from those whose research he or she is directing? For I believe a disinterested viewer would indeed notice a difference. It consists in this. In the midst of the scene of confusion that I have been describing, the director is the one who believes—in the face of all the evidence to the contrary—that the laws of physics continue to apply. The truth, he believes, can be found, and if one remains steadfast it will reveal itself. It is a remarkable affirmation of faith. Sometimes the facts even bear it out.

If this picture of the anguish of the researcher is a little overdrawn, it still comes closer to the realities of doing science than did earlier caricatures, in which a bloodless automaton was seen as having gained access to the scientific method.

Moreover, an important change in perception has occurred. Science has become such a prominent part of our lives that some glimmer of understanding of its subtle nature, as well as its inevitable waste and error, has reached the public.

We continue to do our best, of course, to keep the truth about science a secret by writing our papers as works of fiction in which we claim to have known what we were doing from the outset. Some of us go further and deliver our papers in a monotone so as to disguise our feelings toward our work, which, far from being dispassionate, resemble those of a parent for a child.

It would not matter at all if the actual truth about science—at which I have been hinting—were out. It is good that people realize that in science, as in any other type of knowing, one must fumble in a dim light in order to determine the outlines of things, and must be prepared to revise one's goals as they come into view.

No, what is so damaging is not that the truth is out, but that it is half out. The public senses the confusion that characterizes the voyage of scientific discovery, but fails to appreciate the necessity for it.

There is, as a result, an opening for facile demagoguery, and in my country at least, the air is thick with it. The cry is for a new order in science, an order in which fundamental discoveries will at last be made purposefully, with a view to wealth creation and social betterment. Scientific voyages of discovery are in future to be assessed in advance, on the basis of the geography of the lands they will ultimately discover.

When challenged in the past to say why I studied the motions in newly formed chemical reaction products, I had, I thought, a ready answer. In the first place, I was exploiting a new opportunity offered by nature, and secondly, I was doing it because in my estimation it could teach us something of importance. For the way in which molecules move at the instant of their birth should have things to tell us about the intimate details of the event of chemical reaction. And without chemical reaction we would not exist.

Increasingly, this appeal to the importance of new understanding is falling on deaf ears in Canada. Since understanding is for the long term, it seems to me that we must be in the process of losing faith in our future. . . . rich as we are, we behave like communities under siege. "The time is too late for thought," we appear to be saying. "There is only time for action."

It is relatively easy to get support for an assault on some recognizable enemy (lack of industrial competitiveness, a cure for cancer or for AIDS), but it is ever harder to get it for the vital purpose of reconnoitering to see how that enemy has disposed his forces. . . .

Our problems, those of the physical sciences in my case and the medical sciences in yours, are not so different. They have two sources: ignorance and arrogance (which stems from ignorance). The message of these remarks, beyond my thanks for your kindness, is to say that the process by which we battle ignorance—the process of discovery—is as subtle and as precious as life itself. That is not just hyperbole; from infancy on, discovery is central to our lives. Let us treasure it accordingly.

STUDENT WRITING
KELLY DAVIDSON

SUMMARY/ANNOTATION

Kelly Davidson completed the following summary/annotation of Root's "This Is What the Spaces Say" as part of the same class project for which Marta Currah wrote her annotation of a Peter Elbow essay (see Conversation 3, pages 171–172).

16 November 2002

Root, Robert. "This Is What the Spaces Say." (March 2001): 8 pars. 1 Nov 2002 <http://www.chsbs.cmich.edu/Robert_Root/Background/Spaces.htm>

Robert Root, Professor of English at Central Michigan University, uses spaces and segments both *in* his article and as the *subject* of his article "This Is What the Spaces Say." Root suggests that, like an oratorio or a concerto, "nonfiction need not be one uninterrupted melody, one movement, but can also be the arrangement of distinct and discrete miniatures, changes of tempo, sonority, melody, separated by silences." Root proposes that there should be room for "pause and epiphany" in a piece of academic writing. The "non-fictionist" may use continuous writing, segmenting, or framing to bring about surprises for both the reader and the writer. Root creates an analogy between the use of deliberate spaces in writing and the nature of life: "We learn what we learn, we know what we know, we experience what we live in segments and sections, fragments, moments, movements, periods, disjunctions and juxtapositions." Thus, Root structures his article—both visually and contextually—to show how spaces, asterisks, and jumps in flow and thought can help us to find the truth in our academic writing, much as we seek to find and create truth in our lives through seemingly disjointed, though meaningful and relevant fragments. Root's article, similar in form and concept to a collage, uses a combination of spaces and words as an example of how academic writing is not limited to any one form. Indeed, a scholarly paper does not have to follow a linear model; instead, the truth can come out in bursts of "silence and revelation."

LYNN REICH

INTERVIEW WITH A SCIENCE WRITER

Lynn Reich conducted and wrote up the interview below as a student in a first-year required English course. She used the opportunity of a class assignment to interview someone in a career she was considering pursuing herself (see a similar idea for an essay in Conversation 2, pages 104–105). Apparently Dr. Chacko's description of writing in the sciences did not dissuade her: Reich is now a graduate student in geology.

November 1999

DR. CHACKO, ROCKS, AND WRITING

I knocked on the door and was beckoned in; I passed through a small laboratory, then headed into an office in the back. In the office I found the subject of my interview, Dr. Tom Chacko, sitting at his desk.

My introductory questions revealed Dr. Chacko to have been a professor at the University of Alberta since 1990. His career has a twofold responsibility: research and teaching. I was interested in the research in his field—geology (the study of rocks of the continents)—and how it is related to writing. In response to my inquiry, Dr. Chacko told me "the way of science is through word" or, in other words, "the work is not done until it's written out and understood." He also mentioned that a background of scientific knowledge is imperative to writing effectively, especially in his research papers.

When asked about his writing, Dr. Chacko was moderately surprised at how much writing was involved in his work and personal life. He confessed to writing memos, emails, letters, grant proposals, course outlines, lecture notes, reviews of scientific papers and, most frequently, his own (or collaborative) scientific papers. Most of his writing is done on a computer in his office where he "stares at the computer for an hour" (just as I am doing right now) and slowly writes line by line producing a draft that remarkably resembles his final copy.

One thing I did not expect to get out of the interview is that writing in the field of science is "really, really important." Dr. Chacko began to describe to me that it is not just the data collected in the experiment or the results that prove the hypothesis; it is also how the experiment is presented in his scientific papers. "The writing is just as important as the data"; and it is the writing that is as difficult to compose as the data is to obtain.

After frantically writing everything I possibly could about the presentation of data, I was to learn that there is even more to a scientific paper. Flow was Dr. Chacko's recurring emphasis—how a paper reads. He also emphasized the need for a logical organization of ideas as a framework for the information. As Dr. Chacko explained, "for a paper to be as simple as possible, it must be written in a logical, linear way." This undoubtedly makes sense: if the reader is to learn anything from a paper, he or she has to be supplied with the problem, the facts, the data, then the explanation (in that order). Thus, Dr. Chacko's papers consist of the following: an abstract (summary at the beginning), an introduction, the experimental method, the results, a discussion (analysis), a conclusion and, of course, the references.

The process that Dr. Chacko uses to formulate his paper could be compared to squeezing water out of a rock—it just does not work until you increase the pressure.

When asked if he procrastinates, Dr. Chacko admits "oh God yes" to procrastination of enormous proportions—well, maybe not enormous, but working close to the deadline would describe him. He finds it difficult to write the introduction; conse-quently, he puts it off until the pressure to get the paper done increases. But as Dr. Chacko points out, "if it weren't for the last minute, nothing would get done." Because of his problem with starting papers, he sometimes likes to do an outline of the paper to give him a general idea of where to go with it. This usually helps in my writing as well.

Getting excited about his writing is Dr. Chacko's ultimate tool for writing his sci-entific papers. I asked him why he has to get excited about his writing. He sits back in his chair and looks out the window as if he would find the answer there. Then he replies that when he gets eager to write a paper it is because he "can see the end of it" and the impact it will have on his readers. In general, he finds that it is the "inter-pretation of the data that is the exciting part." Dr. Chacko does, however, reveal that "truth" is what scientific papers should encompass; for this reason, scientific papers are often difficult to write because they have to be "right."

Generally, Dr. Chacko refers to a writing guide for research papers to provide him with the structural elements in his papers, but within the structure he lets the writing lead him. First, Dr. Chacko will outline the problem, why it is important and the solution to the problem; then he puts the main points in sequence to develop the focus. So what is the focus in a scientific paper? Well, to form the focus, there has to be the mass of observations and research organized into a solution to the problem; thus, the focus is the analysis of and conclusions from the research. The shocking part is the amount of research that goes into a paper—usually from one to two years! But keep in mind, research is what gives substance to a paper; research is to a paper as meat and cheese is to a sandwich. Dr. Chacko further explained what is involved in research: surveying other journal articles and books, experimenting in a lab, and/or doing fieldwork.

When the research has been done and the first draft has been written, it is time to revise and edit his paper. "What now, Dr. Chacko?" Since he composes so slowly, he usually has little editing to do. Nevertheless, Dr. Chacko desires to write with more "voice" in his papers. Most often, Dr. Chacko's systematic revision is based on how the paper sounds and how it flows, a practice that would make sense to its future readers who will want the data presented clearly. With resounding certainty, Dr. Chacko explained that another important step is to check the data and references to make sure they are accurate. Lastly, of course, Dr. Chacko allows a colleague to review his paper and welcomes any comments.

I obtained a sample of Dr. Chacko's writing (a scientific paper from 1991), and my initial response was "Huh?" To the average person, Dr. Chacko's papers are for-eign; nonetheless, I managed to decipher the underlying problem in the study. The sample came from a glossy magazine article entitled "Isotopic evidence for involvement of CO_2-bearing magmas in granulite formation"; the article reported the results of a study he had done on carbon isotope compositions of graphite associated with a charnockite dyke from a quarry in South India. Dr. Chacko co-wrote the article with a student for a high-profile scientific journal (Letters to *Nature*), which could explain why he admits that it was challenging to compose. Here is an excerpt from his article:

> It has been suggested that CO_2-bearing magmas play an important part in the formation of granulites. These magmas crystallize directly into granulites, and also expel fluids which promote the development of granulite-facies mineral assemblages in adjacent country rocks.

The purpose of this article was to examine rocks collected during Dr. Chacko's PhD thesis and the phenomenon of their containing graphite. Dr. Chacko and his co-writer wrote the article concisely to make it generally comprehensible to all scientists. In addition, the article had to be "sensational sounding"—well, sensational to scientists and avid readers of scientific articles and journals. This requirement was challenging to meet because Dr. Chacko felt as if the writing had become more important than the science; the abstract had to be flashy and some points were stretched to make the article more exciting. However, Dr. Chacko is happy with the result and feels that beyond the flashiness the "gist of it is still there." It is difficult for technical articles and papers to survive in the world, unless they are spectacular enough for readers to be curious about beyond the abstract. There is no doubt that Dr. Chacko's article has given me a better sense of the writing that is involved in geology.

After Dr. Chacko writes his papers or articles, one would expect that he is relieved to have them finished. He "loves having written" or in other words he is not fond of doing the writing, but he is happy when he has the finished product in front of him. It is the satisfaction of professional accomplishment that stems from "caring about the finished product." This leads to the objective of research—to contribute scientific knowledge or the discovery of a solution to a problem. Just think—Dr. Chacko, an average person in his casual blue shirt and khaki pants, working in his office filled with books and binders of information and rock samples of all sorts, has contributed to a "body of knowledge" and is acknowledged for his writing.

So what did Dr. Chacko say when I asked him what he has learned from writing? His reply was that he learned "how much a part of thinking writing is" and that an essential part of writing is learning from what you write. Dr. Chacko mostly writes about how isotopes can be used to "understand" rocks, so naturally what he knows best is isotopes and rocks. Writing in geology and science is doing the research, then analyzing it, then clearly and logically presenting the results and conclusions.

I gathered my papers and pens and then thanked Dr. Tom Chacko for his time and the invaluable insight he bestowed upon me. I passed though the small laboratory once more, but this time I was leaving with a newfound wealth of knowledge. The subject of my interview told me the ways of writing in science, some of which I had expected and others that had surprised and intrigued me. I had anticipated that the structure and the logical presentation of ideas would be material to writing in geology; however, I did not expect to find that writing in science was as important as the research. I close the office door and take with me not only what I have written down, but also the inspiration to write in my future career as a geologist.

NEW PRACTICES TO TAKE FORWARD

1. **Making Genre and Structure Decisions:** From now on, when you're presented with a writing task, ask yourself the following questions early in the writing process:

    What social action am I being asked to perform?

    What resources can I consult to figure out the traditions and constraints of what I'm being asked to do? Are there people I can talk to? Models of writing I can look at to get a sense of what might be effective and appropriate?

    How can I make this particular writing task my own, even working within the genre constraints that I've figured out?

    What structure might work best for this piece of writing, to accomplish what I need to accomplish? Can I use an existing structure or does the material I'm working with suggest/require a hybrid or new structure of some kind?

    Is there an ongoing conversation that this piece of writing belongs to? And if so, what forms of acknowledgment or citation are appropriate for the occasion, especially if I want to make sure I don't accidentally pass someone else's ideas or words off as my own? Consult the "Note about Citation Styles" in this section or an appropriate handbook as necessary.

2. **Creating an annotated bibliography, part 2:** Take a look at the useful annotated bibliography at the end of Art Young's short online essay, "Writing Poetry in First-Year Composition Courses" (http://www.mhhe.com/socscience/

english/tc/pt/young/young.htm). You've already had an introduction to the genre of the annotated bibliography in Conversation 4; but this time, pay attention to the effect Young's bibliography has on the reader. Suddenly his essay doesn't seem quite so short; it has become a window on a conversation that could claim quite a bit of eavesdropping time. Look back at the student annotations in this volume (Currah on pages 171–172 and Davidson on pages 317–318) and compare them to Young's annotations. Reduce the student annotations to one sentence each: how easy is that to do? If you did an annotated bibliography in Conversation 4 (see the New Practice on page 233), go back to it now and condense each entry to one pithy sentence that captures the essential social action of each item in your bibliography.

ESSAY IDEAS

1. Locate Donald Murray's essay, "Letter to a Young Article Writer" (see the bibliography at the back of this book); then write a short essay of your own giving advice to a young writer. Focus on a particular genre just as Murray does: you could call it "Letter to a Young University Writer" or "Letter to a Young Creative Nonfiction Writer," whatever genre interests you most. Knowing what you know now, what do you want to say to someone just starting out? Can you find the "idea and a half" Murray talks about? What surprises you as you write this letter? Where is the tension, the itch, the edge?

2. Completely rewrite one of your earlier pieces of writing, one that you were bored by. Can you find the cognitive dissonance in it? Can you re-shape it so it has more intellectual suspense, so it can pull a reader through time? Feel free to play with it and transform it into an entirely new genre: turn it into a play (a dialogue between two scholars) or a story. (An example: one of our students used Charles Dickens's *A Christmas Carol* as a model: she became a version of Ebenezer Scrooge, unable to sleep one significant night because she was visited by the ghosts of three scholars who wanted her to re-examine her past, present, and future as a writer). Or write an essay analyzing the structure or genre of a piece you're proud of: describe your writing process in detail, focusing on how you made your genre and organizational decisions.

3. Write an essay analyzing a piece of writing you admire, focusing on its genre and organization. How is it put together? What social action was it meant to perform and how did that influence its structure? How does its structure influence the social action it can perform?

4. Read the articles by MacKinnon and Schryer listed in the bibliography, along with a few other pieces of research on workplace writing. Then write an essay exploring the traditions and constraints of writing in the workplace. Your piece might focus in detail on one of the following questions: How do employees learn to do this writing? How collaborative are their writing processes? How much feedback do they get on early drafts? How do audience constraints shape their writing? How would you describe or categorize the genres you came across in your reading, the social action they are trying to perform? You might also focus your piece primarily on writing you have done in a specific job, drawing on Schryer and MacKinnon and other researchers to point out similarities to or differences from your own experience. Make sure to cite your sources accurately, both in-text and in a list of works cited at the end.

A NOTE ABOUT CITATION STYLES

Handbooks give examples of the various documentation styles we use in academic writing. Since we often have to consult others—to acknowledge their arguments, ideas, or data and to put their arguments, ideas, or data into conversation with our own—we need to make clear whose thinking and writing we have drawn on. Sometimes we quote the exact language of other authors, if it is memorable. Each field of study decides how to document such influences: for example, in psychology and other social sciences, sources are usually documented according to American Psychological Association (APA) style—see the NCTE policy document in Conversation 3 (pages 145–149) for an example of APA style; in English, sources are usually documented according to Modern Language Association (MLA) style.

If your instructor asks you to use MLA style, you'll need to use in-text citations: whenever you summarize, paraphrase, or quote someone else, you will say right in the text where you found that information instead of using a footnote or endnote (footnotes or endnotes are reserved for substantive material; see pages 284, 290, and pages 337–338). For example, if you are using MLA style, you might write,

"[Punctuation] is a learned system, culturally imposed" (Pullum 68).

That code lets your readers know that you took that sentence directly from page 68 in Pullum's book or article (the full information about Pullum's work would be given in a works-cited list at the end of your paper). The square brackets show where you have made a slight change in order to make Pullum's sentence make sense in the context of your own writing; in this case, Pullum's sentence actually was "It is a learned system, culturally imposed." On Pullum's page, the "it" clearly refers to the word "punctuation" in a previous sentence—so you are allowed to make that slight alteration as long as you signal that you've done so by using the square brackets. You could not, of course, insert any word you liked (for instance, "[Football] is a learned system, culturally imposed," would not be acceptable, even if it is true).

If you were asked to use APA style, which emphasizes date of publication, your in-text citations would look slightly different:

> "[Punctuation] is a learned system, culturally imposed" (Pullum, 1991, p. 68).

APA expects you to give your reader not only the author's name and the page number of the sentence you borrowed, but also the year that sentence first appeared in print. (In MLA format, the year of publication usually appears only on the list of works cited at the end of the paper.)

Information like this may be confusing at first, but don't stress about it: no one knows this stuff by heart—we all consult handbooks when we're finishing up our papers, to get the details right and to make sure we have our citations done correctly. Think of each works-cited entry as a sentence constructed in the appropriate code: each punctuation mark carries hidden meaning for people working in that particular community of inquiry. Most handbooks do a good job walking you through the various documentation styles and give lots of examples; of course, you also have lots of examples available for MLA citation style in this volume already. Ask your instructor which documentation style is appropriate for a particular assignment. A reliable online resource is Gordon Harvey's *Writing with Sources* (available at http://www.fas.harvard.edu/~expos/sources/), developed for Harvard students and giving useful guidelines on avoiding unintentional plagiarism as well as giving detailed examples of a range of common citation styles: MLA, APA, CBE (Council of Biology Editors), and CMS (Chicago Manual of Style).

CONVERSATION 7:

Audience, Evaluation, and Response

INTRODUCTION

> Years ago, my father visited a family that included an older daughter still at home. In the evening, the mother took him aside.
>
> "Bill, I don't understand why my daughter never catches anyone's attention."
>
> "I know why," he said. The mother cocked her head.
>
> "You do?"
>
> "When someone speaks to her," my father said, "she leans back, narrows her eyes, and says 'Really?' So the conversation tapers off. It would all be different if she leaned forward, widened her eyes, and said 'Really!'"
>
> They both laughed. A year later the daughter was married and expecting a child.
>
> Kim Stafford, *Northwest Writing Institute Newsletter*, Summer 2002: 1

One of the things that we do manage to find widespread agreement about in the teaching of writing these days is that *students must think about their audience*. Yet there may be times when thinking about audience may not help us discover or create ideas, may not help us get words on the page—may, in fact, silence us if our audience is truly threatening or powerful, able to affect our lives in serious and permanent ways (an audience like a professor known for giving F's and thus preventing students from getting into law school or med school). And thinking about audience might not be useful if it leads us to say things we don't believe just in order to please. As you might expect, the conversation about audience has been going on for a long time and has grown richer and more complicated over the years. The audiences for our writing can be powerful sources of evaluation and response; they can pull writing out of us or shut us down. What, if any, control can we have over audience evaluation and response?

Audience

Wayne Booth wrote a classic and often-cited essay on audience ("The Rhetorical Stance") in 1963 reminding us of our responsibility to our *subject*: we may at times need to say something that a particular audience does not want to hear, in a way that audience does not want to hear it. If, in such a situation, we try instead simply to please a particular audience, we are in essence sell-outs, inconsequential entertainers, and crowd-pleasers. Thinking about one's audience should never mean giving in to them, giving them what they want no matter what, especially if doing so leads us to misrepresent what we believe to be true.

Lisa Ede and Andrea Lunsford's well-known essay, "Audience Addressed/Audience Invoked: The Role of Audience in Composition Theory and Pedagogy," not only gives a useful overview of the conversation on audience (cf. Flower and Hayes, Fulkerson) but also emphasizes that keeping our audience clearly in mind as we write is not as straightforward as it might sound: we are always in part working *to imagine and to create* the kind of audience our writing needs. And audiences often *change* as a result of what they read—in fact, they read in part because they want to change, to be different from what they already are. Part of what writers are supposed to do is change their readers. Negotiating the wide area, full of pitfalls, between giving one's audience what it wants (or what it thinks it wants) versus offending (and therefore alienating) that audience requires a lot more than just "analyzing the rhetorical situation" and then adjusting one's register to suit the audience for each piece. Sometimes it may require, as Peter Elbow suggests ("Closing My Eyes as I Speak: An Argument for Ignoring Audience"), temporarily ignoring audience just so we can hear ourselves think.

And how do we know anything about this abstraction, "our audience," anyway? How many large groups of people do you know of who are all alike? Can you imagine even one room full of readers who share common characteristics? If you were giving a *speech* to a particular group, you might know one specific quality that all members of that group had in common—they might all share a fascination with, say, railroad trains, so you'd feel pretty safe as long as you gave them some absorbing new information about locomotives. But a piece of *writing* won't necessarily go to one specific, known audience. Once it's out of your hands, it can go pretty much anywhere. Putting aside for the moment the most likely situation, that it will go into a pile of similar pieces of writing, all to be read by one instructor under pressure (so he or she can get all the pieces graded and returned by a specific time, before the next batch of papers arrives), imagine it falling into the wrong hands—someone who dislikes you, who disagrees with you, and who might go public (in writing or by speaking to others) about how terrible your piece of writing was.

Perhaps it's a bad idea to imagine this worst-case scenario; but on the other hand, it can also be freeing to acknowledge it. We've had students afraid to freewrite, even though complete privacy was promised, because of demoralizing experiences when they had trusted writing, had turned to it in a time of need, and then had their private writing exposed when a parent or sibling or "friend" found their diary and not only read it, but showed it to others. Such humiliating experiences can be permanently harmful and can change our relationship to language, writing, and audience forever. How do we get beyond them?

Probably the only way is by creating and experiencing, again and again, a different kind of audience for our writing: and this is one reason why inkshedding is such a powerful classroom practice. As Hunt's piece in Conversation 3 makes clear, a major benefit of inkshedding is that when we inkshed within a trusted community of inquiry, we know we are putting words on the page that will be read soon by others who need and want our writing, who are interested in what we have to say, and who are not going to grade it or make dismissive comments about our spelling, usage, or punctuation. Within this community of inquiry, the writing is to stay focused on the investigation itself—which means that people will inevitably disagree and will need to be honest about these disagreements, but always only in the service of attending to the larger issues, attending to the knowledge that the group is trying to build/discover together.

Inkshedding within such a group allows us to develop a rich sense of a *particular* audience—how varied it is, how many different personalities and attitudes and needs and interests and knowledge levels we're writing for all at once. It helps us notice how different an ongoing conversation in a knowledge community is from a one-on-one conversation with a trusted friend—a friend who will always be your ally and who will support you and listen to you no matter what you say or how badly you say it, who will patiently work with you until they're sure they understand what you mean, who will even help you get your thinking clear. Within a community of inquiry, we can sometimes find a *few* allies like that, allies who are so interested in the subject we're working on that they're willing to wade with us through the murky formative stages (or we can *imagine* or *remember* ideal audiences like that, to help us get the writing done—see Atwood in this Conversation).

But the wider community of inquiry will demand to see our ideas in a more developed form. And outside the community of inquiry within which we work, the audience will be even more demanding (or demanding in quite different ways). The model is still a conversation, but keep in mind that a *written* conversation can reach readers/listeners on the other side of the world, at any hour of the day or night; it can draw in participants who could never be all in one room together at the same time.

Evaluation

As it turns out, the inkshedding/conversation model we've just described is not a bad way to imagine one of your most difficult and persistent audiences right now—the instructor who has assigned a piece of writing and whose job it is to comment on it, evaluate it, and perhaps put a grade on it. Your instructor is actually in an unusual and demanding position, trying to be several different kinds of audience at once. In a very real sense, as a teacher, your instructor *wants* to be an ally and coach, someone you want to write for, someone you trust with your thoughts. After all, the instructor's job is to help you become a better writer, not frighten you into becoming a worse one. An instructor wants to be as encouraging and supportive as possible and wants to play the part—at least at times—of the patient listening friend, the ally within the larger community of inquiry, the one who listens to your murky ideas in the formative stages and helps you prepare them for wider consumption.

But if you pursue a thorough **audience analysis** of your instructor, you'll come up against the fact that the university has given him or her another responsibility, a gatekeeping role, that requires all instructors, as employees of the university and representatives of it, to evaluate student work and decide what work will earn university credit, what work is excellent, and what work is unsatisfactory. In a sense, this immediately puts your instructor in the role of that reader across the world who is looking at your writing without any idea who you are or what a nice person you might be or how hard you might have worked to get your chaotic ideas sorted out and typed up. This distant reader has only the words on the page to judge you by: those words will have to stand on their own as he or she decides what they are worth.

No instructor can ignore the gatekeeping responsibility assigned by the university. Think of it as quality control—what value would your university degree have ten years from now if everyone in the world knew your university had no standards, that it just gave everyone high grades no matter how dismal their work was? Yet for almost every teacher we know, this part of the job—the gatekeeping, grading part—is the hardest, primarily because putting grades on student writing doesn't usually improve the teaching/learning environment in the classroom for anyone. What happens when graded essays are handed back in the classroom? Students who get high grades often assume they're better writers than they are and they don't try as hard next time (or they produce the equivalent of Hollywood sequels, always trying to repeat what worked so well before); students who get low grades get discouraged and perhaps give up. And students in the middle can waste a lot of energy feeling dissatisfied, not understanding why so-and-so got a B- while they got a C+, even though they worked longer and harder on their paper than so-and-so did.

Nevertheless, teachers take this part of their work seriously and they try to do it as fairly as they can. So if you're trying to get a bead on this particular audience, you might begin with the image of a busy person with a stack of papers to read, a person who is torn between being an encouraging ally and a judgmental critic, who can't choose one of those roles over the other but must somehow play both of them simultaneously,[1] who would like nothing better than to be sucked into a fascinating paper that clearly deserved high marks but who (if this didn't happen) would sigh and feel obliged to be honest if writing problems were distractingly obvious on the page.

Okay, that image doesn't help much, does it? You pretty much knew that already: be brilliant and you'll do fine; be boring, and your already glaring errors will stand out even more clearly. Or maybe you could try being funny, a class clown, and that would be distracting enough to slow down the instructor's red pen just a little bit? Making an instructor smile—or perhaps even laugh out loud—is a worthwhile goal; but humour, no matter how appropriate in context, can't usually carry a whole paper.

Your audience dilemma wouldn't improve if you read Nancy Sommers's research, showing how instructors often fail to comment productively on student writing. She found that instructors often confused students by responding to rough drafts as if they were final ones: instead of concentrating on substantive issues (like focus, organization, accuracy, and sufficient supporting detail), instructors often wasted time marking surface errors in whole paragraphs that wouldn't even appear in the final draft. Reading articles like Sommers's "Responding to Student Writing" can empower you if it helps you weather difficult experiences with unproductive instructor comments, but it still doesn't help you figure out how to write for audience-as-evaluator. It's all well and good for Wayne Booth to talk about how we shouldn't just pander to our audiences and give them what they want, that we have a responsibility to our subject matter. *He* isn't in the position of writing for grades. Instructors usually get impatient when students ask them directly, "What do you want on this particular paper?"—but it is a reasonable question, after all. When students ask it, they are trying to analyze the rhetorical situation, to understand their audience.

But what if what this particular audience wants is to be surprised? to learn something new? to encounter a student voice that is so absorbed in thinking something through, so responsible to the subject matter of the paper, that the student is no longer focused on giving an instructor what the student *thinks* the instructor wants? What if what instructors *want* is for students to stop worrying so much about what instructors want because the students are so interested in what they're creating/discovering, in what they're finding out as they write? What if instructors are deeply suspicious of and perhaps even distrust student writers who are trying too hard to please, to second-guess them, to give them "what they want"?

You may be feeling at this point that academics are simply the hardest audience to work in the world. But consider this: university teachers have chosen a profession in which they will work very hard and never get rich, in which their work is never done (because knowledge is never-ending and constantly growing and changing), in which they face large groups of new students (apprentice scholars) every year who usually aren't yet sure which communities of inquiry they belong to or want to belong to. Why do instructors do it?

Because they like to use their minds. Because they like intellectual puzzles. Because they live for that moment when a light goes on and they see, in a piece of student writing or in a student's comment in class or in a quiet student's eyes, that something got through. Whatever their own special area of expertise might be, they also share an interest in introducing students to their field in general. So if you can figure out a way to take whatever writing assignment is given to you and make it your own (while still honouring and acknowledging the framework of the assignment as given); if you can figure out a way to care about the work you're doing and the intellectual conversation of which it is a part; if you can figure out a way to explore some new territory, however small—you will have your instructor's undivided attention, even if your language shows signs of stress as it tackles the job. (And, according to David Bartholomae in "Inventing the University," your language is bound to show such signs of stress whenever you try something difficult, whenever you attempt to move into intellectual territory that's new to you.)

Does this seem impossible to you? Do you believe that you're not in a position to teach teachers anything new about a field in which they're experts and you're an apprentice?

This is a good question, so we should take some time to think about it for a moment. You can't pretend to be an experienced member of a knowledge community when you're just learning for the first time that it even exists. Just looking at the selections in this anthology, for instance—even if you managed to read them all—you'd still be aware that many of these pieces (the academic articles in particular) refer to countless other pieces that you've never read and may never read, countless names with which you're unfamiliar. As Bartholomae put it (in his essay in Conversation 4), these pages are "crowded with others." Each of these pieces seems to be connected to a web that never ends, to what LeFevre refers to as an "infinite conversation."

But *none* of us, no matter how many years we participate in it, will ever be able to hear the entire conversation; we can only participate in the conversation or contribute to it as we experience it ourselves, on our own small patch of the infinite web. This applies to your instructor as much as it does to all scholars and scientists and writers. None of us can escape our embeddedness in our context, a context that brings with it both limitations and possibilities (in fact, limitations that simultaneously define or *are* our possibilities). We all have blind spots—things everyone else can see that we can't. But we also all have visions—things we can see that no one else can.

Does this situation mean that we should all throw our hands up and say about everything, "Well, that's just your opinion—my opinion is X and it's just as good as yours." No. Because even if our limited opinions and beliefs and commitments are all we're left with, even if that's all that our collective human knowledge is made of, nevertheless, some opinions carry more weight: some are supported by more evidence, or explain more of the data we've collected, or persuade more of our colleagues than other opinions do. According to historians of science, for instance, the theory of relativity is an elegant opinion that was, for a long time, disconcertingly contradicted by solid experimental data; but the theory of relativity explained so many details about our world that could not be explained so well before that most members of the scientific community became committed to it. As it happened, their commitment turned out to be justified: the "solid" experiments whose results had contradicted it were—many years later—shown to be flawed (cf. M. Polanyi 9–15). Will the theory of relativity itself ever be found wanting and need to be revised? Who knows. But a scientist living today can only participate in the conversation that is going on today, a conversation that is still busy exploring further implications of the theory of relativity. Whatever conversation is coming in centuries ahead *depends* upon the conversation that is going on now, depends on its being as good as it can be.

In most academic fields, scholars are choosy about whose opinions they take the time to consider seriously, especially since everyone has limited time and energy. Scholars in the field of composition and rhetoric, for instance, are most likely to listen thoughtfully to an opinion about the teaching of writing if it shows up in one of their professional journals; that way, they know that editorial boards made up of experienced teachers and scholars have selected the article from the hundreds submitted each year as one that should become part of the ongoing written conversation. They are also likely to listen to an opinion if they know something about the training and the background and the previous work of the person who stands behind that opinion; and, in some cases (luckily, or the field would never advance at all), they're willing to listen to the opinions of someone they don't know much about simply because that person "speaks their language"—that is, not only uses words they recognize as key words in the field, but uses them to explore as-yet-unanswered questions that everyone is eager to think more about. In fact, writers working at the very edge of knowledge in any particular field are irresistible to others in that field. Imagine the opinions of such people as clues in an intensely exciting murder mystery that you can't put down, and you'll have some idea how excited scholars can get over the academic writing of such a person.

You're probably saying to yourself about now, "This is insane—I can certainly see that a paper 'working at the very edge of knowledge' might be irresistible to my prof, but I can't turn myself into someone capable of writing a paper like that. How can I locate a working edge if I don't even understand the body of knowledge behind it, the stuff that everyone in this field takes for granted, that they all know and understand? And I'm also struggling to learn the lingo—I can't pretend to belong to this discourse community, to speak the same language as everyone else, or to contribute to their ongoing investigations."

Maybe not. But the composition and rhetoric field has got one big characteristic in your favour: *you are* the working edge. What scholars in the field are interested in has everything to do with you—with your history with writing, your writing processes, your education, your perception of what helps you get words on the page and what doesn't. Your life experience, your writing experiences (from the time you first picked up a pencil at age four until now), and your experience in school, all of it counts (or perhaps we should say, you can certainly *make* it count, by shaping it and putting it in a significant context).

Scholars in the field are also interested in the actual writing processes of people in all lines of work. If you look at the academic journals, you'll see research on the consulting reports produced by engineers—who, depending on who you talk to, spend anywhere from 25 percent to 80 percent of their work lives writing—and you'll see research on the letters sent out by insurance companies (Schryer), the proposals sent out by business people, the writing done at the Bank of Canada (MacKinnon), the briefs researched by lawyers, or the writing done by doctors and nurses and psychiatrists and veterinarians. If you carefully interview one or more people about the writing they do in a particular occupation, you already may have data that no one else has.

Further, participating in the ongoing conversation depends to a great extent on honest positioning. Think of the listserv analogy again. Members of a listserv would be annoyed if experienced teachers and scholars contributed lengthy and pompous postings that essentially made the same points that several other members had made two months before: it would be rude, a clear sign that the established scholars were only interested in being heard themselves and hadn't bothered to listen thoughtfully to the ongoing conversation of others. But if an apprentice scholar—you, for example—listened in for a while and then asked a modest, specific question based on the conversation you'd been eavesdropping on, letting everyone know your position as a beginner, you'd be likely to discover people ready to offer guidance, to help you locate an answer if they didn't know it themselves.

In a paper written for a university course, positioning means primarily that you acknowledge that a conversation has been going on, that you're a beginner, but that you want to put your ideas and the information you're working with into a meaningful relation with the work done by some of the other scholars you've read. Even if that means your works-cited list consists of only three essays, you've still made an honest start at thinking something through in the presence of these other thinkers: you've entered the endless web of conversation at one particular point. You aren't likely to win a Nobel Prize for this move—but you *are* likely to have your instructor's serious and undivided attention.

Response

We're going to put you in a different position now—all at once, *you are the audience*, you are the one required to respond thoughtfully to the work of someone else. What the new paradigm in the teaching of writing has emphasized (take a look back at Hairston's piece in Conversation 3) is that students often learn much more about writing from each other and from reading and responding to each other's work than they can ever learn from an instructor. In a writing workshop, where members of the class are bringing copies of their work-in-progress to share with others, especially if they are reading their work out loud (either to the whole class or to a smaller peer response group), this learning proceeds especially quickly. First, you learn more by reading your own work out loud to others than you can learn any other way. You *hear* it instantly when your sentences get tangled or when something falls flat; and the reverse is true— you know instantly that something is working if everyone bursts out laughing or if, at a serious moment in your piece, you can hear a pin drop because all your listeners are holding their breath. Second, you notice quickly when things aren't working in the writing of your colleagues—somehow it's easier to see why something doesn't work when the specific example is coming from someone else's piece, not yours.

Yet writing groups are also dangerous. There always seems to be someone who needs the ego boost that comes from tearing everyone else's work to shreds. These days, however, most instructors know how to prepare students to be disciplined and productive participants in a writing group and how to prevent destructive situations from developing. The most important piece of advice is to realize that you are not being asked to "play teacher." You might have heard writing groups referred to as "peer-editing groups," a term that could give the impression that students are supposed to edit or "correct" one another's work. Certainly, peers can be useful to each other during final proofreading—see Conversation 8—but at the moment, we're talking about drafts at a more formative stage when students are quite right to be uneasy if they're put in the position of evaluating or "correcting" the work of a colleague. They know they're not equipped to be telling others what's wrong with their syntax, their imagery, their punctuation, their symbolism, their organization. But students *are* ideally equipped to tell each other things that no one else could—that is, what a particular piece of writing made happen inside one individual heart, one individual mind, one very specific body.

Each individual reader is the *only* person who has the raw data of his or her unique responses. And since most of us need constantly to learn more about our audiences and the effect our writing has on those audiences, that is exactly the information we need.

We'll list here three guidelines for a productive writing group (**peer response group**) and then give fuller explanations in the sections that follow:

1. the author never quarrels with the person giving feedback;

2. the author doesn't apologize or explain—the writing must stand on its own;

3. the reader points first to the passages that should be kept, that have the most heat.

1. Never quarrel with the person giving feedback

Why? It's a complete waste of time. As an author, you should be grateful that anyone took the time to read your work-in-progress at all, let alone to give you detailed responses to it. So you should concentrate on taking in as much of the feedback as you can, jotting it all down to consider later, at your leisure, as you revise. You may eventually decide that this person misunderstood what you were trying to do and that you can't make use of their feedback—fine, that's your decision. But while you're collecting the raw data, your focus should be on making sure you understand fully what that reader is trying to say.[2] After all, if readers are giving honest feedback about what your writing made happen inside them, they are the authority. If they say, "I was so bored by your second page I fell sound asleep," you can't say, "No, you weren't." What would be the point?

If, on the other hand, they are not being honest and disciplined in their responses but are trying to be pompous and tell you how your writing needs to be "fixed," you certainly could quarrel with them. If, for instance, instead of saying that they were so bored by page two that they fell asleep, they had said, "Your second page was boring," their feedback has instantly become unreliable. Why? Because they are trying to make an "objective" pronouncement about your writing itself, not about their reactions to it—and a statement about specific qualities existing in your writing is a statement that you or anyone else in the room could reasonably argue with. *Don't*, however. Invest your limited time and energy instead into translating what they have said as best you can: after all, it's not hard to translate "page two was boring" into "I was bored by page two," so jot it down the second way and make sure you take the information in.

Suppose another student says, "What you need to do on page two is rewrite all of these sentences so they're in active voice and remove all the adverbs and adjectives because the whole page is too wordy." Statements like these are hopeless because they can lead to endless discussions and debates about what good writing *should* be in the abstract—which is an unknowable entity. Good writing is writing that works for readers in a specific situation. The information you need from any decent writing group, therefore, is whether or not your writing is working for them, if it's accomplishing what you hoped it would accomplish. So instead of quarrelling with wrong-headed feedback, ask questions and be persistent in rephrasing so you can get detailed, reliable feedback you can use: "Can you tell me one sentence in particular on page two that made you impatient or bored because it felt wordy and passive to you?"

2. Don't apologize or explain—the writing must stand on its own

You can't usually get good information about what your writing *is* accomplishing if you tell readers ahead of time what you *wanted* it to accomplish: that will bias their reactions. Read your piece clearly and slowly and with as much appropriate emphasis as you can. And then let your listeners/readers tell you what they think the piece is about, what they think the main ideas or characters are, what they think you're trying to do. The feedback sheets in this section give you several ways to give this information quickly to a fellow author (see pages 343–350). One of the simplest and most useful feedback strategies is to inkshed for three minutes your own summary of the piece you just read or heard. We've had students complain that this must be a waste of time—"What use is a summary? She knows what she has in the piece—she wrote it!" But that's just the point. She may know what she *hopes* is in the piece. She may know what she *intended* to put in the piece. She may have a clear idea in her head what she *meant* for that piece to say or do. But until she hears from readers—preferably more than just one or two readers—she won't know *what the piece itself* is saying and doing. Descriptive feedback of all kinds is extraordinarily useful in letting us know what readers heard. If they heard what we hoped they would hear, we're on the right track. If they heard something quite different or even the opposite of what we had hoped, we've got work to do.

Both of the feedback forms included in this chapter allow for comments about craft since so many readers feel they're not being helpful unless they point out something that's not working. Of course, there's no reason why a comment on craft has to be negative—a reader could say, "You seem to have a real knack for dialogue—I found all the conversations in this piece so natural and believable," and that would be an enormously useful piece of feedback: it would let the writer know what skills to build on, what to keep. It's a curious phenomenon that when someone hands us a piece of writing and wants to know what we think, we often feel our responsibility is to tell them what's wrong with it, where their mistakes are. If a friend wrote a song and wanted us to hear it, then played a guitar and sang the song to us, we're unlikely to respond with "Well, that note at the end of the second measure seemed wrong, the refrain isn't working in the third line, and the beat is off in the final stanza." We're much more likely to thank our friend for singing to us and then ask some questions: When did you write it? Why? How did you come up with that amazing image in the second verse?

What is it about writing that makes us behave differently? Elbow's piece in this Conversation makes an important contribution to the conversation about responding to each other's writing when he emphasizes what skill it takes to *like* a piece of writing. We all know it's easier to destroy things than to create them, to blow up in one morning a skyscraper that took many years to design and build, to burn a book that took a decade to write. But for some reason in the academy we assume that people who can tear things apart, poke holes in arguments, or point out what's wrong with a piece of writing are way smarter than people who can do the opposite—who can see potential in a draft, help someone make their argument even stronger, help build a piece of writing by pointing out what's good in it, what should be kept and developed further. *Liking* a piece of writing doesn't necessarily mean we think it's finished or even close—the piece could be a real mess and need lots more work. But if we're able to see what's strong in it, the part that gives it energy, the thinking edge, we can be of genuine use to the author. It's hard work and takes a lot of practice to learn to do this well—but the good news is, if we learn to do it for others, we gradually become better at doing it for ourselves, at noticing and building on the strengths in our own work (and cutting the rest).

3. Point first to the passages that should be kept, that have the most heat

This is your first responsibility, always. These passages need not be things you like—in fact, they could be things that make you angry or things that you disagree with—but they should be the things you're most likely to remember from this piece of writing. *Your right to make any other comments at all about the writing depends on your performing this simple task first.* We call it **pointing** (following the terminology in Elbow and Belanoff's "Sharing and Responding") primarily because you can do it almost as quickly as you can point, as long as you read with a pen or a highlighter in your hand. Simply draw a straight line under (or highlight) the passages that jump out at you. If you find yourself wanting to underline an entire paragraph or page, draw a straight vertical line beside that passage in the margin instead. If this behaviour reminds you of something, that might be because it's what readers regularly do with books they read for pleasure, so they can quickly return to their favourite passages. If when you respond to someone's draft, you have time for nothing else, do this: *this* is the feedback that should never be omitted. Hand the piece of writing back to the author saying, "I've underlined the parts that had the most energy for me." If the writer receives this kind of feedback from several people, the accumulating information is persuasive (if everyone underlines the same passage, for instance, a writer would be crazy to cut it).

Of course, it's essential that everyone understand what these underlines mean. One of us had a student who missed a few classes at the beginning of term and who grew more and more upset as the term progressed; she finally showed up during office hours to complain in exasperation, "I don't know what to do to make you happy—you don't like anything I write! You underline everything, but don't tell me how to make it better." Obviously, that misunderstanding got cleared up quickly, but she'd spent such a long time getting upset that it took her a few weeks to go back, re-read all her drafts, and try to readjust to how good they were.

Often during the first few weeks of term, pointing is the only feedback we allow students to give each other on drafts. Old habits are hard to break, and the minute you're allowed to write comments on someone's paper, you're apt to drift back into evaluative language without realizing it. Even to write "This piece is so well written" is to make an evaluative comment; it would be much more useful to be specific—"Your first two lines caught my attention because they made me expect an answer to something I've wondered about for a long time." However, once everyone has learned to actually enjoy the "pointing" responses to their work (which happens more quickly than you might expect, our need to feel *heard* is so strong) and once members of the group have learned a range of possible descriptive responses, written feedback—especially when focused by a feedback form—becomes invaluable. Customized feedback forms for specific assignments can be designed to include additional criteria or checklists. Also, check out Elbow and Belanoff's "Sharing and Responding," which suggests so many specific ways for students to talk to each other productively about their work-in-progress that we've never had time in any one course for our students to try them all.

Still, *pointing* is the move we emphasize the most; no one gets to criticize a piece of writing until they have earned that right by working to understand it and to see its strengths—and until they have let the writer of the piece know what those strengths are. All of us feel vulnerable at some level about our writing, whether we're trying to describe the death of a friend or the birth of an idea. If accomplished writers like Nancy Mairs can feel devastated by criticism and rejection even after many successes, awards, and publications (see her essay "The Writer's Thin Skin and Faint Heart"), how can we expect unpublished writers to turn to revision with energy after dismissive or hurtful comments from each other or from instructors? Mairs's experience (see the excerpt from "Voice Lessons" in this Conversation) also highlights how debilitating a certain kind of dismissive feedback from one's peers can be—and what a productive writing workshop might look like. No matter how grading is handled in a particular course, the crucial thing is to build a generative writing community in the classroom, a place where—as Kim Stafford puts it—better and better writing can be drawn out of us by "the alchemy of the group's attention" (*NWI Newsletter* Fall 1995:1). And students play a key role in shaping such writing communities—no instructor can do it alone, without student understanding and collaboration.

Notes

[1] Elbow suggests that one way to handle these challenging opposing roles is by trying *not* to do them at the same time. For instance, an instructor could emphasize the gatekeeping role at the beginning and end of term (in the syllabus and in the final evaluation of portfolios or exams and the assigning of a course grade) and then feel free to focus on being a supportive coach throughout the rest of the term. Such a procedure might allow the instructor to be even more supportive and encouraging than might have been possible otherwise—as well as more demanding and critical at the end of term, a tougher grader. Since in many educational systems, these functions are separated (that is, your tutor is primarily an ally, helping you study and prepare for exams given by the university—exams that the tutor neither designs nor grades—or helping you prepare pieces for a portfolio that other faculty will be evaluating), an instructor forced to play both roles might do well to set it up as a Dr. Jekyll/Mr. Hyde dichotomy: that is, the *kind* me will do as much as possible to help you do good work and write papers that will satisfy the *demanding ruthless* me, who will have to evaluate and criticize your work fiercely at the end of term. See "Embracing Contraries in the Teaching Process," which has obviously shaped our discussion of these issues.

[2] See Elbow and Belanoff, who suggest that in receiving feedback we should remember two things: the author is always right (it's your piece, only you know what you want to say) and the reader is always right (only the reader knows accurately what got through and what did not and how it made him or her feel—see "Sharing and Responding" 508). They suggest, when you are listening to or reading feedback, that you should "eat like an owl"—owls eat the whole animal, the whole mouse or whatever, and then let their organism sort it out and get rid of what they can't use. Trust your body and your mind and your heart—your organism will sort it out, will ignore what it can't use and will use what it can. But this may take time. Your first responsibility is simply to take everything in and make sure you are a good listener, that you fully understand why your readers are responding as they are (*Writing Without Teachers* 102–103).

INKSHEDDING PROMPTS

1. As you read Margaret Atwood, Nancy Mairs, and Suzanne LiaBraaten, think about the audiences *you* write for. Inkshed about your worst audience ever or the worst you can imagine, an audience that would paralyze you and make writing feel impossible. Or inkshed about your ideal audience, real or imaginary: are there certain readers (friends, colleagues, teachers, family members) who make you eager to write and who make you feel smart and capable when you write? What is it about them that has that effect on you? Could you reproduce it in other writing situations? Do you have any audience stories like theirs to tell? Are you, as LiaBraaten felt herself to be at times, your own worst audience? How?

2. Inkshed about your experiences with feedback: the worst or most painful feedback you've ever gotten, the best or the most pleasurable, the most useless, the most helpful (even if it was hard to hear). Tell a specific story in detail. You might want to write a follow-up inkshed later, if—when you re-read your feedback story(ies)—you notice any revealing patterns in how you respond to feedback on your writing. You could also inkshed about feedback you've given other writers: feedback that was difficult to give or easy to give; feedback that made you uncomfortable; feedback that made you feel smart and helpful because the writer followed your suggestions, improved the work, and was grateful as a result. In the past have you tended to give descriptive or evaluative feedback or some combination of the two? How would you characterize yourself as a giver of feedback? As a receiver?

3. Inkshed about any differences in tone that you've noticed between feed-back you receive from instructors and feedback you receive from your peers. Or inkshed about audience differences you've noticed as you've been eavesdropping on the conversations in this volume: some essays clearly have only researchers or instructors in mind; others are directed only at students; still others have wider public audiences in view. What specific details did you notice that indicated different registers, tones, vocabularies, styles? A close reading comparing and contrasting two essays in terms of audience could lead to a fascinating essay of your own.

4. As you read Elbow's essay in this Conversation, be alert for the ellipses [. . .]. Do any of them make you suspicious or curious? If so, find a copy of Elbow's full essay and locate some of the missing material. We didn't make any of these cuts for wicked reasons (that is, we weren't trying to misrepresent his argument or hide anything crucial from you—and we also cleared these cuts with him). We were just trying to include as much of the piece as we could, given our space constraints—the size of an anthology, after all, affects students directly, since the longer an anthology is, the more it costs. Inkshed about some of the cuts we made. Why do you think we made them? Do you think we should have kept those cuts? And if so, which other passages should we have cut instead? How many of these cuts seem related to audience issues? (He clearly was not expecting students to read his piece.) How would it have affected your reaction to Elbow's ideas if we had included that material?

5. After reading Mammen's interview with Peter Elbow, try inkshedding a quick imaginary dialogue or interview with one of the other authors in this volume. Ask him or her questions and then make up the answers, based on what you think the author of the pieces you've read *would* say. Even more challenging might be an inkshed putting two or more of the writers you've read into conversation with each other—making one talk with, agree with, argue with, or interview the other. Feel free to bring voices together from different conversations, playing with whatever connections interest you: John Polanyi and Kim Stafford (as sons following closely in their fathers' footsteps), LiaBraaten and Fulwiler, Keller and Mairs, Hunt and Matalene (or, more explosive, Elbow and Bartholomae, based on their essays in Conversation 4). Playing with dialogue allows you to experiment with both voice and audience, so have fun.

6. Read the online University of Alberta document that attempts to explain instructors' comments on student papers ("Learning to Read Instructor

Comments and Marks on Essays"); it's posted at http://www.humanities. ualberta.ca/english/marking.html. You might want to download a copy on your computer or print it out for reference. Did that document surprise you in any way? What particular details stand out as being useful for a university student? What if anything confused you? Are there additional issues about grading and evaluation that you wish the document had addressed? How would you describe the difference between the grid printed on the first page of that document and the feedback sheets included here in Conversation 7? You probably noticed that the grid on the University of Alberta (U of A) document owes a lot to the grid in Elbow's essay in this chapter—but how are the two grids different? Which version would you find more useful for an instructor to fill out in response to one of your final drafts?

Check out the links on the U of A document so you can see the research that influenced it. A strong essay could be written analyzing some of that research, the work done by Elizabeth Hodges and Nancy Sommers in particular, and its impact on the U of A document. What did the U of A document make use of? What did it ignore? Keeping in mind that one of the primary uses of that document is to help train new teachers of writing at a university and to guide their marking of student papers, what does your investigation reveal about the influence of academic research on teaching practice?

Margaret Atwood, from "Communion: Nobody to Nobody—The Eternal Triangle: The Writer, the Reader, and the Book as Go-Between"

Margaret Atwood has lent her considerable international reputation as a novelist to encourage and support Canadian writers and writing. Born in Ottawa, raised in northern Ontario, Quebec, and Toronto, she attended Victoria College at the University of Toronto and then earned her master's degree from Radcliffe College. She has received many awards and honorary degrees during her thirty-five years of writing, including the Booker Prize (for *The Blind Assassin*, 2000) and the Governor General's Award (for *The Handmaid's Tale*, 1985). Although she has published over thirty books, including collections of short stories, poetry, essays, and literary criticism, it is her novels that account for her popularity and the fact that her work has been published in over thirty languages—novels such as *The Edible Woman* (1969), *Surfacing* (1972), *Cat's Eye* (1988), *The Robber Bride* (1993), *Alias Grace* (1996), and *Oryx and Crake* (2003). It is a recent work of non fiction, however—*Negotiating with the Dead: A Writer on Writing* (2002)— from which this selection was taken and in which Atwood reflects on the crucial question of audience: for whom does the writer write?

from COMMUNION: NOBODY TO NOBODY— THE ETERNAL TRIANGLE: THE WRITER, THE READER, AND THE BOOK AS GO-BETWEEN

. . . I will go back to the first question—for whom does the writer write? And I will give two answers. The first is a story about my first real reader.

When I was nine, I was enrolled in a secret society, complete with special handshakes, slogans, rituals, and mottoes. The name of this was the Brownies, and it was quite bizarre. The little girls in it pretended to be fairies, gnomes, and elves, and the grownup leading it was called Brown Owl. Sadly, she did not wear an owl costume, nor did the little girls wear fairy outfits. This was a disappointment to me, but not a fatal one.

I did not know the real name of Brown Owl, but I thought she was wise and fair, and as I needed someone like that in my life at the time, I adored this Brown Owl. Part of the program involved completing various tasks, for which you might collect badges to sew on to your uniform, and in aid of various badge-collecting projects—needlework stitches, seeds of autumn, and so forth—I made some little books, in the usual way: I folded the pages, and sewed them together with sock-darning wool. I then inserted text and illustrations. I gave these books to Brown Owl, and the fact that she liked them was certainly more important to me than the badges. This was my first real writer-reader relationship. The writer, me; the go-between, my books; the recipient, Brown Owl; the result, pleasure for her, and gratification for me.

Many year later, I put Brown Owl into a book. There she is, still blowing her whistle and supervising the knot tests, in my novel *Cat's Eye*, for the same reason that a lot of things and people are put into books. That was in the 1980s, and I was sure the original Brown Owl must have been long dead by then.

Then a few years ago a friend said to me, "Your Brown Owl is my aunt." "Is?" I said. "She can't possibly be alive!" But she was, so off we went to visit her. She was well over ninety, but Brown Owl and I were very pleased to see each other. After we'd had tea, she said, "I think you should have these," and she took out the little books I had made fifty years before—which for some reason she'd kept—and gave them back to me. She died three days later.

That's my first answer: the writer writes for Brown Owl, or for whoever the equivalent of Brown Owl may be in his or her life at the time. A real person, then: singular, specific.

Here's my second answer. At the end of Isak Dinesen's "The Young Man with the Carnation," God's voice makes itself heard to the young writer Charlie, who has been so despairing about his work. "'Come,' said the Lord. 'I will make a covenant between Me and you. I, I will not measure you out any more distress than you need to write your books . . . But you are to write the books. For it is I who want them written. Not the public, not by any means the critics, but Me, Me!' 'Can I be certain of that?' asked Charlie. 'Not always,' said the Lord."

So that is who the writer writes for: for the reader. For the reader who is not Them, but You. For the Dear Reader. For the ideal reader, who exists on a continuum somewhere between Brown Owl and God. And this ideal reader may prove to be anyone at all—any *one* at all—because the act of reading is just as singular—always—as the act of writing.

Nancy Mairs, from "Voice Lessons"

Nancy Mairs (see also Conversation 6, page 301) reflects on genre, gender, and audience in this piece, as she lays out the larger responsibilities that writers have as they read and respond to each other's work: the responsibility to strengthen and energize fellow writers to face the long task of revision; the responsibility to enter into lives and experiences quite different from their own; the responsibility to listen closely, to ask the difficult questions, and to "laugh in all the right places."

from VOICE LESSONS

What else could rouse me to write? What else did I know? *There were the babies, and the blood, the way bread yields and sighs like flesh under your fist, the death of the little dog, so sudden, unlooked for, and the way your tears choked you as you folded him into the pillowcase and heaped dirt over the linen, and then too your body, its betrayal sudden but also its diminishment protracted so that grief, you learn, will actually never end, and the babies gone, and soon the blood as well.* These were the sorts of things I knew, or was learning, and so I tried some of them out on the guys (yeah, it was just them and me that year) in a poetry workshop. "Yech," they said.

And kept on saying. That was a bad time for me, alone with the guys, who knew what writing was because they were doing it, who knew what I was doing, to the extent that they weren't doing it, wasn't writing, not the real thing (muscular, tough-minded, penetrating, gritty), and who didn't mind telling me so. One or another has gone on telling me so ever since. "Stop squandering your time on this feminist stuff," Edward Abbey told me for years. And after he died, a reviewer for *The New York Times* caught up the tune before it faded away: "a waste of a talented voice," he wrote. I don't think that any man has ever suggested I give up writing. It's just that a lot of them want me to write something *else*. (My mother does too, by the way, so I'm using the word *man* pretty loosely.) . . . If I'd been trapped forever by some evil genie in that poetry workshop with all those guys doing the polite equivalent of sticking their fingers down their throats in response to my writing, I can't imagine what would have become of me. . . . As luck would have it, however, I found myself in another poetry workshop altogether, gathered under the pear trees outside a very old farmhouse in New Hampshire on summer Mondays, listening to, reflecting upon, discussing, and celebrating the poems of a small but diverse group of women.

And when (around the same time I began my doctoral work) my poems began to turn into essays about a woman's life, the life of a woman's body, the life of a crippled woman's body, no one at Skimmilk Farm moved to banish me from the Monday workshop. In the ivory phallus, I had found, where poets hardly speak even to fiction writers (let alone the essayists, literary critics, and the like), the genres are like armed camps, and transgressing their boundaries can result in swift expulsion. If I'd started reading an essay in my poetry workshop there, I'd have been cut off and told to register for the nonfiction workshop meeting down the hall. At the Farm, the women simply listened to my essays very hard and laughed in all the right places. Although I have not seen many of them for years now, I still think of them as my audience. They, and all the others like them whom I've never met, are the ones I write for.

And really, what more can we—as writers, as artists, as human beings—do for one another? In the middle of a sentence I'm having trouble with, when my attention strays and I find myself cringing in anticipation of the next inevitable *yech* (and I do cringe; old habits die hard), I say: Let the masters of the written word cling to their bodiless principles. Let them pronounce what is interesting and what is not, what is a poem and what is not, what merits their grudging praise and what does not. For myself, I want another model. I want to hear *this* poem by *this* person on *this* muggy August morning under the pear trees. I want to know what it is doing in the life of her work, and in my life as well. I want to give her the courage to say the next hard thing, without fear of ridicule or expulsion if she strays across the borders of good taste, good sense, or good judgement demarcated by a tradition she has had no part in forming. I want her to do the same for me.

This is what we can *all* do to nourish and strengthen one another: listen to one another very hard, ask hard questions, too, send one another away to work again, and laugh in all the right places.

M. Elizabeth Sargent, Feedback Sheets

M. Elizabeth Sargent (see page 149 in Conversation 3) developed the two feedback sheets in this chapter in order to help her students respond productively to one another's work. Based on suggestions in Elbow's *Writing Without Teachers* and *Writing with Power*, the feedback sheets have helped writers at various levels focus on what they *can* do reliably for each other: *not* correct grammar or usage or style, but *describe* as accurately as possible what the writing made happen in their own hearts, minds, and bodies—and why.

The first feedback sheet can be used to respond to almost any kind of writing; immediately following it is an annotated version, giving detailed explanations and examples. The longer feedback sheet ("Feedback Sheet for an Essay Working with Sources") evolved from the first and still focuses on detailed description; but it provides questions and checklists that can be adapted to a range of writing projects and is particularly useful for academic writing that needs to work with and acknowledge sources. Any questions that arise as you work with the longer version can probably be addressed by reading the annotations for the shorter form.

Both feedback sheets can be photocopied for use in writing groups: writers often find it easier to process responses from multiple readers if the commentary from each reader covers roughly the same territory (i.e., doesn't fail to address key issues) and comes in the same order, organized by the feedback sheets. The feedback sheets essentially serve as heuristics for commentary, pushing readers to think in different ways about what they've just read and to articulate their reactions. The feedback forms also aid memory, keeping readers from forgetting certain crucial kinds of response they should give to a particular draft. Students can make multiple photocopies of the blank feedback sheets for use throughout the term, simply handwriting their responses in the appropriate spaces (and continuing on the back if they run out of room).

The blank forms are also available on this book's website (at http://www.sargent. nelson.com), where they can be downloaded, either to be adapted for a particular assignment or simply to serve as a computer template (some readers prefer typing their responses on the feedback sheet, especially if their handwriting is difficult for others to read).

FEEDBACK (Movies of your mind)

Author: _____

Title: _____

Reader: _____

<u>Pointing</u> (to sentences, paragraphs, word, or phrases):

Straight line (these penetrated my thick skull)—

Wavy line (these bounced off or didn't work for me)—

<u>Summarizing</u>:

Main points or centres of gravity:

Three-minute sum up:

Word in—

Word out—

<u>Telling</u>: Tell the story of what happened to you as you read, as if reading the printout from sensitive machines hooked up to you to measure your heartbeat, pulse, breath, sweat. Were you bored, nervous, anxious, asleep, alert? And if so, when? Identify specific pages/passages/lines in the piece that you link to your body's reactions.

<u>Showing</u> (give at least two metaphors):

<u>Craft</u>:

Feedback Sheet with Annotations

FEEDBACK (Movies of your mind: *a story*—an honest, detailed description of what this piece of writing made happen in you)

Author: <u>the person who wrote the piece</u>
Title: <u>a short title of their piece</u>
Reader: <u>the person filling out this form</u>

<u>Pointing</u> **(to sentences, paragraphs, word, or phrases):** Do most of this pointing on your photocopy of the piece itself, which you should give back to the author along with this form. Make sure your name is on the top right corner of the author's piece (no anonymous feedback).

Straight line (these penetrated my thick skull)—
Put a straight line under (or highlight) the passages that had the most energy for you, the words, phrases, images that you are most likely to remember. You may not agree with them or even like them, but they had the most heat. To highlight an entire paragraph or page, put a vertical line beside it in the left margin. There's no limit on how many lines you can underline, but the feedback is obviously more useful if you don't underline everything! You do have a bottom limit, however—you must underline *something*. When you're done, pick the one to three passages you feel most strongly about, ones you think the author should keep no matter what, and identify them here, on this form.

Wavy line (these bounced off or didn't work for me)—
Put a wiggly line under words, phrases, or passages that hit you the wrong way or that confused you or that bored you. If you think you can explain why you reacted as you did, go ahead—but often we can't explain these reactions well or our explanations are in fact misleading, not capturing the real reasons for our resistance (which we may not know ourselves). So don't feel obligated to explain why it doesn't work for you. Again, when you're done, pick the one to three passages that gave you the most trouble and identify them here. Guideline: you cannot wiggly-line anything until you have straight-lined something. Your goal should be to have more straight lines than wiggly lines, both on the photocopy of the piece and on this form (if that's not possible, limit yourself to equal numbers of each).

<u>Summarizing</u>:

Main points or centres of gravity: State briefly what you think this piece was trying to accomplish. How would you describe the centre of gravity, the heart of the piece? You may be aware from reading it what the author *wanted* the centre of gravity to be, but your experience of it may be otherwise (all your attention may have been off in one paragraph with X, even if the author wanted you to be focusing on Y). Let the author know where the weight fell for you.

Three-minute sum up: Time yourself. If you run out of room here, turn this form over and use the back, but be sure to inkshed for at least three minutes as full a summary of this piece as you can. Your summary will be more useful if you prepare for a few minutes by looking back over the piece of writing first and reflecting on the overall structure. How did it open? What happened next? What was the order of events or arguments or information? How did it end? If you need to pause briefly, once or twice, to look back at the piece, go ahead—just extend your inkshedding time accordingly. Do not try to evaluate the organization of the piece—invest all your time in describing it as you see it, in as much detail as possible (referring to specific pages and passages where the movement turns).

Word in—Choose a word that appears in this piece of writing that seems to you an especially significant or key word, even if it was used only once.

Word out—Choose a word that does *not* appear in this piece but that seems to connect to it in some significant way or to capture something about it. You may or may not feel that this word should eventually make its way into the piece. (Often writers get excellent title ideas from this section of the feedback sheet.)

<u>Telling</u>: **Tell the story of what happened to you as you read, as if reading the printout from sensitive machines hooked up to you to measure your heartbeat, pulse, breath, sweat. Were you bored, nervous, anxious, asleep, alert? And if so, when? Identify specific pages/passages/lines in the piece that you link to your body's reactions.**

Brief example: "I was on the edge of my seat because of your first three sentences. I thought you were going to be exploring X, which is something I've been thinking about for a long time so I was eager to go on. But my pulse slowed by the top of page three because I couldn't follow that top paragraph and by page four, that middle paragraph, I was starting to feel lost and anxious because you had stopped talking about X completely and were totally focused on Y, which made me feel stupid because I couldn't understand it. I ended up disappointed in the last paragraph on page five to realize you still hadn't actually told me anything more about X at all. I'm sorry, maybe this piece wasn't even supposed to be about X, but somehow I got that idea from the opening and I could never let go of it."

<u>Showing</u>: **(give at least two metaphors):**

This is probably the most difficult part of the form because it's the strangest. We're not used to giving metaphors to each other as feedback. And most of us don't get much practice at *making* metaphors. But since metaphor is a major intellectual tool in every field, including science, it's good practice for the person *giving* feedback to have to come up with at least two metaphors. And metaphors can give writers feedback that they could not have gotten or *heard* any other way. Your job here is simply to compare the piece you've just read to something else—a piece of fruit, a type of weather, a sound of voice, an article of clothing, an animal, a way of moving. Don't think too long or too hard about it. But do make yourself come up with at least two metaphors (or similes). Don't worry about explaining them. Sometimes you can explain them and sometimes you can't. For instance, we once had a student write on this part of the feedback form, "this piece was a dark red juicy watermelon with millions of hard black seeds"—but he was clueless, unable to explain why that image had come to him. Later during class, however, he glimpsed a possible explanation and shared it with us: "I loved this piece, it was so tasty and, well, delicious to me—but then it just got to be too much hard work to read it, it was so full of typos and careless mistakes that any spellchecker could have caught that I got distracted and irritated and couldn't enjoy it until I got rid of those things first." We noticed that the author who received that feedback turned in remarkably clean final copy from that day forward!

Craft: Mention here *one* specific thing about the writing that is being handled well or that needs work (or both): "Your dialogue is so natural and believable, but I couldn't follow who was speaking when—I think maybe you need a new line for each new speaker" or "That opening line caught my attention right from the start, especially that powerful parallel structure" or "I felt as if I kept driving off a cliff when I was reading your sentences—somehow the punctuation steered me one way, but the sentence went the other way, especially that last sentence on page five."

Feedback Sheet for an Essay Working with Sources

Name of person giving feedback: _____

Author of draft being responded to: _____

Read the first page of the essay only and then stop—answer these questions before proceeding:

Do you want to read on? (Circle one)   YES   NO   UNCERTAIN
If yes or uncertain, why? What intrigues you?

_____

If no, why not? What puts you off?

_____

Does there seem to be a live question, a felt itch, some perplexity that makes you curious?   YES   NO

Is this "itch" clear to you or are you just getting glimmers of it? (Circle the word "clear" or "glimmers" in the preceding sentence to show your response.) Whether you are getting clear signals or glimmers only, what are they or where do they come from? (give specific words if possible):

_____

_____

State the live question here in your own words: _____

_____

If you don't yet sense any live question, read on—when you're finished, respond to this question:

What could you suggest to the author as a possible live question, a focusing perplexity to heighten or develop early in this piece to give it more intellectual suspense? _____

_____

(Try to point to passages in the paper on which you base this suggestion—give page numbers.)

* * *

Pointing (do this on the draft itself as you read, signing in with your colour of pen or pencil):
Straight line (these are things the author should keep as is)—mention here your **favourite** passage (you may have highlighted many, but choose only one here—give page number):

Wiggly line (try to explain why it's not working if you can)—mention here the **most problematic** passage (explain why it bothers you only if you can—give page number):

Now fill in the following checklist:

1. Has the author **quoted specific lines or phrases** from different voices (that is, different authors)?

(Circle one)   YES   NO

Whose voices? (give authors, short titles, and page numbers as they are given in the essay):
   a)
   b)
   c)
   d)
   e)

2. Is the quoting handled correctly in the text (according to MLA or appropriate format)? If not, make suggestions below. (Circle one)   YES   NO

3. Centre of gravity—what resonates or lingers in your mind? (It may not be what the author of the draft intended as the main point.) Describe it here, telling exactly where it comes in the draft (page and line):

_____

4. Inkshed on a separate sheet of paper for three minutes, writing two to four full sentences summarizing what you think the piece is saying right now and how it is built or put together. (Is there a principle of organization or a genre? Is it a collage, a letter, an argument, an explanation, a prayer, a persuasive essay, a report of research, a narrative? Is it combining or mixing genres? And if so, which ones? Does the form seem appropriate for the content, is there a good fit between them?)

When you've finished summarizing the piece, write two quick possible titles here (they can be goofy suggestions or serious ones, whatever springs to mind after reading the piece).

_____   _____

5. What is the current title? (Remember that a title is required—it helps focus the reader's attention.)

_____

Has the author underlined or italicized his or her own title? or put it in quotation marks? (Circle one)   YES   NO   (Mark it on the draft if so—none of these should be done!)

_____

6. TMM? (Tell Me More . . .) What do you want to hear more about? a childhood memory? a scene? the research data? more support for the main claim being made? one of the authors being quoted?

_____

7. Is there a clear lead-in to each quotation? That is, are we given the full name of the author, the title of the article or book, and a context (a sense of *why* this material is being quoted)? (Circle one)   YES   NO

_____

If not, tell which quotations need fuller and clearer lead-ins (give page and line numbers, if necessary).

_____

Is there a clear unpacking of each long quotation? That is, do we know why it's been used and what the author of this essay wants us to get from the quotation? (Circle one)   YES   NO
(Neither lead-in or unpacking need to be lengthy—but mention if either seems insufficient or confusing.)

8. In this piece of writing, do you get a clear sense of an intellectual conversation going on between voices and between the author of this draft and the quoted voices? (Circle one)   YES   NO   SORT OF

If yes, where do you get the fullest sense of this? (Be as specific as possible.) _____

If no (or only "sort of"), what suggestions do you have for heightening the sense of a lively conversation going on?

_____

9. Give two metaphors for this essay (no need to explain them)—**or** give a read-out of your reactions paragraph by paragraph (an EKG of your reading—see one example on the annotated feedback sheet under "Telling").

Peter Elbow, from "Ranking, Evaluating, and Liking: Sorting Out Three Forms of Judgment"

Peter Elbow (see also page 185, Conversation 4) has focused much of his work not just on audience issues but on issues of evaluation, grading, and assessment. He reluctantly accepts the necessity for course grades, although he did teach for a while at Evergreen, a university in Washington State that has thrived for many years, regularly placing students in good graduate schools, while refusing to assign course grades. However, he does *not* believe it necessary to grade individual papers, finding the practice highly suspect. His extensive work on portfolio assessment, as an alternative practice that supports rather than undermines learning, is well known.

from RANKING, EVALUATING, AND LIKING: SORTING OUT THREE FORMS OF JUDGMENT

The Problems with Ranking and the Benefits of Evaluating

. . . Because ranking or grading has caused so much discomfort to so many students and teachers, I think we see a lot of confusion about the process. It is hard to think clearly about something that has given so many of us such anxiety and distress. The most notable confusion I notice is the tendency to think that if we renounce ranking or grading, we are renouncing the very possibility of judgment and discrimination—that we are embracing the idea that there is no way to distinguish or talk about the difference between what works well and what works badly.

So the most important point, then, is that *I am not arguing against judgment or evaluation.* I'm just arguing against that crude, oversimple way of *representing* judgment—distorting it, really—into a single number, which means ranking people and performances along a single continuum.

In fact I am arguing *for evaluation.* Evaluation means looking hard and thoughtfully at a piece of writing in order to make distinctions as to the quality of different features or dimensions. For example, the process of evaluation permits us to make the following kinds of statements about a piece of writing:

- The thinking and ideas seemed interesting and creative.

- The overall structure or sequence seemed confusing.

- The writing was perfectly clear at the level of individual sentences and even paragraphs.

- There is an odd, angry tone of voice that seems unrelated or inappropriate to what the writer was saying.

- Yet this same voice is strong and memorable and makes one listen even if one is irritated.

- There are a fair number of mistakes in grammar or spelling: more than "a sprinkling" but less than "riddled with."

To rank, on the other hand, is to be forced to translate those discriminations into a single number. What grade or holistic score do these judgments add up to? It's likely, by the way, that more readers would agree with those separate, "analytic" statements than would agree on a holistic score. . . .

The process of evaluation, because it invites us to articulate our criteria and to make distinctions among parts or features or dimensions of a performance, thereby invites us further to acknowledge the main fact about evaluation: that different readers have different priorities, values, and standards.

The conclusion I am drawing, then, in this first train of thought is that we should do less ranking and more evaluation. Instead of using grades or holistic scores—single number verdicts that try to sum up complex performances along only one scale—we should give some kind of written or spoken evaluation that discriminates among criteria and dimensions of the writing—and if possible that takes account of the complex context for writing: who the writer is, what the writer's audience and goals are, who we are as reader and how we read, and how we might differ in our reading from other readers the writer might be addressing.

But how can we put this principle into practice? The pressure for ranking seems implacable. Evaluation takes more time, effort, and money. It seems as though we couldn't get along without scores on writing exams. Most teachers are obliged to give grades at the end of each course. And many students—given that they have become conditioned or even addicted to ranking over the years and must continue to inhabit a ranking culture in most of their courses—will object if we don't put grades on papers. . . . Here are some ways in which I and others use *less ranking* and *more evaluation* in teaching. . . .

(a) Portfolios. Just because conventional institutions oblige us to turn in a single quantitative course grade at the end of every marking period, it doesn't follow that we need to grade individual papers. Course grades are more trustworthy and less damaging because they are based on so many performances over so many weeks. . . .

(b) Another useful option is to . . . . sometimes do a *bit* of ranking even on individual papers, using two "bottom-line" grades: H and U for "Honors" and "Unsatisfactory." I tell students that these translate to about A or A- and D or F. . . . I'm not giving many grades; only a small proportion of papers get these H's or U's (. . . . [and] I could put an OK or S [for satisfactory] on all those middle-range papers). . . . [T]hese holistic judgments about best and worst do not seem as arbitrary and questionable as most grades. There is usually a *bit* more agreement among readers about the best and worst papers. What seems most dubious is the process of trying to rank that whole middle range of papers—papers that have a mixture of better and worse qualities so that the numerical grade depends enormously on a reader's priorities or mood or temperament. . . . Thus there is a huge reduction in the total amount of unreliability I produce. (It might seem that if I use only these few minimal grades I have no good way for figuring out a final grade for the course—since that requires a more fine-grained set of ranks. But I don't find that to be the case. For I also give these same minimal grades to the many other important parts of my course such as attendance, meeting deadlines, peer responding, and journal writing. If I want a mathematically computed grade on a scale of six or A through E, I can easily compute it when I have such a large number of grades to work from—even though they are only along a three point scale.). . .

(c) Sometimes I use an analytic grid for evaluating and commenting on student papers. Here's an example:

Strong	OK	Weak	
			CONTENT, INSIGHTS, THINKING, GRAPPLING WITH TOPIC
			GENUINE REVISION, SUBSTANTIVE CHANGES, NOT JUST EDITING
			ORGANIZATION, STRUCTURE, GUIDING THE READER
			LANGUAGE: SYNTAX, SENTENCES, WORDING, VOICE
			MECHANICS: SPELLING, GRAMMAR, PUNCTUATION, PROOFREADING
			OVERALL [Note: this is not a sum of the other scores.]

I often vary the criteria in my grid (e.g., "connecting with readers" or "investment") depending on the assignment or the point in the semester.

Grids are a way I can satisfy the students' hunger for ranking but still not give in to conventional grades on individual papers. Sometimes I provide nothing but a grid (especially on final drafts), and this is a very quick way to provide a response. Or on midprocess drafts I sometimes use a grid in addition to a comment: a more readerly comment that often doesn't so much tell them what's wrong or right or how to improve things but rather tries to give them an account of what is *happening to me* as I read their words. I think this kind of comment is really the most useful thing of all for students, but it frustrates some students for a while. The grid can help these students feel less anxious and thus pay better attention to my comment.

I find grids extremely helpful at the end of the semester for telling students their strengths and weaknesses in the course—or what they've done well and not so well. Besides categories like the ones above, I use categories like these: "skill in giving feedback to others," "ability to meet deadlines," "effort," and "improvement." This practice makes my final grade much more communicative.

(d) I also help make up for the absence of ranking—gold stars and black marks—by having students share their writing with each other a great deal both orally and through frequent publication in class magazines. Also, where possible, I try to get students to give or send writing to audiences outside the class. At the University of Massachusetts, freshmen pay a ten dollar lab fee for the writing course, and every teacher publishes four or five class magazines of final drafts a semester. The effects are striking. Sharing, peer feedback, and publication give the best reward and motivation for writing, namely, getting your words out to many readers.

(e) I sometimes use a kind of modified *contract grading*. That is, at the start of the course I pass out a long list of all the things that I most want students to do—the concrete activities that I think most lead to learning—and I promise students that if they do them *all* they are guaranteed a certain final grade. Currently, I say it's a B—it could be lower or higher. My list includes these items: not missing more than a week's worth of classes; not having more than one late major assignment; *substantive* revising on all major revisions; good copy editing on all major revisions; good effort on peer feedback work; keeping up the journal; and substantial effort and investment on each draft.

I like the way this system changes the "bottom-line" for a course: the intersection where my authority crosses their self-interest. I can tell them, "You have to work very hard in this course, but you can stop worrying about grades." The crux is no longer that commodity I've always hated and never trusted: a numerical ranking of the quality of their writing along a single continuum. Instead the crux becomes what I care about most: the *concrete behaviors* that I most want students to engage in because they produce more learning and help me teach better. . . .

It's crucial to note that I am *not* fighting evaluation with this system. I am just fighting ranking or grading. I still write evaluative comments and often use an evaluative grid to tell my students what I see as strengths and weaknesses in their papers. My goal is not to get rid of evaluation but in fact to emphasize it, enhance it. I'm trying to get students to listen *better* to my evaluations—by uncoupling them from a grade. In effect, I'm doing this because I'm so fed up with students *following* or *obeying* my evaluations too blindly—making whatever changes my comments suggest but doing it for the sake of a grade; not really taking the time to make up their own minds about whether they think my judgments or suggestions really make sense to them. The worst part of grades is that they make students obey us without carefully thinking about the merits of what we say. I love the situation this system so often puts students in: I make a criticism or suggestion about their paper, but it doesn't matter to their grade whether they go along with me or not (so long as they genuinely revise in some fashion). They have to think; to decide.

Admittedly this system is crude and impure. Some of the really skilled students who are used to getting A's and desperate to get one in this course remain unhelpfully hung up about getting those H's on their papers. But a good number of these students discover that they can't get them, and they soon settle down to accepting a B and having less anxiety and more of a learning voyage.

The Limitations of Evaluation and the Benefits of Evaluation-Free Zones

. . . [But] evaluation harms the climate for learning and teaching—or rather *too much* evaluation has this effect. That is, if we evaluate *everything* students write, they tend to remain tangled up in the assumption that their whole job in school is to give teachers "what they want." Constant evaluation makes students worry more about psyching out the teacher than about what they are really learning. Students fall into a kind of defensive or on-guard stance toward the teacher: a desire to hide what they don't understand and try to impress. This stance gets in the way of learning. (Think of the patient trying to hide symptoms from the doctor.) Most of all, constant evaluation by someone in authority makes students reluctant to take the risks that are needed for good learning—to try out hunches and trust their own judgment. . . .

I find that the greatest and most powerful breakthroughs in learning occur when I can get myself and others to *put aside* this nagging, self-doubting question ("How am I doing? How am I doing?")—and instead to take some chances, trust our instincts or hungers. When everything is evaluated, everything counts. Often the most powerful arena for deep learning is a kind of "time out" zone from the pressures of normal evaluated reality: make-believe, play, dreams—in effect, the Shakespearian forest.

In my attempts to get away from too much evaluation (not from all evaluation, just from too much of it), I have drifted into a set of teaching practices which now feel to me like the *best* part of my teaching. I realize now what I've been unconsciously doing for a number of years: creating "evaluation-free zones."

(a) The paradigm evaluation-free zone is the ten minute, nonstop freewrite. . . .

(b) A larger evaluation-free zone is the single unevaluated assignment—what people sometimes call the "quickwrite" or sketch. This is a piece of writing that I ask students to do—either in class or for homework—without any or much revising. It is meant to be low stakes writing. There is a bit of pressure, nevertheless, since I usually ask them to share it with others and I usually collect it and read it. . . .

(c) For the last few semesters I've been devoting the first three weeks *entirely* to the two evaluation-free activities I've just described: freewriting (and also more leisurely private writing in a journal) and quickwrites or sketches. Since the stakes are low and I'm not asking for much revising, I ask for *much more* writing homework per week than usual. And every day we write in class: various exercises or games. The emphasis is on getting rolling, getting fluent, taking risks. And every day all students read out loud something they've written—sometimes a short passage even to the whole class. So despite the absence of feedback, it is a very audience-filled and sociable three weeks.

At first I only dared do this for two weeks, but when I discovered how fast the writing improves, how good it is for building community, and what a pleasure this period is for me, I went to three weeks. I'm curious to try an experiment with teaching a whole course this way. I wonder, that is, whether all that evaluation we work so hard to give really does any more good than the constant writing and sharing (Zak). . . .

The best argument for evaluation-free zones is from experience. If you try them, I suspect you'll discover that they are satisfying and bring out good writing. Students have a better time writing these unevaluated pieces; they enjoy hearing and appreciating these pieces when they don't have to evaluate. And *I* have a much better time when I engage in this astonishing activity: reading student work when I don't have to evaluate and respond. And yet the writing improves. I see students investing and risking more, writing more fluently, and using livelier, more interesting voices. This writing gives me and them a higher standard of clarity and voice for when we move on to more careful and revised writing tasks—tasks that involve more intellectual pushing and that sometimes make their writing go tangled or sodden.

The Benefits and Feasibility of Liking

. . . Let me start with the germ story. I was in a workshop and we were going around the circle with everyone telling a piece of good news about their writing in the last six months. It got to Wendy Bishop, a good poet (who has also written [many] good books about the teaching of writing), and she said, "In the last six months, I've learned to *like* everything I write." Our jaws dropped; we were startled—in a way scandalized. But I've been chewing on her words ever since, and they have led me into a retelling of the story of how people learn to write better.

The old story goes like this: We write something. We read it over and we say, "This is terrible. I *hate* it. I've got to work on it and improve it." And we do, and it gets better, and this happens again and again, and before long we have become a wonderful writer. But that's not really what happens. Yes, we vow to work on it—but we don't. And next time we have the impulse to write, we're just a *bit* less likely to start.

What really happens when people learn to write better is more like this: We write something. We read it over and we say, "This is terrible. . . . But I *like* it. Damn it, I'm going to get it good enough so that others will like it too." And this time we don't just put it in a drawer, we actually work hard on it. And we try it out on other people too—not just to get feedback and advice but, perhaps more important, to find someone else who will like it.

Notice the two stories here—two hypotheses. (a) "First you improve the faults and then you like it." (b) "First you like it and then you improve faults." The second story may sound odd when stated so baldly, but really it's common sense. Only if we like something will we get involved enough to work and struggle with it. Only if we like what we write will we write again and again by choice—which is the only way we get better.

This hypothesis sheds light on the process of how people get to be published writers. Conventional wisdom assumes a Darwinian model: poor writers are unread; then they get better; as a result, they get a wider audience; finally they turn into Norman Mailer. But now I'd say the process is more complicated. People who get better and get published really tend to be driven by how much *they* care about their writing. Yes, they have a small audience at first—after all, they're not very good. But they try reader after reader until finally they can find people who like and appreciate their writing. I certainly did this. If someone doesn't like her writing enough to be pushy and hungry about finding a few people who also like it, she probably won't get better.

It may sound so far as though all the effort and drive comes from the lonely driven writer—and sometimes it does (Norman Mailer is no joke). But, often enough, readers play the crucially active role in this story of how writers get better. That is, the way writers *learn* to like their writing is by the grace of having a reader or two who likes it—even though it's not good. Having at least a few appreciative readers is probably indispensable to getting better.

When I apply this story to our situation as teachers I come up with this interesting hypothesis: *good writing teachers like student writing* (and like students). I think I see this borne out—and it is really nothing but common sense. Teachers who hate student writing and hate students are grouchy all the time. How could we stand our work and do a decent job if we hated their writing? Good teachers see what is only *potentially* good, they get a kick out of mere possibility—and they encourage it. When I manage to do this, I teach well.

Thus, I've begun to notice a turning point in my courses—two or three weeks into the semester: "Am I going to like these folks or is this going to be a battle, a struggle?" When I like them everything seems to go better—and it seems to me they learn more by the end. When I don't and we stay tangled up in struggle, we all suffer—and they seem to learn less.

So what am I saying? That we should like bad writing? How can we see all the weaknesses and criticize student writing if we just like it? But here's the interesting point: if I *like* someone's writing it's *easier* to criticize it.

I first noticed this when I was trying to gather essays for the book on freewriting that Pat Belanoff and Sheryl Fontaine and I edited. I would read an essay someone had written, I would want it for the book, but I had some serious criticism. I'd get excited and write, "I really like this, and I hope we can use it in our book, but you've got to get rid of this and change that, and I got really mad at this other thing." I usually find it hard to criticize, but I began to notice that I was a much more critical and pushy reader when I liked something. It's even fun to criticize in those conditions.

It's the same with student writing. If I like a piece, I don't have to pussyfoot around with my criticism. It's when I don't like their writing that I find myself tiptoeing: trying to soften my criticism, trying to find something nice to say—and usually sounding fake, often unclear. I see the same thing with my own writing. If I like it, I can criticize it better. I have faith that there'll still be something good left, even if I train my full critical guns on it.

In short—and to highlight how this section relates to the other two sections of this essay—liking is not the same as ranking or evaluating. Naturally, people get them mixed up: when they like something, they assume it's good; when they hate it, they assume it's bad. But it's helpful to uncouple the two domains and realize that it makes perfectly good sense to say, "This is terrible, but I like it." Or, "This is good, but I hate it." In short, I am not arguing here *against* criticizing or evaluating. I'm merely arguing *for* liking.

Let me sum up my clump of hypotheses so far:

- It's not improvement that leads to liking, but rather liking that leads to improvement.
- It's the mark of good writers to like their writing.
- Liking is not the same as evaluating. We can often criticize something better when we like it.
- We learn to like our writing when we have a respected reader who likes it.
- Therefore, it's the mark of good teachers to like students and their writing.

If this set of hypotheses is true, what practical consequences follow from it? How can we be better at liking? It feels as though we have no choice—as though liking and not-liking just happen to us. I don't really understand this business. I'd love to hear discussion about the mystery of liking—the phenomenology of liking. I sense it's some kind of putting oneself out—or holding oneself open—but I can't see it clearly. I have a hunch, however, that we're not so helpless about liking as we tend to feel.

For in fact I can suggest some practical concrete activities that I have found fairly reliable at increasing the chances of liking student writing:

(a) I ask for lots of private writing and merely shared writing, that is, writing that I don't read at all, and writing that I read but don't comment on. This makes me more cheerful because it's so much easier. Students get *better* without me. Having to evaluate writing—

especially bad writing—makes me more likely to hate it. This throws light on grading: it's hard to like something if we know we have to give it a D.

(b) I have students share lots of writing with each other—and after a while respond to each other. It's easier to like their writing when I don't feel myself as the only reader and judge. And so it helps to build community in general: it takes pressure off me. Thus I try to use peer groups not only for feedback, but for other activities too, such as collaborative writing, brainstorming, putting class magazines together, and working out other decisions.

(c) I increase the chances of my liking their writing when I get better at finding what is good—or *potentially* good—and learn to praise it. This is a skill. It requires a good eye, a good nose. We tend—especially in the academic world—to assume that a good eye or fine discrimination means *criticizing*. Academics are sometimes proud of their tendency to be bothered by what is bad. Thus I find I am sometimes looked down on as dumb and undiscriminating: "He likes bad writing. He must have no taste, no discrimination." But I've finally become angry rather than defensive. It's an act of discrimination to see what's good in bad writing. Maybe, in fact, this is the secret of the mystery of liking: to be able to see potential goodness underneath badness.

Put it this way. We tend to stereotype liking as a "soft" and sentimental activity. Mr. Rogers is our model. Fine. There's nothing wrong with softness and sentiment—and I love Mr. Rogers. But liking can also be hard-assed. Let me suggest an alternative to Mr. Rogers: B. F. Skinner. Skinner taught pigeons to play ping-pong. How did he do it? Not by moaning, "Pigeon standards are falling. The pigeons they send us these days are no good. When I was a pigeon . . ." He did it by a careful, disciplined method that involved close analytic observation. He put pigeons on a ping-pong table with a ball, and every time a pigeon turned his head 30 degrees toward the ball, he gave a reward (see my "Danger of Softness").

What would this approach require in the teaching of writing? It's very simple . . . but not easy. Imagine that we want to teach students an ability they badly lack, for example how to organize their writing or how to make their sentences clearer. Skinner's insight is that we get nowhere in this task by just telling them how much they lack this skill: "It's disorganized. Organize it!" "It's unclear. Make it clear!"

No, what we must learn to do is to read closely and carefully enough to show the student little bits of proto-organization or sort of clarity in what they've already written. We don't have to pretend the writing is wonderful. We could even say, "This is a terrible paper and the worst part about it is the lack of organization. But I will teach you how to organize. Look here at this little organizational move you made in this sentence. Read it out loud and try to feel how it pulls together this stuff here and distinguishes it from that stuff there. Try to remember what it felt like writing that sentence—creating that piece of organization.

Do it some more." Notice how much more practical and helpful it is to say, "Do more of what you're doing here," than to say, "Do something *different* from anything you've done in the whole paper."

When academics criticize behaviorism as crude it often means that they aren't willing to do the close careful reading of student writing that is required. They'd rather give a cursory reading and turn up their nose and give a low grade and complain about falling standards. No one has undermined behaviorism's main principle of learning: that reward produces learning more effectively than punishment.

(d) I improve my chances of liking student writing when I take steps to get to know them a bit as people. I do this partly through the assignments I give. That is, I always ask them to write a letter or two to me and to each other (for example about their history with writing). I base at least a couple of assignments on their own experiences, memories, or histories. And I make sure some of the assignments are free choice pieces—which also helps me know them. . . .

Getting a glimpse of them as individual people is particularly helpful in cases where their writing is not just bad, but somehow offensive—perhaps violent or cruelly racist or homophobic or sexist—or frighteningly vacuous. When I know them just a bit I can often see behind their awful attitude to the person and the life situation that spawned it, and not hate their writing so much. When I know students I can see that they are smart behind that dumb behavior; they are doing the best they can behind that bad behavior. Conditions are keeping them from acting decently; something is holding them back. . . . [A]nd the conditions under which we teach sometimes make it difficult for us to like them and their writing. Writing wasn't meant to be read in stacks of twenty-five, fifty, or seventy-five. And we are handicapped as teachers when students are in our classes against their will. . . .

(e) It's odd, but the more I let myself show, the easier it is to like them and their writing. I need to share some of my own writing—show some of my own feelings. I need to write the letter to them that they write to me—about my past experiences and what I want and don't want to happen.

(f) It helps to work on my own writing—and work on learning to *like* it. Teachers who are most critical and sour about student writing are often having trouble with their own writing. They are bitter or unforgiving or hurting toward their own work. (I think I've noticed that failed PhDs are often the most severe and difficult with students.) When we are stuck or sour in our own writing, what helps us most is to find spaces free from evaluation such as those provided by freewriting and journal writing. Also, activities like reading out loud and finding a supportive reader or two. I would insist, then, that if only for the sake of our teaching, we need to learn to be charitable and to like our own writing. . . .

Let me sum up the points I'm trying to make about ranking, evaluating, and liking:

- Let's do as little ranking and grading as we can. They are never fair and they undermine learning and teaching.
- Let's use evaluation instead—a more careful, more discriminating, fairer mode of assessment.
- But because evaluating is harder than ranking, and because too much evaluating also undermines learning, let's establish small but important evaluation-free zones.
- And underneath it all—suffusing the whole evaluative enterprise—let's learn to be better likers: liking our own and our students' writing, and realizing that liking need not get in the way of clear-eyed evaluation.

WORKS CITED [in this selection]

Belanoff, Pat, Peter Elbow, and Sheryl Fontaine, eds. *Nothing Begins with N: New Investigations of Freewriting.* Carbondale: Southern Illinois UP, 1991.

Bishop, Wendy. *Something Old, Something New: College Writing Teachers and Classroom Change.* Carbondale: Southern Illinois UP, 1990.

—. *Released into Language: Options for Teaching Creative Writing.* Urbana: NCTE, 1990.

Elbow, Peter. "The Danger of Softness." *What Is English?* New York: MLA, 1990: 197–210.

Zak, Frances. "Exclusively Positive Responses to Student Writing." *Journal of Basic Writing* 9.2 (1990): 40–53.

Lori Mammen, "When Teachers Are Writers: An Interview with Peter Elbow"

In the following interview with Peter Elbow, Mammen gets Elbow to talk about grading and about "the foundation for [his] teaching," the theory of different audience relationships (see pages 366–370). Mammen wrote this piece when she was editor of *Writing Teacher*, a publication that later joined forces with *THINK* magazine to become an online journal, *r•w•t*™ *magazine (reading, writing, and thinking).* Although *r•w•t*™ *magazine* has ceased publication, material from past issues continues to be available online at http://educyberstor.com. A former classroom teacher, Mammen has written books and articles on teaching reading and writing, including *Writing Prompts Plus, Writing Warm-Ups,* and a range of teachers' guides to the Harry Potter books. As

Editorial Director of ECS Learning Systems, Inc., she continues to be interested in audience issues. The following passage from the November 2002 issue of *r•w•t*™ *magazine* provides an image that suggests why writing requires so much energy and time:

> Writing introduces important "guests" for thinking—the audience—and they require a different kind of thinking.
>
> A gracious host or hostess always prepares for guests: clean house, fresh linens, special recipes, pleasant conversation. The old cliché about "only the best will do" usually applies to our guests, even if we willingly accept less-than-perfect living conditions the rest of the time.
>
> In a similar way, "gracious" writers must prepare for the "guests" to their thinking—and only the best should do. A thinker-writer must consider the audience's needs and practice great discipline throughout the writing process. And just like the organized host/hostess, the wise writer should have a "to-do list" that guides the preparation.

At the top of the list, Mammen suggests, is a question all writers need to ask: "What do I want my audience to know or learn from my writing?"

WHEN TEACHERS ARE WRITERS: AN INTERVIEW WITH PETER ELBOW

Note: The interview is a regular feature of *Writing Teacher*. In this issue, we focus on our recent conversation with Dr. Peter Elbow of the University of Massachusetts. Dr. Elbow is the author or co-author of numerous books on the teaching of writing, which include *Writing Without Teachers*, *Writing with Power*, and *A Community of Writers: A Workshop Course in Writing*. In this interview, Dr. Elbow discusses why teachers should write with their students. Lori Mammen, editor of *Writing Teacher*, conducted this interview.

WT: During the past twenty years, we have seen many changes in writing instruction. One of the more controversial changes recommended by some is that teachers should become writers—not just students. Do you agree with this recommendation?

ELBOW: Yes, I agree. I don't want to sound too exclusionary about it. I don't mean that you have to be a genius, an artist, or some extraordinary person in order to be a teacher. Let me begin with two autobiographical facts.

When I started graduate school, I was having trouble writing, and it just got worse and worse. I couldn't write the papers that I was expected to write, and I had to quit school before

I was kicked out. Through a former teacher, I found a job as a teacher. I was scared to go back into the classroom, but I found I enjoyed teaching. I discovered something too. You can't be a student unless you can write, but not being able to write didn't get in my way as a teacher at all. This seemed a little sad. There is too little reason for teachers to write.

The second piece of autobiography is this. It was my very difficulties in writing that got me interested in writing. When I finally went back to graduate school, I built up a kind of diary of my struggles with writing. I especially tried to write about stuck moments and moments of getting unstuck. These jottings are what eventually grew into *Writing Without Teachers*. I feel as if I often teach out of my own experiences and struggles as a writer.

WT: Do you think these struggles give you a different perspective?

ELBOW: Yes, very often people who teach writing or English are naturally good writers, or at least they learned to write well at an early age. They don't struggle at it so they have a hard time understanding the struggle of students. This reinforces the students' feelings that to be a writer you have to have a special gift or be a special person. They don't realize that writing is just a matter of forcing yourself to get words down on the pages and it means that you have to make a mess. I guess if I could make a rule, I would say that teachers should experience all the difficulties of writing—and still keep on writing.

Writing is a great leveler. I may be an excellent writer, I may be skilled and experienced, and my students may be unskilled and naive, but we can identify with one another as writers. When we write in class and share what we have written, it feels like we are in the same boat. We can see the struggle that we are having. It is good for teachers to be writers because it allows them to identify and understand their students' struggles better than if they didn't write.

If teachers don't write, it becomes too easy for them to think that there is one right way to do it—make an outline first and make it clear, every paragraph must have a topic sentence. When a person doesn't write, especially if the person is a good reader, it is too easy for the person to say, "Why can't the student just do it the right way?" When you write, you realize there is no right way to do it. The process is a mess. One day you have to do it this way; another day you have to do it that way. Some people can do it one way and others can do it another way. If you are a writer, it gives you a respect for the unpredictability, the messiness, and the difficulty of the writing process. I want teachers to experience that.

By the way, writing is more effective than reading as a bridge between students and teachers. For the mental process of reading is more hidden and mysterious. When my students and I read together, it may be difficult for my students to see how I understand certain things. I may not see how they understand things. It takes a good deal of careful detective work to see the complex process of construction that goes on when people work out the meaning of a text. In reality, there is draft making and hypothesis making in reading, but it goes on so fast and inside the head that you can't see it.

WT: Most teachers would not consider themselves to be writers. Why do you think this is true?

ELBOW: It is important to stop and ask what it means to be a writer. In our culture, the word *writer* carries a lot of baggage. It has always been difficult for me to think of myself as a writer even though I have written a bunch of books. I feel uncomfortable when I say that I am a writer because I don't write novels or poetry. It seems like the word *writer* in our culture is reserved for the imaginative artist—the novelist or poet. That is an odd fact, but I do have some ideas about it. There is more magic attached to the activity of writing novels, stories, and poems. We feel that to be a writer is to be someone special, to have a little magic, to be a genius. A writer is not just a regular person. Of course, I want to fight that. On perfectly selfish grounds, I want to consider myself a writer, and I have finally come to insist on it. But there is a cultural tide that says, "Oh well, if you only write non-fiction about teaching or literature, you are not a writer."

I think what I said about fiction and poetry has changed a little bit. During the past ten years the reading public has become very interested in nonfiction. Nonfiction has become as popular as novels. People who have written popular nonfiction are considered real writers. These are writers like Tracy Kidder and Annie Dillard. So in addition to saying that the connotations of the word *writer* involve magic and genius, they also involve getting ideas across to the general public or selling a lot of books. I think it is important to fight this. A long time ago Frank Smith said that a writer is anyone who writes. A writer can be a regular, ordinary person. If the person writes, he or she is a writer.

What's crucial, then, is that this *open* meaning of writer is fed into the advice that teachers should be writers. Teachers don't have to publish novels or take on the mystique of writers—as people who suffer or live by themselves. Teachers do not have to take on that funny cultural role. To be a writer you just have to be a person who cranks out words onto the page. When I ask my students to think of themselves as writers, and to write case studies of themselves as writers, they often bridle at thinking of themselves in this way. I tell them, "Well, you write all these papers in school. You are writers." One of the things that I have discovered is that their unconscious definition of a writer is a person who only writes special, high, deep, wonderful things—who only writes what she wants to write—who only writes "from the soul." It is fun to turn the tables on my students and give them a more realistic definition of a writer. Real writers—especially people who make a living by writing—are people who say, "You pay me, and I will write it."

WT: But isn't a writer someone who publishes?

ELBOW: It is not crucial that teachers publish—although it is wonderful. Publishing is part of our skewed cultural definition of a writer—someone who publishes blockbuster novels and makes millions of dollars. No: writers are people who write.

But there is a crucial kind of publication that is different from normal publication in magazines and books. Or rather we need to think in a more careful and human way about what publication really means. Publication means getting writing to readers. A class "read-around" is publication. The crucial distinction here is between getting *published* and getting *feedback*. When I get published, people read my words; when I get feedback, people tell me which parts worked well or badly for them or give me suggestions.

Sending writing to friends or to a network is publishing. Smart teachers find small groups of friends and share their writing with them. It's not hard to establish a network of acquaintances who care about some of the same issues that we do. It is very powerful, helpful, and fun to produce writing and send it to the fifteen or twenty people that we know and like and say, "Here is something I wrote. It is for you. I'm not looking for feedback; I just want to give it to you."

In short, publishing means being read, not being criticized. If we let publication be defined for us by our current commercial arrangements—to mean *only* official or commercial getting into large scale print—this means we spend all our time getting rejection notices, it means we are prey to what is in fashion, and it is very discouraging. It's crazy to say that my writing cannot go out to readers unless some editor likes it. If God hadn't meant us to get our writing out to readers, she wouldn't have given us computers and desktop publishing.

Anyway, what I'm saying is that all teachers should be writers, but that doesn't mean they have to become special people. They just have to write and give themselves the pleasure of getting it out to friends and allies. They shouldn't sit there and grade papers while their students write. They should take the time for their own writing, too.

By the way, the idea of taking writing time in class is important. When I was in school, if we wrote in class, it was usually punishment. But I have discovered that it is extremely useful to write in class, and not as a punishment. It may be the most productive way to spend class time. But it is crucial that the teacher write along with the students. If the teacher sits and reads papers, the message is not good. It is most valuable if they see me writing, too.

WT: How often do you write with your students?

ELBOW: Just about every day. I take ten minutes of almost every class for writing. On some days I take longer chunks of time.

WT: What kind of writing does this include?

ELBOW: All kinds of writing. But most commonly it is "low stakes" writing. Freewriting, of course, is my bread and butter here—private nonstop writing. The privacy gives safety. But sometimes I ask for a piece of focused freewriting that we will try and share with each other. But it is usually very "low stakes" writing because I am trying to train them to do what is often difficult for them, which is to take risks, fool around, and follow trains of thought and see where they go. It is difficult for students to do this if the stakes are very high. It is also difficult to do this at home because they are alone and their old habits take over. If we are sitting and writing together, I can coach and give them encouragement as we go along.

Of course, if I take class time for writing, it gives *me* some time for writing. All teachers are busy and it is very hard to find time for writing. So much is demanded of them. I am extremely sympathetic to that point. When we take some class time for writing, it gives us a chance to write.

WT: Do you share your writing with your students?

ELBOW: Yes, I share it, but not all of it. It is important to me that some of our writing be private. We have to take chances in our writing. If we have to show everything to everyone, then we can't take as many chances. Students, too. They need to do writing that they don't give to us or to anyone else.

Let me talk for a moment about a point of theory that I care a lot about. In fact, it's the foundation for my teaching. There are *four very different* relationships that a writer can have with an audience. First is no audience—writing that is private. Second, there is writing that goes to an audience, but the writer receives no response or feedback. Third, there is writing that goes to an audience, and the writer receives a response—thoughts, questions, appreciations—but no criticism or advice. Fourth, there is writing that goes to an audience, and the audience gives the full range of feedback, including criticism and advice. Writers need *all four* audience relationships to stay healthy—a balanced diet. But most students have only had the fourth relationship. Everything they write they hand in to a teacher for correction, criticism and evaluation. This is like living on nothing but Twinkies. Writers need the solid food of private writing; they need the nourishment of writing that is shared but receives no response—just shared for the pleasure, the celebration, the communication. They need to write and get simple responses from the reader too: "What did you like? What ideas interested you? What does it make you think about? What else do you want to hear about?"

Elementary school teachers are doing much better about this than the rest of us. They understand about the "read-around." Everyone reads, and that is all. The audience just says, "Thank you." I try and make this happen for my own sake and for modeling with my students. I make sure we have private writing, and I make sure that we do some writing that we share. In this case I will share my own writing. Maybe we will do ten minutes of private writing, but then we do ten minutes of writing that will be public. Of course, it is important to tell people what kind of writing they are doing in advance. I try to give my students a chance to look over what they have written before sharing it with the class.

Some teachers say, "Well, if I give students my writing, they will be intimidated. It is so good." But what we teachers write on the spot is usually not intimidating. It's often fun and encouraging. And what the students write is sometimes *better.* (Maybe this is why some teachers are scared to share their writing.)

WT: How do teachers balance the teaching of writing with their personal writing? Students will need guidance as they write.

ELBOW: The answer comes back to the four audiences. As teachers, we tend to assume that everything that students write should come to us and that we should give some sort of thoughtful guidance—even *grade* it, for goodness sake. That doesn't make sense. We don't have to provide them all their learning. Students learn well from all four audience relationships. From private writing they learn how to have a dialogue with *themselves.* That's probably the main ability that distinguishes a thoughtful, mature, educated person—the ability to have a conversation with oneself and thus to make up one's own mind—not be jerked around by social or institutional pressures, especially peer pressure.

By the same token, students learn enormously from just sharing their writing with each other. When they read their words out loud, they can feel when a sentence works well or badly—through the feeling in their mouth and the sound in their ear. Most writers agree that the mouth and the ear are the main organs through which we learn to write better. And students learn from hearing each other's writing. Notice that there is no instruction: it's all learning and no teaching. Also I get them to "share" their writing with me. That is, I make some assignments where I tell them I'll just collect it and read it and scrawl "Thanks" at the bottom of the paper. Or sometimes I take it one step further and place a straight line in the margin beside sections that I like or that work. But essentially, I am giving no feedback. Students learn a lot from this process. They do not need our feedback to learn. In fact, lots of research shows that students often *completely misunderstand* our feedback. And students can give good feedback to each other that they don't misunderstand. They need help and training in how to do this, but our professional publications are now full of good suggestions about how to set up peer response pairs and groups. The sharing of writing is much more encouraging and much less work for teachers. Even private writing is encouraging although it is more subtle. At first it does not feel encouraging just to sit, write, and not show it to anyone. However, I find that my students find that they appreciate it. I tend to do my freewriting right at the beginning of class. It helps people to settle down and collect their thoughts. When I forget, students often remind me. If teachers would make more use of private and merely shared writing, it would help with the management of the classroom.

WT: You are talking about establishing a community of writers in the classroom.

ELBOW: Yes. It is so helpful when we can tell our students about the struggles we have had. Students don't realize that writing is a mess for all of us, not just for them.

WT: How do you handle the idea of grading and providing the kind of responses that students need for their writing?

ELBOW: I have just begun to think more and more about grading. I think it is a real serious problem, and I see more and more teachers feeling pain about the difficulty and inherent unfairness of grading. It seems to get in the way of the kind of relationship we want to have with our students. To put it bluntly, I think that we shouldn't grade individual pieces of writing. It just doesn't make sense. Note that I'm not saying "anything goes," or "there is no such thing as judgment or quality." I am making a distinction between grading and judging. We can still use judgments. We can still say "This part worked. That part didn't work." But grading is a crude and oversimplified representation of a complex judgment process. You have to sum something up into a single number. Research on evaluation shows that grading is not reliable, not fair. Readers disagree. Even good readers—especially good readers. Readers *can* be trained in a holistic grading session so that they give the same grades, but that's only because of the training. They aren't reading the way they normally read. When readers read normally, we find over and over again that one specific piece of writing is given a whole range of grades by different readers. Readers do not agree. Students are right when they say that a single grade is not fair. The same thing is found at the level of philosophical and literary theory. The best critics cannot agree on a correct interpretation of a text much less an evaluation—and the best theorists tell us that there are no principles to settle such disputes. People can't even agree about what something means much less how good it is.

But just because grades on single papers have no reliability, that doesn't mean that we have to quit our jobs or go on strike against grading. If we are obliged to give a grade at the end of a marking period or semester, it is not as bad. There is so much material to go on by then that a B– at the end of the semester is not such a travesty as giving a B– to a single paper. This doesn't mean we have to give up judgment; we can still judge. We can still talk about strengths and weaknesses in single pieces of writing. A text is a complex entity; it is not simple and unified. We have to talk about different features of it—the meaning, the organization, the style. We have to talk about how it operates differently on different readers. In this way, we can make judgments and can be discriminating. To grade is to be crude and undiscriminating. Many teachers are finding that portfolios are useful for grading. In this case you might have five or six pieces of writing, and you look at them together. Then if a teacher has to give a grade, it makes more sense. And portfolios *encourage* a good learning and teaching climate—instead of undermining it.

WT: So the attention and guidance that teachers give to their students should not be misinterpreted to mean grading?

ELBOW: What a writer needs most is an audience. The writer needs to know how an audience perceives a text and how an audience experiences the text. But this feedback is completely different from a grade.

WT: The idea of "teachers as writers" will be a new idea to some teachers. How can they begin writing with their students?

ELBOW: If it is really new or difficult, the best way to start is with freewriting. This is writing that doesn't matter. They must take the time every period and engage in freewriting with the students.

WT: Can you define freewriting?

ELBOW: Freewriting is an exercise of turning off the judging part and writing without stopping for ten minutes. It is also essential that it be private. When you do frequent freewriting exercises, then you learn to use a kind of "freewriting muscle" in your regular writing. You learn to start writing when you are not in the mood or your thoughts are not clear, you learn how to keep on going even when you hit a tangle. When you think of problems with what you are writing, you tell yourself that you can deal with those problems later. You just keep writing, filling up page after page.

WT: What comes after freewriting?

ELBOW: Next comes the process of finding pieces or passages of freewriting or exploratory writing that you want to develop into something more finished. It can be quite small and not perfect. You should not start out trying to write a novel. The third crucial step is to find some supportive friends and try your ideas on them. It doesn't even require feedback. This must be done with allies, not people who will try to fix you or your writing. Writing will naturally grow from this sequence of activities.

WT: What kinds of problems occur when a teacher begins this process?

ELBOW: As teachers, we have been trained to be *critics* and *correctors* of writing. But writing requires two abilities. One is the ability to produce a lot of words and ideas. The other is the ability to criticize writing. These two mental abilities fight each other. If most of your experience with writing has been to be a critic and corrector, then you will have a hard time. You will see too many things wrong with what you write. When you engage in writing, you are constantly bombarded with feelings that it is no good. You have to realize how deeply embedded those feelings are and push them to the side. You can't get rid of them fast, but eventually you can. You must put up with them and say, "Oh, that's just the editorial voice in my head that wants to criticize everything. I mustn't listen to that right now. I'll listen later on—after I have a draft." And you keep on writing.

WT: What final comments or suggestions would you like to share with our readers?

ELBOW: For the past three summers, I have taught a one-week program for teachers called "Teachers as Writers." We spend most of the week using the first two audience relationships, private writing and sharing. There is very little feedback, no evaluation, and no talk about teaching. We just work on our own writing. It is very easy and pleasing yet I think it is the best teaching I do. The people who take part in it really appreciate it and enjoy being writers. The teachers are not trying to be geniuses; they are not trying to get everything perfect. They are taking pleasure in the act of getting their thoughts and feelings on paper and in a supportive setting where they can show them to others for pleasure. If it is done right, this can have the deepest and most pleasurable effect on our teaching. The most powerful improvement in our *teaching* comes when we can improve our own relationship to writing.

STUDENT WRITING
SUZANNE LIABRAATEN

ESSAY: "NEW BEGINNING"

Suzanne LiaBraaten wrote the following essay as a first-year student in a required writing class, entering into conversation with Bartholomae, Elbow, Fulwiler, Godwin, and Murray.

9 March 1999

I sit down in a chair to start my paper. I take out my notes and other research. I look at the computer screen and I see blank. The blank transfers to my mind and my mind is blank. I have to look over my notes to fill my mind with the things I already know I know. I look at the screen and my mind begins to fill with that blankness again. I stop it by quickly putting my name at the top of the screen. This slows the blankness from running a little, but it's still coming quickly. So I give my paper a title, no matter what it is, anything to stop the blankness. I'm stuck. I'm stuck on the first sentence. So I just begin.

I am my worst enemy when it comes to writing. My inner "watcher" is critical, demanding perfection, shooting down ideas before they have a chance to be realized. Gail Godwin talks about the "Watcher at the Gates" (174). My watcher is a bully to my young ideas. She bullies me. I have always felt as if I am letting myself down when I cannot think of the right words to say. Cautious and timid, I am afraid to let any original or personal ideas out.

> Give yourself a break; what you write today is what you're capable of writing. Strive to improve, but accept what you produce.
>
> (Scanlan, qtd in Murray 46)

That's exactly what I needed to hear. Through all the freewriting I've done lately, I have gained more confidence in myself as a writer and I see that I have the potential to write well. I had to sit down and ask my watcher, "Why are you so hard on me? Why can't you just accept me as I am?" My watcher had a difficult time answering. Perfection may never come, she would have to accept that. So I put my watcher on a "time out" to search through my mind for the treasures I was never able to find. Once I freed myself from some of my watcher's criticism, my freewriting became more personal. I was able to delve into ideas I never could have before. Sure, I make many mistakes. I am a young writer. My writing would only become better if I actually wrote, even if it wasn't perfect: "Sometimes you have to write badly to write well" (Murray 141).

This is what I was never able to accept. Before I could become a better writer, I had to accept my imperfections. If I never accepted anything less than perfect, I could never get started, let alone improve. Once I was able to move past the constant criticism of my writing, I could look thoughtfully at what other writers had to say about writing and their approaches to teaching writing. I was especially interested in the heated debate between Peter Elbow and David Bartholomae. Their discussion on different styles of teaching young writers helped me reflect on the ways I have been taught to write.

Most of my writing in high school consisted of papers where the only motivation was to get a good grade. I have always been more concerned with getting an "A" grade than with expressing any interesting ideas. And now those papers that meant so much for the grade are sitting in a dump or recycling center somewhere. I didn't keep them because they had no meaning. I wasn't writing for me or for intellectual growth; I was writing for my teacher and for that letter in red on the top of the paper. Writing needs to have importance to the writer. Toby Fulwiler says that "freshmen arrive at college with a badly distorted view of writing because they have seldom written anything that mattered to them" (1). If what I write isn't important to me, why should any reader be interested in reading it? I feel sorry for teachers who, day after day, are forced to read papers that don't have meaning for the students who write them. Readers need to feel as if they have received something for the time they spend on reading. So if I don't care about what I write, I shouldn't expect my reader to care about reading it.

Elbow and Bartholomae discuss ways that writing should be taught to first-year university students. On one hand, Bartholomae's argument is strong on teaching students to become academic writers so they can function well in the academic world: "I want them to be prepared to write themselves out of a rhetorical situation in which their roles are already prepared, where they are figured as simple-minded or not-yet-ready-for serious discussion" (86). He wants us as students to be able to prove that we are intellectual enough to join in academic conversation. I appreciate the confidence he has in young students.

Elbow, however, writes about how a focus on academic writing in the first year conflicts with the growth of students as independent writers: "I choose the goal of writer over that of academic" (73). His approach is like building blocks. First, students discover themselves as writers; then, they are able to learn how to effectively join in an academic conversation with new and intelligent ideas.

For anyone who has ever seen the movie *Good Will Hunting*, I would like to make some comparisons. I see Bartholomae as the professor, Jerry, trying to help Will, but he goes about it the wrong way. He is more focused on what Will should do for the sake of others and what is "expected" and "proper" than what Will wants to do. He is focused on the outcome rather than the help Will needs to get there. I see this trait in Bartholomae. He wants student writers to write well in the academic world, but it's as if he expects them to "get it" during a first-year class.

Now, look at Elbow compared to Robin Williams's character, Sean. Sean is focused more on taking the time to help Will discover himself and to work out his problems. He realizes that Will is a genius and has potential. But Will cannot realize his genius until he works out the problems from his past. Just like Will, many freshman students struggle with their writing past. Teacher's standards, formal outlines, spelling and grammar consume our thoughts during the first draft of any paper. Elbow realizes this. His approach is to break down all the structural walls that hinder individual thought, to let students make discoveries about themselves through their writing. Freewriting is a break from any "normal" type of writing. It is raw thought.

Through the freewriting I've done this year, I have been able to move past the physical act of writing and simply put my ideas down on paper. The blankness I experience is created through my fear of failure and imperfection. I realize now that my mind is not blank. That blankness is a wall that covers my thoughts when I start to doubt what I am capable of as a writer. I believe I will look back on this year and see it as a kind of new beginning in the life of my writing. My fears and criticisms are still inside me, but now I know how to handle them.

WORKS CITED

Bartholomae, David. "Writing With Teachers: A Conversation with Peter Elbow." *College Composition and Communication.* 46.1 (Feb. 1995): 62–71.

Elbow, Peter. "Being a Writer vs. Being an Academic: A Conflict in Goals." *College Composition and Communication.* 46.1 (Feb. 1995): 72–83.

Fulwiler, Toby. "Freshman Writing: It's the Best Course in the University to Teach." *The Chronicle of Higher Education.* 31.21 (Feb. 5, 1986): 1–2.

Godwin, Gail. "The Watcher at the Gates." *The Writer's Home Companion: An Anthology of the World's Best Writing Advice, from Keats to Kunitz.* New York: Henry Holt and Company, 1997. 174–177.

Murray, Donald M. *The Craft of Revision.* 3rd Ed. Florida: Harcourt Brace, 1997.

NEW PRACTICES TO TAKE FORWARD

1. **Using feedback sheets:** Make photocopies of the blank feedback sheets on pages 345 and 349–350. Depending on the kind of writing you need to respond to, choose one to fill out the next time you are asked to give thoughtful feedback to a colleague's early draft. If that colleague is unfamiliar with descriptive feedback, make sure to explain it or to include a copy of the annotated feedback sheet along with your response. Keep in mind that descriptive feedback is most useful on early drafts; writers might find it annoying to get it if they have asked for proofreading help alone. On the other hand, if you do help with proofreading as requested but also feel moved to describe your larger responses to the piece, you'll discover that most authors are grateful for those as well, as long as you're not suggesting a major rewrite at the last minute.

   If you need feedback yourself, try giving a blank feedback sheet to your reader, along with the annotated version. Always ask specifically for the kind of feedback you need: don't be shy. Evaluative feedback too early in the writing process can be devastating, especially if you're working with emotionally difficult material. And descriptive feedback too late in the writing process can be useless. It's *your writing*, so ask for what you need and describe it in detail if necessary.

   If someone asks you to give feedback to a piece of theirs, always ask them specifically where they are in the writing process on that particular draft and what kind of feedback they most want and need. Since most people aren't aware that there *are* different kinds of feedback, you may need to explain some of the options.

2. **Writing a feedback report/revision plan:** Next time you receive feedback from several people, take fifteen minutes to inkshed a feedback report before you revise. Here's how. Go through all of the feedback sheets you've received, as well as any notes you might have taken on verbal feedback accompanying the feedback sheets. Go through all of these materials with several highlighters in hand. Use one highlighter to indicate comments that you found useful or that suggested changes that you definitely don't want to forget. Use another colour to indicate comments that you found really annoying or useless for one reason or another. You might want to use a third colour to indicate passages that readers felt you should not change at all, the "keepers."

After you've gone through all of this material, inkshed for fifteen minutes (quickly consulting the feedback sheets and your notes whenever you need to) about what you now plan to do as you revise the next draft. Be as detailed as you can be about the changes you want to make and why—and the changes you *don't* want to make and why. But don't waste time fuming about wrong-headed feedback: your job is to consume feedback like an owl, trusting your body to discard the comments it can't make use of. Feedback is precious: it represents time that readers invested in your work. There's nothing to be gained from arguing readers' reactions away. It's your writing so you don't have to change anything you don't want to change. On the other hand, it can sometimes be useful to make a special effort to understand feedback that gets under your skin or that seems impossibly thick-headed: try ignoring a reader's specific suggestions about how you should change the writing—instead go back to specific passages in your piece and re-read your own sentences, trying hard to figure out how on earth they could have been so misunderstood. Sometimes a light will go on and you'll be able to see what steered readers in the wrong direction; it may require changing something they weren't even aware of, precisely because they were misreading so completely.

Feedback reports are, in fact, a vital part of the publishing industry. Authors are regularly asked to write them after reading through a collection of readers' responses to draft manuscripts at various stages in the process of completing a book. The feedback report is essentially a revision plan, and most editors/publishers will require several such plans as a project moves forward and evolves over a period of months or years.

3. **Using the evaluation grid:** Make several copies of the grid in Elbow's essay (page 353) or of the grid available online in the University of Alberta document, "Learning to Read Instructor Comments and Marks on Essays," located at http://www.humanities.ualberta.ca/english/marking.html—whichever version you prefer. Begin to make a habit of submitting a copy of that blank grid with all your papers in all your courses, along with a polite note asking instructors to please check off your strengths and weaknesses if they have time. Or, if you prefer, submit the grid with a copy of your marked paper after the fact. That is, if you've received a mark that puzzles you or if you simply wish for more detailed feedback on what you could have done to improve a particular paper, politely ask the instructor either in writing or in person if they might be willing to use the grid quickly to check off what the strengths

and weaknesses were in that piece of writing. Since the grid doesn't require the instructor to write any further comments, it won't usually take much time, as long as the paper is still fresh in the instructor's mind and as long as you resubmit a copy of the paper with the instructor's comments and grade on it. Certainly busy instructors might refuse if they don't have time to do this, but if you ask politely, they won't take offence. And they might be willing to hold onto the grid and use it on the next paper of yours that they need to mark.

4. **Writing acknowledgments:** Now that you've learned more about giving and receiving different kinds of feedback from your colleagues, you need to begin the practice of writing acknowledgments at the end of your papers, right before the works-cited list. Of course, any works-cited list is, in a sense, a statement of acknowledgments. But take a look at the end of Hunt's essay on page 140, the NCTE guidelines on using journals on page 149 (a document worked on by a group of people), Reither and Vipond's piece on page 160 (a co-authored article), and Sommers's essay on page 419. Or take a look at the acknowledgments at the beginning of this text. Few writers complete any serious project without help and input from others. Take a moment at the end of any final draft to thank those who have invested time and energy responding to early drafts, assisting you in your research, pointing you to sources or ideas you might not have been aware of otherwise, or proofreading. This statement should be brief and should usually not include the instructor who is going to be marking your writing. If the piece were going to be published later, however, instructors should of course be mentioned if their comments helped you improve the piece for publication (just as we have thanked reviewers who offered criticism and suggestions for improving this book).

    Even readers whose feedback you didn't use or agree with should be mentioned, *anyone* who read your work in draft and took time to write down their honest reactions. Most faculty include acknowledgments when they write up and publish their own work, so they will appreciate your doing the same. But if you're at all uncertain about a specific instructor, especially if great emphasis has been placed in the course on *not* doing collaborative work or on *not* getting feedback or input from others for some reason, check with the instructor ahead of time. A statement of acknowledgment is *not* a statement that others did your research or writing for you, but some instructors may be uneasy if students openly acknowledge assistance they have received on a written project. Some, however, will require or expect acknowledgments, so double-check each time.

5. **Doing an audience analysis:** Before you complete your next writing task, take fifteen minutes to inkshed an audience analysis in as much detail as you can. Reflect on your rhetorical situation. What is this audience like? What are their biases—what do they like, dislike? What can you count on their knowing already? not knowing? What do they need or want to know? What do you want your writing to make happen in their hearts and minds? What do you want them to know or feel or do after reading your writing? How will your very first sentence draw them into your line of thinking and feeling? Keep this inkshed with you as you do your research and reading and as you write. Occasionally read through it and update it if necessary. Read it again right before your final revision and proofreading.

ESSAY IDEA

Conduct an interview of your own and write it up, following the format Mammen has used. You could interview one or two family members about all the different kinds of writing they do, personal and/or academic and/or business or work-related (students are often surprised to find out about the poems or love letters that their parents, grandparents, aunts, or uncles have stashed in a trunk somewhere). Or you could interview one or two professionals in the field you're hoping to enter. Ask them not just about all the writing they do in the course of a day, but also about how they manage to get it done, what their strategies are, what ideas they might have to share about writing well in their profession, what advice they might have for others. Whichever possibility you explore, focus less on their writing *practices* and more on their *theory*—that is, how they think to themselves about writing and its importance in their lives, how they judge the writing of others, how they think about their various audiences and the social action they want their writing to accomplish in the world. (For a related essay idea, see pages 104–105 in Conversation 2.)

Make sure to gather more information than you can actually use in your piece: strong interviews always give a sense that a wealth of additional data lurks in the background somewhere, unstated. And look closely at how Mammen has structured her piece: an opening paragraph that sets a context, then the illusion that her conversation with Elbow is being repeated word for word (though of course she has tightened, edited, cleaned up, and changed the order of their actual spoken sentences). Notice how short her questions are compared to his answers. How does she identify herself as the questioner throughout? Does the interview have a focus, any particular emphasis or shape apart from just one answered question after another? Mammen most likely interviewed Elbow more than once; at least one follow-up interview, after you've written a draft, is always a good idea. She probably also allowed Elbow a chance to read through the piece before publication to see if she had gotten anything wrong or misstated from her notes and to see if her editing, condensing, rewording, and rearranging had inadvertently misrepresented his ideas.

Mammen's interview format is obviously only one possible structure out of many. Check out some contemporary journals and magazines to see what other formats you might prefer—or invent your own, one that seems more appropriate for the material you've collected from your interviewee. Make sure, however, to capture the distinctive voice of the person you interview by quoting at least some of their most striking expressions exactly.

CONVERSATION 8:

Separating Revision from Proofreading

INTRODUCTION

[W]e must frequently revise what we have just written. For beside the fact that thus we secure a better connexion between what follows and what precedes, the warmth of thought which has cooled down while we were writing is revived anew, and gathers fresh impetus from going over the ground again. . . . [W]e love all the offspring of our thought at the moment of their birth; were that not so, we should never commit them to writing. But we must give them a critical revision, and go carefully over any passage where we have reason to regard our fluency with suspicion.

Quintilian, *Education of the Orator*, c. 94 AD, X.iii. 5–7

If I write something down, I don't feel secure about it until I have gone back and read it with the knowledge I have accumulated through having written it down the first time. . . . [R]evision brings a greater richness to the second time through and then the third time and so on. It isn't just the beginning and the end; there are multiple things all the way through. There are dawning realizations as adjustments are made. I can imagine reading and revising an infinite number of times. For me, the language is never set like concrete; it's always like taffy.

William Stafford, "A Witness for Poetry" 59–60

Advice to a beginning writer: don't waste your energy imagining somebody who knows better than you do how to write your book. If this isn't a way of telling yourself you never will, then it's a way of dreaming a shortcut from Draft 3 to Draft 17. But Draft 4 will never be Draft 17, no matter what you do.

Greg Hollingshead, *First Chapter* 51

At some point, all shaping on a draft comes to an end. You have worked hard at gathering your thoughts, doing your research, building a solid piece; you've managed to discover/create an organization that will pull the reader along. In a sense, the analogy from Elbow and Belanoff's *Being a Writer* describes the progression—you've worked at the *bone* level (the overall structure of your essay) and at the *muscle* level (putting meat on those bones, data and detail). You can then shift your attention to what could be called the *skin* level, getting the surface presentable to readers.

But the bone/muscle/skin analogy is useful to us as writers mainly when we're first drafting a piece, when we try to remind ourselves (somewhat morbidly) not to waste time fussing with the make-up and hairdo on a piece that's already DOA: or, to move into the cartoon realm, not to worry about cosmetic surgery on either a pile of skin lying shapeless on the floor (because it has no skeleton) or a sheet of skin hanging limp over a skeleton-like coat rack (because those bones have no muscle on them and are thus rigid, lifeless, incapable of movement). The analogy helps us focus on how to spend our time as we write what Murray would call a **discovery draft**, a piece in which (as William Stafford puts it) we have written "the beginning without knowledge of the end" ("Witness" 60). It helps us focus on how to spend our time as we write what Hollingshead might call Draft 6.

But if we consider the bone/muscle/skin analogy a bit further, it becomes a much more organic and complicated way of talking about writing than it might at first appear. After all, we know that cosmetics and cosmetic surgery can never provide what lots of exercise, a healthy diet, strong bones, and lean muscle mass are much more likely to give: clear, firm, and glowing skin. And we become more aware, year by year, how porous the skin is, how easily toxins can pass through our skin to enter the blood and bone that we assumed the skin would protect.

So how is the analogy useful at all? It reminds us how difficult it is to separate composing from revising and revising from proofreading, even while it is necessary for us to do so, temporarily at least, in order to conceptualize the writing process as we move through it recursively for each unique writing project. The title of this chapter can be a helpful mantra for writers *after* they have a discovery draft to work with: both **revision** and **proofreading** are crucial in the writing process, but they are *not* the same.

Many writers would argue that they are constantly revising even as they compose, and we don't disagree. Thus, this Conversation on revision could have come much earlier in this volume. Yet we've positioned our discussion of revision here in order to contrast it more clearly with proofreading, with which it is often confused. As Nancy Sommers's groundbreaking research made clear, students regularly assume that revising an essay simply means proofreading, working with the surface, the skin, of the essay: cleaning up punctuation and spelling errors, eliminating typos, and finding replacements for words that have been repeated too often. Experienced writers, on the other hand, see "re-vision" as a process of figuring out what they really want to say, having the "vision" over again. Of course, true proofreading and copy editing, preparing final copy for submission to a professor or a publication, are also more time-consuming and difficult—and important—than most of us want to admit. Learning to keep these two moves in the writing process distinct in our minds, to separate revision from proofreading, takes time and practice. It becomes a matter of focus and emphasis rather than complete separation, a matter of moving back and forth between these two processes in a rhythm over time for the greater health of both.

Revision

Revision begins the moment we begin to compose: we're constantly pausing to consider the fit between what we want to say and what has just appeared on the page. Sondra Perl's Composing Guidelines in Conversation 3 encourage us to make precisely this move, to test what we're writing against our body's **felt sense** of what it is we're trying to say—to ask "does this say it?" and "what's missing?" and "why is this topic difficult for me?" If we feel the fit isn't there, we try again until we experience that shift, the "click" (quiet and small though it may be) that lets us know we're on the right track. Even these slight pauses and adjustments could be considered revision—so we're clearly not talking about something we put off until a few hours before a deadline. And it's important to emphasize that the pauses Perl is asking us to make *have nothing to do with proofreading or correcting surface errors*—quite the opposite. One of the reasons she developed the Composing Guidelines in the first place was to help struggling student writers who couldn't keep their attention on *what* they were trying to say because they were constantly stopping to fiddle with *how* they had said it, constantly stopping to copy edit their work too soon, to fix mistakes that could and should be fixed much later in the process, after a writer had managed to get a line of thinking worked out.

Murray's piece in this Conversation (notice the title—"Internal Revision: A Process of Discovery") led him to decide that revision was so central to all writing that he needed to write a book about it. The book that grew from the essay reprinted here, a book we highly recommend, is called *The Craft of Revision*; and carrying his commitment perhaps to extremes, Murray has completely rewritten this little book at least three times. All four editions are good, so take your pick—they are all quite different.

You may have noticed that, as much as Stephen Pinker has to say about grammar and spoken language, he has just one thing to say about how student writing could improve: revision. If students went through more drafts before turning their papers in (that is, if they behaved like experienced writers, according to Sommers's research), their writing would be better. Nothing more mysterious than that (see page 257 in Conversation 5). And just in case you think we're making this up about experienced writers and revision, read what Raymond Carver has to say about revision in this chapter. Carver, a poet as well as one of the greatest short-story writers of the twentieth century, answered an interviewer's question about his writing habits in this way:

> It doesn't take that long to do the first draft of the story, that usually happens in one sitting, but it does take a while to do the various versions of the story. I've done as many as twenty or thirty drafts of a story. Never less than ten or twelve drafts. It's instructive, and heartening both, to look at the early drafts of great writers. . . . [Tolstoy] was always revising, right down to the time of page proofs. He went through and rewrote *War and Peace* eight times and was still making corrections in the galleys. Things like this should hearten every writer whose first drafts are dreadful, like mine are. (Interview, *Paris Review* 203)

Of course, we can imagine situations where too much revision might make a piece worse, take the life out of it. But that's not much of a danger now that we have computers and can keep all of our early versions safe on disk. And please, take our word for it, you *do want* to save your early versions: when you sit down at the computer to revise a piece, give it a new but related name, like "essay OneA," "essay OneB," "essay

OneC." That way, if you feel you've truly ruined something as you revised or have deleted a paragraph that you later decide was working well, you can rest assured that it has not been copied over but still exists on disk in an earlier version and can easily be recovered.

Still, how often have you revised a piece several times and then known for certain that the final version was much weaker than the first? A much greater danger is our not allowing enough time to revise at all. As Carver's comments and Murray's multiple versions of *The Craft of Revision* make clear, a first draft simply stakes out the territory you want to explore. For many writers, that first draft comes fairly quickly. Once you have that draft in front of you, you can begin to get a feel for the lay of the land, what is known and what remains unknown, uncharted. You certainly don't want to eliminate all the energy and surprise from that discovery draft as you revise, but neither do you want to submit for public consumption or evaluation a piece whose implications you don't yet fully understand yourself.

An analogy might be useful here. If you were trying to write an essay about a short story written by someone else—say, Ray Carver's "Cathedral"—you would obviously have to read the story through several times. The first time is simply a discovery read: you're finding out how the story is shaped, where the weight falls, what characters and images and scenes gather emphasis because of the way the story ends. Therefore, when you read the story through a second time, everything looks different: details that you didn't notice before jump out at you because you now know what happens in the final scene; words that seemed casual on a first read-through now seem full of meaning. Knowing the overall movement of the piece changes how you read it. The same is true for your own writing. If you can possibly allow a day or two to pass before you read through your discovery draft, even better: you'll be able to heighten the sense that you're reading someone else's work—you'll be able to get more distance on your writing and a greater ability to sense where it's working for readers and where it isn't. If you have time to get input from others, to get a different set of eyes on your writing, even better: real readers can help as nothing else can, even if all they do is flag what's working (the things we should keep) and put wavy lines wherever they stumbled or got lost.

At this stage, one of the hardest things to face is the possibility that the part we liked best of all or the part we worked on the most might need to be cut. Computers can be a great help here. When you cut such a passage, save it and put it in a separate computer file with a name that clearly identifies it; that way you can always return to it, start another piece with it, or reinstate it later if you change your mind. Usually, we discover these scraps of writing with surprise years later and we hardly ever use them because by then they've lost their hold over us. But saving them makes the initial heart-rending cut much easier.

Proofreading

None of our emphasis on revision is meant to suggest, however, that **proofreading** is unimportant. In fact, your level of proofreading may be the first thing that readers notice about your writing; they may make an instant decision whether to trust you or not based on a first impression, based on how presentable your piece is on the surface.

You may have just written a brilliant essay that could change the course of Western civilization if readers were to take it seriously—but no one *will* take it seriously if, in the end, it looks as if you don't care much about your ideas because you've let them go out in public undressed. Consider how unlikely it is that you would show up at an important job interview, for a position you wanted with all your heart, in rumpled pajamas with your hair uncombed, your teeth unbrushed, your face unwashed—and you'll have some idea how instructors are apt to react when they see a paper that hasn't been carefully proofed. Just because proofreading is something we put off until very late in the writing process doesn't mean it's inconsequential. Everything may depend on it.

We tried an experiment years ago to convince our first-year students of this fact. We asked them to compose a one-page letter giving some information about their work history and education and qualifications, asking for a job interview. They knew that we had found a local banker, a store owner, and a builder who had agreed to read through the printouts quickly and then to make a list of the students they would interview on the basis of the letter alone. The banker and the store owner listed several students they would *definitely* interview and a few they *might* interview, but the list of those they would definitely *not* interview was by far the longest. What upset our students, however, was the fact that the builder—the one many of them had thought would be the easiest employer to please—said he wouldn't consider interviewing *any* of them. When we pushed him for a reason, his reply was unequivocal: "If that's what they do with a comma, what do you think they might do with a nail?" Our point had been made.[1]

Proofreading is often considered the same thing as **copy editing**, although in our experience copy editing is usually done by someone who is not the author, someone who is helping the author prepare a piece for publication—and the copy edits demanded by such a person can often require rewriting entire sentences to make them clear for readers, not merely a cleaning up of typos or surface error. For this reason, we're also not certain whether we think of *Editor* (the software program mentioned by Sargent later in this chapter) as helping most with revision, with copy editing, or with proofreading. At times it has helped us with all three: often, therefore, we've used *Editor* at several different stages with the same piece of writing. A program that could best be described as an interactive handbook offering text-specific commentary on matters of style, usage, and mechanics, *Editor* should not be confused with anything that claims to be a "grammar checker." The two English professors who developed *Editor* (further information is available at http://www.serenity-software.com) understand the word **grammar** in the way that linguists like Stephen Pinker do and realize that no computer program is now or is ever likely to be capable of reliably analyzing human syntax. Certainly, there was some hope for a while that computers would be able to perform at least basic proofreading functions for authors; but that seems less and less likely as the years go by. And don't even get us started on the so-called "grammar checking" incorporated into Microsoft's *Word*; we ask our students to turn off that function because of the misinformation it hands out. It can usefully find excess spaces and two repeated words together and that's about it; on all other matters, it's much more likely to do harm than good.

Spell checkers, however, are a wonderful invention as long as we are aware of their limitations. While we would never submit a piece of writing for publication or evaluation *without* running a spell checker on it first—and we therefore don't accept student papers that have neglected that quick but crucial step in the proofreading process—we also know that there is no substitute for proofreading our own work carefully. Once, in a rush, one of us spell checked a letter to a friend and then mailed it without any human proofreading. The friend was amused to read the first sentence in this long-overdue letter: "Now that I have a few days of relative clam, I'm finally able to answer your note."

Spell checkers simply have no idea what you're trying to say, so any word that actually *is* a word—like "clam"—will pass with flying colours, whether it makes sense in context or not. The trouble is, as David Bartholomae's piece in this Conversation makes clear, many of us lose the ability even to see such problems on the page because we read what we *meant* to say, not what is actually there. As a result of Bartholomae's work, we now have incorporated two practices into our writing and teaching: first, we try to read all our own writing out loud to ourselves or to others when we proofread (this helps to slow our eye down and catch things we might not see otherwise); and second, we ask our students to do the same, sometimes during small group writing conferences in our offices. A couple of useful things happen when students read their work out loud to us: many of them catch mistakes as they read and fix them then and there; many read (as John does in Bartholomae's piece) what they *meant* to say, not what is on the paper in front of them—and that helps us figure out which errors are true errors and which ones are simply accidents of transcription (that is, the student knows the correct form to use but somehow the hand didn't write down the message the brain sent out). There's no point wasting time teaching students things they already know. We might pause to call their attention to the problem on the page, just so they're alert to the proofreading dilemma—but we would quickly move on and focus our attention and energy on other, more important issues in the writing.

Slowing your eye down in order to proofread carefully is not easy. At times, it can even help to read a piece backward (not word by word, but sentence by sentence): doing so helps to break up the patterns of expectation we've established by being too close to that particular piece of writing for the time being. Of course, nothing beats a new set of eyes: we proofread for each other and we often ask our students to do the same. In fact, Sargent's guidelines on preparing final copy (see pages 429–431 in this chapter) emphasize the importance of having someone else proofread your last draft. We develop our skill as proofreaders much more quickly if we proofread for others. This works best, of course, if your proofreader is completely new to a particular piece of writing (since patterns of expectation build up quickly, in readers as well as writers). And few human proofreaders will catch everything—the more caught up they get in *what* you're saying, the more quickly they'll read and the more they'll read what they *expect* to see rather than what is actually there.

What does this mean? That few papers, even published ones, are ever perfectly free of typos and mechanical errors. We just need to get them as close as we can. Ray Carver refers to Evan Connell saying "that he knew he was finished with a short story when he found himself going through it and taking out commas and then going through the story again and putting commas back in the same places" ("On Writing" 15). Revising and proofreading until you reach that point, the point when most of your remaining punctuation decisions have to do with style and emphasis (with the kind of decisions we discuss in Conversation 5), is the goal. Deadlines are a part of life both within the academy and without, and they don't always allow us the time we would like for revising and proofreading our work. But we always want to honour these two distinct elements of the writing process and allow as much time for them as we possibly can, especially for high-stakes pieces of writing.

When Ray Carver describes the one-on-one conferences he had as a student in a class taught by novelist John Gardner, he says,

> We'd discuss commas in my story as if nothing else in the world mat-
> tered more at that moment—and, indeed, it did not. (Foreword, page
> 392 in this chapter)

And Carver suggests elsewhere that we ought to post above our desks a three-by-five index card containing the following line from one of Isaac Babel's short stories: "No iron can pierce the heart with such force as a period put just at the right place" ("On Writing" 15).

But when does a period like that get put in position? during early exploratory writing? during a slower, more deliberate session of composing? during revision? during proofreading? We can imagine it happening at almost any point in the writing process, and part of the art of revision and the art of proofreading is learning what to keep, what to leave just as it is, as well as what to change or fix or cut out. That's why computers are never going to be able to do the job for us. And that's why we must never submit for publication or evaluation a computer printout that we have not read through carefully ourselves, out loud, one last time.

---

[1] See also Hairston, "Not All Errors," and L. W. Beason, whose research into reactions to error in the workplace revealed similar assumptions and dismissive judgments about intelligence and reliability.

INKSHEDDING PROMPTS

1. Raymond Carver, Greg Hollingshead, William Stafford, and Donald Murray are presumably the kinds of experienced writers that Nancy Sommers is talking about in her research on revision, although of course her study included many published academic writers as well. Where do you think you fit in her study? You don't have to categorize yourself as simply "experienced" or "inexperienced" but perhaps somewhere on a continuum between the two (which is probably where most of us writers would show

up). How did you feel as you read her piece—were you irritated at the way she categorized student writers or did her assessment seem fair to you? Inkshed about your attitudes toward revision: which of the two lists in her article describe your current attitudes best? Or tell the story of your changing attitudes toward revision over the years: what are your current practices compared to your practices a year ago, three years ago? What changed them?

2.   When you read Carver and Murray on revision, what jumps out at you? Does anything surprise you in what they say about the role of revision in the writing process? Does your experience with revision contradict theirs? Or, conversely, can you describe one of your own experiences with writing that coincides with theirs—or that their comments help you see in a new light?

3.   Find a paragraph or two of your own in a draft you're working on, paragraphs that don't seem all that lively or strong to you, and try inkshedding an alternative version of them by doing *one* of the following (just play for fifteen minutes to see what happens, not expecting much, writing fast):

> **Add** something (a sensory detail or two or three, a piece of evidence or information or data or a quotation from another source).
>
> **Limit** an element (if you're writing a narrative, limit yourself to a specific hour or even a specific minute; if a location is involved, zoom in and limit yourself to one province/state or one city or one room or one angle—something that could be seen through a camera lens; if quantity is involved, limit yourself to one type, one item in particular).
>
> **Transform** something (transform the time—change the tense throughout the paragraph; transform the genre—turn this paragraph into a letter, a prayer, a poem, or a lab report; transform the point of view—write in a different voice, a different time, from the perspective of one particular person affected by whatever issue you're discussing).

You might, probably will, throw this paragraph away: don't worry about that. The point is to experiment in your inkshed, try out something outlandish just to see where it takes you, just to get you thinking in new ways about your subject. What's worth noticing, however, is that you're *not* working at the lexical or sentence level here, tinkering with the words you already have on the page. You're drafting a completely new paragraph; it's based on the same material, yes, and will include some elements that were in the original—but it comes at that material and combines those elements in a different way. This way of inkshedding gives you a feel for revision, as opposed to copy editing or proofreading.

And who knows, you could end up keeping something from these fifteen minutes of goofing off, even something that wasn't in the inkshed itself, perhaps just an idea that came to you because you wrote it.

It's easy to remember these three strategies for provoking revision—think of the ALT key on your computer keyboard: Add, Limit, or Transform. (For further ideas on revision and the source for this one, see Toby Fulwiler's "Provocative Revision.")

4. Short-story writer Raymond Carver revealed the following about himself as a writer in an afterword to his book *Fires*:

    > I like to mess around with my stories. I'd rather tinker with a story after writing it, and then tinker some more, changing this, changing that, than have to write the story in the first place. That initial writing just seems to me the hard place I have to get to in order to go on and have fun with the story. Rewriting for me is not a chore—it's something I like to do. . . . Maybe I revise because it gradually takes me into the heart of what the story is about. I have to keep trying to see if I can find that out. (218)

    Is he talking about proofreading or revision here? Skin or muscle or bone? If *he* doesn't know what his stories are about, who does? Inkshed about which part of the writing process you prefer and why: reading, researching, interviewing, collecting data? exploratory writing? composing a discovery draft? revising? polishing your sentences? proofreading?

5. How did you react to Bartholomae's description of John's writing in "The Study of Error"? What assumptions would you have made about John if you'd never met him but had just read the paragraph in Bartholomae's essay? Point to specific details that would have made you react this way. What did you think of Bartholomae's analysis of the errors in John's work and the reasons for them? How easy would it be for you to help fellow students by analyzing their errors in this way? How do you think teachers should help you find and eliminate your writing mistakes? Do you *want* to know about these mistakes? Or would you rather that teachers commented on your ideas only, even in final drafts?

6. Donald Murray often emphasizes writing quickly, to "outrun the censor." Doesn't that seem at odds with his commitment to revision? Or do the two things *require* each other, since generating a lot of material at high speed necessitates throwing a lot of writing away later, when the eye of judgment

has cooled? So why not just go more slowly and get it right the first time? Inkshed about your preferred writing method (and it may be different for different kinds of projects). Would you rather work slowly and deliberately from the start? or write a lot and cut/revise a lot later? Which is the more efficient method for you? What if you were like the writer in Camus' novel *The Plague*, agonizing over every word to find *le mot juste* and taking years to get one sentence you could live with?

7.   Have you ever used the "grammar checker" in Microsoft *Word* or any similar program? How was it useful? How was it not useful? Be as detailed as you can be about feedback the program gave you. Did the program help you more with revision or with proofreading?

8.   Once you've used the checklist (on pages 429–431) for preparing final copy, inkshed about the experience. What did you learn? What were your proofreader's strengths? weaknesses? Would this be a good partnership to continue for future papers or do you both need to find someone better at a particular skill you both lack (like locating sentence fragments, for instance)? If you used *Editor* on your essay, write about specific moments when *Editor* was helpful, not helpful, infuriating, confusing—be as specific as possible. Next time, how will you approach *Editor* differently?

9.   Look at Murray's research ideas. Inkshed about some aspect of the writing process you'd like to investigate, a question of your own, and how you'd go about getting some answers (see Conversation 3, Prompt 8).

Raymond Carver, Foreword to John Gardner's *On Becoming a Novelist*

Raymond Carver, now recognized as a major twentieth-century short-story writer, was born and raised in the Pacific Northwest. His father worked in a sawmill, and as a boy Carver always assumed he would too. But after high-school graduation and six months at the mill, he knew something had to change. He married and started a family early, so he and his wife had to struggle with poverty and part-time jobs to earn their college degrees.

After earning his BA (1963) at state universities in California, he headed off to the Iowa Writer's Workshop (like William Stafford before him and Gail Godwin after). But he could afford only one year and returned to California, taking a job as a night janitor so he could write during the day. By the late 1960s, his drinking had become a serious problem; he quit drinking completely a decade later, June 2, 1977, and said in his *Paris*

Review interview, "I'm prouder of that, that I've quit drinking, than I am of anything in my life" (196).

And that's saying a lot. By the time Carver returned to the Pacific Northwest with his second wife, poet Tess Gallagher, he had been a Guggenheim Fellow, a winner of many awards for his poetry and short fiction, and a teacher at numerous universities, finishing his teaching career as Professor of English at Syracuse University. His work had been translated into over twenty languages.

Carver has described some of the three-by-five cards he had taped to the wall beside his desk: "Fundamental accuracy of statement is the ONE sole morality of writing" (Ezra Pound); "Isak Dinesen said that she wrote a little every day, without hope and without despair"; "No cheap tricks" (Geoffrey Wolff). Carver was often described as a minimalist, but there was nothing minimal about the emotional impact or the humour of his late stories. His own words describe the effect of his work better than any critic has ever done: "The words can be so precise they may even sound flat, but they can still carry; if used right, they can hit all the notes." He was known for the care he invested in multiple drafts and revisions:

> Evan Connell said once that he knew he was finished with a short story when he found himself going through it and taking out commas and then going through the story again and putting commas back in the same places. I like that way of working on something. I respect that kind of care for what is being done. That's all we have, finally, the words, and they had better be the right ones, with the punctuation in the right places so that they can best say what they are meant to say. ("On Writing" 15)

Carver died of cancer in 1988, before reaching his fiftieth year.

FOREWORD TO JOHN GARDNER'S *ON BECOMING A NOVELIST*

A long time ago—it was the summer of 1958—my wife and I and our two baby children moved from Yakima, Washington, to a little town outside of Chico, California. There we found an old house and paid twenty-five dollars a month rent. In order to finance this move, I'd had to borrow a hundred and twenty-five dollars from a druggist I'd delivered prescriptions for, a man named Bill Barton.

This is by way of saying that in those days my wife and I were stone broke. We had to eke out a living, but the plan was that I would take classes at what was then called Chico State College. But for as far back as I can remember, long before we moved to California in search of a different life and our slice of the American pie, I'd wanted to be a writer. I wanted to write, and I wanted to write anything—fiction, of course, but also poetry, plays, scripts, articles for *Sports Afield*, *True*, *Argosy*, and *Rogue* (some of the magazines I was then reading), pieces for the local newspaper—anything that involved putting words together to make something coherent and of interest to someone besides myself. But at the time of our move, I felt in my bones I had to get some education in order to go along with being a writer. I put a very high premium on education then—much higher in those days than now, I'm sure, but that's because I'm older and have an education. Understand that nobody in my family had ever gone to college or for that matter had got beyond the mandatory eighth grade in high school. I didn't *know anything*, but I knew I didn't know anything.

So along with this desire to get an education, I had this very strong desire to write; it was a desire so strong that, with the encouragement I was given in college, and the insight acquired, I kept on writing long after "good sense" and the "cold facts"—the "realities" of my life told me, time and again, that I ought to quit, stop the dreaming, quietly go ahead and do something else.

That fall at Chico State I enrolled in classes that most freshman students have to take, but I enrolled as well for something called Creative Writing 101. This course was going to be taught by a new faculty member named John Gardner, who was already surrounded by a bit of mystery and romance. It was said that he'd taught previously at Oberlin College but had left there for some reason that wasn't made clear. One student said Gardner had been fired—students, like everyone else, thrive on rumor and intrigue—and another student said Gardner had simply quit after some kind of flap. Someone else said his teaching load at Oberlin, four or five classes of freshman English each semester, had been too heavy and that he couldn't find time to write. For it was said that Gardner was a real, that is to say a practicing, writer—someone who had written novels and short stories. In any case, he was going to teach CW 101 at Chico State, and I signed up.

I was excited about taking a course from a real writer. I'd never laid eyes on a writer before, and I was in awe. But where were these novels and short stories, I wanted to know. Well, nothing had been published yet. It was said that he couldn't get his work published and that he carried it around with him in boxes. (After I became his student, I was to see those boxes of manuscript. Gardner had become aware of my difficulty in finding a place to work. He knew I had a young family and cramped quarters at home. He offered me the key to his office. I see that gift now as a turning point. It was a gift not made casually, and I took it, I think, as a kind of mandate—for that's what it was. I spent part of every Saturday and Sunday in his office, which is where he kept the boxes of manuscript. The boxes were stacked up on the floor beside the desk. *Nickel Mountain*, grease-pencilled on one of the boxes, is the only title I recall. But it was in his office, within sight of his unpublished books, that I undertook my first serious attempts at writing.) . . .

For short story writers in his class, the requirement was one story, ten to fifteen pages in length. For people who wanted to write a novel—I think there must have been one or two of these souls—a chapter of around twenty pages, along with an outline of the rest. The kicker was that this one short story, or the chapter of the novel, might have to be revised ten times in the course of the semester for Gardner to be satisfied with it. It was a basic tenet of his that a writer found what he wanted to say in the ongoing process of *seeing* what he'd said. And this seeing, or seeing more clearly, came about through revision. He *believed* in revision, endless revision; it was something very close to his heart and something he felt was vital for writers, at whatever stage of their development. And he never seemed to lose patience rereading a student story, even though he might have seen it in five previous incarnations.

I think his idea of a short story in 1958 was still pretty much his idea of a short story in 1982; it was something that had a recognizable beginning, middle, and an end to it. Once in a while he'd go to the blackboard and draw a diagram to illustrate a point he wanted to make about rising or falling emotion in a story—peaks, valleys, plateaus, resolution, *denouement*, things like that. Try as I might, I couldn't muster a great deal of interest or really understand this side of things, the stuff he put on the blackboard. But what I did understand was the way he would comment on a student story that was undergoing class discussion. Gardner might wonder aloud about the author's reasons for writing a story about a crippled person, say, and leaving out the fact of the character's crippledness until the very end of the story. "So you think it's a good idea not to let the reader know this man is crippled until the last sentence?" His tone of voice conveyed his disapproval, and it didn't take more than an instant for everyone in class, including the author of the story, to see that it wasn't a good strategy to use. Any strategy that kept important and necessary information away from the reader in the hope of overcoming him by surprise at the end of the story was cheating.

In class he was always referring to writers whose names I was not familiar with. Or if I knew their names, I'd never read the work. Conrad. Céline. Katherine Anne Porter. Isaac Babel. Walter van Tilburg Clark. Chekhov. Hortense Calisher. Curt Harnack. Robert Penn Warren. (We read a story of Warren's called "Blackberry Winter." For one reason or another, I didn't care for it, and I said so to Gardner. "You'd better read it again," he said, and he was not joking.) William Gass was another writer he mentioned. Gardner was just starting his magazine, *MSS*, and was about to publish "The Pedersen Kid" in the first issue. I began reading the story in manuscript, but I didn't understand it and again I complained to Gardner. This time he didn't tell me I should try it again, he simply took the story away from me. He talked about James Joyce and Flaubert and Isak Dinesen as if they lived just down the road, in Yuba City. He said, "I'm here to tell you who to read as well as teach you how to write." I'd leave class in a daze and make straight for the library to find books by these writers he was talking about.

Hemingway and Faulkner were the reigning authors in those days. But altogether I'd probably read at the most two or three books by these fellows. Anyway, they were so well-known and so much talked about, they couldn't be all that good, could they? I remember Gardner telling me, "Read all the Faulkner you can get your hands on, and then read all of Hemingway to clean the Faulkner out of your system."

He introduced us to the "little" or literary periodicals by bringing a box of these magazines to class one day and passing them around so that we could acquaint ourselves with their names, see what they looked like and what they felt like to hold in the hand. He told us that this was where most of the best fiction in the country and just about all of the poetry was appearing. Fiction, poetry, literary essays, book reviews of recent books, criticism of *living* authors *by* living authors. I felt wild with discovery in those days.

For the seven or eight of us who were in his class, he ordered heavy black binders and told us we should keep our written work in these. He kept his own work in such binders, he said, and of course that settled it for us. We carried our stories in those binders and felt we were special, exclusive, singled out from others. And so we were.

I don't know how Gardner might have been with other students when it came time to have conferences with them about their work. I suspect he gave everybody a good amount of attention. But it was and still is my impression that during that period he took my stories more seriously, read them closer and more carefully, than I had any right to expect. I was completely unprepared for the kind of criticism I received from him. Before our conference he would have marked up my story, crossing out unacceptable sentences, phrases, individual words, even some of the punctuation; and he gave me to understand that these deletions were not negotiable. In other cases he would bracket sentences, phrases, or individual words, and these were items we'd talk about, these cases were negotiable. And he wouldn't hesitate to add something to what I'd written—a word here and there, or else a few words, maybe a sentence that would make clear what I was trying to say. We'd discuss commas in my story as if nothing else in the world mattered more at that moment—and, indeed, it did not. He was always looking to find something to praise. When there was a sentence, a line of dialogue, or a narrative passage that he liked, something that he thought "worked" and moved the story along in some pleasant or unexpected way, he'd write "Nice" in the margin, or else "Good!" And seeing these comments, my heart would lift.

It was close, line-by-line criticism he was giving me, and the reasons behind the criticism, why something ought to be this way instead of that; and it was invaluable to me in my development as a writer. After this kind of detailed talk about the text, we'd talk about the larger concerns of the story, the "problem" it was trying to throw light on, the conflict it was trying to grapple with, and how the story might or might not fit into the grand scheme of story writing. It was his conviction that if the words in the story were blurred because of the author's insensitivity, carelessness, or sentimentality, then the story suffered from a tremendous handicap. But there was something even worse and something that must be avoided at all costs: if the words and the sentiments were dishonest, the author was faking it, writing about things he didn't care about or believe in, then nobody could ever care anything about it.

A writer's values and craft. This is what the man taught and what he stood for, and this is what I've kept by me in the years since that brief but all-important time. . . .

It was his experience—and it has been mine, in my role as a teacher of creative writing—that certain aspects of writing can be taught and handed over to other, usually younger, writers. This idea shouldn't come as a surprise to any person seriously interested in education and the creative act. Most good or even great conductors, composers, microbiologists, ballerinas, mathematicians, visual artists, astronomers, or fighter pilots, learned their business from older and more accomplished practitioners. Taking classes in creative writing, like taking classes in pottery or medicine, won't in itself make anyone a great writer, potter, or doctor—it may not even make the person *good* at any of these things. But Gardner was convinced that it wouldn't hurt your chances, either.

One of the dangers in teaching or taking creative writing classes lies—and here I'm speaking from my experience again—in the overencouragement of young writers. But I learned from Gardner to take that risk rather than err on the other side. He gave and kept giving, even when the vital signs fluctuated wildly, as they do when someone is young and learning. A young writer certainly needs as much, I would even say more, encouragement than young people trying to enter other professions. And it ought to go without saying that the encouragement must always be honest encouragement and never hype. . . .

No teacher or any amount of education can make a writer out of someone who is constitutionally incapable of becoming a writer in the first place. But anyone embarking on a career, or pursuing a calling, risks setback and failure. There are failed policemen, politicians, generals, interior decorators, engineers, bus drivers, editors, literary agents, businessmen, basket weavers. There are also failed and disillusioned creative writing teachers and failed and disillusioned writers. John Gardner was neither of these . . . . My own debt is great . . . . I miss him more than I can say. But I consider myself the luckiest of men to have had his criticism and his generous encouragement.

Donald Murray, "Internal Revision: A Process of Discovery"

Donald M. Murray practises what he preaches: he revised this early essay (published in 1978) into a book called *The Craft of Revision*, a text that he went on to revise completely three times (so far). But probably more important, this call for more research on revision encouraged scholars like Sommers and Bartholomae and many others to continue to focus on the crucial role of revision in the writing process and to publish their findings. The list of possible research questions in this piece, as well as Murray's suggestions for how we might conduct this sort of research, is richly suggestive for further investigations not just into revision but into other aspects of the writing process as well. Characteristically, Murray insists that the conversation about the teaching of writing must always include the expertise and struggles of working writers themselves, many of whom he cites in this essay and in an appendix to the essay that is not included here.

INTERNAL REVISION: A PROCESS OF DISCOVERY

Writing is rewriting. Most writers accept rewriting as a condition of their craft; it comes with the territory. It is not, however, seen as a burden but as an opportunity by many writers. Neil Simon points out, "Rewriting is when playwriting really gets to be fun. . . . In baseball you only get three swings and you're out. In rewriting, you get almost as many swings as you want and you know, sooner or later, you'll hit the ball."

Rewriting is the difference between the dilettante and the artist, the amateur and the professional, the unpublished and the published. William Gass testifies, "I work not by writing but rewriting." Dylan Thomas states, "Almost any poem is fifty to a hundred revisions and that's after it's well along." Archibald MacLeish talks of "the endless discipline of writing and rewriting and rewriting." Novelist Theodore Weesner tells his students at the University of New Hampshire his course title is not "Fiction Writing" but "Fiction Rewriting."

And yet rewriting is one of the writing skills least researched, least examined, least understood, and—usually—least taught. The vast majority of students, even those who take writing courses, get away with first-draft copy. They are never introduced to the opportunities of serious revision.

A search of the literature reveals relatively few articles or books on the rewriting process. I have a commonplace book which has grown from one thin journal to 24 3-inch-thick notebooks with more than 8,000 entries divided into prewriting, writing, and rewriting. Yet even with my interest in the process of rewriting—some of my colleagues would say my obsession—only four of those notebooks are labeled rewriting.

I suspect the term rewriting has, even for many writers, an aura of failure about it. Rewriting is too often taught as punishment, not as an opportunity for discovery or even as an inevitable part of the writing process. Most texts, in fact, confuse rewriting with editing, proofreading, or manuscript preparation. Yet rewriting almost always is the most exciting, satisfying, and significant part of the writing process.

THE WRITING PROCESS

The most accurate definition of writing, I believe, is that it is the process of using language to discover meaning in experience and to communicate it. I believe this process can be described, understood, and therefore learned. Prewriting, writing, and rewriting have been generally accepted as the three principal divisions of the writing process during the past decade. I would like to propose new terms for consideration, terms which may emphasize the essential process of discovery through writing: *prevision, vision,* and *revision.*

Of course, writing will, at times, seem to skip over one part of the writing process and linger on another, and the stages of the process also overlap. The writing process is too experimental and exploratory to be contained in a rigid definition; writers move back and forth through all stages of the writing process as they search for meaning and then attempt to clarify it. It is also true that most writers do not define, describe, or possibly even understand the writing process. There's no reason for them to know what they are doing if they do it well, any more than we need to know grammatical terms if we speak and write clearly. I am convinced, however, that most writers most of the time pass through the following distinct stages.

Prevision. This term encompasses everything that precedes the first draft—receptive experience, such as awareness (conscious and unconscious), observation, remembering; and exploratory experience, such as research, reading, interviewing, and note-taking. Writers practice the prevision skills of selecting, connecting, and evaluating significant bits of information provided by receptive and exploratory experience. Prevision includes, in my opinion, the underestimated skills of title and lead writing, which help the student identify a subject, limit it, develop a point of view towards it, and begin to find the voice to explore the subject.

Vision. In the second stage of the writing process, the first draft—what I call a discovery draft—is completed. This stage takes the shortest time for the writer—in many cases it is written at one sitting—but it is the fulcrum of the writing process. Before this first draft, which Peter Drucker calls "the zero draft," everything seems possible. By completing this vision of what may be said, the writer stakes out a territory to explore.

Revision. This is what the writer does after a draft is completed to understand and communicate what has begun to appear on the page. The writer reads to see what has been suggested, then confirms, alters, or develops it, usually through many drafts. Eventually a meaning is developed which can be communicated to a reader.

THE IMPORTANCE OF DISCOVERY

My main concern in this [essay] is revision. But to be able to understand what I consider the most important task in the revision process, we have to appreciate the fact that writers much of the time don't know what they are going to write or even possibly what they have written. Writers use language as a tool of exploration to see beyond what they know. Most texts and most of our research literature have not accepted this concept or dealt with its implications.

Elie Wiesel says, "I write in order to understand as much as to be understood." The poet Tony Connor gives a recipe for writing a poem: "Invent a jungle and then explore it." William Stafford states, "You don't know what's going to happen. Nobody does." I have included at the end of this chapter forty-seven other quotations from my commonplace book which testify to the essential ignorance writers feel many times about what they are writing.

In teaching writing I often feel that the most significant step is made when a student enters into the writing process and experiences the discovery of meaning through writing. Yet this process of discovery has not been generally explored or understood for a number of reasons. First of all, it has not been experienced by nonwriters or admitted when it is experienced by writers in the less imaginative forms of writing. One professor of philosophy, after reading a text of mine, confessed he had been ashamed of the way he wrote, that he didn't know what to say or how to say it when he sat down to write. He had to write and write and write to find out what he had to say. He was embarrassed and didn't want his colleagues to know how dumb he was. When he read my book he found his activities were legitimate. I suspect such unjustified shame is more prevalent than we like to admit. Another professor told me recently that he makes assignments he could not complete by his own deadline. He explained, "My students are smarter than I am. I have to rewrite and rewrite many drafts." Yet he neither "confesses" this to his students nor allows them the opportunity to perform the writing task essential for them to achieve publication.

Most professors who are aware of the process of rewriting to discover meaning are uncomfortable thinking about it, to say nothing of discussing it in class. Discovery seems the province of the "creative writer," the writer who deals in poetry, fiction, or drama. Such activities are not quite respectable in the academic community, where we too often have a sex manual attitude: it's okay to read about it as long as you don't do it. But I am an academic schizophrenic, a "creative" writer and a "noncreative" writer. As the chairperson of a rather large department, I spend a good deal of my time writing memos to deans and vice provosts. (That's really creative writing.) I also moonlight occasionally as a corporate ghostwriter. I publish texts, novels, poems, and "papers." And in all of these roles I find the process of discovery through language taking place. I do not agree with the educational segregation of functional and imaginative writing, creative and noncreative writing. I know the process of discovery takes place when I write fiction and nonfiction, poetry and memos. To produce letters, reports, novels, essays, reviews, poems, and academic papers that say something, you have to allow language to lead you to meaning.

In drafting this paper I found myself writing, as I attempted to define the writing process, that the writer, after the first draft, is "not dealing with the vision but a fact." The word vision surprised me. It appeared on the page without premeditation. In reading it over I cut the sentence but decided the word was a better term than *writing* to describe the second stage of the writing process and, working from that point, saw the virtue of using the term *revision* for rewriting and then tried on the term *prevision* for size and found it fit, although I can't find it in my dictionary. I'm not sure that this is a discovery of enormous value, but it was fun; and I think this accident of language, this business of using words I didn't know I was going to use, has helped me understand the writing process a little bit better.

I suspect most of us have experienced many similar discoveries, but we feel it a failure: if we had a bit more IQ, we would have known the right word. I find few English teachers are comfortable with the concept of uncalculated discovery. They simply do not believe the testimony of writers when they say they write what they don't know, and this may indeed be an uncomfortable concept if you spend your classroom hours analyzing literature and telling your students exactly why the writer did what he or she did, as if literature resulted from the following of a detailed blueprint. Writing, fortunately for writers, is much more exciting than that. The writer does plan but keeps adapting those plans to what is discovered on the page.

The writer, however, who lives in the academic community—and today most of us do—is surrounded by people who seem to know precisely what happens in a piece of literature. The other night my colleague, the poet Charles Simic, said his favorite poems were the ones he didn't understand, an unsettling confession in a department of English. It is hard to admit that you don't know what you're doing when you write. It seems a bit undignified, perhaps even cause for the removal of tenure. Surely my governor would think I ought to know what I'm doing when I sit down to write—I'm a full professor, for goodness sake—and yet I don't. And hope I never will.

Listening to a lecture the other day, I found myself doodling with language. (The better the lecture the more likely a piece of writing will start to happen on my notebook page.) From where I sat in the lecture hall, I could see an office door, and I watched a person in that office get up and shut the door against the lecture. It was an ordinary act, yet, for no reason I can recall, I found myself writing this on the page:

> I had an office at a university, an inside office, without window or air. The classrooms up and down the corridor would fill up with words until they spilled over and reached the edge of my half-opened door, a confident, almost arrogant mumble I could no longer bother to try to understand. Was I to be like the makers of those words, was I already like the students in my own Freshman sections? Perhaps the only good thing about this position was that Mother was dumbly proud and Father puzzled and angry, "Is this where they put you, an educated man? The union would kill me."
>
> If I hadn't killed a man, my life would have seemed trite. . . .

I have followed this short story for only a couple of pages in the past few days. I am ashamed to reveal the lines above—I don't know if they will lead me to a story—but I'm having fun and think I should share this experience, for it is revealing of the writing process. I did not intend to write a short story. I am working on a novel, a book of poems, and articles such as this one. Short fiction is not on the menu. I did not intend to write an academic short story. I do not like the genre. I do not particularly like the character who is appearing on my page, but I am interested in being within his head. I have not yet killed a man, to my knowledge, and I have never been a teaching assistant, although I have known many.

I want to repeat that there was absolutely no intent in what I was doing. The fact that the character had killed a person came as a total surprise to me. It seems too melodramatic, and I don't like this confessional voice, and I do not like the tense, and I have trouble dictating these words from my notebook to my wife, because they keep changing and leading me forward. I do not know if the killing was accidental or premeditated. I don't know the victim. I don't know the method. I don't know if it was imaginary. I do know the phrase "killed a man" appeared on the page. It may have come there because of what the father said; or, since in the next paragraph I discovered that the young man feels this one act gives him a certain distance from life, a sort of scenic overlook from which to view life, perhaps that idea came from the word "position" in the first paragraph. In my lower middle-class background, even a teaching assistant had a position, not a job. A little more of this kind of thing, however, and the story will never be written.

Writers must remain, to some degree, not only ignorant of what they are going to do but what they are doing. Mary Peterson just wrote me about her novel, "I need to write it before I can think about it, write it too fast for thought." Writers have to protect their ignorance, and it is not easy to remain ignorant, particularly in an English department. That may be one reason we have deemphasized the experience of discovery in writing.

Discovery, however, can be a frightening process. The terror of the empty page is real, because you simply do not know what you are going to say before you say it or if indeed you will have anything to say. I observe this process most dramatically at those times when I dictate early drafts of nonfiction to my wife, who types it on the typewriter. We have done this for years, and yet rather regularly she asks me to repeat what I have said or tell her what I am going to say so that she can punctuate. I don't think, after many books and many years, that she really believes me when I claim I can't remember what I've just said or that I don't know what I'm going to say next.

This process is even more frightening when you engage in the forms of writing that take you inside yourself. "There's not any more dangerous occupation in the world," says James Dickey of poetry. "The mortality rate is very, very high. Paul Valéry once said, 'one should never go into the self except armed to the teeth.' That's true. The kind of poets we're talking about—Berryman, Crane, Dylan Thomas—have created something against which they have no immunity and which they cannot control."

Finally, many expert readers who teach English, and therefore writing, are ignorant of the process of discovery because it is not, and should not be, apparent in a finished work. After a building is finished, the flimsy scaffolding is taken away. Our profession's normal obsession with product rather than process leads us towards dangerous misconceptions about the writing process. I believe increasingly that the process of discovery, of using language to find out what you are going to say, is a key part of the writing process. In light of this I would like to reexamine the revision process.

THE TWO PRINCIPAL FORMS OF REVISION

The more I explore the revision process as a researcher and the more I experience it as a writer, the more convinced I am that there are two principal and quite separate editorial acts involved in revision.

Internal revision. Under this term, I include everything writers do to discover and develop what they have to say, beginning with the reading of a completed first draft. They read to discover where their content, form, language, and voice have led them. They use language, structure, and information to find out what they have to say or hope to say. The audience is one person: the writer.

External revision. This is what writers do to communicate what they have found they have written to another audience. It is editing and proofreading and much more. Writers now pay attention to the conventions of form and language, mechanics, and style. They eye their audience and may choose to appeal to it. They read as an outsider, and it is significant that such terms as *polish* are used by professionals: they dramatize the fact that the writer at this stage in the process may, appropriately, be concerned with exterior appearance.

Most writers spend more time, *much* more time, on internal revision than external revision. Yet most texts emphasize the least part of the process, the mechanical changes involved in the etiquette of writing, the superficial aspects of preparing a manuscript to be read, and pass over the process of internal revision. It's worth noting that it is unlikely intelligent choices in the editing process can be made unless writers thoroughly understand what they have said through internal revision.

Although I believe external revision has not been explored adequately or imaginatively, it has been explored. I shall concentrate on attempting to describe internal revision, suggesting opportunities for research, and indicating some implications for the teaching of writing.

The Process of Internal Revision

After the writer has completed the first draft, the writer moves toward the center of the writing process. E. M. Forster says, "The act of writing inspires me," and Valéry talks of "the inspiration of the writing desk." The writer may be closer to the scientist than to the critic at this point. Each piece of writing is an experiment. Robert Penn Warren says, "All writing that is any good *is* experimental: that is, it's a way of seeing what is possible."

Some pieces of writing come easily, without a great deal of internal revision. The experience is rare for most writers, however, and it usually comes after a lifetime of discipline, or sometimes after a long night of work, as it did when Robert Frost wrote "Stopping by Woods on a Snowy Evening." The important thing to understand is that the work that reads the most easily is often the product of what appears to be drudgery. Theodore Roethke wisely points out that "you will come to know how, by working slowly, to be spontaneous."

I have a relatively short 7-part poem of which there are 185 or more versions written over the past 2 years. I am no Roethke, but I have found it important to share with my students in my seminar on the teaching of writing a bit of the work which will never appear in public. I think they are impressed with how badly I write, with how many false starts and illiterate accidents it took for me to move forward towards some understanding of the climate in a tenement in which I lived as an only child, surrounded by a paralyzed grandmother and two rather childlike parents. The important thing for my students to see is that each word changed, each line crossed out, each space left on the page is an attempt to understand, to remember what I did not know I remembered.

During the process of internal revision, writers are not concerned with correctness in any exterior sense. They read what they have written so that they can deal with the questions of subject, of adequate information, of structure, of form, of language. They move from a revision of the entire piece down to the page, the paragraph, the sentence, the line, the phrase, the word. And then, because each word may give off an explosion of meaning, they move out from the word to the phrase, the line, the sentence, the paragraph, the page, the piece. Writers move in close and then move out to visualize the entire piece. Again and again and again. As Donald Hall says, "The attitude to cultivate from the start is that revision is a way of life."

Discovery and Internal Revision

The concept of internal revision is new to me. This essay has given me the impetus to explore this area of the writing process. The further I explore the more tentative my conclusions. This [essay] is, indeed, as I believe it was meant to be, a call for research, not a report of research. There are many things I do not understand as I experience and examine the process of internal revision. But in addition to my normal researches, I am part of a faculty which includes seven publishing writers, as well as many publishing scholars and critics. We share our work in process, and I have the advantage of seeing them discover what they have to say. I also see the work of graduate students in our writing program, many of whom are already publishing. And I watch the writing of students who are undergraduates at the university, in high school, in middle school, and in elementary school. And I think I can perceive four important aspects of discovery in the process of internal revision.

The first involves *content*. I think we forget that writers in all forms, even poetry, especially poetry, write with information. As English professors and linguistic researchers, we may concentrate on stylistic differences, forgetting that the writer engaged in the process of internal revision is looking through the word—or beyond the word or behind the word—for the information the word will symbolize. Sitting at a desk, pausing, staring out the window, the writer does not see some great thesaurus in the sky; the writer sees a character walking or hears a character speaking, sees a pattern of statistics which may lead toward a conclusion. Writers can't write nothing; they must have an abundance of information. During the process of internal revision, they gather new information or return to their inventory of information and draw on it. They discover what they have to say by relating pieces of specific information to other bits of information and use words to symbolize and connect that information.

This naturally leads to the discoveries related to *form and structure*. We all know Archibald MacLeish said that a poem should not mean but be, but what we do not always understand is that the being may be the meaning. Form is meaning, or a kind of meaning. The story that has a beginning, a middle, and an end implies that life has a beginning, a middle, and an end; exposition implies that things can be explained; argument implies the possibility of rational persuasion. As writers bring order to chaos, the order brings the writers toward meaning.

Third, *language* itself leads writers to meaning. During the process of internal revision (what some writers might call eternal revision), they reject words, choose new words, bring words together, switch their order around to discover what they are saying. "I work with language," says Bernard Malamud, "I love the flowers of after-thought."

Finally, I believe there is a fourth area, quite separate from content, form, or language, which is harder to define but may be as important as the other sources of discovery. That is what we call *voice*. I think voice, the way in which writers hear what they have to say, hear their point of view towards the subject, their authority, their distance from the subject, is an extremely significant form of internal revision.

We should realize that there may be fewer discoveries in form and voice as a writer repeats a subject or continues work in a genre which he or she has explored earlier and become proficient with. This lack of discovery—this excessive professionalism or slickness, the absence of discovery—is the greatest fear of mature, successful writers. They may know too much too early in the writing process.

QUESTIONS LOOKING FOR QUESTIONERS

Speculations about the writing process are fun to propose and entertaining to consider, but we will not understand the writing process unless we employ all of the methods and tools of modern research. Hypotheses suggested, such as the existence of an identifiable process of internal revision, must be subjected to tough, skeptical investigation. We must ask uncomfortable, demanding questions of the writing process. We will certainly not get the answers we expect—many of our pet theories will be destroyed—but the answers will bring new and better questions. Research into the writing process will eventually produce an understanding of how people write, which will have a profound effect on our educational procedures. We now attempt to teach a writing process we do not understand; research may allow us to teach what we understand.

The following are some of the questions researchers must ask:

1. How can the process of internal revision be described? The actual process of internal revision should be described in precise terms so we can understand the steps taken by a broad range of professional and student writers as they use language to discover and clarify the meaning of what they are writing. The process should be broken down and analyzed, defined and documented, so we can begin to understand what happens during internal revision.

2. What attitudes do effective writers bring to the task of internal revision? Attitude precedes and predetermines skill. Too often we attempt to teach skills and fail because we have not taught the attitudes which make the skill logical and obvious. It is important to know the attitude of effective revisors (or is it revisionists?) when they come to their own piece of writing. Do they accept the process of revision as a normal part of the writing process, or do they see it as punishment? Do writers expect their understanding of what they are saying to change as they write?

3. How do writers read their own copy? Writers perform a special, significant kind of reading when they read their own writing in process. Writers must achieve a detachment from their work that allows them to see what is on the page, not what they hoped [would] be on the page. They also must read with an eye to alternatives in content, form, structure, voice, and language. How do they read their own page and visualize the potential choices which may lead to a clarified meaning? How do they listen to the page to hear what is being said and what might be said?

4. What skills does the writer employ during the process of internal revision? There seem to be four distinct areas or types of internal revision. The first involves content, the collection and development of the raw material, the information with which the writer writes. The next is the form or structure of the writing itself. The last two are the voice and the language employed in the clarification of meaning. It is likely that there are overlapping but identifiable skills employed by the writer in each of these areas. The skills need to be observed and described. One unexplored skill which might help our understanding of internal revision is the writer's use of memory. There seem to be two significant forms of

memory employed by the writer: one is the way in which writing unlocks information stored in the brain; the other is the memory of what the writer has previously written within the piece, which influences each choice during the process of internal revision. Another skill might come from the fact some writers say they write with verbs, especially during the process of revision. It might be fruitful to examine how writers use verbs as the fulcrum of meaning.

5. What developmental stages are significant to an understanding of the process of internal revision? Applying our knowledge of how people react to their own world at different ages may help us understand the process of internal revision. There may be significant differences because of sex, levels of intelligence, or social-economic background. Our preconceptions about student willingness to revise may be wrong. Teachers who see rewriting as punishment may believe that students will not rewrite at certain levels of development and may, because of this conviction, discourage rewriting. In fact, their students may wish to revise, to explore the same subject in draft after draft, if they are given the opportunity. There may be a significant relationship between length and revision. Students may want to write longer than their teachers think they can, and the longer pieces students write may have a greater potential for exploration than shorter pieces. There are also indications that considerable familiarity with a subject, experience with a form, and confidence in a voice may increase discovery.

6. What new knowledge may help us understand the process of internal revision? There are significant new discoveries in brain research, for example, which may provide major breakthroughs in how writers write. The most significant article pointing out this new territory is Janet Emig's "The Biology of Writing: Another View of the Process." We also need to apply the latest findings of linguistic studies, rhetorical research, and learning theory to the process of internal revision. We must draw on as many fields as possible to attempt to understand the writing process. What can the teachers of foreign languages teach us? What can we learn from those who are studying the process of creativity in art, in music, in science? What can we learn from those who study the language of mathematics and from those who design and use computers, which employ the language of mathematics to discover meaning in information?

7. What writing tools, habits, environments, or schedules influence the process of internal revision? Most writers scorn the interviewer's questions about what time of day they write and whether they use pen or typewriter. They feel this is trivia, and it may be, but it also may be significant trivia, for writers among themselves often seem obsessed by such matters. Writers are craftsmen who are greatly

concerned with their tools—the texture, weight, size, and tint of paper; the flow of ink and its color; the design of the pen, its feel, and the breadth of its point. Most writers have superstitions about their favorite writing tools, and most of them vary their tools at different stages of the writing process. I write early drafts of poems in longhand (Mont Blanc fountain pen, thin point, permanent black ink, eye-ease green legal ruled paper), but in a stage central to the process of internal revision, I shift to a typewriter so I can see the poem in print. I find that most poets work in this way. Most writers also find certain environments, quiet or noisy, secluded or public, stimulate the writing process. (I hide in a secluded office these days, but I'd work best in a busy restaurant if I could afford to rent a table and if I could be anonymous—an impossibility in a small university town.) Writers usually are compulsive about the hour at which the work seems to go the best. (My present rule is at least 600 words before 9 a.m. every day.) Most writers seem to move towards the extremes of early morning or late at night, when they have the maximum energy or can work best without interruption, or can tap most easily into their subconscious. Writers have rituals or habits—reading or not reading what they have written or stopping in mid-sentence—which stimulate the flow of discovery through writing. These tricks of the trade may be important for students to know, and they may call for different learning styles or curriculum patterns than those normally imposed in school.

8. What subject areas, writing forms, or language patterns stimulate or discourage discovery of meaning through internal revision? We should observe writers at work on the traditionally most creative forms, such as poetry, but also on the less traditionally studied forms, such as technical writing, business letter writing, speech writing, news writing, and so on, to find out how these writers and the forms they use influence the process of discovery of meaning through language. The evidence we have is restricted to very few forms of writing. We need to extend this examination to all forms.

9. How do editors read writing and encourage improvement through the process of internal revision? Editors are highly specialized readers of writing in process who work closely with writers at each stage of the writing process. Yet, as far as I know, there have been no significant studies of how editors read copy, what they discover, and how they communicate with writers. This editing is not proofreading—it is the constructive examination of a draft with directions as to how further drafts may be developed. It should be obvious that editors are highly expert teachers and that they have a great deal to tell us about the writing process and the teaching of that process. They must motivate and employ techniques of communication which will make criticism constructive, which will

stimulate, not discourage, improvement in writing. Their knowledge, attitudes, and skills might be a significant contribution to the understanding of the writing process and the means by which it can be taught.

10. What curricula, teaching environments, and methods encourage the improvement of writing through the process of internal revision? There are increasing numbers of teachers at every level, from preschool through graduate school, who are helping their students learn to write by taking them through the experience of the writing process. We need to observe these teachers at work and see exactly what their students do while they are engaged in the process of internal revision.

Those are just a few of the questions which should be asked of the process of internal revision. Each question will, of course, lead to additional questions. Each answer will produce even more questions, and researchers bringing their own special knowledge to the task will develop new questions. This is an exciting prospect, for the best and most obvious questions about the writing process have, amazingly, not been asked or investigated. We have a frontier ready for exploration.

How We Can Research Such Questions

I can suggest a number of ways to investigate the essential questions of internal revision:

Bring researchers in the writing process closer together with linguists, rhetoricians, and brain or neuroresearchers in teams and seminars to focus their divergent disciplines on an understanding of the writing process.

Examine writers' manuscripts to discover from the evidence on the page how writers read and revise to clarify their meaning for themselves.

Make use of accounts of the writing process—writers' interviews, diaries, journals, letters, autobiographies—to see what writers say they are doing.

Sponsor accounts of writers at work. Encourage writers to keep journals of an evolving piece of work, together with manuscript pages, so that they might become more aware and make others aware of the nature of their concern during the process of internal revision. (Many writers would refuse, of course, but some would not.)

Observe professional writers and editors at work, and interview them to see what they have done. Not many writers will stand still for this, but there may be some who would consent to be observed in a manner similar to the observation of students done by researchers such as Emig (1971) and Donald Graves (1975).

Collect and examine drafts of a number of versions of pieces of writing in many fields, not just examples of "creative writing" but examples of journalism, technical writing, scholarly writing. When I was an editor at *Time*, many copies of every single draft were typed, distributed, and I believe retained. A research project might collect and examine such drafts and perhaps interview the writers/editors who were producing them.

Observe students' writing and follow drafts evolving through the process of internal revision. Perhaps some students, for example, might be willing to read for revision or even revise using a scanner which shows how their eyes follow the text, where they stop and start.

Test the effectiveness of what we find out about the process of internal revision by having our students follow the examples of the writers who read and rewrite to discover what they have to say, and then see if the students' drafts define and refine a meaning more effectively than the early drafts.

These are just a few of the possible methods of researching internal revision. It seems clear, however, that the most productive method of exploring the writing process is the case study. We do not need extensive statistical surveys as much as we need close observation of a few writers and students doing the entire writing process by well-trained observers who follow their observations with intelligent, probing interviews. This method of investigation seems the one which will yield the basic data and concepts which will be tested and developed by other means of investigation.

The Implications for Teaching

If writers don't write what they know, but to learn what they may know, there may be significant implications for teaching, especially in the area of internal revision. Some of them are:

Stupid kids may not be stupid. Students classified as slow may simply have the illusion writers know what they are going to say before they say it. Since they do not know what they are going to write, they may be paralyzed and not write. Such students, once they understand how writers write, may be released from this paralysis. Some slow students may then appear less slow when their writing evolves through/towards a subject.

Many articulate, verbal, glib students who are overrewarded for first-draft writing may be released from the prison of praise and high grades and encouraged to write much better than they ever have before.

Unmotivated students may be motivated to write when they find writing an adventure. In my teaching of "remedial" students, the exploration of a subject through many drafts is the single most significant motivating factor. Teachers constantly make the judgment that their least motivated students will not write many drafts, when in fact they are often the students who most quickly write many drafts once they experience the excitement of exploring a subject with language.

An understanding of the process of prevision, vision, and revision may result in the redesign of writing units so that students spend more time on prevision, far less time on vision, and much more time on revision. Students will have a greater opportunity in such units to discover an area they want to explore and more time to explore it.

Research into the writing process may reveal the process of writing to teachers so they will allow their students to experience it.

Finally, an understanding of the writing process may give literature teachers a new appreciation and understanding of the product we call literature. They may be able to read in a way which will help them discover the full implications of what the writer has done and is doing on the page.

Most of these implications could and should be evaluated by educational researchers. The teaching of writing certainly needs far more professional inquiry than the subjective accounts, anecdotes from the trenches, which so many of us, myself included, have produced in the past.

The new interest in the process of writing, rather than the product of writing, opens the door for important and interesting research which can employ all of the tools of intelligent investigation. It is a job which needs to be done. The process of writing—of using language to discover meaning and communicate it—is a significant human act. The better we understand how people write—how people think—the better we may be able to write and to teach writing.

Nancy Sommers, "Revision Strategies of Student Writers and Experienced Adult Writers"

Nancy Sommers, Sosland Director of Expository Writing at Harvard, has been in the news repeatedly over the past few years as a result of the longitudinal study of four hundred Harvard undergraduates (one-quarter of the class of 2001) that she and her colleagues at Harvard have undertaken. The Harvard Study of Undergraduate Writing—between 1997 and 2001—collected "600 pounds of student writing, 520 hours of transcribed interviews, and countless megabytes of survey data" in an attempt to examine "the role writing plays in a college education and to compose as complete a portrait as possible of the college writing experience." A glimpse of the study's preliminary findings is available online at http://www.fas.harvard.edu/~expos/—click on "Study" and then choose to read further about it or to watch the fourteen-minute film *Shaped by Writing*.

Hired by historian Richard Marius, Director of Harvard's Expository Writing Program at the time, Sommers left Rutgers University to serve as Associate Director of Expos from 1987 to 1993, when she became Director. She is one of the few scholars in the field ever to have won the Braddock Award twice, once in 1983 for her influential piece on "Responding to Student Writing" and then again, ten years later, for a more personal reflection on revision, "Between the Drafts," in which she criticizes the early piece reprinted here for its lack of voice. See if you agree with her. We can imagine a fascinating essay evolving from close examination of Sommers's four best-known early essays: the two mentioned above, the one below, plus "I Stand Here Writing" (1993). Differences in authorial voice, in handling of sources, in presentation of data, in intention—any one of these would be worth analyzing in some detail and could make a serious contribution to the conversation about writing. How does Sommers's writing voice and position and practice change when her physical location changes, when she is no longer trying to *enter* the conversation from the margins but in fact *defines the centre* of the conversation by directing the oldest writing program in North America?

Bookmark the webpage mentioned above: it provides excellent resources on academic writing. Especially useful is *Writing with Sources*, written by Edmonton native and University of Alberta graduate Gordon Harvey, Associate Director of Expository Writing at Harvard.

REVISION STRATEGIES OF STUDENT WRITERS AND EXPERIENCED ADULT WRITERS

Although various aspects of the writing process have been studied extensively of late, research on revision has been notably absent. The reason for this, I suspect, is that current models of the writing process have directed attention away from revision. With few exceptions, these models are linear; they separate the writing process into discrete stages. Two representative models are Gordon Rohman's suggestion that the composing process moves from prewriting to writing to rewriting and James Britton's model of the writing process as a series of stages described in metaphors of linear growth, conception—incubation—production.[1] What is striking about these theories of writing is that they model themselves on speech: Rohman defines the writer in a way that cannot distinguish him from a speaker ("A writer is a man who . . . puts [his] experience into words in his own mind" [15]); and Britton backs his theory of writing on what he calls (following Jakobson) the "expressiveness" of speech.[2] Moreover, Britton's study itself follows the "linear model" of the relation of thought and language in speech proposed by Vygotsky, a relationship embodied in the linear movement "from the motive which engenders a thought to the shaping of the thought, *first* in inner speech, *then* in meanings of words, and *finally* in words" (qtd. in Britton 40). What this movement fails to take into account in its linear structure—"first . . . then . . . finally"—is the recursive shaping of thought by language; what it fails to take into account is *revision*. In these linear conceptions of the writing process revision is understood as a separate stage at the end of the process—a stage that comes after the completion of a first or second draft and one that is temporally distinct from the prewriting and writing stages of the process.[3]

The linear model bases itself on speech in two specific ways. First of all, it is based on traditional rhetorical models, models that were created to serve the spoken art of oratory. In whatever ways the parts of classical rhetoric are described, they offer "stages" of composition that are repeated in contemporary models of the writing process. Edward Corbett, for instance, describes the "five parts of a discourse"—*inventio, dispositio, elocutio, memoria, pronuntiatio*—and, disregarding the last two parts since "after rhetoric came to be concerned mainly with written discourse, there was no further need to deal with them,"[4] he produces a model very close to Britton's conception [*inventio*], incubation [*dispositio*], production [*elocutio*]. Other rhetorics also follow this procedure, and they do so not simply because of historical accident. Rather, the process represented in the linear model is based on the irreversibility of speech. Speech, Roland Barthes says, "is irreversible":

> A word cannot be retracted, except precisely by saying that one retracts it. To cross out here is to add: if I want to erase what I have just said, I cannot do it without showing the eraser itself (I must say: "*or rather . . .*" "*I expressed myself badly . . .*"); paradoxically, it is ephemeral speech which is indelible, not monumental writing. All that one can do in the case of a spoken utterance is to tack on another utterance.[5]

What is impossible in speech is *revision*: like the example Barthes gives, revision in speech is an afterthought. In the same way, each stage of the linear model must be exclusive (distinct from the other stages) or else it becomes trivial and counterproductive to refer to these junctures as "stages."

By staging revision after enunciation, the linear models reduce revision in writing, as in speech, to no more than an afterthought. In this way such models make the study of revision impossible. Revision, in Rohman's model, is simply the repetition of writing; or to pursue Britton's organic metaphor, revision is simply the further growth of what is already there, the "preconceived" product. The absence of research on revision, then, is a function of a theory of writing which makes revision both superfluous and redundant, a theory which does not distinguish between writing and speech.

What the linear models do produce is a parody of writing. Isolating revision and then disregarding it plays havoc with the experiences composition teachers have of the actual writing and rewriting of experienced writers. Why should the linear model be preferred? Why should revision be forgotten, superfluous? Why do teachers offer the linear model and students accept it? One reason, Barthes suggests, is that "there is a fundamental tie between teaching and speech," while "writing begins at the point where speech becomes *impossible.*"[6] The spoken word cannot be revised. The possibility of revision distinguishes the written text from speech. In fact, according to Barthes, this is the essential difference between writing and speaking. When we must revise, when the very idea is subject to recursive shaping by language, then speech becomes inadequate. This is a matter to which

I will return, but first we should examine, theoretically, a detailed exploration of what student writers as distinguished from experienced adult writers *do* when they write and rewrite their work. Dissatisfied with both the linear model of writing and the lack of attention to the process of revision, I conducted a series of studies over the past three years which examined the revision processes of student writers and experienced writers to see what role revision played in their writing processes. In the course of my work the revision process was redefined as *a sequence of changes in a composition—changes which are initiated by cues and occur continually throughout the writing of a work.*

METHODOLOGY

I used a case study approach. The student writers were twenty freshmen at Boston University and the University of Oklahoma with SAT verbal scores ranging from 450-600 in their first semester of composition. The twenty experienced adult writers from Boston and Oklahoma City included journalists, editors, and academics. To refer to the two groups, I use the terms *student writers* and *experienced writers* because the principal difference between these two groups is the amount of experience they have had in writing.

Each writer wrote three essays, expressive, explanatory, and persuasive, and rewrote each essay twice, producing nine written products in draft and final form. Each writer was interviewed three times after the final revision of each essay. And each writer suggested revisions for a composition written by an anonymous author. Thus extensive written and spoken documents were obtained from each writer.

The essays were analyzed by counting and categorizing the changes made. Four revision operations were identified: deletion, substitution, addition, and reordering. And four levels of changes were identified: word, phrase, sentence, theme (the extended statement of one idea). A coding system was developed for identifying the frequency of revision by level and operation. In addition, transcripts of the interviews in which the writers interpreted their revisions were used to develop what was called a *scale of concerns* for each writer. This scale enabled me to codify what were the writer's primary concerns, secondary concerns, tertiary concerns, and whether the writers used the same scale of concerns when revising the second or third drafts as they used in revising the first draft.

REVISION STRATEGIES OF STUDENT WRITERS

Most of the students I studied did not use the terms *revision* or *rewriting*. In fact, they did not seem comfortable using the word *revision* and explained that revision was not a word they used, but the word their teachers used. Instead, most of the students had developed various functional terms to describe the type of changes they made. The following are samples of these definitions:

> *Scratch Out and Do Over Again:* "I say scratch out and do over, and that means what it says. Scratching out and cutting out. I read what I have written and I cross out a word

and put another word in; a more decent word or a better word. Then if there is some-where to use a sentence that I have crossed out, I will put it there."

Reviewing: "Reviewing means just using better words and eliminating words that are not needed. I go over and change words around."

Reviewing: "I just review every word and make sure that everything is worded right. I see if I am rambling; I see if I can put a better word in or leave one out. Usually when I read what I have written, I say to myself, 'that word is so bland or so trite,' and then I go and get my thesaurus."

Redoing: "Redoing means cleaning up the paper and crossing out. It is looking at something and saying, no that has to go, or no, that is not right."

Marking Out: "I don't use the word rewriting because I only write one draft and the changes that I make are made on top of the draft. The changes that I make are usually just marking out words and putting different ones in."

Slashing and Throwing Out: "I throw things out and say they are not good. I like to write like Fitzgerald did by inspiration, and if I feel inspired then I don't need to slash and throw much out."

The predominant concern in these definitions is vocabulary. The students understand the revision process as a rewording activity. They do so because they perceive words as the unit of written discourse. That is, they concentrate on particular words apart from their role in the text. Thus one student quoted above thinks in terms of dictionaries, and, following the eighteenth-century theory of words parodied in *Gulliver's Travels*, he imagines a load of things carried about to be exchanged. Lexical changes are the major revision activities of the students because economy is their goal. They are governed, like the linear model itself, by the Law of Occam's razor that prohibits logically needless repetition: redundancy and superfluity. Nothing governs speech more than such superfluities; speech constantly repeats itself precisely because spoken words, as Barthes writes, are expendable in the cause of communication. The aim of revision according to the students' own description is therefore to clean up speech; the redundancy of speech is unnecessary in writing, their logic suggests, because writing, unlike speech, can be reread. Thus one student said, "Redoing means cleaning up the paper and crossing out." The remarkable contradiction of cleaning by marking might, indeed, stand for student revision as I have encountered it.

The students place a symbolic importance on their selection and rejection of words as the determiners of success or failure for their compositions. When revising, they prima-rily ask themselves: can I find a better word or phrase? A more impressive, not so clichéd, or less humdrum word? Am I repeating the same word or phrase too often? They approach the revision process with what could be labeled as a "thesaurus philosophy of writing"; the students consider the thesaurus a harvest of lexical substitutions and believe that most problems in their essays can be solved by rewording. What is revealed in the students' use of the thesaurus is a governing attitude toward their writing: that the meaning to be communicated is already there, already finished, already produced, ready to be communicated, and all that is necessary is a better word "rightly worded." One student defined *revision* as "redoing"; *redoing* meant "just using better words and eliminating words that are not needed." For the students, writing is translating: the thought to the page, the language of speech to the more formal language of prose, the word to its synonym. Whatever is translated, an original text already exists for students, one which need not be discovered or acted upon, but simply communicated.[7]

The students list repetition as one of the elements they most worry about. This cue signals to them that they need to eliminate the repetition either by substituting or deleting words or phrases. Repetition occurs, in large part, because student writing imitates—transcribes—speech: attention to repetitious words is a manner of cleaning speech. Without a sense of the developmental possibilities of revision (and writing in general) students seek, on the authority of many textbooks, simply to clean up their language and prepare to type. What is curious, however, is that students are aware of lexical repetition, but not conceptual repetition. They only notice the repetition if they can "hear" it; they do not diagnose lexical repetition as symptomatic of problems on a deeper level. By rewording their sentences to avoid the lexical repetition, the students solve the immediate problem, but blind themselves to problems on a textual level; although they are using different words, they are sometimes merely restating the same idea with different words. Such blindness, as I discovered with student writers, is the inability to "see" revision as a process: the inability to "re-view" their work again, as it were, with different eyes, and to start over.

The revision strategies described above are consistent with the students' understanding of the revision process as requiring lexical changes but not semantic changes. For the students, the extent to which they revise is a function of their level of inspiration. In fact, they use the word *inspiration* to describe the ease or difficulty with which their essay is written, and the extent to which the essay needs to be revised. If students feel inspired, if the writing comes easily, and if they don't get stuck on individual words or phrases, then they say that they cannot see any reason to revise. Because students do not see revision as an activity in which they modify and develop perspectives and ideas, they feel that if they know what they want to say, then there is little reason for making revisions.

The only modification of ideas in the students' essays occurred when they tried out two or three introductory paragraphs. This results, in part, because the students have been taught in another version of the linear model of composing to use a thesis statement as a controlling device in their introductory paragraphs. Since they write their introductions and their thesis statements even before they have really discovered what they want to say, their early close attention to the thesis statement, and more generally the linear model, function to restrict and circumscribe not only the development of their ideas, but also their ability to change the direction of these ideas.

Too often as composition teachers we conclude that students do not willingly revise. The evidence from my research suggests that it is not that students are unwilling to revise, but rather that they do what they have been taught to do in a consistently narrow and predictable way. On every occasion when I asked students why they hadn't made any more changes, they essentially replied, "I knew something larger was wrong, but I didn't think it would help to move words around." The students have strategies for handling words and phrases and their strategies helped them on a word or sentence level. What they lack, however, is a set of strategies to help them identify the "something larger" that they sensed was wrong and work from there. The students do not have strategies for handling the whole essay. They lack procedures or heuristics to help them reorder lines of reasoning or ask questions about their purposes and readers. The students view their compositions in a linear way as a series of parts. Even such potentially useful concepts as "unity" or "form" are reduced to the rule that a composition, if it is to have form, must have an introduction, a body, and a conclusion, or the sum total of the necessary parts.

The students decide to stop revising when they decide that they have not violated any of the rules for revising. These rules, such as "Never begin a sentence with a conjunction" or "Never end a sentence with a preposition," are lexically cued and rigidly applied. In general, students will subordinate the demands of the specific problems of their text to the demands of the rules. Changes are made in compliance with abstract rules about the product, rules that quite often do not apply to the specific problems in the text. These revision strategies are teacher-based, directed towards a teacher-reader who expects compliance with rules—with pre-existing "conceptions"—and who will only examine parts of the composition (writing comments about those parts in the margins of their essays) and will cite any violations of rules in those parts. At best the students see their writing altogether passively through the eyes of former teachers or their surrogates, the textbooks, and are bound to the rules which they have been taught.

REVISION STRATEGIES OF EXPERIENCED WRITERS

One aim of my research has been to contrast how student writers define revision with how a group of experienced writers define their revision processes. Here is a sampling of the definitions from the experienced writers:

Rewriting: "It is a matter of looking at the kernel of what I have written, the content, and then thinking about it, responding to it, making decisions, and actually restructuring it."

Rewriting: "I rewrite as I write. It is hard to tell what is a first draft because it is not determined by time. In one draft, I might cross out three pages, write two, cross out a fourth, rewrite it, and call it a draft. I am constantly writing and rewriting. I can only conceptualize so much in my first draft—only so much information can be held in my head at one time; my rewriting efforts are a reflection of how much information I can encompass at one time. There are levels and agendas which I have to attend to in each draft."

Rewriting: "Rewriting means on one level, finding the argument, and on another level, language changes to make the argument more effective. Most of the time I feel as if I can go on rewriting forever. There is always one part of a piece that I could keep working on. It is always difficult to know at what point to abandon a piece of writing. I like this idea that a piece of writing is never finished, just abandoned."

Rewriting: "My first draft is usually very scattered. In rewriting, I find the line of argument. After the argument is resolved, I am much more interested in word choice and phrasing."

Revising: "My cardinal rule in revising is never to fall in love with what I have written in a first or second draft. An idea, sentence, or even a phrase that looks catchy, I don't trust. Part of this idea is to wait a while. I am much more in love with something after I have written it than I am a day or two later. It is much easier to change anything with time."

Revising: "It means taking apart what I have written and putting it back together again. I ask major theoretical questions of my ideas, respond to those questions, and think of proportion and structure, and try to find a controlling metaphor. I find out which ideas can be developed and which should be dropped. I am constantly chiseling and changing as I revise."

The experienced writers describe their primary objective when revising as finding the form or shape of their argument. Although the metaphors vary, the experienced writers often use structural expressions such as "finding a framework," "a pattern," or "a design" for their argument. When questioned about this emphasis, the experienced writers responded that since their first drafts are usually scattered attempts to define their territory, their objective in the second draft is to begin observing general patterns of development and deciding what should be included and what excluded. One writer explained, "I have learned from experience that I need to keep writing a first draft until I figure out what I want to say. Then in a second draft, I begin to see the structure of an argument and how all the various sub-arguments which are buried beneath the surface of all those sentences are related." What is described here is a process in which the writer is both agent and vehicle. "Writing," says Barthes, unlike speech, "develops like a seed, not a line,"[8] and like a seed it confuses beginning and end, conception and production. Thus, the experienced writers say their drafts are "not determined by time," that rewriting is a "constant process," that they feel as if they "can go on forever." Revising confuses the beginning and end, the agent and vehicle; it confuses, *in order to find*, the line of argument.

After a concern for form, the experienced writers have a second objective: a concern for their readership. In this way, "production" precedes "conception." The experienced writers imagine a reader (reading their product) whose existence and whose expectations influence their revision process. They have abstracted the standards of a reader and this reader seems to be partially a reflection of themselves and functions as a critical and productive collaborator—a collaborator who has yet to love their work. The anticipation of a reader's judgment causes a feeling of dissonance when the writer recognizes incongruities between intention and execution, and requires these writers to make revisions on all levels. Such a reader gives them just what the students lacked: new eyes to "re-view" their work. The experienced writers believe that they have learned the causes and conditions, the product, which will influence their reader, and their revision strategies are geared towards creating these causes and conditions. They demonstrate a complex understanding of which examples, sentences, or phrases should be included or excluded. For example, one experienced writer decided to delete public examples and add private examples when writing about the energy crisis because "private examples would be less controversial and thus more persuasive." Another writer revised his transitional sentences because "some kinds of transitions are more easily recognized as transitions than others." These examples represent the type of strategic attempts these experienced writers use to manipulate the conventions of discourse in order to communicate to their reader.

But these revision strategies are a process of more than communication; they are part of the process of *discovering meaning* altogether. Here we can see the importance of dissonance; at the heart of revision is the process by which writers recognize and resolve the dissonance they sense in their writing. Ferdinand de Saussure has argued that meaning is differential or "diacritical," based on differences between terms rather than on "essential" or inherent qualities of terms. "Phonemes," he said, "are characterized not, as one might think, by their own positive quality but simply by the fact that they are distinct."[9] In fact, Saussure bases his entire *Course in General Linguistics* on these differences, and such differences are dissonant; like musical dissonances which gain their significance from their relationship to the "key" of the composition (which itself is determined by the whole), language, specific language (parole), gains its meaning from the system of language (langue) of which it is a manifestation and part. The musical composition—a "composition" of parts—creates its "key" as an overall structure which determines the value (meaning) of its parts. The analogy with music is readily seen in the compositions of experienced writers: both sorts of composition are based precisely on those structures experienced writers seek in their writing. It is this complicated relationship between the parts and the whole in the work of experienced writers which destroys the linear model; writing cannot develop "like a line" because each addition or deletion is a reordering of the whole. Explicating Saussure, Jonathan Culler asserts that "meaning depends on difference of meaning."[10] But student writers constantly struggle to bring their essays into congruence with a predefined meaning. The experienced writers do the opposite: they seek to discover (to create) meaning in the engagement with their writing, in revision. They seek to emphasize and exploit the lack of clarity, the differences of meaning, the dissonance, that writing as opposed to speech allows in the possibility of revision. Writing has spatial and temporal features not apparent in speech—words are recorded in space and fixed in time—which is why writing is susceptible to reordering and later addition. Such features make possible the dissonance that both provokes revision and promises, from itself, new meaning.

For the experienced writers the heaviest concentration of changes is on the sentence level, and the changes are predominantly by addition and deletion. But, unlike the students, experienced writers make changes on all levels and use all revision operations. Moreover, the operations the students fail to use—reordering and addition—seem to require a theory of the revision process as a totality—a theory which, in fact, encompasses the *whole* of the composition. Unlike the students, the experienced writers possess a non-linear theory in which a sense of the whole writing both precedes and grows out of an examination of the parts. As we saw, one writer said he needed "a first draft to figure out what to say," and "a second draft to see the structure of an argument buried beneath the surface." Such a "theory" is both theoretical and strategical; once again, strategy and theory are conflated in ways that are literally impossible for the linear model. Writing appears to be more like a seed than a line.

Two elements of the experienced writers' theory of the revision process are the adoption of a holistic perspective and the perception that revision is a recursive process. The writers ask: What does my essay as a *whole* need for form, balance, rhythm, or communication? Details are added, dropped, substituted, or reordered according to their sense of what the essay needs for emphasis and proportion. This sense, however, is constantly in flux as ideas are developed and modified; it is constantly "re-viewed" in relation to the parts. As their ideas change, revision becomes an attempt to make their writing consonant with that changing vision.

The experienced writers see their revision process as a recursive process—a process with significant recurring activities—with different levels of attention and different agendas for each cycle. During the first revision cycle their attention is primarily directed towards narrowing the topic and delimiting their ideas. At this point, they are not as concerned as they are later about vocabulary and style. The experienced writers explained that they get closer to their meaning by not limiting themselves too early to lexical concerns. As one writer commented to explain her revision process, a comment inspired by the summer 1977 New York power failure: "I feel like Con Edison cutting off certain states to keep the generators going. In first and second drafts, I try to cut off as much as I can of my editing generator, and in a third draft, I try to cut off some of my idea generators, so I can make sure that I will actually finish the essay." Although the experienced writers describe their revision process as a series of different levels or cycles, it is inaccurate to assume that they have only one objective. The same objectives and sub-processes are present in each cycle, but in different proportions. Even though these experienced writers place the predominant weight upon finding the form of their argument during the first cycle, other concerns exist as well. Conversely, during the later cycles, when the experienced writers' primary attention is focused upon stylistic concerns, they are still attuned, although in a reduced way, to the form of the argument. Since writers are limited in what they can attend to during each cycle (understandings are temporal), revision strategies help balance competing demands on attention. Thus, writers can concentrate on more than one objective at a time by developing strategies to sort out and organize their different concerns in successive cycles of revision.

It is a sense of writing as discovery—a repeated process of beginning over again, starting out new—that the students failed to have. I have used the notion of dissonance because such dissonance, the incongruities between intention and execution, governs both writing and meaning. Students do not see the incongruities. They need to rely on their own internalized sense of good writing and to see their writing with their "own" eyes. Seeing in revision—seeing beyond hearing—is at the root of the word *revision* and the process itself; current dicta on revising blind our students to what is actually involved in revision. In fact, they blind them to what constitutes good writing altogether. Good writing disturbs: it creates dissonance. Students need to seek the dissonance of discovery, utilizing in their writing, as the experienced writers do, the very difference between writing and speech—the possibility of revision.

Notes

[1] D. Gordon Rohman and Albert O. Wlecke, "Pre-writing: The Construction and Application of Models for Concept Formation in Writing," Cooperative Research Project No. 2174, U.S. Office of Education, Department of Health, Education, and Welfare; James Britton, Anthony Burgess, Nancy Martin, Alex McLeod, Harold Rosen, *The Development of Writing Abilities* (11–18) (London: Macmillan, 1975).

[2] Britton is following Roman Jakobson, "Linguistics and Poetics," *Style in Language,* ed. T. A. Sebeok (Cambridge: MIT P, 1960).

[3] For an extended discussion of this issue see Nancy Sommers, "The Need for Theory Composition Research," *College Composition and Communication* 30 (Feb. 1979): 46–49.

[4] *Classical Rhetoric for the Modern Student* (New York: Oxford UP, 1965) 27.

[5] Roland Barthes, "Writers, Intellectuals, Teachers," *Image-Music-Text,* trans. Stephen Heath (New York: Hill, 1977) 190–91.

[6] Barthes 190.

[7] Nancy Sommers and Ronald Schleifer, "Means and Ends: Some Assumptions of Student Writers," *Composition and Teaching* 2 (1980): 69–76.

8 "Writing Degree Zero," in *Writing Degree Zero and Elements of Semiology*, trans. Annette Lavers and Colin Smith (New York: Hill, 1968) 20.

9 *Course in General Linguistics*, trans. Wade Baskin (New York, 1966) 119.

10 Jonathan Culler, *Saussure*, Penguin Modern Masters Series (London: Penguin, 1976) 70.

The author wishes to express her gratitude to Professor William Smith, University of Pittsburgh, for his vital assistance with the research reported in this article and to Patrick Hays, her husband, for extensive discussions and critical help.

David Bartholomae, from "The Study of Error"

David Bartholomae won a major award in the field of composition and rhetoric—the 1981 Braddock Award—for the essay from which the following excerpt is taken. "The Study of Error" was judged to be the best essay of the year published in *College Composition and Communication*. This excerpt makes a salutary companion piece to Bartholomae's essay in Conversation 4 (page 186) since it reveals his painstaking and thoughtful ways of working with individual writers and his respect for their intelligence. His emphasis on our need to ask students *why* they're making certain recurring errors comes from Mina Shaughnessy's work with open admissions students in New York City; this particular segment focuses simultaneously on the necessity for and the limits of painstaking proofreading.

from THE STUDY OF ERROR

Let me turn to an example. This is part of a paper that a student, John, wrote in response to an assignment that asked him to go back to some papers he had written on significant moments in his life in order to write a paper that considered the general question of the way people change:

> This assignment call on chosing one of my incident making a last draft out of it. I found this very differcult because I like them all but you said I had to pick one so the Second incident was decide. Because this one had the most important insight to my life that I indeed learn from. This insight explain why adulthood mean that much as it dose to me because I think it alway influence me to change and my outlook on certain thing like my point-of-view I have one day and it might change the next week on the same issue. So in these frew words I going to write about the incident now. My exprience took place in my high school and the reason was out side

of school but I will show you the connection. The situation took place cause of the type of school I went too. Let me tell you about the situation first of all what happen was that I got suspense from school. For thing that I fell was out of my control sometime, but it taught me alot about respondability of a growing man. The school suspense me for being late ten time. I had accummate ten dementic and had to bring my mother to school to talk to a conselor and Prinpicable of the school what when on at the meet took me out mentally period.

One could imagine a variety of responses to this. The first would be to form the wholesale conclusion that John can't write and to send him off to a workbook. Once he had learned how to write correct sentences, then he could go on to the business of actually writing. Let me call this the "old style" response to error. A second response, which I'll call the "investigative approach," would be to chart the patterns of error in this particular text. Of the approximately 40 errors in the first 200 words, the majority fall under four fairly specific categories: verb endings, noun plurals, syntax, and spelling. The value to pedagogy is obvious. One is no longer teaching a student to "write" but to deal with a limited number of very specific kinds of errors, each of which would suggest its own appropriate response. Furthermore, it is possible to refine the categories and to speculate on and organize them according to cause. The verb errors almost all involve "s" or "ed" endings, which could indicate dialect interference or a failure to learn the rules for indicating tense and number. It is possible to be even more precise. The passage contains 41 verbs; only 17 of them are used incorrectly. With the exception of four spelling errors, the errors are all errors of inflection and, furthermore, these errors come only with regular verbs. There are no errors with irregular verbs. This would suggest, then, that when John draws on memory for a verb form, he gets it right; but when John applies a rule to determine the ending, he gets it wrong.

The errors of syntax could be divided into those that might be called punctuation errors (or errors that indicate a difficulty perceiving the boundaries of the sentence), such as

Let me tell you about the situation first of all what happen was that I got suspense from school. For thing that I fell was out of my control sometime, but it taught me alot about respondability of a growing man.

and errors of syntax that would fall under Shaughnessy's category of consolidation errors,

This insight explain why adulthood mean that much as it dose to me because I think it alway influence me to change and my outlook on certain thing like my point-of-view I have one day and it might change the next week on the same issue.

One would also want to note the difference between consistent errors, the substitution of "situation" for "situation" or "suspense" for "suspended," and unstable ones, as, for example, when John writes "cause" in one place and "because" in another. In one case John could be said to have fixed on a rule; in the other he is searching for one. One would also want to distinguish between what might seem to be "accidental" errors, like substituting "frew" for "few" or "when" for "went," errors that might best be addressed by teaching a student to edit, and those whose causes are deeper and require time and experience, or some specific instructional strategy.

I'm not sure, however, that this analysis provides an accurate representation of John's writing. Consider what happens when John reads this paper out loud. I've been taping students reading their own papers, and I've developed a system of notation, like that used in miscue analysis,[11] that will allow me to record the points of variation between the writing that is on the page and the writing that is spoken, or, to use the terminology of miscue analysis, between the expected response (ER) and the observed response (OR). What I've found is that students will often, or in predictable instances, substitute correct forms for the incorrect forms on the page, even though they are generally unaware that such a substitution was made. This observation suggests the limits of conventional error analysis for the study of error in written composition.

I asked John to read his paper out loud, and to stop and correct or note any mistakes he found. Let me try to reproduce the transcript of that reading. I will boldface any substitution or correction and offer some comments in parentheses. The reader might first go back and review the original. Here is what John read:

> This assignment calls on **choosing** one of my incident making a last draft out of it. I found this very difficult because I like them all but you said I **had** to pick one so the Second incident was decide**d on**. Because (John goes back and rereads, connecting up the subordinate clause.) So the second incident was decided on because this one had the most important insight to my life that I indeed learn**ed** from. This insight explains why adulthood **meant** that much as it dose to me because I think it always influences me to change and my outlook on certain things like my point-of-view I have one day and it might change the next week on the same issue. (John goes back and rereads, beginning with "Like my point of view," and he is puzzled but he makes no additional changes.) So in these **few** words **I'm** going to write about the incident now. My exp**eri**ence took place in

my high school and the reason was out side of school but I will show you the connection. The **situation** took place **be**cause of the type of school I went to (John had written "too.") Let me tell you about the **situation** (John comes to a full stop.) first of all what happen**ed** was that I got **suspended** from school (no full stop) for thing**s** that **I felt** was out of my control sometime, but it taught me a lot about **responsibility** of a growing man. The school **suspended** me for being late ten times. I had **accumulated** (for "accumate") ten **demerits** (for "dementic") and had to bring my mother to school to talk to a counselor and **the Principal** of the school (full stop) what **went** on at the meet**ing** took me out mentally (full stop) period (with brio).

I have chosen an extreme case to make my point, but what one sees here is the writer correcting almost every error as he reads the paper, even though he is not able to recognize that there *are* errors or that he has corrected them. The only errors John spotted (where he stopped, noted an error and corrected it) were the misspellings of "situation" and "Principal," and the substitution of "chosing" for "choosing." Even when he was asked to reread sentences to see if he could notice any difference between what he was saying and the words on the page, he could not. He could not, for example, see the error in "frew" or "dementic" or any of the other verb errors, and yet he spoke the correct form of every verb (with the exception of "was" after he had changed "thing" to "things" in "for things that *I felt* was out of my control") and he corrected every plural. His phrasing as he read produced correct syntax, except in the case of the consolidation error, which he puzzled over but did not correct. It's important to note, however, that John did not read that confused syntax as if no confusion were there. He sensed the difference between the phrasing called for by the meaning of the sentence and that which existed on the page. He did not read as though meaning didn't matter or as though the "meaning" coded on the page was complete. His problem cannot be simply a syntax problem, since the jumble is bound up with his struggle to articulate this particular meaning. And it is not simply a "thinking" problem—John doesn't write this way because he thinks this way—since he perceives that the statement as it is written is other than that which he intended.

When I asked John why the paper (which went on for two more pages) was written all as one paragraph, he replied, "It was all one idea. I didn't want to have to start all over again. I had a good idea and I didn't want to give it up." John doesn't need to be "taught" the paragraph, at least not as the paragraph is traditionally taught. His prose is orderly and proceeds through blocks of discourse. He tells the story of his experience at the school and concludes that through his experience he realized that he must accept responsibility for his tardiness, even though the tardiness was not his fault but the fault of the Philadelphia subway system. He concludes that with this realization he learned "the responsibility of a growing man." Furthermore John knows that the print code carries certain conventions for ordering and presenting discourse. His translation of the notion that "a paragraph develops a single idea" is peculiar but not illogical.

It could also be argued that John does not need to be "taught" to produce correct verb forms, or, again, at least not as such things are conventionally taught. Fifteen weeks of drill on verb endings might raise his test scores but they would not change the way he writes. He *knows* how to produce correct endings. He demonstrated that when he read, since he was reading in terms of his grammatical competence. His problem is a problem of performance, or fluency, not of competence. There is certainly no evidence that the verb errors are due to interference from his spoken language. And if the errors could be traced to some intermediate system, the system exists only in John's performance as a writer. It does not operate when he reads or, for that matter, when he speaks, if his oral reconstruction of his own text can be taken as a record of John "speaking" the idiom of academic discourse.[12]

John's case also highlights the tremendous difficulty such a student has with editing, where a failure to correct a paper is not evidence of laziness or inattention or a failure to know correct forms, but evidence of the tremendous difficulty such a student has objectifying language and seeing it as black and white marks on the page, where things can be wrong even though the meaning seems right.[13] One of the hardest errors for John to spot, after all my coaching, was the substitution of "frew" for "few," certainly not an error that calls into question John's competence as a writer. I can call this a "performance" error, but that term doesn't suggest the constraints on performance in writing. This is an important area for further study. Surely one constraint is the difficulty of moving the hand fast enough to translate meaning into print. The burden imposed on their patience and short-term memory by the slow, awkward handwriting of many inexperienced writers is a very real one. But I think the constraints extend beyond the difficulty of forming words quickly with pen or pencil.

One of the most interesting results of the comparison of the spoken and written versions of John's text is his inability to *see* the difference between "frew" and "few" or "dementic" and "demerit." What this suggests is that John reads and writes from the "top down" rather than the "bottom up," to use a distinction made by cognitive psychologists in their study of reading.[14] John is not operating through the lower level process of translating orthographic information into sounds and sounds into meaning when he reads. And conversely, he is not working from meaning to sound to word when he is writing. He is, rather, retrieving lexical items directly, through a "higher level" process that bypasses the "lower level" operation of phonetic translation. When I put *frew* and *few* on the blackboard, John read them both as "few." The lexical item "few" is represented for John by either orthographic array. He is not, then, reading or writing phonetically, which is a sign, from one perspective, of a high level of fluency, since the activity is automatic and not mediated by the more primitive operation of translating speech into print or print into speech. When John was writing, he did not produce "frew" or "dementic" by searching for sound/letter correspondences. He drew directly upon his memory for the look and shape of those words; he was working from the top down rather than the bottom up. He went to stored print forms and did not take the slower route of translating speech into writing.

John, then, has reached a stage of fluency in writing where he directly and consistently retrieves print forms, like "dementic," that are meaningful to him, even though they are idiosyncratic. I'm not sure what all the implications of this might be, but we surely must see John's problem in a new light, since his problem can, in a sense, be attributed to his skill. To ask John to slow down his writing and sound out words would be disastrous. Perhaps the most we can do is to teach John the slowed down form of reading he will need in order to edit.

John's paper also calls into question our ability to identify accidental errors. I suspect that when John substitutes a word like "when" for "went," this is an accidental error, a slip of the pen. Since John spoke *"went"* when he read, I cannot conclude that he substituted "when" for "went" because he pronounces both as "wen." This, then, is not an error of dialect interference but an accidental error, the same order of error as the omission of "the" before "Principal." Both were errors John corrected while reading (even though he didn't identify them as errors).

What is surprising is that, with all the difficulty John had identifying errors, he immediately saw that he had written "chosing" rather than "choosing." While textual analysis would have led to the conclusion that he was applying a tense rule to a participial construction, or over-generalizing from a known rule, the ease with which it was identified would lead one to conclude that it was, in fact, a mistake, and not evidence of an approximative system. What would have been diagnosed as a deep error now appears to be only an accidental error, a "mistake" (or perhaps a spelling error).

In summary, this analysis of John's reading produces a healthy respect for the tremendous complexity of transcription, for the process of recording meaning in print as opposed to the process of generating meaning. It also points out the difficulty of charting a learner's "interlanguage" or "intermediate system," since we are working not only with a writer moving between a first and a second language, but a writer whose performance is subject to the interference of transcription, of producing meaning through the print code. We need, in general, to refine our understanding of performance-based errors, and we need to refine our teaching to take into account the high percentage of error in written composition that is rooted in the difficulty of performance rather than in problems of general linguistic competence.

Let me pause for a moment to put what I've said in the context of work in error analysis. Such analysis is textual analysis. It requires the reader to make assumptions about intention on the basis of information in the text. The writer's errors provide the most important information since they provide insight into the idiosyncratic systems the writer has developed. The regular but unconventional features in the writing will reveal the rules and strategies operating for the basic writer.

The basic procedure for such analysis could be outlined this way. First the reader must identify the idiosyncratic construction; he must determine what is an error. This is often difficult, as in the case of fragments, which are conventionally used for effect. Here is an example of a sentence whose syntax could clearly be said to be idiosyncratic:

> In high school you learn alot for example Kindergarten which I took
> in high school.[15]

The reader, then, must reconstruct that sentence based upon the most reasonable interpretation of the intention in the original, and this must be done *before* the error can be classified, since it will be classified according to its cause.[16] Here is Shaughnessy's reconstruction of the example given above: "In high school you learn a lot. For example, I took up the study of Kindergarten in high school." For any idiosyncratic sentence, however, there are often a variety of possible reconstructions, depending on the reader's sense of the larger meaning of which this individual sentence is only a part, but also depending upon the reader's ability to predict how this writer puts sentences together, that is, on an understanding of this individual style. The text is being interpreted, not described. . . . There is an extensive literature on the question of interpretation and intention in prose, too extensive for the easy assumption that all a reader has to do is identify what the writer would have written if he wanted to "get it right the first time." The great genius of Shaughnessy's study, in fact, is the remarkable wisdom and sympathy of her interpretations of student texts. . . .

This paper has illustrated two methods for gathering information about how a text was created. A teacher can interview the student and ask him to explain his error. John wrote this sentence in another paper for my course:

> I would to write about my experience helping 1600 childrens have
> a happy christmas.

The missing word (I would *like* to write about . . .) he supplied when reading the sentence aloud. It is an accidental error and can be addressed by teaching editing. It is the same kind of error as his earlier substitution of "when" for "went." John used the phrase, "1600 childrens," throughout his paper, however. The conventional interpretation would have it that this is evidence of dialect interference. And yet, when John read the paper out loud, he consistently read "1600 children," even though he said he did not see any difference between the word he spoke and the word that was on the page. When I asked him to explain why he put an "s" on the end of "children," he replied, "Because there were 1600 of them." John had a rule for forming plurals that he used when he wrote but not when he spoke. Writing, as he rightly recognized, has its own peculiar rules and constraints. It is different from speech. The error is not due to interference from his spoken language but to his conception of the "code" of written discourse.

The other method for gathering information is having students read aloud their own writing, and having them provide an oral reconstruction of their written text. What I've presented in my analysis of John's essay is a method for recording the discrepancies between the written and spoken versions of a single text. The record of a writer reading provides a version of the "intended" text that can supplement the teacher's or researcher's own reconstruction and aid in the interpretation of errors, whether they be accidental, interlingual, or due to dialect interference. I had to read John's paper very differently once I had heard him read it.

More importantly, however, this method of analysis can provide access to an additional type of error. This is the error that can be attributed to the physical and conceptual demands of writing rather than speaking; it can be traced to the requirements of manipulating a pen and the requirements of manipulating the print code.[18]

In general, when writers read, and read in order to spot and correct errors, their responses will fall among the following categories:

1. overt corrections—errors a reader sees, acknowledges, and corrects;

2. spoken corrections—errors the writer does not acknowledge but corrects in reading;

3. no recognition—errors that are read as written;

4. overcorrection—correct forms made incorrect, or incorrect forms substituted for incorrect forms;

5. acknowledged error—errors a reader senses but cannot correct;

6. reader miscue—a conventional miscue, not linked to error in the text;

7. nonsense—In this case, the reader reads a non-sentence or a nonsense sentence as though it were correct and meaningful. No error or confusion is acknowledged. This applies to errors of syntax only.

Corrections, whether acknowledged or unacknowledged, would indicate performance-based errors. The other responses (with the exception of "reader miscues") would indicate deeper errors, errors that, when charted, would provide evidence of some idiosyncratic grammar or rhetoric.

John "miscues" by completing or correcting the text that he has written. . . . Reading . . . frees a writer from the constraints of transcription, which for many basic writers is an awkward, laborious process, putting excessive demands on both patience and short-term memory. John, like any reader, read what he expected to see, but with a low percentage of meaning-related miscues, since the meaning, for him, was set, and with a high percentage of code-related miscues, where a correct form was substituted for an incorrect form.

The value of studying students' oral reconstruction of their written texts is threefold. The first is as a diagnostic tool. I've illustrated in my analysis of John's paper how such a diagnosis might take place.

It is also a means of instruction. By having John read aloud and, at the same time, look for discrepancies between what he spoke and what was on the page, I was teaching him a form of reading. The most dramatic change in John's performance over the term was in the number of errors he could spot and correct while re-reading. This far exceeded the number of errors he was able to eliminate from his first drafts. I could teach John an editing procedure better than I could teach him to be correct at the point of transcription.

The third consequence of this form of analysis, or of conventional error analysis, has yet to be demonstrated, but the suggestions for research are clear. It seems evident that we can chart stages of growth in individual basic writers. The pressing question is whether we can chart a sequence of "natural" development for the class of writers we call basic writers. If all non-fluent adult writers proceed through a "natural" learning sequence, and if we can identify that sequence through some large, longitudinal study, then we will begin to understand what a basic writing course or text or syllabus might look like. There are studies of adult second language learners that suggest that there is a general, natural sequence of acquisition for adults learning a second language, one that is determined by the psychology of language production and language acquisition.[21] Before we can adapt these methods to a study of basic writers, however, we need to better understand the additional constraints of learning to transcribe and manipulate the "code" of written discourse. John's case illustrates where we might begin and what we must know.[22]

Endnotes and Sources

. . .

11. See Y. M. Goodman and C. L. Burke, *Reading Miscue Inventory: Procedure for Diagnosis and Evaluation* (New York: Macmillan, 1972).

12. Bruder and Hayden noticed a similar phenomenon. They assigned a group of students exercises in writing formal and informal dialogues. One student's informal dialogue contained the following:

What going on?
It been a long time . . .
I about through . . .
I be glad . . .

When the student read the dialogue aloud, however, these were spoken as

What's going on?
It's been a long time . . .
I'm about through . . .
I'll be glad . . .

See Mary Newton Bruder and Luddy Hayden, "Teaching Composition: A Report on a Bidialectal Approach," *Language Learning*, 23 (June, 1973), 1-15.

13. See Patricia Laurence, "Error's Endless Train: Why Students Don't Perceive Errors," *Journal of Basic Writing*, 1 (Spring, 1975), 23-43, for a different explanation of this phenomenon.

14. See, for example, J. R. Frederiksen, "Component Skills in Reading," in R. R. Snow, P. A. Federico, and W. E. Montague, eds., *Aptitude, Learning, and Instruction* (Hillsdale, N.J.: Erlbaum, 1979); D. E. Rumelhart, "Toward an Interactive Model of Reading," in S. Dornic, ed., *Attention and Performance VI* (Hillsdale, N.J.; Erlbaum, 1977); and Joseph H. Denks and Gregory O. Hill, "Interactive Models of Lexical Assessment during Oral Reading," paper presented at Conference on Interactive Processes in Reading, Learning Research and Development Center, University of Pittsburgh, September 1979.

   Patrick Hartwell argued that "apparent dialect interference in writing reveals partial or imperfect mastery of a neural coding system that underlies both reading and writing" in a paper, "'Dialect Interference' in Writing: A Critical View," presented at CCCC, April 1979. This paper is available through ERIC. He predicts, in this paper, that "basic writing students, when asked to read their writing in a formal situation, . . . will make fewer errors in their reading than in their writing." I read Professor Hartwell's paper after this essay was completed, so I was unable to acknowledge his study as completely as I would have desired.

15. This example is taken from Mina Shaughnessy, *Errors and Expectations: A Guide for the Teacher of Basic Writing* (New York: Oxford University Press, 1977), p. 52.

16. Corder refers to "reconstructed sentences" in "Idiosyncratic Dialects and Error Analysis," in Jack C. Richards, ed., *Error Analysis: Perspectives on Second Language Acquisition* (London: Longman, 1974), pp. 158-171.

. . .

18. For a discussion of the role of the "print code" in writer's errors, see Patrick Hartwell, "'Dialect Interference' in Writing: A Critical View."

. . .

21. Nathalie Bailey, Carolyn Madden, and Stephen D. Krashen, "Is There a 'Natural Sequence' in Adult Second Language Learning?" *Language Learning*, 24 (June, 1974), 235-243.

22. This paper was originally presented at CCCC, April 1979. The research for this study was funded by a research grant from the National Council of Teachers of English.

M. Elizabeth Sargent, "Preparing Final Copy"

M. Elizabeth Sargent compiled this checklist so students would have a clear procedure to follow once they had left their first-year writing course behind and were submitting papers in upper-level courses in their majors. But she also required that some version of this basic checklist be submitted with each final draft (along with printouts from the *Editor* software program). This checklist (which has been revised and updated for this volume) was first published as an appendix to Sargent's "Errors and Expectations," an essay in which she argued that students would never take the preparation of final copy seriously as an essential part of the writing process unless it was *taught*, unless class time was devoted to it. She regularly adapts this basic checklist for different assignments. (See also the introduction to "Strategies for Writing-to-Learn" in Conversation 3.)

    Editor is described briefly in the introduction to this Conversation (see page 383 or visit http://www.serenity-software.com to get an idea how the program works). Although the following checklist assumes that *Editor* is being used at this point in the writing process, steps 4 and 6 below could be skipped if *Editor* is not available.

PREPARING FINAL COPY

A useful procedure for *all* papers to be submitted for a grade or formal evaluation, as long as you add the final step of revising on the computer one last time. NEVER submit as a final draft any computer printout you haven't read yourself. However, use this checklist and follow this procedure *only* if your piece has already gone through a few substantive revisions and rewrites already.

    Before submitting a final draft in this class, go through the steps below. If you have not, the paper will be returned to you unread. You will need to resubmit it, and it will be counted late:

1. Type the paper into the computer if it wasn't composed there. Revise on the screen according to the latest feedback from your editing group and from any

other readers. Save on hard disk and then on at least one removable disk or CD—or send the file somewhere electronically (the essential thing is to make sure you always have another copy of your file to work with if the computer you're working on crashes).

2. Print out this version. Have several people read it (out loud to you, if possible). READ IT YOURSELF (again, out loud). Make any necessary changes on the computer.

3. Spell check (be sure to SAVE the spell checked version before printing). Have a good dictionary with you. No spell checker will catch everything. Please note: *Editor* only works well if you spell check your document first. It does not *replace* spell checkers, although it is designed to catch some spelling errors that a spell checker will not catch.

4. Run *Editor* on your paper for the first time. Get the necessary *Editor* printouts and revise.

5. Read the paper out loud to yourself, at least once forward and then once backward, sentence by sentence, to catch fragments, run-ons, missing words, and typos. In proofreading, the goal is to slow your eye down; don't read for meaning right now as much as for mechanical detail. Double-check all page references and citations for accuracy and for correspondence to MLA form (or whatever citation format this particular paper requires). Make corrections on the computer and save (again, in at least two places).

6. Run *Editor* again, this time saving printouts from both the *Draft* and *Usage* programs to submit with your final copy. (Include *Word Frequency* output only if you found it useful for some reason and state that reason clearly on the printout.) If you disagreed with *Editor* and decided to ignore some of its suggestions, you must explain *why* legibly and briefly on the printout, next to each significant suggestion you ignored. However, no notation is needed on *Editor* "heads-up" commentaries (that is, items *Editor* flags *whenever* they appear, like the homonyms "there," "their," and "they're"), as long as you've double-checked to be sure you've chosen the appropriate form. Please note: numbered sentences must correspond exactly between *Draft* and *Usage* output, so *both programs must be run again, one right after the other, at this point.*

7. Double-space your file now if you haven't done so already. NUMBER all pages and put your name clearly on the first page.

8. Print out two IDENTICAL copies (not similar, but IDENTICAL—this will be crucial in the proofreading conference). If you prefer, photocopy your printout.

9. Get someone in your editing group to proofread IN PENCIL and SIGN one draft. Let them know they are PROOFREADING only at this point, not suggesting major changes (it's way too late in the process for that). They should read slowly and *non-invasively* for detail, putting a small check in the margin only to identify typos or clear problems in wording.

10. In blue or black PEN, enter any corrections you accept from your proofreader clearly on **both** drafts. Again, this step is crucial for the proofreading conference. One copy should contain nothing but your own final decisions, entered as neatly as possible. DO **NOT** GO BACK TO THE COMPUTER TO ENTER CHANGES AT THIS POINT: otherwise I will be unable to evaluate your proofreader's work and unable to quickly identify the choices you've made in response to that work. *On the proofreader's copy only*, write a tiny "NO" above marks you disagree with. If there are major changes to be made or so many small corrections needed that the paper is no longer readable or presentable (say, over fifteen changes), you should go back to the computer and then *repeat steps 8, 9, and 10*. If you rewrite a whole paragraph or more at this point, you should run *Editor* again as well.

11. Submit BOTH IDENTICAL copies, with the SECOND set of *Editor* printouts, not the first: in other words, this printout should be revealing primarily either the kinds of comments from *Editor* that we *should* ignore (such as *Editor's* flagging of homonyms when we have double-checked and know we've chosen the appropriate one) or comments from *Editor* that you disagree with (with your *brief* explanations). Also submit all feedback sheets you received on earlier drafts and include a copy of any drafts on which I wrote comments (at least one early draft must be submitted). Please put all of these items together in a manila envelope with this completed checklist and a one-page cover letter telling me whatever you want me to know about the process you went through in writing and revising this piece.

STUDENT WRITING
STEPHANIE BISHOP

COLLAGE/SEGMENTED ESSAY

Stephanie Bishop drew on the rich material she had produced during a long session of loop writing in order to produce the following segmented essay about her relationship to writing and her worries about becoming an English teacher.

November 2002

***

Lies:

- Writing is easy.

- Junior high students are horrible writers and they don't deserve my help with their writing because they will never learn anyway.

- Teaching writing is a waste of time and will not benefit students in any way.

- I will be a horrible teacher and I will have a bad effect on every student that I teach.

***

Well, here I am in a new school, with a new teacher and a new class. I don't know anyone. Maybe French Immersion was a mistake. Oh God, why did I do this? Maybe I should go back to St. Peter's. I don't belong here. I can't speak French. What happens if I can't make friends? What if they don't like me? OK Stephanie—calm down and relax. You will be fine once the teacher gets here and explains everything. Oh, a girl is waving at me to sit with her. Should I? I guess I'll never make friends if I don't. OK, here I go.

"Hi," a voice says.

"Hi, my name is Stephanie."

"I'm Sarah, this is my twin sister, Jessica, and this is Michelle. Would you like to sit with us?"

"Sure," I find myself saying with ease.

I am making friends already and they seem nice. This won't be so bad after all.

***

Dear Natalie Goldberg,

I am writing to comment on two of your articles, "The Power of Detail" and "Make Statements and Answer Questions." You have made numerous points that I agree with, but there are others that I initially found to be completely ridiculous. But I want to say that you're an excellent writer. The pieces are well-written—I am a university student, so clarity is an important quality I look for when I read.

The first point I would like to address concerns how details in writing help readers feel that they matter. I particularly enjoy it when you say

> We must become writers who accept things as they are, come to love the details, and step forward with a yes on our lips so there can be no more noes in the world, noes that invalidate life and stop these details from continuing (44).

I agree with this point because when I read something, my first instinct is to relate the topic to my life. If details are missing and I am unable to make specific connections, I feel disconnected from the piece and I stop reading.

As I read the section "Make Statements and Answer Questions," at first I thought your points about women's writing were absolutely ridiculous:

> In their sentence structure women were always looking for reinforcement for their feelings and opinions. They didn't just make statements and stand behind them: "This is beautiful." "This is terrible." They needed encouragement from outside themselves (85).

In an attempt to prove this idea of yours invalid, I read a piece of writing that I had completed and compared it to one written by a man. I was amazed to discover my writing validated your argument. Compared to a piece written by a man, my own was full of unneeded statements to obtain exactly what you had noticed: external validation and encouragement. For example, a lot of my sentences start off with "In my opinion" or "I believe that," whereas the piece written by the male was full of forceful statements such as "This is." I now know what you mean by "writing is the act of burning through the fog in your mind" (86). As I look back at my previous writing, I realize I have plenty of fog to get through!

Thank you for these two essays.

Sincerely, Stephanie Bishop

***

These girls are so nice! First they ask me to sit with them and now they're asking me to go to a movie with them tonight. Maybe this won't be so bad after all! Oh, here comes the teacher. Wow, he is tall! And his shoelaces are different colors! Well, I'd better pay attention because he is beginning to speak French.

Oh my—I can't understand a word he is saying. I'd better ask him to speak slowly and explain what he is saying to us.

"Sir?" I say.

He points toward the door and turns angrily at me: "OUT!"

I don't understand. What did I do wrong? Wait a minute—I said "Sir," didn't I? "Excusez-moi, monsieur," I correct myself, laughing.

"OUT!" he says again.

Is he still kicking me out? Why, because I spoke one English word? I am so embarrassed! Everyone is laughing at me. I knew I should have stayed at my old school. I don't belong here. What a disaster.

***

Since high school, my writing has been only for teachers. I have been a perfectionist when it comes to my writing because of my audience. I have always felt the need to be perfect because I do not want to look stupid or silly to anyone who reads my writing. I had also never completed any type of peer editing, and I felt apprehensive when I first tried it. My goal was to have everything flawless, so I was anxious that one of my peers would read something I had written and say "she is so stupid" or "how am I supposed to respond to this piece of writing without telling her that her style is awful." But reading Russ Hunt's piece "What Is 'Inkshedding'?" has helped me to look at my writing in a different way. For example, he talks about how if an individual's audience knows that the piece of writing is inkshedding, it will be read in a different way than if it were a formal polished essay. Hunt says an inkshed is read in what we can characterize as "dialogic" ways—that is, read for what it says, dialogically, not in order to evaluate it or to help the writer improve her text (2).

This has eased my mind about how I feel about peer editing. I can see that we are all on equal ground and are here to help one another, and that it's all right to make mistakes as long as we learn from them and don't humiliate each other in public for them.

***

I was crying in the hallway when my teacher came out to talk with me. He says from now on there is no English to be spoken in the classroom. I tell him that he has embarrassed me in front of a group of strangers, and I feel I can't go back in. He apologizes and says it will never happen again. So, I go back in and the next day, I came back. I continued this until I completed my six years of French Immersion at the top of my class. But being humiliated has affected me throughout my education. It has haunted me and it's something I will never forget.

***

The other part of Hunt's piece that I found had an effect on me is the section about voice. I have always been a shy person, especially when speaking in front of a group of peers. Because of an experience in my youth, I try to avoid situations where I have to do any type of public speaking. However, Hunt talks about how inkshedding can help people like me have their voices heard even if they are intimidated by oral discussion:

> It's also important that ideas, positions, and questions which would not otherwise attain a hearing have a better opportunity to get "on the floor" than they would in an oral discussion (1).

Hunt then quotes Anthony Paré:

> Inkshedding allows each member of the group to "gather" his/her thoughts before they are scattered by that first, articulate, confident person who gets up to say what you weren't even thinking about (1).

These statements are particularly relevant to me. Hunt has given me a new attitude about my writing and how it can help me overcome my lingering fear of public speaking.

***

My heart raced as my teacher handed back the first major essay I had ever written. My hands sweated and I began to shake. What happens if I failed? Will I ever be able to write an essay properly? What if my friends get higher grades than I do? They will laugh at me, I just know it. Oh my God, please, please, PLEASE let me do well. Here she comes. She called out my name. It's in my hand—oh I can't look!
"What did you get?" a voice says behind me.
"I haven't looked at it yet," I say.

Maybe I can open it, cover the grade and read the remarks first. Yes, that sounds like a good idea. Well, this looks OK. I'm going to look. Here I go—Eighty-five percent! I can't believe it!

My teacher tells me afterwards that my essay was one of the best in the class. She says how much she enjoyed reading it. I can't believe it. I feel excited, relieved, and I want to laugh and cry all at once. Wait until my parents see it!

***

Writing has always been a problematic process for me. The essay I am speaking of in the above excerpt was the first major essay I had ever written, and although I received a high grade, I now believe that the way in which I was taught to write it was inadequate. It was an argumentative essay where I had to present both sides and then defend my position with evidence. The reason for the high grade was that the essay followed the structure asked for by the teacher: introductory paragraph with a thesis statement, three paragraphs in the body of the essay, and a conclusion that repeated the thesis statement. Thinking back, revising this piece was the most difficult part of the process for me. I assumed that the meaning was already produced in my writing because when I read the words, I read for sound rather than processing the content in my head. In other words, my focus was on the vocabulary rather than on the content as a whole. Nancy Sommers says it best in her article "Revision Strategies of Student Writers and Experienced Adult Writers":

> The students understand the revision process as a rewording activity. They do so because they perceive words as the unit of written discourse. That is, they concentrate on particular words apart from their role in the text (381).

And the *last* thing on my mind was my audience—I was taught to focus more on the way the words looked on the page than on the content or my audience. According to Sommers's definition, I was clearly a "student writer," and some of this persona is still with me today.

However, I like to think that my writing has evolved since the tenth grade. Now when I write, I try to ask myself what my purpose is, who my audience will be, and if I am making the arguments I want to make. I like how Sommers explains the attitude of "experienced writers":

> they see their revision process as a recursive process—a process with significant recurring activities—with different levels of attention and different agendas for each cycle (386).

Granted, I don't revise this way every time—I'm only midway between a student writer and an experienced writer. I hold qualities of both personas, but I'm becoming a more experienced writer each time I write a piece. It is satisfying to know that I am growing every time my thoughts flow from my pen on to the paper.

***

Truths:

- – Writing takes practice.

- – Junior high students can become writers and deserve my help because they all have enormous potential.

- – Writing is an important skill for students to learn and will be beneficial to them in their future careers.

- – With experience, I will learn to be a successful teacher and have a positive effect on most students I teach.

Works Cited

Goldberg, Natalie. *Writing Down the Bones*. Boston: Shambhala, 1986.

— . "Make Statements and Answer Questions." *Writing Down the Bones*. 85–86.

— . "The Power of Detail." *Writing Down the Bones*. 43–44.

Hunt, Russell. "What Is 'Inkshedding'?" *Inkshed* (May 1999): 27 pars. <http://www.stthomasu.ca~hunt/dialogic/inkshed.htm>.

Sommers, Nancy. "Revision Strategies of Student Writers and Experienced Adult Writers." *College Composition and Communication* 31 (1980): 378–388.

NEW PRACTICES TO TAKE FORWARD

1. **Giving detailed descriptive feedback:** After you've written a discovery draft and then revised until it's close to a final version, work in a small group with two other writers who have close-to-final drafts of similar length. Each person in this group of three should supply the other two with a draft they can mark up. Clearly number the paragraphs in each draft. Then read each draft closely, pointing as you go (see the discussion of pointing on pages 335–337).

On a separate sheet of paper for each essay, you'll be writing two sentences for each paragraph in the essay. You should number each set of sentences, making sure that the numbers correspond to each paragraph in the draft. The first sentence in each set should state briefly but as accurately as possible what that particular paragraph is trying to *say*. Leave plenty of space for another sentence of equal length, but for right now, go on to the next paragraph and do the same. Go through the entire essay writing one detailed sentence for each paragraph, a sentence that tries to sum up the essential *content* of that paragraph. Try not to make evaluative comments; focus instead on describing the *substance* of each paragraph as accurately as you can. Besides, if a paragraph is weak on content or data or detail, something about your sentence will probably make that clear anyway (Example: "P4 cites one phrase from Sommers on revision and then grumbles that it doesn't seem fair to say that students are inexperienced writers since obviously the pressure of too many courses and assignments and deadlines as well as too many extracurricular activities makes it impossible for them to revise the way professional writers do").

Once you have gone through the entire essay that way, go back to the beginning. Now you're prepared to write your second sentence about each paragraph. This sentence should *not* summarize content at all, if possible. Instead, try to describe the *purpose* of this paragraph within the whole paper (something you probably couldn't have done well until you had read through the complete essay at least once). For instance, "This paragraph is trying to grab my attention and make me care about this issue by telling me a sad story." Or, later in the piece, "This paragraph is trying to convince me even further by giving me the results of some research, but it seems to be putting an awful lot of trust in a website that sounds kind of flaky to me; I'm more suspicious than convinced, so P5 might not be accomplishing what I think it wants to accomplish."

When you've read through both essays and completed your sentences, before you give your pages of sentences to the authors, if possible, give them to the other reader. Take time to read through the sets of sentences written by the other reader. Then confer individually with the other reader while the two of you look simultaneously at both sets of sentences and the draft itself. As readers of the same essay, the two of you might expect your sentences to match up pretty well. In fact, it's unlikely that many of them match at all. Discuss the differences. Then take ten minutes to inkshed about those differences individually, about why you think the two of you experienced parts of the paper differently (make clear which parts those were). Now give your sentences *and* your inksheds to the author.

Yes, this takes a lot of time. Thoughtful revision of an academic paper always takes a lot of time. But consider that while you're investing this time and energy into responding to the work of colleagues, they are also investing similar time and energy to let you know exactly how they see the shape of *your* piece, what they think it's saying, and how they resist or go along with your writerly plans to structure reader responses.

Also, notice that they have given you all of this information without ever once telling you exactly what to do or how to fix or change your paper. You could leave your paper exactly as is, especially if their reactions are exactly what you had hoped for. If they aren't, you have some work to do—but at least you have some detailed information about where your essay might be derailing or heading fast in the right direction but without enough cargo. You have some specific ideas about where you need to do more research, gather more data, or where you need to reorganize, cut, or add. In a sense the three of you have given one another a blow-by-blow description of how the paper affected you, what new information you took in, what you misunderstood, where you got lost or irritated. Such information from good readers is invaluable as you revise at a late stage in the writing process.

2. **Using the checklist for preparing final copy**: The next time you submit a paper for final evaluation, use the checklist on pages 429–431. Allow a lot of extra time and find a colleague who can go through the process with you. This process can work well if you're not in the same class, doing the same assignment—when deadlines come at different times, readers are apt to be less stressed proofreading for each other. They also bring a fresh pair of eyes to the piece since they're not familiar with the material or the assignment (but do make sure they understand what the assignment is). Being an outsider helps them limit their involvement to proofreading: they're less apt to misunderstand their role and start telling you how to rethink major sections of your piece from scratch when it's way too late in the process for that. Make sure that you give them your draft only when you've got it as clean as you can make it on your own with the help of a spell checker, a dictionary, and if available to you, *Editor* (you never want to ask a human to waste time doing something a machine could do just as well).

    Keep in mind that the proofreader is unlikely to be 100 percent correct. Also, some proofreaders are way more invasive than others. You may be irritated either way—that is, your proofreader may mark hardly anything, and you may have the feeling that they haven't invested much time or energy in looking for typos and mechanical problems and so on. Or your proofreader may drive you crazy trying to reword every sentence, sentences that were perfectly correct as they were, even if they could have been tighter or clearer. The worst-case scenario is a proofreader who makes things worse, telling you to insert commas into a million places where they shouldn't go. (That's why you never let a proofreader touch your final copy just before you hand it in!)

A useful guideline is to ask the proofreader only to mark places where there are obvious errors, missing words, typos, or things that don't make sense. Make clear that you don't plan to change your writing style from Faulkner to Hemingway at this particular point (even if it might be a good idea at some later point!).

Go through the proofreader's suggestions and, unless you're submitting this piece to a writing instructor who wants to see and comment on the proofreading itself, go back to the computer and enter in only the changes and corrections you agree with. If you have questions or hesitations about any of them, consult someone else. Unfortunately, we can sometimes work with proofreaders who have the exact blind spots we have; if you think that's the case (say, for instance, you've been told you have way too many run-on sentences and your proofreader has, suspiciously enough, not found even one in your essay), you may want to enlist the help of a second proofreader. Don't forget to read your essay out loud, to yourself or to someone else, as well: have a pencil in hand and pause to circle places where you stumble or where you notice a problem that needs fixing. Better yet, ask a friend to read your paper out loud to you and use the pencil to mark where *they* stumble— there's likely to be something missing or confusing at that point, even if it's just a missing punctuation mark.

When all corrections are entered on the computer, make sure to read through your final printout one last time before you submit the paper.

ESSAY IDEA

Complete the research you described in Inkshed Prompt 9 in this chapter (Conversation 8, page 338): write up and share your results.

BIBLIOGRAPHY: OTHER VOICES TO BRING INTO THE CONVERSATION

Abrams, M. H. *The Mirror and the Lamp.* 1953. New York: Oxford UP, 1971.

Allen, Guy. "Language, Power, and Consciousness: A Writing Experiment at the University of Toronto." *Writing and Healing: Toward an Informed Practice.* Ed. Charles M. Anderson and Marian M. MacCurdy. Urbana, IL: NCTE, 2000. 249–290.

Anderson, Chris. "The New Rhetoric and the New Journalism: Reflections on Freewriting as Product." Belanoff et al. 243–257.

Anderson, Chris, and Lex Runciman. *Forest of Voices.* London: Mayfield, 1995.

Atwood, Margaret. *Negotiating with the Dead: A Writer on Writing.* Cambridge: Cambridge UP, 2002.

Bartholomae, David. "Inventing the University." *When a Writer Can't Write: Studies in Writer's Block and Other Composing Problems.* Ed. Mike Rose. New York: Guilford, 1985.

___. "The Study of Error." *College Composition and Communication (CCC)* 31.3 (October 1980): 253–269.

Beason, Larry. "Ethos and Error: How Business People React to Errors." *CCC* 53.1 (Sept. 2001): 33–64.

Belanoff, Pat. "Freewriting: An Aid to Rereading Theorists." Belanoff et al. 16–31.

Belanoff, Pat, Peter Elbow, and Sheryl Fontaine, eds. *Nothing Begins with N: New Investigations of Freewriting .* Carbondale: Southern Illinois UP, 1991.

Bishop, Wendy, ed. *Elements of Alternate Style: Essays on Writing and Revision.* Portsmouth, NH: Heinemann Boynton/Cook, 1997.

___. *The Subject Is Writing.* 3rd ed. Portsmouth, NH: Heinemann Boynton/Cook, 2003.

Bitzer, Lloyd F. "The Rhetorical Situation." *Philosophy and Rhetoric* 1 (1968): 1–14.

Bizzell, Patricia. "The Intellectual Work of 'Mixed' Forms of Academic Discourse." In Fox et al. 1–10.

Booth, Wayne. "The Rhetorical Stance." *CCC* 14 (October 1963): 139–145.

Braddock, Richard. "The Frequency and Placement of Topic Sentences in Expository Prose." *Research in the Teaching of English* 8 (Winter 1974): 287–302. Rpt. in *Cross-Talk in Comp Theory.* Ed. Victor Villanueva. Urbana, IL: NCTE, 1997. 167–181.

Brent, Doug. "Reflections on Inkshed 18." *Inkshed.* Canadian Association for the Study of Language and Learning 19.2 (Autumn 2001): 1–2. <http://www.StThomasU.ca/inkshed/nletta01/brent.htm>.

Bridwell-Bowles, Lillian. "Discourse and Diversity: Experimental Writing Within the Academy." *CCC* 43 (October 1992): 349–368.

___. "Freedom, Form, Function: Varieties of Academic Discourse." *CCC* 46.1 (February 1995): 46–61.

Britton, James, et al. *The Development of Writing Abilities, 11-18.* London: Macmillan, 1975.

Buckley, Joanne. *Checkmate: A Writing Reference for Canadians.* Toronto: Thomson Nelson, 2003.

Calkins, Lucy. *The Art of Teaching Writing.* 1st ed. Portsmouth, NH: Heinemann, 1986.

Carlyle, Thomas. *Latter-day Pamphlets.* 1850. New York: Charles Scribner's Sons, 1898.

Carver, Raymond. Afterword. *Fires.* By Carver. New York: Vintage, 1984. 217–219.

___. Interview. *Paris Review.* Rpt. in *Fires.* 187–216.

___. "On Writing." *Fires.* 13–18. First published as "A Storyteller's Notebook." *The New York Times Book Review*, February 15, 1981.

Caywood, Cynthia L., and Gillian R. Overing. Introduction. *Teaching Writing: Pedagogy, Gender, and Equity.* Albany: State U of New York P, 1987. xi–xvi.

Connors, Robert J. "The Rise and Fall of the Modes of Discourse." *CCC* 32.4 (1981): 444–455.

Connors, Robert J., and Andrea A. Lunsford. "Frequency of Formal Errors in Current College Writing, or Ma and Pa Kettle Do Research." *CCC* 39.4 (1988): 395–409.

Corbett, Edward P. J. "Teaching Style." *The Territory of Language: Linguistics, Stylistics, and the Teaching of Composition.* Ed. Donald A. McQuade. Carbondale: Southern Illinois UP, 1986. 23–33.

Dawkins, John. "Teaching Punctuation as a Rhetorical Tool." *CCC* 46.4 (December) 1995: 533–547.

Denton, Don. *First Chapter: The Canadian Writers Photography Project.* Banff: Banff Centre P, 2001.

Didion, Joan. "Why I Write." *Joan Didion: Essays and Conversations.* Ed. Ellen G. Friedman. Princeton, NJ: Ontario Review P, 1984. 5–10.

Ede, Lisa, and Andrea Lunsford. "Audience Addressed/Audience Invoked: The Role of Audience in Composition Theory and Pedagogy" *CCC* 35 (May 1984): 155–171.

___. *Singular Texts/Plural Authors: Perspectives on Collaborative Writing.* Carbondale: Southern Illinois UP, 1990.

Editor. See Thiesmeyer.

Elbow, Peter. "Closing My Eyes as I Speak: An Argument for Ignoring Audience." *College English* 49.1 (January 1987): 50–69.

___. "The Doubting Game and the Believing Game—An Analysis of the Intellectual Enterprise." *Writing Without Teachers*. 147–191.

___. *Embracing Contraries*. New York: Oxford UP, 1986.

___. "Embracing Contraries in the Teaching Process." *College English* 45 (1983): 327–39. Rpt. in Edward P. J. Corbett, Nancy Myers, and Gary Tate, *The Writing Teacher's Sourcebook*. 4th ed. New York: Oxford UP, 2000. 54–65.

___. *Everyone Can Write: Essays Toward a Hopeful Theory of Writing and Teaching Writing*. New York: Oxford UP, 2000.

___. "Methodological Doubting and Believing: Contraries in Inquiry." *Embracing Contraries*. 254–300.

___. "Reflections on Academic Discourse." *College English* 53.2 (February 1991): 135–155. Rpt. in *Everyone Can Write*. 235–256.

___. "The Shifting Relationships Between Speech and Writing." *CCC* 36.3 (October 1985): 283–303.

___. "Teaching Writing by Not Paying Attention to Writing." *fforum*. Ed. Patricia Stock. Upper Montclair, NJ: Boynton/Cook, 1983. 234–239.

___. "What Is Good Organization in Writing? The Story of the Ant and the Painting." Conference of the American Institute of Graphic Arts. Boston. April 2002.

___. *Writing with Power*. 1981. New York: Oxford UP, 1998.

___. *Writing Without Teachers*. 1973. New York: Oxford UP, 1998.

Elbow, Peter, and Pat Belanoff. *Being a Writer*. New York: McGraw Hill, 2002.

___. "Sharing and Responding." *A Community of Writers: A Workshop Course in Writing*. 3rd ed. New York: McGraw Hill, 2000. 505–557.

Emig, Janet. "Writing as a Mode of Learning." *CCC* 28 (1977): 122–128.

Flower, Linda, and John Hayes. "The Cognition of Discovery: Defining a Rhetorical Problem" *CCC* 31 (February 1980): 21–32. Rpt. in Gary Tate and Edward P. J. Corbett, *The Writing Teacher's Sourcebook*. 2nd ed. New York: Oxford, 1988. 92–102.

Fox, Helen. "Being an Ally." In Fox, Schroeder, and Bizzell. 57–67.

Fox, Helen, Christopher Schroeder, and Patricia Bizzell, eds. *Alt Dis: Alternative Discourses and the Academy*. Portsmouth, NH: Heinemann Boynton/Cook, 2002.

Fulkerson, Richard. "Composition Theory in the Eighties" *CCC* 41 (December 1990): 409–429.

___. "Four Philosophies of Composition." *CCC* 30 (December 1979): 343–448.

Fulwiler, Toby. *The Journal Book.* Portsmouth: Heinemann Boynton/Cook, 1987.

___. "Provocative Revision." *Writing Center Journal* (Spring 1992): 190–204.

___. "Writing Is Everybody's Business." *National Forum: Phi Kappa Phi Journal* 65.4 (Fall 1985): 21–24.

Gage, John. "An Adequate Epistemology for Composition: Classical and Modern Perspectives." In *Essays on Classical Rhetoric and Modern Discourse.* Ed. Robert J. Connors, Lisa Ede, and Andrea A. Lunsford. Carbondale: Southern Illinois UP, 1984. 152–169, 281–284.

Gendlin, Eugene. "How Philosophy Cannot Appeal to Experience, and How It Can." In Levin. 3–41.

___. "Reply to Wallulis." In Levin. 284–285.

Giltrow, Janet. *Academic Writing.* 3rd ed. Peterborough, ON: Broadview, 2003.

Glenn, Cheryl. "When Grammar Was a Language Art." *The Place of Grammar in Writing Instruction: Past, Present, Future.* Ed. Susan Hunter and Ray Wallace. Portsmouth, NH: Boynton/Cook, 1995. 9–29.

Goldberg, Natalie. "The Action of a Sentence." *Writing Down the Bones.* Boston and London: Shambhala, 1986. 87–89.

Graff, Gerald. *Beyond the Culture Wars: How Teaching the Conflicts Can Revitalize American Education.* New York: W. W. Norton, 1992.

Gray, Libba Moore. *My Mama Had a Dancing Heart.* New York: Orchard Books, 1995.

Green, Keith, and Jill LeBihan. *Critical Theory and Practice: A Coursebook.* London: Routledge, 1996.

Hacker, Diana. *A Canadian Writer's Reference.* 2nd ed. Toronto: Thomson Nelson Learning, 2001.

Hairston, Maxine. "Not All Errors Are Created Equal: Nonacademic Readers in the Professions Respond to Lapses in Usage." *College English* 43.8 (1981): 794–806.

Hartwell, Patrick. "Grammar, Grammars, and the Teaching of Grammar." *College English* 47 (1985): 105–127.

Harvey, Gordon. "Writing with Sources." Harvard University Expository Writing Program. 4 June 2004 <http://www.fas.harvard.edu/~expos/sources/>.

Haussamen, Brock. "Public Grammar and Private Grammar: The Social Organization of Grammar." *Syntax in the Schools: The Journal of the Assembly for the Teaching of English Grammar* 17.4 (Summer 2001): 1–4. Revised June 2004 version available at www.sargent.nelson.com.

Hollingshead, Greg. In Denton. 51.

Hunt, Kellogg. "Early Blooming and Late Blooming Syntactic Structures." Cooper, Charles R., and Lee Odell, eds. *Evaluating Writing: Describing, Measuring, Judging.* Urbana, IL: National Council of Teachers of English, 1977. 91–106.

Iyer, Pico. "In Praise of the Humble Comma." *Time.* 13 June 1988: 6.

James, William. 1892. *Psychology: Briefer Course.* New York: Henry Holt & Company, 1920.

Johns, Ann M., ed. *Genre in the Classroom: Multiple Perspectives.* Mahwah, NJ: Lawrence Erlbaum, 2002.

Jungwirth, Darci. Loop collage. In Elbow and Belanoff's *Being a Writer.* 90–93.

Kischner, Michael, and Edith Wollin. *Writers' Choices: Grammar to Improve Style.* Boston: Thomson Heinle, 2002.

Kolln, Martha. *Rhetorical Grammar: Grammatical Choices, Rhetorical Effects.* New York: Macmillan, 1991.

Kreisler, Harry. Interview with Eva Hoffman. Berkeley's Institute of International Studies, 2000. 4 Nov. 2003 <http://globetrotter.berkeley.edu/people/Hoffman/hoffmancon2.html>.

Kurt, Karen. "The Loop Writing Process." Cartoon. Sargent, "Errors and Expectations" 32.

Lamb, Catherine E. "Beyond Argument in Feminist Composition," *CCC* 42 (February 1991): 11–24. Rpt. in Gary Tate, Edward P. J. Corbett, and Nancy Myers, *The Writing Teacher's Sourcebook.* 3rd ed. New York: Oxford, 1994. 195–206.

Lanham, Richard A. *Revising Prose.* 2nd ed. New York: Scribner's, 1987.

Larson, Richard. "The 'Research Paper' in the Writing Course: A Non-Form of Writing." *College English* 44 (December 1982): 811–816.

Lawrence, D. H. "Study of Thomas Hardy." 1936. *Study of Thomas Hardy and Other Essays.* Ed. Bruce Steele. Cambridge: Cambridge UP, 1985. 3–128.

Lefer, Diane. "Breaking the 'Rules' of Story Structure." *The Best Writing on Writing.* Ed. Jack Heffron. Cincinnati: Story Press, 1994. 11–19.

LeFevre, Karen Burke. *Invention as a Social Act.* Carbondale: Southern Illinois UP, 1987. (Based on 1984 diss. at Rensselaer Polytechnic, *Infinite Conversation: A Social Perspective on Rhetorical Invention*).

Levin, David Michael. *Language Beyond Postmodernism: Saying and Thinking in Gendlin's Philosophy.* Evanston: Northwestern UP, 1997.

MacKinnon, Jamie. "Becoming a Rhetor: Developing Writing Ability in a Mature, Writing-Intensive Organization." *Professional Writing and Rhetoric: Readings from the Field.* Ed. Tim Peeples. Toronto: Longman, 2003.

Macrorie, Ken. *Telling Writing.* Rochelle Park: Hayden, 1970.

Mairs, Nancy. "The Writer's Thin Skin and Faint Heart." *Voice Lessons: On Becoming a (Woman) Writer.* Boston: Beacon Press, 1994. 136–149.

Micciche, Laura. "Making a Case for Rhetorical Grammar." *CCC* 55.4 (June 2004): 716–737.

Miller, Carolyn R. "Genre as Social Action." *Quarterly Journal of Speech* 70 (1984): 151–167.

Murray, Donald. *The Craft of Revision.* 1991. 4th ed. Fort Worth: Holt, Rinehart, 2001.

___. "Letter to a Young Article Writer." *The Best Writing on Writing.* Ed. Jack Heffron. Cincinnati: Story Press, 1994. 58–61.

Noguchi, Rei R. *Grammar and the Teaching of Writing.* Urbana, IL: NCTE, 1991.

Paraskevas, Cornelia. "The Craft of Punctuation." *Oregon English Journal* 23 (Spring 2001): 19–25.

___. "The Craft of Writing: Breaking Conventions." *English Journal* 93.4 (March 2004): 41–46.

___. "The Place of Run-ons and Dashes in Writing—The Craft of Breaking Conventions." June 2004 <www.sargent.nelson.com>.

___. "Sentence Fluency, Sentence Craft." *Classmate* (May 2002): 15–17.

___. "Teaching Grammar as Style." *Inland* 20.2 (Winter 1998): 6–9.

Perl, Sondra. "The Composing Processes of Unskilled Writers at the College Level." *Research in the Teaching of English* 13.4 (1979): 317–336.

___. *Felt Sense: Writing with the Body.* With accompanying CD. Portsmouth, NH: Heinemann Boynton/Cook, 2004.

Polanyi, Michael. "Objectivity." *Personal Knowledge: Towards a Post-Critical Philosophy.* 1958. Chicago: U of Chicago P, 1962.

Quintilian, *Education of the Orator,* c. 94 AD, X.iii. (5–7).

Ray, Katie Wood. *Wondrous Words.* Urbana, IL: NCTE, 1999.

Reither, James A. "Writing and Knowing: Toward Redefining the Writing Process." *College English* 47 (1985): 620–628. Rpt. in Edward P. J. Corbett, Nancy Myers, and Gary Tate, *The Writing Teacher's Sourcebook.* 4th ed. New York: Oxford UP, 2000. 286–293.

Rogers, Jaqueline McLeod. "The [Growing]Role of Narrative as Evidence in Academic Writing." Unpublished essay.

Root, Robert. "Beyond Linearity: Writing the Segmented Essay." In Root and Steinberg. 321–328.

Root, Robert, and Michael Steinberg. *The Fourth Genre: Contemporary Writers of/on Creative Nonfiction.* 2nd ed. Toronto: Longman, 2002.

Royster, Jacqueline Jones. "Academic Discourses or Small Boats on a Big Sea." In Fox, Schroeder, and Bizzell. 23–30.

Runciman, Lex, and Chris Anderson. *Forest of Voices.* London: Mayfield, 1995.

Sargent, M. Elizabeth. "Connecting Reading and Writing: Inkshedding-to-Learn." *Teaching Composition.* McGraw-Hill. April 2002 <http://www.mhhe.com/socscience/english/tc/>.

____. "Errors and Expectations: How Composition Scholarship Has Changed the Way I Ask For and Respond to Student Writing." *ADE Bulletin* 109 (Winter 1994): 23–34.

____. "Felt Sense in the Composition Classroom." *ADE Bulletin* 134 (2003): 57–67.

Schryer, C. F. "Walking a Fine Line: Writing 'Negative News' Letters in an Insurance Company." *Journal of Business and Technical Communication* 14.4 (2000): 445–497.

Shaughnessy, Mina P. *Errors and Expectations.* New York: Oxford UP, 1977.

Sommers, Nancy. "Responding to Student Writing." *CCC* 33 (1982): 148–156.

Stafford, Kim. "Director's Notes." *Northwest Writing Institute Newsletter.* Portland, Oregon. (Fall 1995): 1; (Summer 2002): 1.

____. "Writing Daily, Writing in Tune." *The Muses Among Us: Eloquent Listening and Other Pleasures of the Writer's Craft.* Athens: U of Georgia Press, 2003. 1–2.

Stafford, William. "Breathing on a Poem." *You Must Revise Your Life.* 48–51.

____. "A Witness for Poetry." *You Must Revise Your Life.* 58–66.

____. *Writing the Australian Crawl.* Ann Arbor: U of Michigan P, 1978.

____. *You Must Revise Your Life.* Ann Arbor: U of Michigan P, 1986.

Stewart, Donald C. "Some History Lessons for Composition Teachers." *Rhetoric Review* 3 (January 1985): 134–144. Rpt. in Gary Tate and Edward P. J. Corbett, *The Writing Teacher's Sourcebook.* 2nd ed. New York: Oxford, 1988. 16–23.

Thiesmeyer, Elaine C., and John E. Thiesmeyer. 1990. *Editor: A System for Checking Usage, Mechanics, Vocabulary, and Structure.* Windows edition. Serenity Software, 2004 <http://www.serenity-software.com>.

Tompkins, Jane. "Me and My Shadow." *New Literary History*. Autumn 1987. Rpt. in Root and Steinberg. 349–363.

Trimmer, Joseph. *Narration as Knowledge*. Portsmouth, NH: Heinemann Boynton/Cook, 1997.

Truss, Lynne. *Eats, Shoots & Leaves*. New York: Gotham Books, 2004.

University of Alberta English Department. "Learning to Read Instructor Comments and Marks on Essays: A Handout for First-Year English Courses." May 2000. Updated May 2003 <http://www.humanities.ualberta.ca/english/marking.html>.

Wallace, M. Elizabeth, C. Paraskevas, T. Rand, J. Thielsen, and D. Weiss, eds. *What's Happening with Writing at Western Oregon State College?* Monmouth, OR: Western Oregon State College, 1991.

Weathers, Winston. *An Alternate Style: Options in Composition*. Rochelle Park, NJ: Hayden, 1980.

Whitney, Robert. "Why I Hate Freewriting: A Philosophical Self-Study." In Belanoff et al. 214–230.

Young, Art. "Writing Poetry in First-Year Composition Courses." *Teaching Composition*. McGraw-Hill. 4 June 2004 <http://www.mhhe.com/socscience/english/tc/pt/young/young.htm>.

COPYRIGHT ACKNOWLEDGMENTS

INDEX OF NEW PRACTICES

SUBJECT AND KEY TERM INDEX

(Note: Page locators for key terms are in boldface; the locators indicate where that term is defined in the text or used with an added layer of meaning.)